LATIN AMERICAN
POLITICS AND DEVELOPMENT

LATIN AMERICAN POLITICS AND DEVELOPMENT

NINTH EDITION

Edited by

Harvey F. Kline, *University of Alabama (emeritus)*

Christine J. Wade, *Washington College*

Howard J. Wiarda

WESTVIEW
PRESS

Westview Press
Hachette Book Group
1290 Avenue of the Americas
New York, NY 10104
www.westviewpress.com

Printed in the United States of America

Ninth Edition: July 2017

Published by Westview Press, an imprint of Perseus Books, LLC, a subsidiary of Hachette Book Group, Inc.

The Hachette Speakers Bureau provides a wide range of authors for speaking events. To find out more, go to www.hachettespeakersbureau.com or call (866) 376-6591.

The publisher is not responsible for websites (or their content) that are not owned by the publisher.

Print book interior design by Amy Quinn

Library of Congress Cataloging-in-Publication Data
Names: Kline, Harvey F., editor. | Wade, Christine J., editor.
Title: Latin American politics and development / edited by Harvey F. Kline, University of Alabama (emeritus); Christine J. Wade, Washington College.
Description: Ninth edition. | Boulder, CO: Westview Press, 2017. | Includes bibliographical references and index. |
Identifiers: LCCN 2017020912 (print) | LCCN 2017021630 (ebook) | ISBN 9780813350745 (e-book) | ISBN 9780813350509 (paperback) | ISBN 9780813350745 (eBook)
Subjects: LCSH: Latin America—Politics and government—Textbooks. | BISAC: HISTORY / Latin America / General.
Classification: LCC F1410 (ebook) | LCC F1410 .L39 2017 (print) | DDC 320.98—dc23
LC record available at https://lccn.loc.gov/2017020912

ISBNs: 978-0-8133-5050-9 (paperback), 978-0-8133-5074-5 (e-book)

LSC-C

10 9 8 7 6 5 4 3 2 1

CONTENTS

List of Tables and Maps   ix
List of Acronyms   xi
Preface to the Ninth Edition   xiii

PART I

The Latin American Tradition and Process of Development

Harvey F. Kline and Christine J. Wade

Introduction   3
  1   The Context of Latin American Politics   9
  2   A Brief History of Latin America   19
  3   Actors, Interest Groups, and Political Parties   29
  4   State Institutions and Public Policy   47
  5   The Political Economy of Latin America   59
  6   Latin America and the United States   75
  7   The Struggle for Democracy in Latin America   89

PART II

The Political Systems of South America

  8   Argentina: The Economic Tango Continues   103
    Linda Chen
  9   Brazil: The Politics of Elite Rule   123
    Britta H. Crandall
 10   Chile: From Democracy to Dictatorship and Back   141
    Peter M. Siavelis

11 Colombia: Is Guerrilla Violence Near Its End?   169
    Harvey F. Kline

12 Peru: Overcoming the Authoritarian Legacy at Last?   195
    Julio F. Carrión and David Scott Palmer

13 Venezuela: Political Decay amid the Struggle for Regime
    Legitimacy   217
    David J. Myers

14 Uruguay: Balancing Growth and Democracy   245
    Martin Weinstein and Jorge Rebella

15 Paraguay: The Uneven Trajectory   265
    Sebastian A. Meyer

16 Bolivia: Changes, Continuities, and Contradictions   283
    Miguel Centellas

17 Ecuador: Change and Continuity After Ten Years of New Left
    Revolution   299
    Jennifer N. Collins

PART III

The Political Systems of Mexico, Central America, and the Caribbean

18 Mexico: Democratization and Violence   319
    José Luis Velasco

19 Cuba: Revolution in the Balance?   345
    Juan M. del Aguila, Frank O. Mora, and Brian Fonseca

20 Costa Rica   369
    Mitchell A. Seligson

21 Nicaragua: An Uncertain Future   383
    Richard L. Millett

22 El Salvador: Civil War to Uncivil Peace   395
    Christine J. Wade

23 Guatemala: Breaking Free from the Past?   411
    Michael E. Allison

24 Honduras: Democracy in Peril   423
    J. Mark Ruhl

25 Panama: Political Culture and the Struggle to Build Democracy   435
    Orlando J. Pérez

26 The Dominican Republic: Democracy, Still a Work in Progress   449
    Lilian Bobea
27 Haiti: Searching for Democratic Governance   465
    Georges A. Fauriol

    About the Editors and Contributors   477
    Index   483

TABLES AND MAPS

Tables

1.1 Indices of Modernization in Latin America, 2014–2015   13
4.1 Contrasting Foundations of Latin and
     North American Society   48
4.2 Presidential Elections and Terms in Latin America   50
5.1 Export Commodity Concentration Ratios, circa 1913   61
5.2 Export Concentration Ratios and Total Exports, 2014   67
7.1 Freedom House Scores for Latin American Countries   96
11.1 Parties Elected to Congress in 2014 Election   172
11.2 The Changes in Status of Women in Colombia, 1910–2010   174

Maps

South America   102
Mexico, Central America and the Caribbean   318

ACRONYMS

AID	Agency for International Development
ALBA	Bolivarian Alliance for the Peoples of Our America
MERCOSUR	Common Market of the South
CELAC	Community of Latin American and Caribbean States
CAFTA-DR	Dominican Republic-Central American Free Trace Agreement
GATT	General Agreement on Tariffs and Trade
GDP	Gross Domestic Product
GNP	Gross National Product
ISI	import-substitution industrialization
IADB	Inter-American Development Bank
IAF	Inter-American Foundation
IMF	International Monetary Fund
ALASI	Latin American Integration Association
LAPOP	Latin American Public Opinion Project
NAFTA	North American Free Trade Agreement
NGOs	nongovernmental organizations
OAS	Organization of American States
FSLN	Sandinista National Liberation Front
UFCO	United Fruit Company
UNESC	United Nations Educational, Scientific and Cultural Organization
UNASUR	Union of South American Nations

PREFACE TO THE NINTH EDITION

Howard Wiarda had the idea for this book in 1978. The first edition, coedited by Harvey Kline, was published in 1979, the second in 1985, the third in 1990, the fourth in 1996, the fifth in 2000, the sixth in 2007, the seventh in 2010, the eighth in 2014, and now the ninth in 2017. Although Howard Wiarda's death in 2015 means that he did not take an active part in editing this edition, his inspiration will always be with those of us who were his colleagues, his students, or who read his many books.

The issues we have sought to examine in all nine editions include how and why Latin America is different from the United States economically and politically; the extent to which Latin American societies have achieved modernization and development, breaking through their dependent and semi-feudal past; what paths of national development the distinct countries of the area have followed (evolutionary or revolutionary; authoritarian, Marxist, or democratic; capitalist, socialist, or statist); and what developments and difficulties of democracy have been encountered in the region. These are large, weighty issues; their importance goes beyond the geographic confines of Latin America.

Each of the nine editions of the book has reflected the major dynamic changes occurring in Latin America itself. The decade of the 1970s was a period of authoritarianism and repression in much of the region with widespread human rights abuses, all of which resulted in theories about the area—corporatism, dependency theory, and bureaucratic-authoritarianism—that reflected scholars' pessimism about Latin America's future. Following this, the 1980s was a period of democratization throughout Latin America, with greater optimism about its political future (even though the economic prospects continued to be poor) and newer interpretations that stressed transitions to democracy.

In the early 1990s there was considerable agreement on goals for the region (labeled the "Washington Consensus") between the United States and Latin America: democracy, economic liberalism, and free trade. By that point most of the authoritarian regimes of the area had given way, and with the collapse of the Soviet Union, Marxism-Leninism had become less attractive; democracy and economic liberalism therefore seemed the only viable options. But by the end of the 1990s and continuing into the twenty-first century, although democracy, economic reform, and freer trade were still high on the agenda, a number of cracks had appeared in the prevailing consensus. Democracy was still limited and not working well in quite a few countries: much of Latin

America had achieved electoral democracy but not liberal or participatory democracy. Economic reform continued, but the neoliberal agenda had resulted in widespread unemployment and privation in many countries. Trade barriers continued to fall in Latin America, but in the United States protectionist political pressures prevented new trade initiatives. Meanwhile, Latin America moved increasingly away from the United States and followed a more independent policy.

Although Latin America has gone through its political and economic ups and downs over this more than fifty-year period, its society has been massively transformed. These are no longer the "sleepy," "backward," "underdeveloped" countries of cartoon and movie stereotypes. Since 1960, Latin America as a whole has gone from 70 percent rural to 70 percent urban and from 70 percent illiteracy to 70 percent literacy. The old two-class society is giving way, a new middle class is emerging, and poverty is slowly being reduced. These figures reflect the massive social changes underway throughout the area as well as the transformation from a peasant-agricultural economy to a more modern, industrial, and diversified one.

In the mid-1970s seventeen of the region's twenty countries were authoritarian, but today nineteen of the twenty (all except Cuba, and even there changes are possible soon) are democratic—incomplete democracies, but certainly better than the human rights–abusing regimes of earlier decades. Economically, quite a number of the countries are booming, with miraculous or near-East Asian–level growth rates, but others are still mired in underdevelopment. At the same time a host of new issues—rising crime and insecurity, drugs, gangs, social inequality, and globalization—have come to the fore. So, as always, Latin America reflects a mixture of successes and failures, of traditional and modern features, of mixed and often crazy-quilt regimes in an always-changing, dynamic context.

Latin America is one of the most exciting regions of the globe for the comparative study of economic, social, and political change. In previous decades, the choice of developmental models seemed wide open, representing diverse routes to modernization, but by now the democratic, mixed-economy route seems the main one conceivable, although still with great variation among the countries of the region. But populist regimes dedicated to redistribution also came to power, with varying degrees of success. In most countries, the state plays a major role in the economy, and the private sector is weaker than in the United States. Virtually every social, economic, and political issue, process, and policy present in the world can be found in Latin America. It thus remains an exciting, innovative, ever-changing, and endlessly fascinating living laboratory for study, travel, and research.

Not only is Latin America an interesting area to study, but it has also become increasingly important to the United States. After Canada, Mexico is now the United States' second largest trading partner in the world. Hispanics have become the largest minority in the United States and are voting in increasing numbers. On a host of new, hot issues—including oil, natural gas, drugs, trade, immigration, tourism, energy, pollution, investment, the environment, democracy, and human rights—the United States and Latin America have become increasingly intertwined and interdependent. Yet conflict persists in US relations with Cuba, Venezuela, and other countries. At the same time, both Europe and Asia are also increasing their trade with and interest in

Latin America and as a result, are often competing with the United States for influence. So is Iran.

This book offers in its first part a broad, region-wide overview of the patterns and processes of Latin American history, politics, society, and development. It then proceeds to a detailed country-by-country treatment of all twenty Latin American countries. Major countries like Argentina, Brazil, Chile, Colombia, Cuba, Mexico, Peru, and Venezuela receive extended coverage, and the smaller countries receive complete but somewhat briefer treatment. Each country chapter is written by a leading specialist in the field. To facilitate comparisons between countries we have asked each of our authors as far as it is feasible to use a common outline and approach. We emphasize throughout both the unique features of each country as well as the common patterns and processes that exist. Instructors thus have maximum flexibility in the selection of which countries to study and which themes or developmental models to emphasize.

Latin American Politics and Development has throughout its previous editions emerged as one of the most durable yet innovative texts in the field, and we hope that this ninth edition will intrigue new students of Latin America as it has stimulated two generations of earlier ones. Many of these students have now gone on to careers in business, academia, private agencies, or foreign policy; it is always rewarding to meet, hear from, or run into these former as well as current students. We hope that some of our enthusiasm for the subject continues to inspire them.

The editors wish to thank our contributors, both new and old. In this edition, in addition to the new co-editor, there are nine new contributors. Seven of the contributors are from Latin America, the highest number of any of the editions. We also wish to thank Raquel Gómez Fernández for her research assistance.

Finally, we wish to thank acquisitions editor Katharine Moore of Westview Press for encouraging this new edition and shepherding it through the publication process.

Harvey F. Kline
Christine J. Wade

PART I

The Latin American Tradition and Process of Development

Harvey F. Kline
Christine J. Wade

INTRODUCTION

Latin America is not a single, homogeneous region. Although the region's countries offer discernible patterns of political and economic development, its diversity is a key factor in explaining variances in these patterns. In this book we use the term "Latin America" to mean the twenty countries south of the United States in which the people speak a language that evolved from the Latin brought by Romans to France and the Iberian Peninsula. This diversity is reflected in the twenty independent countries selected for this book. Hence there is one country that was a colony of France (Haiti), one that was a colony of Portugal (Brazil), and eighteen that were colonies of Spain. Although the Latin American countries share to some degree a common basis in law, language, history, culture, sociology, colonial experience, and overall political patterns, which enables us to discuss the region in general terms, we must recognize that each country is different and becoming increasingly more so.

Unity amid diversity is a theme that runs throughout this book, to some extent affecting institutions, economies, and social relationships. Accelerated economic and social change, democratization, and globalization are having an impact, often incompletely and unevenly. Latin America still has abundant poverty, malnutrition, disease, poor housing, and the worst distribution of income in the world; its economic and political institutions often fail to work well or as intended; and social and political reforms are still strongly needed. However, at least some of the countries—generally the larger, more stable, and richer ones—are making what appears to be a definitive breakthrough to democracy, and many of the small countries are changing as well.

During the past twenty years a consensus seems to have emerged: namely democracy in the political sphere; a modern, mixed, and in some cases social-democratic economy; and greater integration with the rest of the world. Today there are more Latin American countries with elected leaders than ever before. Democracy is the preferred form of government in Latin America, even though it does not always work well or quickly enough. Democracy takes forms that are often different from that of the United States and it is still threatened by upheaval, corruption, and vast social problems. Globalization affects Latin America in all areas of life: culture, society (behavioral norms), politics (democracy), and, above all, economics. Latin America is now part of a global market economy. It has little choice but to open its markets to global trade and investment. That said, the Latin American countries vary greatly in how they manage development policy, and they are still debating their choices about the basic model to follow.

As Latin American countries have become more democratic and their economies more open, they have balanced outside pressures and domestic, often traditional, ways of doing things. Modernity and tradition often exist side by side in Latin American countries—the most traditional agricultural methods alongside the most modern skyscrapers—reflecting the mixed, often transitional nature of Latin American society. Patronage considerations often remain as important as merit and electoral choice. Moreover, as democracy has come to the region, it has often been a more centralized, executive-centered form of democracy rather than one of separate and equal executive, legislative, and judicial branches. At the same time, despite privatization and neoliberalism, the state has remained a strong force in economic and social programs, closer to the European tradition than to the US laissez-faire model. Thus development in Latin America has represented a fascinating blend of US, European, and historical Latin American ways of doing things.

A FRAMEWORK FOR ANALYSIS

This book has two chief objectives: Preliminary chapters offer brief overviews of Latin American history, parties and interest groups, government, political economy, relations with the United States, and the struggle for democracy. The chapters of parts II and III give in-depth analyses of the twenty countries.

In order to better understand the changes and continuities of Latin American development, the coeditors asked the authors of the twenty country chapters that follow to keep in mind the following questions. Although the coeditors recognized that Latin American countries are so different that not all questions would be relevant in all countries, we believe this framework can provide a deeper understanding of Latin American political development; it is also fundamental to the comparative analysis that is at the heart of this book.

Changes in Political Culture

Has the political culture changed? Until the 1930s, Latin America had often been feudal and medieval in its thinking, but then education increased, literacy expanded, and radio and television brought new ideas to even the most isolated areas. To what extent have the old fatalism and passivity faded? How have people become mobilized, and have new and challenging ideas of democracy and socialism arisen? More recently, the digital age and its accompanying technologies—computers, the internet, smartphones, and social media—have transformed communications and improved access to information. As countries and technologies have democratized, has the relationship between state and citizen changed? Have fundamental beliefs, ideas, and attitudes toward governments and institutions shifted over the past two decades?

In the country chapters that follow the authors will analyze among which groups these ideas are changing, how deep and extensive the changes are, and what impact a changing, more democratic and participatory political culture has had on institutions and policy. The authors will also describe how people feel about government, as well as how they perceive their relationship to it.

Economic Change

Are Latin America's economies now more diversified, and are most no longer dependent on one export crop? Are these economies larger, more complex, and more integrated into world markets? Have they shifted away somewhat from the state control and mercantilism of the past toward a system of open markets, freer trade, and greater efficiency, and have more modern businesses, industries, and services replaced the subsistence and plantation agriculture of the past? How have these changes created new jobs and opportunities, or given new dynamism to the economies of the area? These changes have reduced poverty throughout the region, although in many cases the gap between the rich and the poor is greater than before. As a result of this uneven development, are some groups and countries doing much better than others? All of these changes, the positive and the negative, carry important political and policy implications that vary from country to country. What is the role of the state in reducing inequality and alleviating poverty in this post-neoliberal era? How free are states to craft their own economic policies given global realities?

Social Change

Have social changes taken place, and have they been accompanied by an increase in political pluralism and tolerance? To what extent do these changes support the development of democracy in the country? Is the old landed oligarchy giving way to a more diverse panoply of business, industrial, commercial, banking, and other elites? A sizable middle class has grown up in every country, ranging from 20 to 50 percent of the population. Labor unions have organized, peasant groups have mobilized, and in some countries the urban employed poor are becoming politicized. In addition, there are new women's groups, community organizations, civil society organizations, and indigenous movements. Some of the older groups such as the military are also undergoing change, becoming more middle class, less elitist, and more professionalized. Roman Catholicism is being challenged in many countries by Protestant evangelicalism, which often involves quite different values and attitudes toward work, social policy, and the role of family. In the last half century Latin America has gone from being mostly rural to two-thirds urban. Have these changes been accompanied by an increase in political pluralism and tolerance? To what extent do these changes support the development of democracy in the country?

Political Institutions

Have all these social changes and the far greater social pluralism led to changes in political institutions? Have elections become more routinized and more honest, and are they generally accepted as the only legitimate route to power? Are other governing institutions being modernized as well? Are political parties better organized than in the past, with a real mass base and real programs and ideology, as compared with the small, personalist, and patronage-based parties of the past? Are there many more interest groups, NGOs, and civil society organizations than ever before, whose agendas need to be satisfied? Finally, is there growing pressure on government agencies and institutions to modernize, increase efficiency, reduce corruption, and deliver real goods and services?

There are other trends that suggest that Latin America's transition to democracy is perhaps less than complete. Do legislatures and court systems generally remain less powerful than the executive branch? Even in the post-*caudillo* era, does the government remain dominated by a strong president who has a number of enhanced powers not typically associated with separation of powers systems? Has this tension between democracy and authoritarianism become increasingly prevalent in recent years, as populist leaders from the left and right have sought to extend their time in power? Although the military and police operate under civilian rule throughout most of the region, is the military increasingly assuming new security functions? Are the armed forces among the most trusted state institutions, and are they more trusted than civilian institutions? Finally, have decentralization and the strengthening of local governments enhanced democratization?

In each country chapter the author will consider the level of democracy in the country. To do so the authors will consider four key dimensions posited by authors who have written about democracy in Latin America: (1) Are the head of government and the legislature elected in fair and open competitive elections? (2) Does the great majority of the population have the right to vote? (3) Are political and civil rights protected, including freedom of the media, freedom of speech, and freedom to organize? (4) Do the elected officials exercise real governing power and are not overshadowed by the military or other nonelected groups?

Public Policy

Is the government being called upon to provide a host of new public policy programs and reforms? These may address agriculture, family planning, education, economic development, the environment, housing, health care, or lesbian, gay, bisexual, and transgender (LGBT) rights, among other areas. Although patronage and clientelism remain prevalent in many countries, there is increasing pressure on the government to offer real policy solutions to real problems. Is the government dealing with a host of complicated policy issues, including reducing inequality, addressing climate change and environmental resource issues, confronting crime and drug trafficking, and dealing with migration? What factors shape public policy responses? How effective are the region's governments in addressing their most pressing problems?

To what extent are laws passed by the national government enforced throughout the country? Are public policies applied throughout the country or are there areas where they are not because of the challenges of geography—the mountains, the tropical rain forests, the distances between the national capital and the outlying regions? Does another difficulty come from the Iberian heritage of passing laws that, either intentionally or unintentionally, are simply unenforceable? Do the legal systems include enough properly trained police officers to investigate crimes and detain lawbreakers, and is the court system too understaffed (or inexperienced) to carry out trials against the ones who are arrested? Does this situation engender lack of respect for the laws, and are prisons overcrowded with individuals awaiting trials? Do such insufficient rule of law and impunity undermine the quality of democracy and erode public confidence in institutions?

The International Environment

For centuries, Latin America was isolated from the world, but now some countries are becoming more closely integrated—politically, culturally, and economically—into it. Has globalization come to the country? Have the values of the citizens, especially of young people, become more democratic, less authoritarian, less religious, and less traditional? Is the country now a part of the global economy, with good consequences (increased trade, commerce, jobs, affluence) and negative ones (currency uncertainties, fluctuating market demands, capital flight)? Has the country signed new trade agreements and courted new, international investors, notably China? Or is the country looking inward, cultivating economic relationships within the region? Is the relationship of the country with the United States less antagonistic than in the past, and has the country increasingly demonstrated a more independent, less subservient attitude in dealing with its neighbor to the north?

CONCLUSION: THE CRUCIAL QUESTIONS

All of the trends reflected in these questions have had a profound effect on Latin America, but they vary between countries and within institutions and even individuals, which continue to show complex mixes of traditional and modern attitudes and practices. In the second decade of the new millennium, we need to know just how democratic Latin America in general and individual countries are. Are the changes sufficient to provide a firmer basis for pluralism and democracy? Equally important, how can we better understand the nature and meaning of democracy in Latin America? How successful are the reforms in favor of free trade and open markets, and to what extent have they improved living standards in the region? How responsive are political parties, interest groups, and government institutions? Now that the Cold War is over, can US–Latin American relations be put on a normal, more mature basis, and what of Latin America's relations with the rest of the world? These are some of the crucial questions that this book tries to answer.

I

THE CONTEXT OF
LATIN AMERICAN POLITICS

INTRODUCTION: THE LAND AND THE PEOPLE

Latin America is a region of great linguistic, ethnic, geographic, and economic diversity, both within and between countries. Despite this diversity, Latin American countries share a history of political turmoil and a pattern of political development.

Including South America, Central America, Mexico, and the Caribbean island countries of Cuba, Haiti, and the Dominican Republic, Latin America encompasses 8 million square miles (21 million square kilometers), about one fifth of the world's total land area. Its population is about 600 million, almost twice that of the United States. The former Dutch and British colonies in the area are also interesting and worthy of study, and although they are part of the *geographic* region of Latin America, they are not culturally, socially, religiously, or politically "Latin" American. For this reason, they are not included in this book.

The social and racial composition of Latin America is exceedingly diverse and complicated. At the time of Columbus's "discovery" of America in 1492, some areas (Mexico, parts of Central America, Andean South America) had large numbers of indigenous people, whereas other areas did not. Even today the assimilation and integration of indigenous people into national life remains one of the great unsolved problems of these countries. Where there were few indigenous people or they died out, and when the climate was right for plantation agriculture (such as in the Caribbean islands, northeast Brazil, and some coastal areas), large numbers of African slaves were brought in. White Europeans formed the upper class and blacks were enslaved; indigenous people worked for the Europeans who had the responsibility to care for and Christianize them, and many worked on the land, either in small landholdings or as workers on large estates. Social and race relations in northeast Brazil, the Caribbean islands, and other coastal areas would then be written mainly in terms of the relations

9

between whites and blacks. On the rest of the mainland the major socioracial components remained white and indigenous. The cultures of the Spanish colonies in the Caribbean and the Portuguese in Brazil, because of the African influence, were often different from those in the other Spanish-speaking countries. In some countries, all three major racial strains (indigenous, black, white), as well as Asian and Middle Eastern, are now present.

In contrast to North America, where the colonists arrived with their wives and families to settle and farm, the conquest of Latin America was a military campaign (no women initially), and widespread mixing between whites and indigenous people, whites and blacks, blacks and indigenous, and their offspring, took place right from the beginning. This gave rise to a mulatto (white and black) element in the Caribbean and Brazil and a *mestizo* (white and Indigenous) element in the mainland countries of the Spanish empire, with endless social and racial gradations based on color, hair, and facial features. Although there is racial prejudice, because of these many variations and gradations, Latin Americans tend not to typecast people as "black," "white," or "indigenous" based solely on color as North Americans do. Indeed, in many of the Central American and Andean countries of South America, one is considered an *indio* mainly if one speaks a native language other than Spanish. Once a person moves to a city, becomes educated, and speaks Spanish, the person would probably no longer be called "indigenous." In Bolivia, long considered the Latin American country with the highest percentage of indigenous people, after urbanization, many no longer consider themselves to be *indios*. As such, the concept of race is more fluid in Latin American than in the United States.

The economies of the area are similarly diverse. A few countries (Argentina, Brazil, Uruguay) have vast, rich agricultural lands comparable to the Midwest of the United States, whereas in most of the others subsistence agriculture has predominated. Because of climate, only the southern South American countries can grow the kind of grains grown in more temperate climates; hence sugar, bananas, coffee, cacao beans, and fruits have predominated. Mexico and the larger South American countries have considerable mineral wealth and some have oil, but others have few natural resources and are likely to remain poor, regardless of whether they call themselves capitalist or socialist. Based on their resources, some countries—generally the bigger ones with large internal markets (Argentina, Brazil, Chile, Colombia, Mexico)—are "making it" in the global economy and becoming competitive with the most efficient countries. The same is true of the smaller countries of Panama and Uruguay. Another group of Latin American countries is doing moderately well economically and improving their condition. However, a number of countries (Bolivia, Paraguay, Ecuador, El Salvador, Guatemala, Haiti, Honduras, Nicaragua) are not doing well at all, and in fact are mired at the lower end of the rankings with the world's poorest nations.

The Latin American countries differ not only in people and economics, but also in geography. The continent contains the world's second-highest mountain range, the Andes (over 20,000 feet), which runs like a vertical spine up and down the Pacific Coast. Latin America also has some of the world's largest river systems (Amazon, Orinoco, Plate) but few of these connect major cities with agricultural areas or provide the internal transportation networks formed by the rivers and Great Lakes of North America. In many countries, mountains come right down to the sea, leaving little coastal land for settlement and agricultural development. Much of the interior land is similarly unsuitable for cash crops, and although some countries have iron ore, few have coal, thereby making it difficult to produce steel, one of the keys to early industrial development. Hence, although nature has been kind to Latin America in some resources, it has been stingy in others, and although a few countries are resource-rich, others are stunningly poor. The rise of commodity prices has helped benefit the resource-rich countries, but those prices could fall again—boom and bust.

One of the most startling features of South America is the vast Amazon basin, stretching nearly two thousand miles in all directions. Largely uninhabited until recently, the Amazon rain forest produces upward of 40 percent of the world's oxygen supply. Environmentalists seek to preserve this area, but Brazil and other countries on its perimeter see the Amazon's resources as the keys to their future development. Most of South America's great cities are located on the ocean coast; only in recent decades have efforts been made to populate, develop, and exploit the vast interior.

Geographically, Latin America is a land of extremes: high mountains that are virtually impassable, lowlands that are densely tropical and also difficult to penetrate, and such extremes of heat, rainfall, and climate that make living and working difficult. Latin America largely lacked the resources that the United States had during its great march to modernization in the nineteenth century, one of the key reasons it lagged behind. The mountainous, chopped-up terrain made internal communications and transportation difficult, dividing Latin America into small, isolated villages or regions and making national integration extremely difficult. Only now, with the advent of modern communications and transportation, have the Latin American countries begun to become better integrated and to develop their vast potential.

LATIN AMERICA'S ECONOMIC DEVELOPMENT

The Latin American economies were founded on a basis that was rapacious and exploitative. Under the prevailing economic theory of mercantilism, colonies such as those of Spain and Portugal existed solely for the benefit of the mother countries. The considerable gold, silver, and other resources of the colonies were drained away by the colonial powers. Latin America was cast in a position of dependency to the global powers.

The most characteristic feature of colonial Latin America was the feudal or semi-feudal estate, patterned after the European model, with Spaniards and Portuguese as the overlords and indigenous people and blacks as peasants and slaves. Even after independence, Latin America remained mainly feudal; only slowly did capitalism and an entrepreneurial ethic develop. However, the economic situation of the colonies varied considerably: The Caribbean islands and northeast Brazil were areas of large-scale sugar plantations, and Mexico, Central America, Colombia, Peru, Bolivia, and other areas of Brazil were valued for their mineral wealth. Argentina, Uruguay, and other farm areas were settled later because at the time there were better ways than agriculture to get rich quick.

The vast territory was divided among the Spanish and Portuguese conquerors, who exploited the indigenous labor living in it. Each Spanish and Portuguese *conquistador* could live like the feudal nobility: haughty, authoritarian, exploitative, and avoiding manual labor. These large estates were mainly self-sufficient, with their own priests, political authority (the landowners themselves), and social and economic life. Few areas in Latin America (Chile and Costa Rica come closest) were founded on a productive, family-farm basis.

It was only in the second half of the nineteenth century that these feudal estates began to be converted into more modern, export-oriented capitalist enterprises producing intensively for a world market as well as for domestic consumption. Foreign investment further stimulated this conversion process. From this period of economic growth onward, indigenous people and peasants were exploited even more than in the past or pushed off their communal lands into the infertile hillsides. The result was class polarization and, in Mexico, a violent revolution in 1910.

Production for the export market brought Latin America into the world economy for the first time, with both positive and negative consequences. Greater affluence led to greater political stability and new economic opportunities from roughly the 1890s to 1930s, but it also made Latin America subject to global economic forces over which it had no control, particularly in countries where 60 percent or more of export earnings depended on one crop. Price fluctuations could have dire consequences, especially during the 1929–1930 world market crash, when not only did the bottom drop out of all the Latin American economies, but their political systems collapsed as well. Almost every country in the area had a military coup d'état associated with the depression; Colombia and Mexico were exceptions.

Industrialization began in Latin America in the 1930s precisely because the countries had insufficient export earnings to purchase imported manufactured goods and therefore had to produce them on their own. Most of the heavy industries—steel, electricity, petroleum, and manufacturing—were established as state-owned industries, reflecting the weakness of entrepreneurialism and the history of mercantilism. This system of state capitalism was the beginning of Latin America's large but often bloated, inefficient, and patronage-dominated state sector.

During World War II and the postwar period, Latin America developed rapidly on the basis of this import-substitution-industrialization (ISI) model. However, growing demand for new social programs outstripped the countries' ability to pay for them, and then came the massive oil price increases of the 1970s and the debt crisis of the 1980s. Latin America was unable to pay its obligations and many countries slipped into near bankruptcy. Economic downturn again helped produce political instability in the 1960s and 1970s as it had in the 1930s.

In the 1990s and continuing in the new millennium, the Latin American economies began to recover, but in many countries the growth was anemic and debt continued to be a burden. Nevertheless, there was recovery throughout the region and many countries began to reform their economies. In an effort to become competitive in the global economy, many countries sold off inefficient public enterprises, opened previously protected economic sectors to competition, emphasized exports, and sought to reduce or streamline inefficient bureaucratic regulation. They also tried to diversify their economies internally and sought a wider range of trading partners. However, their reform efforts often produced mixed results because, although it was economically rational to reduce the size of the state, that conflicted both with social justice requirements and the political patronage demands of rewarding friends and supporters with cushy state jobs.

Chile, Brazil, and Mexico were the chief leaders and beneficiaries of the new, free-market economic policies. Several countries did moderately well as middle-income countries, but others remained poor and backward, as shown in Table 1.1. Then, the global economic crisis of 2009 brought renewed pressures for state-led growth.

Table 1.1   Indices of Modernization in Latin America, 2014–2015

Country	Population in millions	Population growth rate*	Gini index 2013	GDP growth rate*	Inflation (consumer prices)*	Life expectancy	Infant mortality****
Argentina	43.42	1	42.3	0.5	10.6	76	13
Bolivia	10.72	1.5	48.1	5.5	4.1	69	38
Brazil	207.8	0.9	52.9	0.1	9	75	14
Chile	17.94	1.1	50.5	1.9	4.3	82	8
Colombia	48.23	0.9	53.5	4.6	5.0	74	16
Costa Rica	4.80	1.1	49.2	3.5	0.8	80	10
Cuba	11.39	0.1	..	2.7***	..	80	6
Dominican Republic	10.52	1.2	47.1	7.3	0.8	74	31
Ecuador	16.14	1.5	47.3	3.7	4	76	22
El Salvador	6.12	0.3	43.5	2	−0.7	73	17
Guatemala	16.34	2	52.4**	4.2	2.4	72	29
Haiti	10.71	1.3	60.8**	2.7	9.0	63	69
Honduras	8.07	1.4	53.7	3.1	3.2	73	20
Mexico	127.01	1.3	48.1**	2.2	2.7	77	13
Nicaragua	6.08	1.1	40.5	4.7	4	75	22
Panama	3.92	1.6	51.7	6.2	0.1	78	17
Paraguay	6.63	1.3	48.3	4.7	3.1	73	21
Peru	31.37	1.3	44.7	2.4	3.6	75	17
Uruguay	3.43	0.3	41.9	3.5	8.7	77	10
Venezuela	31.10	1.4	39**	−4	121.7	74	15

Source: World Bank. World Development Report 2014.

*Annual percentage.
** 2011–2012 data.
*** 2013 data.
**** Mortality rate, under five, per one thousand live births.

CLASSES AND SOCIAL FORCES

During the colonial period, Latin America was structured on a fundamentally two-class basis. There was a small, white Hispanic or Portuguese elite at the top, and a huge mass of indigenous people, black slaves, and peasants at the bottom, with almost no one in between. The two-class system was a reflection of feudal Spain, of the medieval Christian conception of each person being fixed and situated in his or her station in life, and of slavery. This strict social hierarchy was assumed to be immutable and in accord with God's ordering of the universe; in Latin America, the rigid class structure was further reinforced by racial criteria. Over time, as miscegenation progressed, a considerable number of mixed-race mulattos and mestizos emerged, often forming a small middle class.

The onset of economic growth in the late nineteenth century and industrialization in the twentieth century eventually gave rise to new social forces, although for a long time they did not change the basic two-class structure of society. In the early stages of economic growth in the nineteenth century, a new business-commercial class began to emerge alongside the traditional landed elite, but this new class thought like the old elite, intermarried with it, and adopted the same aristocratic, haughty ethos. Similarly, as a large middle class of shop owners, small businesspeople, government workers, and professionals began to emerge in the 1930s and thereafter, it too acquired conservative attitudes, disdained manual labor, and often allied with a repressive military to prevent left-wing and lower-class movements from acquiring power. Emerging new social movements were co-opted by the elites and the two-class society was generally preserved.

During the 1930s as industrialization began, a working class also developed in Latin America; by the 1950s and 1960s peasant groups appeared; and in the 1970s and thereafter women, indigenous elements, community and neighborhood groups, and other social movements and civil society also organized. At first the elite groups (large landowners, the church, and the army) that had long dominated Latin America tried either to co-opt these groups as they had others in the past or to send the army out to repress, kill, and intimidate them. The co-optation/repression or carrot-and-stick strategies worked when these new groups were small, heading off revolution or even democracy and enabling the old power structure to survive. However, as the labor movement, peasant elements, and other civil society groups grew in power, the old techniques of co-optation/repression proved less successful. These processes then produced a variety of outcomes in Latin America: dictatorships in some countries, democracy in others, revolution in still others, and in most alternation or muddling along between rival alternatives.

Latin America today is much more pluralistic and democratic than before. There is still an old, landed, oligarchic class in most countries, but it has been largely supplanted by business, banking, industrial (including agro-industrial), and commercial groups. There is now a larger middle class that, depending on the country, may comprise 20 to 50 percent of the population. In many countries, the business and middle classes, rather than the old oligarchies, dominate. These groups tend to favor a stable democracy both because it serves their interests and because the global international community now demands it.

Since 2003 there has been rapid economic growth in most Latin American countries. Higher overall income plus some redistribution of wealth have led to growth in the middle-income sector of most countries. Recent analysis by World Bank economists is that overall, from 2003 to 2013, the percentage of people in extreme poverty declined from 24.1 percent to 11.5 percent. As a result of these changes, the extremely poor are no longer the majority; rather the largest group is made up of people who are "sandwiched between the poor and the middle class . . . who appear to make ends meet well enough as not to be counted among the poor but who do not enjoy the economic security required for membership in the middle class," a group that might be best called "the vulnerable."[1] Important questions are whether this middle sector has become a "middle class" (stable, prosperous, peaceful, democratic) in any sense and how this still vulnerable sector might have changed its politics.

At lower-class levels, important changes are also occurring. Labor is organizing; peasants are mobilizing and sometimes marching on private lands; new neighborhoods and community groups are forming. Protestantism is growing, especially evangelical groups; and women's organizations, racial and ethnic groups, and many nongovernmental organizations (NGOs) are becoming more active. At grassroots levels, many of these civil society groups have organized to get things done, often bypassing the traditional political parties, bureaucratic agencies, and patronage systems. In many countries, however, there are rivalries between these newer, more pluralistic civil society groups and the traditional, patronage-dominated ones. We must also remember that Latin America's pluralism is still more limited than US interest-group pluralism, more state-controlled, and therefore less participatory and democratic. The number of groups is small, the elites and/or the state still try to co-opt and control them, and interest group lobbying as seen in the US system is often absent. Nevertheless, Latin America is sufficiently pluralist that it is harder now to govern dictatorially, and that means a stronger base for democracy's survival.

CHANGING POLITICAL VALUES

The basic values and ideas that dominate in a society vary from country to country and from region to region. An analysis of the political values of a society includes its religious orientation, historical experience, and standard operating procedures. Political values can be determined and analyzed using literature, music, and other variables that shape the general culture. To speak of political culture, we increasingly rely on information from public opinion surveys. Political culture may change, although usually slowly. There may be two or more political cultures within a given society, and the diverse views and orientations that compose political culture may be in conflict.

Whereas the political values of the United States are mainly democratic, liberal (believing in the classic freedoms of the Bill of Rights), and committed to representative government, those of Latin America have historically been more elitist, authoritarian, hierarchical, corporatist, and patrimonial.

Latin American elitism stems from the Iberian tradition of nobility, the feudal landholding system, and a powerful tradition in Spanish-Portuguese political theory that holds that society should be governed by its "natural" elites. Authoritarianism in Latin America derived from the prevailing elitist power structure, biblical precepts and medieval Christianity's emphasis on top-down rule, and the chaotic and often anarchic conditions in Latin America that seemed to demand strong government.

The notion of a hierarchy among people derived from early Christian political ideas as well as the social/power structure of medieval Spain and Portugal that was carried over to Latin America. God was at the top of this hierarchy, then archangels, angels, and so on until we reach mankind. Rulers received their mandate from God; land, cattle, military prowess, and high social and political status were similarly believed to derive from the "Great Chain of Being," God's unchanging design for the universe. Proceeding down through society, one eventually reaches workers and peasants, who have some, though limited, rights. In the New World, indigenous people and Africans were thought to be barely human. After a long debate, the Roman Catholic Church decided that indigenous people also had souls; as a result, they were given to Spanish conquerors in *encomiendas*, through which they would work for the Spanish, who had the duty of "civilizing" and "Christianizing" the less-fortunate indigenous people. The church fathers initially decided, on the other hand, that Africans did not have souls and could therefore be enslaved, having no rights at all. It is obvious that this hierarchical conception is profoundly inegalitarian and undemocratic.

Another feature of Latin American political values is corporatism, or the organization of the nation's interest groups under state regulation and control rather than on the basis of freedom of association. The main corporate groups in Latin America have been the church; the armed forces; the landed and business elites; and, more recently, the trade union movement, peasants, women, and indigenous elements. Corporatism, which is largely unknown in US politics, is a way of both organizing and controlling interest group activity. Corporatism is thus often associated with authoritarianism and an illiberal society, and it reinforces the other undemocratic traits previously mentioned.

Patronage is another feature of traditional—and present-day—Latin American society and politics. In Latin America, patronage historically has been based on a system of mutual obligation: a favor for a favor. This is also a quasi-feudal concept with roots in Greek and Christian philosophy. Patronage manifests itself in various ways, including votes in return for gifts or money, votes in return for a government job, government contracts for friends or relatives, special access to those with good connections, and sometimes whole programs or government offices doled out in return for critical political support. At high levels patronage verges on and is corruption; at low levels, it constitutes the "grease" that keeps the machinery of government working. Patronage is inherently uneven and undemocratic: some are patrons or godfathers, others are humble petitioners.

These features of historical Latin American political values—elitism, authoritarianism, hierarchy, corporatism, and patrimonialism—remained largely intact over three centuries of colonial rule and became deeply embedded in the region's customs and political processes. However, when Latin America became independent in the nineteenth century, a new set of political values emerged based on representative institutions, even while the old political values remained strong. The result was two sets of political values, one authoritarian, the other liberal, existing side by side and vying for dominance throughout the nineteenth century and much of the twentieth. The two sets also had different social bases: the more traditional one centered in the church, the landed elite, and the military; the newer, liberal one concentrated in urban areas among intellectuals, students, the emerging middle class, and some business elements. With no one set of political values being dominant, Latin American politics were often unstable and torn by frequent civil strife between the two.

A third set of values—socialist, Marxist, social-democratic—emerged in the 1930s, particularly among students, trade unionists, and intellectuals. Some of these groups favored a full-scale Marxist-Leninist regime, others wanted a socialist redistribution of wealth, and still others advocated only greater social welfare. The common themes among them included a strong role for the state in directing change, leftist ideology, and anti-imperialism. Fidel Castro and the Nicaraguan Sandinista revolution were representative of groups during the Cold War, which in the past often looked to the Soviet Union for support. Although the collapse of the Soviet Union and of Marxist-Leninist movements and regimes worldwide led to a sharp decline in support for Marxism, leaders of a reinvigorated left, including Venezuela's Hugo Chávez and Bolivia's Evo Morales, adopted social-democratic and populist platforms in opposition to neoliberal reforms.

Meanwhile, these historical political values, or at least some of their aspects, are fading. The older notions of authority, hierarchy, and elitism, although still often present, are no longer the dominant political values. At the same time, the traditional groups that were the strongest (the church, the landed oligarchy, the army) are either changing internally or are losing influence. However, patronage and patrimonialism remain.

Latin America has modernized, democratized, and become part of the global economy. Rising literacy, urbanization, social change, immigration, globalization, and democratization are all changing the appearance and culture of Latin America. Public opinion polls reveal that a majority of citizens in most countries supports democratic rule; none of the alternatives (authoritarianism or Marxism-Leninism) has much support. And yet these same polls show that Latin Americans want effective government that delivers genuine social and economic reform.

Democracy and economic liberalism are still weak and unconsolidated in Latin America. They could still be upset in some of the weaker, poorly institutionalized countries. Moreover—and this is what makes Latin America so interesting—the form that democracy takes there is often quite different from democracy in the United States. It is more organic and centralized and still has powerful patronage and corporatism features. Latin America now has formal, electoral democracy; whether it has genuinely liberal democracy may be quite another thing. Although the changes have been vast, the continuities from Latin America's past remain powerful.

CONCLUSION: AN ASSESSMENT

Latin America's geography, economic underdevelopment, dependency conditions, socio-racial conditions, and political culture traditions have historically retarded national unity, democracy, and development. However, the great forces of twentieth and twenty-first century change—urbanization, industrialization, modernization, democratization, and now globalization—are breaking down the historical barriers and altering the foundations of traditional Latin American societies. Latin America is experiencing many of the same revolutionary transformations that the United States, western Europe, and Japan went through in earlier times. Latin America has commenced the process, but there the changes are occurring more quickly than they did in those places. The outcome is likely to include a great variety of political systems rather than some pale imitation of the United States. To us that is healthy, invigorating, challenging, and interesting.

Although the changes have been immense and often inspiring, many problems still remain. Poverty, malnutrition, and malnutrition-related disease are still endemic in many areas; too many people are ill-housed, ill-fed, ill-educated, and just plain ill. Wages are too low, the economies and democracies are often fragile, and the gap between the rich and the poor is greater than in any other area in the world. The political systems are often corrupt and ineffective; the standards of living of the rural and urban poor are woefully inadequate; and crime, violence, drug activity, and general personal insecurity are increasing. Social and economic changes often occur faster than political systems can handle them; fragmentation, ungovernability, and collapse are still lurking.

SUGGESTIONS FOR FURTHER READING

Black, Jan Knippers, ed., *Latin America: Its Problems and Promise*. 4th ed. Boulder, CO: Westview Press, 2005.

Clawson, David L., *Latin America and the Caribbean: Lands and Peoples*. New York: Oxford University Press, 1996.

Keen, Benjamin. *A History of Latin America*. 9th ed. Boston: Wadsworth, 2013.

Kicza, John E., ed. *The Indian in Latin American History: Resistance, Resilience, and Acculturation*. Wilmington, DE: Scholarly Resources, 1993.

Klein, Herbert S., and Ben Vinson. *African Slavery in Latin America and the Caribbean*. 2nd ed. New York: Oxford University Press, 2007.

Langley, Lester. *The Americas in the Modern Age*. New Haven, CT: Yale University Press, 2005.

Wiarda, Howard J. *The Soul of Latin America*. New Haven, CT: Yale University Press, 2001.

NOTES

1. Francisco H. G. Ferreira, Julian Messina, Jamele Rigolini, Luis-Felipe López-Calva, Maria Ana Lugo, and Renos Vakis, *Economic Mobility and the Rise of the Latin American Middle Class*, (Washington DC: World Bank, 2013), 1–2.

2

A BRIEF HISTORY OF LATIN AMERICA

INTRODUCTION

Latin America was exploited and pillaged by the colonial powers. Spain, Portugal, England, France, Holland, and most recently the United States have all taken advantage of Latin America. Colonialism and imperialism devastated the area. At many levels and throughout history, Latin America was brutalized, exploited, and robbed of its resources. It was an isolated dependency of the great powers, an exploited periphery kept apart from global modernizing movements, with a history of suffering.

THE CONQUEST

The conquest of the Americas by Spain and Portugal was the extension of a "reconquest" of the Iberian Peninsula that had been occurring in the mother countries for the preceding seven centuries. In the eighth century AD, the armies of a dynamic, expansionist Islam had crossed the Strait of Gibraltar from North Africa and conquered most of present-day Spain and Portugal. In the following centuries, the Christian forces of Spain and Portugal gradually retook these conquered lands, until the last of the Islamic Moors were driven out in 1492, the same year that Columbus "discovered" America. Because of the long military campaign against the Moors, which was also a religious crusade to drive out the Islamic "infidels," Spanish and Portuguese institutions tended to be authoritarian, intolerant, militaristic, and undemocratic. These same practices and institutions were carried over to Latin America.

The conquest of the Americas was one of the great epic adventures of all time; its impact was worldwide. The encounter with the New World vastly expanded humankind's knowledge, exploration, and frontiers; led to a period of prolonged European world dominance; and helped stimulate the Industrial Revolution. It also led to the brutalization, death, and isolation of much of the indigenous population.

At the time of Columbus's landing in America there were only three million indigenous people in all of the area north of Mexico, but some thirty million in Latin America. In Latin America, they were organized into large civilizations, especially the Aztec in Mexico, the Maya in southern Mexico and Central America, and the Inca in Peru and Bolivia, with five to seven million persons each. The Maya Empire, centered in the tropical lowlands of what is now Guatemala, reached the peak of its power around the sixth century AD. The Mayans excelled at agriculture, pottery, hieroglyph writing, calendar-making, and mathematics, and left behind an impressive architecture and symbolic artwork. Most of the Maya cities were abandoned by 900 AD, however, and since the nineteenth century scholars have debated what might have caused this dramatic decline.

When the Spanish arrived at Tenochtitlán, modern Mexico City, in 1519, the Aztec capital had between 100,000 and 200,000 inhabitants. During the same time period, Paris had 200,000 people while Venice, Naples, and Milan each had 100,000 and London had 60,000. In comparison, most of the North American indigenous people lived in small tribal, nomadic bands.

Whereas in North America the indigenous people were often eliminated, pushed farther west, or confined to reservations, in Latin America the large numbers and organizations of indigenous groups called for a different strategy. The Spanish tactic was usually to capture or kill the indigenous leaders, replace them with Spanish overlords, and rule them by dominating their own power structure, meanwhile seeking to Christianize and assimilate them into European ways. That was the strategy for more than five hundred years, but recently indigenous groups in such countries as Mexico, Guatemala, Colombia, Ecuador, and Bolivia have been raising the issue of indigenous rights and seeking new degrees of autonomy from the nation-states that Spain and Portugal left in their wake.

The degree of colonial influence varied from place to place. The first area impacted by Spanish colonial rule was Hispaniola, the Caribbean island that later was divided between the two independent countries of Haiti and the Dominican Republic. Here Spain carried out its first experiments in colonial rule: a slave-plantation economy, a two-class and caste society, an authoritarian political structure, and a church that served as an arm of the conquest. But Hispaniola had little gold and silver and, as the Indian population was decimated, largely by disease, Spain moved on to more valuable conquests.

Next came Cuba and Puerto Rico, but when the scarce precious metals and Indian labor supply were exhausted there also, Spain moved on to conquer Mexico and explored Florida and the North American Southeast. The conquest of Mexico by Hernán Cortés was fundamentally different from the earlier island conquests. First, Spain found a huge native civilization, the Aztecs, with immense quantities of gold and silver and a virtually unlimited labor supply, and second, Mexico's huge mainland territory finally convinced the Spaniards that they had found a new continent and not just scattered islands on the outskirts of Asia. Mexico therefore became a serious and valuable colony to be settled and colonized by Spain, not just some way station en route to somewhere else.

From Mexico, the lieutenants of Cortés fanned out to conquer Central America and the American Southwest. In the meantime, Vasco Núñez de Balboa had crossed the Isthmus of Panama to gaze out upon the Pacific, and other Spanish conquistadores had explored both the east and west coasts of South America. From Panama in the 1530s the Pizarro brothers, using the same methods Cortés had used in Mexico, moved south to conquer the vast Inca empire that stretched from southern Colombia in the north, through Ecuador and Peru, to Chile in the south. Meanwhile, Portugal had gained a foothold on the coast of Brazil that extends toward Africa. Other Spanish explorers spilled over the Andes from Peru to discover and subdue Bolivia and Paraguay and sailed down-river to present-day Buenos Aires, which had been explored in the 1530s but was not settled until the 1580s. Chile, where the Indian resistance was especially strong, was conquered in the 1570s, and other previously unconquered territories were then explored and subdued.

In less than a hundred years from the initial discovery, Mexico, the Caribbean, Central America, and all of South America, east to west and north to south, had been conquered. Spain had most of the territory; Portugal had Brazil. It was a remarkable feat in a short period of time, especially when one considers that it took North American settlers almost three hundred years to cross the continent from the Atlantic to the Pacific.

COLONIAL SOCIETY

The institutions that Spain and, less aggressively, Portugal brought to the New World reflected the institutions that had developed in the mother countries during their centuries-long struggles against the Moors and their efforts to form unified nation-states out of disparate social and regional forces. These institutions included a rigid, authoritarian political system, a similarly rigid hierarchical class structure, a statist and mercantilist economy, an absolutist church, and a similarly closed and absolutist educational system.

In the New World, the Spanish and Portuguese conquerors found abundant territory that they could claim as feudal estates; abundant wealth that enabled them to live like grandees; and a ready-made "peasantry" to exploit, in the indigenous Indian population or imported African slaves. The men who accompanied Columbus and other explorers to the New World were often the second and third sons of Spanish and Portuguese aristocrats, and under Spanish law they were prohibited from inheriting their father's land, which went to the first son. But in the New World they could acquire vast territories and servants and live like feudal overlords. The oligarchies of Latin America, then as now, were haughty, aloof, authoritarian, and disdainful of manual labor and those forced to work with their hands.

The economy was feudal and exploitative; the wealth of the colonies, in accord with the prevailing mercantilism, was drained off to benefit the mother countries and not used for the betterment of the colonies themselves. Similarly, the social structure was basically feudal and two-class, with a small group of Spaniards and Portuguese at the top, a large mass of Indians and Africans at the bottom, and almost no one in between.

Ironically, Latin America's precious metals little benefited the mother countries, but instead flowed through Spain and Portugal to England and Holland, where they helped launch the Industrial Revolution. As in the Americas, the north of Europe then forged ahead while the south fell farther behind.

Under feudalism, the land, wealth, and people were all exploited; there was almost no effort to plow back the wealth of the land into development or to raise living standards. In accord with the feudal ethic and then-prevailing values, the total social product was fixed, and people had a duty to accept their station in life. The whole system was imperialistic and exploitative.

The Roman Catholic Church reinforced royal authority and policy in the colonies and was similarly absolutist and authoritarian. Its role was to Christianize the indigenous population and thus serve the Crown's assimilationist polices. Some individual clergy sought to defend the Indians against enslavement and maltreatment, but the church was primarily an arm of the state. Intellectual life and learning, monopolized by the church, was based on rote memorization, deductive reasoning, and unquestioned orthodoxy.

ROOTS OF INDEPENDENCE

Spanish and Portuguese colonial rule lasted for more than three centuries, from the late fifteenth through the early nineteenth centuries. It was a remarkably stable period, with few revolts against the colonial system, a testimony to its efficiency. However, in the late eighteenth century the first serious cracks began to appear in this monolithic colonial structure. Under the impact of the Enlightenment, ideas of liberty, freedom, and nationalism began to creep in; the examples of the United States (1776) and French (1789) revolutions also caused tremors in Latin America. In addition, the rising Latin American commercial class sought to break the monopolistic barriers of Spanish mercantilism so as to trade freely with other countries. One of the main sources of the desire for independence was the growing rivalry between creoles (persons of Spanish background born in the colonies) and *peninsulares* (officials sent by the Spanish crown to govern the colonies). The creoles had growing economic and social influence, but the peninsulares monopolized all administrative positions. Denied the political power to go along with their rising prominence, many creoles began to think of doing away with the inconvenience of Spanish colonialism and moving toward independence.

The immediate causes of Latin American independence were precipitated by events in Europe. From 1807 to 1808 the forces of Napoleon Bonaparte invaded the Iberian Peninsula, occupied both Spain and Portugal, ousted the reigning monarchs, and placed Napoleon's brother Joseph on the Spanish throne. The Latin American creoles opposed this usurpation of royal authority by Napoleon's army and, operating under longtime medieval doctrine, moved to hold power until the legitimate king could be restored. This was, in effect, an early declaration of independence. A few years later Napoleon's forces were driven from the peninsula and the Spanish and Portuguese monarchies restored. However, when the Spanish king accepted the principle of limited monarchy and a liberal constitution, the conservative creoles in Latin America moved for independence.

The independence struggles in Latin America waxed and waned before succeeding in the 1820s. The first revolt in Argentina in 1807 was quashed by Spanish authorities, but independence fervor was also growing in Colombia, Mexico, Venezuela, and other countries. Independence sentiment waned for a time after 1814 when the Spanish monarchy was restored, but resumed again in 1820 as a result of the king's shortsighted policies.

Simón Bolívar, the "George Washington of Latin America," led the struggle against Spanish forces in Venezuela, Colombia, and Ecuador. José de San Martín liberated Argentina, then crossed the Andes to drive the Spanish forces from Chile. The key to the independence of the rest of South America was Lima, Peru, one of the most important Spanish viceroyalties and home of a sizable Spanish garrison. Bolívar came south overland and San Martín north by ship, and in the key battle of Ayacucho Bolívar's lieutenant Antonio José de Sucre defeated the royalist forces, ending Spanish authority in South America. The other main viceroyalty was Mexico City, but by 1821 independence forces were in control there, also. Once Mexico was freed, Central America, as part of the same administration, was liberated without much actual fighting. By 1826, all Spanish forces and authority were removed from mainland Latin America. Two islands, Cuba and Puerto Rico, remained Spanish colonies until 1898.

Haiti and Brazil were also special cases. In Haiti, a successful slave revolt in 1795 drove out the French colonial ruling class, destroyed the plantations, and established Haiti as the world's first black republic, unloved and unwelcome by the rest of the world (including the United States), which still practiced slavery. Brazil was a different story. When Napoleon's troops occupied Portugal in 1807, the royal family fled to Rio de Janeiro, the first reigning monarchs to set foot in Latin America. In 1821 the king, Dom João, was called back to Lisbon, but he left his son Pedro in charge of the kingdom of Brazil. The following year Pedro was also called back to Portugal, but he refused to go and declared Brazil an independent monarchy. Thus, Brazil gained independence without the upheaval and destruction of the other countries and was a monarchy for its first seventy years. Brazil escaped the tumult that soon enveloped its Spanish-speaking neighbors.

THE NEW COUNTRIES AFTER INDEPENDENCE

The independence movements in Latin America had almost all been conservative movements of separation from the mother countries rather than full-scale social or political revolutions. Led and directed by the white, aristocratic, creole elite, they were aimed at holding power for the deposed monarch and in defense of the old social hierarchy. After they later became movements for independence, they retained their elitist, conservative orientation. When social revolution raised its head, it was either isolated and despised as in Haiti or brutally repressed as in Mexico, where large-scale Indian protests had been part of the independence struggle.

The same conservative orientation was present in the laws, constitutions, and institutions established in the new republics. The franchise was extremely limited: only male literates and property owners (less than 1 percent of the population) could vote, if and when there were elections. Thus, the feudal landholding and class system was kept intact, before and after independence. The church was given a privileged position, and Catholicism in most countries remained the official religion. However, a new, similarly conservative force was added: the army, which replaced the crown as the ultimate authority. Although Latin America adopted constitutions modeled after the

United States, in reality, checks and balances, human rights, and separation of powers existed mostly in theory. The laws and constitutions of the new Latin American states enshrined the existing power structure and perpetuated paternalistic, top-down, elite rule.

With independence, the Latin American economies also went into decline, and social structures were severely disrupted. Many countries fell into chaos and the disintegrative forces set loose by independence continued. The former viceroyalty of New Granada split up into the separate nations of Colombia, Ecuador, and Venezuela; the viceroyalty of Rio de la Plata divided into the separate countries of Argentina, Paraguay, and Uruguay; and the Central American Confederation disintegrated into Guatemala, El Salvador, Honduras, Nicaragua, and Costa Rica. Within the new nations further fragmentation and confusion occurred. Only Brazil under its monarchy and Chile under a stable oligarchy escaped these divisive, disruptive, and disintegrative early postindependence forces.

Deprived of their Spanish markets but still lacking new ones, many of the countries slipped back to a more primitive barter economy, and living standards plummeted. Similarly, the old Spanish/Portuguese social-racial categories were formally abolished in most countries but were resurrected informally; at the same time the levels of education, literacy, and assimilation were so low (in many countries the majority of the population did not speak the national language, participate in the national economy, or even know that they were part of a nation-state) that pluralist and participatory democracy seemed only a distant dream. In the absence of political parties, organized interest groups, civil society, or well-established institutions of any kind, the Latin American countries sank into dictatorship or anarchy, usually alternating between the two. Internationally, Latin America was isolated and cut off from the modern, Western world. Hence the immediate postindependence period, from the mid-1820s until the mid-1850s, was in most countries a time of turbulence and decline.

EARLY ECONOMIC CHANGE

By the 1850s a degree of stability had begun to emerge in many Latin American countries. Some of the more vexing questions of early independence—sovereignty and borders, federalism versus unitarianism, church-state relations—had been resolved. By this time also the first generation of postindependence dictators had passed from the scene. Agriculture began to recover; a degree of order returned.

With increased stability at midcentury came foreign investment and greater productivity. The first banks in the region were chartered. British capital invested in the area provided a major stimulus for growth. New lands were opened to cultivation and new exports (sugar, coffee, tobacco, beef, and wool) began to restore national coffers. The first highways, railways, and port facilities were built to transport the exports to foreign markets. The telephone and telegraph were introduced. The opportunities available in Latin America began to attract immigrants from Europe, who often brought knowledge and entrepreneurial skills with them. They opened small shops and started farms and prospered; often this new wealth intermixed with older landed wealth.

As Latin America's prospects began to improve, the area attracted other investors: France, Germany, Italy, and most important, the United States, which began to replace

England as the largest investor in the area. These changes, beginning at midcentury but accelerating in the 1870s and 1880s, brought prosperity for the landed and business elites and stimulated the growth of a middle class. Peasant and Indian elements, however, often were left behind or had their lands taken from them for the sake of greater production for global growth. The changes also increased political stability, although not in all countries.

Three patterns may be observed. The first, in Argentina, Brazil, Chile, Peru, and other countries, involved the consolidation of power by an export-oriented landed oligarchy whose leaders rotated in the presidential palace over a thirty- to forty-year period. The second, in Mexico, Venezuela, and the Dominican Republic, involved the seizure of power by strong authoritarian dictators who provided both long-term stability and development. A third pattern emerged slightly later, in the first decades of the twentieth century, in the smaller, weaker, resource-poor countries of Central America and the Caribbean. It involved US military intervention and occupation and the carrying out by the Marines of many of the same policies as the order-and-progress oligarchs and dictators: pacification, infrastructure development (roads, communication, port facilities), and overall nation-building.

Two subperiods are discernible here. The first, 1850 to 1890, established the preconditions for Latin America's economic growth: greater stability, banks, investment, population increase, and infrastructure development. The second, 1890 to 1930, was the economic takeoff itself, the most stable and prosperous period in Latin American history. Under more stable regimes and exporting for the first time for a world market, Latin America began its development process, not at the rapid rate of the United States and Europe during the same period, but slowly and steadily.

Although Latin America's development was often impressive, it came under nondemocratic leadership: oligarchs, order-and-progress dictators, and US military occupations. Hence the potential for future problems was also present even amid the growing prosperity. Before the 1930s market crash caused the entire edifice to come crumbling down, in 1910 the order-and-progress dictator Porfirio Díaz was overthrown in Mexico, precipitating a bloody ten-year social revolution out of which Mexico's present political system emerged. In 1912 in Argentina and in the early 1920s in Chile a rising middle class challenged and eventually wrested political power away from the old oligarchs. These changes in some of the more advanced countries of Latin America provided a foretaste of what would occur in the other countries in later decades.

UPHEAVAL AND RESTRUCTURING

When the stock market crashed in the United States in 1929 and in Europe the following year, the effects were global. The bottom dropped out of the market for Latin America's exports, sending the economies of the area into a tailspin and crashing their political systems as well. Between 1930 and 1935 there were coups d'état in fourteen of the twenty Latin American countries, not just the usual substitution of one colonel for another but real transforming changes. The immediate causes of this collapse were economic, but deep-rooted social and political issues were also involved. By this time Latin America had a business class, a middle class, and a restless trade union movement, but power was still monopolized by the old landowning oligarchs and something had to give. The chasm between traditional holders of power and the new social and political forces clamoring for change had grown wider; the new forces were demanding change and democratization while the older elites clung to their privileges at all costs.

The 1930s Depression was the catalyst that collapsed the prevailing political as well as economic structure. The decade was thus, in the words of David Collier and Ruth Berins Collier, a "critical juncture" in Latin American history, a period in which a variety of alternative developmental models—authoritarian, quasi-fascist, populist, single party, democratic—were tried out and came to power in various Latin American countries.[1] Once the Latin American political systems had collapsed, the question was what the new regimes would be. A variety of solutions were tried. Some countries, after a brief interruption in the early 1930s, reverted to restoring oligarchic rule. In others, new, tough dictatorships (Fulgencio Batista in Cuba, Anastasio Somoza in Nicaragua, Rafael Trujillo in the Dominican Republic, Jorge Ubico in Guatemala) brought the new business and middle classes into power and stimulated development, but under authoritarian auspices. Mexico replaced the old regime with a one-party authoritarian-corporatist regime that monopolized power for the next seventy years.

In Argentina and Brazil, the regimes of Juan Perón and Getúlio Vargas, respectively, borrowed some semi-fascist features from Mussolini's Italy in an effort to bring labor unions into the system even while imposing strict controls over them. Other countries borrowed selectively from European corporatism and fascism while maintaining a democratic façade. Populism was still another option, whereas other countries—Chile and Uruguay followed by Costa Rica, Colombia, and Venezuela—moved toward democracy. The revolutionary alternative (as in Cuba and Nicaragua) came later.

Some countries rotated among several of these options or tried to combine them. Many countries are still strongly shaped by the choices made and the directions taken during this period. The Depression years of the 1930s and the later war and postwar years of the 1940s were thus a time of both uncertainty and upheaval; although the old, stable, oligarchic order had come crashing down, what would replace it was not altogether clear.

As the demand for their products rose again during World War II, the Latin American economies began to recover from the devastation of the Depression; they were also stimulated by industrialization. The postwar period continued this economic growth, enabling some countries to move toward greater prosperity and democracy while others continued under dictatorship. Although gradual economic growth was occurring throughout the region in the 1940s and 1950s and stimulating further social change, the political systems of Latin America remained divided, full of conflict, and often unstable.

A key turning point in the region and in US–Latin American relations was the Cuban revolution of 1959. Cuba became the first openly socialist country in Latin America, the first to ally itself with the Soviet Union, and the first to openly turn its back to the United States. The revolution initiated improvements in health care, education, and other social programs, although over time its economic policies proved a failure and its political system was hardly democratic.

After a brief democratic interlude in the late 1950s and early 1960s, by the late 1960s and throughout the 1970s Latin America had succumbed to a new wave of militarism.

By the mid-1970s, fourteen of the twenty countries were under military-authoritarian rule, and in three others the military was so close to the surface of power that authoritarianism ruled even if civilians were still technically in office. That left only Colombia, Costa Rica, and Venezuela as democracies, and even they were elite-directed regimes.

The causes of this throwback to military authoritarianism were basically two: economic and political. By the 1960s, Latin America's economies had become less competitive in global markets, the strategy of import-substitution-industrialization (ISI) was not working, the terms of trade had turned unfavorable (it cost Latin America more in exports of sugar, bananas, coffee, or other goods to pay for its imports than before), and the economies of the area could not pay for all the programs its citizens were demanding. Politically, the 1960s was a period when workers, peasants, and left-wing guerrillas were all mobilizing; the traditional wielders of power (elites, military) felt threatened by the mass mobilization and they thus turned to the army to keep the lower classes in check. This was called "bureaucratic-authoritarianism" rule by the institutional armed forces and their civilian supporters, as distinct from the man-on-horseback leaders of the past.

CONCLUSION

By the late 1970s, most of these military regimes were having serious difficulties and Latin America began to reverse course and return to democracy. The armed forces had often proved just as corrupt and inefficient at running governments as their civilian predecessors; they were notorious human rights abusers and thus despised by their own people, and the international community led by the United States put pressure on them to return to their barracks. There followed one of the most amazing transformations in Latin American history. By the turn of the millennium, nineteen of the twenty Latin American countries were ruled by the "third wave" of democratization that affected the entire world and surely constituted one of the most significant events of the late twentieth century.

Yet this did not mean that the Latin American countries were to have democratic governments like those of the United States and western Europe, that human rights would be respected in all the countries, or that their economies would flourish as never before. In the first decade and a half of this century, many changes have been more incremental than revolutionary. Some economies have gone through periods of boom and bust; a new form of authoritarianism has appeared. Latin America has continued to change constantly, raising new questions for scholars. Those changes are the subject of the following chapters.

SUGGESTIONS FOR FURTHER READING

Burkholder, Mark, and Lyman Johnson. *Colonial Latin America*. 8th ed. New York: Oxford, 2012.

Collier, David, ed. *The New Authoritarianism in Latin America*. Princeton, NJ: Princeton University Press, 1980.

Malloy, James, ed. *Authoritarianism and Corporatism in Latin America*. Pittsburgh: U. of Pittsburgh Press, 1977.

Skidmore, Thomas E., Peter H. Smith, and James N. Green. *Modern Latin America*. 8th ed. New York: Oxford University Press, 2013.

Veliz, Claudio. *The Centralist Tradition in Latin America*. Princeton, NJ: Princeton University Press, 1980.

Wiarda, Howard J., ed. *Authoritarianism and Corporatism in Latin America—Revisited*. Gainesville, FL: University Press of Florida, 2004.

NOTES

1. David Collier and Ruth Berins Collier, *Shaping the Political Arena: Critical Junctures, the Labor Movement, and Regime Dynamics in Latin America* (Princeton, NJ: Princeton University Press, 1991).

3

ACTORS, INTEREST GROUPS, AND POLITICAL PARTIES

INTRODUCTION

Latin American political parties and interest groups are involved in the region's current conflict between its corporatist past and a newer system based on pluralism and democracy. Since the beginning of the 1990s the conflict has been between two different views of what the political rules of the game should be. On one side are new forces that desire majority rule, human rights, and freedom of association. On the other side are those that favor traditional ways of doing things, where the emphasis was often on creating an administrative state above party and interest-group politics, and in which such agencies as the church, the army, the university, and perhaps even the trade unions were often more than mere interest groups, forming a part of the state system and inseparable from it.

Of particular importance is the nature of relationships between the government and interest groups. Although these traditionally ranged from almost complete governmental control to almost complete freedom, as under liberalism, the usual pattern involved considerably more state control over interest groups than in the United States, and this helped put interest group behavior in Latin America in a different framework than was the case in the United States. As Charles Anderson has suggested, at least until the 1980s Latin America never experienced a definitive democratic revolution—that is, a struggle resulting in agreement that elections would be the only legitimate way to obtain public power.[1] In the absence of such a consensus, political groups did not necessarily work for political power by seeking votes, the support of political parties, or contacts with elected representatives. The groups might seek power through any number of other strategies, including coercion, economic might, technical expertise, and controlled violence. Any group that could mobilize votes was likely to do so for electoral purposes, but because that was not the only legitimate route to power, the result of any election was tentative. Given the varying power of the competing groups and the incomplete legitimacy of the government itself, the duration of any government was uncertain. Political competition was a constant, virtually permanent struggle and preoccupation.

Further, group behavior in Latin America was conditioned by a set of unwritten rules that Anderson called the "living museum." Before a new group could participate in the political system, it had to demonstrate both that it had a power resource and that it would respect the rights of already existing groups. The result was the gradual addition of new groups under these two conditions but seldom the elimination of the old ones. The newest, most modern groups coexisted with the oldest, most traditionalist ones, often leading to gridlock.

A related factor was the practice of co-optation or repression. As new groups emerged as potential politically relevant actors, already established actors (particularly political parties or strong national leaders) sometimes offered to assist them in their new political activities. The deal struck was mutually beneficial to each: the new group gained acceptance, prestige, and some of its original goals, and the established group or leader gained new support and increased political resources. In some circumstances, new groups refused to be co-opted, rejecting the rules of the game. Instead, they took steps indicating to established groups and leaders that they might act in a revolutionary fashion against the interests of the established elites. In the case of a group that violated the ground rules by employing mass violence, for example, an effort was made by the established interests to repress the new group, either legally by refusing it legal standing or in some cases through the use of violence. Most commonly, such repression proved successful, and the new group disappeared or atrophied, accomplishing none of its goals. The general success of repression made co-optation seem more desirable to new groups, because obtaining some of their goals through co-optation was preferable to being repressed. In a few cases the established political groups failed to repress the emergent groups, and the latter came to power through revolutionary means, proceeding to eliminate the traditional power contenders. These are known as the true, genuine, or social revolutions in Latin America and include only the Mexican Revolution of 1910–1920, the Bolivian Revolution of 1952, the Cuban Revolution of 1959, and the Nicaraguan Revolution of 1979. Examples of the reverse process—utilization of violence and repression to eliminate the newer challenging groups and to secure in power the more traditional system—were Brazil in 1964 and Chile in 1973. Both led to the elimination of independent political parties, student associations, and labor and peasant unions as power groups.

Before the late 1980s we viewed the politically relevant groups of Latin America in this context of a historically patrimonial, corporative, and co-optive tradition. Since then, with the movement toward liberal democracy, some individuals and groups have favored the new regime while other people and organizations have preferred the historical one, and throughout Latin America there has been conflict between the new supporters of democracy and the supporters of the traditional system. Peru and Guatemala hold special interest in this regard, as both are cases where presidents tried to govern within the old, unwritten rules rather than the new, written ones incorporated in constitutional and democratic precepts.

THE TRADITIONAL OLIGARCHY

After independence, three groups that comprised what can be called the nineteenth-century oligarchy were predominant in Latin America: the military, the Roman Catholic Church, and the large landholders. Through the process of economic growth and change new groups emerged: first commercial elites; later industrial elites, students, and middle-income sectors; then industrial labor unions and peasants; and most recently groups representing indigenous people, women, consumers, nongovernmental organizations, and many others. Political parties have existed throughout the process. Particularly since the end of the nineteenth century, the United States has been a relevant force in the domestic politics of the Latin American countries.

The Armed Forces

During the wars for independence, the Spanish American countries developed armies led by a great variety of individuals, including well-born creoles, priests, and people of humbler backgrounds. The officers did not come from military academies but were self-selected or chosen by other leaders. Few of the officers had previous military training, and the armies were much less professional than armies today.

Following independence, the military element continued as one of the first important power groups. The national army was supposed to be preeminent, and in some countries national military academies were founded in the first quarter century after independence. Yet the national military was challenged by other local or regional armies. The early nineteenth century was a period of limited national integration, with regional subdivisions of the countries often dominated by local landowners or *caudillos*, charismatic leaders who had their own private armies. One aspect of the development of Latin America was the struggle between the central government and its army on one hand and the local caudillos on the other, with the former winning in most cases. One of the unanswered questions about Latin American politics even today is the extent to which outlying areas of the countries, in the mountains or jungles, are effectively covered by the laws made in the national capitals.

The development of Brazil varied somewhat from the norm because Portugal was the colonizing power and because there was no war for independence. The military first gained prominence in the Paraguayan War (1864–1870). Until 1930, the Brazilian states had powerful militias, in some cases of comparable strength to the national army.

Although Latin American militaries varied in the nineteenth century, two general themes applied. First, various militaries, including the national one, became active in politics. At times, they were regional or personal organizations; at others, they were parts of political parties that were participants in the civil wars frequently waged between rival factions. However, national militaries also often played the role of a moderating power, staying above factional struggles and preferring that civilians govern, but taking power temporarily when the civilians could not rule effectively. Although not emerging in all countries, this moderating power was seen in most, and especially in Brazil, where, with the abdication of the emperor in 1889, the military became the chief moderator in the system.

As early as the 1830s and 1840s in Argentina and Mexico, and later in the other Latin American countries, national military academies were established. Their goal was to introduce professionalism into the military, requiring graduation rather than elite family connections for officer status. These academies were for the most part successful in making entry to and promotion within the officer corps proceed in a routinized manner, and by the 1950s Latin American officers were appointed as generals, with potential political power, only after a career of some twenty years.

Through professionalization, the military career was designed to be a highly specialized one that taught the skills for warfare but eschewed interest in political matters. Being an officer would supposedly absorb all an individual's energy, and officers' functional expertise would be distinct from that of politicians. Civilians were to have complete control of the military, which would stay out of politics. However, this model of professionalism, imported from western Europe and the United States, never took complete root in Latin America. In the absence of strong civilian institutions, the military continued to play politics and to exercise its moderating power, and coups d'état continued.

By the late 1950s and early 1960s a change had occurred in the nature of the role of the military in Latin America. The success of guerrilla revolutions in China, Indochina, Algeria, and Cuba led to a new emphasis on the military's role in counterinsurgency and internal defense functions. In addition, Latin American militaries—encouraged by US military aid—began to assume responsibility for civic action programs, which assisted civilians in the construction of roads, schools, and other public projects. The new professionalism, with its emphasis on counterinsurgency, was a product of the Cold War and may have been more in keeping with Latin American political culture than the old professionalism had been. Military skills were no longer viewed as separate or different from civilian skills. The military was to acquire the ability to help solve national problems that might lead to insurgency, a task that was in its very essence political rather than apolitical. The implication of the new professionalism was that, besides combating active guerrilla factions, the military would ensure the implementation of social and economic reforms necessary to prevent insurgency if the civilians proved incapable of doing so. The new professionalism in Latin America led to more military intervention in politics, not less.

The end result of this process was bureaucratic authoritarianism, the rule of the military institution on a long-term basis.[2] Seen especially in Argentina, Brazil, Chile, Peru, and Uruguay, this new form of military government involved the institution as a whole—not an individual general—and was based on the idea that the military could govern better than civilians. The bureaucratic authoritarian period, during which the military often governed repressively and violated human rights, lasted from the mid-1960s through the late 1970s.

Since the 1980s the Latin American militaries have begun transitions to subservience to civilian control and support of democratically elected presidents. The transformation has had its difficulties, with militaries supporting a president who dismissed congress and the courts (Peru), playing a key role in overthrowing a president who attempted the same maneuver (Guatemala), putting down coups d'état against chief executives (Venezuela), helping civilian groups to depose unpopular presidents (Ecuador), and failing to intervene even though key elements of public opinion and the US ambassador apparently favored getting rid of the elected president (Colombia).

It has always been difficult to compare the Latin American militaries cross-nationally. Similarly, trying to distinguish "civilian" and "military" regimes was a difficult task at best and sometimes a meaningless one. Often military personnel temporarily resigned their commissions to take leadership positions in civilian bureaucracies or as government ministers. They often held military and civilian positions at the same time. In some cases, an officer resigned his commission, was elected president, and then governed with strong military backing. In almost all instances, coups d'état were not just simple military affairs but were supported by groups of civilians as well. It was not unheard of for civilians to take a significant part in the ensuing governments. Sometimes civilians actually drew the military into playing a larger political role. In short, Latin American governments were often coalitions established between certain factions of the militaries and certain civilian factions in an attempt to control the system.

We suggest that several dimensions of military involvement in politics be considered in the chapters about individual countries that follow. First is whether the military still forcefully removes chief executives, an activity that now has become a thing of the past in most countries. The second is the extent to which military leaders have a say in non-military matters. Although in the past generals have protected their large-landowner friends and relatives, that phenomenon may also be passing. The last is the extent to which the role of moderating power still obliges the military to step in and unseat an incompetent president or one who has violated the rules of the game.

The Roman Catholic Church

All Latin American countries were nominally Catholic, although the form of that religion varied from country to country. The Spanish and Portuguese came to "Christianize the heathens" as well as to seek precious metals. In areas with a heavy concentration of indigenous peoples, religion became a mixture of pre-Columbian and Roman Catholic beliefs. To a lesser degree, Catholicism later blended with African religions, which also existed on their own in certain areas, especially in Brazil and Cuba. Religion in the large cities of Latin America is similar to that in the urban centers of the United States and western Europe, while in the more isolated small towns, Roman Catholicism is still of fifteenth-century vintage.

The power of the church hierarchy in politics also varies. The church traditionally was one of the main sectors of Spanish and Portuguese corporate society, with rights and responsibilities in such areas as care for orphans, education, and public morals. Beginning in the nineteenth century, some laypeople wanted to strip the church of all its temporal power, including its lands. Generally speaking, the conflict over the role of the church ended in most countries by the first part of the twentieth century.

Between the 1960s and the 1980s the church changed, especially if by "church" we mean the top levels of the hierarchy that control the religious and political fortunes of the institution. These transformations were occasioned by the new theologies of the previous hundred years, as expressed through various papal encyclicals, Vatican II, and the conferences of the Latin American bishops at Medellín, Colombia, in 1968 and Puebla, Mexico, in 1979. Significant numbers of bishops (and many more parish priests and members of the various orders) subscribed to what was commonly called liberation theology. This theology stressed that the church was of and for this world and should take stands against repression and violence, including the demeaning and life-threatening institutionalized violence experienced by the poor of the area. Liberation theology also stressed the equality of all believers, laypeople as well as clerics and bishops, as opposed to the former stress on hierarchy. The end result, in some parts of the region, was new popular-level churches with lay leadership and only minimal involvement of priests.

It would be a mistake to assume that all, or even most, members of the Latin American clergy ever subscribed to liberation theology. Many believed that the new social doctrine had taken the church more into politics than it should be. Some were concerned with the loss of traditional authority that the erosion of hierarchy brought. The various countries of Latin America differ substantially in church authority and adherence of the bishops to liberation theology.

As a result of these changes, the clergy is no longer uniformly conservative; rather, its members differ on the role that the church should play in socioeconomic reform and on the nature of hierarchical relations within the church. At one extreme of this conflict is the traditional church elite, usually with social origins in the upper class or aspirations to be accepted by it, still very conservative, and with close connections to other supporters of the status quo. At the other end of this conflict are those priests, of various social backgrounds, who see the major objective of the church as assisting the masses to obtain social justice. In some cases, these priests have been openly revolutionary, fighting in guerrilla wars. Other priests fall between these two extremes of political ideology, and still others favor a relaxing of the rigid hierarchy, giving more discretion to local parish priests.

Liberation theology had its critics outside of Latin America. The Congregation for the Doctrine of the Faith, headed by German cardinal Joseph Ratzinger (later Pope Benedict XVI), strongly opposed certain elements of liberation theology. In both 1984 and 1986 the Vatican officially condemned liberation theology's acceptance of Marxism and armed violence. In 1985 Leonardo Boff, a Brazilian leader in the liberation theology movement, was "condemned to 'obsequious silence' and was removed from his editorial functions and suspended from religious duties." Although some argue that liberation theology weakened as the Marxist world disappeared, it did not disappear. In mid-2007 the Vatican strongly criticized the work of the Jesuit father Jon Sobrino, who was born in Spain but had been working in El Salvador since the 1980s. The Congregation for the Doctrine of the Faith warned pastors and all other Catholics that Father Sobrino's work contained "erroneous or dangerous propositions."[3] The church still participates in politics to defend its interests, although in most cases its wealth is no longer in land. Certain church interests are still the traditional ones: giving religious instruction in schools, running parochial high schools and universities, and occasionally attempting to prevent divorce legislation and to make purely civil marriage difficult. At times the church has been a major proponent of human rights, especially when military governments deny them. A touchier issue has been that of birth control, and in most cases the Latin American hierarchies have fought artificial methods. However, in the face of the population explosion many church officials have assisted in family planning clinics, turned a blind eye when governments have promoted artificial methods of birth control, and occasionally even assisted in those governmental efforts.

Some analysts feel the Roman Catholic Church in Latin America is no longer a major contender. They argue that on certain issues its sway is still considerable but that the church is no longer as influential politically as the army, the wealthy elites, or the US embassies. Modernization, urbanization, and secularism have also taken their toll on church attendance and the institution's political power. However, that has not prevented church leaders from making statements in recent years in opposition to abortion and same-sex marriage.

On March 13, 2013, Jorge Mario Bergoglio, an Argentine Jesuit whose parents were of Italian background, was elected the 266th pope of the Roman Catholic Church. Choosing the name of Francis, he was the first pope from Latin America. The new pope has been progressive in many of his statements; however, to this point there has been little change in Latin America.

In recent decades, Protestant religious groups have grown rapidly in Latin America. In some countries, Protestants constitute 25 to 35 percent or more of the population. The fastest-growing of these sects were the evangelical ones, not the older mainline churches. In Guatemala, a Protestant general, Efraín Rios Montt, became dictator for a time. Two Protestant evangelicals, Jorge Serrano Elías and Jimmy Morales, have served as president of Guatemala. El Salvador's first evangelical president, Tony Saca, was also the first to be sworn in by a Protestant pastor. Protestantism has been identified with a strong work ethic, obliging its members to work hard and save, and social conservativism. Until recently, however, the Protestant groups have generally not become politically active.

Large Landowners

In all the countries of Latin America except Costa Rica and Paraguay, the colonial period led to the establishment of a powerful group of individuals who had received large tracts of land as royal grants. With the coming of independence, these landowners wielded more influence than before and developed into one of the three major power groups of nineteenth-century politics.

This was not to say that they operated monolithically; sometimes they were pitted against each other. In recent times, such rifts have remained among the large landowners, usually along the lines of crop production. However, the major conflict has been between those who have large tracts of land and the many landless people. In those circumstances the various groups of large landowners tend to coalesce. Sometimes there is an umbrella organization to bring all of the various producer organizations together formally; at other times the coalition is much more informal.

In the 1960s the pressures for land reform were considerable, both from landless peasants and from foreign and domestic groups who saw this type of reform as a way to achieve social justice and to avoid Castro-like revolutions. In some countries, such as Mexico, land reform had previously come by revolution; in others, such as Venezuela, a good bit of land had been distributed by the government to the landless; in still others, the power of the landed, in coalition with other status quo groups, led to merely the appearance of land reform rather than actual changes. In some Latin American countries, especially those in which the amount of arable land is limited and the population has exploded, the issue of breaking up large estates will continue for the foreseeable future.

Since the 1960s, with Latin America rapidly urbanizing, the rural issue has become less important. The traditional landowners still dominate in some countries, but in others power has passed to newer commercial and industrial elites. Although land reform may still be necessary in some areas, with large percentages of the population moving to the cities many of the main social issues have become urban rather than rural.

OTHER MAJOR INTEREST GROUPS

Commercial and Industrial Elites

Although not part of the traditional oligarchy, commercial elites have existed in Latin America since independence; one of the early political conflicts was between those who wanted free trade (the commercial elites and allied landed interests producing crops for export) and those who wanted protection of nascent industry (industrial elites with allied landed groups not producing for export). In recent decades, the strength of these commercial and industrial groups has steadily grown.

With the exception of Colombia, the real push for industrialization in Latin America did not come until the Great Depression and World War II, when Latin America was cut off from trade with the industrialized world. Before those crises industrial goods from England and the United States were cheaper, even with transportation costs and import duties, than locally produced goods.

Between the mid-1930s and the mid-1980s, Latin American countries experienced import-substitution industrialization (ISI)—that is, producing goods that formerly were imported from industrialized countries. This was the case in light consumer goods; in some consumer durables, including assembly of North American and European automobiles; and in some other heavy industries such as cement and steel. Because import substitution necessitated increased foreign trade to import capital goods, there was no longer much conflict between commercial and industrial elites: expanded trade and industrialization go together.

Since the 1980s neoliberal presidents in Latin America have been pushing for more foreign commerce in a world with trade barriers that are lower or do not exist at all. In this internationalization of the Latin American economies, foreign trade is of utmost importance. Hence so are the commercial elites. Mexico entered a free trade association with the United States and Canada in 1994 through the North American Free Trade Agreement (NAFTA), Central America and the Dominican Republic entered into a similar association with the United States in 2005 through the Central American Free Trade Association (CAFTA), and in separate agreements Colombia and Peru began free trade agreements with the United States in 2011. The goal is to have a free trade association covering all of the Americas, from Alaska to Tierra del Fuego.

A complicating factor is the industrial elite's relationship with the landed elite. In some countries, such as Argentina, the early industrialists were linked to the landed groups; later, individuals who began as industrialists invested in land. The result was two intertwined groups, a marriage of older landed and newer moneyed wealth, with only vague boundaries separating them and with some families and individuals straddling the line. All these groups were opposed to agrarian reform.

Industrialists and commercial elites, who are strategically located in major cities of Latin America, are highly organized in various chambers of commerce, industrial associations, and the like. They generally favor a status quo that profits them. They are often the driving forces in Latin American economic development; for this reason and because they are frequently represented in high official circles, no matter what government is in control, they are very powerful. Neoliberalism and globalism have made these groups even more essential to the functioning of the economy, and hence also to the political system.

The Middle Sectors

With economic growth, the percentage of Latin Americans who are in the middle class has increased, with some suggesting that a majority of Mexicans are now in that group. Although the Latin American countries began independence with a basically two-class system, there have always been individuals who fell statistically into the middle ranges, neither very rich nor abjectly poor. These few individuals during the nineteenth century were primarily artisans and shopkeepers; later this group included doctors and lawyers. The emergence of a larger middle sector was a twentieth-century phenomenon, associated with urbanization, technological advances, industrialization, and the expansion of public education and the role of the government.

All of these changes necessitated a large number of white-collar, managerial workers. New teachers and government bureaucrats constituted part of this sector, as did office workers in private businesses. In addition, small businesses grew, particularly in the service sector of the economy. Many of these new non-manual-labor professions have been organized, including teachers, small-business owners, lawyers, and government bureaucrats. Military officers, university students, political party officials, and even union and peasant group leaders are usually considered middle class.

The people who filled the new middle-sector jobs were the product of social mobility, with some coming from the lower class and others "fallen aristocrats" from the upper class. Their numerous and heterogeneous occupations temporarily impeded the formation of a sense of common identity as members of a middle class. Indeed, in some of the Latin American countries this identification has yet to emerge.

In those countries of Latin America in which a large middle-sector group first emerged, certain generalizations about its political behavior can be made. In the early stages of political activities, coalitions tended to be formed with groups from the lower classes against the more traditional and oligarchic groups in power. Major goals included expanded suffrage, the promotion of urban growth and economic development, a greater role for public education, increased industrialization, and social welfare programs.

In the later political evolution of the middle sectors the tendency was to side with the established order against rising mass or populist movements. In some cases the middle-class movements allied with landowners, industrialists, and the church against their working-class partners of earlier years; in other cases, when the more numerous lower class seemed ready to take power on its own, the middle sectors were instrumental in fomenting a middle-class military coup, to prevent "premature democratization" (a democratic system that the middle sectors could not control).[4] Because the status of the middle class varies greatly in Latin America, a number of factors should be considered when reading the chapters about individual countries, including the size of the middle-income group, its cohesion and relationships with political parties, and the degree of self-identification as members of a "middle class." Only time will tell whether the middle sectors will serve as a new, invigorated social base for democracy or whether they will continue to imitate the upper class and thus perpetuate an essentially two-class and polarized social structure.

Labor Unions

From its inception, organized labor in Latin America has been highly political. Virtually all important trade union groups of the area have been closely associated with a political party, strong leader, or government. On some occasions labor unions have grown independently until they were co-opted or repressed. In other cases, labor unions have owed their origins directly to the efforts of a party, leader, or government.

Latin American unionism was influenced by ideological currents that came from southern Europe, including anarchist and Marxist orientations. In addition, three characteristics of the Latin American economies favored partisan unionism. First, unions came relatively early in the economic development of the region—in most cases earlier than in the United States and western Europe. Second, the labor pool of employables has been much larger than the number who can get the relatively well-paid jobs in industry. An employer in that situation could almost always find people to replace striking workers unless they were protected by a party or by the government. Finally, inflation has been a chronic problem in Latin America, making it important for unions to win the support of other political groups in the continual renegotiation of contracts to obtain higher salaries, which often need governmental approval.

The Latin American legal tradition required that unions be officially recognized by the government before they could bargain collectively. If a group could not obtain or retain this legal standing, it had little power. Labor legislation, in addition, varied greatly, including codes mandating that labor organizers be employed full-time by the industry they were organizing, limiting the power of unions that lacked leaders who were paid full salaries to spend part of the working day in union activities. This was only one of the many governmental restrictions placed on labor unions.

Some union organizations were co-opted by the state; others remained outside the system. Key questions to consider when reading the country chapters include the extent to which workers are organized, how the labor code is used to prevent or facilitate worker organization, the nature of the relationships between labor and the political parties or between labor and the government, and the extent to which unions have been co-opted or repressed. Are the unions a declining or growing interest in Latin America?

Peasants

The term *peasant* refers to many different kinds of people in Latin America. Some prefer the Spanish term *campesinos* (people who live in the *campo,* the countryside) rather than the English term with its European-based connotations. The major groups of campesinos, who vary in importance from country to country, include indigenous groups who speak only their native language or who are bilingual in that language and Spanish; workers on the traditional haciendas, tilling the fields in return for wages or part of the crops, with the owner as a patron to care for the family or, more frequently, a manager-patron who represents the absentee owner; workers on modern plantations, receiving wages but remaining outside of the older patron-client relationship; individuals with a small landholding, legally held, of such a size that a bare existence is possible; people who cultivate small plots but have no legal claim to that land, perhaps moving every few years after the slash-and-burn method and the lack of crop rotation deplete the soil; and those who have been given a small plot of land to work by a landowner in exchange for labor on the large estate.

What all of these campesinos have in common, in the context of the extremely inequitable distribution of arable lands in Latin America, is a marginal existence due to their small amount of land or income and a high degree of insecurity due to their uncertain claims to the land they cultivate. It was estimated in 1961 that more than 5 million very small farms (below 30 acres, or 12 hectares) occupied only 3.7 percent of the land, while, at the other extreme, 100,000 holdings of more than 1,500 acres (607 hectares) took up some 65 percent of the land. Three decades later, the situation had changed little. At least eighty million people still lived on small landholdings with insufficient land to earn even a minimum subsistence, or they worked as agricultural laborers with no land at all. For many of these rural people their only real chance of breaking out of this circle of poverty was to move to an urban area, where they faced another—in some ways even worse—culture of poverty. For those who remained on the land, unless there was a dramatic restructuring of ownership, the present subhuman existence was likely to continue. Moreover, as commercial agriculture for export increased in many countries, the campesinos were increasingly shoved off the fertile lands into the sterile hillsides, where their ability to subsist became more precarious.

Rural peasant elements have long been active in politics, but only recently as independent, organized interest groups. The traditional political structure of the countryside was one in which participation in national politics meant taking part in the patronage system. The local patrons, besides expecting work on the estate from the campesino, expected certain political behavior. In some countries, this meant that the campesino belonged to the same political party as the patron, voted for that party on election day, and, if necessary, served as cannon fodder in its civil wars. In other countries, the national party organizations never reached the local levels, and restrictive suffrage laws prevented the peasants from participating in elections. In both patterns, for the peasants there was no such thing as national politics, only local politics, which might or might not have national party labels attached to the local person or groups in power.

This traditional system still exists in many areas of Latin America. However, since the 1950s signs of agrarian unrest and political mobilization have been more and more evident. In many cases, urban political parties, especially those of the Marxist left, organized major agrarian movements. Some of these peasant movements were based in revolutionary agrarianism, seeking to reform and improve the land tenure system and to significantly reform the entire power structure of the nation. They employed strategies that included the illegal seizure of land, the elimination of landowners, and armed defense of the gains thus achieved. Less radical were the movements that sought to reform the social order partially through the elimination of a few of the most oppressive effects of the existing power structure, but without threatening the power structure itself.

EMERGING GROUPS

Many newly influential groups have appeared in Latin America in recent decades. Three of particular importance are indigenous groups, women's groups, and nongovernmental organizations (NGOs).

Indigenous Groups

Indigenous peoples constitute about 8 percent of the total population of Latin America, or an estimated forty million people. In some four hundred distinct groups, they are concentrated in southern Mexico, parts of Central America, and the central Andes of South America. In these states, they make up between 10 to 70 percent of the population. Some individual language groups have more than one million members. A dozen groups have more than a quarter million members, in total making up some 73 percent of the indigenous population of the region. Finally, two groups have less than one thousand members.

In the 1970s, Indian populations in Latin America began to mobilize politically in unprecedented ways to protect their lands and cultures from the increasing influence of multinational companies, colonists, the state, and other intruders. In the 1980s, they placed a greater emphasis on the recuperation of ethnic identities and the construction of a pan-indigenous cultural identity. Contemporary Latin American indigenous organizations seek equal status for their cultures, forms of social organization and laws to advance their interests, and the means to facilitate and control their economic development. Their ultimate goal is the transformation of what they view to be a discriminatory, homogeneous state into a "plurinational state," one whose institutions reflect the cultural diversity of society. In the 1990s, seven Latin American states—Bolivia, Colombia, Ecuador, Mexico, Nicaragua, Peru, and Paraguay—recognized a milder version of this claim, declaring their societies "pluricultural and multiethnic." At the same time, many individuals of indigenous background continue to follow the traditional assimilationist strategy of seeking to integrate themselves into Hispanic culture.

The main component of rising indigenous nationalism is the struggle for territorial, political, economic, and cultural autonomy. Until 1987 only the Kuna of Panama enjoyed what could be described as territorial and political autonomy. In 1987, the Nicaraguan government established two multiethnic autonomous regions to accommodate claims of the Miskitu and other smaller groups that had joined the anti-Sandinista counterrevolutionary guerrilla movement supported by the United States. Although the autonomous regions were largely a failure in terms of indigenous peoples' aspirations, their establishment inspired indigenous organizations throughout Latin America to make similar claims.

Only Colombia's indigenous population has achieved politico-territorial autonomy. The 1991 Colombian constitution elevated indigenous reservations to the status of municipal governments; recognized indigenous traditional leaders as public authorities and, with some restrictions, indigenous customary law as public and binding; and provided guaranteed representation in the national senate. The governments of Bolivia, Ecuador, Guatemala, and Mexico considered some type of politico-territorial autonomy arrangements following constitutional reforms or peace agreements with armed groups concluded in the 1990s.[5] The most notable cases of members of indigenous groups taking part in national politics were the election of Alejandro Toledo in Peru in 2001 and the election of Evo Morales in Bolivia in 2006. Although the Toledo presidency was troubled (see Chapter 12), the Morales presidency is still a work in progress (see Chapter 16).

Women's Groups

Women in Latin America are making progress in ascending to leadership positions in government, politics, and civil society. Many women's groups played a prominent role in the struggles against authoritarian rule in the 1970s and 1980s. The consolidation of democracy was expected to promote greater participation of women in the formulation and execution of laws governing their lives. From 1994 to 2004 women's participation rose, on average, from 9 to 14 percent in the executive branch (in ministerial positions), from 5 to 13 percent in the senate, and from 8 to 15 percent in the lower house or unicameral parliament.[6] In that decade women's presence in the public spheres of the economy and society also grew. Such growth is a reflection of social changes such as women's entry into the labor force, rising educational levels, and changing attitudes about the role of women.

During the past two decades, more women have been elected to high-ranking positions. Most notably, six women were elected presidents in their countries: Violeta Barrios de Chamorro in Nicaragua in 1990, Mireya Moscoso de Gruber in Panama in 1999, Michelle Bachelet in Chile in 2006 and 2013, Cristina Fernández de Kirchner in Argentina in 2007 and 2011, Dilma Rousseff in Brazil in 2010, and Laura Chinchilla in Costa Rica in 2010.

As of 2014, women held approximately 26 percent of cabinet positions in the region. In some countries, such as Bolivia and Nicaragua, women held more than 30 percent of cabinet positions. Colombia requires at least 30 percent of administrative positions to be held by women. On average, women hold between 23–25 percent of seats in national legislatures. In 2016, women occupied more than 40 percent of seats in one or both houses in Bolivia, Cuba, Mexico, Ecuador, and Nicaragua. Only the Nordic countries had a higher regional average. By comparison, women held only 19.4 percent of seats in the United States Congress.

Between 2001 and 2011 the number of female judges increased from 10 percent to 22.6 percent. Although women tend to be better represented as trial judges, approximately 22 percent of supreme court judges in the region were women. In countries, such as Venezuela, Costa Rica, Colombia, and Nicaragua, women represented more than 30 percent of supreme court judges. In the developing world, only Central and Eastern Europe had a higher percentage of women in the judicial system.[7]

Figures on women's representation in politics show that their opportunities to exercise leadership are greater outside the main centers of power, in the lower levels of organizational hierarchy, outside the capital city area, and in less powerful governmental agencies.

One important consequence of women's organizing has been the adoption of quota laws, intended to increase women's representation in political office. After pressure from organized women's groups, Argentina, Bolivia, Brazil, Costa Rica, the Dominican Republic, Ecuador, El Salvador, Mexico, Nicaragua, Panama, Peru, and Uruguay have passed national laws requiring political parties to reserve 20 to 50 percent of legislative candidacies for women. Of course, that women are nominated does not necessarily mean that they are elected. Colombia enacted a law making it mandatory that mayors have women as one-third of their appointed officials, but the law is not always followed.

Despite the growth of women's representation, the women's movement has appeared to some observers to be increasingly fragmented and to have lost its visibility and capacity for political intervention. The obstacles to women's full participation in Latin American democracies and economies stem from women's weaker social position, traditional gender roles and the cultural expectations and stereotypes built around these roles, and blatant sex discrimination. Few Latin American countries have made efforts to make motherhood and work compatible. No Latin American country has a comprehensive child care policy. Although most countries have laws requiring businesses that employ twenty or more women to have on-site day care facilities, these laws are rarely enforced. Pregnancy discrimination is widespread in the region, with some companies requiring a pregnancy test or a sterilization certificate as a condition of employment. Some fire women once they become pregnant. Although both actions are against the law, the laws are seldom enforced. Access to abortion remains controversial. Chile, El Salvador, the Dominican Republic, Haiti, Honduras, and Nicaragua have total bans on abortion, meaning there is no provision for rape, incest, or to save the life of the mother. In El Salvador, abortion is criminalized, with lengthy jail terms for women and abortion providers. In many countries, emergency contraception is also banned. Although cultural changes coming from women's improving position will help erode such discriminatory barriers, this is likely to happen only in the very long run.

Nongovernmental Organizations

Nongovernmental organizations (NGOs), a newer type of group, are increasingly important actors in Latin American politics. Although some are specific to individual countries, others are based on a general theme and have offices in many Latin American countries. Some NGOs are transnational, with headquarters in one country and activities in many countries. Amnesty International, the Environmental Defense Fund, and the Red Cross are transnational NGOs that have influenced recent events in Latin America. Local NGOs are shaping contemporary politics too. For example, NGOs are providing community services in Mexico, raising racial consciousness in Brazil, extending credit to poor people in Colombia, defending indigenous peoples in Bolivia, and asserting women's rights in Argentina. Unlike interest groups, NGOs do not focus their activities exclusively on governments. They also work to change the policies of international institutions such as the World Bank, the practices of private businesses and entire industries, and the behavior of individuals and society as a whole.

POLITICAL PARTIES

In Latin America, political parties have often been only one set of groups among several, probably no more (and perhaps less) important than the army or the economic oligarchy. Elections were not the only legitimate route to power, nor were the parties themselves particularly strong or well organized. They were important actors in the political process in some of the more democratic countries, representing the chief means to gain high office. But frequently in other countries the parties were peripheral to the main focal points of power and the electoral arena was considered only one among several. Many Latin Americans have viewed political parties as divisive elements and hence they are not held in high esteem. This increasingly seems to be the case in recent years as candidates use the mass media rather than parties to get elected.

Many of the groups described earlier in this chapter have often joined into political parties in their pursuit of governmental power. As a result, there has been a myriad of political parties in the history of Latin America. Indeed, someone once quipped that to form a political party all you needed was a president, vice president, secretary-treasurer, and rubber stamp. (If times were bad, you could do without the vice president and the secretary-treasurer!) Peter Smith shows that during the period of democracy since 1978 there have been more political parties in most Latin American countries than there were during the 1940–1977 period.[8] Nevertheless, there have been certain characteristics common to parties, although the country chapters that follow show great national variation.

The first parties were usually founded by elite groups in competition with other factions of the elite. Mass demands played only a small role, although campesinos were sometimes mobilized by the party leaders, often to vote as they were instructed or to serve as cannon fodder. In many cases the first cleavage was between individuals in favor of free trade, federalism, and anticlericalism (the liberals) and those who favored protectionism for nascent industry, centralism, and clericalism (the conservatives). In most countries, these original party divisions have long since disappeared, replaced by other cleavages.

With accelerating social and economic change in most countries of Latin America, the emergence of new social strata in the 1920s and 1930s led to the founding of new political parties. Some of these attracted the growing middle sectors, which were quite reformist in the early years but later changed as they became part of the system. In other cases, new parties were more radical, calling for a basic restructuring of society and including elements from the working classes. Some of these originally radical parties were of international inspiration; most of the countries where they emerged have had Communist and socialist parties of differing effectiveness and legality. Other radical parties were primarily national ones, albeit with ideological inspiration traceable to Marxism.

One such party, founded in 1923 by the Peruvian Víctor Raúl Haya de la Torre, was the American Popular Revolutionary Alliance (APRA). Although APRA purported to be the beginning of a new international association of like-minded democratic-left individuals in Latin America, this goal was never fully reached. At the same time, inspired by Haya and APRA, a number of similar national parties were founded by young Latin Americans. The most successful APRA-like party was Democratic Action (AD) in Venezuela, but many of the same programs have been advocated by numerous other parties of this type, including the Party of National Liberation (PLN) in Costa Rica and the National Revolutionary Movement (MNR) in Bolivia, as well as parties in Paraguay, the Dominican Republic, Guatemala, Honduras, and Argentina. Only in Venezuela and Costa Rica did the APRA-like parties come to power more than temporarily, and in a much less radical form. They favored liberal democracy, rapid reform, and economic growth. In most cases the APRA-like parties were led by members of the middle sectors, and they received much of their electoral support from the middle and lower classes. APRA came to power in Peru in 1986, although founder Haya was no longer living.

A newer group of political parties was the Christian-Democratic ones, particularly successful in Chile, Venezuela, Costa Rica, Nicaragua, and El Salvador. These parties often call for fundamental reforms but are guided by church teachings and papal encyclicals rather than Marx or Engels, even though they are nondenominational and open to all. The nature of the ideology of these parties varies from country to country.

Other parties in Latin America have been based on the leadership of a few people or even a single one, and hence do not fit into the neat party categories just described. Quite often the caudillo was more important than the program of a party. This tradition was seen in Brazil, where Getúlio Vargas founded not one but two official political parties; in Ecuador, where personalistic parties have been strong contenders for the presidency; and in Communist Cuba, where in the 1960s the party was more Castroist than Communist. In Venezuela, former military coup leader Hugo Chávez personalized not only a presidency but an entire change of government structure.

The system of co-optation further complicates the attempt at classification. How is one to classify a political party that is traditional in origin and includes at the same time large landowners and the peasants tied to them, as well as trade union members organized by the party with the assistance of segments of the clergy? How does one classify a party such as Mexico's Institutional Revolutionary Party (PRI), which until the mid-1990s made a conscious effort to co-opt and include all politically relevant sectors of the society?

With the increasing number of popularly elected governments in Latin America in the 1990s, political parties generally became more important than before. Democracy exists only if there is real competition between candidates, and throughout the world political parties have been the organizations that have presented such rival candidates. However, in some Latin American countries (Peru and Venezuela, for example) political parties are held in such low esteem that attempts have been made to have democracy without parties. In addition, as pointed out in Chapter 7, political parties have less importance when countries move to delegative democracy.

In addition to the traditional questions posed about parties in Latin America (the number of major parties, their programs and policies, the nature of electoral laws, the relationships between parties and the military), we need to ask questions posed in democracies all over the world. How are parties funded? Do they come up with programs and follow them after the elections? Are voters well informed about political party activities by the mass media? Are those countries that are trying to have democracy without parties having any success?

CONCLUSION AND IMPLICATIONS

The preceding discussion has indicated that there have been many politically relevant groups in Latin America and that they use various means to secure and retain political power. Yet at least two other themes should be introduced that tend to complicate the picture.

First, it should be noted that the urban poor outside the labor unions have not been included in the discussion. This shows one of the biases of the system. Because traditionally a necessary first step in attaining political relevance is being organized, potential groups, especially poorly educated and geographically dispersed ones such as peasants and the urban poor, face difficulties in becoming politically relevant because they have trouble organizing themselves or being organized from the outside. The poor and the vulnerable tend to be the weakest groups in politics, although in most countries they are numerically the largest.

Second, not all politically relevant groups fall into the neat categories of this chapter. Anthony Leeds's research in Brazil has shown (at least in small towns, probably larger cities, and even perhaps the whole nation) a politically more relevant series of groups to be the patronage- and family-based *panelinhas* ("little saucepans").[9] The same kinds of informal family-based networks exist in other countries. These groups are composed of individuals with common interests but different occupations—say, a doctor, a large landowner, a lawyer, and a government official. The panelinha at the local level exercises control at that level and endeavors to establish contacts with the panelinha at the state level, which might have contacts with a national panelinha. Of course, at the local level there are rival panelinhas, with contacts with like-minded ones at the state level, which in turn have contacts in the national patronage system as well. As is generally the case with such patrimonial-type relations, all interactions (except those within the panelinhas themselves) are vertical, and one level of panelinha must take care to ally with the winning one at the next higher level if it wants to have political power.

Similar research in other countries has revealed a parallel pattern of informal, elitist, familial, patronage politics. Whether called the panelinha system, as in Brazil, or the *camarilla* system, as in Mexico, the process and dynamics are the same. The aspiring politician connects himself with an aspiring politician at a higher level, who is connected with an aspirant at a yet higher level, and so forth, up to an aspiring candidate for the presidency. If the person in question becomes president, the various levels of camarillas prosper; if he remains powerful without becoming president, the camarillas continue functioning in expectation of what will take place at the next presidential election; but if the aspiring candidate is disgraced, is dismissed from the official party, or dies, the whole system of various levels of camarillas connected with him disintegrates. The camarilla system operates outside of but overlaps the formal structure of groups and parties described here.

This discussion of panelinhas and camarillas raises the question of whether US-style interest groups and political parties are operating and are important in Latin America, or if they are operating in the same way. The answer is that they are and they aren't. In the larger and better-institutionalized systems, the parties and interest groups are often important and function not unlike their North American or European counterparts. However, in the less institutionalized, personalistic countries of Ecuador, Paraguay, and the Central American nations (and even behind the scenes in the larger ones), family groups, cliques, clan alliances, and patronage networks frequently are more important, often disguised behind the appearance of partisan or ideological dispute. One must be careful, therefore, not to minimize the importance of a functional, operational party and interest-group system in some countries, while recognizing that in others it is often the less formal network through which politics is carried out.

SUGGESTIONS FOR FURTHER READING

Anderson, Charles. *Politics and Economic Change in Latin America: The Governing of Restless Nations*. Princeton, NJ: Van Nostrand, 1967.

Collier, David. *The New Authoritarianism in Latin America*. Princeton, NJ: Princeton University Press, 1980.

———— and Ruth Collier. *Shaping the Political Arena: Critical Junctures, the Labor Movement, and Regime Dynamics in Latin America*. Princeton, NJ: Princeton University Press, 1991.

Lewis, Paul. *Authoritarian Regimes in Latin America*. Blue Ridge Summit, PA: Rowman & Littlefield Publishers, 2005.

Loveman, Brian, and Thomas M. Davies Jr. *The Politics of Antipolitics: The Military in Latin America*. Wilmington, DE: Scholarly Resources, 1999.

Offutt, Stephen. *New Centers of Global Evangelicalism in Latin America and Africa*. New York: Cambridge University Press, 2015.

Schwaller, John Frederick. *The History of the Catholic Church in Latin America: From Conquest to Revolution and Beyond*. New York: NYU Press, 2011.

NOTES

1. Charles W. Anderson, *Politics and Economic Change in Latin America: The Governing of Restless Nations* (New York: Van Nostrand, 1967), especially Chapter 4.

2. See David Collier, ed., *The New Authoritarianism in Latin America* (Princeton, NJ: Princeton University Press, 1979).

3. On Boff: http://leonardoboff.com/site-eng/lboff.htm. On Sobrino: Congregation for the Doctrine of the Faith, "Notification on the Works of Father Jon Sobrino, SJ," 2006. Zenit: The World Seen from Rome, www.zenit.org/article-19147?l=english (accessed August 10, 2013).

4. José Nun, "The Middle Class Military Coup," in *The Politics of Conformity in Latin America*, ed. Claudio Véliz (London: Oxford University Press, 1967), 66–118.

5. This section is based on Donna Lee Van Cott, "Latin America: Indigenous Movements," *Encyclopedia of Nationalism*, vol. 2 (San Diego: Academic Press, 2000).

6. Mala N. Htun, "Women's Political Participation, Representation, and Leadership in Latin America," Women's Leadership Conference of the Americas issue brief, www.iadiaglo.org/htunpol.html (accessed September 22, 1999).

7. Mayra Buvinic and Vivian Roza, "Women, Politics and Democratic Prospects in Latin America," Inter-American Development Bank, December 2004.

8. Peter H. Smith, *Democracy in Latin America: Political Change in Comparative Perspective* (New York: Oxford University Press, 2005), 176.

9. Anthony Leeds, "Brazil Careers and Social Structure: A Case Study and Model," *American Anthropologist* 66 (1964): 1321–1347.

4

STATE INSTITUTIONS AND
PUBLIC POLICY

INTRODUCTION

With few exceptions, Latin American countries have state institutions like those of
the United States. That said, the functions and effects of those institutions may vary
significantly from country to country—or even by administration. Robert Keohane
defined institutions as "persistent and connected sets of rules that prescribe behavioural
roles, constrain activities, and shape expectations."[1] Understanding variances in institutional design can not only help explain the differences in policy outcomes between
countries, but can also illuminate the variations in relationships between citizen and
state. As such, institutional design can also affect legitimacy and effectiveness.

A BRIEF HISTORY OF INSTITUTIONAL DEVELOPMENT

The institutions established by Spain and Portugal in Latin America reflected and reinforced the medieval system of the mother countries. At the top was the king, who
claimed absolute power; his authority came from God (divine-right monarchy) and
was therefore unquestionable. Below the king was the viceroy (literally "vice king"),
similarly with absolute power and serving as the king's agent in the colonies. Below
the viceroy was the captain-general, also absolute within his sphere of influence; next
came the landowner who enjoyed absolute power within his own estate. Originally
there were two viceroyalties, Nueva España in Mexico, established in 1535, and the
Viceroyalty of Perú, established in 1542. Later the Viceroyalty of Nueva Granada was
established in Bogotá, first in 1717 and permanently in 1739, and in 1776 the Viceroyalty of the Río de la Plata was established in Buenos Aires.

The founding principles and institutions of Latin America were essentially medieval, pre-1500. In contrast, by the time the North American colonies were established,

the back of feudalism had been broken in England, and hence the thirteen colonies that would later form the United States were organized on a more modern basis. By that time, the idea of limited government rather than absolutism had emerged, the Protestant Reformation had destroyed the older religious orthodoxy and given rise to religious and political pluralism, the Industrial Revolution was occurring, mercantilism was giving way to commerce and entrepreneurship, the scientific revolution was breaking the hold of the old scholasticism, and a new multiclass society was beginning to emerge. Founded on these principles and changes, North American society was modern from the start, whereas Latin America continued to be plagued by feudalism. These differences also explained why from the start the United States was able to forge ahead while Latin America lagged behind. Table 4.1 summarizes these contrasting foundations of US and Latin American society.

Table 4.1   Contrasting Foundations of Latin and North American Society

Institutions	Latin America, 1492–1570	United States, Seventeenth Century
Political	Authoritarian, absolutist, centralized, corporatist	More liberal, early steps toward representative and democratic rule
Religious	Catholic orthodoxy and absolutism	Protestant and religious pluralism
Economic	Feudal, mercantilist, patrimonialist	Emerging capitalist, entrepreneurial
Social	Hierarchical, two-class, rigid	More mobile, multiclass
Educational and Intellectual	Scholastic, deductive reasoning	Empirical

The period following independence was an uncertain one. Without experience in self-governance, most Latin American countries adopted institutional models similar to those found in the United States and France, though old patterns of authoritarianism and exclusion persisted. Those institutions persisted across regime changes. In many cases, authoritarian regimes moved into the structures of democratic institutions during the 1960s and 1970s. Although region-wide democratization has resulted in the modernization of those institutions during the past few decades, some elements of the authoritarian legacy remain.

BRANCHES OF GOVERNMENT

The Presidency

Power in the Latin American systems has historically been concentrated in the executive branch, specifically the presidency. Terms like *continuismo* (prolonging one's term of office beyond its constitutional limits), *personalismo* (emphasis on the person of the president rather than on the office), and, particularly, *machismo* (strong, manly authority) are all now so familiar that they form part of our own political lexicon. The present-day Latin American executive is heir to an imperial and autocratic tradition stemming from the absolute, virtually unlimited authority of the Spanish and Portuguese crowns. Of course, modern authoritarianism has multiple explanations for its origin (a reaction against earlier mass mobilization by populist and leftist leaders, the result of stresses generated by modernization, and the strategies of civilian and military elites for accelerating development) as well as various forms (caudillistic and more institutionalized arrangements). In any case, the Latin American presidency (or prime minister, as is the case with Haiti) has long been an imperial presidency in ways that no president of the United States ever conceived.

The formal authority of Latin American executives is extensive. It derives from a president's powers as chief executive, commander in chief, and head of state, as well as from the broad emergency powers to declare a state of siege or emergency, suspend constitutional guarantees, and rule by decree. This concentration of power in the hands of the president is referred to by some as hyperpresidentialism. The presidency was a chief beneficiary of many twentieth-century changes, among them radio and television, concentrated war-making powers, and broad responsibility for the economy. In addition, some Latin American chief executives serve simultaneously as heads of state and presidents of their party machines. If the potential leader's route to power was the army, the president also has the enormous weight of armed might for use against foreign enemies and domestic foes. Considerable wealth, often generated because the lines between private and public wealth are not so sharply drawn as in North American political society, may also become an effective instrument of rule.

Perhaps the main difference lies in the fact that the Latin American systems, by tradition and history, are more centralized and executive-oriented than those in the United States. It is around the person occupying the presidency that national life swirls. The president is responsible not only for governance but also for the well-being of society as a whole and is the symbol of the national society in ways that a US president is not. Not only is politics concentrated in the office and person of the president, but it is by presidential favors and patronage that contracts are determined; different clientele are served; and wealth, privilege, and social position are parceled out. The president is the national *patrón*, replacing the local landowners and men on horseback of the past. With both broad appointive powers and wide latitude in favoring friends and those who show loyalty, the Latin American president is truly the hub of the national system. Hence, when a good, able executive is in power, the system works exceedingly well; when this is not the case, the whole system breaks down.

Various gimmicks have been used to try to limit executive authority. Few have worked well. These range from the disastrous results of the experiment with a plural executive in Uruguay (nine-person government-by-committee) to the varied unsuccessful efforts at parliamentary or semiparliamentary rule in Chile, Brazil, Cuba, and Costa Rica. Constitutional gimmickry has not worked in limiting executive rule because it is an area-wide tradition and cultural pattern, not simply some legal article. Spreading democracy in Latin America is now forcing most presidents to work within a constitutional framework.

The architects of democratization in the region were also leery of presidential power, particularly following extended authoritarian rule. Initially, some countries sought to mitigate this by implementing term limits on the executive. In some countries, such as Mexico, Guatemala, and Paraguay, presidents may be limited to a single term. Other countries limit presidents to two terms, which may either be served consecutively (Argentina, Bolivia, Brazil, and Ecuador) or non-consecutively (Costa Rica, Dominican Republic, Panama). In some cases, presidents may serve unlimited terms so long as they are non-consecutive (Chile, El Salvador, Peru, Uruguay). In recent years, several presidents have tried to extend their terms in office; some successfully (Bolivia, Honduras, and Nicaragua) and others not (Colombia and Ecuador). Only in Cuba, Nicaragua, and Venezuela may presidents seek indefinite reelection.

Presidents are chosen by popular elections. In some a simple plurality is enough to be elected. In others, an absolute majority is required and, if no candidate receives that, a second-round election is held between the two top candidates (see Table 4.2). Variations also exist in Costa Rica, where a candidate can win on the first round with only 40 percent of the vote, and Argentina, where a candidate is elected if he or she receives 45 percent of the vote, or 40 percent plus more than a 10 percent lead over the second-place candidate.

Table 4.2   Presidential Elections and Terms in Latin America

Country	Election	Years	Reelection
Argentina	Second round if no candidate has more than 45 percent of vote	4	One successive term
Bolivia	Congress chooses the president from among the top three candidates if no candidate receives a majority	5	One successive term
Brazil	Majority; Second round	4	One successive term
Chile	Majority; Second round	6	Unlimited non-consecutive terms
Colombia	Majority; Second round	4	No reelection
Costa Rica	Second round if no candidate receives more than 40 percent	4	Non-consecutive terms
Dominican Republic	Majority; Second round	4	One successive term
Ecuador	Majority; Second round	4	One successive term
El Salvador	Majority; Second round	5	Non-consecutive terms
Guatemala	Majority; Second round	4	No reelection
Haiti	Majority; Second round	5	One successive term
Honduras	Plurality	4	Reelection; details pending
Mexico	Plurality	6	No reelection
Nicaragua	Plurality	5	indefinite reelection

Table 4.2 Presidential Elections and Terms in Latin America, *continued*

Country	Election	Years	Reelection
Panama	Plurality	5	Two non-consecutive terms
Paraguay	Plurality	5	No reelection
Peru	Majority; second round	5	Non-consecutive terms
Uruguay	Majority; second round	5	One non-consecutive term
Venezuela	Plurality	5	indefinite re-election

Sources: Inter-American Dialogue, "Overview of Latin American Electoral Systems," http://pdba.georgetown.edu/Elecdata/systems.html; Daniel Zovatto, "Latin America: re-election and democracy," Open Democracy, www.opendemocracy.net/daniel-zovatto/latin-america-re-election-and-democracy, March 2014.

Legislatures

Most Latin American countries have bicameral legislatures; only the countries of Central America, Cuba, and Venezuela are unicameral. Legislatures are elected through proportional representation in all countries except Cuba, Haiti, and Mexico. Depending on the party system in the country, presidents may not enjoy a legislative majority. This may be particularly true in countries where there are non-concurrent elections. Not only does this potentially promote gridlock, but it may further prompt presidents to use extraordinary powers.

In most countries, the role of the congress has not historically been to initiate or veto laws, much less to serve as a separate and coequal branch of government. Congress's functions can be understood if we begin not with the assumption of an independent branch but with one of an agency that has historically been subservient to the president and, along with the executive, a part of the same organic, integrated state system. The congress's role was thus to give advice and consent to presidential acts (but not much dissent), to serve as a sounding board for new programs, to represent the varied interests of the nation, and to modify laws in some particulars (but not usually to nullify them). The legislature also was a place to bring some new faces into government as well as to pension off old ones, reward political friends and cronies, and ensure the opposition a voice while guaranteeing that it remained a minority. In recent years, however, the congress in several Latin American countries has acquired newfound power and autonomy.

In some countries (Chile, Colombia, Costa Rica) the congress has long enjoyed considerable independence and strength. A few congresses have even gone so far as to defy the executive—and gotten away with it. In 1992–1993, congresses in both Brazil and Venezuela removed the president from office for fiscal improprieties. The Brazilian congress used corruption allegations to oust Dilma Rousseff in 2016. The congress may serve as a forum that allows the opposition to embarrass or undermine the government, as a means of gauging who is rising and who is falling in official favor, or as a way of weighing the relative strength of the various factions within the regime.

Courts

Many of the same comments apply to the courts and court system. First, the court system has not historically been a separate and coequal branch, nor was it intended or generally expected to be. Many Latin American supreme courts would declare a law unconstitutional or defy a determined executive only at the risk of embarrassment and danger to themselves, something the courts have assiduously avoided. Second, within these limits the Latin American court systems have often functioned fairly. Third, the courts, through such devices as the writ of *amparo* (Mexico and Argentina), popular action and *tutela* (Colombia), and *segurança* (Brazil), have played an increasingly important role in controlling and overseeing governmental action, protecting civil liberties, and restricting executive authority even under dictatorial regimes.

The court system had its origins in the Iberian tradition. The chief influences historically were Roman law; Christianity and the Thomistic hierarchy of laws; and the traditional legal concepts of Iberia, most notably the *Siete Partidas* of Alfonso the Wise. In Latin America's codes, lists of human rights, and hierarchy of courts, the influence of the French Napoleonic Code has been pronounced. In the situation of a supreme court ruling (in theory at least) upon the constitutionality of executive or legislative acts, the US inspiration is clear. At present the courts in various countries are increasing in power and beginning to assert themselves, but they often face problems of incompetence, corruption, and lack of adequate training.

It should be remembered, however, that what has made the system work is not so much the legislature or judiciary but the executive. The formally institutionalized limits on executive power in terms of the usual checks and balances are still not extensive and frequently can be bypassed. More significant has been the informal balance of power within the system and the set of generally agreed-upon understandings and rules of the game beyond which even the strongest of Latin American presidents goes only at severe risk to his regime's survival. Nevertheless, the growing importance of congress and courts in many countries is a subject for further study.

REGIONAL AND LOCAL GOVERNMENT

Over the last quarter of a century, the relevance of local governments (states in federal systems, provinces or departments in centralized systems, and municipalities in all) in Latin America has been increasing. The process started with a wave of decentralization, particularly in the education and health sectors, followed by an increase in other responsibilities of local governments and their accompanying budgets. In the first decade and a half of the new century this was topped off by the allocation of additional investment resources fueled by the commodities boom. In some countries, half of the national budget is now allocated to lower levels of government.[2]

Federalism in Latin America emerged from exactly the reverse of the situation that existed in the United States. In the United States in 1789 a national government was reluctantly accepted by thirteen self-governing colonies that had never had a central administration. In Latin America, by contrast, a federal structure was adopted in some countries (Argentina, Venezuela, Mexico, Brazil) that had always been centrally administered.

Although these four nations were federal in principle, the central government reserved the right to intervene in the states. As the authority of the central government grew during the 1920s and 1930s, its inclination to intervene also increased, thereby often negating the federal principle. Over a long period, these major countries were progressively centralized with virtually all power concentrated in the national capital. Nevertheless, the dynamics of relations and tensions between the central government and its component states and regions, who still have some independent autonomy, make for one of the most interesting political arenas. Recently there have been pressures to decentralize, but in all countries the central state remains dominant.

The Latin American countries were structured after the French system of local government, with virtually all power concentrated in the central government and its ministries, and authority flowing from the top down. Local government was ordinarily administered through the ministry of interior, which is also responsible for the national police. Almost all local officials historically were appointed by the central government and served as its agents at the local level. Some Latin American countries, however, now have elections for governors and legislative bodies of provincial states or departments and for mayors and municipal councils.

Local governments had almost no power to tax or to run local social programs. These activities are generally administered by the central government according to a national plan. This system of centralized rule also is a means of concentrating power in oftentimes weak and uninstitutionalized nations.

Yet even though the theory has been that of a centralized state, the reality in Latin America has always been somewhat different. The Spanish and Portuguese crowns had difficulty enforcing their authority in the interior, which was far away and virtually autonomous. With the withdrawal of the Crown early in the nineteenth century, centrifugal tendencies were accelerated. Power drained off into the hands of local landowners or regional men on horseback, who competed for control of the national palace. With a weak central state and powerful centrifugal tendencies, a strong de facto system of local rule did emerge in Latin America, contrary to what the laws or constitutions proclaimed.

Thereafter, nation-building in Latin America often consisted of two major tendencies: populating and thus "civilizing" the vast empty interior and extending the central government's authority over the national territory. Toward the end of the nineteenth century, national armies and bureaucracies were created to replace the unprofessional armed bands under the local *caudillos*, national police agencies enforced the central government's authority at the local level, and the collection of customs duties was centralized. Authority became concentrated in the central state, the regional isolation of the *patria chica* broke down as roads and communications grids were developed, and the economy was similarly centralized more under the direction of the state.

In most of Latin America the process of nation building, begun in the 1870s and 1880s, is still going forward. Indeed, that is how development is often defined throughout the area. A developed political system is one in which the central agencies of the state exercise control and regulation over the disparate and centrifugal forces that comprise the system. In many countries, this process is still incomplete, so in the vast interior, in the highlands, in diverse indigenous communities, and among some groups (such as landowners, large industrialists, the military, and big multinationals), the authority of the central state is still tenuous. Even today isolated areas (especially those in the rugged mountains or tropical jungles) often have little governmental presence. Local strongmen—sometimes guerrillas, paramilitary groups, or drug traffickers—may be more powerful than the national government's representatives. Indeed, the efforts of the central government to extend its sway over the entire nation constitute one of the main arenas of Latin American politics. Conversely, the local units (be they regions, towns, parishes, or indigenous communities) still attempt to maintain some degree of autonomy. Centralization and decentralization are often in conflict.

FOURTH BRANCH OF GOVERNMENT: THE AUTONOMOUS STATE AGENCIES

One of the primary tools in the struggle to centralize power in Latin America from the 1930s to the 1980s was the government corporation or the autonomous agency. The growth of these agencies gave the central government a means to extend its control into new areas. These agencies became so large and so pervasive that they could be termed a separate branch of government. Some Latin American constitutions even recognized them as such.

The proliferation of these agencies was such that in some countries they numbered in the hundreds. Many were regulatory agencies, often with far broader powers than their North American counterparts, with the authority to set or regulate prices, wages, and production quotas. Others administered vast government corporations, among them steel, mining, electricity, sugar, coffee, tobacco, railroads, utilities, and petrochemicals.

Still other governmental agencies were involved in social programs: education, social security, housing, relief activities, and the like. Many more participated in the administration of new services that the state had been called upon to perform, such as national planning, agrarian reform, water supplies, and family planning. The purposes for which these agencies were set up were diverse. Some, such as the agrarian-reform or family-planning agencies, were established as much to please the US government and to qualify a country for US and World Bank loans as they were in fact to carry out agrarian reform or family planning. Others were created to bring a recalcitrant or rebellious economic sector (such as labor or the business community) under government control and direction. Some were used to stimulate economic growth and development, to increase government efficiency and hence its legitimacy, or to create a capitalist structure and officially sanctioned entrepreneurial class where none had existed before. They also enabled more job seekers to be put on the public payroll.

The common feature of these myriad agencies was that they tended to serve as agents of centralization in that historic quest to bring order to what was a vast, often unruly, near-empty territory with strong centrifugal propensities. The growth of these agencies, specifically the government corporations, meant that the degree of central state control and even ownership of the means of production increased significantly as well.

This phenomenon had important implications. It meant that the stakes involved in the issue of control of the central government, with the vast resources involved, were very high. It also implied that very rapid structural change was readily possible. In countries where between 40 and 60 percent of the GNP was generated by the public sector and where so much power was concentrated in the central state, the transformation from a state-capitalist to a state-socialist system was relatively easy and could happen almost overnight (as in Cuba, Ecuador, or Venezuela). All that was required was for a left or socialist element to capture the pinnacles of these highly centralized systems.

The growth of all these centralized state agencies had another implication deserving mention. Although established as autonomous and self-governing bodies, the state corporations had in fact become highly political agencies. They provided a wealth of sinecures, a means to put nearly everyone on the public payroll. They were giant patronage agencies by which one rewarded friends and cronies and found places for (and hence the loyalty or at least neutrality of) the opposition. They also became centers of corruption, often on a massive scale. Many of the agencies were woefully inefficient, and the immense funds involved provided nearly endless opportunities for private enrichment from the great public trough. In performing these patronage and spoils functions, the state agencies preserved the status quo because large numbers of people, indeed virtually the entire middle class, were dependent upon them for their livelihood and opportunities for advancement. It is not surprising that a significant part of the debt problems faced by many Latin American countries came from state agencies—not the national governments—receiving foreign loans.

PUBLIC POLICY TODAY

As Latin American institutions have evolved over the past thirty years, policy makers have faced a variety of public policy challenges. Some of the issues of half a century ago, such as land reform, are no longer as important. Other issues, such as poverty and inequality, persisted. Meanwhile, new challenges, such as inefficiency, corruption, and crime, emerged for the new democracies.

With the neoliberal reforms of the 1990s, governments reduced the number and role of decentralized agencies. Many that were involved in productive activities were privatized. In the process the benefits for poorer people in the countries have been reduced, as well as the number of jobs available to be passed out to political supporters. But in the recent economic downturn these state agencies have again increased in size.

Although it varies from country to country, public policy seems to be heading in two different directions. One the one side, many Latin American governments are getting out of the energy and telecommunications fields by selling their state companies to private businesses. The change began in the 1990s. At the beginning, all petroleum-producing countries in Latin America permitted limited participation of the private sector in the oil and gas industry. The general rule was that the participation was through some form of association with the state-owned oil company with the outside investor bearing all exploration risk. The governments received resources from service fees and taxes or from profits and taxes. As the decade progressed, the Latin American countries, to varying degrees, introduced policy or legal reforms to allow more private sector participation in the industry. Privatization and deregulation were in vogue. Some countries went as far as dismantling or selling off their state-owned oil companies (Bolivia, Argentina, and Peru).[3]

In the opposite direction, many Latin American countries are developing new social programs to target poverty and inequality—in part a response to the retraction of the state during the early years of neoliberalism. In recent years, conditional cash transfer programs (CCTs) have emerged as the predominant public policy approach in this fight. CCTs began in Brazil and Mexico in the 1990s. Within the next decade, Argentina, Bolivia, Chile, Colombia, Costa Rica, Dominican Republic, Ecuador, El Salvador, Guatemala, Honduras, Nicaragua, Panama, Peru, and Uruguay would also launch CCT programs, though those in Brazil and Mexico were the largest by far, reaching some eighty million beneficiaries. By providing cash transfers to heads of household of poor families, usually female, based on conditions that require the household to seek particular health and education services, these programs not only seek to improve living standards in the short term, but in the long term they also strengthen the capacity of households to break the intergenerational transmission of poverty.

Conditional cash transfer programs involve billions of dollars, and constitute a massive financial program reaching more than 20 percent of Latin America's poorest people. Because the intended beneficiaries are economically vulnerable, some governments have created mechanisms to prevent households in need from being wrongfully excluded from program rolls, discourage clientelism and abuse of programs for political and private gain by state actors, and strengthen the potential of the programs to reach their objectives and most effectively serve their intended beneficiaries.[4]

In these changing times, Latin American governments are under pressure to get out of some programs and establish others. Although neoliberal reforms resulted in a reduction in the size of the state, governments are increasingly being called upon to provide public policy programs in the fields of education, economic development, the environment, housing, health care, lesbian, gay, bisexual, and transgender (LGBT) rights, drug consumption, and others. But state capacity to address these issues was limited in many cases. In the Northern Triangle countries of El Salvador, Guatemala, and Honduras, poverty, low growth, and one of the world's most serious crime epidemics has undermined the state's ability to effectively address other policy issues.

The tradition of corruption also poses a significant challenge to effective public policy and state capacity. Transparency International publishes a yearly report on corruption in the nations of the world, giving scores between 0 (the most corrupt) to 100 (the least corrupt). In 2016, the Latin American countries with the worst scores were Venezuela (17), Haiti (20), Nicaragua (26), Guatemala (28), Paraguay (30), Honduras (30), Mexico (30), Dominican Republic (31), Ecuador (31), and Bolivia (33).[5] In some countries, such as Guatemala and Honduras, corruption and impunity have been serious enough to lead to the creation of internationally supported bodies to help combat the problems.

CONCLUSION

Although patronage and clientelism remain prevalent in many countries, there is increasing pressure on the government to offer real policy solutions to real problems. With so many political officials, including presidents, benefiting from corrupt behavior, the important question is how government policy can address it. Beyond this, there are serious problems to address that affect the entire region, including increasing crime, the effects of the drug trade, and the environment. If officials are unable to adequately meet the people's needs, public confidence in democracy and government institutions will continue to erode.

SUGGESTIONS FOR FURTHER READING

Diaz-Cayeros, Alberto. *Federalism. Fiscal Authority, and Centralization in Latin America*. New York: Cambridge University Press, 2016.

Geddes, Barbara. *Politician's Dilemma: Building State Capacity in Latin America*. Oakland, CA: University of California Press, 1996.

Keohane, Robert. *International Institutions and State Power: Essays in International Relations Theory*. Boulder, CO: Westview Press, 1989.

Kurtz, Marcus J. *Latin American State Building in Comparative Perspective: Social Foundations of Institutional Order*. New York: Cambridge University Press, 2013.

Stein, Ernesto, Mariano Tommasi, Carlos Scartascini, Pablo Spiller, eds. *Policymaking in Latin America*. Cambridge MA: David Rockefeller Center for Latin American Studies, 2008.

Vellinga, Menno. *The Changing Role of the State in Latin America*. 2nd Revised ed. Edition. Boulder, CO: Westview, 1997.

NOTES

1. Robert Keohane, *International Institutions and State Power: Essays in International Relations Theory*. (Boulder, CO: Westview Press, 1989), 3.

2. Arturo Herrera Gutierrez, "What are we talking about when we talk about 'subnational' governments?" World Bank, https://blogs.worldbank.org/latinamerica/prospects/taxonomy /term/14196, September 1, 2015.

3. Jose L. Valera, "Changing oil and gas fiscal and regulatory regimes in Latin America," Oil and Gas Journal, December 3, 2007, www.kslaw.com/Library/publication/O&GJ_Changing Oil&GasLA_Valera.pdf.

4. Transparency International, "Conditional Cash Transfers in Latin America: Promoting Equality through Transparency and Accountability," June 30, 2016, www.transparency.org /whatwedo/publication/conditional_cash_transfers_in_latin_america_promoting_equality _through_tran.

5. http://www.transparency.org/news/feature/corruption_perceptions_index_2016.

5

THE POLITICAL ECONOMY
OF LATIN AMERICA

INTRODUCTION

It is impossible to understand the patterns of Latin American politics without under-standing the region's economic development. From the time of the conquest, Latin America's economy was developed to primarily benefit entities outside of the region, whether that be the Spanish crown, the British empire, the United States, or mul-tinational corporations from across the globe. Uruguayan author Eduardo Galeano described Latin America as "the region of open veins. Everything from the discov-ery until our times, has always been transmuted into European—or later—United States—capital, and as such has accumulated on distant centers of power. Everything: the soil, its fruits and its mineral-rich depths, the people and their capacity to work and to consume, natural resources and human resources."[1]

In this chapter, we consider the characteristics of the Latin American economies and identify patterns of development from colonialism to the present. We conclude by looking at issues of sustainable development in the region's political economy, includ-ing poverty and inequality, the informal economy, and the environment.

THE COLONIAL ECONOMY

The colonial economies in the Americas could best be described as extractive and ex-ploitative. Under the mercantilist system, the colonies existed for the economic benefit of the colonizing power. All of the precious metals that were found in the Americas (gold in Colombia, silver in Mexico, Peru, and Bolivia) were sent to Spain. In the later colonial period, agricultural products were also exported to the colonizing power: Haiti sent sugar to France, while the Caribbean countries sent it to Spain and Brazil to Por-tugal. Conversely, colonies in Latin America were required to purchase all commodities from their colonial powers. Spain and Portugal, however, were unable to fully meet demand with their own markets, which resulted in contraband trade with other colonial powers in the region.[2] Spain's Bourbon Reforms in the eighteenth century, just as mercantilism was declining in popularity, were intended to improve administration and tax collection, reduce contraband trade, and limit the power of the emerging Latin American elite (the *creoles*). The reforms alienated creoles, and led many to support the independence movement out of a desire to increase their income by trading with other countries.

The Spanish crown established the *encomienda* system, large tracts of land for Spanish citizens to develop (not own) with indigenous labor in exchange for a portion of its output—known as the *repartida*. The *encomenderos* were supposed to care for and Christianize the indigenous people living in their territory, but abuse was common. The system was abolished in early eighteenth century and replaced with the *latifundia*, large, feudal estates dedicated primarily to export agriculture. Workers received small plots of land for subsistence agriculture and were then tied to the estates in a form of debt peonage. In rural areas workers were often tied to *haciendas* for generations.

The wars of independence in Latin America (1810–1824) were costly and destabilizing. In addition to the political disarray, the economic output of some of the new countries declined from what it had been during the colonial period. Landholding patterns developed during the colonial era remained largely intact following independence, resulting in a sizable gap between rich and poor, with landed elites controlling the vast majority of land and resources. Mining and agricultural production were monopolized by wealthy landowners. The great majority of inhabitants of the new countries were poor, working the poorest lands and without education and health care. They had no importance in politics, with the exception of being the foot soldiers as directed by their patrons in civil wars.

LIBERALISM AND THE DEVELOPMENT OF EXPORT COMMODITIES

As political and territorial disputes were settled by the mid-nineteenth century, economies began to recuperate. Generally speaking, the political elites followed Adam Smith's idea of basing their exports on comparative advantage; that is, producing the products that their country could most efficiently produce. As Colombian Treasury Secretary Florentino González stated in 1847:

> In a country rich in mines and agricultural products, which can sustain a considerable and beneficial export trade, the latter should not attempt to encourage industries that distract the inhabitants from agricultural and mining occupations. . . . We should offer Europe raw materials and open our doors to her manufactures, to facilitate trade and the profit it brings, and to prove the consumer, at a reasonable price, with the products of the manufacturing industry.[3]

Following this idea, Latin American countries produced agricultural or other primary goods that were traded with the more developed countries of the North for industrial goods. As such, economic development policy focused largely on promoting a few exports. By the end of the nineteenth century, Latin America's monocrop economy was well-established. Many Latin American countries concentrated on only one or two primary goods: coffee and bananas for many Central American countries, sugar for Cuba and the Dominican Republic, coffee for Colombia and Brazil, cacao in Ecuador, and nitrates and copper for Chile. As demonstrated in Table 5.1, primary and secondary commodities accounted for well more than half of total exports for most countries. In some cases, such as Cuba, El Salvador, and Guatemala, more than 90 percent of their exports were concentrated in two commodities. Although some countries might have a comparative advantage in those primary products, the national economies suffered when there was a world oversupply of them and were also vulnerable to crop failures and to quotas fixed by the industrial nations.

Table 5.1   Export Commodity Concentration Ratios, circa 1913

	Primary Product	Percentage	Secondary Product	Percentage	Total Percentage of Exports
Argentina	Maize	22.5	Wheat	20.7	43.2
Bolivia	Tin	72.3	Silver	4.3	76.6
Brazil	Coffee	62.3	Rubber	15.9	78.2
Chile	Nitrates	71.3	Copper	7.0	78.3
Colombia	Coffee	37.2	Gold	20.4	57.6
Costa Rica	Bananas	50.9	Coffee	35.2	86.1
Cuba	Sugar	72.0	Tobacco	19.5	91.5
Dominican Republic	Cacao	39.2	Sugar	34.8	74.0
Ecuador	Cacao	64.1	Coffee	5.4	69.5
El Salvador	Coffee	79.6	Precious metals	15.9	95.5
Guatemala	Coffee	84.8	Bananas	5.7	90.5
Haiti	Coffee	64.0	Cacao	6.8	70.8
Honduras	Bananas	50.1	Precious metals	25.9	76.0
Mexico	Silver	30.3	Copper	10.3	40.6
Nicaragua	Coffee	64.9	Precious metals	13.8	78.7
Panama	Bananas	65.0	Coconut	7.0	72.0
Paraguay	Yerba mate	32.1	Tobacco	15.8	47.9
Peru	Copper	22.0	Sugar	15.4	37.4
Uruguay	Wool	42.0	Meat	24.0	66.0
Venezuela	Coffee	52.0	Cacao	21.4	73.4

Source: Adapted from Victor Bulmer-Thomas, *The Economic History of Latin America Since Independence* (New York: Cambridge University Press, 1994), 59.

Export promotion was key to regional growth during the second half of the nineteenth century. The region's raw materials supported Europe's Industrial Revolution. Latin America's economies grew rapidly from 1880–1910 as light industry, such as textile factories, emerged in the region. But the region's economies were also subject to cycles of boom and bust due to fluctuations in the global economy. The first shocks to the system came with the outbreak of World War I in 1914 and the Great Depression of the 1930s, when international commerce ground to a halt and prices on primary products fell significantly. Although trade quickly recovered, World War II had a particularly devastating effect on Latin American economies, as the European market was virtually cut off. In 1938, before the war, Europe had consumed 55 percent of the region's exports and supplied 45 percent of imports.[4] One consequence of this was a growing trade relationship with the United States, which had previously made up a small portion of Latin America's trade.

Of course, the US had economic interests in the region prior to the wars, particularly in sugar and bananas in Central America and the Caribbean basin. In addition to agribusiness, US corporations later entered the extractive field (petroleum, copper, coal, iron ore). Among the most influential companies, the United Fruit Company (UFCO) had significant investments in the region. The company acquired significant land and built transport and telecommunications companies. The enclave economies it established were virtual states within a state. The company's investments gave it considerable political influence, including the 1954 coup in Guatemala detailed in Chapter 6. Although this is one of the more extreme examples, US corporations in Latin America often entered into the politics of their host countries, bribing public officials, undervaluing assets, or threatening to cut off a country's products if certain policies were approved by its government.

IMPORT-SUBSTITUTION AND STATISM

The US emphasis on postwar reconstruction in Europe resulted in a decline in intraregional trade and investment. Latin America's postwar growth was modest. As a result, debate over Latin America's economic model emerged. Argentine economist Raul Prebisch and the United Nations Economic Commission on Latin America and the Caribbean (ECLAC) undertook a study of Latin American economic development. The study revealed that Latin America suffered from unfair terms of trade, wherein the value of Latin America's exports steadily declined while the cost of imported manufactured goods from the US and Europe increased. To overcome this disadvantage and promote diversification, Prebisch and ECLAC advocated import-substitution industrialization (ISI). Rather than importing manufactured goods, the Latin American country imported capital goods and technology, which it then used to produce the goods that formerly were imported.

Further, to lessen the dependence on one crop, the governments made tax and credit decisions that would encourage production of goods other than the traditional ones for export. This vision of a new, economically developed society became one in which more goods of greater variety were produced for export, while fewer manufactured goods were imported. Increased trade was an important facet of this policy, because hard currency was needed for the purchase of these capital goods. These policy recommendations gave the state a strong role in managing the economy, imposing tariffs, establishing state-owned enterprises, and encouraging domestic investment.

The policies were in stark contrast to the prevailing liberal economic discourse of the time, but scholars (particularly from the developing world) had become increasingly critical of the failures of modernization. Dependency theorists (*dependistas*), who were influenced by Marxism and neocolonialist arguments of the 1960s, argued that Latin America's lack of development was the result of political and economic patterns established during the colonial era. The extraction of resources and wealth to support outsiders—first colonial powers and later industrializing powers—meant that the Latin American economy had been systematically developed to benefit outsiders rather than the region itself. Whether countries could develop under such conditions was a point of contention between dependency theorists. Some, like Andre Gunder Frank, argued that underdevelopment was a *process*, a result of capitalism, while others argued that dependent development was possible. Although dependency theory as an explanation of development (or underdevelopment) fell out of vogue relatively quickly, the concepts of dependency and dependent development continued to dominate discourse in the region for decades to come.

In addition to adopting import-substitution, some countries also joined regional trade schemes, capitalizing on intraregional trade that emerged during the war years. ECLAC promoted regional integration as a means to expand domestic markets while protecting them from international competition, by eliminating tariff and non-tariff barriers among member countries while erecting barriers for non-member countries. Perhaps the most successful of these was the Central American Common Market (CACM), comprising Costa Rica, El Salvador, Guatemala, Honduras, and Nicaragua, though it was in decline by the early 1970s.

Latin America's economy grew an average of 5.4 percent during the 1950s and 1960s, but weaknesses of the model were exposed by the late 1960s. Goods produced locally were expensive and of poor quality. This was not only bad for local consumers, but also meant that that the region's economies remained dependent on exporting primary goods, as their manufactured products weren't competitive. Additionally, the jobs lost in the agricultural sector were not replaced by the new industrial sector, resulting in growing unemployment. Many of those who migrated from rural areas to cities in search of employment joined the ranks of the un- and underemployed in the informal sector. During this time period, Latin Americans also lost out because the prices of industrial goods rose more than those of primary goods. Because of this "terms of trade" problem, over time it took more bags of Colombian coffee beans, to use one example, to purchase a tractor or most other industrial goods. Thus, the model altered the nature of dependency rather than eliminating it.

DEBT AND LATIN AMERICA'S "LOST DECADE"

During the 1960s and 1970s, Latin American governments borrowed heavily to finance development projects, trade deficits, military expenditures, and capital flight. Interest rates were generally low, which made reliance on credit attractive. Interest rates increased significantly between 1979–1981, which resulted in economic recession and left many countries unable to repay their debts. By the early 1980s, many Latin

American countries had a debt crisis. In August 1982, Mexico was forced to declare a moratorium on its debt payments. Others followed Mexico's default, and a deep recession overtook the region during Latin America's "lost decade." The crisis was greatly exacerbated by enormous capital flight, which reduced growth, degraded the tax base, and increased inequality. Between 1973 and 1987 capital flight totaled US$151 billion, the equivalent of 43 percent of total external debt.[5] Though not the most extreme case, capital flight from Mexico equaled roughly half of the country's GDP between 1979 and 1982.

A complicating factor in the 1970s was the increase of petroleum prices by the Organization of Petroleum Exporting Countries (OPEC). The only Latin American petroleum-exporting countries were Venezuela, Mexico, and Ecuador. The other, importing countries realized that more of their earnings from exports would have to be used to import petroleum. The debt crisis was caused by the energy crisis in two ways. First, all Latin American countries found, by the late 1970s, that private banks, recycling petrodollars invested by OPEC members, were willing to lend money at real interest rates (corrected for inflation) that were near or even below zero. The debts were impossible to repay, however, because recession in the industrial world in the early 1980s resulted in fewer Latin American exports being bought. Second, the oil-exporting countries (especially Mexico and Venezuela) contracted debts under the assumption that the price of petroleum would continue increasing. By 1982, however, the oil glut led to much lower prices for their exports.

Although the debt crisis affected countries throughout the globe, the crisis was most acute in Latin America, which held 37 percent of the world's total debt in 1988. In 1975, Latin America's total external debt was approximately US$75 billion. By 1989 Latin America's debt totaled US$434.1 billion, approximately 54 percent of the region's GNP.[6] The region's average income per capita declined 1 percent annually, and was more than 8 percent below its 1980 level in 1989.[7] Although several of the region's larger economies (Argentina, Brazil, Chile, Mexico, Peru, Venezuela) held the majority of the debt, the crisis was particularly acute in smaller economies (Bolivia, Ecuador, Costa Rica) where debt comprised a higher percentage of debt relative to GDP or export earnings. Inflation and hyperinflation were rampant. Hyperinflation in Argentina was persistent throughout the crisis, averaging 335.5 percent from 1980 to 1985 and 1,392 percent from 1986–1989. In other countries, hyperinflation was more episodic. In Bolivia, inflation averaged 2,251.5 percent from 1980–1985, reaching 60,000 percent from May to August 1985 before dropping to 28.7 percent in 1986–1989.

Debt rescheduling allowed borrowers to receive new loans while paying interest on old loans. In exchange for the loans, the International Monetary Fund (IMF) required borrowers to reorganize their economies, known as *conditionality*. The exact reforms were negotiated between individual governments and the IMF, but the structural adjustment policies (SAPs) followed a policy prescription known as the "Washington Consensus." Although the term is often seen as synonymous with "neoliberalism" and "globalization," economist John Williamson, who coined the term, said that it meant much more:

1. Fiscal discipline
2. A redirection of public expenditure priorities toward fields offering both high economic returns and the potential to improve income distribution, such as

primary health care, primary education, and infrastructure
3. Tax reform (to lower marginal rates and broaden the tax base)
4. Interest rate liberalization
5. A competitive exchange rate
6. Trade liberalization
7. Liberalization of inflows of foreign direct investment
8. Privatization
9. Deregulation (to abolish barriers to entry and exit)
10. Secure property rights[8]

Since its implementation, the phrase "Washington Consensus" has become a lightning rod for dissatisfaction amongst anti-globalization protesters, developing country politicians and officials, trade negotiators, and numerous others. To a certain extent, the neoliberal economic system is like the traditional one, emphasizing products in which a nation had a comparative advantage. However, it also included privatization of government-owned enterprises and ending subsidies for the poor through pricing products at international levels. In the short run, at least, these new policies led to more unemployment and a greater disparity of income. The neoliberal leaders urged patience, but some politicians paid more attention to the cries of large numbers of suffering people. Hence, in recent years the conflict was between the neoliberals and the supporters of a government-controlled economy.

There has been a fair amount of resistance to neoliberal policies in the region, ranging from protests to uprisings. Some of the strongest protests have been in response to the privatization of public goods and services, including water, health care, and utilities (telecommunications, energy). Part of the opposition to neoliberal policies is derived from the costs or perceived costs of privatization, including increasing costs and unemployment. Another part of the opposition to privatization is philosophical and grounded in the region's history—should multinational corporations be allowed to profit from the sale of a country's natural resources back to its own people, especially when those resources are vital to human life? In Cochabamba, Bolivia a "water war" broke out in 2000 after the Bolivian government approved a law privatizing the country's state-owned water utility. A severe rate hike by the multinational Aguas de Tunari resulted in widespread, and sometimes violent, protests in the region.

Although most economies stabilized by the mid- to late 1990s, the burden of debt service for some poor countries inhibited economic growth. In 1996, the IMF and World Bank announced the Heavily Indebted Poor Countries initiative (HIPC), providing a measure of debt forgiveness to some of the world's poorest countries. To qualify for full or partial relief, countries had to demonstrate that their debt was unsustainable based on debt-to-export and debt-to-revenue numbers. They also had to demonstrate that they had attempted fiscal reforms to prevent future debt crises. In Latin America, only Bolivia, Haiti, Honduras, and Nicaragua qualified for HIPC relief.

FREE TRADE, GLOBALIZATION, AND THEIR DISCONTENTS

As a part of the Washington Consensus, in the 1990s leaders of the countries of the Americas embraced the idea that market regimes and democratic governance were more likely to stimulate economic growth and raise standards of living than state-run regimes. To encourage this reform, in June 1990, President George H. W. Bush announced his Enterprise for the Americas Initiative, which envisioned debt relief in exchange for continued economic reform and proposed free trade from "the tip of Alaska to the tip of Argentina." This initially ignited an enormous wave of enthusiasm and goodwill toward the United States throughout the region.

The first step in implementing the trade portion of the initiative between the United States and a Latin American country was the negotiation of the North American Free Trade Agreement (NAFTA) in 1992. NAFTA, a free trade agreement between Canada, Mexico, and the United States, went into effect on January 1, 1994. One of the most obvious outcomes of NAFTA was the decline of US manufacturing and the proliferation of the manufacturing industry in Mexico. *Maquiladoras*, assembly plants, expanded throughout Mexico's border states, enticing investors with low-wage labor, tax incentives, and lax labor and environmental standards. The *maquilas* became synonymous with globalization. What Mexico gained in manufacturing, it lost in other sectors. Mexican farmers found it difficult to compete with US-subsidized agriculture.

In 1994, the thirty-four hemispheric leaders attending the Miami Summit agreed to negotiate by 2005 a comprehensive Free Trade Area for the Americas (FTAA) that was patterned on NAFTA. However, events in the US and throughout Latin America impeded progress on the FTAA. Instead, the United States pursued other free trade agreements with Latin American countries. The Central America-Dominican Republic-United States Free Trade Agreement (CAFTA-DR) was signed on August 5, 2004.[9] Though ultimately approved by the region's governments, there was significant citizen opposition to the agreement. On February 27, 2006, the United States and Colombia announced they had concluded their work on a free trade agreement. Bilateral agreements were later signed with other countries, including Chile, Colombia, and Peru.

One of the problems for the FTAA was the growing anti-neoliberal sentiment in the region. The Bolivarian Alliance for the Peoples of Our America (ALBA) was founded in December 2004 by Venezuelan president Hugo Chávez and Cuban president Fidel Castro as an alternative to neoliberal policies such as the FTAA. Additional members include Bolivia, Ecuador, Nicaragua, and several Caribbean island nations. Honduras was a member from August 2008 to December 2009. ALBA, described as a "political, economic, and social alliance in defense of independence, self-determination and the identity of peoples comprising it," encourages trade between member countries, and provides low-cost oil and low-interest loans for development initiatives through the Petrocaribe bank.[10] Given the tenuousness of Venezuela's political and economic situation at the beginning of 2017, it was unclear whether ALBA would be able to continue its generous oil subsidies to members.

One of the results of globalization has been increased foreign investment in the region. This has aided the diversification of the region's economy, particularly the expansion of the service sector. US and other foreign corporations have expanded beyond agribusiness and mining into retail, the services industry (accounting firms, computer outfits), communications (telephones, telegraphs, computers), and retailing (fast food, clothing).

Table 5.2 shows that most Latin American countries in 2014 had much more diversified exports than at the beginning of the twentieth century (as shown in Table 5.1). Only Venezuela depended overwhelmingly on one product for its exports, with more than 90 percent of exports concentrated in two products, while only Bolivia, Colombia, Costa Rica, Ecuador, and Haiti had more than half of their export earnings from the top two products. Additionally, many countries had first or second exports that are manufactured goods, with the employment and value-added that comes with them. Significant shifts have occurred in the Caribbean Basin, where agribusiness was once dominant. Costa Rica no longer depends on coffee or bananas for its export earnings; instead its leading exports were integrated circuits and office machine parts. That free trade has changed other Latin American economies is also shown in the maquila exports from other Central American and Caribbean countries (T-shirts and electrical capacitors from El Salvador and T-shirts and sweaters from Haiti).

Table 5.2   Export Concentration Ratios and Total Exports, 2014

Country	Primary Export	Percentage	Secondary Export	Percentage	Primary and Secondary Total	Total Exports (US$B)
Argentina	Soybean meal	17.2	Delivery trucks	5.6	22.8	69.0
Bolivia	Petroleum gas	44.8	Gold	10.0	54.8	13.4
Brazil	Iron ore	11.8	Soy beans	10.3	22.1	228.0
Chile	Refined copper	23.3	Copper ore	21.5	44.8	77.3
Colombia	Crude petroleum	45.5	Coal	13.4	58.9	56.5
Costa Rica	Integrated circuits	36.2	Office machine parts	14.6	50.8	21.3
Dominican Republic	Gold	15.7	Medical instruments	11.3	27.0	10.7
Ecuador	Crude petroleum	49.6	Bananas	11.8	61.4	27.4
El Salvador	Knit T-shirts	18.1	Electrical capacitors	5.4	23.5	5.52
Guatemala	Raw sugar	8.5	Bananas	7.6	16.1	11.7
Haiti	Knit T-shirts	42.4	Knit sweaters	17.6	60.0	1.06
Honduras	Knit sweaters	11.5	Coffee	10.5	22.0	8.66
Mexico	Crude petroleum	9.2	Cars	8.2	17.5	400.0

Table 5.2   Export Concentration Ratios and Total Exports, 2014, *continued*

Country	Primary Export	Percentage	Secondary Export	Percentage	Primary and Secondary Total	Total Exports (US$B)
Nicaragua	Insulated wire	13.4	Coffee	8.1	21.5	5.41
Panama	Passenger and cargo ships	12.1	Refined petroleum	12.0	24.1	4.62
Paraguay	Soybeans	29.8	Soybean meal	15.0	43.8	7.71
Peru	Copper ore	17.4	Gold	14.7	32.1	39.8
Uruguay	Frozen bovine meat	11.3	Soybeans	9.8	21.1	9.2
Venezuela	Crude petroleum	76.0	Refined petroleum	17.3	93.4	63.0

Source: A.J.G. Simoes, C.A. Hidalgo. "The Economic Complexity Observatory: An Analytical Tool for Understanding the Dynamics of Economic Development." Workshops at the Twenty-Fifth AAAI Conference on Artificial Intelligence. (2011) http://atlas.media.mit.edu/en/profile/country/.

But trade and investment have not necessarily generated sufficient employment or economic opportunity in the region. For some, the failure to find work at home resulted in emigration in search of work. More than 20 million Latin Americans live outside of their country of birth. The money they send home, known as remittances, has become an important source of income for millions of families throughout the region. Most recipients of remittances use the funds to cover basic needs, including food, medicine, schooling, and consumer goods. In some circumstances, remittances are invested to increase productivity and income. This might include, for example, the purchase of fertilizer in agricultural areas or establishing a restaurant. In countries such as Mexico and Haiti, hometown associations (HTAs) make communal decisions about the investment of remittances.

Remittances have also become a vital source of foreign exchange for the region's economies, sometimes offsetting the costs of neoliberal policies. In 2001 migrants sent home US$23 billion in remittances. By 2015 remittances to Latin American and the Caribbean totaled US$68.3 billion.[11] Although Mexicans send back the highest amount of remittances (US$24.77 billion in 2015), their remittances are only equivalent to 1.9 percent of GDP. In other countries, *migradollars*, as they are sometimes known, increasingly account for a higher percentage of GDP. In El Salvador, Haiti, and Honduras, remittances are approximately 20 percent of annual GDP. In 2014 Haiti received more than twice as much in remittances (US$2.2 billion) as it did in exports (US$1.06 billion), while El Salvador's remittances totaled 78 percent of exports.

Remittances are 10 percent of GDP in Guatemala and Nicaragua. If remittances were to dry up, it would have significant consequences for remittance-dependent economies.

Globalization has also brought new players to Latin America's economy. China's role in the Latin American economy has expanded significantly in recent years. China is the primary destination for exports from Brazil, totaling about US$40.9 billion compared to US$27.3 billion to the US. China imports approximately 75 percent of Brazil's soy exports, displacing the European Union as the top destination of Brazilian soy within the past decade. China is a major investor in Peruvian mining and a major importer of minerals, receiving 58 percent of Peru's copper and 48 percent of its gold in 2014. Not only have trade volume and foreign investment increased, but Chinese banks have surpassed US banks in lending. Chinese loans to Latin American governments totaled US$29 billion in 2015, more than the World Bank and Inter-American Development Bank combined.[12] Chinese loans have sustained Venezuela and others with poor access to international credit in recent years.

But China's economic relationship with Latin America reveals dangerously familiar patterns: the development of export commodity primarization while providing a market for finished goods from China. This potentially leaves China's regional trading partners in a vulnerable position as its economy slows down or as commodity prices decline. In 2015, foreign investment declined by 9.1 percent from the previous year, dropping to US$179.1 billion, the lowest level since 2010. This was largely due to the decline in investments in mining and hydrocarbons.[13]

TOWARD SUSTAINABLE DEVELOPMENT

Amid the criticisms and shortcomings of the neoliberal model to address various issues related to development, most notably poverty and inequality, a discourse began to emerge on sustainable development. In 1992 representatives from 178 governments and civil society representatives from around the globe gathered in Rio de Janeiro for the United Nations Conference on Environment and Development. The goal of the Rio Summit was to articulate a response to the United Nations World Commission on Environment and Development's 1987 report, *Our Common Future*. Also known as the Brutland Report, the document offered a definition of sustainable development: "development which meets the needs of the present without compromising the ability of future generations to meet their own needs." The United Nations outlines seventeen goals of sustainable development, including reducing poverty; addressing income and gender inequality; and promoting sustainable economic growth, employment opportunities, protection of natural resources, and actions to combat climate change.[14] We discuss some of these issues below.

The emphasis on sustainable development was reinforced when, in 2000, the United Nations established eight Millennium Development Goals (MDGs) to be reached by 2015: (1) Eradicate extreme poverty and hunger; (2) Achieve universal primary education; (3) Promote gender equality and empower women; (4) Reduce child mortality; (5) Improve maternal health; (6) Combat HIV/AIDS, malaria, and other diseases; (7) Ensure environmental sustainability; and (8) Develop a global partnership for development.[15] By 2015 Latin America had reached the targets of halving extreme poverty and reducing the under-five mortality rate by two-thirds; reached water target early; and had almost reached the target of halving the proportion of the population without basic sanitation. There was also progress on reducing the prevalence of hunger and malnourishment, expanding access to primary education, and reaching gender parity in primary education. That said, there were notable differences in several categories between Latin America and the Caribbean, where hunger and poverty are greater and education enrollments lower. Although the coverage of protected natural resources increased, 3.6 million hectares per year were still lost over the period from 2005 to 2010.[16]

Poverty and Inequality

Important strides have been made toward reducing poverty and inequality in recent years, though Latin America still has the most unequal income distribution in the world. The region's Gini index, which measures inequality, declined from .56 to .51 from 2000 to 2012.[17] Much of the decline was the result of significant increases in social spending, including conditional cash transfers (CCTs) as discussed in Chapter 3. According to the Inter-American Development Bank, social spending grew at a faster rate than GDP, reaching almost 19 percent of GDP in 2012.[18] The middle class grew from 21 percent of the population in 2000 to 34 percent in 2012. Additionally, extreme poverty decreased from 19.3 percent in 2002 to 12 percent in 2014. Despite reductions in poverty and a growing middle class, the UNDP estimates that nearly 200 million Latin Americans (38 percent) are vulnerable to falling into poverty.[19] These so-called vulnerables find themselves somewhere just above the poverty line, but far enough above to be able to weather a crisis. As the 2008 economic recession demonstrated, Latin American countries remain highly vulnerable to fluctuations in the global economy.

Among the Millennium Development Goals, there were positive signs for gender equality in the region. In addition to achieving gender parity in primary education, more girls are enrolled in secondary education than boys. Latin America also has the highest share of women in parliament in the developing world. Women are nearing parity in wage-earning jobs in the nonagricultural sector (45 of every 100), though women's wages remain lower. That said, there is a persistent poverty gap between women and men, maternal mortality rates in the region remain high (77 per 100,000 in Latin America and 190 per 100,000 in the Caribbean in 2013), as does the rate of adolescent pregnancy (73 per 1,000 in 2015).[20] Data on indigenous women suggests they fare more poorly in most categories than non-indigenous women. Women's economic vulnerabilities also may also make them more vulnerable to violence. Gender-based violence, including inter-partner violence, remains a serious problem. ECLAC estimates that as many as 40 percent of women in the region have been victims of violence.[21] Femicide, the deliberate murder of women, has been a growing problem in the region, notably in countries such as El Salvador, Guatemala, and Mexico. Though many governments have now established femicide laws, impunity rates remain high.

The Informal Sector

One of the UN's sustainable development goals focuses on full and "decent" employment, meaning fair wages and workplace protections, as a means of addressing poverty. The failure of Latin America's economic policies to generate sufficient employment or wealth has resulted in a large informal sector. Although access to education has expanded over the years, the quality of education remains poor in some areas. This not only limits prospects for higher quality jobs but also has hindered the adoption of new technologies.[22] According to the International Labour Organization, as many as 46.8 percent of Latin Americans were employed in the informal sector in 2014, including more than half of the working vulnerables. Youth unemployment is particularly high, with some 27 million working in the informal sector. Moreover, women are overrepresented in the informal sector and underrepresented in formal employment. The growth of the informal sector was particularly acute during the debt crisis, though it has continued to expand in recent years. In Latin America, many participants in this sector work in construction, domestic service, transport, as street vendors, or in many other legal jobs. However, some also include illicit activities, such as prostitution or drug trafficking, as part of the informal sector. Jobs in the informal sector are characterized by low pay, low quality, and a lack of protection of labor laws. Workers don't receive benefits or the security associated with formal employment. Most working in the informal sector do so for survival rather than profit.

The Environment and Development

Latin America is a region of abundant natural resources: minerals, oil deposits, arable land, and extensive forested areas rich in biodiversity. The temptation to leverage those resources to advance economic development is a problem that many developing countries face. Whether and how to protect those resources has become a topic of significant debate in the region. Although some see growth potential in protecting and promoting the environment, such as the development of eco-tourism in Costa Rica or biofuels in Brazil, others have welcomed the development of their natural resources by multinationals. Multinational corporations, foreign investment, and demand for commodities threaten the region's environment through activities such as mining and logging. Some governments have taken steps to legally protect their resources, embracing the philosophy of *buen vivir* ("good living") as an alternative to capitalist extractive policies. In 2008 Ecuador became the world's first country to guarantee constitutional rights to nature. Bolivia's 2012 Law of Mother Earth grants nature equal rights under the law. However, both governments have come under fire from activists for continuing to allow extractive practices, including oil extraction in Yasuni National Park in Ecuador, considered the most biodiverse place on earth. Other governments have targeted specific industries. In March 2017, El Salvador became the first country in the world to ban all metal mining after long-term dispute with Canadian-Australian firm OceanaGold.

Additionally, clashes between citizens and the state and/or corporations over resources have been contentious and sometimes deadly. Latin America is the most dangerous region in the world for environmental land rights activists. Activists opposing hydroelectric dams in Honduras and Guatemala, activists demanding land rights that conflict with palm plantation developers in Honduras, anti-mining activists in Peru, and anti-mining and agribusiness activists in Colombia have been subject to harassment and assassinations. More than 150 environmental activists were killed in Brazil between 2012 and 2016, including 50 in 2015 alone. Many of the assassinated activists were indigenous or Afro-descendant.

The need to protect environmental resources from degradation is underscored by the threat posed by climate change and natural disasters, both of which are exacerbated by human factors such as land degradation and shoddy construction. Weather patterns such as El Niño have resulted in both severe droughts and flooding. In 2016 more than 3.5 million people were food insecure in Central America's so-called "Dry Corridor" as a result of the region's worst drought in thirty years. In Guatemala alone, a country with one of the highest child malnutrition rates in the world, nearly 1 million people were considered food insecure in 2015. Parts of Central America are still recovering from Hurricane Mitch, which killed as many as 20,000 people, most of them in Honduras and Nicaragua, in 1998. Millions were left homeless and billions of dollars of crops were destroyed. Shrinking glaciers in the Andes have left some large cities, like La Paz, in severe water shortages. In other countries, El Niño has brought heavy rains, which have resulted in extensive flooding and landslides. As many as 30,000 were killed in floods and mudslides in Caracas, Venezuela, in December 1999. In 2017 Peru suffered from widespread flooding that displaced thousands. Of course, not all of the region's natural disasters were climate-related. Between 100,000–200,000 were killed in Haiti's 2010 earthquake, which followed devastating hurricanes in 2008 and 2009.

Increasing temperatures and decreasing precipitation in coming decades could result in decreased food production, decreasing water supply in more arid areas and flooding in urban areas, the loss of bio-diverse ecosystems, the spread of disease, the loss of coastal areas, and increases in poverty and inequality.[23] Those living in poor urban households, two-thirds of the region's poor, may be particularly susceptible to the impact of climate change and natural disasters.[24] Pollution, flooding, and exposure to contaminated waste are merely a few of the environmentally related health risks for urban dwellers in informal, or precarious, settlements. This enhanced risk is, of course, the result of development failures.

CONCLUSION

Latin America's economies are more complex than they were half a century ago. Although agribusiness remains prominent throughout the region, many countries have successfully diversified to manufacturing and services. Brazil, the world's second largest beef exporter, is also one of the world's largest exporters of airplanes. Foreign investment no longer means resources coming from the northern countries to Latin America. China, a developing country, is fast becoming one of the largest investors in the region. Local elites and industrialists are themselves becoming investors. Colombian industrialists invest not only in their own country but also in other Latin American countries and the United States. Significant gains have been made toward reducing poverty and inequality in the region thanks to a dramatic increase in social spending.

Yet not all is rosy. The vicissitudes of climate and supply and demand make the economies of those countries very vulnerable. Despite reductions in poverty, many remain only just above the poverty line, eking out a living in the region's informal sector. Precious natural resources continue to be developed and extracted by foreign entities, much as they were hundreds of years ago. The new Trump administration in the United States also introduces a measure of uncertainty. If large numbers of undocumented immigrants are deported, the remittances to their countries will be reduced. If NAFTA is renegotiated, it will have serious effects on the Mexican economy. Thus, although Latin America's economic prospects are improving, the region remains vulnerable.

SUGGESTIONS FOR FURTHER READING

Bulmer-Thomas, Victor. *The Economic History of Latin America Since Independence.* New York: Cambridge University Press, 1994.

Cardoso, Eliana, and Ann Helwege. *Latin America's Economy: Diversity, Trends and Conflicts.* Cambridge, MA: The MIT Press, 1995.

Frank, Andre Gunder. *Capitalism and Underdevelopment in Latin America.* New York: Monthly Review Press, 1967.

Franko, Patrice, *The Puzzle of Latin American Economic Development.* Lanham, MD: Rowman and Littlefield, 2007.

Hershberg, Eric, and Fred Rosen. *Latin America After Neoliberalism: Turning the Tide in the 21st Century?* New York: The New Press, 2007.

Kingstone, Peter. *The Political Economy of Latin America: Reflections on Neoliberalism and Development.* New York: Routledge, 2011.

Reyes, Javier, and W. Charles Sawyer. *Latin American Economic Development*, 2nd ed. New York: Routledge, 2016.

Silva, Eduardo. *Challenging Neoliberalism in Latin America.* New York: Cambridge University Press, 2009.

NOTES

1. Eduardo Galeano, *Open Veins: Five Centuries of the Pillage of a Continent.* (New York: Monthly Review Press, 1973), 2.

2. Victor Bulmer-Thomas, *The Economic History of Latin America Since Independence* (New York: Cambridge University Press, 1994), 24.

3. Quoted in Miguel Urrutia, *The Development of the Colombian Labor Movement* (New Haven: Yale University Press, 1969), 6–7.

4. Bulmer-Thomas, *The Economic History of Latin America Since Independence*, 240.

5. Manual Pastor Jr., *Capital Flight and the Latin American Debt Crisis* (Washington DC: Economic Policy Institute, 1989), 4.

6. Eliana Cardoso and Ann Helwege, *Latin America's Economy: Diversity, Trends and Conflicts.* (Cambridge, MA: The MIT Press, 1995), 111.

7. Ibid., 110–111.

8. "Washington Consensus," Global Trade Negotiations Homepage, Center for International Development at Harvard University, April, 2003, www.cid.harvard.edu/cidtrade/issues/washington.html

9. See Rose J. Spalding, *Contesting Trade in Central America: Market Reform and Resistance.* (Austin: University of Texas Press, 2014).

10. ALBA-TCP, What is ALBA? 2010 www.alba-tcp.org/en/contenido/alba-tcp-eng.

11. Manuel Orozco, Laura Porras, and Julia Yansura. "The Continued Growth of Family Remittances to Latin America and the Caribbean in 2015." Washington, DC: Inter-American Dialogue, February 2016.

12. Margaret Myers, Kevin Gallagher, and Fei Yuan, "Chinese Finance to Latin America: Doubling Down" (Washington, DC: The Dialogue, February 2016). www.thedialogue.org/wp-content/uploads/2016/02/Dialogue-LoansReport-v4-lowres.pdf.

13. ECLAC, Foreign Direct Investment in Latin America and the Caribbean 2016. http://repositorio.cepal.org/bitstream/handle/11362/40214/6/S1600662_en.pdf.

14. United Nations, "Transforming our world: the 2030 Agenda for Sustainable Development" (A/RES/70/1), September 2015.

15. United Nations General Assembly, "United Nations Millennium Declaration," September 18, 2000, A/Res/55/2 www.un.org/millennium/declaration/ares552e.pdf.

16. United Nations, Millennium Development Goals Report, 2015: Regional Backgrounder Latin America and the Caribbean, July 6, 2015. www.un.org/millenniumgoals/2015_MDG_Report/pdf/backgrounders/MDG%202015%20PR%20Bg%20LAC.pdf.

17. The Gini coefficient measures inequality of income distribution on a scale of 1 (perfect equality) to 100 (perfect inequality).

18. Inter-American Development Bank, The Labyrinth: How Can Latin American and the Caribbean Navigate the Global Economy (Inter-American Development Bank, Washington, DC: 2015), 51. https://publications.iadb.org/bitstream/handle/11319/6850/2015-Latin-American-and-Caribbean-Macroeconomic-Report-The-Labyrinth-How-Can-Latin%20America-and-the-Caribbean-Navigate-the-Global Economy.pdf;jsessionid=47AECF5F9D7804A8FEC952C0091AA5C0?sequence=1.

19. United Nations Development Program, "One third of Latin Americans risk falling into poverty, says UNDP," August 26, 2014. www.latinamerica.undp.org/content/rblac/en/home/presscenter/pressreleases/2014/08/26/un-tercio-de-los-latinoamericanos-en-riesgo-de-caer-en-la-pobreza-dice-el-pnud/.

20. United Nations, Millennium Development Goals Report, 2015: Regional Backgrounder Latin America and the Caribbean, July 6, 2015. www.un.org/millenniumgoals/2015_MDG_Report/pdf/backgrounders/MDG%202015%20PR%20Bg%20LAC.pdf.

21. Comisión Económica para América Latina y el Caribe (CEPAL), ¡Ni una más! Del dicho al hecho: ¿Cuánto falta por recorrer?, October 2009 www.cepal.org/mujer/noticias/noticias/2/37892/niunamas2009.pdf.

22. Inter-American Development Bank, The Labyrinth: How Can Latin American and the Caribbean Navigate the Global Economy (Inter-American Development Bank, Washington, DC: 2015), 55. https://publications.iadb.org/bitstream/handle/11319/6850/2015-Latin-American-and-Caribbean-Macroeconomic-Report-The-Labyrinth-How-Can-Latin%20America-and-the-Caribbean-Navigate-the-Global.

23. Economic Commission on Latin America and the Caribbean, "The economic impact of climate change in Latin America: Paradoxes and challenges of sustainable development." (Santiago, Chile: United Nations, 2015), 24. http://repositorio.cepal.org/bitstream/handle/11362/37311/S1420655_en.pdf.

24. Lucy Winchester and Raquel Szlachman, "The Urban Poor's Vulnerability to Climate Change in Latin America and the Caribbean," http://siteresources.worldbank.org/INTURBANDEVELOPMENT/Resources/336387-1342044185050/8756911-1342044630817/V2Chap28.pdf.

6

LATIN AMERICA AND THE
UNITED STATES

INTRODUCTION

It is difficult to overstate the role that the United States has played in shaping Latin American politics and development. From the early nineteenth century, when the US first identified the region as its "backyard," through the Cold War, it has wielded enormous power and influence. As a result, Latin America's political and economic development was often tied to US security interests. Although relations in the post–Cold War era have created new opportunities for regional cooperation, the legacy of United States intervention has loomed large in the minds of Latin Americans.

RELATIONS IN THE EARLY YEARS

The primary concern of the United States during the period following the independence of the Latin American nations was that the new nations might fall under the control of European powers. The Monroe Doctrine (1823) was originally a defensive statement, proclaiming that further efforts by European nations to colonize land or interfere with states in the Americas would be viewed as acts of aggression and would require US intervention. The doctrine effectively established the region as the United States' own backyard. In fact, the United States had little ability to enforce that threat. At the same time, the doctrine noted that the United States would neither interfere with existing European colonies nor meddle in the internal concerns of European countries.

From 1823 until 1845, relations between the governments of the Americas were good but very weak as the new nations consolidated independence. British sea power dominated and the US government took no action to enforce the Monroe Doctrine when the British asserted their authority over the Falkland (Malvinas) Islands in

December 1832. The US government also took no action during this time when the French and British set up blockades around Argentina.

US aspirations of territorial conquest during the mid-nineteenth century were driven by "Manifest Destiny," the belief that the United States had the right to spread across the continent to the Pacific Ocean. In 1845 President James Polk annexed Texas and issued the first change to the Monroe Doctrine. The Polk Corollary declared that the United States was opposed to "any European interference" in the Americas, even "by voluntary transfer." Shortly thereafter, war between Mexico and the United States (1846–1848) resulted in Mexico losing about one-third of its territory, including nearly all of present-day California, Utah, Nevada, Arizona, and New Mexico.

By 1860 the government of the United States was more concerned with internal matters than with Latin America, first because of the US Civil War (1861–1865) and reconstruction, and then because of internal development, both in the consolidation of the West and the growth of large businesses. When Austria and France invaded Mexico in 1863, making Maximilian emperor of the country, the United States was too involved in its own internal problems to enforce the Monroe Doctrine.

By contrast, the years between 1890 and 1933 were ones of active intervention by the United States government in Latin America. During an 1895 boundary dispute between Venezuela and Great Britain's colony of British Guiana, Britain accepted the United States' intervention to force arbitration of the disputed territory under the Olney Doctrine. Crafted by Secretary of State Richard Olney, the doctrine claimed the United States' right to intervene under the Monroe Doctrine. Shortly after, the United States became involved in the Spanish-American War, beginning with the sinking of the battleship Maine in Havana Harbor and ending with the 1898 Treaty of Paris, which allowed the United States to take temporary control of Cuba, and ceded ownership of Puerto Rico, Guam, and the Philippine islands.

Through the Platt Amendment (1901), the United States government laid down eight conditions to which the Cuban government had to agree before the withdrawal of US forces and the transfer of sovereignty could begin. Among them, the Cuban government was prohibited from entering into any international treaty that would compromise Cuban independence or allow foreign powers to use the island for military purposes. The United States also reserved the right to intervene in Cuban affairs in order to defend Cuban independence and to maintain "a government adequate for the protection of life, property, and individual liberty." Under that last clause, the United States sent troops to Cuba three different times.

Theodore Roosevelt was the most active president during this period. During his presidency, the two most notable interventions were the backing of a rebellion in the Colombian area of Panama and the Roosevelt Corollary to the Monroe Doctrine, which led to US military intervention in the Dominican Republic, Haiti, and Nicaragua.

A French company had begun attempts to dig a canal through Panama in 1882, but failed to complete the project. In 1902, Roosevelt negotiated the rights to the property for US$40 million and started negotiations with Colombia for a treaty. After the Colombian senate refused to ratify the treaty, the president joined with those holding business interests in Panama to stage a revolution. After US military actions prevented the Colombian army from fighting the insurgents, Panama gained independence on

November 3, 1903. The Hay–Bunau-Varilla Treaty signed gave the United States rights to the zone around the canal "as if it were sovereign." The forty-eight-mile Panama Canal opened in August 1914.

The Roosevelt Corollary was an addition to the Monroe Doctrine articulated by President Roosevelt in his State of the Union address in 1904 after the Venezuela Crisis of 1902–1903. Under international law at the time, the government of a country had the right to intervene in a country that owed money to its businesses. The corollary stated that the United States would intervene in conflicts between European countries and Latin American countries to enforce legitimate claims of the European powers, rather than having the Europeans press their claims directly. US presidents cited the Roosevelt Corollary as justification for US interventions in Cuba (1906–1909), Nicaragua (1909–1910, 1912–1925, and 1926–1933), Haiti (1915–1934), and the Dominican Republic (1916–1924). In those cases, US civilians were sent to collect customs duties (the major source of governmental revenue in the countries). US Marines were sent to protect those civilians and in some cases to enter into active combat against opposition groups.

This interventionist policy continued until 1933 with President Franklin Roosevelt's Good Neighbor Policy. Its main principle was that of non-intervention in the domestic affairs of Latin America. Under this new policy, the Platt Amendment was rescinded, and US custom receivers and military troops were removed from Haiti, the Dominican Republic, and Nicaragua. The treaty with Panama was revised, giving more rights to the Panamanian government.

At least part of this pivot could be explained by changes in geopolitical affairs. The rise of Adolf Hitler in Germany necessitated a shift in resources. As such, the Good Neighbor Policy was based on the "economy of force doctrine," which was based on three principles: (1) Money and time can only be used once; (2) Latin America was not as important to the United States as other parts of world; and (3) The US government needed an inexpensive policy for Latin America so resources could be used in other places. The new policy was carried out in three ways. The United States started giving foreign aid for economic projects. However, the loans were "tied," meaning that the money had to be spent in the United States. Instead of sending US troops to the countries, the United States trained Latin American troops. And the US government supported compliant political leaders, that is, ones that the US government could rely upon to carry out policies favorable to the United States. Often those leaders were dictators (Fulgencio Batista in Cuba, Rafael Trujillo in the Dominican Republic, and Anastasio Somoza García in Nicaragua). During World War II, Latin American countries in general cooperated with the United States and the Allies, although Argentina, able to sell beef and wheat to both sides, declared war on the Axis Powers only slightly before it had to in order to be a charter member of the United Nations.

THE COLD WAR

The United States emerged from World War II more powerful, and with a renewed interest in expanding its influence in Latin America. Both the Inter-American Treaty of Reciprocal Assistance (the "Rio Treaty") of 1947 and the establishment of the Organization of American States (1948) were collective security arrangements, meaning that an attack against one was an attack against all. The OAS Charter recognized the territorial integrity of sovereign states by prohibiting intervention. As conflict increased with the Soviet Union and later the People's Republic of China, along with the development of nuclear weapons and intermediate-range missiles, for the security of the United States it became more important that the communist countries have no allies in the Western Hemisphere. The US government carried out a number of diplomatic and military interventions to protect its economic interests and national security.

The first case was in Guatemala, a country that had traditionally been dominated by military rule. After the military overthrew the dictator in 1944, two presidents were elected. During the presidency of the second, Jacobo Árbenz (1951–1954), the national congress passed a land reform program expropriating uncultivated lands and redistributing those lands to peasants. The largest landowner in the nation was the United Fruit Company, and both US secretary of state John Foster Dulles and his brother, CIA director Allen Dulles, had previous connections with that multinational. The Central Intelligence Agency developed a psychological warfare program and enlisted Guatemala exile Carlos Castillo Armas to overthrow Árbenz. A small number of troops trained by the CIA and led by Castillo invaded the country and the CIA carried out bombings. Árbenz was forced to resign by the military in June 1954.

The second case came in Cuba in 1959, when the guerrillas led by Fidel Castro overthrew the military dictatorship of Fulgencio Batista. Relations between the United States and Cuba worsened when the Castro government began nationalizing US businesses and established diplomatic relations with the Soviet Union, signing an agreement that Soviet oil would be sent to the island to be refined. When US companies on the island refused to refine Soviet crude, the Cuban government seized them in June 1960. In retaliation, the following month the US government ended the quota through which Cuba could sell sugar in the United States above the international market price and in October 1960 began an economic embargo on the island. In January 1961, in his final month in office, President Eisenhower suspended diplomatic relations.

In April of 1961, the United States government sponsored the Bay of Pigs invasion by Cuban exiles who were armed and trained in Central America by the CIA. The Cuban military repelled the invasion. The attempts to remove Castro from power after the Bay of Pigs included an assassination attempt involving an exploding cigar, as well as another that was laced with LSD and another that was poisoned; poisoned pens and diving suits; and a hit by Mafia agents on the island. In addition, the United States put diplomatic pressure on Cuba by ending economic relations and by having the Organization of American States exclude Cuba.

The experience in Cuba resulted in a shift of the economy of force doctrine under President John F. Kennedy. The US government began encouraging democratic solutions as an antidote to leftist revolutions. The "Alliance for Progress," which built upon Eisenhower's loan program, was designed to foster economic development through loans, reduce poverty, and promote democracy. This, it was believed, would undercut support for leftist guerrillas in the region. Despite the funding allocated to the project, some US$18 billion during the 1960s, the program failed to stimulate growth. But the economy of force doctrine remained the same in other ways. In some cases, the Central Intelligence Agency attempted to remove right-wing autocrats, one of whom was dictator Rafael Trujillo in the Dominican Republic. Trujillo was assassinated in 1961, although apparently not by a plot carried out by the CIA.

By the mid-1960s it was clear that US Cold War policy in the region would favor military dictatorships over leftist regimes, as was the case with the 1964 coup in Brazil. The perceived threat of Communist subversion resulted in military governments in many countries in Latin America. One such case was Chile, a country that had traditionally been democratic and was one of the showcases during the Alliance for Progress years. In 1970 Salvador Allende, a member of the Socialist Party, was elected president by a simple plurality—despite US efforts to sway the vote. Even prior to the election, the CIA planted false stories in the Chilean media, hoping to frighten voters about the consequences of voting for Allende. Allende won a plurality of the votes but not an absolute majority. Under the Chilean constitution, in such a case the Senate would choose the president. The US government used various tactics to sway the vote away from Allende, but the Senate followed tradition and elected him nonetheless.

After his inauguration, Allende began to restructure Chilean society along socialist lines while retaining the democratic form of government and respecting civil liberties and the due process of law. In 1971, Chile expropriated the US-owned copper companies without compensation. At the same time, the US government increased its activities to destabilize the Chilean government, including decreasing economic aid while increasing military aid to the country. On September 11, 1973, the Chilean military overthrew Allende, replacing him with a military dictatorship led by Augusto Pinochet. Although the actions of the US government assisted in the end of the democratic government and the CIA apparently had prior knowledge of the coup, in a conversation with President Nixon, Henry Kissinger stated, "We didn't do it. We helped them."

While other South American countries fell to military dictatorships, Central America was also a region in crisis. Revolutionary movements emerged in El Salvador, Guatemala, and Nicaragua in response to socioeconomic exclusion and political repression. The Alliance for Progress had failed to deliver any meaningful change to the region. The United States had a long-standing interest in Nicaragua. Following the occupation of US marines (1912–1933), the United States created the feared National Guard. The head of the National Guard, Anastasio Somoza García, and his sons ruled Nicaragua for more than four decades with significant support from the US government. The Somoza family controlled some 60 percent of the national economy and constructed a democratic façade, using the repressive National Guard to maintain order. In 1962 students and intellectuals created a movement to defeat the dictatorship, naming it Sandinista National Liberation Front (FSLN) after nationalist revolutionary leader Augusto César Sandino, who had been assassinated by Somoza's National Guard in 1934.

By 1974 the guerrillas were capable of initiating attacks throughout the country. In 1978 Pedro Joaquín Chamorro, director of the national newspaper *La Prensa* who had opposed Anastasio Somoza Debayle, was murdered. His murder resulted in protests against the regime and increased support for the FSLN. More than a year of general strikes and guerrilla activity eventually forced Somoza from power as thousands of guerrillas and civilians entered the Plaza de la República on July 19, 1979.

The Carter administration initially maintained diplomatic relations with the FSLN government while attempting to strengthen the private sector, giving it economic aid. But the election of Ronald Reagan in 1980 resulted in a significant shift in policy. Reagan ordered an economic blockade in 1981 in an effort to cripple the country's economy. The remnants of the Somoza National Guard, settled in Honduras, Costa

Rica, and Miami, soon received clandestine financial support from the US government and organized a group of counterrevolutionaries known as the Contras. The war with the Contras had a devastating impact on Nicaragua's people and its economy. The US Congress attempted, with limited success under the Boland Amendment (1982, 1984), to prevent the Reagan administration from giving military assistance to the Contras.

In neighboring El Salvador, junior officers in the Salvadoran military carried out a reformist coup in October 1979 in hopes of preventing a civil war. The country's military government had become increasingly repressive and fraudulent elections prevented any peaceful means of political participation. The Carter administration sent the new regime an aid package of considerable size. Death squad activity, however, continued and hardliners took over the governing junta. Between 1977 and 1980, many priests were tortured, beaten, and exiled, and eleven were murdered. El Salvador's archbishop, Óscar Romero, was murdered by death squads in March 1980 for his calls to end state repression. Later that year, four American churchwomen were raped and murdered by El Salvador's National Guard. In response, Carter temporarily suspended military aid only to restore it two months later.

The assassination of Archbishop Romero resulted in growing support for the Farabundo Martí National Liberation Front (FMLN) guerrillas. The FMLN launched its "final offensive" on January 10, 1981, hoping to take power before Ronald Reagan took office. Their offensive surprised government forces but failed to overwhelm them. Reagan took a tough stand against the FMLN. When the president wanted to increase military and economic aid to El Salvador, Congress voted in January 1982 to require certification by the Reagan administration that El Salvador was making progress in curbing abuses by the military. Reluctantly, the administration accepted the certification requirement and proceeded with its policy of a military buildup against the FMLN, while urging El Salvador's government to end death squad activity. As the war dragged on, the US government funneled nearly US$5 billion into its efforts to defeat the FMLN on the battlefield. The United States also pursued a political strategy in El Salvador: supporting elections with a US-friendly candidate. Jose Napoleon Duarte, who lost the 1972 presidential election due to fraud, won the 1984 presidential elections. His victory gave the Reagan administration a cosmetically acceptable civilian president, but he was unable to curb death squad activity or military abuses.

By the late 1980s, both El Salvador and Nicaragua had been devastated by US-sponsored wars. As the Cold War waned, the US lost interest in military victories in the region. In 1990 US-backed coalition candidate Violeta de Chamorro defeated the FSLN's Daniel Ortega in the presidential elections. The two sides soon began to negotiate the end of the conflict. In El Salvador in 1992 and in Guatemala in 1996, opposing forces signed UN-mediated peace agreements. Between 400,000 and 500,000 people had died in the wars in El Salvador, Guatemala, and Nicaragua.

SINCE THE END OF THE COLD WAR

After the collapse of the Soviet Union and the end of the Cold War in the late 1980s, the focus of relations between the government of the United States and those of Latin America shifted from security to economic and political issues. US policy in the post–Cold War era was more pragmatic and less ideological. It was also less interventionist and more cooperative. Although there were notable shifts across administrations, US policy was generally characterized by remarkable continuity. This section addresses three major issue areas that have persisted across recent administrations: democracy, drugs, and immigration. Free trade and US-Cuba relations, two other key issues, are covered extensively in Chapters 5 and 19.

Democracy

Despite the rhetoric, promoting democracy was not always a top US priority in Latin America. Though its commitment to supporting democracy improved following the end of the Cold War, US support for democracy and human rights proved to be uneven across administrations. In 1991 the Organization of American States (OAS) adopted Resolution 1080, which declared that "representative democracy is an indispensable condition for the stability, peace, and development of the region"[1] and provided for high-level meetings in the event of an interruption of a country's constitutional process. The first test of the resolution and the US commitment to democracy in the region came in September 1991 when newly elected Haitian president Jean-Bertrand Aristide, a former Roman Catholic priest popular among the poor, was overthrown in a military coup d'état. President George H. W. Bush called for the restoration of democracy, and worked with the Organization of American States (OAS) to impose a trade embargo on all goods except medicine and food. The OAS denounced Haiti's illegitimate government for three years, though it would ultimately take the use of force by the United States in 1994 to bring military rule to an end. President Aristide returned to Haiti in October 1994. He was removed from office again via coup in 2004. Aristide, who was in exile until 2011, claimed that the George W. Bush administration had kidnapped him.

US resolve to support Resolution 1080 came into play in response to four other cases: Peru (1992), Guatemala (1993), Paraguay (1996), and Honduras (2009). Although the overall record on democratic defense was mixed—the hemisphere's governments might have been more forceful in dealing with some of these situations—the OAS nonetheless reacted swiftly and positively on all four occasions. That said, there clearly were limitations to this approach. Following Peruvian president Alberto Fujimori's 1992 "self-coup," in which he suspended the constitution, closed the congress, and took over the courts, the OAS invoked Resolution 1080 and the United States government applied sanctions to express US disapproval. However, once the Fujimori administration held new elections in November 1992, international pressure substantially diminished. One reason for that was the effective anti-drug policy of the Peruvian government.

From the beginning, the Clinton administration (1993–2001) claimed to attach high value to promoting liberal, representative democracy along the lines of the US model. This commitment to supporting democracy and promoting hemispheric cooperation was most clearly expressed at the first Summit of the Americas, a hemispheric meeting of democratically elected leaders in Miami in 1994. The resulting "Declaration of Principles" and "Plan of Action" documents identified twenty-three areas of cooperation, including strengthening democracy and improving human rights, economic integration, and security.[2] However, in the latter years of the 1990s, new leaders challenged the Clinton administration's model for liberal representative democracy. The changing political climate in Latin America and unpopular economic policies also created public dissatisfaction with this democracy promotion model in the region.

Among these new leaders, Venezuelan president Hugo Chávez in particular challenged the conventional concept of democracy held by US officials. Chávez, a former lieutenant colonel and a populist elected in 1998, appealed directly to the people, bypassing democratic institutions such as political parties. He also gave a greater role in public works and development projects to the armed forces. He publicly repudiated the idea of representative democracy and the importance of checks and balances, which he saw as responsible for the country's ills. His message captivated the Venezuelan people, at least the mass of poor who overwhelmingly supported him.

The Clinton administration maintained a wait-and-see posture in response to Chávez—one not unrelated to considerable US oil interests in Venezuela—preferring to permit Chávez to exercise his rhetorical excesses as long as his actions fell strictly within constitutional and legal bounds. The George W. Bush administration, however, preferred other methods. In addition to openly criticizing Chávez, the National Endowment for Democracy (NED) channeled considerable funds to Chávez's opposition.

On April 11, 2002, the Venezuelan military overthrew President Hugo Chávez. Three days later Chávez was reinstated after his supporters rioted in Caracas. After the coup, Chávez asserted numerous times that United States government officials knew about plans for a coup, approved of them, and assumed they would be successful and alleged that two military officers from the United States were present in the headquarters of coup plotters.[3] Rear Admiral Carlos Molina, a central leader of the coup, later said that the coup leaders felt they were acting with US support. President George W. Bush denied the involvement of the United States, and blamed Chávez's provocations for the "change of government."[4] Meanwhile, Latin American leaders condemned the coup, ultimately prompting the administration to change its position.

The coup in Venezuela set the stage for more acrimonious relations not only between the Bush administration and Chávez, but also between the United States and a wave of new leftist presidents throughout the region who increasingly challenged US hegemony. The lack of US credibility in democracy promotion and US policy priorities elsewhere led to a decline in US influence in the region.

President Obama initially represented a welcomed change in the eyes of the region's leaders. Less interventionist than his predecessor, the administration generally shied away from expressing support or opposition for leaders in the region. But Obama otherwise represented continuity on most key issues in the region. Critics charge that his response to the 2009 coup against President Manuel Zelaya in Honduras was weak, taking days to refer to events as a coup in comparison to the immediate, widespread condemnation by Latin American presidents. Honduras was suspended from the OAS until an agreement was reached for Zelaya's return to the country in 2011, long after US aid and diplomatic recognition had been restored. For a second time, Latin American presidents led the United States in the support for democracy.

Drugs

In 1971 President Nixon declared a war on drugs, and in 1973 reorganized the various federal drug law enforcement agencies into the Drug Enforcement Agency (DEA). Even after many organizational changes over the years, the strategy of the US government continued to be to disrupt the market for illegal drugs in a way that both reduces the profitability of the drug trade and increases the costs of drugs to consumers. In their best year, the DEA working together with foreign governments seized about one percent of the worldwide drug crop, leaving 99 percent free to supply the United States.

Latin America has historically been and remains the closest source of illicit drugs coming into the United States and, as such, has been much of the focus of United States anti-drug policy. In 1975, the Mexican government launched a major crackdown on drugs, particularly marijuana, as a result of US pressure. Afterwards, Colombia became the center of marijuana production in the hemisphere. Drug dealers, especially those from Medellín, soon realized that there was more money to be made in cocaine. They invested their marijuana profits in cocaine, with the raw material, coca, coming from Bolivia and Peru. This provided start-up cash for drug entrepreneurs. Two of these, Carlos Lehder Rivas and Jorge Luis Ochoa, decided that instead of using "mules" (individuals carrying small amounts of drugs) and trying to make money by selling cocaine in small quantities at high prices, they would go for lower prices and higher volume. They did this by using airplanes, having their pilots fly in slowly at low altitudes, employing traffic lanes already used by others, for example, oil-rig pilots. This led to the so-called Medellín cartel, led by Pablo Escobar.

One ambitious effort to stop the drug trade was Plan Colombia (described in Chapter 11), agreed to in 1998–1999 when Colombian President Andrés Pastrana and US President Bill Clinton agreed on the United States giving military aid as part of an anti-cocaine strategy. The plan would come to define the increasingly militarized, re-securitized approach to US drug policy in the region. As a result of the plan, Colombia became the third largest recipient of military aid in the world. Originally the money was for the training of troops, fumigation of drugs, and capture of drug dealers. After the terrorist attacks of September 11, 2001, and the election of Álvaro Uribe as Colombian president in 2002, that focus was broadened to include the Marxist guerrilla groups (relabeled as "narcoterrorists") that had been operating in the country since the 1960s. Although the plan did lead to diminished guerrilla violence, it had little effect on the quantity of drugs produced in Colombia. By 2015, Colombia produced more coca than any other country (420 metric tons), followed by Peru (345 metric tons) and Bolivia (230 metric tons).[5] Coca production continued increasing during 2016 and 2017.

A significant recent shift was a change in the route for moving cocaine from Colombia and the Andes to the United States, as well as the growing prominence of Mexican drug cartels. During the 1970s and 1980s, much of the US drug interdiction focus was on the Caribbean. As enforcement efforts grew, Colombian cartels increasingly sought to move product through Mexico. As Colombian cartels declined, Mexican drug cartels, such as the Zetas, Sinaloa, and Gulf Cartels, came to dominate cocaine trafficking. Another consequence of the shift to Mexico is that Central America has become a major transshipment hub between Colombia and Mexico, adding to the region's woes. In 2007 the US, Mexican, and Central American governments announced the launch of the Mérida Initiative, also known as "Plan Mexico" among critics for its similarities to Plan Colombia. The plan authorized US$1.6 billion over three years (2007–2010) to provide technical assistance and military equipment, as well as funding for judicial reform and improving institutional capacity. By 2014 Mexico had received US$2.35 billion with little evidence of improvement. Rule of law remained a serious concern and there were ongoing concerns about human rights abuses by Mexican security forces, particularly following allegations of state involvement in massacres in 2014.[6]

Immigration

The story of Latin American immigration to the United States is too complicated to discuss in full here, so this section offers a brief overview of US-Latin American immigration history with a focus on more recent issues. In particular, unauthorized immigration has been a key policy issue for US administrations for the past several decades. In 2014 there were approximately 11 million unauthorized immigrants in the United States; approximately half of those were from Mexico. Unauthorized immigration from Mexico declined between 2007 and 2014, just as unauthorized immigration from Central American countries increased.

US expansion into the West meant that immigration was relatively fluid for decades. It wasn't until 1875 that the United States began to place restrictions on immigration, and those generally weren't aimed at Latin Americans. Only with the Great Depression did the US begin to target immigrants from the region. But even that policy was amended in 1942, when the US government enacted the Bracero program, ultimately employing some 4.5 million Mexicans to fill jobs left by the US war effort. There were many charges of abuse, exploitation, and discrimination against Mexican workers. US citizens complained that the migrant workers were crowding US citizens out of the job market, and the program was terminated in 1964.

Between 1964 and 1986, there was relatively little policy movement on unauthorized immigration from Latin America. In 1986 the Immigrant Reform and Control Act (IRCA) sought to address the issue by fining employers who hired unauthorized immigrants and increasing border security. The IRCA also included an amnesty for those living in the United States prior to January 1982; that amnesty extended to approximately two million Mexicans. Provided they met certain criteria, undocumented immigrants could apply for temporary and later for permanent legal status, including citizenship. In the end, the effort was ineffective. It would be more than a decade before the US government would undertake another major policy initiative.

Amnesty and asylum in US immigration policy were themes repeated throughout the 1980s and 1990s. Central Americans, primarily from El Salvador and Guatemala, began entering the United States in increasing numbers as a result of wars in the region. Unlike Cubans, who had long benefited from a preferential asylum policy under the 1966 Cuban Adjustment Act, Central Americans were not eligible for asylum. The Reagan administration maintained that the Central Americans were "economic migrants" as acknowledging the repression could have jeopardized US aid to the Guatemalan and Salvadoran governments. Some became eligible for Temporary Protected Status (TPS) in 1990, which provides temporary residency status to those fleeing war, natural disaster, and other "extraordinary circumstances." A similar disparity emerged in the 1990s when emigration from Haiti surged following the 1991 coup against Aristide. Intercepted Haitians were detained or returned, first under George H. W. Bush and then under Clinton. Thousands of Cuban émigrés, who were fleeing the island following the economic collapse of the Soviet Union, were still subject to the 1966 policy. That changed in 1995, when the Act was amended to state that those Cubans intercepted at sea would be returned, while those who made it to land could stay in the US, a policy known as "wet-foot, dry-foot."

The next major attempt at immigration reform was the 1996 Illegal Immigration Reform and Immigrant Responsibility Act (IIRIRA), which aimed to improve and expand border control and crack down on human smuggling. The law also outlined removal and detention procedures, limited judicial authority in removal considerations, and restricted access to public assistance. It established penalties for unlawful presence in the United States, barring individuals from obtaining visas for re-entry for a period of between three and ten years. The IIRIRA effectively criminalized undocumented immigration by establishing penalties for illegal entry, document fraud, and false claims of citizenship. Additionally, foreign nationals (including both documented and undocumented immigrants) convicted of even misdemeanor offenses became eligible for expedited removal. Although the law failed to reduce undocumented immigration (and by some accounts magnified the problem), it did result in a wave of mass deportations and mass incarcerations.

One notable consequence of the law was the deportation of thousands of young men to Central America, thousands of whom took their street gang culture with them. Once resettled in their countries of origin, they developed transnational street gangs and criminal networks throughout El Salvador, Guatemala, and Honduras (the "Northern Triangle"). Soon gang violence, drug trafficking, and other criminal activity resulted in the highest homicide rates in the world. By 2014 it was clear that the region's violence was the driving factor in record migration from the region, particularly among unaccompanied minors.

Following the September 11, 2001, terrorist attacks, the Immigration and Naturalization Service (INS) was moved from the Department of Justice to the Department of Homeland Security and most of its functions were moved to new bureaucracies, including US Citizenship and Immigration Services (USCIS) and US Immigration and Customs Enforcement (ICE). The change dramatically increased funding for border control and redefined immigration as a national security issue.

The failure of IIRIRA and other immigration policies to sufficiently address border control and undocumented immigration has made it a politically polarizing issue, particularly in border states. Although there have been numerous proposals in Congress over the past decade, none have been approved by both houses. One proposal, the Development, Relief, and Education for Alien Minors (DREAM) Act, would provide legal residency and a path to citizenship for undocumented immigrants aged 12–35— many of whom were brought into the country by their parents—who graduate from US high schools and have been accepted into an institution of higher education. Though the bill failed to pass both houses, in 2014 President Obama signed two executive actions based on the bill. Deferred Action for Childhood Arrivals (DACA) and Deferred Action for Parents of Americans and Lawful Permanent Residents (DAPA) would delay deportation for millions of undocumented immigrants and their parents. In June 2016, the Supreme Court split 4–4 on a twenty-six-state lawsuit against Obama's amnesty decrees, leaving in place a 2015 injunction blocking the decrees.

The controversy over the decrees and the issue of undocumented immigrants in general became a major focal point of the 2016 US election. Democratic Party nominee Hillary Clinton pledged to undo some of her husband's policies and develop a path to citizenship, but Republican Party nominee Donald Trump pledged to establish new immigration controls, engage in mass deportations, and to build "an impenetrable physical wall on the southern border, on day one," which he claimed Mexico would pay for.[7] Tensions over president Trump's insistence that Mexico pay for a border wall led

Mexican president Enrique Peña Nieto to cancel a meeting with Trump during his first weeks in office.

CONCLUSION

The nature of the relationships of the US government with the governments of the Latin American nations have been defined by cycles of conflict and cooperation. US attempts to extend its dominance over the region began in the nineteenth century and continue to the present day. Though the end of the Cold War resulted in a less interventionist approach to the region, the terrorist attacks of September 11, 2001, provided a new basis for re-securitizing US policy in Latin America.

Although the Obama administration offered rapprochement on several issues, including re-establishing diplomatic relations with Cuba and intervening less in domestic affairs, it continued the practice of mass deportations and made little headway on other issues, such as drugs, crime, and economic relations.

It seemed likely that US relations with Latin America would change with the inauguration of Donald Trump on January 20, 2017, but the exact nature of that change remained unclear at the time of this writing. The campaign had focused its attention on the region almost exclusively on immigration and trade agreements, leaving much unknown about policy stances toward Cuba, the war on drugs (which some Latin American leaders believed should be changed), and support for democracy and human rights. That lack of clarity and perceived interest could also mean that, as many times in the past, relationships with Latin America would be secondary to those with other "more important" parts of the world.

SUGGESTIONS FOR FURTHER READING

Crandall, Russell. *The United States and Latin America After the Cold War*. New York: Cambridge University Press, 2008.

Grandin, Greg. *Empire's Workshop: Latin America and the Roots of U.S. Imperialism*. New York: Henry Holt, 2006.

Holden, Robert H., and Eric Zolov. *Latin America and the United States: A Documentary History*. 2nd ed. New York: Oxford University Press, 2010.

LaFeber, Walter. *Inevitable Revolutions: The United States and Central America*. 2nd ed. New York, NY: W. W. Norton, 1993.

Pastor, Robert. *Exiting the Whirlpool: U.S. Foreign Policy Toward Latin America and the Caribbean*. 2nd ed. Boulder, CO: Westview Press, 2001.

Schoultz, Lars. *Beneath the United States: A History of U.S. Policy Toward Latin America*. Cambridge, MA: Harvard University Press, 1998.

Schlesinger, Stephen, and Stephen Kinzer. *Bitter Fruit: The Story of the American Coup in Guatemala*. Revised edition. Cambridge, MA: David Rockefeller Center for Latin American Studies, 2005.

Sigmund, Paul. *The Overthrow of Allende and the Politics of Chile, 1964–1976*. Pittsburgh: University of Pittsburgh Press, 1977.

Smith, Peter. *Talons of the Eagle: Latin America, the United States, and the World*. 4th ed. New York: Oxford University Press, 2012.

Weeks, Gregory. *U.S. and Latin American Relations*. 2nd ed. Hoboken, NJ: Wiley-Blackwell, 2015.

NOTES

1. Organization of American States, "Representative Democracy," AG/RES 1080 (XXI-O/91) www.oas.org/juridico/english/agres1080.htm.

2. "Summit of the Americas Plan of Action," Miami, Florida, December 9–11, 1994, www.summit-americas.org/miamiplan.htm.

3. Juan Forero, "Documents Show C.I.A. Knew of Coup Plot in Venezuela," *The New York Times*, December 3, 2004, www.nytimes.com/2004/12/03/washington/world/documents-show-cia-knew-of-a-coup-plot-in-venezuela.html?_r=0.

4. US Department of State, "Venezuela: Change of Government," April 12, 2002, https://2001-2009.state.gov/r/pa/prs/ps/2002/9316.htm

5. Office of National Drug Control Policy, "Coca in the Andes," www.whitehouse.gov/ondcp/targeting-cocaine-at-the-source.

6. Michael Hoopes, "The Merida Initiative at 7 Years: Institutional Improvement Amidst Increased Militarization." *Small Wars Journal*. September 16, 2015.

7. "Immigration," Trump/Pence Campaign Website, www.donaldjtrump.com/policies/immigration/.

7

THE STRUGGLE FOR DEMOCRACY IN LATIN AMERICA

INTRODUCTION

In 2017, of the twenty Latin America countries, only Cuba did not have a democratically elected chief executive, which seemed to suggest that democracy had finally arrived as the dominant political system in Latin America. Although we maintain that Latin America became more democratic after the late 1970s, it is important to draw attention to the characteristics of democracy, a term that is really quite complex, and to the difficulties that Latin American countries have had in achieving and maintaining constitutional governments. In this chapter, we discuss the ongoing conflict between three models of government in the area: the traditional "living museum" form discussed in Chapter 3; liberal democracy; and an apparent combination of the two called "delegative democracy," a form of populism that at its extreme might better be considered "semi-authoritarian" instead of democratic.

THE DEMOCRATIC WAVE

The 1980s and 1990s brought remarkable change to the world in general and in Latin America in particular. Communism collapsed in the Soviet Union, which then had elections and disappeared as a political entity, replaced by a smaller Russia. In some countries of Asia and Africa, dictatorships disintegrated and elections ensued. In South America, military dictatorships ended in Brazil, Ecuador, Bolivia, Argentina, Uruguay, and Chile. In Paraguay, Alfredo Stroessner—the longest in power of the Latin American caudillos—fell to a military coup whose leaders immediately called for elections.

Changes also occurred in the Central American countries. In Nicaragua internationally monitored elections saw the defeat of the candidate of the ruling Sandinista

party, and even more remarkably that revolutionary party allowed the opposition candidate Violeta Barrios de Chamorro to take office. In Panama, with the assistance of an
armed intervention by the United States, strongman Manuel Antonio Noriega fell and
the previously elected Guillermo Endara occupied the presidency.

Latin America had earlier periods of democratic rule. The first was between 1847
and 1883, the second between 1901 and 1922, and the third between 1944 and 1957.
The third ended with coups related to the Cold War. The current period is the longest
in Latin American history and it might be considered the most important change in
Latin American politics since the wars of independence.[1]

Yet this is not to indicate that all is going well. As Freedom House reported in 2012,
"the dominant recent story has been the steady decline of a critical mass of countries
in the region, a process that has accelerated over the past five years." The countries that
have retreated from records of relatively impressive democratic performance could be
lumped into three categories:

- Countries governed by regimes of what Jorge Castañeda called the "irresponsible
  left." Venezuela under Hugo Chávez was the most notable case, followed by Ecuador, Nicaragua, Bolivia, and, to a less clear-cut degree, Argentina.
- Countries where criminal violence, often driven by drug-trafficking rivalries, was
  so completely out of control as to have weakened press freedom, the rule of law,
  and other democratic indicators. Mexico was the principal example, as Colombia
  had been in the 1980s and 1990s. Drug-related violence also retarded the growth
  of democratic institutions in El Salvador, Guatemala, Honduras, and the Dominican Republic.
- Countries that experienced less-than-democratic leadership upheavals. The main
  examples were Honduras, still recovering from a 2009 coup that removed President Manuel Zelaya from office, and Paraguay, where President Fernando Lugo
  was ousted in an impeachment process that lasted barely twenty-four hours.[2]

THE LATIN AMERICAN CONTEXT FOR DEMOCRACY

As the democratic wave arrived in Latin America, difficulties came from six sources:
the Iberian tradition and history, the misuse of "democracy" before the 1980s, pockets
of underdevelopment along with serious inequities of income distribution, the aftereffects of recent civil wars, and the absence of governments that could effectively implement policies for the nation as a whole.

Challenges to Democracy from the Iberian Tradition and History

Constructing and maintaining a democracy is not an easy matter anywhere. As the
Latin American countries faced a possible democratic future, difficulties arose from a
political tradition unfavorable to limited government, as shown in Chapters 1 and 2.

It might be anticipated that the groups that benefited from the old system would
resist democracy, and if Latin American history since the 1980s is any guide, the two
major groups uncomfortable with the new rules of the game were the military and the
economic elite. Although evidence suggested that the civilian elites now saw democracy
as the best hope for stability, it still seemed possible that, if elected governments in

Latin America faced serious economic difficulties, some members of the military would think of the traditional way of disposing of misbehaving governments—the military coup. There were two attempts to overthrow the elected president of Venezuela in the early 1990s, and the *New York Times* reported in January 1994 that many Brazilians were ready for the military to return to power because of economic problems and rampant corruption among civilian politicians. With each passing year, the probability of a military coup seemed lower. However, in the first fifteen years of the new millennium they occurred in Ecuador, Bolivia, Honduras, and Paraguay.

Previous Misuse of "Democracy"

Some Latin American countries called themselves "democracies" before 1989, although they were not in fact. Various Latin American dictators, including Anastasio Somoza Debayle in Nicaragua and Rafael Trujillo in the Dominican Republic, among many others, had already shown that an electoral facade could make a country appear to be democratic, although fraud made the claim hollow.

Within a cultural tradition that favored strong leadership more than institutional constraints on power, the region has often had elections without having democracy. Historically this came about for four basic reasons: the limitation of suffrage on gender, educational, or economic grounds; the restriction of voting rights of parties opposing the one in power; the limitation of the power of the elected executive by some other body, usually the military or foreign governments and multilateral institutions; and excessive executive power. But even if those four conditions are met, a consolidated democracy means much more than elections.

In the first case, suffrage was sometimes restricted by either literacy or property ownership. Of course, in many countries the landless and uneducated tended to be indigenous people, blacks, mulattos, and mestizos, but there were also many whites who had the misfortune to fall into that category. Regarding female suffrage, Latin American countries tended to be later than the United States in the enfranchisement of women. However, by the 1960s there were no Latin American countries in which suffrage was not at least theoretically open to all.

Second, many Latin American countries denied the vote to some on the basis of political loyalties. At times this was done by not allowing members of one political party to vote, while allowing members of another the prerogative to vote more than once (e.g., Colombia in the 1950s). In other cases, the ability to vote as one pleases was constrained when the voting process was watched closely by the military (e.g., Venezuela in the early 1950s). Likewise, there have been instances when press freedoms were so restricted that opposition parties could not effectively get their views out to the electors. The opposition to Hugo Chávez stated that the same happened in 2012 in Venezuela.

Third, there were countries in which all citizens apparently had the right to vote and there were few constraints on any candidate during the electoral process. However, afterward the elected president was greatly restricted in his policy options by the military. Hence, in the 1960s, the Guatemalan military allegedly informed President Julio César Méndez Montenegro that he could do anything that did not affect either the military or the large landowners. In the 1990s the Sandinistas in Nicaragua placed similar restrictions on Violeta Barrios de Chamorro, protecting Sandinista labor unions and the military upon agreeing to let her assume the presidency after her election in 1990.

Sometimes the constraint might come from some foreign government or international organization.

In addition, while internally very democratic in some ways, some Latin American governments were constrained in their economic policies, especially those having to do with foreign businesses, by the US government, the World Bank, or the IMF, or a combination of the three. The most notable instance in the 1970s was the government of Salvador Allende in Chile.

After the 1990s the outside constraints had more to do with the continuation of democracy. In 1992, for example, the United States reduced aid to Peru after President Alberto Fujimori suspended the congress and the judicial system. This policy was tempered in the new millennium, especially after terrorism became a priority of the US government. However, the Organization of American States used its influence at times to maintain democracy, as seen in the cases of Ecuador and Paraguay. The Inter-American Democratic Charter, passed by the OAS in 2001, recognized that the countries of the region might confront critical political situations that could lead them to request OAS intervention. After assessing the situation, representatives of the OAS member states can collectively take the necessary diplomatic initiatives, with the support of the General Secretariat, to prevent or confront an alteration of the constitutional regime, thus protecting or restoring democratic institutions.

The fourth aberration of democracy in some elected governments was the excessive power of the president, with no real separation of powers or checks and balances. Hernando de Soto and Deborah Orsini analyzed decision making in Peru before the presidency of Alberto Fujimori (although this could have described other Latin American countries), stating that the "only element of democracy in Peru today is the electoral process, which gives Peruvians the privilege of choosing a dictator every five years." Once in power the president made decisions in a vacuum, enacting 134,000 new rules and regulations every five years (or about 106 a day), with no checks on his power.[3]

Even with this strong executive power, President Alberto Fujimori found that he could not do all that he wished and disbanded congress and the courts in 1992, leading to international condemnation for ending "democracy." Guatemalan President Jorge Serrano tried to do the same in 1993. In this case the president failed for lack of support from the armed forces and was removed from power by them. Both cases show that, even though excessive executive power detracts from democracy in Latin America, on occasion the chief executive has nevertheless attempted to increase his already overwhelming power.

Pockets of Underdevelopment and Income Inequality

Although very modern in many ways, all Latin American countries have large pockets of people living in abject poverty. The neoliberal economic changes, the end of protective tariffs, the privatization of state-owned industries, and the reduction of support for the poor that occurred in the area in the last decade of the twentieth century increased, at least in the short run, the number of poor people through the unemployment caused when previously protected industries went bankrupt. In addition, some people with slightly higher living standards, such as owners of small businesses and bureaucrats, opposed further change because they once benefited from the traditional state-capitalist economic system.

These socioeconomic inequalities seemed to some to make democracy unlikely in Latin America. Robert Wesson, for example, after listing the problems of ethnic divisiveness, low standards of living, disdain for politics, a weak press that is not free, poorly organized and narrow parties, unfair elections, politically powerful armies, weak institutions of higher education, traditions of strong leadership, the paternalistic state, and clientelist politics, argued that "one basic condition may account for most of the rest, and it is probably a sufficient condition to explain the difficulty of democracy in Latin America, although by no means the sole cause. This is inequality, the separation of the rich from poor or top from bottom, of educated from ignorant or illiterate, or refined and proud elite from despised masses."[4] The difficulty that this inequality creates for democracy is that "to expect the cultured and well-off would accede to major social changes because they are outnumbered and outvoted in elections of dubious honesty by the ignorant and impoverished—many of whom are undernourished and diseased—is unrealistic. That would require a society of saints with an unlikely degree of loyalty to democratic principles."[5]

Ironically, because neoliberals see democracy and economic reform as interdependent, the poor and others who benefited from the mercantilist system may use the new democratic political regime to elect presidents and members of national congresses that are opposed to neoliberalism. This happened in the elections of Hugo Chávez in Venezuela, Evo Morales in Bolivia, and Daniel Ortega in Nicaragua, among others.

The Legacy of Civil Wars

In many Latin American countries, thousands have died in recent civil wars. Tension exists between conflict and consensus in any democracy, by its nature a system of institutionalized competition for power. As Larry Diamond argues, "Hence the paradox: Democracy requires conflict—but not too much; competition there must be, but only within carefully defined and universally accepted boundaries. Cleavage must be tempered by consensus."[6] Many Latin American countries have suffered years of war before learning this lesson. Nowhere has the problem of conflict been more serious than in Mexico (although not since the 1920s) and Colombia, where there have been bloody civil wars between parties. Other countries have had civil wars at the beginning of their independent history but then moved on to less violent modes of competition. In the 1960s, Marxist guerrilla groups chose armed conflict when faced with a lack of genuine electoral competition, and the resulting civil wars created a series of related problems for Latin American democracies.

It is especially difficult for a democratic government to deal with revolutionaries with different ethical standards. As Gustavo Gorriti has argued about countries with guerrilla movements:

A well-planned insurgency can severely test the basic assumptions of the democratic process. While they provoke and dare the elected regime to overstep its own laws in response to their aggression, the insurgents strive to paint the very process they are trying to destroy as a sham. If ensnared in such perverse dynamics, most Third World democracies will find their legitimacy eroding, and may eventually cease to be democracies altogether.[7]

Democracy is abandoned altogether when a government under this pressure becomes involved in a "dirty war." A number of countries have had such wars, in which thousands of people have been murdered or simply "disappeared"—Argentina and Chile in the 1970s, El Salvador and Guatemala in the 1980s, Peru in the 1980s and 1990s, and for the last fifty years in Colombia. In these cases, the government, or at least the military, has been involved. Once the dirty war is over and democracy is restored, the question becomes to what extent violators of human rights in the previous period should be punished. Punishing the guilty (from the military, predominantly) may in turn threaten the democracy. As did Raúl Alfonsín in Argentina in the 1980s, civilian presidents may pardon alleged violators of human rights rather than risk making the military so angry as to intervene again.

Although during the 1960s most Latin American countries faced guerrilla threats, by 2016 only Colombia continued grappling with the problem. As described in Chapter 11, in 2016 the Colombian government and the largest guerrilla group, the Revolutionary Armed Forces of Colombia (FARC), reached a peace agreement. It has yet to be implemented and negotiations with the second largest guerrilla group began in February 2017. The Shining Path (*Sendero Luminoso*) still existed in Peru, but with much less importance than before, and guerrillas were still present in the southern part of Mexico. Where civil wars have only recently ended, the difficult task is to achieve consensus among erstwhile enemies. As has become apparent in El Salvador and Colombia, even though a government may grant amnesty to guerrillas, the people who suffered at their hands may not be ready to forgive and forget.

The Ability to Govern

As Charles Tilly has argued, "No democracy can work if the state lacks the capacity to supervise democratic decision making and put its results into practice."[8] Although the degree of state weakness varies in Latin America, few governments have been able to enforce their decisions throughout their countries. As relatively poor countries with serious problems of transportation and communication, many Latin American countries have never been able to ensure the rule of law for the entire nation. Although they might be quite democratic in the way in which their leaders are elected and their laws are written, they at best govern only the major cities.

This weakness of government was exacerbated in Latin American countries with the emergence of the drug trade in the 1970s. Especially affected in this regard were Colombia, Peru, Bolivia, and Mexico. In Peru the Shining Path Marxist guerrilla group along with the drug traffickers of the Upper Huallaga valley destabilized politics for ten years. In Colombia, the Medellín and Cali cartels dominated the drug trade until the 1990s. After the cartels' demise small drug groups, paramilitary bands, and the guerrilla groups continued to control parts of the country. Mexico, given its size and apparent stability, at times seemed less affected. However, its location made it a transit point to the United States and some drug interests have infiltrated its government much as they have in Colombia. By 2008 Mexican drug groups had replaced Colombian ones as the chief suppliers to the market in the United States. Conflicts between rival Mexican groups made murder and kidnapping rates sadly reminiscent of Colombia in the 1980s.

THE PERIOD OF DEMOCRACY SINCE 1978

At no time in history have the Latin American countries had elective presidents as frequently as they have since the democratic wave began in 1978. However, this does not mean that "liberal democracy" has arrived in all the Latin American countries. Also, "delegative democracy" has replaced the liberal variety in some countries.

Liberal Democracy

Peter Smith gives simple definitions of liberal democracy. If a country has free and fair elections, it is an "electoral democracy." If the country also provides extensive guarantees of civil liberties, it is a "liberal democracy." However, an electoral democracy that provides partial or minimal guarantees is an "illiberal democracy."[9]

Philippe Schmitter and Terry Lynn Karl also suggest that elections are not the only criterion for liberal democracy. They add ten characteristics[10]: First, constitutionally elected officials must effectively control government decisions. Second, the elections for those officials must be frequent and fair. Coercion cannot exist on a large scale if the criterion of free elections is going to be met. Third, almost all adults must have the right to vote in these elections and, fourth, likewise they must have the right to run in them. There must be no danger in either voting or running for public office. Fifth, citizens must have the right to express themselves about politics without fear of punishment. Sixth, they also must have the right to seek alternative sources of information, and such sources must exist and be protected by law. This suggests that the media must be allowed to publish and broadcast, unlike many cases in the past when states of siege or emergency have led to censorship. Seventh, citizens must have the right to form independent organizations and groups, including political parties, civil societies, and interest groups. The stipulation of "independent" suggests that the government should not favor certain interest groups over others (as was characteristic of the ones that had been successfully co-opted), and should neither reward some with financial assistance nor punish some by using violence against them. Eighth, the officials who are elected must be able to govern constitutionally without the veto power of unelected officials, such as the military. Ninth, the same officials must be able to act independently without outside constraints. Tenth, power must not be controlled by one branch of government alone; rather, there should a system of checks and balances.

In addition, some argue that a full democracy should also have a considerable degree of egalitarianism, a sense that all people are full citizens, not victims of class, racial, or gender discrimination. Everyone should have a sense of participation, social and economic programs that are more or less just, and a certain civic consciousness that all people deal with each other in fair, impartial, and just ways. So, although some of the Latin American countries may have the institutional apparatus of democracy, in many respects they are still far from having democratic societies.

A democracy is consolidated when people consider it "the only game in town." This means that, no matter how bad things get, the only option is to behave in a democratic way—that is, wait for the next election, contact representatives in government, use (if available) other constitutional methods such as recall elections. It does not mean occupying key roads and bridges (as happened in Argentina in 2000–2002), using the military to overthrow a president who is disliked (as in Ecuador several times in the first decade of the new millennium), or using economic power to get rid of a president, or at least pressure him to change policies (e.g., Venezuela in 2002).

One of the goals of this book is to compare the level of democracy of the twenty Latin American countries. Two recent attempts have been by Freedom House and by political scientists Mainwaring and Pérez-Liñán.

Freedom House, an independent organization set up in 1942, which each year evaluates the degree of democracy. Freedom in the World 2016 evaluated the state of freedom in 195 countries and 15 territories during calendar year 2015. Each country and territory was assigned between 0 and 4 points on a series of 25 indicators, for an aggregate score of up to 100. These scores are used to determine two numerical ratings, for political rights and civil liberties, with a rating of 1 representing the freest conditions and 7 the least free. A country or territory's political rights and civil liberties ratings then determine whether it has an overall status of Free, Partly Free, or Not Free. The average of a country's or territory's political rights and civil liberties ratings is called the Freedom Rating, and it is this figure that determines the status of Free (1.0 to 2.5), Partly Free (3.0 to 5.0), or Not Free (5.5 to 7.0)

Freedom in the World assigned the designation "electoral democracy" to countries that have met certain minimum standards for political rights. According to the methodology, an electoral democracy designation requires a score of 7 or better in the Electoral Process subcategory and an overall political rights score of 20 or better. Freedom House's term "electoral democracy" differs from "liberal democracy" in that the latter also implies the presence of a substantial array of civil liberties. In Freedom in the World, all Free countries can be considered both electoral and liberal democracies, while some Partly Free countries qualify as electoral, but not liberal, democracies.

According to the Freedom House rankings on political rights, Argentina, Brazil, Chile, Costa Rica, El Salvador, Panama, and Peru were "Free." The "Partly Free" Latin American countries were Bolivia, Colombia, the Dominican Republic, Ecuador, Guatemala, Haiti, Honduras, Mexico, Nicaragua, Paraguay, and Venezuela. Cuba occupied the "Not Free" category by itself.[11]

Not content with the ordinal (more or less) categories of the Freedom House, political scientists Mainwaring and Pérez-Liñán took the organization's rankings from 1978 to 2010 and, as shown in Table 7.1, gave each country an interval level measurement score. In that way, they ranked Costa Rica as the most democratic and Haiti as the least. Cuba was not ranked.[12]

Table 7.1   Freedom House Scores for Latin American Countries

Country	First year of competitive regime	Average FH Score, 1978–2010
Costa Rica	1949	11.7
Uruguay	1985	11.2
Chile	1990	10.8
Panama	1990	9.9
Argentina	1983	9.6

Table 7.1   Freedom House Scores for Latin American Countries, *continued*

Country	First year of competitive regime	Average FH Score, 1978–2010
Dominican Republic	1978	9.4
Ecuador	1979	8.9
Brazil	1985	8.9
Venezuela	1959	8.5
Bolivia	1979	8.4
El Salvador	1984	8.3
Honduras	1982	8.2
Mexico	1988	7.9
Peru	1980	7.7
Colombia	1958	7.6
Paraguay	1984	7.5
Nicaragua	1984	6.6
Guatemala	1986	6.6
Haiti	1991	3.0

Source: Rescaled Freedom House scores, Aníbal Pérez-Liñán and Scott Mainwaring, "Regime Legacies and Levels of Democracy: Evidence from Latin America," *Comparative Politics* 45, no 4 (July 2013): 379–397.

We believe that such numerical comparisons of democracy in the Latin American countries are valuable. However, it is also our opinion that democracy is such a complex phenomenon that it is essential to describe its nuances in each of the twenty countries.

Delegative Democracy

One of those complexities is a paradox of democratization in Latin America. On one hand, there have been more elected presidents in more nations than ever before. For the first time, there is near universal suffrage. But on the other hand, there have been limitations and shallow democratic practices. Scholars have come up with adjectives such as "low-intensity democracy" and "schizophrenic democracy." The most common, however, has been "delegative democracy." They all suggest that the initial euphoria surrounding the demise of military dictatorships has changed to a growing dissatisfaction regarding the ambiguous character and quality of new civilian regimes.[13]

Guillermo O'Donnell's idea of a "delegative democracy" includes four major characteristics. First, the president is the embodiment of the nation and the main custodian of the national interest, which it is incumbent upon him to define. Second, what he does in government does not need to bear any resemblance to what he said or promised during the electoral campaign—he has been authorized to govern as he sees fit.

Third, because this paternal figure has to take care of the whole nation, it is almost obvious that his support cannot come from a party; his political basis has to be a movement, the supposedly vibrant overcoming of the factionalism and conflicts that parties bring about. Typically, and consistently, winning presidential candidates in delegative democracies present themselves as above all parties; that is, both political parties and organized interests. How could it be otherwise for somebody who claims to embody the whole of the nation?

Finally, in this view, other institutions—such as congress and the judiciary—are nuisances that come attached to the domestic and international advantages of being a democratically elected president.[14]

Although such executive domination is far from new in Latin America, in the first decade of the new millennium liberal democracies became delegative ones in Venezuela (Hugo Chávez), Bolivia (Evo Morales), Ecuador (Rafael Correa), and, perhaps to a lesser degree, Colombia (Álvaro Uribe). In all cases, necessary constitutional changes were accepted by the voters through referendums or by the national congress through constitutionally mandated procedures.

Some scholars, however, think that these governments are not democratic in any way, not even a delegative one. In a study of Venezuela and Paraguay, Paul Sondrol argued that calling them "democracies" with modifiers failed to capture their authoritarian nature and that they were unlikely, given time, to become democracies.[15]

These are, Sondrol says, democratically disguised dictatorships, a particular regime type whereby formal democratic institutions mask and legitimate de facto authoritarian political control. They have four major characteristics: (1) blocking mechanisms limiting electoral transfers of power; (2) democratic trappings and weak institutionalization; (3) policy disconnect between economic and political liberalization, controlled and manipulated by regime elites, and (4) limits to civil society empowerment.

Sondrol concluded that Venezuela's Hugo Chávez represented the new type of revolutionary, messianic strongman, elected by citizens "with eyes wide open." They were "alienated by traditional politics and lured by simple, appealing, populist solutions to cut through the red tape of confusing, corrupt, and tedious pluralist politics." Therefore, "Perhaps it is time to stop thinking in terms of the 'democratic transitions' paradigm, and to start calling these semi-dictatorships what they really are."[16] The fourth consecutive election of Venezuelan President Hugo Chávez in October 2012 suggested that Sondrol is correct.

The death of Chávez from cancer in 2013, however, showed the inherent weakness of a regime built on one person. The difficulties that might follow the demise of the leader have been shown in the last four years in Venezuela during the government of Nicolás Maduro, whom Chávez had chosen to follow him. More of these complications are analyzed in Chapter 13.

CONCLUSION

As the following chapters of this book demonstrate, many Latin American countries have a coexistence of the old system of "living museum" politics, liberal democracy, and delegative democracy. Some might best be called "semi-authoritarian." To the extent that the living museum system exists, the paradigm suggested by Charles Anderson (and presented in Chapter 2) is still useful. If liberal democracy, delegative democracy, or semi-authoritarianism has become the dominant system, new paradigms for interpreting Latin America must be developed. In assessing which system prevails in a country, the characteristics of liberal democracy and of delegative democracy will be helpful.

Two concerns should be kept in mind as one evaluates the politics of the Latin American nations. First, the systems are very dynamic, with change occurring constantly. A valid conclusion made on one date might soon change. Second, judgment about the factors of liberal and delegative democracy is very difficult; many times, sources in the United States do not include adequate information. If Latin American sources are consulted (and many are readily available on the Internet), often information comes from both governments and their opposition and is intentionally reported incorrectly.

SUGGESTIONS FOR FURTHER READING

Camp, Roderic. *Democracy in Latin America*. Wilmington, DE: Scholarly Resources, 1999.

Dominguez, Jorge. *Democratic Politics in Latin America and the Caribbean*. Baltimore: Johns Hopkins University Press, 1998.

———— and Abraham Lowenthal, *Constructing Democratic Governance*. Baltimore: Johns Hopkins University Press, 1996.

Drake, Paul W. *Between Tyranny and Anarchy: A History of Democracy in Latin America, 1800–2006*. Stanford, CA: Stanford University Press, 2009.

Huber, Evelyne, and John D. Stephans, *Democracy and the Left: Social Policy and Inequality in Latin America*. Chicago: University of Chicago Press, 2012.

Mainwaring, Scott, and Aníbal Pérez-Liñán, *Democracies and Dictatorships in Latin America: Emergence, Survival, and Fall*. New York: Cambridge University Press, 2013.

Millett, Richard, Jennifer Holmes, and Orlando Perez, eds. *Latin American Democracy: Emerging reality or Endangered Species?* 2nd ed. Routledge, 2015.

Needler, Martin. *The Problems of Democracy in Latin America*. Lexington, MA: Lexington Books, 1987.

Pastor, Robert. *Democracy in the Americas*. New York: Holmes and Meier, 1989.

Seligson, Mitchell, and John A. Booth. *The Legitimacy Puzzle in Latin America: Political Support and Democracy in Eight Nations*. New York: Cambridge University Press, 2009.

Smith, Peter. *Democracy in Latin America: Political Change in Comparative Perspective*. Oxford: Oxford University Press, 2005.

NOTES

1. Scott Mainwaring and Aníbal Pérez-Liñán, *Democracies and Dictatorships in Latin America: Emergence, Survival, and Fall* (New York: Cambridge University Press, 2013), 71–73.

2. Freedom House, Latin America's Wavering Democracies, September 2012. https://freedomhouse.org/blog/latin-america%E2%80%99s-wavering-democracies).

3. Hernando de Soto and Deborah Orsini, "Overcoming Under-Development," *Journal of Democracy* 2, no. 2 (Spring 1991): 106.

4. Robert Wesson, *Democracy in Latin America: Promise and Problems* (New York: Praeger, 1982), 125.

5. Ibid., 130–131.

6. Larry Diamond, "Three Paradoxes of Democracy," *Journal of Democracy* 1, no. 3 (Summer 1990): 49.

7. Gustavo Gorriti, "Latin America's Internal Wars," *Journal of Democracy* 2, no. 1 (Winter 1991): 86–87.

8. Charles Tilly, *Democracy* (Cambridge: Cambridge University Press, 2007), 15.

9. Peter Smith, *Democracy in Latin America: Political Change in Comparative Perspective.* (Oxford: Oxford University Press, 2005), 9–11.

10. Calling anything with elections democracy, despite fraud, was labeled "electoralism" by Philippe C. Schmitter and Terry Lynn Karl, "What Democracy Is . . . And Is Not," *Journal of Democracy* 2, no. 3 (Summer 1991): 78.

11. Freedom House, Americas, www.freedomhouse.org/regions/americas.

12. Aníbal Pérez-Liñán and Scott Mainwaring, "Regime Legacies and Levels of Democracy: Evidence from Latin America," *Comparative Politics* 45, no. 4 (July 2013): 379–397.

13. Kenneth M. Roberts, *Deepening Democracy? The Modern Left and Social Movements in Chile and Peru* (Stanford: Stanford University Press, 1998), 1.

14. Guillermo O'Donnell, "Delegative Democracy?" Kellogg Institute Working Paper #192 (April 1993), http://kellogg.nd.edu/publications/workingpapers/WPS/172.pdf, page 7.

15. Paul Sondrol, "Semi-Authoritarianism in Latin America," www.allacademic.com//meta/p_mla_apa_research_citation/0/9/8/8/8/pages98880/p98880-1.php 1-2.

16. Ibid, 25.

PART II

The Political Systems of South America

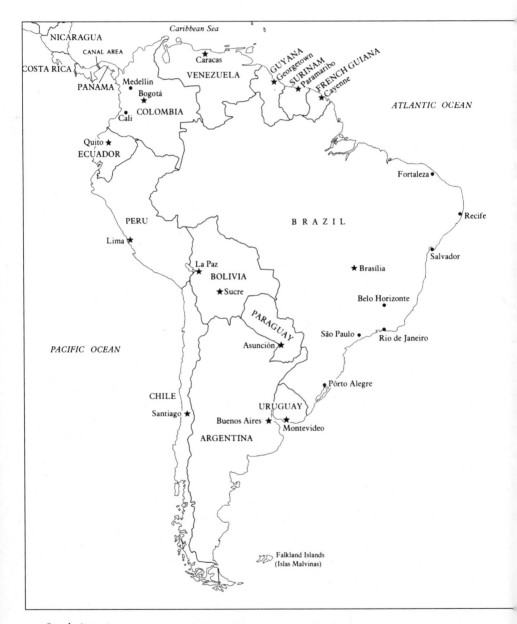

South America

8

ARGENTINA: THE ECONOMIC TANGO CONTINUES

Linda Chen

INTRODUCTION

As the second largest economy in South America, just after Brazil, Argentina presents an interesting study in economic policy and weak political institutionalization. Twelve years of government under Néstor Kirchner and Cristina Fernández de Kirchner came to an end in 2015. *Kirchnerismo*, as their political movement was called, oversaw Argentina's economic recovery from the disastrous policies of neoliberalism and an unprecedented era of economic growth. At the same time, the Kirchners exacerbated the problems of weak political institutionalization by widely expanding the powers of the executive branch. The current president, Mauricio Macri, elected in December 2015, appears to be continuing this practice of hyper-presidentialism. Inheriting the problems of an economy that is experiencing sluggish growth and increasing inflation, the questions for Macri are whether he can use the powers of the presidency to arrest the declining economic situation, and how long Argentines will be willing to give his administration a chance to succeed.

HISTORICAL BACKGROUND

Argentina's history has been shaped by conflict and division. The period after independence in 1816 from Spain was characterized by conflicts over whether Argentina should have a centralized government centered on Buenos Aires and free trade, as represented by Bernardino Rivadavia and his Unitary Party, or a decentralized system whereby the interior provinces would be free to run their own affairs under a federalist system. Juan Manuel de Rosas resolved this conflict by establishing a federalist system with Buenos Aires as its center. A powerful rancher who represented the cattle interests of the interior, Rosas ruled with an iron fist and personified the image of the *caudillo* (military strong man) that characterized power relations in Latin America in that era. He was ousted in 1852 by a combination of rebellious rival caudillos and exiles.

From 1852–1916, Argentina was governed by a liberal oligarchy that adopted a constitution patterned closely after that of the United States. Its liberal principles included the separation of powers, checks and balances, the right to private property, and guarantees of free speech and press. It also encouraged the government to support European immigration. In practice, the liberal oligarchy controlled electoral outcomes and governed by fraud and corruption. Foreign trade grew rapidly, and the profits were plowed into domestic developments: roads, bridges, ports, and public education. New methods of agriculture were adopted, cattle breeding and pasturage were improved, and new lines of production were introduced: grain growing and sheep raising. Foreign capital invested in the railroads, telephone and telegraph, gas and electric power, the refrigerated steamship, modern meat packing, and modern sanitation. With the commercial boom also came an increase in banking, insurance, and construction. The port of Buenos Aires became one of the busiest in the world, and the city was transformed from a dull colonial outpost into a modern European-style capital whose broad boulevards and imposing buildings reminded travelers of Paris.

The twentieth century saw the rise of mass politics in Argentina as the agricultural oligarchy's political dominance was contested by the emergence of urban middle-class sectors and a huge working-class population, fueled by immigration mostly from Southern Europe. By 1914, Argentina's population had mushroomed to 7.8 million; Buenos Aires had grown to 1.5 million, with fully half of its population being foreign born. As the agricultural oligarchy found itself losing its monopoly on power, Argentina saw the emergence of middle-class sectors and working-class interests. Political reforms accelerated this trend as new political parties formed, the most prominent of which was the Radical Civic Union (UCR); a universal suffrage law was passed; the secret ballot was instituted; and labor unions representing socialist, syndicalist, and anarchist persuasions proliferated. The Radical Civic Union, representing middle-class business interests, dominated the politics of Argentina from the early twentieth century through the Great Depression. The rise of urban middle-class interests would clash with growing labor union activism.

The era of the Great Depression and the 1930s brought profound changes to Argentina. With the economic dislocation brought about by declining demand and prices for Argentina's commodity exports, the political situation destabilized. Responding to oligarchical interests and their own sense of nationalist pride, a new political era began for Argentina as the military entered domestic politics and a new political phenomenon, Peronism, would seize the day.

The Peronist Watershed

The political scene in Argentina in the early 1940s was dominated by the external events of World War II. The army, many of whose officers were German-trained, supported an alliance with the Axis powers. A group of high-level officers conspired to install a government modeled after Mussolini's Italian fascist regime. Calling themselves the Group of United Officers (GOU), they successfully took power in 1943. Among their members was a little-known army colonel named Juan Domingo Perón. When the events of World War II made it clear that the Axis powers were losing, the military establishment in power searched for an exit strategy.

Meanwhile, in 1943 Perón had asked to take over the management of the Secretariat of Labor and Social Welfare. Previously he had served as Minister of War, a position he used to build a support base within the army. As minister of labor, Perón began to settle disputes in labor's favor. He reversed long-standing anti-labor legislation and actively promoted legislation to improve workers' lives. Old-age pensions, accident and health insurance, annual paid vacations, factory safety codes, and minimum wage and maximum hour legislation all were expanded and enforced. Labor unionists were given positions in his ministry; others were freed from jail. Employers who had fought the creation of labor unions were now forced to accept them. Perón's support base among labor grew.

Some within the military began to view Perón's policies with alarm. The conservative elites and industrial groups were also resentful and suspicious of Perón's overtures to workers. The growing opposition to Perón led a group of officers to oust him from all government posts and put him under arrest on a naval base in the La Plata River. What happened next is still the stuff of Peronist legend. Labor unions and workers' organizations mobilized to protest Perón's jailing. Thousands of workers descended on the capital of Buenos Aires and converged on the Plaza de Mayo demanding Perón's release. Not having an alternative, the military finally agreed to release Perón. On October 17, 1945, Perón appeared on the balcony of the Casa Rosada (Office of the President) and saw the results of his hard work organizing the working classes. Gesturing in victory to thousands of workers cheering him, it was clear that the working classes had forced their way into the political arena. The Peronist Era had begun.

The election of 1946 passed the mantle of power and legitimacy to Perón. In the run-up to the election Perón founded his own political party, the Labor Party, which organized his many supporters under his leadership. He had the solid support of the labor unions, many of which had formed within the past three years; factions of the military from whose ranks he came; and the Catholic Church, which Perón had won by promising to retain the church's right to control education and to prevent divorce legislation. The Conservative Party, landed elites, urban industrialists, middle-class radicals, and an array of socialists and communists were opposed to Perón. Nevertheless, Perón's victory in the 1946 election was decisive: 1,479,517 votes for the Labor Party compared to 1,220,822 for the opposition Democratic Union, a coalition of anti-Peronist interests. Perón's allies also swept the two houses of congress, the provincial governorships, and all but one of the provincial legislatures.

Perón came to power with a number of factors in his favor. He had won a fair and open election with the support of a broad coalition of groups, including elements of the military and the Catholic Church. The state treasury was full, as Argentina had been able to capitalize on the sale of supplies to the Allies during World War II. Furthermore, international prices of food and raw agricultural materials were rising relative to industrial goods. His development policies focused on expanding basic industrialization, expanding social welfare benefits, some redistribution of wealth, and promoting nationalism.

Perón continued to pursue his pro-labor policies by promulgating legislation covering all aspects of workers' lives. Real wages and fringe benefits went up. Under the Secretariat of Labor and Social Welfare Perón created an extensive network for the administration of labor affairs. He gradually concentrated labor matters under the General Direction of Labor and Direct Social Action (DGTASD). All aspects of labor relations, including collective bargaining, labor law enforcement, union registrations and dues, workplace conditions, and employer-union conflicts came under the purview of the DGTASD. To ensure labor compliance with Peronist policies, the General Confederation of Labor (CGT) was given monopoly control over labor unions. The CGT was the only legally recognized labor confederation in the country, and any union that wished to be legally recognized had to fall under its control and oversight. In classical corporatist fashion, the CGT was the vehicle by which Perón transmitted his policies down to labor rank and file.

Perón's pro-labor policies were part of his economic project to further industrialization. Profits from the agricultural sector were transferred to the industrial sector. Agriculturalists were forced to sell all their commodity exports to a government agency called the Argentine Institute for Production and Trade (IAPI) at government-set prices. The idea was for IAPI to buy at the lowest possible price and then sell the goods on the world market at the highest possible price. The profits would then be used to finance industrialization.

Perón's industrial project sought to expand import substitution industrialization. To that end, he nationalized the central bank, railroads, telephone, electricity and gas, and urban transport. The state began development of aviation and steel industries. Compensation for the nationalizations came from state treasury funds, leading to a severe depletion of state funds for promoting industrialization beyond that of light manufactured goods. As a result, capital-intensive industrialization never really took off. Parallel to the CGT controlling labor, Perón set up the General Economic Confederation (CGE) to represent industrialists, merchants, and agriculturalists.

Perón's political style was clearly populist, as he continued to direct his words and deeds to the working classes. With his wife, Eva Duarte de Perón, he sought to elevate the working classes from their historic second-class status. Eva Perón (Evita), in particular, served as an effective interlocutor between Perón and the people. Her own biography, emphasizing her illegitimate upbringing in a dusty provincial town and her rise to political fame, served as an inspiration to millions of working-class and poor Argentines. Adopting a glamorous style, Eva Perón took an active part in dispensing social welfare funds to the working class and poor.

Perón's populism, though, also had its authoritarian side. Soon after taking office he changed the name of the Labor Party to the Peronist Party so as to solidify his own personal power base. He and his allies set about purging Argentine politics and society of anyone who opposed Perón, whether they were independent-minded labor leaders or newspaper publishers. Political parties other than the Peronist Party were harassed and repressed. Perón used censorship and outright strong-arm Mafioso tactics to reinforce his power. Political corruption was endemic, as the Peróns surrounded themselves with relatives and friends, many of whom saw access to the Peróns as an invitation to seek personal and material gains. In many ways, Peron's authoritarianism resembled that of a modern-day caudillo.

From 1946 to 1949 the Peronist project produced economic growth and a substantive improvement in people's lives. The real incomes and quality of life of Argentine workers and the middle classes increased, and for all the loathing the economic elites expressed toward Perón, they did not suffer much under his redistributive policies. Regardless, industrialization did not lead to sustained economic growth, and by 1950 the state treasury was running out of money to continue supporting its own state-run, inefficient industries and its expanded social welfare expenditures. When Eva Perón died from cancer in 1952, Perón's decline began.

Facing pressure from a deteriorating economic situation, Perón sought even greater controls over society. He attacked the Catholic Church, an early Perón supporter, when they refused to canonize his wife as a saint despite popular demonstrations on her behalf. Then the clergy provoked a confrontation when it began to organize Christian Democratic trade unions in competition with Peronist unions. Perón went on the attack, forbidding religious processions and expelling priests. Street clashes escalated until finally, on the night of June 16, 1955, Peronist fanatics set fire to several downtown churches, including the cathedral and the Archbishop's palace. Meanwhile, anti-Peronist opposition had been growing in the military. The navy had always been a center of resistance, but now the army, one of Perón's main pillars of support, was restive. Its professionalism was insulted by mandatory courses in Peronist political indoctrination at the Military Academy and by the regime's new program of encouraging the sergeants and enlisted men to join the Peronist Party. The officers feared that their own men would be encouraged to spy on them. With the Catholic Church and important factions of the military allied against Perón, a military coup, led by General Eduardo Lonardi, forced Perón from office in September 1955. Perón initially took refuge in Paraguay and ultimately made his way to Spain. The first Peronist experiment was over.

The legacy Perón left Argentina in 1955 was expanded group interests vying for political power. The Peronist Party–supported labor unions and working classes vied for political power alongside the agricultural elites, the armed forces, the urban middle-class interests, and industrialists. To the state, he left a huge bureaucracy with responsibilities to nationalized industries and social welfare policies. To the economy, he left a depleted state treasury and a shaky industrial base. Perón neither destroyed the power of the traditional economic elites nor did his government gain enough strength to check their power. Rather, the next eighteen years would see attempts to defeat Peronism, all of which would fail at high social and political cost.

Peronism in Exile

The period from 1955–1973 was one of political and economic turmoil. The military regime that came to power in 1955 sought to de-Peronize Argentine society by outlawing the Peronist Party and attacking the labor unions that were its stronghold. In 1958, the military called elections but the Peronist Party was prohibited from fielding candidates, so the civilian government, elected under the Radical Civic Union, failed to establish its legitimacy. A military coup in 1966 did little to bring an end to Peronism, especially as Perón continued to assert his influence from exile in Spain. The military called elections in 1973, still prohibiting the participation of Perón. To circumvent the ban on Perón, his trusted secretary, Héctor Cámpora, ran for president. He prevailed, and a few months later, he resigned to pave the way for Perón's return to the presidency. However, Perón could not manage the disparate forces that had emerged during his time in exile. Students, organized as the Montoneros, who had agitated for his return by using urban guerrilla tactics were summarily rejected by Perón; labor union leaders who had built power bases independent of Perón were wary of his intentions; and sectors of the military became increasingly concerned with his erratic decision making. Perón's death in 1974 ushered in further domestic chaos as his widow, Isabel, took over the helm of government. When she proved unable to govern, the military once again stepped into power. On March 26, 1976, to most Argentines' relief, Isabel was removed from power in a military coup.

Military-Sponsored Terror

The coup of March 1976 heralded a return to military rule, one that would be a departure from past military interventions. Calling its mission the "Process of National Reorganization" (El Proceso), the military junta, made up of representatives of the army, navy, and air force, with Army General Jorge Rafael Videla as its head, committed itself to ending the political chaos and to setting the economy on a stable course. To achieve the former, the military undertook draconian measures to purge Argentine society of subversive elements that were impeding Argentina's development. It was not enough to rout the guerrilla forces that had plagued Argentine society for the past decade; what was needed was to attack the root causes of Argentina's political instability. According to the military junta, Argentina's woes went beyond the problems of Peronism and an intransigent labor movement. To the military junta, the entire fabric of Argentine life had been poisoned and diseased by leftist subversion, leading to a sick society rent with chaos and corruption. The solution was a concerted campaign to purge Argentina of those subversive elements and to reassert the "true" values of Argentine life. One of the self-proclaimed mottoes of the military junta was "Tradition, Family, and Property," borrowed from the ultraconservative Catholic Opus Dei organization that was popular with some in the military. The Argentine Catholic Church hierarchy became a staunch supporter of the junta.

The methods used by the military junta are by now infamous. Green Ford Falcons with no license plates chauffeured by nondescript men sped through the streets of Buenos Aires both day and night in search of specific individuals believed to be subversives. Illegal detention centers were set up all over the country, equipped with both sophisticated and primitive means of torture. Basic civil liberties were severely restricted as Argentine society found itself gripped with fear and terror by the military junta's actions. All groups representing civil society (political parties, labor unions, civic associations) were repressed and their leadership went underground.

Although no sector of Argentine society was immune from this war against subversion, the hardest hit were the working classes, students, labor-movement activists, and urban professionals. The words "the disappeared ones" (*los desaparecidos*) entered the Argentine lexicon to signify that persons were "being disappeared" by shadowy forces rather than disappearing of their own accord. Most of the disappeared were never found (all told, an estimated 30,000 persons lost their lives between 1976 and 1983), although mass graves are periodically uncovered in contemporary Argentina, filled with skeletons that show signs of violent deaths such as bullet holes, bashed-in skulls, and broken bones. In addition to dumping torture victims in mass graves, people were burned alive in ovens, and others were thrown into the La Plata River in the hopes that their bodies would be eaten by sharks. Some remains, however, would end up on the beaches of the river. Among those who were kidnapped and disappeared were women who were pregnant. It is estimated that approximately four hundred babies were born in captivity to women who were subsequently killed after giving birth. The babies were adopted by the families of military men or were sold on the black market. The whereabouts of these children of the disappeared continues to be an issue in contemporary Argentina.

Although all sectors of Argentine society were repressed, it is noteworthy that a group of women whose children were disappeared organized to defy the military junta's policies. The Mothers of the Plaza de Mayo captured the imagination of the international media beginning in 1977, when a few brave women decided to demonstrate publicly against the repressive policies of the regime. Covering their heads with white scarves and holding up placards with pictures of their missing children, the Mothers held weekly marches around the Plaza de Mayo, calling attention to the regime's human rights abuses. Several of the original founders of the group were themselves disappeared, but the group persevered and was an important voice in ensuring that the human rights abuses of the junta not be ignored once it left power.

Part of the motivating drive for the repression was the military junta's economic priorities. Under the direction of José Martínez de Hoz, Argentina's economy was to be "reorganized" so as to promote growth, competitiveness, and global integration. Argentina's economy suffered from too much state intervention and the dominance of trade unions. In order to fix Argentina's economy, labor unions needed to be tamed and state-run industries needed to be privatized. In these ways, foreign investment could be attracted so as to restart the Argentine economy.

With respect to the organized labor movement, the military junta attacked the central labor confederation, the CGT, and jailed many prominent labor leaders. Factory floors were occupied by military men to coerce laborers to work. Trade union activity was banned, union elections were disrupted by the military, and control over union dues reverted to the government. Organized labor's fortunes were also eroded due to the free-market policies of the regime that led to the closing of state-run and inefficient industries, thereby causing massive unemployment.

The long-term impact of Martínez de Hoz's policies was disastrous. Economic growth did not occur nor was inflation tamed, and by 1980 Hoz's days were numbered. As the economic situation took a downturn, the military junta sought ways to maintain power. In 1981 General Videla ceded power to General Roberto Viola, who in turn was replaced by General Leopoldo Galtieri at the end of the year. By this time human rights groups in Argentina and newly radicalized labor unions began to agitate against the military regime. To quell the rising domestic discontent, Galtieri took Argentina into the ill-conceived war against Great Britain for control of the Falklands—or the

Malvinas, as the Argentines call this group of islands in the South Atlantic. It was hoped that inflaming a longtime conflict with Great Britain would rally Argentine nationalism toward the regime. What Galtieri did not bargain for was Great Britain's response: it sent its famed naval fleet and Royal Air Forces to retake the islands. Argentina's defeat led to the hurried exit of the military junta from political power.

Transition to Democracy

The election of Raúl Alfonsín to the presidency in December 1983 was a pivotal event in Argentina's political history. For the first time in a freely contested election, the Peronists did not win. The people's preference for the Radical Civic Union candidate, who himself had been jailed under the military, signaled a desire for a fresh start in Argentine politics, one that was a clear repudiation of past authoritarian regimes. During the electoral campaign Alfonsín promised to bring the Proceso's top military officers to trial for violating human rights, a promise he made good on once elected. Alfonsín appointed a special investigative commission whose report *Never Again* was used as the basis for trials held in 1985. For several months in early 1985, victims and families of victims testified to the extent of the human rights violations. General Videla was handed a life sentence and the other junta leaders were given long prison terms. The military, fully discredited due to their disastrous performance in the Falklands War, had little recourse to protest. However, when courts and prosecutors began to indict lower-level officers, military rebellions occurred. Three military rebellions took place between 1987 and 1988, events that led to the curtailing of the human rights prosecutions. A "full stop" law was enacted, which limited the time period when cases could be brought to the courts, all but stopping prosecutions against military personnel. The "due obedience" law then absolved from prosecution those who were "just following orders." Human rights organizations, including the Mothers of the Plaza de Mayo, vigorously opposed this legislation.

Alfonsín and his economic team embarked on a number of strategies to curb rampant inflation, which had reached a yearly rate of 6,900 percent by 1985. Alfonsín introduced a reform package called the Austral Plan that consisted of wage and price freezes, spending cutbacks, and hikes in utility rates. Although the plan was initially successful, it did not prevent a resurgence of hyperinflation. Attempts to fix the Austral Plan came to nothing, and in the 1987 congressional elections the Radicals were roundly defeated by the Peronists. Two years later Alfonsín himself left office early due to his government's inability to manage the economic crisis. At the time of his resignation in June 1989, inflation had roared back to 4,900 percent, the gross domestic product had contracted, real wages had fallen, and the external debt had reached a record US$63,314 million.

Peronism Without Perón

One indicator of democratic stability is an electoral transition where one political party passes power to another political party. The election of 1983 signaled the end of military rule and a return to democratic norms. The election of 1989, with the Peronist Party candidate, Carlos Menem, as its winner, signaled that Argentine democratic norms had perhaps become institutionalized. A former governor of La Rioja province, Menem ran on the traditional Peronist Party platform of championing the working classes. Once in office, his administration took a sharp turn to the political right as he embraced the neoliberal economic policies that favored foreign capital, free trade, and privatization of state-owned industries. Menem's economic policies followed the thinking of the Washington Consensus, which privileged market mechanisms for economic development.

Integrating Argentina's economy into global markets, characterized by the inflow of capital and external competition, led to an initial period of economic stability and growth. Menem used his success in economic policy making to lobby for a change in the Constitution to allow his reelection. The Argentine Constitution, at the time, limited a president to one term of six years. In a move to extend his time in office, Menem successfully lobbied to have that changed to two four-year terms. Menem easily won re-election in 1995. However, his administration was increasingly beset by scandals, many related to the sale of state-run industries, and allegations of political corruption. Furthermore, Menem's highly public divorce from his wife, his penchant for consorting with movie stars and celebrities, and his use of family members as political advisors who were accountable to no one further compromised his reputation. Finally, the economic consequences of the Washington Consensus saw economic stability replaced by the impoverishment of millions, as Argentine industries were driven out of business by foreign competition and massive unemployment ensued.

The economic chaos unleashed by the failure of neoliberal economic policies saw Peronism's defeat at the polls in the presidential election of 1999, this time at the hands of a coalition consisting of the Radical Civic Union and the Front for a Country in Solidarity (FrePaso). The latter was a political party formed in 1994 by disaffected Peronists and persons from left-of-center political parties. Calling themselves the "Alianza," Fernando de la Rúa (head of the Radicals) was elected on a platform of promising to end political corruption and to ameliorate the suffering of millions of Argentines whose economic livelihoods were destroyed by the neoliberal policies of the 1990s. However, the Alianza was short-lived as political differences between the Radicals and FrePaso led to a fracturing of the alliance and instability in the de la Rúa coalition. Economic policy making failed to arrest the deepening decline of economic productivity, and poverty rates increased.

By the end of 2001 the political and economic situation was chaotic. De la Rúa resigned from the presidency, thereby plunging Argentina into its worst political crisis since the era of military rule. A succession of three presidents rotated into the presidency over a two-week period. Peronist politician Eduardo Duhalde, the third president, served in the position until 2003.

Kirchnerismo

Néstor Kirchner was elected to the presidency in 2003. The Peronist governor of the small Patagonian province of Santa Cruz, Kirchner gave notice to the International Monetary Fund and international creditors that his priorities would focus on alleviating the economic hardships of Argentines first and meeting its international financial obligations second. With world commodity prices being high, Kirchner was able to effectively carry out economic policies to rebuild the Argentinian economy from the tatters of failed neoliberal reform. Acting very much as a traditional Peronist, Kirchner focused on social welfare spending. He was particularly successful at reaching out to the human rights community by reopening the trials for military men accused of abuses during the last military dictatorship. During his time in office, Argentina more fully confronted its military past.

Riding a wave of popularity, Kirchner stepped aside in 2007 to enable his wife, Cristina Fernández de Kirchner, herself a senator, to run for the presidency. She won handily. It was widely believed that having Cristina run for the presidency would enable Néstor to make a run in 2011 and beyond, thereby cementing the dominance of Kirchnerismo. However, these hopes were dashed with Néstor's untimely death due to a heart attack in October 2010.

Fernández de Kirchner easily won reelection in 2011. She continued the economic policies that were the hallmark of Kirchnerismo—even as economic growth began to slow. Her second term was marred by increasing inflationary pressures, and a downturn in the international economy that adversely effected Argentine commodity prices and other exports. Social unrest erupted among sectors of the population as the economic situation started to stagnate. Fernández de Kirchner's response was to ignore and suppress the less-than-favorable economic indicators. Corruption scandals tied to her administration continued to crop up and her attempt to change the constitution to allow her to run for a third term was thwarted in the midterm elections of 2013, where her political rivals gained enough seats to prevent such a move. Being term limited, Fernández de Kirchner could not run for another term. The 2015 presidential elections saw a swing back to what promises to be a resurrection of neoliberal economic policies.

Macri and the End of Kirchnerismo?

In an election largely devoid of significant differences among the three leading candidates, Argentina elected Mauricio Macri, a well-known businessman who was the mayor of Buenos Aires. This election was significant in several ways. For the first time since the return to democracy in 1983, a runoff election was required as no candidate received 45 percent of the vote on the first ballot. Macri was also the first elected president since 1946 who was neither a Peronist nor a Radical. Macri won under the political coalition Republican Proposal, consisting of disaffected Radicals and others. Macri is identified with business interests and once owned Boca Juniors, one of the national soccer teams of Argentina. Although he has espoused his support for neoliberal economic policies, his electoral campaign stressed that he was a pragmatist and problem-solver. During the campaign, Macri avoided specifics on which policies he would change and which he would keep; he instead emphasized that Argentina would prosper under his guidance. This message succeeded with the electorate, as he was elected with 51 percent in the second round of the popular vote. Macri took office on December 10, 2015.

SOCIETY

Argentina's population of just over forty-two million is overwhelmingly urban (92 percent), with approximately one third living in the greater Buenos Aires metropolitan area. It is also overwhelmingly of European descent—mainly Spaniards and Italians—and also Roman Catholic, at least nominally. Infant mortality stands at eleven per one thousand live births, life expectancy is seventy-four years for males and eighty years for females, and the literacy rate is 97 percent for Argentines fifteen years and older.

Argentina's ethnic mix—97 percent European, 3 percent mestizo and others—is a product of its unusual pattern of settlement. As a colony, it produced little wealth for the Spanish crown and therefore remained sparsely settled. The indigenous population was made up of small, nomadic, hostile tribes that were gradually driven off the Pampa by the settlers, down into Patagonia. By the end of the nineteenth century they were practically eliminated. At the same time, Argentina's cattle-raising culture required minimal importation of African slaves to work the ranches (*estancias*). Then, in the last two decades of the nineteenth century, there was an enormous influx of European migrants that significantly reconstituted the population, drawn by the attraction of vast tracts of cheap land. Today, in addition to Spanish and Italian surnames, French, German, English, Irish, Slavic, Jewish, and Arabic last names are common.

Social structure in Argentina has allowed for movement both upward and downward. The upper classes consist of two kinds of elites. First is the traditional large rancher/farmer *estanciero* elite. Although very wealthy, this is by no means a closed aristocracy. Many successful immigrants joined it during the late nineteenth and early twentieth centuries. Alongside and overlapping with it is the more modern group of bankers, merchants, and industrialists. The two elites mingle socially in the highly prestigious Jockey Club and tend to congregate in the fashionable neighborhood of Barrio Norte in Buenos Aires.

The middle classes range from a very well-to-do upper stratum that is positioned just below the elites to a petite bourgeoisie consisting of small farmers and businesspeople, white-collar professionals, and lower-level bureaucrats. Top military officers, Catholic clergy, lawyers, doctors, and managers of corporations form the upper middle class.

The upper levels of the working classes consist of white-collar workers (*empleados*) and skilled laborers (*obreros calificados*). Skilled laborers often make more money than white-collar workers, but they lack the latter's social status. Empleados go to work in a coat and tie (but they may own only one of each) and they do not get their hands dirty. Obreros, on the other hand, do sweaty work. Most working-class parents dream of getting their children enough education to move them up the social scale from obrero to the empleado category, if not into the middle class. Below these two groups are the semi- and unskilled urban workers, and below them are the unskilled rural workers. Joining them are the members of the informal labor force, or *cuentapropistas*. These are unregistered workers who work part- or full-time in economic activities that official statistics do not capture. The ranks of these workers in the informal economy have exploded in the past twenty years, with some estimating that they now constitute nearly half of all workers in the country.

POLITICAL PARTIES AND INTEREST GROUPS

For much of the twentieth century, when the military was not in power, Argentina was essentially a two-party system. The Radical Civic Union, a political party founded in 1889, represented middle-class urban interests. The Peronist Party (officially the Justicialist Party) founded by Juan Perón in 1946 originally represented labor unions. Both political parties competed against each other during most of the twentieth century, alternating in political power. The demise of military rule in 1983 brought the UCR to power to lead the transition to democracy. It was voted out of power in 1989, on the heels of an economic crisis, where the voters decided to give the Peronist candidate, Carlos Menem, a chance. The UCR regained the presidency in 1999 only to see its fortunes go down in ruin during the financial crisis of 2000–2001.

On balance, it is the Peronist Party that has weathered the political and economic misfortunes of the past twenty-five years. The institutional development of *Justicialismo* was marked by the fact that it began as Perón's personal vehicle, the Peronist Party. Even so, the party has often been a coalition of various interests. Besides the trade union movement, its membership consisted originally of dissidents from the Radicals who liked Perón's statist program as well as right-wing authoritarians with fascist leanings. When Perón granted women the vote, Evita Perón helped form a women's wing of the party. Translated into practical terms, Justicialismo was a version of the corporatist state, in which business, farmers, labor, the professions, and students were required to belong to officially sanctioned organizations. Its highly regulated economy aimed at national self-sufficiency encouraged the growth of three powerful interests that became the permanent basis for the Peronist coalition: a highly centralized trade union movement, a class of rent-seeking capitalists living off state subsidies and protection, and a large government bureaucracy. In the 1970s the left-wing Montoneros guerrillas added themselves temporarily to the Peronist coalition, so that ideologically its supporters spanned the entire political spectrum, from extreme left to extreme right. In the 1990s President Carlos Menem moved the Justicialist Party decisively to the right with his neoliberal program, doing so at the cost of alienating a large number of working-class supporters.

President Néstor Kirchner resurrected some traditional populist rhetoric during his term in office, but at the same time he did not fully reverse the neoliberal reforms of Carlos Menem. He did, however, pay more attention to the social needs of the population and challenged international lending agencies to be more cooperative. Cristina Fernández de Kirchner largely followed the same trajectory. Elected to office in 2007 and again in 2011, she won the 2011 elections with 54 percent of the vote. Many analysts interpreted this win as indicating wide public sympathy due to the untimely death of her husband. However, the fact that her electoral coalition, called the Front for Victory, managed to gain an absolute majority in both chambers of Congress, having lost that majority in the 2009 by-elections, seemed to indicate that the depth of support for her ran deeper than just sympathy. Much of her campaign rhetoric of unity and dialogue appealed to middle-class sectors that had grown increasingly alienated by her husband's authoritarian proclivities. A large student movement, dubbed *La Cámpora*, named for former president Héctor Cámpora, who had supported the urban guerrilla group the Montoneros in the 1970s, was an important political base of Cristina Fernández de Kirchner's support, especially during her second term. However, both Kirchners did little to build party unity.

The election of Mauricio Macri signaled the first time in post-1946 politics that neither a Peronist nor a Radical candidate would head the executive branch. Rather, Macri won with a coalition of his Republican Proposal (PRO) party with the lingering remnants of the UCR, which formed the Let's Change Alliance. Macri's victory came from support in the most economically dynamic regions of the country, including Greater Buenos Aires and the central regions of the country.

Rather than signaling the beginning of a new political realignment, the 2015 presidential elections are seen by many as evidence of the further erosion of Argentina's political parties. Charismatic personalities rather than well-honed policy platforms have won elections, enabling politicians to promote their own agendas and individual brands with little regard for party discipline. The Kirchners sought to establish their own brand with Kirchnerismo. However, with term limits preventing Fernández de Kirchner from running for a third term, there were few alternatives within her party to carry on her political legacy. The three main candidates running in the 2015 election represented a patchwork of differing alliances and political party factions that even political professionals had trouble keeping straight. In addition, alliances between political party factions or groups often do not continue once an election is over. Switching from one party alliance to another is common practice in Argentine politics, even among coalitions on the winning side. Complicating matters is the fact that party alliances are not necessarily replicated at the provincial or local levels. Factions allied at the national level often may be rivals at lower levels of the federalist system. The weakness of political parties is a main contributing factor to a weak legislature.

GOVERNMENT, STATE POWER, INSTITUTIONS

With some revisions, the 1853 constitution still basically is the law of the land. It was modeled after that of the United States and provides for a federal republic with twenty-three provinces and a federal district. The national government is divided into three branches: the executive, a bicameral congress, and a judiciary. There is a strict separation of powers and a classic system of constitutional checks and balances. The constitution also contains a lengthy section outlining citizens' rights and guarantees, including the rights to petition, assembly, free speech, and free press. Freedom of religion is guaranteed, as is the right to own private property. An individual may not be arrested without a warrant, may not be forced to testify against him- or herself, and has a right to a lawyer and to a speedy and fair trial. The sanctity of the home and personal privacy are protected rights.

There is often a wide gap, however, between the written constitution and how Argentina is actually governed. For example, rights and guarantees may be suspended in times of emergency. Serious domestic conflict or the threat of a foreign attack may be used by the president to justify declaring a state of siege. Although the president is supposed to obtain the senate's approval, which is given only for a limited time and only for specific purposes, in practice both dictatorial and democratic governments have found it relatively easy to evade these restrictions, especially if the president has a congressional majority.

Despite the tripartite division of powers at the national level, the president dominates the political system. Neither congress nor the courts have developed as powerful, independent institutions. At various times, both have been abolished, suspended, or ignored. Congress consists of two houses, a Senate and a Chamber of Deputies. Each of Argentina's twenty-three provinces has three senators, as does the federal district of Buenos Aires, for a total of seventy-two. Since 2001, they have been directly elected for six-year terms, with one third of the seats up for reelection every two years. The Chamber of Deputies is based on population, and it currently has 257 members, directly elected for four-year terms, with one half up for reelection every two years. Seats are distributed on the basis of proportional representation.

The Argentine congress historically has been weak, and during the present era of democracy dating from 1983 it has delegated a great deal of power to the executive in the form of "emergency powers" that have enabled the president to enact budgetary and regulatory laws without congressional oversight. Very few politicians appear to make a career out of serving in congress, and the result is that its institutional capabilities are quite underdeveloped. There are few experienced legislators in congress, committees are weak, technical expertise is low, and oversight bodies are ineffectual. Legislation may originate in either house, except for bills that deal with taxes or appropriations, which must start in the Chamber of Deputies. Bills must pass both houses, after which they go to the president for his approval. The bills become laws if presidents sign them, but if he vetoes them in whole or in part (he has a line-item veto), only a two-thirds majority of both houses can override him. The weak political party system exacerbates the ineffectiveness of the congress to serve as a check on presidential power.

The president and vice president are directly elected by the voters for a four-year term. Presidents may be reelected once. Their patronage powers are wide ranging: judges, ambassadors, cabinet officers, and the top military posts require senate approval, but lower administrative officials are appointed by the president alone. Beyond that, they are charged with seeing that the laws are faithfully executed, acting as commander-in-chief of the armed forces, and opening each annual session of congress with a state-of-the-union message.

The primary source of the president's dominance lies in certain extraordinary powers, which presidents traditionally have interpreted in such a way as to overwhelm the other branches of government. First, there is the state-of-siege power, which can temporarily release a president from constitutional restraints. Second, the power to intervene in the provinces has enabled presidents to cancel the mandates of their opponents. Third, the president may issue rules and instructions that are "urgent and necessary" for the execution of the laws. This innocuous phrase has been the source of presidents' increasingly common use of executive orders to bypass the regular legislative process. Nor does the congress usually act as a watchdog over such overexpansion of executive power. For President Néstor Kirchner, coming into office in the midst of one of Argentina's worst economic crises enabled him to demand—and get—from congress extraordinary emergency powers to issue legally binding decrees. Cristina Fernández de Kirchner centralized greater legislative and fiscal authority within the executive branch. She used the relative weakness of the legislature to gain emergency powers to make key economic policies. She also used her office to censure and/or oust political foes. Within days of assuming the presidency, Mauricio Macri started dismantling Kirchnerist policies by using emergency decree powers. He, too, seems to be using the typical Argentine playbook to skirt the legislature in making policy decisions. Hyper-presidentialism continues apace in contemporary Argentina.

DEMOCRATIC STABILITY

It is worth noting that when Argentina experienced its severe economic crisis of 2000–2002, the military was not called back into power, nor did it even suggest a willingness to assume that role. For a country that had seen its share of military coups throughout the twentieth century, the lack of any serious discussion of a military solution speaks to how far Argentina's democracy has advanced. That being said, the twelve years of the Néstor and Cristina Fernández de Kirchner administrations present a very mixed record on the health of Argentine democracy.

Néstor Kirchner's election to the presidency engendered a number of political reforms that in many ways strengthened Argentina's political institutions and civil society. He reformed the Supreme Court by overturning the changes made by former President Carlos Menem, who had packed the court with political cronies. Kirchner forced the resignation of six out of nine justices and replaced them with respected jurists. He eventually reduced the Supreme Court to its original five members as a show of support for the court's independence. A major commitment of his presidency was the repeal of amnesty laws that had all but shut down prosecutions of military leaders from the 1976–1983 era of military rule, a period of unprecedented human rights violations. Kirchner had the pardons of the military leaders annulled, a longtime demand of the human rights community, which paved the way for new trials. Prominent human rights organizations saw their long years of hard work vindicated and the legitimacy of their demands recognized by the government. Additionally, Kirchner appeared to respect civil liberties, allowed for clean elections, and built greater public trust in the government. He served his entire term in office, a noteworthy feat considering the long history of civilian presidents forced from office either by military coup or economic crisis.

On the negative side, Néstor Kirchner, like his predecessors, concentrated power in the executive. After the legislative elections of 2005, which gave him huge majorities, he strong-armed congress into granting him vast discretionary authority over budget decisions in the "superpowers law." He used his power to intervene in the once independent state statistical agency, INDEC, by firing technocrats and manipulating the procedures by which inflation was measured. And, in a blatant attempt to prolong his presidency, Kirchner had his wife run for the presidency in 2007. The plan was to have Néstor run for the presidency again in 2011 and hopefully serve two terms through 2019.

Cristina Fernández de Kirchner was elected in 2007, largely because of the popularity of her husband's economic policies. Her contributions to democratic viability veered from social progressivism to authoritarianism. During her first term, she sponsored a *Universal por Hijo*, roughly translated as Universal Benefit for Children, that gave cash payments to poor families who ensured that their children went to school and had the proper vaccinations. This program was designed to lift families out of poverty while ensuring children received the education and health care they needed to grow. Approximately five million children were covered under this program, which in its first year yielded a reduction in poverty rates. Another progressive social policy Fernández de Kirchner endorsed was the legalization of same-sex marriage, which occurred in 2010. Both social welfare policies created the hope that civil rights (the right to an education and the right to marry) would strengthen the social fabric of Argentine society. Fernández de Kirchner also continued the prosecution of former military men involved in the 1970s Dirty War.

On the negative side, Cristina Fernández de Kirchner used her office to attack her political foes and to ignore widespread corruption within her government. One example was her attack on several media conglomerates that had criticized her and her husband's policies. Initially introduced in 2009, the Media Law was designed to break up the oligopolies that had long existed in the Argentine media sector by restricting the number of media licenses per company and allocating greater shares of these to the government and other entities. Although on its face the law appeared to bring greater openness and access to the media, it was clear from the beginning that the Kirchners were targeting the *Clarín* Media group, a former ally that had become critical of the increasing heavy-handedness with which the Kirchners wielded national power. The conflict with *Clarín* became personal when the government sought to compel the adopted children of *Clarín's* owner, Ernestina de Noble, to undergo DNA tests to determine whether they were illegally adopted children of the disappeared.

Political corruption dogged Fernández de Kirchner's presidency during and after her term. A number of cabinet ministers were indicted on allegations of money laundering and diverting funds from public works to private hands, and most famously, her administration was implicated in the mysterious death of a former federal prosecutor, Alberto Nisman. He allegedly committed suicide, one day before he was to have testified before congress that Fernández de Kirchner was involved in covering up Iran's role in the 1994 bombing of an Argentine Jewish community center. The allegations regarding the Nisman suicide have never been proven, but conspiracy theories have a long shelf life in Argentina.

The administration of Mauricio Macri has also come under scrutiny. His name surfaced in the famous Panama Papers leak that uncovered dealings with offshore companies set up to evade financial regulations. Ethical concerns also have been raised about his energy minister's owning shares in Royal Dutch Shell. Many critics of Macri claim his neoliberal economic reforms are serving to mainly benefit his business associates, both domestic and international.

The concentration of presidential power and the engrained culture of political corruption are symptoms of the lack of accountability and countervailing institutional powers. As mentioned, the Argentine legislature is weak and does not have the structural means to serve as a check on the executive. The judiciary has often been viewed as highly politicized and under the control of whomever is in power. Investigations into wrongdoing often occur once an individual has left office, and the persons under investigation often make allegations that the judiciary is itself corrupt and cannot be impartial. Until Argentina can establish a stronger legislature and a truly independent and impartial judicial branch, the concentration of power in the hands of the executive branch will continue.

PUBLIC POLICY: THE DOMINANCE OF THE ECONOMY

The dominant issue in Argentine policy making is the economy. Argentina has a sophisticated economy based on plentiful natural resources (especially oil); a highly skilled labor force; an efficient, export-oriented agricultural sector; and a great variety of industries. Its exports consist mainly of wheat, corn, soy, beef, and oilseeds. Argentina's chief trading partners are Brazil, the United States, and Italy. In 1991 it joined Brazil, Paraguay, and Uruguay to form a regional trading bloc called the Common Market of the South (MERCOSUR), which has proven to be an important boost to foreign trade. Economic growth in the early 1990s averaged between 6 and 8 percent a year, following a period in the 1980s of economic contraction and hyperinflation. Unfortunately, that period also left Argentina saddled with a huge foreign debt that continues to plague the Argentine economy. As structural problems, international crises, and domestic policies all worked to undermine Argentina's ability to grow and prosper, the Argentine recovery of the early 1990s did not last. By the late 1990s the economy was in recession and the years from 2000 to 2002 saw the Argentine economy contract and economic crises take hold. The situation began to improve starting in 2003 as the administration of Néstor Kirchner managed to arrest Argentina's decline and steer it on the road to recovery.

The precipitating cause of the economic collapse of 2000 was the neoliberal reforms instituted by President Carlos Menem designed to insert Argentina into the global economy on terms promoted by the United States and international lending agencies. These reforms, commonly known as the Washington Consensus, advocated cutbacks in government spending, privatization of state-owned industries, and liberalization of trade. The linchpin of Menem's neoliberal economic project was the "convertibility plan," which pegged the peso's value to the dollar so that one peso equaled one dollar. Although early results from the convertibility plan were positive and international creditors and lending agencies were impressed, the plan's structural flaws became evident after 1994. The overvaluation of the Argentine peso meant that Argentine goods were not competitive on the world market. The plan also depended on access to available credit, a situation that would turn sour after the Mexican financial crisis of 1994 caused a decline in external investment. Along with problems of political corruption, infighting in Menem's government, profligate spending by the provincial governments, and the chronic problem of tax evasion, by the end of the 1990s the Argentine economy was headed toward crisis.

Argentina's 2001 debt default plunged the country into economic and political chaos. Neoliberal reforms were in shambles. The next two years saw an unprecedented contraction of the economy and the severe impoverishment of the Argentine population. Between 1999 and 2002 the GDP shrank by 20 percent, unemployment reached record-high levels of 18 percent, and more than 50 percent of the population saw their lives descend into poverty. International lending agencies all but abandoned the country.

The election of Néstor Kirchner to the presidency effectively brought a halt to Argentina's economic decline. In a departure from and perhaps rejection of the Washington Consensus, Kirchner reasserted the role of the state in managing economic policy and promoted a nationalist-tinged argument for economic recovery. In what is often referred to as neodevelopmentalism, Kirchner sought to prioritize social welfare spending with the continued need for global integration. During his four-year term ending in 2007, Argentina's economy rebounded. Economic growth averaged 9 percent per year and private consumption increased by 52 percent. Unemployment and poverty rates saw sharp declines. Unemployment declined from a high of 20 percent in 2002 to 9 percent in 2007. Poverty rates went from a high of 50 percent in 2002 to 27 percent by the end of 2007. Kirchner also resuscitated collective bargaining among labor unions, and workers saw a rise of 70 percent in real wages. Without a doubt, the economic reforms pushed forward by Kirchner brought much relief to millions of Argentines. Kirchner's ability to carry out such drastic reforms was facilitated by a period of high prices for Argentine exports, especially in commodities, fuels, and processed agricultural goods. The Argentine peso also enjoyed relatively favorable terms on global exchange markets. Tax revenues increased and foreign investment began to flow back into the country. Kirchner also succeeded in renegotiating Argentina's foreign debt with positive terms for Argentina.

Cristina Fernández de Kirchner's election in 2007 coincided with the global downturn in the economy. In her first year in office, she fought the agro-export sectors in her quest to raise tax revenue. Inflation began creeping into the economy and export prices began to decline. Her decision to nationalize billions of dollars of private pension funds set off new concerns about the government's fiscal solvency. In addition to the pension funds, Fernández de Kirchner embarked on a series of nationalizations—Aerolineas Argentina, the airline, and most prominently the oil industry, in which the Spanish firm Repsol had a majority interest. Many outside analysts saw Fernández de Kirchner's policies as a turn toward protectionism. Import controls put in place in early 2012 just reinforced this perception.

As Fernández de Kirchner headed into her second term, the economy worsened. Commodity prices were declining in world markets and the slowing Chinese economy undermined Argentina's ability to continue spending heavily on maintaining its nationalized industries as well as subsidizing energy and transportation costs for the population. Argentina, with its huge shale oil deposits in Patagonia, was affected by the global downturn in oil prices. Inflation grew and popular discontent led to demonstrations and strikes.

The 2015 presidential election was largely decided on how voters viewed the economy. Post-election results showed that Macri won among urban, older, and economically better off voters. These voters were concentrated in Buenos Aires and its surrounding regions. These voters believed the economy was floundering and that change was needed. Daniel Scioli, the Peronist standard-bearer, did better among the more rural and less well-off regions. In these regions, voters felt the economy was doing pretty well so they sought to stay the course.

Interestingly, the electorate did not appear to want a total reversal of Kirchnerismo. Rather, in sensing a decline in economic performance, voters were signaling that they wanted the situation to stabilize and improve. Voters generally believed that the government should regulate prices for necessities and basic utilities, that it should redistribute wealth to reduce inequality, and that it should control major industries. The fact that Macri campaigned on promises to maintain social welfare spending and was particularly vague about what changes he would make attests to the validity of this interpretation of the electoral mood.

It is perhaps surprising then, that upon assuming office, Macri swiftly enacted presidential decrees aimed at dismantling many of Kirchner's economic policies. He devalued the peso by lifting currency controls, slashed education spending, cut subsidies to electricity and gas, and ordered thousands of public-sector layoffs. The result has been mass demonstrations throughout Macri's first year in office.

GLOBALIZATION AND FOREIGN RELATIONS

The Kirchners' foreign policies reflected the twenty-first century trend among Latin American countries to emphasize independence from the United States and closer relations with governments of the region. Argentina was a founding member of the MERCOSUR, which has seen a significant increase in trade among its member countries. Néstor Kirchner maintained friendly relations with the leftist president Hugo Chávez of Venezuela, president Lula da Silva of Brazil, and the government of Cuba. Safeguarding national sovereignty in the face of external pressures continued as a popular refrain of the Cristina Fernández de Kirchner administration. Her administration's nationalization of the oil company, YPF, which was majority owned by the Spanish company Repsol, garnered criticism from the European Union.

The dominant issue of the past fifteen years has been the aftermath of Argentina's 2001 default on its US$95 billion external debt, which plunged the country into economic and political chaos. The Néstor Kirchner administration responded by taking a hard line against the demands of the IMF and external creditors for debt restructuring. Whereas the IMF called for debt servicing and international creditors demanded to be paid, Kirchner focused on domestic economic recovery, aided by the advantage of high commodity prices and a stable peso. Against all the naysayers in the international financial community, Kirchner's state-directed policies resulted in a remarkable economic recovery for Argentina. By 2005, Argentina had paid off its debt to the IMF, which itself had received scathing criticism for the way it had handled the Argentine debt crisis. Argentina also subsequently negotiated a steep "haircut" on its debt to private creditors, but a few bond holders refused to accept the terms of debt restructuring. Their demands for better compensation led Fernández de Kirchner to label these companies "vultures" intent on holding the Argentine economy for ransom.

This militancy toward the IMF and international creditors did not come without cost. Argentina could not access international credit and interest rates were phenomenally high. It continued to be pilloried by the leading financial media, which were brutal in their criticism of the Kirchner government's protectionist policies. Legitimate criticisms over the doctoring of economic statistics and the increasing authoritarianism of the Kirchner administration continued to dominate international coverage of Argentina.

The election of Mauricio Macri seems to have changed Argentina's global position overnight. Macri quickly rescinded a number of protectionist policies and signaled eagerness to encourage foreign investment. He attended the World Economic Forum at Davos, a sign that showed Argentina's willingness to rejoin the international economic community. Most importantly, for the global economic community, Macri succeeded in settling the fifteen-year dispute between the Argentine government and a group of bondholders over debt payments stemming from the Argentine collapse of 2001. Whether this economic tango toward international capital will benefit Argentines remains an open question.

CONCLUSION: PROSPECTS FOR THE FUTURE

Since its transition to democracy in 1983, Argentina has experienced periods of political stability marked by free and open elections, the smooth transition of power from one political party to another, and after some initial tensions, military willingness to subordinate itself to civilian control. In many ways, Argentina continues to be a robust democracy, with a politically engaged civil society, respect for civil liberties and rights, and continued national support for democracy. Despite these gains, Argentina remains a country where the economy plays a disproportionate role in the functioning of political institutions. Political institutions are often subordinated to the will of an ever-powerful presidency, rules of the political game change with every crisis, and policy-making is erratic. With a new government in power in a context of worsening domestic economic conditions, Argentina continues to face challenges to its democracy.

SUGGESTIONS FOR FURTHER READING

Auyero, Javier. *Flammable: Environmental Suffering in an Argentine Shanty Town*. New York: Oxford University Press, 2009.

Bonner, Michelle. *Sustaining Human Rights: Women and Argentine Human Rights Organizations*. University Park: Penn State University Press, 2007.

Cleary, Matthew, and Susan Stokes. *Democracy and the Culture of Skepticism: Political Trust in Argentina and Mexico*. New York: Russell Sage Foundation, 2006.

Epstein, Edward, and David Pion Berlin, eds. *Broken Promises? The Argentine Crisis and Argentine Democracy*. Lanham, MD: Lexington Books, 2006.

Fiorucci, Flavia, and Marcus Klein, eds. *The Argentine Crisis at the Turn of the Millennium: Causes, Consequences and Explanations*. Amsterdam: Aksant, 2004.

Helmke, Gretchen. *Courts Under Constraints: Judges, Generals, and Presidents in Argentina*. New York: Cambridge University Press, 2004.

Levitsky, Steven, and Maria V. Murillo, eds. *Argentine Democracy: The Politics of Institutional Weakness*. University Park: Penn State University Press, 2005.

Lopez-Levy, Marcela. *We are Millions: Neo-Liberalism and New Forms of Political Action in Argentina*. London: Latin America Bureau, 2004.

Nouzeilles, Gabriela, and Graciela Montaldo. *The Argentina Reader: History, Culture, and Politics*. Durham, NC: Duke University Press, 2002.

Spiller, Pablo, and Mariano Tommasi. *The Institutional Foundations of Public Policy in Argentina*. New York: Cambridge University Press, 2007.

Tedesco, Laura. *The State of Democracy in Latin America: Post-transition Conflicts in Argentina and Chile*. New York: Routledge, 2004.

Veigel, Klaus. *Dictatorship, Democracy, and Globalization: Argentina and the Cost of Paralysis, 1973–2001*. University Park: Penn State University Press, 2009.

Wright, Thomas. *State Terrorism in Latin America: Chile, Argentina, and International Human Rights*. Lanham, MD: Rowman and Littlefield, 2007.

9

BRAZIL: THE POLITICS OF ELITE RULE

Britta H. Crandall

INTRODUCTION

"We are living through one of the best periods of our nation's life," exulted the newly inaugurated Brazilian president, Dilma Rousseff, in January 2011. "Millions of jobs are being created; our growth rate has more than doubled and we have ended a long period of dependence on the International Monetary Fund, at the same time as overcoming our external debt."[1] In addition to Brazil's macroeconomic success, Rousseff and the governing Workers Party (PT) took credit for launching millions of Brazilians out of extreme poverty, while helping millions more join the coveted *Clase C*, or the middle class.

Rousseff's optimism was questioned by few. Aptly described as a "country of superlatives,"[2] Brazil occupies nearly half of South America, has vast oil reserves, boasts the world's largest sugar-based ethanol industry, and is richer in fresh water per capita than any other country in the world. With its history of military rule, hyperinflation, populist governance, and the debt crisis well behind it, Brazil in 2011 seemed to have finally gotten both its political and economic acts together. The vast country was apparently able to shed the vestiges of its previous instability and sustainably harness its endless potential—no longer condemned to being the eternal "country of the future."

Fast-forward just five years, and the picture couldn't be more dissimilar: Brazil's economy was in disarray in 2016, struggling through its worst recession in eighty years; President Rousseff had been impeached; wasteful government spending on a barely pulled-off Olympics was still resented by millions of Brazilians; and the country remained embroiled in the largest corruption scandal ever uncovered in a democracy. Indeed, the euphoria of 2011 was a distant memory, reminding us how far and quickly Brazil had fallen from grace. It also left many Brazilians and outsiders alike wondering what on earth had happened.

The catalyst for this sudden decline was an ostensibly benign increase in the price of government-regulated bus fares by a mere 20 centavos in June 2012. But for a population reliant on bus transportation, some precariously hanging on to the middle class, most frustrated with an absence of government accountability, it was the proverbial straw that broke the camel's back. Protests began in the city of São Paulo and mushroomed into the largest outpouring of civil discontent in Brazil's history—even dwarfing that demanding the end of military rule thirty years prior. Calling themselves the Free Fare movement, on June 20, 2012, more than one million Brazilians protested in eighty cities throughout the country. These protests continued, with varying size and intensity, for the next several years, revealing a latent discontent with much more than just public transportation, encompassing official corruption, the recent economic slowdown, dysfunctional public health care, an inadequate education system, and wasteful spending on Olympics infrastructure, among other complaints. As previous environment minister, senator, and presidential candidate Marina Silva explained, "In these twenty cents, which is the symbol of the protest, are included the hospital that does not work, the problem of security, and the lack of channels to know what the strategic agenda of the country is."[3]

Not affiliated with any political party or interest group, the protests represented a mandate for change, representation, accountability, and transparency. It was a mass edict from a middle class for whom increased consumption was no longer enough— who now demanded more from the bloated and unresponsive political system that was Brazil's government. Though not clear at the time, these protests represented the end of the PT's thirteen years in power. And for a country loath to change suddenly—they held the possibility to represent the end of governance as we know it in Brazil.

HISTORICAL FRAMEWORK FOR ANALYSIS

Brazil's beginnings were marked by continuity and peace. The western world discovered Brazil in 1500 through Portuguese nobleman Pedro Cabral and his fleet—by mistake, the story goes, as they were aiming for India and got blown off course. Greeted by a group of nomadic natives, forests of red-hued timber dubbed "brazil wood," and a lack of any obvious precious metals, Cabral's expedition left after just eight days; Brazil, as it was later called, was largely ignored by Europe for the next thirty years. However, this began to change beginning in 1530 in response to the increasing presence of the French along the coast of Brazil, as well as the increase in global sugar production for which Brazil was aptly suited. The Portuguese returned, and governance of the new colony was initially administered by twelve *donatários*—wealthy and politically connected individuals who each received a portion of the country to manage and profit from. This initial experiment in state capitalism, however, was short-lived, as only two of the fifteen captaincies were profitable, leading the Portuguese Crown in 1549 to shift to a more traditional royal governor model.

The seeds for the colony's independence were sown in 1808 when Napoleon's Iberian invasion forced the Portuguese court to resettle to Brazil—at that point, the Crown's largest and wealthiest colony. Prince João arrived in Rio de Janeiro with his mentally ill mother and the entire royal court packed into some three-dozen ships. Before he was called back to Portugal in 1821, he was able to establish in Brazil the trappings of a developed economy, including a printing press, higher schools of medicine and law, a national bank, and a world-class botanical garden. He also created a strong central-ized bureaucracy; Brazil's "patrimonial state"—a bureaucratic power serving its own interests—had begun.[4]

Brazil's swift and nonviolent independence from Portugal in 1822 certainly seemed like a good omen. Dom João had left his son Pedro in power after returning to Lisbon. Pedro proved to be more Brazilian than Portuguese, refusing to submit to Portugal's subsequent attempts to undermine the strength and autonomy of Brazil's central gov-ernment. When Dom Pedro also rejected Lisbon's demands that he return to the main-land, the Brazilian empire was born. The moment of independence was uneventful (consisting of Pedro drawing his sword and proclaiming "Independence or death!"). And by regional standards, the war of independence that ensued was modest. It lasted just two years and involved limited physical destruction and no widespread violence. Dom Pedro declared himself Emperor of this newly independent country, making Bra-zil the only country in the Americas (save Canada) to adopt a monarchy for any signifi-cant amount of time after independence. The monarchical political system modernized and became more politically inclusive; the continuity of Portuguese rule also meant that Brazil enjoyed a smooth transition from colonial to independent power.

Thus began a pattern in Brazil that has held constant through the centuries—the country has avoided dramatic political and social ruptures, opting instead for incre-mental change or in some cases, little change at all. At no point in Brazil's history has it experienced a dramatic revolution or social uprising that has prompted meaningful or sustained transformation of its existing social structures. This has made for a peaceful existence—aside from regional uprisings in its early years, Brazil has never had a civil war or gone to war with any of its neighbors. It has also meant that in terms of elite dominance over political and economic institutions, not much has changed since the days of the Braganza monarchy.

Brazil was the last country in the Western world to abolish slavery, in 1888. Even then, the country's abolitionist "Golden Act" was promulgated by Princess Isabel while Dom Pedro was traveling in Europe. Final abolition, therefore, did not come about from a disruptive civil war as in the United States; rather, it was facilitated economically by the advent of cheap labor from European immigrants. The long-lasting institution of slavery in Brazil meant that the Brazilian state didn't invest in the education, health, or development of poorer Brazilians for centuries. And the sheer magnitude of the slave trade—an estimated four to five million slaves came to Brazil from Africa—made the longevity of slavery that much more corrosive to any semblance of republican rule after the end of the empire. Slavery left a deeply ingrained class hierarchy in which the white elite was educated and wealthy, and the darker-skinned slaves and working class were poor and neglected. Indeed, the legacy of slavery was to be felt for centuries to come.

Abolition itself is credited with hastening the fall of the empire in 1889, as conserva-tive and politically powerful coffee barons shifted their support away from the crown.

In true Brazilian fashion, however, the political transition brought little upheaval. The overthrow of the monarchy led to the country's first attempt at republican democracy, modeled after the US example. But in this constitutional democracy, elections were rigged and the landed oligarchs ruled. The *café com leite* (coffee with milk) power-sharing arrangement emerged, whereby the presidency would alternate between Brazil's two largest states—São Paulo and Minas Gerais (respectively coffee and dairy producers). This system consolidated the power and influence of the old monarchical elite.

Raymundo Faoro, a Brazilian intellect best known for his 1958 tome *Os Donos do Poder*, described the keepers of power from pre-colonialism until the Getúlio Vargas period in the 1930s. He wrote that a combination of military, nobility, and bureaucrats attempted to use state power not to govern, but rather to stay in power, intentionally preventing the masses from ruling for the public good.[5] Faoro's framework has held up beyond the Vargas years. In fact, independent of its point in history, power in Brazil has been concentrated in the so-called bureaucratic estate or patrimonial order. As we have already established, this was true during the shift from colonialism to independent nation, and from empire to republic. Not even in 1930 when Getúlio Vargas took power in a coordinated regional revolt, nor in his 1937 coup that ushered in the "New State," an eight-year repressive, corporatist regime, did the elite's grip on power weaken. The 1964 military coup was no exception. "The coming to power of Vargas or the military," asserts Riordan Roett, "merely meant that different members of the elite were to occupy key decision-making positions."[6] The new men in power had one thing in common with their predecessors: they agreed on the importance of preserving their own status.

Brazil's military regime, prior to 1964, had assumed a moderating power in Brazil's politics. The armed forces intervened frequently in the political process to serve as a stabilizing influence, initiating multiple coups in the early to mid-twentieth century, but quickly receded back to the barracks once the conflict had been resolved. This changed in 1964, when an unprecedented degree of political polarization and economic uncertainty led the military to intervene and this time stay in power for twenty-one years. The coup was part of a wave of military takeovers that swept through Latin America during this period. However, Brazil's military regime differed from its South American counterparts. Although repressive, its "dirty war" didn't reach the level of mass disappearances of Chile or Argentina. And Brazil's military regime was a quintessential "bureaucratic-authoritarian regime," with changing leaders, as opposed to the more personalistic military rule of, say, Chile's Pinochet or Peru's Velasco.

After a gradual period of controlled political opening beginning in the late 1970s, the Brazilian military finally stepped down amid economic chaos and social unrest in 1985, paving the way for Brazil's current period of participatory government. The patrimonial order remained intact, though, through the first several democratically elected presidents. This changed, ostensibly, with the election of Luís Inacio da Silva (Lula) in 2002. A shoe-shine boy turned union leader, championing labor rights and more equal distribution of wealth, Lula represented Brazil's first real challenge to the patrimonial order. Starting in 1989, he unsuccessfully ran for president in three elections, falling short due to his radical leftist rhetoric and rough-cut appearance. But for the 2002 elections, he softened both his message and his image, campaigning in a suit and tie with polished teeth, and espousing a more moderate pro-poor, pro-growth message.

Promising to clean up politics in Brasília, he was elected president by a landslide. For the first time in Brazilian history, the PT held the presidency, and it appeared that the ruling elite had at last lost its grasp on political power.

Lula completed two terms as president, and undeniably oversaw a broadening of political participation from 2002 to 2010. High commodity prices for Brazil's principal exports coupled with robust social welfare programs resulted in a meaningful reduction in poverty levels and a growth of the middle class. As opposed to scaring investors, Lula became the darling of the international financial market for his commitment to low inflation and fiscal spending limits. At the same time, his successful anti-poverty programs made him beloved by Brazil's poor.

During the halcyon days of Lula's two administrations, Brazil had the Midas touch. In addition to its macroeconomic stability, weathering the 2009 global economic downturn virtually unscathed, and international prestige, it served as a model to the developing world in balancing the needs and demands of both São Paulo financiers as well as its indigent poor. President Obama admiringly referred to Lula as "my man . . . the most popular politician on earth."[7] Increases in the public payroll outpaced public investment in infrastructure by more than tenfold, the tax burden remained the highest among emerging markets, and overdue political and labor reforms remained untouched. But these were mere footnotes in Brazil's larger success narrative.

Constitutionally banned from seeking a third term, Lula left office the most popular president in Brazil's history. Thus, his hand-picked successor, Dilma Rousseff, had it made. A relatively unknown figure in national politics, she had never held elected office before. But as energy minister and then Lula's chief of staff, she was known as a tough and competent administrator; more importantly, she had Lula's blessing and was eager to continue his agenda.

The world now realizes how significant these blemishes actually were. The PT was indeed able to increase the incomes of millions of Brazilians. Pushing the labor agenda through an unwieldy congress came at a cost, however, of joining the patrimonial state that it once shunned. Rather than change the status quo in which politicians' principal goal was to retain their own power, the PT joined in and even upped the ante by initiating and sustaining a multi-billion-dollar bribery scheme. Those who were revolutionaries became conservative; the result was a failed opportunity to sustainably alter the structural causes of inequality and inefficiency in Brazil.

POLITICAL INSTITUTIONS AND CULTURE

Voting is mandatory in Brazil. Although Brazilians (between the age of eighteen and seventy) are required to cast a ballot, they can submit a null or blank vote. This voting behavior has grown in recent elections: according to the Superior Electoral Court (TSE), 7.1 million voters (21.6 percent of the electorate) abstained from the second round of elections in October 2016. When combined with those who voted blank or null, the number surpassed 32 percent of the electorate. In the city of Rio de Janeiro, more than 24 percent of citizens abstained (risking the small fee), and an excess of 17 percent of ballots were blank or null. The increase in both abstentions and spoiled ballots reflected a general dissatisfaction with the political system in Brazil—and certainly a disenchantment with both the Workers Party as well as its competitors.

That said, elections in Brazil are fair and generally accepted as the only legitimate route to political power. And Brazilian politicians have thus far avoided the regional temptation of populist leaders from both the left and right to extend their time in power through sidestepping term limits. On the national level, the strongest political parties are the Workers Party (PT) and the Brazilian Social Democratic Party (PSDB). But Congress is fragmented. Since the return of democracy in 1986, Brazil has had a multiparty political system facilitated by open-list proportional representation. In this voting system, voters can either vote for individual leaders or the party as a whole. Seats are then allocated to parties based on the total number of votes won by their candidates. In practice, it means that anonymous candidates can win elections and party identity is weak. For example, in 2010, a professional clown named Tiririca received 1.3 million votes. Seen as a protest vote against government corruption and inefficiency, his success brought in others from the little-known Brazilian Republic party. The proportional representative system also makes it that much harder for the electorate to punish legislators for corruption. Each state comprises a single electoral district; so, for example, Minas Gerais has fifty-three deputies that represent the entire state. There are thirty-five registered political parties in Brazil, twenty-seven of which are represented in the lower house of Congress, many of which are redundant and lack any ideology. One thing these parties do have in common, however, is the pursuit of their own longevity, wealth, and influence.

An outcome of the multiparty system is the necessity for coalition building in order to get legislation passed. This reality has its upsides: the building of coalitions provides for more stable government through the ongoing act of negotiation; repeated compromise tends to steer policy away from the radical populism seen in neighboring countries. However, coalition support comes at a price in Brazil. Politicians need to be paid—either with money or with influence, often in the form of cabinet posts. When Dilma Rousseff took office in 2011, she constructed the largest governing coalition since the end of the military regime, encompassing twelve different parties from across the political spectrum. Before she was impeached, her cabinet reached a size of thirty-nine, compared to seventeen in the United States. "Coalitional presidentialism" had been taken to an extreme.

CORRUPTION

Official corruption has deep roots in Brazil. The 2005 *mensalão* ("monthly payment") scandal implicated high-level members of the then-ruling PT party in a widespread operation of paying lawmakers monthly payments in return for voting in favor of government programs. As much as this tainted the reputation of the PT, it paled in comparison to its successor—the *Lava Jato* ("Carwash") money-laundering operation, which was uncovered in 2014. Investigators discovered that over several years, a group of Brazilian companies conspired to overcharge Petrobrás (Petróleo Brasileiro), the government-run oil company, by between 1 and 3 percent on contracts. These monies—totaling billions of dollars—were then funneled back to Petrobrás officials and members of the ruling PT coalition. For a country inured to official corruption, the Petrobrás scandal was shocking for its magnitude. By late 2016, 239 people had been charged with criminal offenses related to the operation and ninety-three had been convicted. Prosecutors had levied approximately US$10 billion in fines.

Not all related directly to Lava-Jato, 60 percent of the members of Congress faced some sort of criminal investigation in mid-2016. Eduardo Cunha, head of the lower house who led the charge to impeach Rousseff, was expelled from office in September 2016, and arrest warrants were out for the Senate president, former president José Sarney, and other high-ranking party leaders. Lula himself had been detained in a corruption probe, and Dilma Rousseff, although not facing personal corruption charges, was impeached in September 2016 for a fiscal irregularity in the previous budget. President Michel Temer, Rousseff's vice president who became president after her impeachment, was shown scheming to gain the presidency, and his new minister of transparency was forced to resign after proof emerged that he advised the senate president about how to dodge his own corruption investigation. This grim reality begged the question: is every politician corrupt in Brazil?

Before one can analyze the illegal personal enrichment and siphoning of public money by Brazil's government leaders, it is important to understand the *legal* inefficiencies built into Brazil's political system. According to journalist and Brazil scholar Michael Reid, the "voracious cupidity of a predatory class of professional politicians" has resulted in a norm of high salaries, and perks such as free health insurance and subsidized flights. Tellingly, cites Reid, the total public payroll increased by 30 percent in the decade before 2012; two-thirds of the increase took place in state and municipal governments.[8] The proliferation of municipalities also reveals this trend: approximately 1,200 new municipalities have been created since 1990 by dividing existing ones, all supporting well-paid municipal legislators. Further, cabinet members and federal legislators can only be tried by the Supreme Court, providing them a certain degree of immunity. Reversing their initial roles, Rousseff named Lula as her chief of staff in March 2016 in a perceived effort to shield him from federal prosecution surrounding the Petrobrás scandal. She backed down only after additional protests erupted.

These built-in inefficiencies exacerbate the propensity toward graft inherent to Brazil's fragmented multiparty Congress. The sad result was that rather than transform a government of the elite ruling for the elite, during its thirteen years in power, the PT had become like any other political party in Brazil. Its promises of cleaner governance became farcical as it broke all records for kickbacks, embezzlement, and liberal appointments to garner favors. Lula was so successful moving his agenda through Congress precisely because he was paying people off. As Marina Silva lamented in 2016, "I hope things get better, but I don't have much hope. Even when good people get to power, the money corrodes them and they end up forgetting the Brazilian people."[9]

Rousseff's impeachment itself revealed the self-serving nature of the congress. Her supporters emphasize that Rousseff was never accused herself of personal enrichment and was brought down by a commonly practiced fiscal irregularity. The true motivation for many members of Congress who voted for her impeachment was to draw attention away from their own corruption investigations. In this manner, Dilma's impeachment reflected not congressional power, but rather the weakness of Brazil's party system. Fernando Henrique Cardoso, president from 1995 to 2003, aptly described a broken political system suffering from a "crisis of legitimacy."[10]

The events of 2016 established without a doubt that Brazil's political institutions were not functioning as intended. However, the world also saw a significant discrepancy among institutions in Brazil. The shining light was clearly the public prosecutors' office, also called the "fourth branch" of government in Brazil. It operates independently of the other three branches, and it is defending the public good in an unprecedented manner in Brazil. A group of brave young prosecutors have been willing to apply the law, use plea bargains, and send the economic and political elite to jail. For example, Justice Sérgio Moro who oversaw the Lava Jato case, and Joaquim Barbosa, the Supreme Court justice who tried the mensalão case, reached rock-star status among Brazilians for their independent and relentless pursuit of justice in these trials. Complaints emerged in 2016 that the Lavo Jato case had become overly politicized; but with the public clamoring for accountability and transparency, prosecutors were increasingly seen as the best hope for Brazil to emerge from the crisis, perhaps even stronger for it.

Interestingly, and perhaps not surprisingly, political turmoil and the weakness of the congress, presidents, and political parties have caused many Brazilians to look again to the military as the ultimate stabilizer. Others have pushed for a return to the monarchy. It is to the credit of the military that it has not taken advantage of the situation to reenter the political arena as it did in the chaos of 1964. However, both in terms of funding and strategic goals, Brazil's military is unrecognizable from its Cold War self, focusing instead on the Amazon and international peacekeeping missions.

ECONOMIC EVOLUTION

Brazil's economy has experienced boom and bust cycles similar to those of other Latin American countries, but its experience differs from its neighbors in that its natural resource exports have changed over time, and have originated from different regions.

Sugar was Brazil's most important and lucrative export during the first century of the colonial period—facilitated by the productive slave plantations in Brazil's northeast. At its peak, sugar comprised 30 percent of exports in the early-mid 1600s. However, it began a long, slow decline after increased production in the Caribbean prompted a drop in global sugar prices. A mineral boom followed in the mid-eighteenth century, in which Brazil was at one point the largest producer of gold in the world. This boom was followed by coffee. Starting in the early nineteenth century following independence, coffee was grown principally for domestic consumption. However, the high world prices of the late 1820s to 1830s catalyzed Brazil's export market. In 1901, Brazil produced three-quarters of the total world supply of coffee, and the commodity brought in half of the country's foreign exchange. Brazil's economic prospects hinged on the global price of coffee, whose price was particularly volatile given that only three countries (the United States, Britain, and Germany) purchased 75 percent of world sales. Finally, a rubber boom took off after 1880, catalyzing a push to exploit the Amazon region. Rubber reached a third of all exports from 1900 to 1913; however, when the British began to get in on the trade, Brazil's advantage disappeared.

The natural commodity boom and bust cycles ended near the end of the twentieth century as Brazil began to diversify exports. Following the Great Depression, the Brazilian government introduced a series of nationalist economic policies, taking ownership of many of the country's largest companies. Getúlio Vargas, Brazil's first dictator, who was brought down by the military in 1945 then resurrected as an elected president in 1950, created Petrobrás and other state-owned-enterprises. Next, Juscelino Kubitschek, president from 1956 to 1961, initiated an ambitious public works program as part of his pledge to initiate "fifty years' progress in five." His presidency saw a dramatic increase in the government's involvement in promoting new industry, including ship-building, petrochemicals, motor vehicles, and aircraft. Kubitschek's state-led development also included the penetration of Brazil's interior through moving the country's capital from coastal Rio de Janeiro to Brasília in 1961. Brazil's armed forces that overthrew the weak and polarized João Goulart presidency in 1964 promised stability and unity, and initially embarked on a radical downsizing of the government bureaucracy and opened the economy to foreign investment. However, after a few years the indisputable importance of a robust government role in economic management returned.

Several industries—the Brazilian Aeronautical Enterprise (Embraer) being one of the best known—owe their success to this Import Substitution Industrialization (ISI) era. Government spending was also the catalyst for the economic "miracle" years from 1967 to the late 1970s, a time of unusually rapid economic growth. However, the overriding legacy of this supersized state role in the economy was a tumultuous period of debt, chronically high levels of inflation, and a decline in living standards in the late twentieth century.

For more than twenty years the government response was a system of indexing virtually all transactions in the economy to the inflation rate. This mass synchronization of prices had the intended result of protecting individuals' real salaries and savings (those, that is, in the formal economy); it also had the warping effect of institutionalizing persistent price increases, building in the expectation of continuous and inevitable inflation. Multiple efforts at stamping out inflation throughout the 1980s and early 1900s failed, helping bring down presidents with them. For example, President Fernando Collor took office in 1990 promising to "kill the tiger of inflation with only one shot." He implemented two failed currency stabilization plans before being impeached and forced to resign in 1992. His and other attempted solutions involved a combination of price and asset freezes, replacement of the existing currency (with a newer more appreciated one), and other heterodox measures aimed at stopping the inexorable increase in prices. What they all failed to address, however, was the fiscal problem. Without a meaningful reduction in government spending, any new currency package was bound to fail, as fiscal deficits were a major component of inflation.

It wasn't until 1994 with the introduction of the "Real Plan" that the Brazilian government won its decades-long battle against inflation. Its author was newly tapped Finance Minister Fernando Henrique Cardoso, a sociologist rather than an economist, but who was well-acquainted with a group of highly qualified economists from the University of São Paulo and Rio's Catholic University; they had been working intensively on strategies to break the inflationary cycle, and found a receptive ear in Cardoso. Rather than relying on the quick fix of a price freeze, their plan focused on the introduction of a virtual currency that was tied to the US dollar. This virtual currency stabilized expectations and facilitated the smooth transition to yet another new currency, the *real*. But the lynchpin in the success of the Real Plan was meaningful fiscal adjustment. Reining in government spending was the first component of the successful stabilization plan, and actually passed the beleaguered congress.

The Real Plan was not perfect. Brazil struggled in subsequent years with an overvalued currency and debilitating high interest rates. However, it accomplished the core goal of eradicating the inflation that had decimated the savings and purchasing power of the poor, while stymying investment and growth. The stabilizing effect of Cardoso's policies also set the stage for a renewed period of economic growth at the turn of the twenty-first century.

When Lula was elected president in 2002, he became the first left-wing candidate to hold the presidency in almost fifty years. He entered office promising sweeping reforms to Brazil's economic and political institutions, and vowed to reduce poverty and eliminate hunger. But to quell nervous investors fearful of a radical turn to socialism, he also pledged to maintain his predecessor's commitment to fiscal and monetary restraint. This policy balance, timed with a sustained increase in world commodity prices of Brazil's exports (principally iron ore and soy) proved to be the winning ticket. During Lula's two presidential terms, Brazil's economy experienced positive growth each year. His *Bolsa Familia* conditional cash transfer program, which provided a monthly stipend for poor Brazilians who kept their children in school along with an increase in the minimum wage, helped push millions of Brazilians out of poverty and into the middle class. Petrobrás's 2006 discovery of massive deep-water oil reserves off Rio's coast was considered the largest oil discovery of the century, even referred to by Lula as a "second independence" for Brazil.

Euphoria surrounded Brazil as it emerged seemingly unscathed from the 2009 global downturn. Lula triumphantly announced before the G20 Summit in London that for the first time, an international financial crisis had been caused by "white, blue-eyed bankers."[11] Loaded with foreign exchange reserves, an active development bank, and finally a creditor to the International Monetary Fund, Brazil could be part of the solution, not the problem. The city of Rio de Janeiro successfully won its bid to host the 2016 Olympics—the first time that event had been held in South America—bringing with it the promise for increased international exposure and investment. Finally, Brazil was uniquely poised to benefit from the explosive economic growth of the massive Chinese economy. China replaced the United States as Brazil's largest trading partner, as it gobbled up Brazil's beef, iron ore, soya, and oil. One scholar called this time, in economic terms, "the best moment in the entire history of Brazil."[12] Brazil's success certainly seemed to confirm Lula's patriotic claim that indeed, "God is Brazilian."

When China's economy began to slow in mid-2015, Brazil's China-led commodities boom again went bust. In 2016, Brazil experienced economic contraction with inflation—not unlike the stagflation experienced in the United States in the 1970s. Making matters worse, the Petrobrás scandal discredited its politicians as well as democratic institutions. The result was the country's worst recession since the 1930s, causing unemployment levels to exceed 11 percent.

China was only part of Brazil's problems. Critics point out that Dilma strayed from balanced budgets and inflation targeting in favor of policies aimed at spurring economic growth and expanding social programs. Expecting the commodities boom to continue, the PT government effectively began spending expected oil windfalls before they were actually realized. The Brazilian Development bank (BNDES) offered cheap credit, the government subsidized energy consumption, and it financed multi-million dollar stadiums for the 2014 World Cup and 2016 Olympics. The fiscal deficit increased from 2 percent in 2010 to 10 percent in 2015, bringing total government debt to more than 70 percent of GDP. Moreover, Dilma's administration failed to prioritize the difficult reforms most needed in Brazil, such as social security and tax reform, that would have been much easier to pass and implement when times were good.

In full, Brazil's twenty-first century economy was much larger, more diversified, and more integrated into world markets. But there had not been a sustained policy shift toward a system of open markets, freer trade, or greater efficiency. For its size, it remained a closed economy, relying on import protection and restrictions on foreign investment to drive domestic demand. Moreover, the Brazilian economy still exhibited boom and bust qualities; although natural commodities comprised a much smaller percentage of GDP, they remained drivers of economic performance. A 2016 Morgan Stanley report indicated that no other country had a tighter correlation between commodity prices and growth.[13]

SOCIAL STRUCTURES

Brazil's post-military government enshrined its egalitarian ideals in the 1988 constitution, such as the constitutional right to health care. However, in practice these rights were more often than not overwhelmed by the elitist nature of Brazil's society. Indeed, Brazil's deeply institutionalized official corruption is mirrored in day-to-day interactions among its citizens. One often hears the phrase in Brazil, "Do you know who you're talking to?" In other words, "How dare you question my authority?" All too often, social status is more important than the law, the latter of which does not apply equally to all Brazilians. The notion that entitlement is based in one's social status is part of Brazil's social fabric, and the resulting impunity in turn erodes faith in the law in Brazil. Brazilians often say there is only one law that is always respected when you are rich or well-connected: "the law of impunity."[14]

The social dualism that defined Brazil's colonial and postindependence years is intact today. In spite of the lip service paid to inequality reduction by the ruling PT, there remains a disconnect in Brazil between a large and increasingly vocal civil society who want the trappings of liberal democracy, such as better health care and education, and the political class who has always had those things. Revealed by the massive public demonstrations beginning in 2012, Brazil's old patronage system began clashing with movements for change. These forces included a growing middle class, an independent media (including the widespread use of social media), a strong cadre of independent prosecutors, and a growing evangelical church.

The most time-tested manifestation of Brazil's income inequality are the states of the northeast. Although this region was the first to be discovered and colonized by the Portuguese, it has lagged in development since the beginning of the empire due in part to its devastating periodic droughts. Poverty disproportionately affects Brazilians living in the northeast in spite of generations of development commissions, working groups, and initiatives to try to promote economic growth. For example, the Kubitschek government created an agency specifically for the area's development: Superintendence for the Development of the Northeast (SUDENE). However, the agency was seen as a symbol of leftism, and its mandate of change threatened the status quo of local elites. SUDENE's aid, similar to other development programs, ended up serving only as a tool by local politicians to maintain power.

At the turn of the twenty-first century, the northeast experienced a decade of GDP growth higher than the national average. Although helped by Bolsa Familia and *Brasil sem Miseria*, the latter a PT-led social assistance program aimed at eradicating extreme poverty in Brazil, it was the private sector that spurred growth in the region. More than one hundred different companies moved to the northeast during this period, attracted by tax breaks, investment in infrastructure, and the seemingly endless Chinese demand for Brazil's exports. But growth slowed in line with China's downturn; without any sustained investment in education, the region lacked an educated workforce. Its rural population relied predominately on subsistence farming, and an uneven land distribution revealed that the predominant political power of landowners had not changed.

Nowhere is Brazil's income inequality more glaring than the city of Rio de Janeiro, where world-class boutiques and hotels butt up against the *favelas* or shantytowns occupying the city's steep hillsides. The state historically ignored the favelas, which lacked any stable police presence or public services. Rio became a city starkly divided between the *morro* (the hill) and the *asfalto* (the asphalt)—a reality that *Cariocas* (natives of the city of Rio de Janeiro) became quite used to.[15] Strategies to deal with favelas varied from razing the ramshackle housing and forcefully relocating their residents, to investing millions of dollars in domestic and international official aid resources to try to integrate these haphazard communities into mainstream society. In more recent history, several of these favela communities have shared in the rising economic prosperity of Brazil, driving improved living standards for many, while at the same time creating the double-edged sword of gentrification and pricing out the very families who had lived there for generations. Conversely, the advent of the 2014 World Cup and 2016 Olympics saw a repeat of the military regime's strategy of "disappearing" these unsightly neighborhoods. As pressure emerged to beautify Rio and take advantage of prime locations to build new sports venues, government authorities began the age-old pattern of attempting to solve the "favela problem" through forced eradication.

Land reform in Brazil had a different history from the rest of Latin America. In spite of highly skewed land holding, a legacy of the Portuguese captaincies system, land was not as defining a political issue in the turbulent 1960s as it was in regional neighbors such as Chile or Mexico. Political mobilization surrounding land reform in Brazil did not take hold until the end of the military regime. But by the turn of the twenty-first century, Brazil was home to one of the world's strongest land reform movements. The *Movimento Sem Terra* (MST, Landless Movement) was officially organized in 1984. The organization fought for more equal land distribution through "invading" and squatting on unused land, armed by the 1988 constitution, which mandates that land must fulfill a "social function." According to the 1988 constitution, at least 80 percent of one's land must be used effectively, and must meet environmental and labor standards. The MST has successfully contested and won title to more than 7.5 million hectares of land since 1980. Shunning the option of becoming a political party, the movement heightened the visibility of the problem of land inequality in Brazil, but was unable to dislodge Brazil's stubborn patrimonial order.

Finally, one cannot understand income inequality in Brazil without addressing the issue of race. Brazilians do not classify themselves into neat black and white categories; rather, along the white-black continuum, there are upward of 135 different terms describing skin color. However, Brazil's official census institute classifies Brazilians into five different racial categories (white, brown, black, yellow, and indigenous). Afro Brazilians, or those that identify themselves as black or brown, comprised 51 percent of the total population according to the last census in 2010. One-third of marriages in

Brazil are interracial; however, the quixotic notion of a Brazilian "racial democracy" is a myth. In Brazil, it is often noted, the color of poverty is black. Almost 70 percent of Brazilians living in extreme poverty are black; blacks earn an estimated 42 percent less than their white counterparts; they are less educated and die younger—often due to violence. President Temer appointed an all-white male cabinet in 2016. However, an aggressive and controversial affirmative action program initiated in 2012 sets aside a percentage of public university seats and government positions for Brazilians of color. And the government affirmed land rights for several *quilombos*, settlements of runaway slaves. Although critics see these efforts as no more than window-dressing on an entrenched problem of racism in Brazil, supporters applaud the government's efforts to right a historic wrong.

Newly energized religious groups represent yet another element prompting change to Brazil's social hierarchies. Since the Portuguese colonized Brazil, it has been predominantly Catholic; with an estimated 123 million Catholics (64.6 percent of the total population), Brazil still is home to more Catholics than any other country in the world. However, the percentage of Brazilians who identify themselves as Catholic has dropped steadily since the 1970s, reflecting a particularly intense competition between Catholicism and Protestant evangelicalism. The latter typically holds more progressive attitudes toward social policy and work, and has attracted Brazil's poor in droves. However, the inauguration of Pope Francis in 2013—the first Pope hailing from Latin America—helped the Roman Catholic church regain lost ground in the region, particularly among its youth. Father Marcelo Rossi, a middle-aged Brazilian priest and former aerobics instructor with celebrity status, is also emblematic of this new Catholic church in Latin America. His masses can include upward of ten thousand worshipers, engaging in gospel rock and aerobics—clearly symbolizing an effective response to the Pentecostal movement's popularity in Brazil.

VIOLENCE

In absolute numbers, Brazil was the deadliest country in the world outside Syria in 2016 and was responsible for 10 percent of the world's murders.[16] A 2015 Mexican report also showed that Brazilian cities dominated the list of the fifty murder capitals of the world. Brazil's violence stems from a toxic combination of income inequality, poverty, the drug trade with its ever-sophisticated weapons, and the lack of an effective state presence in pockets of the country.

When the global cocaine trade boomed in the 1980s, Brazil became a key transit country from Colombia to Europe and the United States. This status gave birth to its drug gangs, which control portions of Brazil's cities with near impunity. The *Comando Vermelho* (Red Command), one of Brazil's largest and most powerful criminal organizations, actually has its roots in the military regime. On a remote island, political prisoners suspected of trying to overthrow the regime (including priests, urban guerrillas, student leaders, and union organizers) were imprisoned alongside delinquents and criminals; a simple prison gang was born, which evolved to be one of Brazil's most terrifying drug gangs in recent years.[17] The Red Command, along with other criminal organizations, has expanded its influence across the country and into neighboring Paraguay and Bolivia, engaging in drug trafficking, extortion, and robberies, among other crimes. The drug gang presence was particularly felt in Brazil's favelas, where drug traffickers controlled entire communities and the only police presence consisted of sporadic and deadly raids. Vigilante militias fighting the drug gangs increased the violence levels all the more.

Beginning in 2008, Governor Sérgio Cabral of Rio de Janeiro state introduced a bold experiment to improve the relationship between the police and favela residents and to also sustainably reduce crime in favelas. Under his community-policing program, "Pacifying Police Units" known as UPPs attempt to "pacify" these lawless areas through sustained police presence. Replacing the brutal raids that defined police activity before, UPP officers would instead first establish order and then would actually establish a permanent presence within the favelas to consolidate security gains. By the 2016 Olympics, Brazil had expanded the UPP program to approximately a quarter of Rio's favelas. The results were impressive—homicides and robberies were down significantly in the pacified favelas, as well as the city of Rio as a whole. The UPP's record, however, was not flawless. Homicides were often replaced by other types of violent crime; as the stabilizing force of drug gangs had been removed, the culture of police violence persisted; and the program's labor-intensive design made the initiative expensive and subject to budget cuts along with the national economic slowdown.

THE INTERNATIONAL ENVIRONMENT

Brazil has traditionally been critiqued for lacking a true foreign policy. An oft-repeated anecdote involves Secretary of State Henry Kissinger's 1976 visit to meet with his Brazilian counterpart, Antônio Azeredo da Silveira. Upon admiring the modern Itamaraty (Foreign Affairs) building in Brasília, Kissinger quipped, "It's a magnificent building, Antônio, now all you need is a foreign policy to go with it." Apart from an aversion to unilateral action and standing apart from the United States, it remained unclear what Brazil stood *for*.

Lula attempted to change this perceived ambivalence, establishing an ambitious foreign policy during his two terms. He strengthened regional ties as well as cooperation among developing countries, successfully pushed for a larger voice for the developing world in international financial governance, and generally extended Brazil's presence on the world stage. But his ventures into global diplomacy often got him into trouble. For example, in March 2010, Lula went head to head with the US State Department over Iran's nuclear program. In his search for a diplomatic solution and opposition to UN sanctions, which Brazil saw as a prelude to intervention, Lula negotiated a side agreement with Iran and Turkey. The negotiators had revived a proposed deal that had been offered by the United Nations the previous year. But much had changed since this first version, and Lula's plan was seen as watered down and overly lenient. The agreement fell apart, the UN Security Council proceeded with sanctions, and Brazil was left looking naive and inexperienced.

Brazil has also been a leader of the BRICS forum. This grouping of large emerging economies includes Brazil, Russia, India, China, and South Africa (the last added in 2010). It began as a simple acronym coined by the then-chairman of Goldman Sachs in 2001 to describe the world's largest emerging economies, and the shift in global economic power they represented. The BRIC countries initially had little in common, but the group fit well with Lula's goal to foster cooperation among the global South; member countries began meeting regularly in 2009, and increased the forum's reach and agenda, including the prospect of a BRICS development bank.

Brazil was also instrumental in the creation of the IBSA Dialogue Forum (India, Brazil, South Africa) in 2003. At the local level, Brazil continues to flex its muscles as a regional leader through the now dysfunctional Common Market of the South (MERCOSUR) customs union and the regional group Union of South American Nations (UNASUR), the latter representing Brazil's goal of creating a unified political and economic entity in South America. Brazil's PT government also served as a middle man of sorts between the radical left in countries like Ecuador and Venezuela, versus the more moderate left in Chile and Uruguay.

However, the south-south focus for Brazil has come at the cost of closer economic and political ties with the United States. Brazil's relationship with its northern neighbor is less antagonistic than in the past, but it is still fraught with tension and marred by distrust.[18] The two countries are in many ways natural allies, and Brazil certainly does not want to challenge the US worldview. But it also comes to the table as a developing country with a history of dependence and a discomfort with US influence in its "backyard."

CONCLUSION

Journalist Larry Rohter described two separate Brazils during the military regime, "one official but unreal, the other real but hidden behind subterfuge," and questioned how a society could function "with such a sharp contrast between outer and inner realities."[19] In too many respects, these two Brazils have outlasted the military government—a testament to the tenacity of a patronage-based political system averse to change. The official Brazil is a democratic and diverse country, having achieved global status for its massive economy, significant gains in poverty reduction, and serving as an effective champion for the less-developed world. In contrast, the real Brazil is divided by race and class, rooted in systemic corruption and patronage, and saddled with substandard education, health care, and infrastructure.

The Portuguese phrase *rouba mas faz* (translating to "steals, but gets things done") was originally associated with Ademar de Barros, mayor and later governor of São Paulo state in the 1960s. It alludes to the decades-old reality that corrupt politicians could be tolerated as long as they provided for their constituents. In recent years, however, tolerance by both Brazil's citizens as well as its justice system for official corruption has drastically diminished. An optimist might argue that with the political crisis of 2016, those two Brazils are finally beginning to merge. The growth of the middle class during Lula's presidency was real and had political consequences. These Brazilians now expected more than just a boost in their paycheck, demanding instead increased transparency and accountability in government operations. Unstaffed hospitals, sewage-infested water, and poor public education (to name just a few issues) were no longer acceptable—especially in the midst of such egregious theft of public finances by its elected politicians.

Political and economic crises in general are often the optimal times to implement long overdue structural reforms. Fernando Henrique Cardoso was able to make dramatic fiscal and monetary changes in 1994 because he came to power at a national moment of desperation; Brazilians were ready to do anything if it meant the end of inflation. Brazil might currently be at a similar point, yet instead of hyperinflation being the boogey man to eradicate all costs, it is now corruption and impunity. Indeed, voters in Brazil seem to more accepting of structural change. A billboard in Brasília's airport, financed by the National Confederation of Industry (CNI), demands, "Pension Reform Now!" making public its push for an end to the inefficient and expensive pension scheme that allows Brazilians to retire at an average age of fifty-five. The millions of protesters filling the streets of Brazil's cities demanded Rousseff's impeachment, but they also expressed their right to transparency and functioning institutions. President Michel Temer began to attack byzantine labor and tax laws and implement social security reform upon taking office in 2016. But these problems are much more intransigent than, say, inflation. Further, meaningful spending cuts are limited by the 1988 constitution and other legislation that prohibits cuts on 90 percent of fiscal spending. Dilma Rousseff tried to reform the social security system, for example, but lacked the political capital to get anything through congress.

Societal forces for change provide hope that Brazil is slowly and painfully going through the process of becoming not just an electoral, but a *liberal* democracy with effective political institutions. The private sector is one of the most effective forces. It remains a bright magnet for Brazil's economic recovery; Brazil's aggressive media are another component of the solution; and the country's public prosecutors at both the state and national level are armed with the power and the will to stop impunity for official corruption. Most importantly, Brazilians are demanding change to politics as usual, taking these complaints to the streets with unprecedented numbers and longevity. The biggest challenge, then, will be to continue with reform even when Brazil's economy inevitably begins to improve. The Temer administration and its successor will need to accomplish what no president has—to continue with the reform agenda even after the urgency has subsided, and political appetite for reform invariably dies down.

SUGGESTIONS FOR FURTHER READING

Baer, Werner. *The Brazilian Economy: Growth and Development*, 7th ed, Boulder, CO: Lynne Rienner Publishers, 2013.
Barbosa, Juliana. *Dancing with the Devil in the City of God: Rio de Janeiro on the Brink*. New York: Touchstone, 2015.
Crandall, Britta. *Hemispheric Giants: The Misunderstood History of U.S.-Brazilian Relations*. Lanham, MD: Rowman and Littlefield, 2011.
Perlman, Janice. *Favela: Four Decades of Living on the Edge in Rio de Janeiro*. Oxford University Press, 2011.
Reid, Michael. *Brazil: The Troubled Rise of a Global Power*. New Haven, CT: Yale University Press, 2014.
Roett, Riordan. *Brazil: Politics in a Patrimonial Society*, 5th ed. Westport, CT: Praeger, 1999.
Rohter, Larry. *Brazil on the Rise: The Story of a Country Transformed*. New York: Palgrave Macmillan, 2012.
Skidmore, Thomas. *Brazil: Five Centuries of Change*. 2nd ed. New York: Oxford University Press, 2009.
Vargas Llosa, Mario. *War of the End of the World*. Picador, 2011.

NOTES

1. Dilma Rousseff's inauguration speech, January 3, 2011. Brazil's Ministry of Foreign Relations.

2. Michael Reid, *Brazil: The Troubled Rise of a Global Power* (New Haven, CT: Yale University Press, 2015), 5.

3. "Agenda estratégica do país cabe nos 20 centavos, diz Marina." Instituto Humanitas Unisinos, June 21, 2013.

4. The concept of Brazil's patrimonial state is well developed in Riordan Roett's *Brazil: Politics in a Patrimonial Society*, 5th ed. (Praeger, 1999).

5. Raymundo Faoro, *Os Donos do Poder: Formaçao do Patronato Político Brasileiro*, 3rd ed. (Porto Alegre: Editora Globo, 1976).

6. Roett, *Brazil*, 23.

7. "Brazil's Lula: The Most Popular Politician on Earth," *Newsweek*, September 21, 2009.

8. Reid, *Brazil*, 275.

9. "At the Birthplace of a Graft Scandal," *New York Times*, June 10, 2016.

10. "Brazil Politics Stuck in Crisis of Legitimacy," *The Financial Times*, Interview with Fernando Henrique Cardoso, May 19, 2015.

11. "Brazil's Lula Raps 'White' Crisis," BBC News, March 27, 2009.

12. Marcelo Neri of the Fundação Getulio Vargas, "Lula's Legacy," *The Economist*, September 30, 2010.

13. John Lyons and David Luhnow, "Brazil's Giant Problem," *Wall Street Journal*, April 22, 2016.

14. Augusto Zimmermann, "The Rule of Law as a Culture of Legality: Legal and Extra-legal Elements for the Realisation of the Rule of Law in Society," *Studies* (1990): 19.

15. Zuenir Ventura, *Cidade Partida*, Companhia das Letras, 1994.

16. "Brasil registra 10% dos homicídios no mundo, segundo pesquisa do Ipea," *Globo*, March 22, 2016.

17. For an excellent account of the history and rise of the Red Command, see Juliana Barbassa, *Dancing with the Devil in the City of God: Rio de Janeiro on the Brink* (Touchstone, 2015).

18. For more, see: Britta Crandall, *Hemispheric Giants: The Misunderstood History of U.S.-Brazilian Relations* (Rowman and Littlefield, 2011). Also, Matias Spektor, *Kissinger e o Brasil* (Zahar, 2008).

19. Larry Rohter, *Brazil on the Rise: The Story of a Country Transformed* (New York: Palgrave Macmillan, 2010, 2012), 3.

IO

CHILE: FROM DEMOCRACY TO DICTATORSHIP AND BACK

Peter M. Siavelis

INTRODUCTION

Chile is a geographically unique country. At 2,670 miles, it is roughly as long as the United States is wide, yet it is only 217 miles across at its widest point, bounded by the sea and the Andes Mountains. However, more than for its geography, Chile has received outsized attention as a political case study because it has consistently stood out among its neighbors. Historically, it was unique in the region as a long-standing and durable democracy with strong political parties and institutions and a reputation for probity in politics. There were brief civil wars in 1851 and 1891 and some limited military involvement in politics between 1924 and 1932, but in both cases the military did not assume power and returned to the barracks after a brief period. With the election of Salvador Allende in 1970, Chile was the first country in the world to inaugurate a freely elected, self-avowed Marxist president. After the brutal military coup that followed, with thousands disappeared and exiled, dictator Augusto Pinochet inaugurated a period of political and economic restructuring that became a model (for better or worse) of neoliberal economics, guided by the ideas of Milton Friedman and Chile's notorious Chicago Boys. Chile's eventual democratic transition that formally began in 1988 was also lauded as a model of consensus building and pacted democracy (a democracy with a tacit agreement to respect the fundamental interests of all sides) with lessons for other transitional polities in Latin America and Eastern Europe. The twenty years of stable center-left governments that followed were also praised for their careful management of the economy and the rapid economic growth they spawned, leading many to dub Chile as the Latin American economic "tiger" of the time.

Thus, despite its relatively small size, with seventeen and a half million people, Chile has received outsized attention as a political and economic model. However, Chile is at a crossroads. Chile's model democratic transition, clean government, and remarkable stability made it the poster child of democracy for the first decade and a half following the transition to democracy. In sharp contrast to this image, Chile now makes headlines with the emergence of scandal after scandal, almost constant protests by students and other active social movements, plunging levels of public confidence in political parties and state institutions, and a generalized sense of permanent political crisis without exit. Much of this crisis is tied to inequality, a sense of injustice in the distribution of the fruits of the country's economic success, and the unfinished business of the democratic transition.

This represents something of an enigma, which this chapter will analyze by asking three major questions. First, how and why was Chile able to develop and maintain long-standing civilian rule through most of its history in stark contrast to many of its neighbors? Second, given this record of stability and longevity, why did democracy break down? Finally, what are the roots of the crisis of democracy facing Chile today? The chapter will conclude by looking forward, considering whether the current challenges facing Chile can and will successfully be addressed by future governments and what institutional reforms might stem the emerging crisis of representation in the country.

OLIGARCHIC POLITICS AND THE ROOTS OF CHILEAN DEMOCRACY

Chile's pattern of early political development mirrors much of the rest of Latin America, where postindependence conflict generally boiled down to either armed or political conflict between Liberals and Conservatives. Soon after independence in 1810, conflicts between two oligarchic factions known as the *pelucones* (big wigs) and *pipiolos* (greenhorns—or inexperienced ones) emerged. In a general and somewhat simplistic sense these two factions later coalesced into the Conservative and Liberal parties. However, this evolution unfolded gradually over several decades of political conflict and instability, because early on neither political group had well-defined political organizations or ideologies, beyond a general desire for a decentralized parliamentary republic on the pipiolo side and a strong centralized presidential republic on the pelucón side. Despite the existence of two party options, both were extraordinarily oligarchic and had generalized orientations rather than concrete ideologies, which centered on common interests rather than commonality of political purpose. Notwithstanding the fluidity of these divisions, they were serious enough to lead to civil war in 1829 and the victory of conservative factions, who would dominate Chilean politics for the next thirty years. Even with this victory modern political parties failed to coalesce. Part of the reason was constitutional.

The influential Minister of Interior Diego Portales who served President Joaquín Prieto was influential in drafting the 1833 constitution, which gave extraordinary powers to the president. Portales, often credited as the "father" of the Chilean state, was instrumental in establishing this strong presidential system, as well as centralized state institutions governed by the rule of law. Chile's early commitment to democratic rule, albeit oligarchic like other democracies of the time, was reinforced during the presidency of Manuel Bulnes (1841–1851). Bulnes was the hero of the 1836–1839 War of the Confederation with Peru and Bolivia, which was central to the formation of a strong sense of Chilean national identity and helped underwrite support for political institutions in the country. Bulnes, often referred to as the George Washington of Chile, also established the early precedent of voluntarily stepping down from the presidency after two terms, whereas across the region early presidents often clung to power via authoritarian means.

Chile's subsequent party development was unique in the region, and in many senses followed a more European pattern, with divisions related to class, religion, and region being central to the foundation of parties. This situation contrasts markedly to other Latin American countries where parties were clientelistic, personalistic, and corrupt. In addition, suffrage expansion progressed gradually in Chile, responding to and incorporating new groups. The first such division in Chile, the clerical/anti-clerical divide, led to the formal foundation of the Liberal and Conservative parties. The story began with the spread of liberal ideas from Europe with the encouragement of Bulnes and the foundation of the University of Chile in 1842, which provided a breeding ground for younger, secular intellectuals. The "Generation of 1842" that arose from the University's foundation formed the base of the Liberal Party (PL), founded in 1849. The express intent of the Liberal party was to reform the most authoritarian elements of the 1833 Constitution. This reformist program found its roots in the new message of liberalism sweeping the country, which focused on the ideas of social pluralism and civil liberties growing from the British liberal tradition. The Liberal party also took on the power of the church.

Manuel Montt (president from 1851–1861), though a Conservative, continued this perceived anti-clerical trend, creating divisions in his own party with legislation extending state authority into areas previously controlled by the church. The church felt under siege by liberal forces, and by the secular conservatives of the Montt administration. The issue similarly divided the country's oligarchy, and eventually Montt would leave the Conservative Party. Church officials and conservative religious elites opposing Montt's government reacted strongly against this growing secular tide. From this point on, the Conservative party became a strong defender of the Catholic Church and would remain so for decades, advocating for a church role in all aspects of political and social life.

The resulting divide quickly fractured the Chilean political elite into four parties. The existence of four parties suggests a more complicated scenario than just a division between pro-Catholic and secular forces. The clerical-secular divide splintered the right into two groups, the Conservative Party and the National Party, a short-lived party headed by Montt and other conservative and nationalist dissidents who were more hostile to the Church. These fissures on the right put the Liberals in a position to dominate politics until 1891, a period known as the Liberal Republic (1861–1891) given the succession of five Liberal presidents after 1861. However, government was characterized by shifting alliances often based on the tactical interests of leaders rather than any programmatic affinity among parties. Indeed, common opposition to Montt led to a shaky coalition between the Liberals and Conservatives from 1861–1873.

Despite general Liberal predominance at the time, the status of the Church also divided Liberals. A group of breakaway Liberals was more vehemently anti-secular, advocating the complete separation of church and state, an idea at odds with the Liberal party's emphasis on permitting an official state church, albeit with state supremacy. These dissidents formed the Radical Party (PR) in 1863, advocating constitutional reform, administrative decentralization, the expansion of suffrage, educational reform, and anti-clericalism. The Radical Party would become a major force in Chilean politics, at first representing lower-middle-class intellectuals, small merchants, Masons, and members of reform-minded social clubs.

Party differences faded into the background with the War of the Pacific (1879–1883). Chile's victory was significant to the political and economic development of the country in many ways. It further solidified a sense of unified national identity among elites on different sides of the partisan divide, but perhaps more importantly, increased Chile's national territory by one third, granting it the nitrate- and copper-rich areas that make up northern Chile today.

A central turning point in Chile's political development came with the civil war of 1891. The causes of the war were multidimensional, involving economic crisis and political extremism. Chile's booming nitrate trade filled government coffers, but also created inflation and economic uncertainty. The Radical-Liberal alliance that elected President José Manuel Balmaceda (1886–1891) took measures to depreciate the currency, encourage small land holding, and extend state control over British-controlled nitrate deposits. Balmaceda passed a series of vehemently anti-clerical laws and employed questionably democratic means to ensure large congressional majorities, which in turn alienated Conservatives who began to abstain from elections in the early 1880s. As he ruled with an increasingly iron fist, Balmaceda alienated even his own supporters, as Radicals and Liberals in congress abandoned him. In 1891 congress refused to approve Balmaceda's budget, and the president responded by decreeing the enactment of the previous year's budget. As the conflict played out, congressional forces engaged the Navy, encouraging outright rebellion, and Balmaceda engaged the Army in opposition. With the victory of congressional forces came the ultimate victory of parties over presidential power, and the advent of the "Parliamentary Republic" (1891–1925).

THE PARLIAMENTARY REPUBLIC (1891–1925)

Though called the Parliamentary Republic because of the victory of congressional forces in the civil war and the new and expanded powers of the parliament (referred to as a parliament rather than a congress given changes to its power and position during this period), the system was actually semi-presidential, with a substantially weakened president elected every five years. The chaotic period of the Parliamentary Republic introduced more complexity, with an explosion of new parties based on the power and influence of local caudillos. Governing came down to quickly shifting coalitions, based on politicians' efforts to gain personal advantage. Power shifted from the presidency to the congress, and weakened presidents presided over a series of unstable governing coalitions, with 121 different cabinets formed during the thirty-three years of the Parliamentary Republic.

From independence until the end of the Parliamentary Republic, Chilean politics remained an extraordinarily oligarchic affair. With growing mobilization of the middle and new working class, however, powerful movements began to challenge the authority of the oligarchy. As nitrate, coal, and copper production expanded, so too did the demand for workers. A shortage of workers in the north provided fertile ground for labor organization. Working-class consciousness and organization was further galvanized by the 1907 Santa María School Massacre, when more than two thousand striking nitrate workers and their families were brutally killed by the military. Luis Emilio Recabarren became a driving force behind the organization of the left. Elected to congress in 1906, he was denied his seat because he refused to be sworn in using a Bible, citing his atheistic convictions. He went on to found the Chilean Socialist Workers Party in 1912, which would later become the Communist Party of Chile (PCC) following its 1922 party congress (the current day Socialist Party, PS, would be founded later in 1933 following the short-lived Socialist Republic).

The instability and constant cabinet turnover of the Parliamentary Republic made Chile difficult to govern. Further, the development of synthetic nitrates during World War I dealt a serious blow to export earnings. Amid political instability and economic crisis, Arturo Alessandri Palma tapped into public discontent to lead a new Liberal coalition to the presidency in 1920, determined to fundamentally reform the political system. He proposed an end to the parliamentary system, definitive separation of church and state, the establishment of social welfare measures, and the complete administrative reorganization of the country. However, an intransigent Senate blocked his initiatives. As the country's economic situation continued to deteriorate, congress stymied Alessandri's efforts at reform and repeatedly refused to approve the president's budget. Ultimately in 1924 the military as an institution intervened for the first time in a century. It held power for five months, only to have the initial officers replaced by a younger group of reformist officers that called Alessandri back. Alessandri returned to the country, and ruling by decree, set to fundamentally reform the Chilean political system, and most importantly, to promulgate the 1925 Constitution.

THE 1925 CONSTITUTION, THE *ESTADO DE COMPROMISO,* *TRES TERCIOS,* AND THE GAME OF SHIFTING ALLIANCES (1925–1973)

The end of the Parliamentary Republic ushered in Chile's modern political era, with the 1925 Constitution setting the stage for the development of Chile's notably strong party-based democracy. However, it also planted the seeds for its eventual demise. In terms of formal powers, constitutional designers sought to avoid the instability of the Parliamentary Republic by establishing a strong presidential system with a president with a six-year term. Senators and deputies were elected via proportional representation and served eight and four years respectively. Elections were not always concurrent, meaning that presidents were often faced with a legislature elected at a different time, making it less likely that they could rely on congressional majorities.

However, Chile's great democratic period had inauspicious beginnings, with a series of coups and the advent of the Carlos Ibáñez dictatorship, which lasted from 1927–1931. Though he was backed by the military, the traditional parties of the right did not support Ibáñez. Rather, tending toward corporate fascism, Ibáñez eschewed political parties and instead sponsored a civic movement called the Republican Confederation for Civic Action. The economic consequences of the Great Depression brought an end to the Ibáñez government and ushered in a period of instability characterized by several military coups, a naval revolt, the declaration of a short-lived Socialist Republic, and nine different governments, all in the course of fifteen months.

Democracy returned with a system of elected governments in late 1932, and the military largely withdrew from politics until the 1970s. As the left grew during the 1930s, strong Socialist and Communist parties would emerge. The combination of the consolidation of the PC and the PL into a bloc on the right and the pressure on the Radical Party's ideological left forced it into a new center position around which coalitions would be built. Thus, as Chile entered the modern era of politics with a substantially expanded electorate, coalitional competition in Chile was structured around three large, similarly sized ideological pillars of the center, left, and right, with shifting alliances pairing contiguous ideological pillars, or particular pillars governing alone. This system, often referred to as the pattern of *tres tercios* (or "three-thirds"), characterized competition from the middle of the last century until the democratic breakdown in 1973.

Chile was able to sustain democracy during this period, even given the difficulty in building and sustaining coalitions, because of two central realities: (1) a pattern of shifting and fluid party alliances that allowed presidents to form governments; and (2) a social pact known as the compromise state (*estado de compromiso*). The demise of these factors would also bring the eventual demise of Chile's democracy.

On a political level this balance was held together by Chile's continuing pattern of alliance-making at the congressional and presidential levels. Only between 1961 and 1963 did a president enjoy a majority in congress, meaning that presidents had to consistently engineer agreements between parties in order to govern. For most of Chile's modern democratic period, these coalitions revolved around Radical presidents reaching out to parties of the right and left in order to cobble together working legislative alliances. In this sense, the Radical Party was the center fulcrum on which coalitions were built. Patronage greased the machine of government with generous incentives for coalition-building and maintenance. Candidates of the center were elected with the support of the center in 1938 and 1946, with support of both sides in 1952, and with the support of the right in 1932 and 1964. Indeed, some of the Radical party cabinets of the 1940s included both parties of the left and the right. On only two occasions did the presidency go to candidates of the right or left without centrist support: Jorge Alessandri, who led a government of the right in 1958, and Salvador Allende heading up a coalition of only the left in 1970. This alliance pattern was central in allowing presidents to govern.

To understand the evolution of democracy in Chile it is also essential to analyze the underlying social arrangements that underwrote politics. Chile's permissive proportional representation system ensured that many party options were also represented in congress. Political actors quickly realized that no party or social force could garner a majority, as the partisan options tended to crystallize along three poles, and shifting coalitions of the center, right, and left. These three options also represented fundamentally different social sectors with different opinions and commitments concerning the most fundamental questions facing Chilean society.

Such a highly divided system held together from the mid-1930s until the mid-1960s because Chilean party elites struck a tacit bargain known as the *estado de compromiso* ("compromise state"). In essence, the estado de compromiso emerged as a consensus on the basic outlines of Chile's socioeconomic structure that included the protection of private property and business interests combined with state-led industrialization and a limited welfare state. It emerged from the recognition that no one social class had the ability to impose its will on the others, and a de facto agreement of accommodation gradually developed. The right remained in the game as it was assured that fundamental property interests would be protected. The left remained in the game because it was assured that social reform would continue apace with the expansion of the social welfare state.

The combination of this new coalitional game and the estado de compromiso emerged as Alessandri returned to power in 1932, with a less populist and more conservative ideological bent than had characterized his previous period as president. However, Alessandri fell victim to a perennial problem in Chilean politics, where the combination of staggered elections and a proportional representation legislative election system made it difficult for him to garner majorities and pass legislation.

As a response to the perceived failure of the Alessandri administration on the left, and in line with developments in Spain and France and instructions from the Communist International (COMINTERN), Chile's left advocated the adoption of a popular front strategy. In 1938 Pedro Aguirre Cerda led the Popular Front coalition of Radicals and Socialists (and with the support of the Communist Party, which had moderated its ideological rhetoric) to a victory in that year's presidential election. Aguirre Cerda expanded the social welfare state, but arguably his most important accomplishment was the creation of the Chilean Development Corporation (CORFO), which substantially expanded the role of the state in the economy. In line with the widespread adoption of the Import Substitution Industrialization (ISI) strategies in Latin America, CORFO's main role was to support the development and expansion of industry and to spur economic growth. CORFO oversaw an expanded role for the state in the mining, oil, power, steel, and sugar industries, in addition to the development of the country's transport infrastructure.

Though the Popular Front drew to a close in 1941, Radical Party presidents would dominate politics until 1952, with the return of the familiar military strongman Carlos Ibáñez, who was elected in that year in a populist reaction to the perceived corruption of the Radical administrations. The inability of Ibáñez to deliver on his promises, combined with rising inflation and revelations of meetings with potential coup conspirators, brought the traditional parties back to center stage. However, the party landscape had begun to transform with the emergence of a new Christian Democratic Party (PDC) in 1958. Though Conservative Jorge Alessandri would win the 1958 presidential election with 32 percent of the vote (he was selected by congress, which was the constitutional norm in cases where candidates lacked a majority), in surprisingly strong showing, the Christian Democratic Candidate Eduardo Frei Montalva succeeded in splitting the vote of the center and edging out the Radical Party. The Radical candidate polled only 16 percent to Frei's 21 percent. The rapid emergence of the PDC signaled a sea change in party politics in Chile, though the three-thirds dynamic persisted. Over the coming decades, the PDC would replace the Radicals as the main party of the center.

DUAL CRISES: THE END OF THE COALITIONAL
GAME AND THE *ESTADO DE COMPROMISO*

As Chile moved into the 1960s, the game of shifting alliances was transformed and the country experienced the end of the estado de compromiso. Just as these elements helped hold Chile's sometimes fractious democracy together, their end would be central to explaining the breakdown of democracy. Three transformations help to explain the end of Chile's game of coalition politics in sustaining democracy: the growth in leftist ideology, decline in support for the parties of the right, and the rise of the Christian Democrats.

In addition to a worldwide political shift toward the left in the mid to late 1960s, changes in Chile's left also led to increasing support for this sector. After being outlawed between 1948 and 1958, the Chilean Communist party returned to electoral politics and saw its support grow. In addition, the beginning of the 1960s saw the cementing of unity on the left under the leadership of Salvador Allende.

The right experienced decline in support for a number of reasons. The explosion of the electorate diluted support for the right in relative terms. In 1932 only 15 percent of the voting age population participated in elections. By 1973, this figure was 69.1 percent. This more inclusive electorate tended to support Chile's traditionally oligarchic parties less. Massive migration from rural to urban areas also undermined support for parties of the right. Between 1932 and 1971, Santiago went from comprising 25 percent to 40 percent of Chile's total population. Not only was the right traditionally strong in rural Chile, but the power of clientelism induced even the rural poor to support the conservative parties of their wealthy patrons.

However, the most important development of the 1960s was the rise of the Christian Democratic Party, which transformed the ideological bases of Chilean parties and the pattern of coalition formation at the heart of Chile's consensual democracy. The party traced its roots to the union of the Falange and Conservative Social Christian Party in 1957, and the PDC rapidly grew, becoming Chile's majority party by 1965. This rapid rise took a toll mainly on Conservative parties. The PDC's roots in the Church allowed it to cultivate the right's electoral base and bring it into the center. Moreover, in a real sense the church also abandoned conservatives, with the development of a more progressive brand of Catholicism during the 1950s and 1960s. This new orientation was reflected in a general liberalization of the Church after Vatican II and the formation of the more liberal Latin American Council of Bishops (CELAM). Finally, the Radical Party's strong anti-clericalism forced many religious though potentially more centrist voters into the hands of the Conservatives (and after 1966 the National Party). The PDC's embrace of the Church, on the other hand, transformed it into a new centrist party without the Radicals' anti-clerical baggage. Decline in support for the right and the powerful emergence of the Christian Democrats, which diluted the Conservative Party's claim to be representatives of the church, led the Liberals and Conservatives to merge in 1966, forming the National Party (PN).

The 1964 presidential election, which was contested by the Socialist Salvador Allende, Christian Democrat Eduardo Frei, and Radical Julio Durán, was a crucial turning point. It revealed that the new center was different than the old center. The Radicals played the game of building alliances around the middle, finding common cause with the left and the right and greasing the wheels of deal-making with clientelistic relationships and particularistic agreements that sustained coalition politics. However, in the presidential election of 1964 for the first time in contemporary Chilean history a president achieved an outright majority, with Eduardo Frei's 56.1 percent, suggesting that the emergence of a majority party finally meant that the game of three-thirds might be over. The 1965 parliamentary election reinforced this notion, with the PDC garnering a majority in the Chamber of Deputies without having to rely on a coalition, which had been the norm for decades. These victories convinced the PDC that it could rule as a "third way" force, and most importantly, a single party. The PDC was convinced that its appeal lay in its centrist purity and unwillingness to strike particularistic deals, blazing a new and modern trail in Chilean politics.

This new view of an ideological center party was a crucial ingredient in the eventual breakdown of democracy. Although the PDC is often blamed for failing to bridge the ideological divide by forming an alliance with the left or right, the right is also to blame. In 1964, the right had been willing to accept an alliance with the PDC in order to avoid a leftist victory. By 1970 the right's newly developing project and bitterness between it and the PDC led the newly forged PN to avoid such an alliance.

Seeing himself as a third-way centrist, Frei countered the left's revolutionary rhetoric by proposing a "revolution in liberty" under the leadership of the Christian Democrats. However, Frei faced difficulties with his reform agenda, given his lack of a majority in both houses of congress produced by the staggered dates for elections. What is more, despite a successful three years in office, inflationary pressures and an increasingly hostile congress created an atmosphere of economic instability and uncertainty. Against this backdrop, in 1969 President Frei had to put down the first military insurrection since the 1930s.

Despite growing political uncertainty, the PDC remained confident that it had achieved majority status and could again capture the presidency in 1970. The right was similarly confident that it could win with Jorge Alessandri, who came from a prominent Chilean political family. Meanwhile, Allende had cobbled together a Socialist-Communist alliance with splinter groups from the divided Christian Democratic and Radical parties under the banner of Popular Unity (UP). The results of the 1970 presidential election surprised most observers, with Allende achieving a narrow 36.2 percent victory over Alessandri's 34.9 percent and the PDC's Rodimiro Tomic's 27.8 percent of the vote. The combination of a weak PDC candidate and a deeply divided country produced a result that threw Chile into a political crisis.

Elections had produced similar outcomes on three separate occasions since 1932, including in 1958 when former President Alessandri had been chosen by congress after garnering only 31.6 percent of the vote. However, the reality that Chile faced the prospect of the first popularly elected avowedly Marxist president created international consternation and opposition from Chile's right and center parties. The political situation was further complicated by the launch of a clandestine CIA propaganda campaign urging members of congress to select Alessandri over Allende. The killing of General René Schneider, who opposed the movement to block Allende's election, during a botched kidnap attempt exacerbated the climate of uncertainty. The combination of suspicions of CIA intervention and the killing of Schneider gave members of congress a strong incentive to respect Chile's constitutional tradition and select

Allende, to both appear as defenders of democracy and avoid being perceived as tools of an interventionist foreign power. Allende's election was ratified by 153 of the 200 sitting members of congress.

Allende's rule was fraught with difficulties. Questions of legitimacy abounded given that more Chileans had voted against him than for him, that his margin of victory in the general election was a little more than 39,000 votes, and that he lacked a majority in congress. Despite these realities, Allende felt he had a mandate to transform Chile and limited time to undertake the social transformations promised during his campaign. Thus, Allende was aggressive in his transformational goals. He moved to nationalize US-owned copper mines in 1971—one of his only initiatives that was supported across the political spectrum and despite the negative impact it would have on relations with the United States. In line with his campaign promises, Allende simultaneously instituted large wage increases while establishing strict price controls. The temporary economic boom that resulted buoyed Allende's UP coalition. The coalition was provided what it perceived as additional evidence of support for its project when it garnered more than 50 percent of the vote in the 1971 municipal elections. Allende believed policies could be financed through higher taxes on the wealthy and the expropriation of large businesses that could fill government coffers.

By 1972, Allende's policies had caused runaway inflation and the country was increasingly polarized. To this day arguments abound as to the sources of the economic instability of the Allende years. His critics tie economic instability, sagging growth, and runaway inflation to poor policy-making. Supporters contend that the combination of an "invisible blockade" by the United States and the activities of producer groups tied to the opposition intentionally created shortages of basic necessities, resulting in hoarding and runaway inflation. What is undeniable is that class hostility, rural violence, street conflicts, and economic instability ushered in a deep crisis in the country. What is more, because Allende lacked a majority in congress and the opposition lacked the two-thirds majority of congressional votes to impeach him, an effective deadlock with no institutional exit quickly emerged. The overlong six-year presidential term led many to conclude that the conflict, polarization, and violence would be long-lasting and some type of end game was necessary.

The election of Salvador Allende also signified the end of the estado de compromiso. Allende challenged fundamental property relations with proposals for land reform and the nationalization of industries. Elements on the left including the Popular Unitary Action Movement (MAPU) and Movement of the Revolutionary Left (MIR) became increasingly radicalized, while sectors of the right moved more and more into anti-democratic positions. Although this may have opened up more space in the political center, the reality that the PDC was no longer willing to play a balancing role as the centrist coalition kingmaker left few majority generating options.

The ability of the right to defend the estado de compromiso electorally and through participation in coalitions and in congress also broke down. As noted, sociodemographic changes had eroded popular support for the right. The right also lost its ability to defend its interests in congress through participation and partnership within government, because the system of coalition building broke down. Parties of the right became increasingly convinced that the left would drag Chile down the path of an undesirable Cuban-style revolution. This pushed the right into a reactive position. The

National Party opposed Allende on every front in congress, with the exception of its support for the nationalization of the copper industry. The traditional right that had long prided itself on its democratic credentials increasingly turned to anti-democratic rhetoric and activities. Although the opposition to Allende began among the wealthy, middle-class groups and military sectors increasingly joined. The right became more nationalistic, with the traditional right joining forces with smaller radical groups it previously eschewed like Fatherland and Country (PyL) to oppose Allende with an ever more insurrectional rhetoric.

Allende attempted to reach out to the opposition in congress with little success. By the March 1973 parliamentary elections, the sense of crisis had intensified and congress divided into pro- and anti-Allende forces, with the center-right Democratic Confederation winning 55 percent of the vote and the Popular Unity Coalition winning 43 percent. With only 87 of the 150 deputies, the Democratic Confederation still lacked the votes to impeach the president. Extremists on both sides, including the leftist MIR and the right-wing PyL, responded by inciting violence and carrying out kidnappings, assassinations, and bombings.

Although the military officially remained committed to democratic constitutional rule, discord in the ranks and divisions between constitutionalist and non-constitutionalist officers were increasingly evident. Carlos Prats served Allende as commander-in-chief and was the most vocal and visible representative of the faction defending constitutional rule. A humiliating protest of army wives vocally declaring him a coward outside of his home on August 22, 1973, convinced Prats that he had lost support of his officers, prompting his resignation. Allende appointed Augusto Pinochet as commander-in-chief of the armed forces, believing he was a loyalist officer. This would prove incorrect.

THE MILITARY COUP OF 1973

On the morning of September 11, 1973, Allende received news that the Navy had taken control of the port of Valparaiso. The military had been put on high alert, and the army moved to occupy the La Moneda presidential palace as members of the Carabineros national police who traditionally stood guard left the building and surrounding area. Backup from the Air Force arrived, strafing the presidential palace with the Air Force's Hawker Hunter jet aircraft in central Santiago. Though Pinochet was late to join other generals in the planning and initiation of the coup, he did come to eventually heartily support it and play a central role in its execution.

With La Moneda palace under siege, Allende made an emotional farewell speech, filling the waves of Radio Magallanes with audible gunfire and explosions in the background. Allende stated that his commitment to Chile prevented him from taking an easy way out, and that he refused to be used as a propaganda tool by "traitors" (he refused an offer of safe passage out of the country), clearly implying he intended to fight to the bitter end. Speaking of himself in the past tense, Allende emotionally averred: "Workers of my country, I have faith in Chile and its destiny. Other men will overcome this dark and bitter moment when treason seeks to prevail. Go forward knowing that, sooner rather than later, the great avenues will open again where free men will walk to build a better society." After years of arguments over whether Allende was shot or committed suicide, a government-ordered exhumation and autopsy in 2011 confirmed that he had shot himself in the head with an AK-47 that was a gift from Fidel Castro. Chile's long and proud history of democracy had come to an end.

Simplistic explanations abound surrounding the root causes of the coup. However, its sources were complex and multi-dimensional. First, the coup played out against the general backdrop of the social, political, and ideological processes outlined here. It had become increasingly difficult to sustain the estado de compromiso in an international environment characterized by the radicalization of the left worldwide throughout the 1960s and its concomitant polarization in Chile. The right's ideological extremism in reaction to this trend and the center's unwillingness to bridge the ideological gap also undoubtedly played a role.

However, there is also an institutional dimension related to presidentialism. Despite the success of coalition-making in Chile, the combination of presidentialism and a multiparty system is difficult, often providing few incentives for cooperation between congress and the president when they are of different parties or where presidents lack congressional majorities. In this sense, multiparty presidentialism exacerbated the deadlock that helped lead to the demise of Chilean democracy. Had Chile had a parliamentary system with the possibility of a vote of no confidence, Allende might not have been elected, and if he had been, there would have been an institutional means to remove him.

Finally, one of the most common explanations for the coup's origins comes from scholars, principally on the left, who point to Chile's coup as the quintessential example of US intervention to unseat a democratically elected government perceived as hostile to its Cold War geopolitical interests, and the interests of US multinational corporations. The truth is more complex, and this view often ignores Chile's domestic political dynamics that set the stage for the coup. Declassified documents and a 1975 Senate investigation provided strong evidence of a CIA propaganda war and its support for Allende's opponents, including extreme right-wing groups, and striking truckers determined to destabilize the government by creating shortages and a generalized sense of crisis. However, the CIA did not single-handedly overthrow the government, although it undoubtedly took advantage of Chile's domestic political context to unseat Allende.

MILITARY RULE AND POLITICAL AND
ECONOMIC TRANSFORMATION

There was significant support for the coup in Chile, including Christian Democratic leaders and sectors of the Catholic Church. This was due to a widespread supposition that the military would only remain in power for a few months, stabilizing the economy and quickly calling for new elections. This was clearly not the case, as the military engaged in a seventeen-year project aimed at fundamentally transforming Chilean politics, economics, and society.

In the most immediate political sense, the regime set out to eradicate the threat of the left. Later investigations would reveal at least 35,000 victims of human rights abuses: 28,000 tortured, 2,279 executed, and 1,248 missing. More than 100,000 Chileans were forced into exile, and tens of thousands lost their jobs for political reasons. Immediately following the coup, congress was shut down, and parties and trade unions were outlawed. A state of siege was declared and a curfew was imposed. Universities where shuttered indefinitely. The military immediately opened torture and detention centers throughout the country aimed at eradicating opponents and perceived opponents of the regime.

In terms of leadership, even though Pinochet was late in joining the coup initiative, he was named the first leader of the junta because the army was the oldest branch of government, giving the general seniority. Pinochet completely ignored the constitution he pledged to defend in taking power, ruling by decree. Initially, coup leaders planned to rotate leadership of the junta. However, through a series of institutional and personal machinations, Pinochet managed to transform his rule into a one-man dictatorship. A June 1974 decree law anointed him as president of the republic and supreme leader of the nation. Pinochet consolidated all intelligence branches under one unit named the National Intelligence Directorate (DINA). The DINA was widely feared, overseeing a domestic reign of terror, with tentacles that spread violence across borders. With help from the CIA and the collaboration of like-minded agents of the Argentine secret police, the DINA assassinated exiled General Prats and his wife on September 30, 1974, in Buenos Aires. It also orchestrated the car bombing of Allende's former ambassador to the United States, Orlando Letelier, in central Washington, DC, on September 21, 1976. Investigations revealed that both assassinations were committed by the American expatriate and Chilean citizen Michael Townley.

With respect to its longer-term transformational project, the military government also sought to remake Chile's economy. It engaged in one of the most significant monetarist and liberal free-market experiments in the world. Policy makers relied on the so-called Chicago Boys, a set of Catholic University economists and technocrats influenced by Milton Friedman and the Chicago school of economics. Key economic advisors like Sergio de la Cuadra and economics minister Jorge Cauas advocated a monetarist restructuring program, including cuts in government spending, the sale of state industries, the removal of price controls, slashing state employment, and a lowering of tariffs, which exposed previously protected industries to brutal foreign competition. Much of the nationalized property was returned to previous owners, though the state-owned copper company would remain under state control.

These policies sent the Chilean economy into a tailspin, experiencing a drastic contraction, widespread unemployment, negative growth, and the bankruptcies of numerous previously protected businesses. Nonetheless, in the late 1970s the economy began to recover, when analysts began to describe the "Chilean economic miracle" with growth rates of between 6 and 8 percent a year between 1977 and 1981. With some of the lowest tariffs in the world and a fixed exchange rate of thirty-nine pesos per dollar, cheap foreign goods flooded the country, and the economy diversified with increasing fruit, wine, lumber, salmon, and wood pulp production. This brought the share of foreign exchange generated by copper down to 40 percent from the 80 percent it had comprised at the onset of the dictatorship.

The dictatorship also sought to transform Chile's traditionally state-directed policies of social provision, which it termed the "modernization" of social policy. The government privatized education, establishing a three-tiered system of private, semi-private, and limited and underfunded public primary education. Primary education was transferred to the local level based on contracts between local governments and private educational corporations, effectively stripping teachers of their civil servant status and their right to tenure. For the first time, privately owned universities were permitted and tuition was drastically raised at state universities, given the dramatic cut in state subsidies. The state established a system of loans to finance higher education. Private, profit-making universities and professional institutes, many of questionable quality, proliferated.

The government reorganized and decentralized the National Health Service (FONASA) and established a system of private health-care providers known as Health Institution Providers (ISAPRES). Thirty percent of the Chilean population eventually would dedicate their state-mandated health payment deductions to ISAPRES, while poorer Chileans would continue to rely on the substandard and poorly funded FONASA.

In line with the ideas of the Chicago Boys, Chile's social security system was also privatized under the leadership of José Piñera, Secretary of Labor and Pensions. Chile's traditionally state-run system was changed to a capital-funded system run by individual companies managing investment funds, with payroll deductions contributed to private pension providers known as Pension Fund Administrators (AFPs). The state retained a poorly funded social security safety net for those who were unable to contribute to AFPs, though with the passage of time most workers contributed to the AFP system. In essence, in the area of social provision the regime established a two-tier public/private system, with private options superior in quality and service and available to only the wealthiest Chileans. Poorer Chileans were forced to rely on lower-funded and lower-quality social services.

Once the military had met its initial political goals of establishing and retaining power and eliminating the most immediate threat of the left through torture, killings, and repression, it turned to its long-term transformational project for Chile's political system. The military sought to eliminate the left and root out what it termed the "Marxist cancer," transform the fractious party system, and provide a blueprint for "protected democracy."

A central component of the formula for Chile's political transformation included a 1980 plebiscite that combined the question of Pinochet's continued rule with the simultaneous approval of a new constitution. The plebiscite, undertaken within a context of a completely controlled state media and under conditions of questionable probity, approved a blueprint and timeline for the return of civilian rule. However, it also provided a formula for Pinochet to remain in power until 1990 and potentially beyond. The timeline included another plebiscite scheduled for 1988, with a yes/no vote on Pinochet's continued rule. A victory of the "yes" forces would mean eight more years of Pinochet rule, while a "no" victory would provide an end to the regime and open democratic elections in 1989. If Pinochet lost the plebiscite, he was guaranteed to remain Commander in Chief of the Armed forces by the transitory provisions of the constitution. The constitution also provided him a life-long senate seat (and immunity from prosecution) following his retirement from the military.

Although the 1980 constitution provided a formula for transition, it also created an effective constitutional straightjacket for democratic authorities, leading scholars and politicians to characterize Chilean democracy as "limited," "low intensity," "protected," or "tutelary." The constitution established a National Security Council (COSENA) that included the President of the Republic, the President of the Senate, the President of the Supreme Court, the Comptroller General of the Republic, and the four Commanders in Chief of the Armed Forces and National Police. Given the council's composition, military officers and conservative appointees had the required majority to make decisions and adopt agreements. However, most importantly, the COSENA was empowered to convene in times of crisis and "make known" its concerns to the government with respect to any "event, act, or subject matter, which in its judgment gravely challenged the bases of the institutional order or could threaten national security." The vagueness of the wording regarding its role left the door wide open for military interference in domestic politics.

The regime also effectively packed the senate with its own supporters on the right. In addition to thirty-eight elected senators, the constitution provided for nine appointed senators. The president would appoint two (one had to be a former university president and one a former Minister of State). The Supreme Court named three, and the National Security Council four (each required to be a former Commander of the Army, National Police, Navy, and Air Force, who had held that post for at least two years). The first ones would be appointed by the Pinochet government, meaning that all the original senators were regime sympathizers. However, the influence of the right would prove to linger for years, given that the high levels of the armed forces were staffed with officers who could not be removed, and the Supreme Court was also packed with Pinochet appointees.

The constitution also provided important guarantees for the military. At the time of the transition, currently serving military officers (including Pinochet) could not be removed by the president. Though the president retained the authority to name the commanders in chief of the armed forces, they were required to be chosen from among the five most senior officers in each of the services (also all Pinochet appointees). In addition, the military organic law granted each branch of the armed forces all powers over promotions, hiring, firing, training, internal affairs, and military justice, making Chile a constitutional outlier with respect to the subordination of the military to civilian authorities.

Constitutional tribunals exist around the world as a check on the constitutionality of law. The 1980 constitution provided for the establishment of a constitutional tribunal in Chile. However, unlike most other similar bodies, the Chilean Constitutional Tribunal (TC) is constitutionally empowered to determine the constitutionality of proposals at any point in the legislative process—even before legislation is considered by congress. The composition of the seven-member TC was also determined by bodies packed with Pinochet appointees.

One of the most essential elements of the military government's exercise in constitutional engineering was the design of a new legislative elective system aimed at transforming the party system and reducing the influence of the left. The text of the 1980 constitution established that the electoral law that would be employed would be set down in a later organic law. Thus, the military regime set out to design the election system following defeat in the 1988 plebiscite. The military considered a single member district system like that of the United States and UK, but knew that having received only about 40 percent of the vote in the 1988 plebiscite, it risked the exclusion of the right from congress with such a system. However, with a proportional system, its goal of minimizing the representation of parties of the left and limiting the number of political parties would be undermined, potentially prompting the rebirth of the fractious and polarized multiparty system that historically existed. Thus, the military opted for a two-member district system (or a binomial system). Electoral rules provided that each coalition could present two candidate open lists. Though voters chose a candidate, votes were pooled to determine whether lists won one or two seats. The highest-polling coalition in a district could only win both seats if it more than doubled the vote total of the second-place list—providing effective thresholds of 33 percent for a one-seat victory and 66 percent for a two-seat victory. The military regime knew that any post-authoritarian opposition that would grow from the "no" forces in the plebiscite would likely be unable to reach this threshold, given that the "no" forces only garnered 54 percent of the vote nationwide. Thus, with the eventual development of two alliances based on pro- and anti-Pinochet forces (which the military expected), if neither the right nor the center-left could reach the 66 percent threshold, effectively one seat would go to each alliance. In addition, because of the thresholds of the system, a coalition that lost support in a district could conceivably go from a level of 65 percent support to 35 percent without losing the congressional seat. The system would also marginalize any small party that failed or refused to strike an electoral bargain with one of the two major coalitions, effectively achieving the goal of preventing the proliferation of parties and excluding small, extreme left-wing parties, two additional important goals of the military's exercise in electoral engineering.

An additional check on democratic authorities was the establishment of high quorums for legislating and reforms. For "Constitutional Organic Laws" a 4/7 majority was required, while for "Constitutional Reforms" or "Laws Interpreting Constitutional Precepts" a 3/5 majority was necessary. When coupled with the distorting nature of the binomial system and the existence of appointed senators, these quorums made reforms to the constitution and organic laws virtually impossible.

Although some of these constitutional features stand out for their blatant intention to limit representation or favor the right (e.g., COSENA and appointed senators), others may seem not too far removed from constitutional norms in a cross-national perspective. Nonetheless, in Chile it was the *combination* of all these features that provided a constitutional straightjacket for democratic authorities, one that made it both difficult to govern and legislate and almost impossible to reform the constitution.

THE DEMOCRATIC TRANSITION

With a sense that Pinochet had achieved many of his goals of transformation, and facing domestic and international opposition, political elites in and outside the regime realized the inevitability of an eventual transition back to democracy. Pinochet had successfully put off this transition, pointing to the timeline for reform set down in the 1980 constitution.

Two major attempts at unifying the opposition predate the ultimate establishment of what would become the opposition coalition. Both the "National Accord for a Full Transition to Democracy" of 1985 and the "Civic Assembly" of 1986 fell victim to political divisions and the half-hearted participation of the centrist (and relatively more conservative) elements of the opposition (mostly the PDC). However, Pinochet's framework for a controlled transition unwittingly set the stage for more coordinated opposition to the military.

Part of the dilemma for the opposition was whether to give legitimacy to the constitution and entire process by participating in the plebiscites the regime organized. Despite initial opposition to the 1988 plebiscite, the Communist Party eventually permitted its members to register and participate. Still, at this point in the process the Communist and Socialist parties remained illegal, prompting the Socialists to create and register a new party entitled the Party for Democracy (PPD). Both of these parties were joined by fifteen other center and left parties to form the Command for the No, while two conservative parties backed the "yes" vote with the support of some smaller conservative and regional parties. Unlike the 1980 contest, the 1988 plebiscite was transparent and fair, monitored by international and domestic observers and undertaken with a guarantee of advertising time on state media for both sides. A vigorous campaign ensued, with "yes" forces arguing for Chile's success under the dictatorship, with a not-so-subtle message that a "no" vote would result in a return to the chaotic Allende years. Rather than focusing on human rights abuses and the dictatorship's damage to Chile's social fabric, the "no" forces painted a positive view of what a democratic future would hold, adopting the slogan *"La alegría ya viene"* (happiness is on its way). The "no" vote ultimately triumphed, 54 percent to 43 percent against the "yes" vote, paving the way for the return to democracy.

THE RETURN OF DEMOCRACY AND
CONCERTACIÓN GOVERNMENTS

In essence the regime committed a strategic error by casting the 1988 ballot as a "yes" or "no" vote on Pinochet's continued rule. Had Pinochet opted for a simple presidential election in which he would be a candidate, the fractionalized opposition would have had the likely impossible task of selecting a unifying party standard-bearer to face off against Pinochet. With a plebiscite, rather than discussing and agreeing upon candidates and platforms, all the parties of the center-left needed to do was agree that they opposed Pinochet. The forces of the "no" vote parlayed their support into the formation of a new coalition in 1989 that would contest all elections through the present day. Though the "no" forces were victorious, it really was a mixed win. Although the center-left unseated the regime, it was forced to operate within the confines and constraints of the 1980 constitution. Similarly, though the Pinochet forces lost the plebiscite, they were able to impose their will and retain veto power, because it was in essence their constitution under which democratic authorities had to govern.

Two multiparty coalitions have contested the six presidential and congressional elections since the return to democracy. The center-left *Concertación* coalition, which grew from the 1988 plebiscite's "no" forces, comprised the Christian Democratic Party (PDC), the Socialist Party (PS), the Party for Democracy (PPD), and the smaller Radical Party (PR) and Social Democratic Party (PSD). The latter two parties merged in 1994 to form the Radical Social Democratic Party (PRSD). In 2013, the alliance was renamed *Nueva Mayoría*, and continued to have the four traditional parties (PDC, PS, PPD, PRSD), but also included the Communist Party of Chile (PCC), Citizen Left (IC), and the Wide Social Movement (MAS). The right-wing coalition is the *Alianza,* composed of two major parties, National Renewal (RN) and the Independent Democratic Union (UDI). In the 1993 election, the Union of the Center (UCC) also joined the Alianza. The UDI was more closely associated with allies of the dictatorship and is considered more conservative than RN, whose roots lie in Chile's traditional aristocratic right.

Demonstrating remarkable unity, the Concertación led what were arguably the most successful governments in Chilean history, electing two Christian Democratic presidents, Patricio Aylwin (1990–1994) and Eduardo Frei Ruiz-Tagle (1994–2000), and two Socialists, Ricardo Lagos (2000–2006) and Michelle Bachelet (2006–2010 and 2014–2018). The right would assume power only after twenty years of Concertación governments, under the leadership of National Renewal's Sebastián Piñera (2010–2014), only to see the return of the Concertación (now called Nueva Mayoría) with the second Bachelet government.

It is important to note that this pattern of competition between two alliances was reinforced by the binomial legislative election system analyzed above. Undeniably the election system did provide important coalitional glue that held both alliances together, because the failure to reach coalition agreements could result in the exclusion of parties from congress. On the other hand, the military's electoral engineers were successful in predicting the effects the system would have. Because the Concertación's level of electoral support hovered around 55 percent and the Alianza's at around 40 percent for most of the transitional period as expected by electoral engineers (given the information they had from the 1988 plebiscite), the coalitions consistently divided seats in most districts, providing the predicted electoral bonus for the right while also marginalizing small non-aligned parties.

Patricio Aylwin (1990–1994)

On December 14, 1989, Chileans elected the first post-authoritarian government with Christian Democrat Patricio Aylwin as its standard-bearer. Aylwin assumed office in March 1990 for an initial four-year term. However, Pinochet remained as the commander in chief of the armed forces for eight years. In this sense, Aylwin really was forced into a balancing act between the armed forces, who were loath to see any transformations to Pinochet's legacy, and sectors of the left who were bent on promoting deep, far-reaching transformations.

Aylwin succeeded in walking this fine line, overseeing sustained economic growth, while respecting the fundamentals of the Pinochet neoliberal market model. During his tenure, economic growth averaged 7 percent per year and health spending increased by 75 percent between 1990 and 1997, a process he initiated. The Aylwin presidency saw significant reductions of the percentage of the population living in poverty (though progress on this front continued through all Concertación governments), with the percentage of the population living in poverty declining from 39 percent in 1987 to 23 percent at the end of Aylwin's presidency.

The president also moved quickly but carefully in the area of human rights. Despite demands for the prosecution of human rights offenders, Aylwin pursued a route of reconciliation through the establishment of the Commission on Truth and Reconciliation in April of 1990, headed by former Radical Party Senator Raúl Rettig. Aylwin realized that a prosecutorial path would risk inciting Pinochet and the military, potentially eliciting another coup if the fundamental interests of the armed forces were deemed threatened. In an effort to ensure that the truth be known regarding the dictatorship's human rights abuses, and to avoid the possibilities that human rights deniers would be able to gain traction, Aylwin and his advisors settled on pursuing complete investigations of the abuses without naming or trying perpetrators. The comprehensive Rettig Commission Report provided meticulous details on the military's human rights abuses using the power of moral suasion and documentation to provide an accurate account of abuses and lay the foundation for later reparations for victims' families.

Aylwin faced serious challenges from the military. Indeed, in the hindsight of success, one forgets significant challenges to civilian authority, including two military mobilizations (the *"ejercicio de enlace"* of 1990 and the *"boinazo"* of 1993). The assassination of right-wing senator and founder of the UDI party Jaime Guzmán by members of the Manuel Rodríquez Patriotic Front also created tensions with the army. Still, Aylwin navigated Chile through some of the toughest moments of the transition with careful leadership and balanced judgment.

Eduardo Frei Ruiz-Tagle (1994–2000)

Christian Democrat Eduardo Frei Ruiz-Tagle (Frei Montalva's son) was at the helm of the second Concertación administration. Frei sailed to victory with a record 58 percent of the vote against the Alianza's Arturo Alessandri, nephew of the former president. Frei's administration represented continuity in policy and approach with the Aylwin administration. Economic policy making remained conservative, and the free-market approach continued to prevail. Frei expanded Chile's engagement in the world economy, with the negotiation of several bilateral and multilateral trade agreements.

Like Aylwin, he took a piecemeal approach to challenging the institutional legacy of the dictatorship, including the proposal of an electoral reform, elimination of the institutional senators, and attempts to modernize and reform the judicial system. Nonetheless, the veto powers embedded in the 1980 constitution prevented any significant political reform.

With respect to civil-military relations, human rights challenges were immediately on the table again when Frei assumed office. Judicial changes permitting the jurisdiction of civilian courts over human rights cases in certain situations were completed at the end of the Aylwin administration. In 1993, retired general and former head of the DINA Manuel Contreras and his assistant, Pedro Espinoza, were tried and convicted for participation in the Letelier assassination, and eventually served sentences in jails specifically built and designed to house military officers.

However, Frei's biggest challenge was dealing with Pinochet's October 1998 arrest in London. By 1998, Pinochet's term as armed forces commander in chief had ended, and he assumed his constitutionally guaranteed senate seat and the immunity that came with it. The aging dictator had little time to get involved with senate business, travelling to London for back surgery shortly after assuming his seat. On October 16, while recovering in the hospital, he was detained by Scotland Yard based on an extradition request from Spain in connection with the torture of Spanish citizens in Chile during the military regime, as well as for acts of "genocide, terrorism, and torture." Pinochet was put under house arrest in an elegant suburban mansion outside London, and received visits by former Conservative Prime Minister Margaret Thatcher, who credited Pinochet with saving Chilean democracy and battling the spread of international Marxism.

The Pinochet arrest put the Frei government in a difficult political bind. On the one hand, Concertación governments were no friend of Pinochet. On the other hand, national sovereignty arguments were advanced across the political spectrum, with the contention that Chilean authorities had original jurisdiction over crimes committed on Chilean soil. A sixteen-month legal battle ensued in the House of Lords, the UK's highest court. Pinochet's attorneys claimed that he was immune from prosecution as a former head of state based on the UK's State Immunity Act of 1978. Lawyers for the government contended that heinous crimes like torture were not subject to the Act's protections. Ultimately, the Lords ruled that Pinochet was only subject to prosecution for crimes committed after 1988, the year that the UK implemented the UN Convention Against Torture. Though the cases deemed admissible by the court were not the most serious instances of human rights abuses committed by the regime, on October 8, 1999, the court ruled that Pinochet should be extradited to Spain to stand trial for charges in those cases. Ultimately however, as the process of extradition unfolded, it was clear that the eighty-three-year-old dictator's health was rapidly deteriorating. The UK's Home Secretary Jack Straw ultimately accepted arguments by Pinochet's lawyers and the Chilean government that Pinochet was unfit to stand trial and he was released, returning to Chile on March 3, 2000.

This was not the end to Pinochet's problems, as charges on fifty-eight cases of human rights abuses awaited him. In a signal that Chile's political context had been transformed by the international and domestic light shed on Pinochet's crimes as a result of the arrest, authorities finally had the wherewithal to bring charges against him and investigate other atrocities. Judges took up cases like the notorious "Caravan of Death" (the brutal murder of regime opponents in northern Chile), the General Prats murder, and a series of cases thrust onto the national stage as investigations into the dictatorship's crimes proceeded. Upon his return to Chile, Pinochet was stripped of his senate seat and congressional immunity. A cascade of well-documented accusations followed, including illegal arms dealings, tax fraud, and the existence of illegal bank accounts in the United States. Although these revelations tarnished Pinochet's image even for his former supporters, consistent rulings regarding his physical unfitness to stand trial prevented prosecution for any of his many crimes.

Ricardo Lagos (2000–2006)

The 1999 and 2000 presidential elections represented a historic turning point, with the election of Ricardo Lagos, a Socialist who had served under both Allende and the first two Concertación governments. The campaign was riddled with accusations by the right that Lagos's election would represent a return to the violence and instability of the Allende era. The right supported former Pinochet government minister Joaquín Lavín of the far-right UDI. A combination of the fear of what a Socialist victory might mean for Chile and a well-funded campaign with a charismatic leader on the right brought Lavín within 34,000 votes of defeating Lagos in the first round of the election on December 12, 1999. In the second round, mandated by the constitution when a candidate does not receive a majority, Lagos successfully culled the votes of supporters of the Communist Party candidate in the first round to outpace Lavín with a 2.6 percent margin.

The expectation that Lagos might return to the policies of the Allende government proved completely unfounded. Lagos oversaw a moderate, and some would argue conservative, administration with economic policy making largely respecting the broad outlines of the reigning neoliberal economic model, while engaging in piecemeal reforms. Lagos did, however, undertake a significant reform to the privatized health-care system, extending guaranteed health-care coverage irrespective of ability to pay for a series of conditions.

Chile's economy, buffeted by the world crisis of the 1990s, recovered dramatically under Lagos's administration. Not only did the price of Chile's mainstay product, copper, soar, but foreign investment reached an all-time high, the government and the private sector worked to diversify fruit, forestry, and wine production, and Chile moved into position as the second largest exporter of salmon in the world. The country, which already had signed free trade agreements with Mexico and Canada during the previous administration, added the United States, the European Union, and South Korea. Chile's successful war on poverty continued during the Lagos administration, reducing poverty to 13.7 percent by 2006, though income inequality remained little changed. These successes turned a president who was once seen as a potential enemy of the business sector into one who enjoyed widespread support.

President Lagos also oversaw the most significant constitutional reforms since the return of democracy. The most egregiously authoritarian aspects of the constitution were reformed in September 2005 with the support of the right. The reforms eliminated the positions of appointed senators, reduced the powers of the National Security Council, reestablished presidential authority to remove the commanders-in-chief of the armed forces, and reduced the presidential term from six to four years. These reforms prompted president Lagos to declare that the Chilean democratic transition was finally complete. The right's acceptance of reform grew from the reality that increasingly the power of appointment of these authorities fell to Concertación governments and had increasingly come to work to the center-left's advantage. Although Lagos also proposed an end to the binomial legislative electoral system, he like his two predecessors was stymied by the staunch rightist opposition to such a reform.

Michelle Bachelet (2006–2010)

Despite the success of the Lagos administration, and a 70 percent approval rating, the Concertación faced a turning point as his government drew to a close. It was difficult to sustain a message of change after three successive Concertación governments. The Concertación was able to do so with the choice of Lagos's former Minister of Defense, Michelle Bachelet. The virtually unknown Bachelet, who began her career as a public health pediatrician often working among the poor, was appointed as minister of health in 2000, and in the wake of her success in that position, as Latin America's first woman minister of defense in 2002. The daughter of Air Force General Alberto Bachelet, who died in government custody after torture for non-compliance with the Pinochet government, she and her mother also were detained and tortured by military authorities. As an avowed agnostic and a divorced single mother, in a country that had only legalized divorce in 2004, Bachelet did not fit the traditional mold of Chilean presidential candidates. She portrayed herself as an everyday Chilean and the candidate of change, despite the fact that she represented a coalition that had been in power for sixteen years.

The Bachelet government seemed to get off to a good start, but the honeymoon was short-lived. Campaigning on a platform of reducing inequality and confronting the problems faced by real people, she suggested that the Chilean political class was seriously out of touch. During her first one hundred days in office she moved quickly to implement thirty-six campaign pledges, many aimed at everyday voter concerns. True to her word, Bachelet moved decisively to increase state pensions by 10 percent and improve health coverage for senior citizens. She succeeded in passing legislation that increased the number of state-run nurseries and provided additional employment programs for the neediest Chileans. She also introduced a series of laws to improve education and promote vocational training. In addition to social legislation, Bachelet presented bills that would create a new Ministry of the Environment and a Ministry of Public Safety, and enable legislation to reform the constitution.

Nonetheless, the president was buffeted early in her term by a series of unpredicted events and her response led to questions concerning her decisiveness and leadership. The first was a crisis in the implementation of the newly developed Transantiago transport system, whose inauguration produced long lines, stalled traffic, and frustrated commuters. However, the most serious crisis was the rapid escalation of student protests. In late April 2006, only weeks into Bachelet's term, high school students staged a small-scale demonstration in response to a price increase for the college aptitude test and rumored limitations on the use of the free student transport pass. Protests quickly escalated into demonstrations over inequality and the generally dismal state of public education. More than six-hundred students were arrested and several were injured. Accusations of heavy-handedness by the police and the haughty response of Education Minister Martín Zilic added fuel to an already explosive situation as citizen reaction took the government by complete surprise. On May 30, an estimated half-million students participated in a new protest, and in subsequent protests in early June the numbers swelled to more than 700,000 as high school students were joined by parents, university students, and unions. The students rejected as inadequate Bachelet's initial offer of US$60 million in emergency education spending. Ultimately the president agreed to include an additional US$200 million in the annual education budget, a 2.78 percent increase. She agreed to maintain free bus passes for students, and to make university entrance exams free except for the richest 20 percent of students. Finally, Bachelet announced the formation of a commission to study and recommend reforms aimed at reducing inequality and improving the educational system. Nonetheless, this would only be the beginning of what would become an issue plaguing the two subsequent administrations.

Bachelet was lauded for her handling of the economy. Working with Finance Minister Andrés Velasco, she resisted social demands to spend Chile's copper reserve fund, which had swelled during the years of high copper prices. With the onset of crisis and the plummeting of world copper prices, the government was able to draw on this surplus to keep the economy afloat and to provide a safety net for the poorest Chileans.

Despite early crises in her government, Bachelet left office with an approval rating of 72 percent, an unprecedented level for any president. Yet, it was largely her personal popularity rather than the popularity of the Concertación coalition that explained these numbers. This reality, and the reality of the nomination of former president Frei as the coalition standard-bearer in combination with a lackluster campaign provided an opportunity for the right.

Sebastián Piñera (2010–2014): *The Right Returns*

The right chose Sebastián Piñera of National Renewal—the more moderate party of the Alianza—to head up the presidential ticket for the 2009–2010 campaign. One of the main objectives of Piñera's campaign was to build what he termed a "new right and a new social majority," both inserting an implicit criticism of the right as it had existed and suggesting that this new right would be attractive to many more Chileans. To do this, Piñera based his campaign on two themes, and markedly moved certain key policy positions toward the center. The first was a negative one aimed at the Concertación. Piñera had to be cautious. Bachelet left power with the highest approval rating of any modern president. Therefore, rather than attacking personalities or policies, Piñera focused his campaign on the idea that the Concertación had failed, was out of gas, and had not fulfilled its campaign promises. He criticized the politics of the Concertación and the growing sense that political power was distributed based on political connections rather than talent. In terms of the more positive elements, he argued that Chile needed a new form of government based on efficiency and expertise and not on political connections.

In addition, Piñera tacked remarkably toward the center during the campaign in order to pick up centrist voters, and this was particularly the case with respect to social issues. Because this was a three-way race, with dissident candidate Marco Enríquez Ominami competing on the left, Eduardo Frei, the Concertación candidate, had the most difficult position—attempting to attract voters from the left. This opened up a wider competition for centrist voters for Piñera. He played up his family's Christian Democratic roots and the fact that he had voted against a continuation of the Pinochet regime in the 1988 plebiscite. Perhaps most important, with respect to economic policy, Piñera really simply stole the Concertación's thunder, advocating for much of the outline of the broad policy positions of the Concertación, with a pledge to create a million jobs, eliminate poverty, and to make Chile a developed country.

Piñera ultimately succeeded in promoting this message and was sworn in on March 11, 2010, having received 44 percent of the vote in the first round against Frei's paltry 29.6 percent and a majority of 51.6 percent in the second round. Two weeks before Piñera's inauguration, one of the largest recorded earthquakes in history struck southern Chile. Though the quake caused relatively little damage, especially considering its massive size, it did kill 156 Chileans, most of whom perished in the tsunami that followed the earthquake. The Bachelet government was charged with having had a slow response to the disaster as well as having provided insufficient warning regarding the potential destructive force of the tsunami. These issues would come back to haunt her when she would run for reelection.

As the first democratic government of the right since 1958 in Chile, Piñera's government represented both change and continuity. He appointed a cabinet made up of mostly business leaders rather than the traditional career politicians that characterized Concertación cabinets. Nonetheless, the outlines of broad economic policy remained the same and the specter of student protests continued to haunt him throughout his administration. A high point, after which his popularity soared, was the dramatic rescue of thirty-three miners who had been trapped deep below ground for more than two months in northern Chile. His popularity was short-lived however, as he and his government were sharply criticized for their handling of resurgent student protests. By this point university student protesters had elevated their demands to include free university education for all students. This demand clashed head on with the right's predominant ideology and view of the state.

Michelle Bachelet (2014–2018): "La Presidenta" Returns

Michelle Bachelet was largely expected to return to Chile to run for the presidency again in 2013. She had spent most of Piñera's term in New York serving as the head of the United Nations agency on women. The Concertación was redubbed the Nueva Mayoría coalition and organized internal primaries to choose its presidential candidate. Bachelet led early and her victory was never in doubt, sweeping the June 2013 primaries with 73 percent of the vote, and besting her three competitors.

On the right, Laurence Golborne, who represented the farthest right party, the Independent Democratic Union, led in the polls as a result of his role overseeing the rescue of the trapped miners as Minister of Mining. He was dramatically forced to resign following evidence of his involvement in a credit card scandal and the discovery of US$30 million in a tax-exempt offshore account. The UDI rushed to replace Golborne with Pablo Longueira, a more traditional candidate more closely associated with the former dictatorship. He obtained a surprising 51.37 percent of the primary vote, narrowly defeating Andrés Allamand, the candidate of the more moderate right-wing party National Renewal. Following Golborne's unexpected resignation, another surprise was in the wings. Within three weeks of his primary victory, Longueira's family announced that he would abandon the race due to severe depression. This sent the right into complete disarray and left the Alianza with the unhappy task of nominating a new candidate with the presidential race in full swing. Lingering tensions from the primary led the UDI to reject Allamand as the new candidate, and instead pushed Evelyn Matthei into the presidential race. Her nomination was not just remarkable because two women would face off in the election, but also because Bachelet and Matthei were childhood friends, given that both women's fathers were former military officers. This set the stage for a dramatic race, which was joined by seven additional populist and independent candidates.

Chileans resoundingly returned Bachelet to office on December 15, 2013. Bachelet campaigned and won the election on a much more transformational platform than the first time around. Three of her centerpiece policies included educational and tax reform and reform of the binomial electoral system and constitution. The government has succeeded in reforming holdover educational policies from the dictatorship that first sparked the ongoing waves of protests in 2006. Student demands for basic reforms regarding fees and transportation rapidly escalated to include the removal of any profit motive from education and free higher education for all Chileans. Although falling short of students' demands, Bachelet's education reforms prohibit state-supported educational establishments from making a profit. Free higher education is guaranteed for the poorest 50 percent of students attending state-certified institutions, with a promise to eventually expand free education to 70 percent of the lowest-income earners.

These changes cost money. Such an ambitious overhaul of the educational system could not be financed without a rewrite of the tax code. Early in her term, Bachelet overcame staunch resistance from the right to pass a progressive tax reform, increasing tax revenues by about 3 percent of gross domestic product, drawn almost exclusively from the top 1 percent of Chile's earners.

The third major item on Bachelet's reform agenda involved institutions and elections. In 2014, Bachelet took advantage of escalating protests to build consensus around electoral reforms that would return Chile to a system broadly paralleling its pre-authoritarian proportional representation formula for the 2017 elections. The electoral reforms also ended Chile's status as an outlier in the region when it comes to gender quotas and female representation in politics, by stipulating that no more than 60 percent of a party's candidates could be of the same sex.

Bachelet also turned her sights on the Pinochet constitution. On broader constitutional reform, Bachelet has proposed an eight-step reform process, including a program of civic education and popular dialogue followed by the formulation of a mechanism to draft a new constitution. However, the choice of the actual mechanism has been delayed and will ultimately be determined by the National Congress. Bachelet's constitutional reform path is strategic, because each proposal has its critics. Advocates of a constituent assembly contend that congressional-led constitutional reform will fail to address the demands of social movements and won't include language that somehow expands socioeconomic rights to respond to Chile's glaring inequalities. Opponents of a constituent assembly fear the opposite: that such an assembly will fall victim to a populist dynamic similar to that of Hugo Chávez in Venezuela, creating chaos and threatening Chile's successful economic model. Still, Bachelet has put Chile on the road to finally do away with the constitutional legacy of the dictatorship.

EVALUATING CONTEMPORARY CHILEAN DEMOCRACY

As noted in the introduction to this chapter, Chile has been a model country in so many ways—and certainly for its consensus transition and economic performance. The question becomes how to evaluate contemporary Chilean society and where it is headed.

Importantly, the armed forces are no longer a significant political actor in the country. During Chile's protracted transition, civilian governments had to deal with several direct military challenges to their authority and the very tense moments following Pinochet's 1998 London arrest. In each of these cases, democratic authorities faced down threats yet resisted antagonizing the military. The public eventually lost patience with the political machinations of the military, and even parties of the right came to support the subordination of the armed forces to civilian authorities.

The economic record of post-authoritarian governments has also been quite good. The most recent chapter of the common Chilean economic story is that the country has remained economically stable because democratic presidents (even the Socialist ones), have been simple policy clones of the military government. Once again, the real story is more complex. Concertación governments were cautious at the outset, eager to woo the business community and avoid the potential backlash that might come with significant divergence from the military's economic model. However, successive governments carefully and prudently managed economic policy with an eye toward sustaining growth while addressing Chile's pressing social problems. Between 1990 and 2005 there was a tenfold increase in government spending on health, and just under a tenfold increase in spending on education. The Concertación's poverty eradication programs were impressive, with the percentage of the population living in poverty decreasing from 38.6

percent in 1990 to less than 14.4 percent in 2013. The percentage in extreme poverty fell from 13 percent to under 5.7 percent during this period. Effective private and public investment in infrastructure in a relatively corruption-free environment underwrote successful growth and poverty reduction. Despite these changes the broad outlines of the neoliberal economic model have not been significantly transformed.

Post-transitional governments also made progress on a wider human rights agenda, though the record remains mixed. The conservative nature and power of the Catholic Church has stymied a progressive agenda in the areas of women's rights and reproductive health. Chile was the last country in the Western Hemisphere to legalize divorce in 2004, and abortion remains illegal, with Chile being one of only five countries in the world that allows for imprisonment of both doctors who perform abortions and women that receive them. Several laws have been proposed to liberalize abortion law, but all have gone down to conservative opposition. In 2012 President Piñera signed into law a wide-ranging anti-discrimination law providing protection for LGBTQ individuals, following the brutal killing of a gay man in a hate crime. In 2014 Chile legalized same-sex legal unions, but fell short of approving gay marriage.

In addition, unlike other countries in the region, Chile has few protections for indigenous people and communities. Chile has been criticized for lacking the kind of constitutional recognition of indigenous peoples that exists in other countries, as well as significant barriers for indigenous people in receiving titles for ancestral territories. Conflicts over land and water use remain and the government has consistently relied on anti-terrorism laws to rein in protests that have regularly emerged regarding the rights and status of indigenous people in the country.

Despite the reality that for years Chile was defined as a "model" in so many different ways—for its democratic transition, for its economic model, and for its dynamic of consensus politics—now media coverage of Chile is characterized by depictions of crisis. This crisis is characterized by seemingly unending student protests and occupations of university faculties, social activism and repression of indigenous people, street mobilization, escalating corruption, declining support for political parties and the two-coalition model of transition, and plummeting popularity numbers for the second Bachelet administration.

The causes for this state of affairs are likely a combination of factors. First, corruption for the first time has emerged as a serious problem. The pace of scandals and allegations of political wrongdoing consistently increased during Concertación governments and recently has reached a fevered pitch. The list is extensive even over just the last five years, and includes the Kodama case where the Ministry of Housing and Urban Planning was ready to make a payment to building contractor for almost four times the value of the work done, the Penta case regarding irregular financing of political candidates, as well as the related SQM case, where the SQM Lithium company was accused of submitting false invoices to rationalize payments of the type undertaken in the Penta case. Finally, accusations of corruption reached Bachelet's own door in the CAVAL case, where a real estate company partly owned by the president's daughter-in-law made an outsized profit based on classified information and influence peddling.

Second, in a certain sense the Concertación (now Nueva Mayoría) was a victim of its own success. A combination of constitutional and legal measures and the delicacy of the transition deeply shaped the pattern of government. The Concertación created elaborate power-sharing arrangements among parties to ensure widespread representation and avoid conflict. Party elites understood the difficulty of generating the majorities necessary to govern in a presidential system characterized by many parties. Cabinets and legislative slates were filled by multiple parties, but were negotiated at the elite level. In order to avoid antagonizing the opposition, the alliance engaged in extensive consultation with the opposition and with potential veto players (especially in the business community) that might derail the transition. Candidates for public office were in large part chosen by parties. All of these arrangements left the Chilean public out of the representational equation. When combined with the reality that the binomial legislative election system essentially resulted in the two coalitions winning one seat in each district, even voting came to be seen as irrelevant.

These political dynamics also had profound consequences for the reach of policy. The Concertación consistently governed with an eye to avoiding potentially destabilizing policies. This resulted in a piecemeal reform process. For example, presidents never challenged Pinochet's fundamental economic model for fear of the potential backlash it might cause. All of these realities made the Chilean transition a success. However, ultimately many of these patterns of governing and policy making that were created to respond to the exigencies of the transition came back to haunt the Concertación in the form of the popular discontent and protest that have been sweeping the country in recent years.

In essence, the twenty-year Concertación period was characterized by the tension of achieving social progress within the confines of an economic model that adhered to the principles set down by a neoliberal dictatorship, which privatized social services as far as possible, reduced the size of the state, and limited its tax base. Although the Concertación can be lauded for maintaining economic stability and growth, it also demonstrated a lack of audacity in engaging in real reforms to the Pinochet model that could make Chile a more just and equitable society.

CONCLUSION

Democracy is multidimensional, involving trade-offs between its various elements. At its core, democracy should be representative, with the policy preferences of elected officials reflecting those of the electorate. However, democracy also entails accountability. Voters must be provided opportunities via elections to award or punish (i.e., reelect or remove) the elected based on the quality and nature of the representation provided. Finally, democracy needs legitimacy, with the citizenry seeing democratic outcomes and institutions as the accepted arbiters of conflict. In essence, legitimacy grows from the successful functioning of the other dimensions of democracy.

At its core, the argument of this chapter is that in terms of institutions Chilean political leaders consistently opted for stability and governability with a high cost for representation, accountability, and ultimately legitimacy. This is perhaps the best way to characterize the challenges to representation facing Chile today: a crisis of legitimacy of the institutions of the dictatorship and the political model of the transition.

The potential remedy for the representational challenges facing Chile today is uncertain. Constitutional reform and the new election system are essential. However, without deeper changes to the socioeconomic system it is doubtful whether a simple change in the constitution will solve challenges to representation in Chile and satisfy deeper demands for reform. In this sense, constitutional reform remains a necessary, though perhaps not sufficient, prescription to change Chile. Constitutions are frameworks within which policy change is made. They set the framework for balancing the various dimensions of democracy, including representation, accountability, and legitimacy. They also determine the policies that are within the realm of the possible and who has a voice in policy making. In this sense, in order to transform the sources of Chile's representational challenges on a deeper level, constitutional change is a necessary first step. Institutional reforms alone will not be enough to restore faith in Chilean democracy, but without them it is doubtful that it can be reset at all.

SUGGESTIONS FOR FURTHER READING

Barros, Robert. *Constitutionalism and Dictatorship: Pinochet, the Junta, and the 1980 Constitution.* New York: Cambridge University Press, 2002.

Borzutsky, Silvia, and Gregory Weeks, eds. *The Bachelet Government.* Gainesville: University Press of Florida, 2010.

Chile, National Commission on Truth and Reconciliation. *Report.* Trans. Phillip E. Berryman. Notre Dame, IN: University of Notre Dame Press, 1994.

Drake, Paul, and Ivan Jaksic, eds. *The Struggle for Democracy in Chile, 1982–1990.* Lincoln: University of Nebraska Press, 1995.

Franceschet, Susan. *Women in Politics in Chile.* Boulder, CO: Lynne Rienner, 2005.

Huneeus, Carlos. *The Pinochet Regime.* Boulder, CO: Lynne Rienner, 2007.

Kornbluh, Peter. *The Pinochet File.* New York: New Press, 2003.

Loveman, Brian. *Chile: The Legacy of Hispanic Capitalism.* 3rd ed. New York: Oxford University Press, 2001.

Scully, Timothy. *Rethinking the Center: Politics in Nineteenth-and Twentieth-Century Chile.* Stanford, CA: Stanford University Press, 1992.

Siavelis, Peter, and Kirsten Sehnbruch, eds. *Democratic Chile: The Politics and Policies of a Historic Coalition.* Boulder, CO: Lynne Rienner, Press, 2014.

Sigmund, Paul E. *The Overthrow of Allende and the Politics of Chile, 1964–1976.* Pittsburgh: University of Pittsburgh Press, 1977.

Valenzuela, Arturo. *The Breakdown of Democratic Regimes: Chile.* Baltimore: Johns Hopkins University Press, 1978.

Verdugo, Patricia. *Chile, Pinochet and the Caravan of Death.* Miami, FL: North-South Center Press, 2001.

Weeks, Gregory. *The Military and Politics in Postauthoritarian Chile.* Tuscaloosa: University of Alabama Press, 2003.

11

COLOMBIA: IS GUERRILLA VIOLENCE NEAR ITS END?

Harvey F. Kline

INTRODUCTION

On June 23, 2016, the Colombian government and the Revolutionary Armed Forces of Colombia (FARC) announced a detailed plan to gather FARC fighters in twenty-eight zones to lay down arms. The insurgency's combatants were then to begin civilian life, ending a war that had begun in May 1964. Those fifty-two years of armed conflict led to more than two hundred and twenty thousand deaths and forced more than six million people to flee their homes, and resentments were likely to linger. A final peace deal, unveiled on August 24, resolved the last disputes and brought together earlier agreements negotiated in Havana, Cuba, in negotiations that began in October 2012. Those agreements also included an ambitious scheme of transitional justice; a plan to improve life in rural Colombia; some ways to open up the country's democracy; and a program that, with FARC help, would replace coca cultivation with licit crops.

Although all indications were that the government of Juan Manual Santos had negotiated a treaty that would end the long guerrilla war, the Colombian people put a halt to the process on October 2, 2016. On that day, with 37 percent of the potential voters participating in the plebiscite, 50.22 percent voted "no" on the treaty while 49.78 percent voted "yes." With 13,066,047 people voting, the peace treaty lost by 53,894 votes. After government leaders met with leaders of the groups that had opposed the agreement, delegates from the government and the FARC began negotiations again in

Havana without representatives of the groups who supported the "no" vote. On November 13, a new agreement was announced and it was signed in Bogotá on November 23. On November 29 and 30 the two houses of congress approved the treaty, and on December 10 Juan Manuel Santos was awarded the Nobel Peace Prize. In a country historically characterized by violence, an important step had apparently been taken.

This chapter is an analysis of the enigma named Colombia. It begins by describing the country's demographic, topological, and economic characteristics. Following sections consider the characteristics of the political system, the political history of the nation until 1974, and the increasing violence since those years from guerrilla groups, paramilitary squads, and drug dealers. The efforts to end that violence are the subject of the next section, followed by a final section on the other political issues that have been overshadowed by the violence.

DEMOGRAPHIC, TOPOLOGICAL, AND ECONOMIC CHARACTERISTICS

Colombia is the third most populous country of Latin America with a population of approximately 49.5 million people. It has five very distinct natural regions: the Andes, covering the three branches of the mountains; the Caribbean coast; the Pacific coast; the plains in the Orinoco River basin along the border with Venezuela; and the Amazon rainforest. About three-quarters of the population of the country is in the Andean region, while slightly below 20 percent live in the Caribbean coastal area.

As historian David Bushnell argued about the colonial period, "Certainly no part of Spanish America had so many natural obstacles to unity—so many obstacles to transportation and communication per square kilometer—as New Granada, with a population scattered in isolated clusters in various Andean ranges, not to mention other settlements along the coast." The separation of geography, Bushnell continued, reinforced socioeconomic and cultural differences. The result was "an intense sectionalism that vastly complicated the first efforts at political organization."[1] Because of the geographic diversity of the country, considered by some to be one of the most challenging of the world, Colombia has never been completely economically or politically integrated.

Colombia's urban population is less concentrated in the national capital than in many other Latin American countries. In 2015 the capital city Bogotá was the largest, with 9.765 million inhabitants or about 15 percent of the total, followed by Medellín with 3.911 million, Cali with 2.646 million, Barranquilla with 1.991 million, Bucaramanga with 1.215 million, and Cartagena with 1.092 million.[2]

The rich ethnic mixture of the Colombian people includes those from Spanish forebears, indigenous people, and those from Africa who were brought to the country as slaves, as well as mixtures of those three. Almost all Colombians speak Spanish, with indigenous people living in isolated areas and speaking native languages making up no more than 5 percent of the population. Recognizing the impossibility of objective racial classification and not wishing to emphasize ethnic or racial differences, national censuses dropped references to race after 1918. After that, any figures cited were only guesses. The 2005 census allowed citizens to identify their race if they wanted to; of the people choosing to define their races, 10.6 percent defined themselves as Afro-Colombian and 3.4 percent as indigenous. Within the lower and middle social sectors, questions of race have much less importance than they do in the United States.

In general, the richer and more powerful people are usually of pure or nearly pure Spanish background. According to the Economic Commission for Latin America the top 1 percent of the Colombian population receives 20.5 percent of the total income of the country, the highest percentage in Latin America.[3] The Colombian middle class grew from 15 percent of the population in 2002 to 28 percent in 2011, almost equal to the 27.8 percent of the population that the World Bank says lives in "poverty." Another 8 percent of the Colombian population lives in "extreme poverty."[4]

Colombia is a free market economy with major commercial and investment ties to the United States. The economy has responded more to economic conditions outside of the country than to those inside it. The relevant external factors lie in the developed economies of the world: in the nineteenth century, European countries; between 1900 and 1969 the United States; and since 1970 the United States, Japan, the European Economic Community countries, and now the People's Republic of China.

The Colombian government has followed sound economic policies and in recent years has promoted free trade. Avoiding external shocks, real GDP growth was more than 4 percent per year between 2012 and 2014. However, the country's dependence on energy and mining exports made it vulnerable to the recent drop in prices, especially for petroleum and coal. Colombia is the world's fourth largest coal producer and the fourth largest petroleum producer in Latin America. Although the security situation has fewer economic consequences than it once did, development is still impeded by inadequate infrastructure.

The US-Colombia Free Trade Agreement went into effect in May 2012. Colombia has signed or is negotiating more than a dozen other free trade agreements, as the Santos administration based its foreign policy on increasing commercial ties and domestic investment. Colombia is a founding member of the Pacific Alliance, through which since 2012 it has promoted regional trade and economic integration together with Chile, Mexico, and Peru. In 2013 Colombia began the process of joining the Organization for Economic Co-operation and Development (OECD). In 2013 the level of foreign direct investment, especially in the oil and gas sectors, reached a high of US$16.8 billion.

In 2014 Colombia was the fifty-third largest export economy in the world, exporting US$56.5 billion. The top exports were crude petroleum (US$25.7 billion), coal (US$7.59 billion), refined petroleum ($2.77 billion), coffee ($2.66 billion), and gold ($1.76 billion). After natural gas became abundant through fracking and petroleum and coal prices fell, Colombian exports decreased in the first nine months of 2016, down US$10.824 billion from 2015. The extractive industries fell to US$22.232 billion, down 30 percent, while exports of manufactured goods fell 12.9 percent in the same period.

CHARACTERISTICS OF THE POLITICAL SYSTEM

After changes from federalism to centralism in the first years of independence, the centralist constitution of 1887 was in effect until 1991. Under the 1887 constitution, the president named all governors, who in turn named all mayors. That regime made presidential elections very important as the party that won would control executive positions throughout the country, as well as the composition of the bureaucracy, predominantly based on patronage and not merit, and the commanders of the national police and military.

The constitution of 1991 made changes that were designed to make the country more democratic and strengthen the judicial system. The constitution made congress more important than previously and the government less centralized. Nevertheless, the executive branch in Bogotá continued to be dominant. The president is elected for a four-year term. A constitutional amendment in 2005 added the possibility of a second term, but it was changed back to a single term in 2015. Members of congress are elected to four-year terms and can be reelected indefinitely. Congress is bicameral, with the departments' representation in the lower house based on their population and chosen in proportional representation elections. One hundred members of the senate are chosen by proportional representation, with the entire country as the electoral district. Indigenous groups choose another two. The 1991 constitution gives certain powers to congress, some of which are divided between the two houses, and creates a balance between the congress and the president in others.

Judicial institutions include the Constitutional Court, the Supreme Court, the Council of State, the Superior Council of the Judiciary, local courts, and judges. A military criminal justice system also exists. Congress chooses judges at the national level; local judges are appointed. The judicial system also includes a prosecutor general and an inspector general. Each department has an elected governor and an assembly; each municipality has an elected mayor and council. The election of departmental and municipal executives is relatively recent: mayors in 1983 and governors in 1991. Neither governors nor mayors can be reelected.

POLITICAL PARTIES AND INTEREST GROUPS

From their founding in the mid-nineteenth century until the 1990s, the Liberal and Conservative parties were dominant. The 1991 constitution made it easier to create new political parties. As a result, many politicians left traditional parties to form their own movements that had very few elected representatives and vague ideologies. Also, paramilitary groups developed many regional political parties in order to elect public officials. In 2002, nearly eighty parties had representation in congress, most of them with only one or two congressmen.

Under the 2003 Political Reform, any party that does not get at least 2 percent of the vote for the senate or chamber loses its legal status. As a result, the number of parties went down from almost eighty in 2006 to twelve in 2010. Table 11.1 shows the representation of parties in congress after the 2014 election.

Table 11.1   Parties Elected to Congress in 2014 Election

Party	Percentage Chamber	Seats Chamber	Percentage Senate	Seats Senate
Social Party of National Unity	16.05	39	15.58	21
Liberal Party	14.13	37	12.22	17
Conservative Party	13.17	27	13.58	18

Table 11.1   Parties Elected to Congress in 2014 Election, *continued*

Party	Percentage Chamber	Seats Chamber	Percentage Senate	Seats Senate
Radical Change	7.74	16	6.96	9
Democratic Center	9.47	12	14.29	20
Green Party	3.35	6	3.94	5
Civic Option	3.26	6	3.68	5
Alternative Democratic Pole	2.89	3	3.78	5
Independent Movement of Absolute Renovation	2.87	3	2.28	0
For a Better Huila	0.51	1	n/a	n/a

Source: Colombian parliamentary election, 2014, https://en.wikipedia.org/wiki/Colombian _parliamentary_election,_2014.

The table shows that the traditional Liberal and Conservative parties are not as dominant as they once were. The *Partido de la U* (or Social Party of National Unity) was founded in 2005 by Juan Manuel Santos as a party to support President Álvaro Uribe. Most of its members left the Liberal Party. The Radical Change Party (CR) was founded in 2000 by members of the Liberal Party who wanted a party to stand against corruption and the drug trade. It supported Uribe in the 2002 presidential election. Its platform was the continuation of Uribe's policy of democratic security and was part of President Uribe's congressional coalition. Its leader, Germán Vargas Lleras, finished third in the 2010 presidential election. The party then joined the Liberal Party and the Conservative Party to form the National Unity Pact that supported the Santos government. Vargas was vice president during Santos' second term until March 2017 when he declared his candidacy in the 2018 presidential election.

The Democratic Center was founded by former President Uribe. It is a coalition of individuals opposing the Santos negotiations with the FARC, with members from many political backgrounds. Smaller parties include the Green Alliance (AV), Civic Option, and the leftist Alternative Democratic Pole (PDA).

Since the late 1950s, a few economic interest groups have been as powerful as the traditional political parties in Colombia. All economic sectors of the upper- and middle-income groups are organized. The most powerful seem to be those "peak" organizations of economic activities, the National Federation of Coffee Growers (FEDECAFE) and the National Association of Industrial Producers (ANDI). Other major producer associations are the National Association of Financial Institutions (ANIF), the Colombian Chamber of Construction (Camacol), the Colombian Federation of Ranchers (Fedegán), and the National Federation of Merchants (FENALCO).

All of them come from the upper sector; they all seek to maintain the status quo. In general, most elements of the private sector have been anti-military, and some of the organizations were important in the 1957 fall of military dictator Gustavo Rojas Pinilla. Although they might sometimes disagree with the policy of a government, they have supported the political regime. With the growth of the executive branch, the associations have developed strong ties with that branch.

Hundreds of human rights groups exist at the national, regional, and local levels. Formerly, paramilitary groups threatened them and at the beginning of the twenty-first century, guerrillas and the new criminal bands targeted them. In May 2008, President Álvaro Uribe suggested that some nongovernmental organizations (NGOs) had received money from international sources that they used to violate the human rights of persons with whom they did not agree.

The status of women in Colombia has changed dramatically in the last one hundred years (see Table 11.2). Their traditional Hispanic role—in the home, taking care of the children while the men made all the decisions—is no longer the rule. These changes came slowly; women were able to enter universities only in 1933 and obtained the right to vote in 1954. The number of children per woman decreased for several reasons, including their entering the work force, their having more education, and the availability of artificial birth control methods.

Table 11.2   The Changes in Status of Women in Colombia, 1910–2010.

	1910	2010
Percentage working outside of household	ND	33.4%
Right to own property	no	yes
Right to vote	no	yes
Number with higher education	none	56% of entering students are women
Average pay for work	Salary went to husbands	Make 25% less than men doing same job
Percentage of public positions held by women	0	14%
Percentage of women who are heads of household	ND	56.8%
Number of children per woman	7.3	2.4

Source: *Semana*, no. 1505 (March 7–14, 2011): 80.

As in other countries, Colombian women are paid less for doing the same jobs, and although they are 51 percent of the population, they made up only 16 percent of the senate and only 13 percent of the lower house of congress in 2011. Of the thirty-two departments in Colombia, only one had a female governor. Of the 1,102 municipalities, only ninety-nine were headed by women. In appointive positions, Law 581 of 2000 required that women have a minimum of 30 percent of the positions in maximum decision-making posts and other directive posts at the national, departmental, and municipal levels. Yet this law was not followed in all parts of the country. In Cali in 2004, for example, of the nineteen posts only three went to women.

Women have not been as organized in Colombia as in some other Latin American countries. However, some active organizations include the Casa de la Mujer, which since 1982 has defended, promoted, and protected women's rights in Colombia. This feminist organization works in twenty departments across Colombia to form and strengthen collectives of women who have been impacted by the conflict. Other women's groups include the Women's International League for Peace and Freedom Colombia (LIMPAL Colombia), a branch of the Women's International League for Peace and Freedom (WILPF). As the Nobel Women's Peace Initiative states, "LIMPAL Colombia works to reconstruct bonds of solidarity that have been broken due to the internal conflict, strengthen women's rights processes and support grassroots projects that work to build alternative economic markets based on fair trade." The Initiative of Colombian Women for Peace (Alianza IMP) is an alliance of twenty-two women's organizations, including indigenous, academics, feminists, Afro-Colombians, and others.[5]

POLITICAL HISTORY OF THE NATION THROUGH 1974

Colombia had fewer Native Americans than Mexico, Guatemala, Bolivia, and Peru when the Spanish arrived. Six different linguistic groups existed, perhaps totaling as many as three to four million people. Some were warlike hunters and fishers, including the Caribs and Arawaks. Many had developed agriculture, as well as gold work that attracted the Spanish conquerors. By far the most "advanced" Indian group was the Muiscas, who populated the highland areas of today's departments of Cundinamarca and Boyacá. They were the wealthiest and had established thickly settled agricultural communities in a well-developed social and political organization led by two leaders, the Zipa and the Zaque.

The first Spaniard to reach Colombia was Alfonso de Ojeda in 1500. Cartagena (1533) and Santa Marta (1535) were the first permanent Spanish settlements. In 1538 Gonzalo Jiménez de Quesada founded the city of Santafé de Bogotá.

The colonial years were ones of ineffectual government and regionalism. The captaincy general was formally part of the viceroyalty of Peru, centered in the far-off city of Lima. The area was not a backwater of Spanish colonization, but neither was it a principal center like Lima or Mexico. Cartagena developed into a major port through which all trade with South America was supposed to flow, including the silver of Peru. A small number of Spanish colonizers came for natural riches, especially gold and emeralds. The *encomienda* system, in which the Spanish conquerors used the labor of indigenous people while Christianizing them, existed in some parts of the area, but the lack of relatively advanced and peaceful Native Americans limited this institution to highland regions, especially the area of the Muiscas. African slaves were brought into rich sugar areas of the Caribbean Coast and the gold-mining areas of Antioquia and Chocó. Mixed-race relationships became common throughout the captaincy general.

In 1739 Bogotá became the capital of the new viceroyalty of Nueva Granada, including today's countries of Colombia, Panama, Venezuela, and Ecuador. The area then had relatively more importance for the few years before the independence movement. After the French invasion of Spain, on May 22, 1810, Cartagena declared its independence. Patriots spurred the population of Bogotá into protests against Spanish rule on July 20, 1810. Under pressure the viceroy was forced to agree to allow for a limited independence. The following year the United Provinces of Nueva Granada was formed with Camilo Torres as its first president. Yet independence did not last. In 1815–1816 Spanish troops reconquered Nueva Granada. Final independence only came on August 7, 1819, when troops led by Simón Bolívar and Francisco de Paula Santander defeated the Spanish in the Battle of Boyacá.

In the first years of independence, the present-day countries of Colombia, Venezuela, and Ecuador were united as Gran Colombia. Following its dissolution in 1830, Colombia experienced a brief period of instability, ending when the Liberal and Conservative parties were founded in the 1840s. The Liberals favored free trade, federalism, and a limit to the role of the Roman Catholic Church in secular matters. The Conservatives were for protectionism and central government, and were pro-clerical. Although the parties reached compromises on the first two issues, they never compromised on their differing ideas for the proper role of the church. Power went back and forth between the two parties in the nineteenth century and they changed constitutions according to their ideologies.

Three key sets of choices in the first years of independent Colombia came from the weak state and made it weaker. The first decision was not to construct a strong law enforcement branch of government, because it might be a threat to civilian government, allowing private groups to take the place of official law enforcement. The federalist period of nineteenth-century Colombia (1853–1886) was one of even less central authority, with law enforcement rights and duties reverting to the states.

The second key decision was the use of violence in politics, often in the name of political parties. This violence intensified when religion became a component of the partisan conflict, even though nearly all Colombians were Catholic. The consequences of using violence were potentially less serious for individuals at certain times when the state amnestied partisan violence. As a result, political competition in Colombia has never been limited to peaceful means. There were eight civil wars during the nineteenth century, six of which pitted all or part of one of the two parties against the other party.

The violence continued into the twentieth century, first with a short period of partisan violence in 1932 and then culminating in *"La Violencia,"* a particularly bloody war between the Liberal and Conservative parties, beginning in 1946 and ending in the early 1960s. As a result of this system of violence, other cleavages, such as social class and region, became secondary to the primary party one. Third parties were notably unsuccessful until the early 1990s. Violence became the normal way to handle things.

The final key decision in the first years of independence had to do with the rules for the elite within Colombian democracy. Although the members of the parties were encouraged to take up arms against the members of the other party, the party leaders came from the same economic groups, belonged to the same exclusive social clubs, and at times entered into governing coalitions. On twelve occasions between 1854 and 1949, one political party at the elite level entered into a coalition with all or part of the other political party. These elite coalitions tended to take place when presidents assumed dictatorial powers, when party hegemonies shifted, and, especially in this century, when elite-instigated violence got out of control. The most notable coalition was the National Front (1958–1974).

Colombia was unusual in Latin America, having only one brief military government in the nineteenth century and one in the twentieth. The latter took place in the context of the systemic breakdown of La Violencia. On June 13, 1953, President Laureano Gómez attempted to remove the military commander, Lieutenant General Gustavo Rojas Pinilla. Rojas staged a coup that ended the Gómez presidency and democratic government until 1958. Members of the elite factions of both political parties welcomed the Rojas coup, with the exception of the deposed Gómez Conservatives. This bipartisan support was to last for several years, although Rojas, who considered himself a Conservative, received his most active support from the moderates of that party.

Rojas's first measures included a pardon and amnesty for political prisoners and for all who were fighting, as well as restoring the freedom of the press that Gómez had ended. The amnesty was a success and deaths from La Violencia fell. He made an effort to depoliticize the national police force by transferring it to the armed forces. In addition, the government started an extensive series of public-works projects and improved the system of credits for small farmers. To an extent, the Colombian dictator patterned himself after Juan Perón of Argentina. An organization called the National Secretariat of Social Welfare (SENDAS) gave clothing and food to poor people. The dictator's daughter, María Eugenia Rojas, was in charge of SENDAS.

Rojas did not carry out any structural realignment of Colombian society and the lull in La Violencia was only temporary. The elites of the two parties became increasingly restive, especially after Rojas called a national convention to draft a new constitution. He began talking about a "third force," a vague idea about a coalition of all groups of society, also patterned after the Perón experience in Argentina. It also became increasingly clear that Rojas was not going to hold the 1958 presidential election, and there were abuses of government that were blamed on the dictator. Press censorship returned. By early 1957, most organized groups were opposed to Rojas and leaders of the parties were planning a coalition government. On May 10, 1957, the top military leaders asked Rojas to leave the country. After his departure, these leaders formed a caretaker military junta to govern until August 7, 1958.

The longest, most formal coalition followed the Rojas government. The National Front was an agreement in which the Liberals and Conservatives shared power equally. It was approved in a national referendum and later a constitutional amendment. The agreement was that for sixteen years the two parties would alternate the presidency between the Liberal and Conservative parties, and no other party would be legal. All legislative bodies would be divided equally between the two parties, as well as executive cabinets at all levels, governors, mayors, and non-civil-service bureaucrats. On August 7, 1974, the National Front ended.

THE INCREASING VIOLENCE

New forms of violence appeared in Colombia as the National Front was ending the old bipartisan form. First were Marxist guerrilla groups, followed almost immediately by "self-defense" or "paramilitary" groups, and several decades later by drug dealers. Colombia entered a period that was so complex that its best characterization might be "the enemy of my enemy is my friend."

The Guerrilla Groups

The influence of Marxist revolutionary groups in the countryside went back to the final years of La Violencia. The first such group to emerge was the pro-Castro Army of National Liberation (ELN). It arose after a group of Colombian scholarship students went to Cuba and asked for and obtained military training. The ELN was officially born on July 4, 1964, and initially comprised primarily university students.

In 1966, the Communist-dominated Revolutionary Armed Forces of Colombia (FARC) was founded, although Communist-oriented peasant defense groups predated it by more than fifteen years. In 1964, the Colombian military tried to wipe out a small guerrilla group in the Tolima department. The government termed this an "independent republic" and President Guillermo León Valencia vowed on more than one occasion, "Tomorrow we are going to capture Tirofijo." The effort failed and the guerrillas fled, officially forming the FARC two years later. Tirofijo, one of the aliases of Pedro Antonio Marín Marín, who was also known by his *nom de guerre* Manuel Marulanda Vélez, was the leader of the group until he died of a heart attack in 2008.

In 1967, the Maoist wing of the Colombian Communist Party founded an armed organization, the People's Liberation Army (EPL). In the 1960s and 1970s, it was especially active in the Santander Department, an area of the country traditionally affected by disputes over land between landless *campesinos* and large landowners. In the mid-1970s, the guerrilla group began using kidnapping and extortion to finance its activities.

A final guerrilla group was the 19th of April Movement (M-19). It appeared after the presidential elections of April 19, 1970, in which former General Rojas Pinilla appeared to have won, only to have later government returns show that he had lost. The M-19 was always somewhat of a romantic, Robin Hood–type movement. It carried out several urban guerrilla activities, stealing a sword that belonged to liberator Simón Bolívar; kidnapping all the guests (including the US ambassador) during a cocktail party at the embassy of the Dominican Republic in 1980; kidnapping and executing a missionary from the United States in 1981; and on the morning of November 6, 1985, seizing the Palacio de Justicia in downtown Bogotá. The army reestablished control the following day, but only after more than one hundred deaths, including eleven of the twenty-four Supreme Court justices, and the gutting of the palace by fire.

Paramilitary Groups

Private justice began early in Colombian history. In the nineteenth century, paramilitary groups first appeared as large landowners established their own justice systems on their lands. Private justice appeared in a different form in the twentieth century during La Violencia. The first self-defense groups to organize themselves were the peasant self-defense groups in Tolima and in the 1950s, similar groups appeared in other places.

In 1965, as Marxist guerrilla groups were emerging, President Guillermo León Valencia issued Decree 3398, the stipulations of which became law in 1968 through Law 48. The decree and the law gave legal status to private armed groups by stating that the government could use any citizen in activities to reestablish normalcy. In this way, the weak state could enlist the help of private groups to battle the guerrillas. The military furnished weapons to and trained the private individuals, and close ties developed between many such groups and the armed forces. This was an extremely important decision by the government, one that might have made sense in the short run but in the long run caused the state to have even less power.

In the 1970s, with the growth of the FARC and its increasing hostility toward ranchers and large farmers who could pay protection money, many adopted the self-defense structure to repel the guerrilla attacks. Numerous self-defense groups arose in response to the constant demands of the guerrillas because it was clear that the government could not guarantee to protect them. During the presidency of Virgilio Barco (1986–1990), paramilitary groups experienced a dramatic change. Earlier the groups had been comprised of individuals who produced legal agricultural products. However, as the drug lords became wealthy, they bought more land. Although at first they bought land to become "gentleman farmers," later they used the land to grow coca. Soon, drug money began supporting paramilitary squads. Two other important things occurred by the end of the Barco presidency. First, according to some sources, the number of deaths attributed to paramilitary group activity exceeded those from guerrilla activities. Second, while the connection between the Colombian military and the paramilitary groups officially ended, the relationship continued to exist, at least to a degree.

Drug Dealers

The final ingredient in the violence was the drug trade. The country began a major role in the international marijuana trade in the 1970s but developed its key function in drug trafficking when Medellín drug leaders decided to export cocaine. As a result, a new economic group grew up around the illicit drug industry. Although the cartels of Medellín, led by Pablo Escobar, and Cali, led by brothers Gilberto and Miguel Rodríguez Orejuela, later became internationally known, as early as December 1981 the Colombian drug industry held a secret national convention, at which 223 drug-gang bosses created a death squad called Death to Kidnappers (MAS). The Mafiosi pledged US$7.5 million to the squad, whose goal was to kill all kidnappers and to end the guerrilla practice of kidnapping people, including the drug gang bosses, for ransom.

On November 6, 1986, a group that came to be called *Los Extraditables* ("The Extraditable Ones") issued a communiqué. Using the motto of "better a tomb in Colombia than a jail in the United States," they later carried out a campaign of terrorism to end the possibility of their extradition to the United States. On August 24, 1988, Los Extraditables began a bombing campaign that continued for two years. They stated that they were declaring total and absolute war on the government, on the industrial and political oligarchy, on the journalists who had attacked and ravaged them, on the judges who had sold out to the government, on the presidents of unions, and all those who persecuted and attacked them.

Notable terrorist acts included the November 27, 1989, bombing of a commercial airplane flight from Bogotá to Cali, causing more than one hundred deaths; the December 6, 1989, bombing of the headquarters of the Administrative Department of Security (DAS), killing sixty-three and wounding six hundred; and bombings in major cities the Saturday before Mother's Day, 1990. In the latter, bombs in upper-middle-income sectors of Bogotá killed fourteen, including four children shopping for gifts for their mothers.

On July 3, 1991, Los Extraditables announced their plan to demobilize, stating in a communiqué that the decision was due to the Constituent Assembly vote to eliminate extradition. Members of this group were accused of the assassinations of a number of judges and of four hundred members of the Medellín police force, as well as for the series of bombings. Hence, the organization of Los Extraditables ended. In their first message in November 1986 they had demanded the end of extradition of Colombians. They gained that through the prohibition of extradition in the 1991 Constitution.

The Enemy of My Enemy Is My Friend

There was an interrelationship among the various armed actors. The drug dealers had connections with paramilitary groups, as did the government officially until the Barco years and in practice much later. In addition, guerrilla groups developed relationships with drug dealers, first by protecting their fields and factories, later by "taxing" them, and in some cases by entering the drug enterprise directly. Criminality reached high levels. To the extent that they had existed before, the norms of coexistence and justice collapsed. The national homicide rate, which had declined from 32 per 100,000 (1960–65) to 23 (1970–75), rose steeply to 32 (1985), to 63 (1990), and to 78 (1991–93). The rate did fall to 56 (1998) only to rise again to 63 (1999–2000). Impunity increased. Although the number of deaths by violence increased from four thousand in 1960 to thirty thousand in 1993, the number of individuals charged remained unchanged. Of the reported homicides, 97 percent went unpunished.[6]

There seems to be little doubt that drug groups entered into politics, not only in congress but also by influencing the presidency. Paramilitary groups also entered into "legitimate" politics by financing candidates for elective offices.

EFFORTS TO END VIOLENCE

From the 1960s until today Colombian governments have been most concerned with ending the endemic violence of the country. Although their efforts have been complicated by the interactions of the three groups, in chronological order the first efforts were to end the guerrilla violence, then the drug trade, and finally the paramilitary violence. This chapter considers them in the order of their successes rather than chronologically.

The Drug Trade

The violence from the drug trade was the first to be dealt with successfully. At the beginning the government was tentative and weak in its reaction to the drug trade. The governments of Belisario Betancur (1982–1986) and Virgilio Barco (1986–1990) cooperated with the US Drug Enforcement Administration, destroying crops and factories, capturing some drug dealers, although not the "big fish" leaders, and extraditing a few to the United States.

During the Barco government, a series of "total wars" between the government and the *narcos* took place, all coming immediately following the assassinations of notable governmental officials. The first was after the December 17, 1986, killing of Guillermo Cano Isaza. Cano, editor of the Liberal Bogotá daily *El Espectador*, was long a leading critic of the drug trade. The second came after Colombia's attorney general, Carlos Mauro Hoyos, was killed on January 25, 1988. Hoyos, who had been a supporter of the drug traffickers' extradition to the United States, was killed the day after the traffickers declared total war on anyone who favored extraditing Colombians to face drug charges in the United States.

The third Barco total war came after the August 18, 1989, assassination of Luis Carlos Galán, leader of the New Liberalism movement, who was leading in the polls for the 1992 presidential election. Galán's opposition to the drug trade went back to 1981, when the people of Antioquia elected Pablo Escobar as an alternate member of congress for the Liberal party. Galán then started a campaign to get the narcos out of Liberal politics. In 1984, the narcos assassinated his friend and colleague in New Liberalism, Minister of Justice Rodrigo Lara, increasing Galán's opposition. On August 18, 1989, two assailants shot him down at close range immediately after he rose to the speaking platform in a rally with some seventeen thousand in attendance. Galán was one of three presidential candidates assassinated by the Medellín drug cartel during the presidential election.

At his August 7, 1990, inauguration, President César Gaviria made it very clear that he considered the drug-dealer problem the most important in the country. In the early days of his administration some thought that because Gaviria's mentor Luis Carlos Galán had been murdered by the narcos, he was sure to continue the Barco policy of total war and extradition. This seemed to be the case when, on August 11, 1990, the elite unit of the national police killed Gustavo de Jesús Gaviria, first cousin of Pablo Escobar and second-in-command of the Medellín mafia.

The new government arrived at the conclusion that bargaining was possible with the drug groups. In the process that followed between the government and the leaders of the Medellín drug group, the principals never sat together at a table. Instead, the government issued decrees and the drug leaders reacted to them. Each decree was more specific and met some of the demands of the drug leaders.

At the end of November 1990, Los Extraditables announced that because of the election for a constituent assembly, they had decided to declare a truce. Then, in December Fabio Ochoa surrendered, surprising the Gaviria government, which had thought that their decrees would appeal primarily to second-level narcos. Fabio Ochoa had written to the minister of justice, stating his intention, and asking for more detail on the decrees. His principal concern was avoiding extradition to the United States. A number of governmental decrees followed, culminating with Decree 2047. It stated that there would be no extradition for any crime committed before September 5, 1990, if the person had confessed a crime that had him in prison.

By January 1991, Pablo Escobar and his lawyers were working on three items. First, they were concerned about the date when the decree would lose force. They preferred that it be at the time of the surrender. Second, they would ask that the Constituent Assembly form a committee to consider forbidding the extradition of nationals in the constitution. Finally, they were studying the "strategy of confession." In practice, all the problems could be reduced to one single point: Escobar wanted a legal guarantee that he would not be extradited, and the word of the Colombian president was not enough. For Escobar, the international pressures to have him extradited were so strong that he would only be content if that possibility were completely eliminated. It was likely that the new constitution would consecrate the principle of no extradition; therefore, it was anticipated that Escobar would wait until that happened before surrendering.

On June 18, 1991, at 5:11 in the afternoon, Pablo Escobar surrendered. At 1 p.m. that afternoon the Constituent Assembly had decided that the new constitution would prohibit extradition. On July 3, 1991, Los Extraditables announced their plan to demobilize. In principle, the Medellín cartel had ended. In practice, Escobar continued drug exports from prison. Accounts of those continued criminal activities began to surface in the media, which prompted the government to attempt to move him to a more conventional jail on July 22, 1992. Escobar discovered the plan in advance and escaped. He spent the rest of his life evading the police and was killed on December 2, 1993, in Medellín.

President Ernesto Samper (1994–1998) allegedly received money from the Cali cartel during his 1994 presidential campaign. Nevertheless, it was during his presidency that the Cali cartel was ended. Between June and July 1995, six of the seven heads of the organization were arrested. Gilberto Rodríguez was arrested in his home and a month later Miguel Rodríguez was apprehended during a raid. It was widely believed that the cartel continued to operate and run trafficking operations from within prison.

The end of the two cartels did not mean the end of the Colombian cocaine trade. It was followed, first, by small micro-cartels and later by some of the paramilitary groups. After their demobilization, the drug trade came under the influence of what the Colombian government called the "New Criminal Bands."

The Paramilitary Groups

In May 1989, Minister of Government César Gaviria stated that the government was incapable of eradicating the violence in recently colonized areas such as Urabá, Magdalena Medio, Arauca, and Caquetá. The paramilitary groups had become as important as the guerrillas in their effect on Colombian society. The implications of this for the government were very serious. The peace initiative presented by Virgilio Barco on September 1, 1988 was undoubtedly incomplete in the face of the dimensions of the new force the government had to face. When he launched the peace initiative, the government's own figures indicated that more Colombians had been killed in the previous year by paramilitary groups than by guerrillas.

The government continued its theory of cause and effect, according to which the paramilitary groups were a result of the guerrilla groups and, therefore, focusing the peace initiative on the latter would take care of the problem in the long run. But by this time, it needed to realize that the paramilitary violence needed its own solution. In addition, until the government demonstrated concrete results with the paramilitary groups, there was no real possibility of a guerrilla demobilization.

The Gaviria government used the same decrees as it had with the drug dealers to encourage the surrender of members of the paramilitaries. The self-defense groups argued that, after their organizations were formed by military men, they were then abandoned to their own devices after having lent enormous counterinsurgency services to the army. They demanded to be treated like the guerrillas, who were allowed to turn in their arms, demobilize, and enter into national political life. They assured the government that they had nothing to do with the narcos.

Although a number of paramilitary troops did demobilize during the Gaviria government, their presence became even more evident during the government of Ernesto Samper. In 1995, Carlos Castaño began the work of convincing each one of these solitary units of the necessity of a union, with one commander, one insignia, one uniform, and one policy. In this way, Castaño's personal paramilitary group became the model in both political and military structure. It began with about three thousand troops, but was soon to grow. The United Self-Defense Forces of Colombia (AUC) was founded in 1997.

The influence of the paramilitary squads was seen when President Pastrana began talks with the FARC on January 7, 1999. FARC leader Manuel Marulanda Vélez (a.k.a Tirofijo) did not appear at the first meeting. FARC leader Raúl Reyes stated that security conditions were not sufficient for the leader to appear in public. Two members of the FARC National Political Commission stated that the organization had detained two men who had violated security measures and who were ready to attack Tirofijo. The leaders refused to give additional details or to confirm that the attackers had been sent by paramilitary leader Carlos Castaño in retaliation for attacks on AUC headquarters.

Less than a month into the presidency of Álvaro Uribe in August 2002, the government offered amnesty and pardon to guerrilla and paramilitary members who entered into ceasefires and demobilized. During the first months of 2003, paramilitary leaders met with congressional representatives, members of the Catholic Church, and the "Exploratory Commission of Peace," named by the government on December 22, 2002, with the charge of making contacts with the paramilitary groups that had publicly proclaimed a ceasefire and indicated that they wanted to enter a peace process.

In May 2003, President Uribe announced that he would submit a bill to congress that would not punish members of paramilitary groups, even if they had committed atrocious crimes. AUC leaders Carlos Castaño and Salvatore Mancuso had already made it clear that there could be no progress in the process unless the government eliminated the possibility of extradition. In August 2003, Minister of Interior and Justice Sabas Pretelt de la Vega presented a bill of "penal alternatives" in the Senate to cover groups. He stated that this was not to be a law of "pardon and amnesty"; rather it was a plan of investigation and sanctions for crimes that could not be pardoned and was directed to both the guerrilla and paramilitary groups. Under the proposal, individuals would receive the benefits of the law under six conditions: a ceasefire by the group to which the individual belonged, turning in of arms, promising not to take up arms again, accepting a punishment other than jail, making reparations to victims, and promising not to commit an "intentional crime" in the future.

On June 22, 2005, the Chamber of Representatives approved the Law of Justice and Peace. The major clauses of the law decreed that alternative punishment would consist of suspending traditional imprisonment and replacing it with a sentence in exchange for a contribution to peace and reparation to the victims. Confinement of persons convicted of atrocious crimes like massacres would be between five and eight years, in places designated by the governmental prison authority, which could be agricultural colonies. To be eligible one had to surrender goods, minors recruited, and victims of kidnapping; further the group must not have been organized with the specific goal of drug trafficking or of illegal enrichment. The members of armed groups who benefited from the law would have the obligation of repaying the victims of the actions of which they were guilty. If they found no victims, the payment would go to the national reparation fund.

In all, 31,617 people who allegedly had been in the paramilitary groups returned to civilian life by the end of 2006, a number larger than that estimated by the government at the beginning of the process and that was stated by the AUC several times during it. Although this ended the violence associated with paramilitary groups, it did not terminate their penetration into the economic and political facets of Colombian life.

The Guerrilla Groups

Every Colombian president since 1982 has attempted to end guerrilla violence through negotiations. All efforts before that of President Juan Manuel Santos were failures. The Santos negotiations with the FARC did lead to an agreement. That is not the case, however, with the ELN.

In the first six weeks after Belisario Betancur became president on August 7, 1982, he announced that he would name a Peace Commission. Law 35 of 1982 granted amnesty to all those in armed conflict with the government before November 20, with the exception of those who had committed non-combat-related homicides, those who had committed homicides including "cruelty," and those whose victims had been in a position of "inferior strength." Guerrillas already imprisoned for the pardoned crimes would be released. In the first three months, some four hundred guerrillas accepted the amnesty.

The Betancur government based its peace initiatives on the assumption that guerrilla violence was the product of objective circumstances of poverty, injustice, and the lack of opportunities for political participation. As a result, it reached agreements with three guerrilla groups—the M-19, the FARC, and the ELN. In all cases, there were truces, which a national dialogue was supposed to follow. The dialogue was never very well defined and did not take place.

In negotiations between the government and the FARC in April 1984, the president announced an agreement that included a ceasefire for one year; the creation of a high-level commission to verify compliance with the agreement; the granting of a series of juridical, political, and social guarantees to facilitate the transition of the guerrilla forces back to civilian life; and a rehabilitation program for peasant areas affected by the violence. The government signed similar truces the following month with the M-19 and the EPL. By May 1984, only the ELN had not signed a truce.

By the end of 1985 only the FARC truce continued. Leaders of the other two guerrilla groups accused the government of causing the break, while the government faulted the subversives. Casualties increased, culminating on the morning of November 6, 1985, when the M-19 seized the Palacio de Justicia in downtown Bogotá. The FARC truce was still formally in place at the end of the Betancur government. However, in fact hostilities had also resumed between that group and the government.

In addition, the political party set up by the FARC during the truce, the Patriotic Union (UP), suffered greatly from assassinations of its candidates and members. Not only was one presidential candidate assassinated, but in 1991 UP leaders stated that more than one thousand of its members had been killed in three years.

President Virgilio Barco announced no new peace initiative at his inauguration on August 7, 1986, although the violence continued. It was not until the last two years of the Barco government that changing circumstances led the government and several guerrilla groups to bargain. For the government, the context had changed because the growth of paramilitary attacks gave a negotiation higher priority. Several guerrilla groups also faced different conditions. This was especially the case for the M-19, which was militarily weak, had less legitimacy after the Palacio de Justicia attack, had never had a coherent revolutionary ideology, and had suffered rapid leadership turnover.

In March 1989, the government and the M-19 signed the Declaration of Cauca, expressing their intentions to begin the process of the reintegration of the guerrilla group. Under the declaration, the subversive group would occupy an area in the mountains of Cauca where the Colombian military would protect them. Five hundred soon arrived. "Working tables" were to be set up immediately so that the two sides could arrive at agreements to bring the guerrilla group into the political process.

On July 17, 1989, the M-19 and the government signed a pact that would lead to demobilization and disarming of the guerrillas over the following six months, during which time the working tables would continue. Later there was difficulty in the process when congress failed to pass a constitutional reform suggested by President Barco; however, in January 1990 a joint declaration of the government and the guerrilla group indicated that, although the disarmament and pardon would not be on the agreed-upon date, they would look for ways to make the peace formula viable.

During the government of César Gaviria, there were negotiations with the guerrilla groups who had entered a coalition through the Simón Bolívar Guerrilla Coordinator (CGSB). Representatives of the Colombian government met with ones of the CGSB in Cravo Norte in the department of Arauca in May 1991; in Caracas, Venezuela, from June to November of 1991; and in Tlaxcala, Mexico, in March of 1992.

Although in the last year of the Gaviria presidency there were some successes with small guerrilla groups, the peace process with the CGSB was a failure. Problems included different ways of conceptualizing peace, belief on the part of some participants on both sides that they could still win the war, the economic strength of the guerrilla groups, the lack of viable proposals from both sides, and the lack of unity on both sides.

The peace process was far from complete when Ernesto Samper replaced César Gaviria on August 7, 1994. Samper did little in peacekeeping efforts, largely because of his need to defend himself constantly against accusations regarding the alleged drug money in his campaign. His government also faced a new strategy from the FARC. At its eighth national conference in 1993, the guerrilla group decided to construct a guerrilla army capable of defeating the armed forces in places of strategic value. To that end, the FARC created fronts and strengthened regional commands.

Following this strategy, the FARC carried out major attacks from April 1996 to November 1998, all leading to serious defeats of the Colombian military. They were the El Billar attack, important because it was against an elite group of soldiers with counterinsurgency training, demonstrating that the army was not capable of detecting or preventing the mobilization of nearly eight hundred guerrilla fighters; the Miraflores attack, which occurred only four days before the inauguration of Andrés Pastrana and after he had begun discussions with the FARC leaders about peace talks; and the Mitú attack, which showed that the FARC was capable of capturing a departmental capital, even if it was one of the smallest and most remote. Clearly, the Samper years saw the FARC at its military zenith and the Colombian armed forces at their all-time low.

Andrés Pastrana was elected in 1998 promising to negotiate with the guerrilla groups. From January 1999 until February 2002 his government and the FARC held a series of meetings. The government did not insist that the FARC enter into a ceasefire before the process began; indeed, the ceasefire was one of the matters to be negotiated.

To encourage the FARC to negotiate, the Pastrana government granted a demilitarized zone to the guerrilla group, an area of 41,440 square kilometers (16,000 square miles) and pledged that the insurgents would have complete control of the area during the dialogues. That promise was honored.

The conversations between the Pastrana government and the ELN differed from those with the FARC from their very beginning in 1998 until their end in August 2001. The talks were between the ELN and "civil society" (never clearly defined). Yet that process was similar from its beginning in that only procedural agreements were made.

In the end, both processes were failures. The FARC was strong militarily and the government was the weaker bargainer. The ELN insisted on having a "National Convention" inside the country. The government was willing to do that but paramilitary groups blocked it.

Yet Pastrana contributed to peace in Colombia, even though that would not be clear for some years after his presidency. This contribution came through an agreement with the government of the United States for a massive military assistance program. Although Plan Colombia talked about strengthening the economy and making the country more democratic, it also stressed combating the narcotics industry and promoting the peace process. Because the narcotics industry to a large degree was being run by the FARC, Plan Colombia from its beginning had at least an implicit anti-guerrilla theme, as noted by the FARC at the negotiating table. Colombia became the third largest recipient of US military aid in the world, following only Egypt and Israel.

In his inaugural speech on August 7, 2002, Álvaro Uribe Vélez announced that he would search for dialogue with groups only if they had entered into ceasefires. Later the policy had much greater specificity. There would be a program of stimuli for the demobilization and disarming of guerrilla and paramilitary troops.

The Uribe policies also included changes to the Colombian military. Assuming that the origin of violence was in the historic weakness of the state and its inability to exercise its authority, and using the money from Plan Colombia, the size of the regular Colombian military was increased while their weapons, training, and communication equipment were improved. New military units included "High Mountain Battalions," and "soldiers from our town" to assist the police. The High Mountain Battalions were professional soldiers trained in special skills. The "soldiers from our town" were an addition to the armed forces comprising as many as fifteen thousand volunteers recruited by regional commanders in small towns. Considered soldiers and hence subject to the same professional code of conduct, they were uniformed, but unlike regular soldiers lived in their homes and combined their military duties with other activities such as study or work. After three months of training, they received rifles that they were not allowed to take home. They guarded bridges or other infrastructure of their region and reported on strange movements. They also assisted the regular army and were always accompanied by a patrol of the armed forces made up of regular and professional soldiers and police agents.

The result was that the armed forces took the offensive against the guerrillas. With massive investments in the forces, Uribe launched *Plan Patriota*, the first phase of which was "Operation Liberty I" in Cundinamarca, the department around Bogotá, through which the army achieved the destruction of many FARC fronts. The second stage of the plan took place in the south of the country, the heart of FARC military operations and coca growing.

During the first Uribe administration, there seemed to be the beginning of a real peace process with the ELN. After each side made proposals that led nowhere, serious efforts to initiate a peace process began first in Cuba between August and December of 2002 and afterward through Mexican facilitation between June 2004 and April 2005. Both attempts failed. With the transfer of imprisoned ELN leader Francisco Galán to the Casa de Paz in Medellín, and the implementation of a formal exploratory phase in Cuba after December 2005, a dialogue process opened up that resulted in the joint publication of the pamphlet "Documents of the Exploratory Dialogue between the Government and the ELN," in May 2006.

Abortive attempts of the first Uribe government to have a peace process with the FARC included the possibility of a general peace agreement. However, most of the discussion had to do with a meeting to devise an exchange of hostages held by the FARC for captured FARC guerrillas. The idea was to exchange around five hundred FARC members in Colombian prisons for forty-five hostages, including politicians, soldiers, and police officers, as well as three US military contractors, in the hands of the insurgent group. Perhaps the only real accomplishment of the Pastrana peace process was such a swap. In the Uribe case, according to a Colombian historian, the result of all the discussion was "the collision of two obstinate sides."[7]

During the second Uribe administration, the government was not able to reach a peace agreement with either guerrilla group. There were dialogues with the ELN but the government and the FARC were not able to agree to conversations.

The negotiations of the government of Juan Manuel Santos (2010–present) with the Revolutionary Armed Forces of Colombia went through five stages. The first two were secret, first through intermediaries within Colombia and second in an "Exploratory Encounter" in Havana, Cuba, between February 23 and August 26, 2012. After the Havana talks the two sides agreed to a "General Agreement on the Termination of the Conflict," in which they agreed that the agenda would contain five items: agrarian development, political participation, the end of the conflict, illicit drugs, and victims. The third stage was a "Table of Conversations" in Oslo, Norway, in October 2012. The fourth was the "Dialogue Table" that began in Havana on November 15, 2012, beginning with a consideration of the first topic of comprehensive agricultural development policy.

On May 26, 2013, the two sides announced the first agreement, calling it "Towards a New Colombian Countryside: Comprehensive Rural Reform." Under the agreement seven million acres (three million hectares) of land would be distributed to two hundred and fifty thousand campesinos. It also gave campesinos the same guarantees that city dwellers had of health benefits, work, education, infrastructure, and housing. All of this would take place over a period of ten years.

Political participation was the second item, a complicated task of coming up with ways that the FARC could participate legally. The theme had three subthemes: the rights and guarantees for the exercise of opposition and for new movements that might appear after they signed the final agreement; democratic mechanisms for citizen participation; and means to promote greater political participation at all levels with guarantees of security. The agreement had three parts: First, there would be a new law establishing the rights of the opposition. Second, political parties would be convened and social organizations would be heard to finalize the content of this statute. Third, the government, within the framework of the end of the conflict, would promote the issuance of the relevant regulations.

The third item on the agenda was illicit drugs. The agreement had five major points:

1. The government would stop its fumigation program and would stress voluntary manual eradication of drug crops.
2. The FARC would participate in the removal of antipersonnel mines.
3. The government agreed that solutions were needed for the estimated sixty thousand families that made their living through the cultivation of illicit drugs.
4. With the creation of the Comprehensive National Program for the Substitution of Illicit Crops (PNIS), the government would enter into areas with illegal crops and guide the community in their voluntary eradication and replacement with legal crops.
5. The government acknowledged that consumers needed treatment and should not be juridically pursued.

The discussions then turned to victims, a transitional justice system, and the specifics of demobilization. All of them were important in the debates before the plebiscite and in the negotiations that followed.

The agreement spelled out the end of the armed conflict in great detail. In a maximum of one hundred and eighty days after the treaty entered into effect, the FARC would turn over their arms to representatives of the United Nations and begin developing ideas for their position within the democratic process. The new political party set up by the FARC would have special privileges: between 2018 and 2026 it would have a minimum of five senators and five representatives in the lower house of congress, regardless of the number of votes it receives in elections. In addition, sixteen special districts, based on the areas with the most conflict, would be established for the lower house. In effect, people in those areas would have double representation. The agreement included rules and organizations to guarantee the safety of the members of the new party set up by the FARC. This was to avoid the murder of its members, as had happened when the FARC set up a party under the agreements reached with President Betancur.

The second major agreement at the end of the negotiations dealt with amnesty and justice. To combine justice with the amnesty necessary to end the armed conflict, the agreement established a transitional justice system. The agreement began with the statement that Colombians had been victims of the guerrilla group, the state military and police, paramilitary groups, and individuals who supported the paramilitary groups. The agreement included the following specific elements:

1. A Commission for the Clarification of Truth, Coexistence, and Non-Repetition made up of eleven persons would hear the confessions of responsible people over the course of three years.

2. A Special Jurisdiction of Peace (JEP), the highest court of which would be made up of twenty-four judges, six of whom would be foreigners, would judge those responsible for the conflict.
3. There would be complete amnesty except for crimes against humanity and war crimes. General definitions of those crimes would be used and would include kidnapping, the recruitment of minors, military operations against civilian targets, torture, sexual violence, and disappearances.
4. Punishment for crimes against humanity and war crimes would be applied through transitional justice if and only if the accused had made a truthful confession. The sanctions of the Special Jurisdiction of Peace would include the restriction of movement within an area and community work, the removal of antipersonnel mines, and agricultural work. People punished by the JEP would not lose their political rights. If the crime came from following orders, the punishment would be for two to five years. If the person had ordered crimes, the punishment would be for five to eight years.
5. People who did not confess would fall under the usual procedures of criminal law and would lose their political rights. For crimes against humanity or war crimes, the punishments would be of fifteen to twenty years.
6. To determine the responsible people, FARC leaders would give a list of their members and the actions for which they might be judged.

As mentioned before, the Colombian people put a halt to the process on October 2, 2016, when 50.22 percent voted "no" on the treaty while 49.78 percent voted "yes." Negotiations in Havana started again after the plebiscite failed. After sixty different issues were discussed, on November 12 a second final peace treaty was announced, with many changes arising from the new negotiations. The changes included:

1. The entire treaty would not become part of the Colombian constitution, as the first treaty had stated. Only those elements dealing with human rights and international humanitarian law would be added.
2. Decisions of the Special Jurisdiction of Peace could be appealed to the Constitutional Court. Some of the "no" groups wanted to delete the JEP.
3. More specific limits were established for the areas for punishments.
4. All of the members of the JEP would be Colombians. There would be no foreign judges.
5. The political party established by the FARC could not offer candidates in the sixteen transitional electoral districts. That political party would receive governmental funds under the same formula as other political parties.
6. When disarming was complete, the FARC would present a complete inventory of their goods and assets for reparation for the victims.[8]

On November 29, the Colombian Senate approved the treaty in a vote of 75–0. The treaty then went to the Chamber, which approved it the next day.

In the end, however, making the treaty with the FARC might be much easier than implementing it. Even before its approval, questions were raised about the source of the funds for the many reforms. Another question was whether real willpower existed to carry out the changes, or if one or both sides had never truly intended to follow through. Would it be another case of Colombia living in the way of the Spanish colonial period, when laws and agreements were respected but not followed?

OTHER PUBLIC POLICY ISSUES

After the approval of the FARC peace treaty, major public policy issues in Colombia fell into three categories: other forms of violence, the rights of women and gay people, and corruption, all salient policy questions that had been on the back burner during the years spent resolving the various conflicts.

Other Forms of Violence

Even if the negotiations with the FARC are finally successful, other notable forms of violence will continue to plague Colombia, including conflict with the ELN, antipersonnel mines, the so-called BACRIM (emerging criminal bands), gang violence, and domestic violence.

In October 2016, the government and the ELN agreed to have peace talks in Quito, Ecuador. The government stated the condition, however, that negotiations could not begin until all kidnapping victims were released, one of whom was Odín Sánchez. Sánchez voluntarily went into ELN custody in April 2016 to take the place of his brother Patrocinio, who had fallen ill after three years in captivity. The ELN insisted that at no time had they agreed on liberating Sánchez as a precondition, but that it would be discussed during the first phase of the conversations. The ELN and the government began their talks in February 2017.

A second problem is that after more than five decades of armed conflict, it was estimated that there were 52 million square kilometers (22 million square miles) of antipersonnel mines. In the previous twenty-six years, there had been 11,460 known victims of them, 39 percent of whom had been civilians. In 2014 only Afghanistan had more victims from these mines than Colombia, and in 2016 Colombia was in sixth place worldwide in number of victims. The mines had been placed by guerrilla groups and the military, their exact location was often unknown, and removing them will be a huge task.

A third problem was the emerging criminal bands (BACRIM) that appeared after the paramilitary demobilization. The government said that they were a new phenomenon, different because their chief reason for existence was the drug trade. They were not anti-guerrilla groups, and even cooperated with the Marxists in the drug trade at times, and they had no national organization.

A 2008 study by an NGO concluded that there were one hundred criminal gangs in the country, with twenty-one different names and about eight thousand members. The Atlantic coast was most affected, with 40 percent of the BACRIM members. They were in 246 of the 1,102 municipalities of the country. In 2015 a National Prosecutor's Office official said that there were 1,005 BACRIM in the country.

A similar problem is the growth of youth gangs in the cities. The National Institute of Prisons (Inpec) estimated that the number of members was three thousand times greater in 2015 than it was in 2005. The cities most affected are Barranquilla, Bogotá, Cali, Cartagena, and Medellín, with 109, 149, 105, 86, and 90 gangs respectively. In addition to lacking a complete picture of this complex phenomenon, the government has been incapable of ending it.

Rights of Women and Gay People

Another form of violence, not directly related to the political dimension, is domestic and spousal abuse. In 2014 Martha Ordóñez, Presidential Advisor on Equality for Women, stated that every thirteen minutes a woman was the victim of violence and every four minutes one of them died at the hands of her partner. In 2013, 1,007 women were murdered and there were 37,991 cases of violence against women by their partners and 16,088 cases of sexual violence against them.

In November 2016, the United Nations Commission on Human Rights issued a report about Colombia. Its conclusion was, "The State should intensify its efforts to prevent, combat, and punish all the violence against women and sexual violence and offer attention and full compensation to the victims. Particularly, it should ensure the facilitation of accusations by victims: all the incidences of violence against women and sexual violence should be investigated promptly, completely, and impartially." In addition, the Commission called for the full circulation of information on the right to legal abortion and effective plans to end mistreatment of persons, especially girls.[9]

Since a Constitutional Court ruling in 2006, abortion is legal only in three circumstances: the continuation of the pregnancy constitutes a danger to the life or health of the mother; there are life-threatening fetal malformations; or the pregnancy is the result of rape, non-consensual artificial insemination, or incest. The Catholic Church nonetheless condemned all abortions and protesters gathered outside hospitals to oppose the procedure.

In 2016 the Zika virus made abortion an important issue. Colombia is one of few Latin American nations that allow abortion in the case of a birth defect that makes a fetus unable to survive outside the womb. Although reliable statistics do not exist, anecdotal evidence suggests that few Colombian babies were born with microcephaly when the virus hit the country because their mothers chose abortion.

In a landmark ruling that eliminated a glaringly discriminatory policy, the Constitutional Court ruled in 2015 that gay individuals and couples may adopt children. In a 6-to-2 decision, the court found that barring gay people from adopting had unreasonably deprived children of the right to be raised by families. The decision was the latest victory for gay activists in Colombia, who have challenged discriminatory policies in a string of smartly litigated cases. In 2016 the Constitutional Court ruled that gay couples could marry. The estimate was that since 2013, 450 same-sex couples had celebrated "solemn unions." Those couples were now considered legally married.

Corruption

In Colombia, corruption occurs at the highest levels of the political system. Several high-ranking officials, including two of the last four presidents and 25 percent of the congress, have been recently investigated for political misconduct and abuse of power. Despite some prosecutions, however, more than 25 percent of public administration

officials reported that government officials and members of congress still exercise irregular influence in the activities of the civil service. During the presidency of Álvaro
Uribe, Colombia's domestic intelligence agency was illegally wiretapping and monitoring judges, journalists, politicians, and human rights activists considered to be his
opponents. The November 2016 report of the United Nations Commission on Human
Rights criticized the Colombian government for those illegal wiretaps.

The country faces structural corruption challenges from the collusion of the public
and private sectors, clientelism and policy capture by organized crime, lack of state
control and weak service delivery in remote areas of the country, and the inefficiency
of the criminal justice system. In addition, while the growth of extractive industries in
the country boosted the economy, the lack of adequate regulation and accountability
mechanisms were concerns.[10]

Transparency International's 2015 Corruption Perception Index ranks Colombia
83rd out of the 176 countries and territories assessed, with a score of 39 on a scale of
0–100, where 0 means that a country is perceived as highly corrupt and 100 means
that a country is perceived as very clean. Citizens also perceive corruption to be widespread in the country.[11] The data from the Global Corruption Barometer (2010/2011)
indicated that 56 percent of respondents perceived that the level of corruption in Colombia in the previous three years had increased. The institutions identified as the most
corrupt in this study were the political parties and the congress, with an average score
of 4.2, on a 1 (not at all corrupt) to 5 (extremely corrupt) scale. Other institutions with
high corruption scores were the police and public officials (4.0), the judiciary (3.8), and
the military (3.4). Forty-six percent of respondents rated government actions against
corruption as ineffective while 35 percent saw them as effective.[12]

The survey conducted by the Latinobarómetro in 2011 revealed that Colombians
thought that the most important reforms to strengthen their democratic system would
be reducing corruption (63 percent) and improving the transparency of the state (54 percent). Fifty-four percent of respondents found that committing procedural irregularities
"to get things done" damages democracy (51 percent), and only 13 percent agreed with
bribing as means to achieve the same purpose. Consistent with these findings, the data
from the Global Corruption Barometer 2010/2011 revealed that 24 percent of respondents had paid a bribe within the previous twelve months. From those that had contact with the police, 31 percent paid a bribe. Of the respondents who had contact with
the judiciary or registries, 18 percent and 17 percent respectively paid a bribe. Thirty-
eight percent of those paying bribes did so to receive a service they were entitled to.[13]

CONCLUSION

Having observed Colombia for more than fifty years and having lived there some fifteen times, this author has both positive and negative conclusions. On the positive
side, the country has progressed economically, not only in total wealth but also in the
lessening of income disparity. Different kinds of violence have ended, first from the
two traditional parties and later from the drug dealers, the paramilitary squads, and
now perhaps from the largest guerrilla group. No longer does Colombia lead the world
in homicide rates; indeed, it is not even first in Latin America. Since the coalition of
the National Front ended in 1974, the country has been more democratic, although

improvements can be made. Law enforcement is better, in part because of the assistance of the United States in Plan Colombia.

Yet there are still negative aspects. In addition to the corruption already mentioned, at times there is a general disrespect for law. The government is unable to enforce the law in isolated parts of the country. This was clear when Unión Patriótica members were murdered in the 1980s, and again in 2016 there were indications that the ELN, the BACRIM, and other groups were moving into areas that the FARC left. Other forms of violence exist, in elementary schools, on the streets, and within families. Many individuals and groups believe that the only way to get the attention of the government is through violent activities.

And the drug trade continues. Statistics from 2016 suggested that, as the government ended aerial spraying in part because of the negotiations with the FARC, coca production increased. Some Colombian officials argue that the drug trade is a more serious problem than the guerrilla groups.

Finally, there is the economy. It prospered during the first decade of the new millennium because of high prices for petroleum and coal. Indeed, a mild form of the "Dutch Disease" (increase in the economic development of natural resources and a decline in other sectors like the manufacturing sector or agriculture) began affecting industry. The question now, with the falling prices of coal and petroleum, is what will be the growth engine of the economy.

SUGGESTIONS FOR FURTHER READING

Bushnell, David. *The Making of Modern Colombia: A Nation in Spite of Itself.* Berkeley: University of California Press, 1993.

Kline, Harvey F. *Chronicle of a Failure Foretold: The Peace Process of Colombian President Andrés Pastrana.* Tuscaloosa: University of Alabama Press, 2007.

———. *Fighting Monsters in the Abyss: The Second Administration of Colombian President Álvaro Uribe Vélez, 2006–2010.* Tuscaloosa: University of Alabama Press, 2015.

———. *Showing Teeth to the Dragons: State-Building by Colombian President Álvaro Uribe Vélez, 2002–2006.* Tuscaloosa: University of Alabama Press, 2009.

LaRosa, Michael J., and Germán R. Mejía. *Colombia: A Concise Contemporary History.* Lanham, MD: Rowman & Littlefield Publishers, 2012.

Palacios, Marco. *Between Legitimacy and Violence: A History of Colombia, 1875–2002.* Durham, NC: Duke University Press, 2007.

Safford, Frank, and Marco Palacios. *Colombia: Fragmented Land, Divided Society.* Oxford: Oxford University Press, 2002.

Uribe Vélez, Álvaro. *No Lost Causes.* New York: Celebra, 2012.

NOTES

1. David Bushnell, *The Making of Modern Colombia: A Nation in Spite of Itself* (Berkeley: University of California Press, 1993). (Kindle Locations 527–531).

2. Central Intelligence Agency, "Colombia," World Factbook, www.cia.gov/library/publications/the-world-factbook/geos/co.html.

3. "La desigualdad en Colombia es mayor de lo que se piensa," *El Economista*, 28 de marzo de 2016, www.eleconomista.net/2016/03/28/la-desigualdad-en-colombia-es-mayor-de-lo-que-se-piensa.

194 HARVEY F. KLINE

4. World Bank, "Colombian Middle Class grows over past decade," November 13, 2012, www.worldbank.org/en/news/feature/2012/11/13/colombia-middle-class-grows-over-past-decade.

5. Nobel Women's Initiative, "Women's peace organizations in Colombia," April 29, 2016, http://nobelwomensinitiative.org/womens-peace-organizations-in-colombia/

6. Marco Palacios, *Between Legitimacy and Violence: A History of Colombia, 1875–2002*, 2nd print. (Durham: Duke University Press, 2007), 243.

7. Confidential interviews, Colombian historian, Bogotá, July 5, 2007.

8. "Los 10 cambios fundamentales que trae el nuevo acuerdo," *Semana*, noviembre 12, 2016.

9. "Informe de la ONU sobre derechos humanos en Colombia," *El Tiempo*, noviembre 7, 2016.

10. Hernán Gutiérrez "Colombia: Overview of corruption and anti-corruption, March 15, 2013, www.transparency.org/files/content/corruptionqas/373_Colombia_Overview_of_corruption_and_anti-corruption.pdf.

11. Transparency International, "Corruption by Country: Colombia," www.transparency.org/country#COL.

12. Ibid.

13. Gutiérrez "Colombia: Overview."

12

PERU: OVERCOMING THE AUTHORITARIAN LEGACY AT LAST?

Julio F. Carrión and David Scott Palmer

INTRODUCTION

For most of Peru's nearly 200 years of independence, politics alternated between one form of authoritarian rule or another, with occasional forays into formal democracy. But since 2000, this Andean nation has enjoyed the longest period of uninterrupted democratic rule in its history. Impeccable contests in 2001, 2006, 2011, and 2016 have routinized the role of elections in determining the chief executive. Similar progress has been achieved at the subnational level: decentralization policies continue and regional and local elections have been held in 2002, 2006, 2010, and 2014. We may be witnessing the end of the authoritarian legacy at last, but serious economic, social, and institutional problems still remain.

Peruvians are still divided by the legacy of Alberto Fujimori's government (1990–2000), a highly controversial elected regime that provided the benefits of pacification and economic stabilization on the one hand, but autocratic governance and pervasive corruption on the other. The continuing appeal of his legacy was revealed in the highly contested 2016 presidential election, which Fujimori's oldest daughter, Keiko, came very close to winning.

At the same time, continued improvement in sociodemographic indicators and economic growth since the early 2000s have prompted many to wonder if Peru is on the brink of a significant developmental leap. Nevertheless, some also question the sustainability of an economic model that relies heavily on commodity exports. In addition, citizens bitterly complain about failing public schools, rampant citizen insecurity, corrupt state officials, ineffective political institutions, and an archaic and ineffectual judicial system. Although there is much to celebrate about Peru's embrace of political democracy since 2000, significant challenges still need to be addressed. In many respects, Peru's democracy is still a work in progress.

POLITICAL HISTORY AND CHANGES IN POLITICAL CULTURE

Peru exhibits a deeply ingrained Hispanic tradition as the South American center of the Spanish Empire. This tradition contributed, after a reluctant independence (1821–1824), to instability, military regimes, and authoritarian governments for most of Peru's history as a republic. But there are clear indications that this legacy might be fading. Since 2000 Peru has been enjoying its longest period of democratic rule.

Early Political History and Military Rule

Unlike much of Latin America during the nineteenth century, Peru was divided politically less by a conservative-liberal cleavage and more by the issue of military or civilian rule. By the 1860s, partisans of civilian rule were beginning to organize themselves into a *civilista* movement. The War of the Pacific (1879–1883), in which Chile fought and defeated Peru and Bolivia, dramatically demonstrated the need for professionalization of the Peruvian military and helped provoke the formal establishment of the Civilista Party, as well as a number of more personalistic contenders. The eventual result was Peru's first extended period of civilian rule, starting in 1895. The civilian democratic interlude, however, did not last, and was even briefly interrupted by military intervention in 1914. Augusto B. Leguía, after ruling constitutionally during his first presidency (1908–1912), ended once and for all the shaky civilian democracy in 1919. Rather than work out a behind-the-scenes accommodation with opposition elements in 1919 after he had won democratic election, he led his own successful coup and ruled without open elections until ousted by the military in 1930.

Peru's embrace of new political ideas came with the creation of the Socialist Party by José Carlos Mariátegui and the organization of the American Popular Revolutionary Alliance (APRA) party. Although founded in Mexico by exiled student leader Víctor Raúl Haya de la Torre in 1924, APRA became Peru's first mass-based political party with a fully articulated ideology. By most accounts, APRA was strong enough to determine the outcome of all open elections after 1931. For more than fifty years, however, the military ensured that the party would never rule directly. Outside of Lima, APRA absorbed most of the newly emerging social forces in the more integrated parts of the country between the 1920s and the 1950s, particularly labor, students, and the more marginal middle sectors of the north coast. But opposition to the party from Lima's middle and upper classes was strong. For a good part of the twentieth century, Peruvian politics was defined by the *aprista-antiaprista* cleavage. Between 1956 and 1982 APRA became a center-conservative party willing to make almost any compromise to gain greater formal political power. Although such actions discredited the party for many, APRA remained Peru's best organized and most unified political force.

On October 3, 1968, with a bloodless coup led by General Juan Velasco Alvarado, the armed forces began long-term, institutionalized military rule in Peru. This marks an important moment in Peru's history as the regime's rhetoric and practice helped change Peru's political culture. Embracing a nationalistic discourse, the military government exalted Peru's Andean and indigenous roots, in contrast with previous governments that stressed the European legacy. An August 29, 1975, coup, led by General Francisco Morales Bermúdez and supported by the military establishment, gently eased out the ill and increasingly erratic General Velasco. By 1977 mounting economic and political pressures prompted the military regime to initiate a gradual return to civilian rule.

Transition to Democracy

The Constituent Assembly elections in 1978 opened the transition process to democratic rule. They also represented another political milestone in the changing political culture by including the participation of an array of leftist parties, most of them Marxist. These garnered an unprecedented 36 percent of the vote, even though APRA won the most seats. The Assembly itself was led by APRA founder Haya de la Torre—another first, given the long-term animosity of the military. The Assembly produced the Constitution of 1979, which set up national elections every five years and municipal elections every three years, and included universal suffrage for the first time, another historic milestone. No longer was there a literacy requirement, which had long excluded much of Peru's large indigenous population.

The return of electoral politics in 1980 under the new constitution also returned Fernando Belaúnde Terry to the presidency. Unexpectedly, the transition to democracy coincided with the eruption of a major domestic insurgency. The Shining Path guerrilla movement, originally based in the isolated south-central sierra department of Ayacucho and headed by former professors and students from the local University of Huamanga, advocated a peasant-based "New Democracy" forged through revolution. The Belaúnde administration did not take the group seriously for almost three full years. Only in December 1982 did the government declare Ayacucho an emergency zone and send the military to deal with the problem. By the end of Belaúnde's term thousands had perished in the violence, human rights violations had skyrocketed, and more than US$1 billion in property damage had occurred. The emergence in 1984 of a new guerrilla group, the Túpac Amaru Revolutionary Movement (MRTA), added to popular concerns over spreading political violence.

Economic and political difficulties substantially weakened popular support for Belaúnde and his Popular Alliance (AP) party. In the 1985 presidential vote the AP candidate was routed, gaining only 6 percent of the total vote. The largely Marxist United Left party (IU) garnered 21 percent for its candidate, Alfonso Barrantes, and a rejuvenated APRA won with 46 percent for its youthful (thirty-six-year-old) standard bearer Alan García Pérez (1985–1990). The García victory was doubly historic: after a fifty-five-year struggle APRA had finally gained both the presidency and a majority in both houses of congress. Additionally, for the first time since 1945 and only the second time since 1912, an elected civilian president handed power over to an elected successor. The 1986 municipal elections also saw substantial APRA gains, including for the first time ever, the mayoralty of Lima.

The Fujimori Era

When Peruvians went to the polls in 1990, they faced the choice between the novelist Mario Vargas Llosa, who had galvanized popular concern over President García's failures, and Alberto Fujimori, a political newcomer. Fujimori's victory was explained as the product of popular frustration with politics-as-usual and Vargas Llosa's overidentification with politicians of the right.

Peruvians did not know it at the time, but the country was headed toward electoral authoritarianism. In response to political deadlock, on April 5, 1992, Fujimori, with the support of the military, carried out a presidential coup, also known as the *autogolpe* (self-coup), shutting down congress, suspending the constitution, and purging the judiciary. President Fujimori's government did engage in multiple machinations to remain in office, but he also had a broad base of popular support. Such approval stemmed largely from his government's ability to drastically reduce political violence and to restore economic and political stability. This support was manifested in his successful bid for reelection in 1995, when he obtained 64 percent of the vote. Over the course of the Fujimori decade, political parties were further undermined by a combination of their own limitations and government actions. Independent groups, including the president's, proliferated and dominated the 1995 national elections and the 1995 and 1998 municipal votes. No traditional party except APRA received more than 5 percent of the vote in the 1995 national elections—a dramatic turnaround from the 1980s.

Forcing an unconstitutional third term by running for reelection in 2000 proved to be a disastrous decision, for events soon revealed the pyrrhic quality of Fujimori's electoral "victory." Fujimori faced a unified opposition in the second round of the election, and confronted mounting popular protests against his continuation in office. The leak of a video showing his security advisor, Vladimiro Montesinos, bribing a congressman to switch parties quickly turned into a regime-ending political crisis.

The End of Fujimori and the Return of Competitive Elections

The current wave of democracy that Peru is enjoying today was inaugurated by the transitional government led by president of congress and longtime AP representative Valentín Paniagua, who took the oath of office on November 22, 2000. The Paniagua interim presidency (2000–2001), though only nine months in duration, was surprisingly effective in righting the ship of state and putting it back on course. Peru's continuing democratic process owes much to the Paniagua-led transition. Amid multiple new revelations of official wrongdoing during the Fujimori years, hundreds of former high-level civilian and military leaders were tracked down and arrested for corruption and abuse of position, including Montesinos himself from his refuge in Venezuela.

New elections in April 2001 were as free and fair as those of 2000 were tainted. A hard-fought first round between Lourdes Flores Nano of National Unity (UN) on the right, and Alejandro Toledo of Peru Possible (PP) and APRA's García on the center-left saw Toledo (with 37 percent of the vote) and García (with 26 percent) having edged out Flores (24 percent) in the first round. Here, García's efforts to cast himself as a wiser and more experienced leader fell short. Toledo, who had led the opposition to Fujimori in the aftermath of the 2000 electoral debacle, won with 54 percent of the vote, though without a majority in congress.

The Toledo administration stumbled from the start and disappointed more than it pleased, but Toledo tried to restore citizen confidence in institutions and, to his credit, presided over what turned out to be the beginning of a decade of sustained economic growth. Despite his extremely low levels of popularity, the continuation of democracy was never in question. The elections of 2006 did create a moment of tension as unresolved developmental problems, lingering issues of inequality and social exclusion, and political discontent fueled the candidacy of Ollanta Humala, an outsider and former military officer who waged a left-populist campaign and secured first place in the first round of elections, while Alan García came from behind to finish second.

The fear of a president closely aligned with Hugo Chávez, and García's assurances that he had learned from the mistakes of his disastrous first presidency, tipped the scale in his favor, although he won a much narrower victory over Humala than polls had predicted (53 to 47 percent). In a graphic demonstration of the political center's neglect of the periphery, however, almost all sierra and jungle departments favored Humala, while the entire coast went for García. These were the first Peruvian elections to show such geographical polarization.

Although in his inaugural address President García (2006–2011) proclaimed his determination to deliver a major "economic shock" to develop the sierra, his administration fell far short on actual delivery. He turned out to be genuinely reinvented in his second term as a promoter of continued economic liberalization, including the ratification of a free trade agreement (FTA) with the United States in 2007. However, most of the highlands saw few benefits. For all of its success in the macroeconomic arena, the García government repeated the pattern of inattention and both inappropriate and belated responses to the needs and demands of the population of Peru's periphery.

The 2011 Presidential Elections

The next round of presidential elections in 2011 confirmed that Peru's democracy, although unable to solve some of the pressing issues of inequality, was becoming increasingly routinized. Humala declared his candidacy again, and the question was whether additional years of economic growth had undermined his appeal among the poor and whether Peruvians would opt instead for a more moderate, democratic, and market-oriented figure. But the Humala of 2011 was quite a different candidate. Acknowledging that to have a credible chance at winning the runoff election he needed to appeal to the center, he decided to moderate both his image and message. Instead of praising the virtues of Hugo Chávez and Bolivarian government, as he had done in 2006, Humala embraced the more moderate approach followed by Brazilian President Lula da Silva. Mixing a message of social inclusion, moderate economic reform, and social conservatism (he opposed gay marriage and abortion rights), he came in first place in the first round but failed to obtain an absolute majority.

With the center-right vote split among three different candidates (Toledo, Pedro Pablo Kuczynski, known to Peruvians as PPK, and Luis Castañeda, leader of National Solidarity, or SN), Keiko Fujimori, oldest daughter of the former president, was able to secure a place in the June 5, 2011, runoff. As the campaign for the runoff started, Humala further moderated his proposals, announcing a "road map" that would guide his government if elected. Decidedly different from his original platform entitled "The

Great Transformation," the new platform promised to respect the independence of the Central Bank, keep inflation low, and foster economic growth while embracing social inclusion rather than radical reform. After former president Toledo announced that he would support Humala in the second round, key members of his economic team became Humala's advisors. This further cemented Humala's move to the center.

With a few notable exceptions, most of Peru's establishment and media rallied behind Keiko Fujimori due to their concerns over the populist and anti-democratic elements of Humala's candidacy. The runoff polarized Peru once again, exposed the fault lines of its society, revealed the still prevalent racism, and unmasked the authoritarian predilections of some members of the establishment. For many voters, the election posed an extremely difficult choice between a candidate who might restore the authoritarian practices of her father's regime and another who might undo the significant gains made in the economy and the rule of law.

When Peruvians finally went to the polls on June 5, they elected Humala with a very slim margin: 51.4 percent went for Humala and 48.6 percent supported Keiko Fujimori. Fewer than 500,000 votes, out of 16.5 million votes cast, separated the two. Notably, the narrow margin did not produce a political crisis, as actors accepted both the fairness and the outcome of the contest. Humala was able to secure the presidency because he won in all the departments he carried in 2006 plus four that he had not: Ancash, Ica, Pasco, and Ucayali. For the first time since 1980, the winning candidate was able to claim victory without carrying the capital.

Defying both the expectations of some and the fears of others, Humala eschewed the wave of left-wing populism that had afflicted other Andean countries. This was quite remarkable, considering that Peru exhibits many elements that might favor such a development: namely, a tradition of populist rule, the lack of a strong party system, widespread discontent with the political class and institutions, and finally an economic bonanza that increased state coffers that could fund social programs to benefit a potential populist project.

Humala tried to deliver on his promises of greater social inclusion through new social policies, but those efforts were overshadowed by persistent inefficiencies and the lack of an overarching vision. Moreover, they failed to have an impact on people's perceptions of the effectiveness of the government, as Humala confronted numerous social conflicts emanating from controversial mining projects. He was also unable to curtail a growing concern over citizen insecurity, and had to deal with the consequences of economic slowdown produced by the end of the commodities boom.

For most of the second half of his administration, Humala was castigated in public opinion polls by his perceived passivity and his overreliance on his wife's counsel, who was described by many as virtual co-president. Public dissatisfaction with political institutions and the judiciary deepened, as high-profile cases of corruption involving regional presidents and other local authorities exposed continuing institutional fragilities.

The 2016 Presidential Elections

As Peru approached a new presidential contest in 2016, it was evident that Keiko Fujimori would once again be a serious contender for the presidency. Her party, now renamed Popular Force, had obtained the second largest congressional representation in 2011, but due to frequent defections in the ruling majority, it became the largest by 2015.

The campaign for the April 10, 2016, presidential election revealed both the growing strength of Peru's democracy and its glaring institutional deficits. Keiko was holding a firm lead in the polls by mid-February, closely followed by Julio Guzmán, candidate of All for Peru, a US-trained policy analyst outsider with no previous experience in politics. Guzmán's sudden rise—he was barely registering in the polls in December 2015—was yet another manifestation of voters' yearning for outsiders.

On March 9, 2016, the National Electoral Board (JNE), in a surprising decision, disqualified Guzmán's candidacy for failing to fully comply with the regulations established in the law of political parties. Similarly, it disqualified César Acuña for extending cash payments to participants in his rallies in violation of a recently enacted electoral law. Acuña, leader of the Alliance for Progress (APP) party and owner of a chain of for-profit universities, had also had a meteoric rise in the polls. However, by March 2016, his electoral standing had greatly diminished due to accusations of plagiarism and spousal abuse.

The decision of the JNE to disqualify both candidates generated widespread criticism, because it seemed, especially in Guzmán's case, to put greater emphasis on the minor technical aspects of the law than on the general principle of open political participation. The distrust was deepened when, shortly after, the Board refused to disqualify Fujimori, who had also been accused of distributing money at one of her rallies. The severity of the sanction against Acuña and the leniency toward Keiko led many to believe that the JNE was not acting impartially.

With Guzmán out of the race, his supporters gravitated toward Pedro Pablo Kuczynski, whose standing in the polls began to rise. But in another twist, Veronika Mendoza, the young and charismatic leader of the left-wing Broad Front (FA), began to grow in the polls at the end of March, threatening Kuczynski's hopes to make it to a runoff election to confront Keiko. Mendoza capitalized on the disappointment of many Peruvians of humble origins, especially those residing in the southern sierra, who had voted for Humala because of his promises of social inclusion. Mendoza reactivated a political left that had been considered moribund by many observers, and rattled the nerves of an establishment perhaps too complacent over Peru's economic gains. As Peruvians went to vote, the big unknown was who would face Keiko in the second round, Kuczynski or Mendoza. The first-round results favored Kuczynski over Mendoza (21 percent to 18.7 percent), with Fujimori finishing first, as expected, with 39.9 percent.

The runoff election on June 5, 2016, polarized Peru in a fashion that was reminiscent of the old divide between apristas and antiapristas, only now between fujimoristas and antifujimoristas. Fujimori tried initially to soften her image by removing some figures associated with her father's administration and promising a strict defense of the constitutional order. But the revelation that the US Drug Enforcement Administration was investigating Joaquín Ramírez, Secretary General of her party, for money laundering, created a political firestorm. In an effort to control the damage, José Chlimper, Fujimori's running mate, leaked an audio recording that purportedly exonerated Ramírez, which caused an even bigger scandal when the audio turned out to have been doctored. That Fujimori's running mate would engage in such manipulations, and that the Secretary General of her party might be involved in drug trafficking and money laundering, reminded many Peruvians of the excesses of her father's regime and reversed her second-round electoral momentum.

When the runoff's final results were tabulated, Kuczynski had eked out the narrowest victory in the electoral history of Peru. Of more than 17 million votes cast, Kuczynski won by just over 41,000 votes, a mere 0.24 percent margin. Despite the close outcome, Fujimori quickly accepted the results and congratulated the winner.

For the first time in its history, Peru has held four free and fair presidential elections in a row, an impressive accomplishment. Even so, President Kuczynski has a congress in which the opposition Popular Force party holds a majority of the one hundred thirty seats. The successful continuation of Peru's unprecedented period of electoral democracy depends to a significant degree on how the executive and the legislative branches will manage their unavoidable conflicts.

ECONOMIC CHANGE

Peru has a long-standing dependence on primary product exports, but with a more diverse base than most countries of the region. Still, there is a growing consensus that Peru needs to expand and diversify both export and import markets, and initiatives have been taken in that regard. As in many other Latin American countries during the 1980s, Peru experienced severe economic difficulties during the first years of its new democratic era. The second Belaúnde administration (1980–1985) suffered from increased inflation, which rose from 60 percent in 1980 to more than 100 percent by 1984. A recession deepened as well, with a decline in GDP of more than 10 percent in 1983, and an erosion in real wages of more than 30 percent by the end of Belaúnde's administration.

The election of Alan García in 1985 seemed to augur different economic times. Domestic initiatives, especially in agriculture, contributed to long-overdue economic growth at rates of 9 percent in 1985 and 7 percent in 1986. But the recovery ran out of steam in 1987. The second half of García's term was an unmitigated disaster. Inflation skyrocketed to 1,722 percent in 1988, 2,600 percent in 1989, and 7,650 percent in 1990. The economy declined by more than 20 percent during this period. By the end of the García government in 1990, total foreign debt with arrearages was more than US$23 billion.

Alberto Fujimori, elected in 1990 amid economic chaos, tackled the crisis by embracing the Washington Consensus of economic liberalization. He abolished state subsidies, freed the exchange rate, and embarked on a process of state-owned enterprise privatization. In the short run, his drastic measures accelerated inflation to historic highs, further reduced domestic economic activity (28 percent in 1990), and pushed twelve to fourteen million more Peruvians below the poverty line (60 to 70 percent of the population).

By early 1992, these crisis-driven initiatives began to produce results. Inflation was sharply reduced. International economic reinsertion moved forward after foreign debt payments were resumed in late 1990, along with negotiations with the international financial institutions (IFIs). Signs of economic recovery started to appear as well. In addition, the United States increased bilateral economic assistance in October 1991, plus its first substantial military aid in more than twenty years.

By the mid-1990s, Peru's economy has turned around. Inflation virtually ended (dropping from 139 percent in 1991 to 3 percent by 2000), and with economic liberalization and reinsertion into the international financial community, Peru's economic growth averaged more than 7 percent from 1994 through 1997. Between 1993 and 1998, Peru received more than US$10 billion in new investment and US$8 billion in new loans, and it signed the Brady Plan with foreign creditors, which reduced foreign debt by more than US$5 billion to just under US$19 billion by 1997. A variety of innovative local rural micro development initiatives reduced extreme poverty by more than half from 1991 through 1998 (31 percent to 15 percent) while also creating hundreds of new community organizations that began by administrating these projects.

Although the return to democracy in the 1980s was accompanied by a severe economic crisis, the post-Fujimori democratic era has reflected a much different situation. Between 2001 and 2013, Peru experienced a remarkable period of economic growth. The economy grew by 9.8 percent in 2008, the second highest rate in Latin America that year, slowing to 0.9 percent as a result of the global economic meltdown, but recovering in 2010. Such growth was unprecedented and was based largely on the extended expansion of commodity exports at high international prices. Domestic results included increased tax revenues, public investment, and a rapidly growing internal market, along with growing domestic and foreign investor optimism. According to the Economic Commission for Latin America and the Caribbean (ECLAC), Peru's direct foreign investment levels more than doubled between 2003 and 2011 ($3.5 million to $7.7 million).

Between 2011 and 2014 the economy grew but at an increasingly slow pace, and although growth in 2015 was higher than in 2014, it is clear that Peru can no longer rely on exports of minerals to sustain its impressive economic performance. Nevertheless, more than a decade of solid economic growth has resulted in an improvement of wages and average monthly incomes. The National Statistics office reports that the average national income for workers grew 37.8 percent between 2004 and 2015. Polls also reflect more positive public perceptions of the economic situation. In 2006, 72.9 percent of respondents described their personal economic situation as either "good" or "fair." Six years later, that figure had improved to 84.9 percent. In the same 2006 poll, 27 percent described their personal economic situation as "bad" or "very bad"; by 2012 that figure had dropped to 15.1 percent. Even income inequality has shown improvement: according to World Bank statistics, the Gini index fell from 51.4 in 2007 to 44.1 in 2014.

Peru exhibits today one of the most open economies in South America, a process that began with the adoption of market reforms in the 1990s by the Fujimori governments. These reforms plus long-term modernization processes have changed Peru's economic structure in important ways. Three in particular merit attention. First, agriculture's contribution to GDP has declined markedly (from 11 percent in 1950 to 5.2 percent in 2015), but has been more than replaced by expanding mining and oil production. Second, state participation in the economy has declined significantly, from a high of 21 percent in 1975 (during the reformist military government) to 6 percent in 2000, even below 1950 figures of 7 percent. Third, foreign capital has become much more important, contributing 28 percent of GDP in 2000 compared with 10 percent in 1950. Clearly Peru now embraces a liberal economic model where private investment, both domestic and foreign, plays a much larger role.

Despite such significant changes, Peru's economy continues to be dependent on the export of commodities and thus subject to the demands and vagaries of international markets. As a result, this recent economic growth is masking the structural weakness of relying too much on mining exports. Some economists argue that Peru is currently suffering a case of "Dutch Disease," where high profitability in mining discourages investment in other sectors such as manufacture and construction. These may be less profitable but they are also less vulnerable to external shocks. Moreover, the massive influx of dollars associated with mining and oil exports tends to overvalue the national currency, with deleterious effects (e.g., more expensive exports) for overall long-term economic prospects. In response to this challenge, the Humala administration developed the National Plan of Productive Diversification, creating institutions in charge of fostering technological innovation and developing new foreign markets. Progress in diversification, however, is modest so far.

Another concern is the large informal sector in the economy, which continues to account for some 50 percent to 60 percent of Peru's economic activity. This includes such illegal practices as drug production and trafficking as well as extensive unauthorized logging and gold mining. Besides depriving the government of tax revenue, such informal economic activities are producing serious environmental degradation, especially in Peru's vast but vulnerable Amazon basin jungle areas.

SOCIAL CHANGE

Peruvian society began to change in the 1950s, but social and economic change has accelerated dramatically in the last thirty years. In the 1950s, Peru experienced a dramatic surge in internal migration, as people from the sierra moved to Lima. This mobilization had lasting consequences. From a primarily rural society in the early 1960s, Peru is now largely urban: almost 80 percent of the population lives in cities today (and about 50 percent of the total population resides in cities of 100,000 inhabitants or more). Migration has also changed the population's geographical distribution. Today the majority (57 percent) lives on the coast, and three out of ten Peruvians reside in Lima.

The Velasco military government was a significant catalyst for social change. Most notable was the enactment of a large-scale agrarian-reform program, which effectively eliminated large, private landholdings; in the process, it reconfigured a rural landscape that was archaic and exploitative. About 360,000 farm families received land between 1969 and 1980, most as members of farm cooperatives. Commitment to cooperatives illustrated the regime's concern for popular participation at various levels. Neighborhood organizations, worker communities, and cooperatives of several types proliferated after 1970, as did various coordinating bodies.

Government initiatives in the rural highlands and jungle areas to counter guerrilla activities in the 1980s and 1990s have further changed the social landscape. The organization of community civil defense groups (*rondas campesinas*) was encouraged in areas where they did not exist, and supported in others where they had a long-established presence. Similarly, and especially during the Fujimori administration, control over microdevelopment programs was given to communities. These, along with regular district-level elections, have contributed to local empowerment as well as organized social protests over issues such as official corruption and environmental degradation by mining investments.

Indeed, the social landscape of the sierra has been marked by frequent instances of social conflict related to mining, where local communities opposing the expansion of mining activities have resorted to violence to stop them. One dramatic example of these tensions is the Conga conflict in the northern department of Cajamarca. In late 2011, Newmont Mining Company announced that the Peruvian government had approved the company's plans for a US$4.8 billion investment in the Conga mines, which would be the largest single foreign investment in the country's history. Area residents, with the backing of the regional president, objected to the plan. They criticized the proposed investment's environmental impact and called for a regional strike. Soon the conflict gathered national attention, given the magnitude of the investment at risk and the death of five people in clashes between police and local residents in July 2012. This confrontation forced the Humala government to suspend constitutional guarantees in Cajamarca by declaring a state of emergency. Among many other ongoing conflicts fueled by local opposition to mining projects in both the sierra and jungle are those in Apurímac (Las Bambas), Arequipa (Tía María), and Loreto (Lote 192).

Sustained economic growth in the recent past has improved key indicators of well-being. Probably the two most important consequences for social change have been the reduction in poverty and the growth of the middle class. Total poverty has dropped from 58.5 percent in 2004 to 21.8 percent in 2015. Urban unemployment fell from 9.4 percent in 2002 to 4.5 percent in 2014. According to one report of the Inter-American Development Bank, the middle class increased from 26 percent of the population in 2005 to 49 percent in 2011. Even though other reports show different figures, what is indisputable is that the middle class today is larger than it was in 2000. This growth is reflected in the changing nature of provincial cities, the burgeoning service sector, and the proliferation of malls and supermarkets in areas that were considered until recently too poor to support this kind of economic activity.

Perhaps the indicator that best illustrates both the growth of the middle class and the expansion of communications infrastructure is the penetration of cable television. In 2005, only 10.3 percent of all Peruvian households enjoyed this service; by 2014 the proportion had tripled to 35.9, and in Lima, to 60 percent. Possession of a television set is almost universal: 80 percent of all households, 91 percent in urban areas, and 96 percent in Lima. Peruvians are highly interconnected: the possession of at least one cell phone in the household went from 16.4 percent in 2004 to 75.2 percent in 2011. In 2014, 90 percent of all urban households had a cell phone, and even a bit higher in Lima.

The demographic changes have been no less impressive. In little more than three decades, Peru has more than doubled its population, from 13 million in 1972 to 28 million in 2007, the year of the last census. According to the projections of Peru's National Office of Statistics and Informatics (INEI), Peru surpassed 31 million inhabitants in 2015. The rate of growth of the population was significant in the 1960s and 1970s, and has slowed somewhat since then.

Two significant demographic trends merit attention: first, life expectancy continues to rise. Between 1950 and 1955 life expectancy was 43.9 years; by 2007, Peruvians could hope to live, on average, 76 years. Second, fertility has also declined, with women having fewer children than ever. In 1977–1978, women had on average 5.4 children. In 2004, the number more than halved to 2.4.

Likewise, although infant mortality continues to be high in comparison with countries such as Chile and Argentina, this indicator has changed dramatically in the last decade. In 2000, 40.6 of every 1,000 children born alive died before they reached their first birthday. By 2015, the rate had dropped to 15.

POLITICAL INSTITUTIONS

A variety of forces and events have transformed the political landscape over recent decades. The Velasco military government enacted significant social and economic changes between 1968 and 1980 that would significantly shape subsequent events. It increased state influence and control over the economy; new ministries, agencies, and banks were established; basic services were nationalized, as were some large foreign companies in mining, fishing, and agriculture, and state enterprises or cooperatives established in their place. Important areas of heavy industry were reserved for the state, new investment laws placed various controls on the private sector, and government employment mushroomed.

It is against this backdrop that Peru gradually returned to democratic politics, first with elections for a constitutional assembly, which drafted a very progressive Constitution in 1979 and general elections in 1980. With universal adult suffrage and full civil and political rights granted in the new constitution, the 1980s were years of democracy, with traditional parties and Marxist organizations competing for political power. The election of Alfonso Barrantes, leader of a coalition of Marxist parties, as mayor of Lima in 1983 was emblematic of the openness of the new political system.

But the decade was also affected by political violence and economic recession. The administrations of Fernando Belaúnde and Alan García unsuccessfully grappled with these problems, and their failures contributed in great part to the demise of the party system that had emerged in the post-military decade. By 1990, the economy was in freefall and central government institutions had all but collapsed, with political violence reaching epidemic proportions in the context of the growing radical Maoist Shining Path guerrilla movement. Many local governments and peasant communities in the sierra were hollowed out, abandoned, or incorporated into the guerrilla model of "generated organisms of the New Democracy."

With the restoration of civilian rule in 1980, parties and unions regained their pre-1968 roles, largely supplanting the military's model. Vigorous political participation through a score of parties covering the entire ideological spectrum characterized the 1980s, with power alternating between center-right and center-left groups at the national executive level and with substantial representation in congress by the Marxist left. In municipal elections, political organizations won shares of district governments at different times, with pluralities shifting from Popular Action (AP) to United Left (IU) to APRA and back to IU. An unanticipated legacy of long-term reformist military rule, then, was to usher in a historically unprecedented level of partisan politics, institutionalized to a degree that few people foresaw and proceeding apace in spite of profound domestic economic difficulties and a substantial guerrilla movement.

However, with the breakup of IU in 1988–1989 and widespread popular disappointment with party politics as successive elected governments failed to respond to citizen needs, political independents came to dominate national and local elections in the 1990s, and union membership declined. Alberto Fujimori's 1990 election as an outsider and his 1992 autogolpe reflected the shift to "anti-party" politics, as did the independent-dominated 1992 congressional/constitutional assembly elections and the 1993 local elections. The result was a progressive deinstitutionalization of electoral politics and a return to more personalistic approaches at the center. Another outcome was a dramatic increase of popular organizations at the local level, as citizens sought to fill the newly available political space. However, the Fujimori governments, against all odds, were successful in righting the economy, ending the guerrilla threat, and modernizing government, all while maintaining an anti-party political agenda.

In a manner all too familiar to Latin American politics, however, success bred hubris. Claiming to be facing a national emergency and an obstructionist congress, Fujimori declared the "temporary suspension" of democracy on April 5, 1992. This action drew immediate and almost universal international condemnation but received strong approval in public opinion polls. Fujimori, chastened by the intensity of the international response but knowing that he enjoyed domestic support, agreed immediately to prompt electoral restoration.

This was accomplished with national elections under Organization of American States (OAS) oversight for a new, smaller, one-house congress-cum-constitutional convention in November 1992 and municipal elections two months later. Results included marginalization of traditional parties, greater concentration of power in the presidency, and a congressional majority that supported Fujimori. The new constitution was narrowly approved (52 to 48 percent) in an October 1993 referendum. It recentralized government authority, set the bases for privatization and economic liberalization, and allowed for the immediate reelection of the sitting president.

After a clear mandate in 1995 (64 percent of the valid vote and a majority in congress) President Fujimori called for "direct democracy without parties or intermediaries" and increased expenditures for local development as well as initiated monthly stipends directly to municipal governments. However, his government also changed the political rules—often arbitrarily and unconstitutionally—to keep a robust political party system from reemerging and to undermine the opposition's electoral campaigns. Intimidation tactics included wiretaps, physical assault, and character assassination campaigns orchestrated by the Peruvian National Intelligence System (SIN), directed by Fujimori's closest ally and confidant, Vladimiro Montesinos. The regime also thwarted a 1998 national referendum on a third term (for which 1.4 million signatures had been secured) through a congressional vote denying its validity.

As discussed earlier in the chapter, having rigged electoral machinery and procedures in his favor, President Fujimori surprised no one by deciding to run for a third, constitutionally dubious term in the 2000 elections. Unlike 1995, however, he did not secure an absolute majority in the first round, nor did his supporters win a congressional majority. He was forced into a runoff with second-place finisher Alejandro Toledo, a US-educated economist from a humble indigenous background without political experience. The best efforts of the international community, led by the OAS Election Observer Mission, to ensure a free and fair voting process for the runoff were not successful. Both Toledo and the OAS withdrew in protest, and the incumbent won with just 52 percent of the valid vote (about one-third of all ballots cast were spoiled in protest).

Inaugurated amid massive protests and tear gas in July, Fujimori was gone by November. Precipitating his downfall was the videotaped revelation that SIN director Montesinos was bribing elected representatives of the opposition to ensure a pro-Fujimori majority in congress. In spite of President Fujimori's desperate moves to maintain control—including firing and forcing Montesinos into exile and calling for early elections in which he would not be a candidate—popular indignation overwhelmed his maneuverings. By early November opposition parties had regained control of congress. They refused to accept Fujimori's letter of resignation from Japan, where he had fled in ignominy, but declared the presidency vacant instead on grounds of "moral incapacity."

After Fujimori's fall, Peru has managed the successful completion of four consecutive rounds of presidential elections in 2001, 2006, 2011, and 2016. Such a historic achievement needs to be celebrated, for it signals the consolidation of free and fair elections in Peru. However, out of the four presidents elected since 2001, only one (Alan García, 2006–2011), represented a traditional political organization. All the others emphasized personality over ideology or party platform.

Peru did have a developing party system during the 1980s, with AP and the Popular Christian Party (PPC) on the right, IU on the left, and APRA in the middle of the ideological spectrum. This process was cut short by several developments. First, the AP-PPC and APRA governments performed dismally when in office. Second, the rampant and prolonged economic crisis and the violence of Shining Path and the MRTA provoked a severe decline in civil society organizations. Third, the rise of Alberto Fujimori (1990 2000) as a hegemonic political actor in the 1990s and his administration's concerted effort to undermine any source of opposition to his regime fostered an antipolitical mentality that further undermined traditional parties. The 2000 presidential election saw the emergence of new political organizations to contest Fujimori's grip on power. However, the systematic smear campaign waged against the main candidates challenging his bid for a third term contributed to their inability to consolidate as full-fledged parties.

Even so, APRA continues to be a functioning party worthy of that name, although it has become much weaker in recent years. Increasingly, Popular Force (FP) is emerging as another political organization that may well deserve the label of party as well. To her merit, this group's leader, Keiko Fujimori, used her time after her 2011 defeat to build a national organization. She traveled frequently to the provinces to recruit local leaders, and her political efforts paid off nicely in the 2014 regional elections when her party fielded candidates in most regions, in a context where most other national parties did not compete. Such impressive ground work was repeated in the 2016 congressional elections, in which FP candidates won a majority of the seats.

Other new parties have had trouble planting roots in society. Toledo's PP had the greatest chance, but the shortcomings of his administration and his unsuccessful bid for reelection in 2011 have weakened the party; in the 2016 congressional vote, they failed to elect a single candidate. PP suffered significant defections in the wake of revelations that Toledo may have been involved in shady real estate dealings using money of unclear origin.

Other parties had even more difficult times. We Are Peru (SP) and its leader Alberto Andrade failed to develop as a strong party after Andrade finished his term as Lima's mayor and tried to enter national politics, with uneven success. After a dismal performance in the 2006 election and the death of Andrade in 2009 the party faded even further. Luis Castañeda, leader of National Solidarity (SN), was elected mayor of Lima in 2002 and then reelected in 2006. Despite success as mayor, Castañeda has been unable to expand his party nationally.

Humala's Nationalist Party (PN) barely survived its stint in government between 2011 and 2016. Not only did PN lose deputies while in office but its current leader, the former First Lady Nadine Heredia, is facing investigations for alleged corruption and money laundering. As with every single governing party since 2001, PN failed to field a candidate for the presidency following a term in office.

These organizations have not been able to consolidate into national parties in large part because they are personalistic vehicles devoid of ideology that rely on the charisma of their leaders and their potential access to state resources to support clientelistic and patronage networks. If deprived of political office, these parties struggle to survive. When Toledo finished his first term, he left the country and his party went into hibernation only to be resurrected again in 2011 and 2016 when he ran for reelection. Luis Castañeda basically initiated his political career from his position as a government bureaucrat, following his appointment by Fujimori as head of the National Institute of Public Health (1990–1996) and then as president of the Fishermen's Pension Fund (1997–1999), after which he founded SN. In short, Castañeda needed to be visible in office to continue his viability as a political figure. This may well have motivated him to spearhead an ill-advised recall election in 2013 against Susana Villarán, mayor of Lima, in the hope that he would be able to run again for the office himself and thus keep his party afloat. He ran again for mayor in 2015, successfully, but not as a candidate for president again in 2016.

There is an additional reason that might explain the inability of these parties to develop into solid national organizations. In 2002 President Toledo organized regional elections for the first time. The objective was to elect twenty-three regional presidents (one for each of Peru's departments, with the exception of Lima and Callao) under an electoral law allowing participation by local and independent slates that did not have to be registered as national political parties. Regional elections took place in 2002, 2006, 2010, and 2014, but further eroded national parties by facilitating the participation of independent lists. A conservative count of the electoral performance of these independent lists clearly illustrates the declining importance of national parties: in 2002, independent lists accounted for 21.9 percent of votes cast, steadily increasing to 40.2 percent in 2006, 56.4 percent in 2010, and 65 percent in 2014.

A recent study of political parties in Peru shows that many of the local and regional organizations are nothing but coalitions of independents, who pool resources to compete in the electoral arena and then disband or reassess their options after elections. However, a few organizations are emerging as more institutionalized regional parties, as subnational elections become routinized.

The lack of party coherence has been evidenced in the phenomenon of "party jumping": representatives are elected under one ticket and then switch to another or create their own congressional groups once elected. This phenomenon also includes people who run for office under different party banners in different election cycles. Although the existing law of political parties has tried to minimize this problem, no effects have been felt as yet. More recently, in 2016, the fujimorista delegation in congress succeeded in passing a bill sanctioning *transfuguismo* (as party jumping is known in Peru). According to this law, representatives who renounce their party or are expelled by it cannot join another congressional delegation, become members of the congressional leadership team, or be part of important committees. The law has been criticized, but also represents an effort to increase party coherence and continuity.

The assessment of the level of democracy in today's Peru is largely positive: civil and political freedoms are fully operational and elected officials do have governing power, as the military has accepted a subordinate role. Nevertheless, serious institutional flaws remain, most notably a lack of organized and institutionalized parties, a dysfunctional and inefficient judicial system, a deeply untrusted congress, and growing instances of corruption affecting regional governments and some national figures as well.

PUBLIC POLICY

The size and scope of the state in Peru has ebbed and flowed over the years. Until the 1960s, government employees constituted a small proportion of the workforce and were usually selected on the basis of party affiliation, family ties, or friendship. Ministry bureaucracies were concentrated in Lima. Government presence in the provinces was limited to prefects and their staffs, military garrisons in border areas, small detachments of national police, schoolteachers, and a few judges, all appointed by authorities in Lima. This was consistent with a state whose size was one of the smaller in Latin America.

The government's size and scope increased considerably during the first Belaúnde administration (1963–1968) with the establishment of new government agencies. Total government employment increased by almost 50 percent between 1960 and 1967 (from 179,000 to 270,000), and the public sector's share of GDP grew from 8 percent to 11 percent.

However, the most dramatic changes in the size and scope of the state machinery occurred between 1968 and 1980 under the reformist military regime, which dramatically expanded government involvement in order to accelerate development. Existing ministries were reorganized and new ministries and autonomous agencies were created. By 1975 total government employment had increased by almost 70 percent over 1967 (to 450,000), and the public sector's share of GDP had doubled to 22 percent. Even with such a rapid expansion of the state, however, central government activities remained concentrated in Lima. Official funding tended to go toward construction, equipment, and white-collar employment in the capital rather than for activities in the provinces.

The political and financial crises of 1975 and the change of government brought to an end the dynamic phase of public sector reforms. Resource limitations, growing popular opposition, and the inability of the military regime to act effectively to implement its own decrees prevented full implementation of the corporatist model articulated between 1971 and 1975. The 1979 constitution, however, drawn up by an APRA-IU majority, retained the statist orientation of the Peruvian political system even as it set the bases for civilian rule.

With the return to democracy in 1980 President Belaúnde announced his intention to restore the dynamism of the private sector and to reduce the role of government. However, continuing economic problems and substantial public resistance made these changes difficult to carry out. The first García government (1985–1990) moved quickly to implement long-standing APRA decentralization goals, including regional development corporations, expanded agricultural credit, and regional legislatures, while working simultaneously to win the confidence of domestic entrepreneurs. Initial successes were substantial, but by the end of García's term, they had been overwhelmed by an ill-advised nationalization of domestic banks, soon reversed, and by Peru's worst economic crisis in one hundred years. Central government employment expanded from six hundred thousand employees in 1985 to one million in 1990—but with half the budget!

The Fujimori administrations, after implementing drastic shock measures to stop Peru's economic hemorrhaging, began to move the country toward economic liberalization. This process involved selling off state enterprises created or nationalized under the 1968–1980 military regimes, retiring many government employees and reorganizing ministries to be able to dismiss thousands more, and overhauling the legal framework to favor private property and investment. Tax collection was also reorganized so that the government could begin to pay its own way again. Collections increased from less than 4 percent of GDP in 1989 to 14 percent by 1995.

Over the course of the 1990s, more than one hundred former state enterprises and agencies were privatized, generating around US$8 billion in new foreign investment. The 1993 constitution incorporated these changes but further concentrated power in the presidency and in central government as well. New government agencies, several designed to emphasize microdevelopment projects in Peru's poorest districts, began to operate in the early 1990s, as did a municipal fund to transfer resources to local governments. Overall, the state did not become smaller during the Fujimori years, but was dramatically changed and reorganized.

The origins of Peru's contemporary social and economic policies can be traced back to the Fujimori regime. The National Office of Revenue Administration (SUNAT) rapidly became a powerful tax agency that increased revenue exponentially. Tax revenues jumped 400 percent in 1991 in comparison with 1990. In 1995, tax receipts grew 55 percent in relation to the previous year. Fujimori also established the Commission for the Promotion of Private Investment (COPRI), which was given the task of managing the privatization of state-owned enterprises. Similarly, this government established agencies to foster and fund microdevelopment projects (e.g., MIBANCO, FONCODES), to alleviate extreme poverty (PRONAA), and to promote gender issues (Ministry of Women and Human Development).

Especially during the last half of his administration, Fujimori built a powerful security apparatus that was used to intimidate, harass, or buy opponents. He also created an oversized Ministry of the Presidency that was given the task to manage social programs which, beginning in 1998, shifted their mission toward buying votes to secure yet another term in office. With the failure of Fujimori to continue as president after his fraudulent 2000 re-reelection, successive legitimate civilian governments have introduced a variety of post-conflict initiatives, decentralization policies, and social programs.

A Truth and Reconciliation Commission (CVR) was established in 2001 to document the human rights abuses committed during Shining Path's "people's war." Attempts to bring Fujimori back from exile in Japan to face Peruvian justice were unsuccessful, however, as it turned out that he had Japanese citizenship and could not be extradited. In another disastrous decision, Fujimori left Japan in late 2005 to go to Chile, perhaps in an effort to drum up popular support for a possible candidacy in 2006. Chile detained him and after a request from Peru, Chile's Supreme Court agreed to extradite him in 2007 to face charges of corruption and human rights violations. Fujimori was eventually sentenced to a twenty-five-year prison term for the crimes he committed.

Initiatives related to decentralization include the creation of regions in 2002 during the Toledo administration (2001–2006). Initially each department became a region, but the goal was the creation of regions that would aggregate contiguous departments, an initiative that eventually failed in a referendum held in 2005. Regional elections were also held for the first time in 2002, and then every four years. Toledo also initiated the transfer of activities and resources from executive agencies to regional governments. The second García administration (2006–2011) engaged in further reorganization but also sustained the center's commitment to strengthening regional and local governments with additional funding (e.g., an increase in the Mineral Tax) and expansion of personnel. Nevertheless, even with such reinforcement and support, regional governments in particular have been slow to implement meaningful development programs in their areas of responsibility.

The Humala government (2011–2016) tried to deliver on promises of greater social inclusion with the establishment of the Ministry of Development and Social Inclusion to host a variety of existing and new social programs. These included Strong Child (for school breakfasts and lunches), All Together (for conditional cash transfers), Crib Plus (for day-care centers), Pension 65 (a retirement program for low-income seniors), and the Inter-Amazon Services Program (PIAS; for bringing state services by riverboat to remote Amazonian localities). Humala also established Scholarship 18 (for making higher education affordable), and expanded access to health services through Whole Health Insurance. Impressive as they are, such efforts are overshadowed by persistent inefficiencies and the lack of an overarching vision of a modern, inclusive state devoted to fostering both economic growth and institutional renewal.

Another issue of public policy that is increasingly salient for Peruvians is citizen insecurity. Between 1989 and 1993, homicides increased to a peak of 17.2 per 100,000 inhabitants, due largely to the Shining Path insurgency. This group's decline coincided with a sharp reduction in homicides, to 4.25 in 2002. Since then, however, violent crime has jumped significantly to 18.58 homicides per 100,000 inhabitants in 2010, even higher than peak rates during the worst years of the political violence. In addition, Peruvians report high levels of crime victimization. The 2014 Americas Barometer survey placed Peru first in the region in the percentage of people who say they have been victims of delinquency in the previous year and first in their perceived levels of insecurity. Not surprisingly, then, Peruvians cited violence and insecurity as the country's most important issues in 2014, even above poverty, unemployment, and the economy. In fact, the proportion of respondents who said violence and insecurity were the most pressing problems quadrupled from 2006 to 2014 (10.2 percent to 46.7 percent).

Finally, citizen distrust of political institutions and their skepticism about democracy itself needs to be addressed as a public policy issue. Polls have documented the contradiction between sustained economic growth and widespread political discontent. A 2015 study placed Peru among the bottom third in support for the political system among the Latin American countries where polls conducted. In the same poll, Peru is among the lowest four countries in support for the idea of democracy and trust in the judicial system. It is therefore not surprising that about 13 percent of those interviewed in 2012 said they had participated in a protest the previous year, among the three highest rates in the region.

THE INTERNATIONAL ENVIRONMENT

The combination of deep domestic economic crisis and changing international realities contributed to a dramatic shift in Peru's foreign economic policies in the 1990s. Privatization and economic liberalization opened up the country once again to private investment. Economic nationalism receded rapidly as a cornerstone of Peru's foreign relations. Over the 1990s, scores of public enterprises were privatized, tariffs slashed, foreign debt repayments resumed, and legal foundations for private investment restored. Foreign investment more than doubled—from about US$4 billion in 1993 to more than US$9 billion in 1998. Peru led efforts to reconstitute the Andean Pact as the Andean Group on terms much more favorable to private sector activity. In addition, the international financial community became a major source of government development programs once again. Although foreign debt increased to more than US$30 billion by 1998, with scheduled repayments running at about half of export earnings, most specialists continued to see Peru as a good credit risk.

Perhaps Peru's most significant foreign policy success in recent decades was the successful negotiation with Ecuador of a definitive border settlement in 1998. The Peru-Ecuador boundary dispute had been Latin America's longest-lasting and had provoked almost two dozen armed clashes between the countries even after the issue was supposedly resolved by treaty (the Rio Protocol) in 1942. The most violent was the major confrontation between January and March 1995, which cost the two countries more than US$1 billion and hundreds of casualties.

Full normalization of relations with its neighbors was bolstered by a resolution of the United Nations International Court of Justice located in The Hague over a maritime dispute with Chile. Peru had brought the case to the Court, arguing that the maritime border had not been delimited. Despite Chile's objections, the Court agreed to hear the dispute, and its ruling on January 28, 2014, established a boundary that largely sided with Peru's claims. Although tensions between the two countries were reduced as a result, Chile protested Peru's 2015 decision to create a new administrative district in Tacna, claiming it included land that is Chilean, part of former Peruvian territory gained in the War of the Pacific.

The role of US public and private engagement with Peru has always been quite complex. Private investment grew rapidly in the early twentieth century but was almost exclusively in isolated enclaves on the north coast (oil and sugar, then later cotton and fish meal) and in the sierra (copper, other minerals, and later iron). Successive governments encouraged such investment. Even during the reformist military government, in spite of some expropriations and a conscious attempt to diversify sources of foreign investment, substantial new US investment took place, particularly in copper (Southern Peru Copper Company) and oil exploration and production (Occidental Petroleum Company).

The Belaúnde government's policy toward private investment was more open but only partly successful owing to international and domestic economic problems. The first García administration's nationalistic posture in a context of growing economic and political difficulties discouraged most new investment, both domestic and foreign, between 1985 and 1990. Fujimori's shift to privatization and economic liberalization began slowly, given Peru's grave problems, but gathered momentum beginning in 1993 with several hundred million dollars in portfolio and direct investments.

Between 1993 and 1998, more than one hundred public enterprises were privatized and more than US$6 billion in new foreign investment generated. Spanish investment was the largest, with US$2.4 billion of the US$9.8 billion total as of 1998; US second, with US$1.6 billion; and British third, with US$1.2 billion. Policies favorable to foreign investment continued during both the Toledo and the second García governments, with the 2007 Free Trade Agreement with the United States offering added incentives. Even so, there is concern among some sectors of the public over the negative environmental effects of some investments, especially those in mining.

The US role in anti-drug programs in Peru since the mid-1990s has been quite controversial. Funds for eradication and alternative development have had an impact on cocaine production, but interdiction of planes that appeared to be transporting drugs was suspended after a US missionary's plane was mistakenly shot down in 1999. During the latter years of the increasingly undemocratic Fujimori administration, US policy favored anti-drug activity over pressure to maintain democratic practice. With both the Toledo and the second García governments, continuing counternarcotic activity has contributed to significant increases in organized resistance by coca growers as well as new activity by a Shining Path remnant, posing additional challenges for Peruvian authorities. American concerns over narcotics issues have been less salient recently; therefore, the Humala administration did not have to confront difficult choices that could have stirred domestic unrest.

CONCLUSION

Peru as an independent nation has had great difficulty in overcoming its authoritarian legacy. For about three-fourths of its history, nondemocratic governments have ruled the country. The legacy of Spanish colonial rule was an important factor impeding the evolution of liberal-democratic institutions in the nineteenth century. In the twentieth, additional considerations—including international market forces, the incorporation of more and more of the population into the national political and economic system, and political leadership perceptions and actions—prevented the emergence of a stable institutional structure.

The reformist military governments of 1968 to 1980 tried but failed to construct a new participatory model of community-based politics and a new economic model based on a leading role for the state. Their failure had its origin in their inability to appreciate the boundaries within which reformers must operate in order to accomplish development objectives. In particular, they did not grasp the degree to which political leaders in a country like Peru are hemmed in by forces largely beyond their control.

Then, although full electoral democracy established in 1980 began with great enthusiasm and promise, it soon fell prey to some of the same problems that had undermined its authoritarian predecessors. It also had to cope with Latin America's most radical and violent guerrilla organization, the Shining Path, and it handled that challenge poorly for almost a decade before major changes in approach brought success. A combination of circumstances and political leadership predispositions led to the dismantling of democracy in 1992 with Fujimori's autogolpe. Nevertheless, President Fujimori succeeded where his civilian predecessors had failed by pursuing a new strategy to deal with Shining Path and by implementing a new economic liberalization model that ended hyperinflation and restored economic growth. These successes gave him the popular support necessary to set up a new political system under the constitution of 1993. This system contained democratic forms and procedures, but numerous mechanisms as well that concentrated power in the presidency.

Although many new government agencies and programs worked to benefit the less privileged at the periphery, the quality of democracy and democratic discourse in the center was progressively eroded. Most of the media were cowed, and opponents were often harassed and intimidated. Peru became a prime example in Latin America of a government that manipulated democratic procedures to ensure its own continuance in power. The result was democratic in form but authoritarian in substance—Peru's latest manifestation of its long authoritarian tradition.

After the fall of Fujimori in late 2000, however, elected presidential succession has become the new normal. Competitive democracy has returned, and the progressive normalization of democratic politics is a praiseworthy development. In addition, Peru's economy has grown impressively in the last fifteen years, although less vigorously beginning in 2013. Along with democratic procedures and economic growth, sociodemographic changes are also transforming the nation in significant ways. Today, most Peruvians are healthier and live longer, reside in urban centers, enjoy smaller families, and are highly interconnected.

However, the process of modernization is uneven and has left unresolved longstanding issues of economic development and inequality. Peru is confronting, painfully and slowly, the legacy of an authoritarian past, an economic model that relies too heavily on the exports of primary products, and a state that frequently ignores the plight of the indigenous population. At the same time, the country is trying to chart a future of democracy and development in the midst of pent-up demands and unmet needs. Peru's democracy could become stronger and more inclusive, or it could succumb once again to the enormity of the task.

Democratic practice under Toledo was chaotic and problematic, even in the midst of sustained economic growth; at the same time, his government showed that democracy can survive an unpopular president. The second García administration surprised many by stabilizing the democratic process in spite of some continuing issues that have not been handled well. The trajectory of Humala, to the surprise of many of his early detractors, indicated that Peru was not ready to travel the path of radical and authoritarian populism of some of the Andean nations. Defying predictions, the vituperative 2016 election campaign and Kuczynski's narrowest of victories over Keiko Fujimori did not create a political crisis but was quickly accepted by all.

Concerns remain, however, over deep citizen dissatisfaction with institutions that have failed to provide them with physical security and are still affected by unacceptable levels of corruption and impunity. Likewise, the ongoing absence of well-organized parties that can channel popular protests in a local climate of disquiet and unrest undermine citizen trust in the ability of democracy to provide order and tranquility. This is especially true when government agencies and officers are seen as not being responsive to drug production and trafficking, other illegal activities, and important local issues as they emerge. There is much to celebrate about Peru's continuing embrace of democracy but no cause for complacency, for serious problems remain.

SUGGESTIONS FOR FURTHER READING

Burt, Jo Marie. *Political Violence and the Authoritarian State in Peru: Silencing Civil Society*. Basingstoke: Palgrave Macmillan, 2008.

Carrión, Julio F., ed. *The Fujimori Legacy: The Rise of Electoral Authoritarianism in Peru*. University Park: Pennsylvania State University Press, 2006.

——— and Patricia Zárate. *Cultura política de la democracia en el Perú y las Américas: Gobernabilidad democrática a través de 10 años del Barómetro de las Américas*. Lima: Vanderbilt University-Instituto de Estudios Peruanos, 2015.

Conaghan, Catherine. *Fujimori's Peru: Deception in the Public Sphere*. Pittsburgh, PA: University of Pittsburgh Press, 2005.

Fumerton, Mario. *From Victims to Heroes: Peasant Counter-Rebellion and Civil War in Ayacucho, Peru, 1980–2000*. Amsterdam: Thela Publishers, 2002.

Levitt, Barry. *Power in the Balance: Presidents, Parties, and Legislators in Peru and Beyond*. South Bend, IN: University of Notre Dame Press, 2012.

Mares, David, and David Scott Palmer. *Power, Institutions, and Leadership in War and Peace: Lessons from Peru and Ecuador, 1995–1998*. Austin: University of Texas Press, 2012.

McClintock, Cynthia, and Fabian Vallas. *The United States and Peru: Cooperation—At a Cost*. New York: Routledge, 2003.

Murakami, Yusuke. *Perú en la era del Chino: La política no institucionalizada y el pueblo en busca del un Salvador*. 2nd ed. Lima: Instituto de Estudios Peruanos, 2012.

Palmer, David Scott, ed. *Shining Path of Peru*. 2nd ed. New York: St. Martin's Press, 1994.

———. "Countering Terrorism in Latin America: The Case of Shining Path in Peru," in James J. C. Forest, ed. *Essentials of Counterterrorism*. Santa Barbara, CA: ABC-CLIO, 2015, 251–270.

Pásara, Luis, ed. *Perú ante los desafíos del siglo XXI*. Lima: Fondo Editorial Pontificia Universidad Católica del Perú, 2011.

Plaza, Orlando, ed. *Cambios sociales en el Perú 1968–2008. Homenaje a Denis Sulmont*. 2nd ed. Lima: Fondo Editorial-Pontificia Universidad Católica del Perú, 2012.

Quiroz, Alfonso W. *Corrupt Circles: A History of Unbound Graft in Peru*. Baltimore: Johns Hopkins University Press, 2008.

Schuldt, Jürgen. *Bonanza macroeconómica y malestar microeconómico*. Lima: Universidad del Pacífico-Centro de Investigación, 2005.

St John, Ronald Bruce. *Toledo's Peru: Vision and Reality*. Gainesville: University Press of Florida, 2010.

Stern, Steve J., ed. *Shining and Other Paths: War and Society in Peru, 1980–1995*. Durham, NC: Duke University Press, 1998.

Zavaleta, Mauricio. *Coaliciones de independientes: Las reglas no escritas de la política electoral*. Lima: Instituto de Estudios Peruanos, 2014.

13

VENEZUELA: POLITICAL DECAY AMID THE STRUGGLE FOR REGIME LEGITIMACY

David J. Myers

INTRODUCTION

On December 7, 2016, the Executive Secretary of the opposition Democratic Unity Table (MUD), Jesús "Chúo" Torrealba, called a national press conference. He announced that the MUD would not participate in the next scheduled meeting of the dialogue with the government of Nicolás Maduro, set for January 13, 2017. In short order, several leaders of the most important political parties belonging to the MUD issued statements supporting Torrealba's position. One party leader, Julio Borges of Justice First (PJ), stated that there would be no participation by the opposition on that or any other date if government did not deliver on promises made to the opposition as prerequisites for entering into dialogue.

President Maduro laid down his government's conditions for entering into structured talks with the opposition in mid-October 2016. Most important, he demanded that the opposition call off public demonstrations aimed at forcing him to resign. In late October, the MUD complied. The MUD also pulled back from putting President Maduro on trial in the National Assembly for abandonment of his constitutional responsibilities. In addition, the MUD muted its demand for a recall referendum prior to January 13, the date after which a successful recall would allow the Chavista vice president, a follower of President Hugo Chávez, to serve out the remainder of the vacant presidential term. A recall election prior to that date would have triggered a new presidential election. Public opinion polls indicated that the opposition would succeed in the recall and that in all probability the opposition candidate would win the presidential election. Nicolás Maduro responded to the MUD's pullback with promises to accept MUD conditions for dialogue. First, he agreed to allow for the importation of food and medicine—both in short supply. Second, he agreed to release political prisoners. Finally, he agreed to develop a timetable for elections that would allow voters to decide if he should remain in office.

The MUD demanded that the Supreme Tribunal of Justice (TSJ) respect the National Assembly's constitutional powers. At issue were control over the central government's budget and the Assembly's right to determine the validity of its members' election credentials. The strong salience of this demand sprang from the results of the December 2015 National Assembly elections. Opposition political parties won those elections and made one of their own President of the Assembly. The Chavistas, however, controlled the TSJ. Before the new Assembly had constituted itself the TSJ invalidated the election of three opposition deputies from the state of Amazonas. When the Assembly refused to accept the TSJ ruling, the court deprived the Assembly of its legislative powers.

Torrealba stated at his press conference that the MUD had honored all conditions set by President Maduro for government participation in the dialogue, and charged that the President had reneged on his promises. Thus, there was no good reason for the MUD to continue dialoguing with the government.

The chief government negotiator, Caracas mayor Jorge Rodríguez, disagreed. He opined that President Maduro was arranging for the entry of more food and medicine into the country. He pointed out that the government had released several prisoners and that additional negotiations would yield an electoral timetable. Rodriguez also argued that the 1999 constitution gave the TSJ authority to determine if the actions of other branches of government were in violation of the constitution.

In summary, Venezuelan politics were deadlocked at the close of 2016. Political paralysis and economic misery presaged serious turbulence for 2017.

BACKGROUND

Geography and history have shaped contemporary Venezuelan politics. Nestled in the northeastern quadrant of South America between 1 and 13 degrees north of the equator, Venezuela is hot and tropical. Cool temperatures predominate only at altitudes above 3,280 feet (1,000 meters). The country's 31.8 million inhabitants live in an area of 352,150 square miles (912,050 square kilometers), roughly the size of Texas and Oklahoma combined. Stretching some 1,750 miles (2,816 kilometers) along the Caribbean Sea and the Atlantic Ocean, Venezuela extends south into continental South America. It encompasses snow-covered mountains rising to 16,427 feet (5,007 meters, Pico Bolívar) and reaches into the Orinoco and Amazon jungles. Some 3,000 miles (4,800 kilometers) of continental borders form frontiers with Colombia, Brazil, and Guyana. The Orinoco River, one of the largest and most navigable in the world, drains four-fifths of the country. But the mountains, not the river or the plains, have historically been Venezuela's most influential geographical features. The dominant colonial settlements, agricultural estates, and urban centers are nestled in cool mountain valleys, and until 1925 when petroleum extraction became Venezuela's most important economic activity, these valleys formed the unchallenged heartland of the nation.

Geographers divide Venezuela into five regions: the Guyana Highlands, the Orinoco Lowlands, the Northern Mountains, the Maracaibo Basin/Coastal Lowlands, and the numerous small islands along the Caribbean coast. These regions vary immensely in size, resources, climate, population, and historical input.

The Guyana Highlands, encompassing 45 percent of the national territory, is the largest region. Historically remote, poor, and sparsely populated, Guyana became a symbol in the 1950s of the nation's drive to industrialize. Guyana's industrial and mining centers remain oases of modern civilization surrounded by tropical forests. Until the 1950s Guyana exerted little influence on national affairs, but subsequent government investment in the region has made Guyana's industrial infrastructure central to Venezuela's development aspirations.[1]

Lying between the southernmost part of Venezuela and the coastal mountains are the great grassland prairies (*llanos*) of the Orinoco Lowlands. Occupying 33 percent of the national territory, the llanos support 20 percent of the population. For six months of the year this vast, featureless plain, 620 miles (1,000 kilometers) long and 400 miles (645 kilometers) wide, is subject to rainfall so heavy that much of it lies under water. As the ensuing dry season progresses, the mud turns to deep layers of dust, the heat becomes intense, and streams dry up. Although the region is far from ideal for raising cattle, a type of culture based on that industry has grown there and continues to be managed by a rough—and for many years lawless—breed of man (*el llanero*).

The Northern Mountains is the third major geographical region. Although they encompass only 12 percent of Venezuela's land area, the mountains support roughly two-thirds of the country's population. The principal mountain chain consists of the coastal range and the Sierra Nevada de Mérida. In the coastal range are found the capital city of Caracas, the Valencia-Maracay industrial center, large coffee holdings, sugar *haciendas*, and rich farmlands surrounding Lake Valencia.

The high and rugged Sierra Nevada de Mérida is a spur of the Andes. With peaks rising to 16,400 feet (5,000 meters), the region's early inaccessibility discouraged great agricultural estates (*latifundios*). The Venezuelan Andes were thus characterized by medium-sized landholdings and populated by small clusters of people, both *mestizos* and Indians. Despite the presence of an influential university in the city of Mérida, Andean Venezuela remained isolated until the rise of coffee as a commercial crop.

Ten percent of Venezuela's national territory consists of a narrow, partly arid, partly swampy belt of lowland lying between the steeply rising coastal mountains and the Caribbean Sea. This region comprises the Maracaibo Basin and the Coastal Lowlands. Much of Venezuela's oil is found in the Maracaibo Basin, and the region's drained swampland has been transformed into rich farms and cattle ranches. However, more than 80 percent of the Basin's inhabitants are classified as urban. Most reside in Greater Maracaibo, the country's second largest metropolitan region. Tourism is the most important economic activity of the eastern Coastal Lowlands. Here are located the best Caribbean beaches, and the climate is clear and dry. African influence is stronger in this region than anywhere else in Venezuela.

Most Venezuelans are an amalgam of Caucasian, indigenous, and black. They have a common culture, predominantly Hispanic but with important indigenous and African strands. Overwhelmingly Roman Catholic (85 percent) and Spanish-speaking, Venezuelans view themselves as members of a single ethnic mixture. The national census does not classify according to race or ethnicity (except for indigenous people in the Orinoco and Amazon jungles), so it is only possible to make educated guesses. Pure Caucasians comprise between 10 to 15 percent of the total population. Perhaps 10 percent of Venezuelans are black, less than 3 percent are pure indigenous, and between 70 and 80 percent are of mixed ancestry. Ethnic mixing has occurred at all social levels. Nevertheless, Caucasian features are valued, and their predominance is greater among the higher social and economic strata.

Internal migration since World War II has transformed Venezuela from a rural society into one that is highly urbanized. Initially, Caracas received a disproportionate number of these migrants, mushrooming from a metropolitan region of about five hundred thousand in 1945 to a diverse metropolis of more than five million in 2015. Four other cities—Maracaibo, Valencia, Barquisimeto, and Barcelona-Puerto/La Cruz—boast populations of more than one million. In contrast, large areas of rural Venezuela are depopulated. Census estimates in 2015 placed the total urban population at just over 80 percent of the total national population.

CULTURE CLASH AND POLITICAL CONFLICT

Two political cultures coexist uneasily in post-Chávez Venezuela. A single political culture permeates followers of Hugo Chávez, the Chavistas. Some Chavistas support the government of President Nicolás Maduro (2013–present). Others believe he should be replaced—either because Maduro's continuance in office threatens the survival of Hugo Chávez's Bolivarian Revolution or because Maduro is seen as having betrayed that revolution. The political culture of Chavismo's opponents is more diverse. It encompasses groups and leaders that the Chavistas displaced during the years (1999–2007) when they were dismantling the liberal democracy (known as Punto Fijo) that had ordered Venezuelan political life between 1958 and 1998. The liberal democrats ranged from free marketers to Christian and Social Democrats, and included radical socialists. Hugo Chávez's destruction of Punto Fijo forced liberal democrats into a heterogeneous alliance. Despite ideological differences they coordinate their political efforts to survive and in hope of ending Chavista rule. Opponents of Chavismo also share the preference for some form of a pluralistic democracy.[2]

Examining political culture helps in five ways to understand Venezuelan politics. First, it frames the context in which politics occurs. Second, it links individual and collective identities by identifying significant connections between the fate of individuals and the group. Third, it defines group boundaries by organizing actions within and between them. Fourth, culture provides a framework for interpreting the actions and motives of others. Finally, culture supplies resources for political organization and mobilization.[3] We probe these five components when we examine the political culture of the Chavistas and their opponents.

Framing the Political Context

The environment that framed the political culture of Chavismo's opponents was struggle against General Pérez Jiménez's dictatorship. Those who overthrew Pérez Jiménez imposed Punto Fijo, which lasted forty years. Its hallmark, the Pact of Punto Fijo, was an agreement to share power. The primary beneficiaries were the three victorious political parties—Democratic Action (AD), the Christian Democrats (COPEI), and the Democratic Republican Union (URD). Their leaders also agreed to share economic policy making with the traditional oligarchy and permitted the Roman Catholic Church to retain an important role in education. Punto Fijo's dominant elites viewed power sharing as their best shot at preventing the return of military dictatorship. The Pact of Punto Fijo did not include the Venezuelan Communist Party (PCV).

The PCV and leftist factions in AD, COPEI, and URD reacted against the Pact of Punto Fijo by joining the PCV in an insurgency that lasted for more than a decade. In the early 1970s Punto Fijo elites defeated the insurgency. They allowed their vanquished rivals to participate in electoral politics as long as they abstained from guerrilla warfare. AD and COPEI tilted the electoral playing field to benefit themselves. Unprecedented income to the Venezuelan state from the sale of petroleum ensured that even minor political parties could develop clientelistic networks.

The PCV and other radical leftists never fully accepted Punto Fijo's legitimacy. When the petroleum income roller coaster took a downward turn in the 1980s, political parties could not sustain their clientelistic networks. State-controlled industries went bankrupt, bureaucracies were starved for resources, and military funding contracted. Unemployment increased. Corruption had been tolerated in times of plenty, but it fueled outrage when the economy contracted. Blame for political, economic, and moral decay delegitimized AD and COPEI.

The youthful and charismatic Lt. Col. Hugo Chávez Frías became the agent for political change. He attempted an unsuccessful military coup on February 4, 1992. President Rafael Caldera pardoned the imprisoned lieutenant colonel after he took office in 1994. Hugo Chávez went on to win the presidential election of December 6, 1998. He promised to replace Punto Fijo with a regime that would empower "the People." A new political culture coalesced that directed its ire at liberal democracy. It elevated the Punto Fijo's oppressed masses to the status of *El Soberano* (the Sovereign Ones). El Soberano should wield absolute political power.

Linking Individual and Collective Identities

The second component of the political culture approach, to repeat, links the fate of individuals sharing a culture to the fate of groups. In Venezuela, Chavista and opposition political cultures have distinctive linkages. Identifying these linkages leads to an understanding of how the sense of a common destiny among Chavistas and among their opponents shapes collective action. Shaping involves two distinct elements: the strong reinforcement between individual and collective identity that renders culturally sanctioned behavior rewarding and the attitude that outsiders will treat oneself and other members of one's group in similar ways.

The sense of shared identity is stronger among Chavistas. The most important Chavista shared identity is that of having escaped oppression. They are no longer

victims of corrupt and immoral Punto Fijo democracy. Punto Fijo allowed the ruling classes to steal Venezuela's petroleum wealth. They used that wealth for their own
selfish ends. Under the leadership of Hugo Chávez, the exploited and downtrodden,
as we have seen, became El Soberano. Members of El Soberano are expected to give
preference to each other. They unite to prevent the return to power of Punto Fijo elites.
However, division exists between shantytown residents who view themselves as the
soul of Chavismo and bureaucrats who distribute resources and implement government
rules. The political institution for aggregating the interests of Chavismo is the United
Socialist Party of Venezuela (PSUV).

The glue that binds government opponents is affection and nostalgia for the alleged
freedom and limited pluralism of Punto Fijo politics. Even while recognizing the regime's shortcomings, the opponents of Chavismo view Punto Fijo as having been more
democratic than Chavismo. The opposition, however, includes groups with diverse interests that often conflict. Some would barely be on speaking terms if they did not view
the power and behavior of Chavismo as a threat to their very existence. Their umbrella
political institution, the MUD, is a survival alliance. MUD leaders can never be sure
if their strategic decisions will be supported by all factions of the alliance. However, as
the government of President Nicolás Maduro has become more authoritarian, cohesion
inside the MUD has increased.

Defining Group Boundaries

The third dimension of political culture defines group boundaries and organizes actions within and between them. This process specifies expectations concerning patterns
of association within and between groups. All Chavistas are expected to join the revolutionary political party, the PSUV. Democratic centralism marks decision making
inside the PSUV. The boundary between the PSUV and the government is perme-
able. Venezuelan President Nicolás Maduro is president of the PSUV. Other important
Chavista institutions that strengthen the movement's hold on power are the Community Councils and the Francisco Miranda Front. For them, advancing revolutionary
priorities takes precedence over compliance with the law and regulations. Government
positions at all levels are reserved for Chavistas, as are contracts to supply economic
goods. Active opposition to the government justifies the denial of government benefits
ranging from medical attention to housing.

The political culture uniting MUD factions holds that citizens should be equal before the law whether they are Chavistas, active opponents, or supporters of neither.
Groups sharing this political culture initially believed that they could coexist with
the Chavistas. They assumed that Chavistas would play by rules that differed little
from those in force during the Punto Fijo era. The decree laws that President Chávez
issued in November 2001 shattered those expectations. In response, opponents resorted
to demonstrations, violence, and electoral boycott to drive Chávez from office. These
efforts failed. This allowed advocates of electoral democracy to gain control of the opposition. In the 2006 presidential election, won by Hugo Chávez, government and opposition both participated. It appeared that agreement was developing regarding rules
of the political game.

After winning the 2006 presidential election Chavistas set in place the most exclusionary tenets of their political culture. After suffering a reverse in the 2007 referendum

to reform the constitution by infusing basic tenets of Chavismo into the constitution, the government imposed these tenets incrementally, over a period of seven years. This deepened loyalty and partisanship among the adherents of each political culture. It also widened the chasm between Chavistas and their opponents. Advocacy of power sharing in political institutions with adherents of the opposing political culture was viewed as the betrayal of core values.

Interpreting the Actions and Motives of Others

The fourth dimension of political culture is the framework it provides for interpreting the actions and motives of others. Actions, like words, are highly ambiguous. There is a need to invoke available "scripts" and "narratives" to help people make sense of ambiguous but emotionally salient situations. One galvanizing script that Chavistas invoke is betrayal. In this script, the political parties of Punto Fijo, especially AD and COPEI, are the villains. Instead of instituting revolutionary policies after overthrowing General Pérez Jiménez, AD and COPEI purged revolutionaries from their parties and waged a brutal war against them. A second galvanizing Chavista script portrays the party-dominated governments of Punto Fijo as corrupt and self-serving. The third script criticizes Punto Fijo elites as having sold out Venezuela to imperialists in the United States and western Europe. These scripts cultivate feelings of righteous indignation. Chavista political culture also views the motives and actions of opposition groups as subterfuge to restore Punto Fijo degeneracy.

The scripts uniting Chavista opponents see Punto Fijo in a different light. One portrays the actions of AD and COPEI upon attaining power in 1958 as heroic. Against all odds leaders of these parties established a liberal democracy that reconciled previously hostile groups and interests. This script justified the military campaign against radical leftists, who they portray as tools of communist imperialism. Another opposition political culture script claims that toleration of dissent marked Punto Fijo. It argues that once leftist insurgents abandoned efforts to overthrow liberal democracy by force, they enjoyed freedom of speech and participated in electoral politics.

The opposition political cultural script assessing the policies and behavior of Punto Fijo governments after 1973 resembles that of Chavismo. Both agree that AD and COPEI became self-absorbed and that allied economic elites made major mistakes in managing the economy. The two political cultures point to crony capitalism in the private sector and decry corruption in the central bureaucracy. They disagree when assessing efforts by Punto Fijo reformers to correct the abuses. Opposition scripts argue that reforms were made in good faith and proved beneficial. They also assert that efforts were made to work with Chavistas to deepen reforms after Hugo Chávez's election in December 1998, but that his government wanted no input from any groups associated with Punto Fijo. Chavismo emerges in the opposition narrative as fostering pervasive partisanship.

Providing Assets for Political Organization

Fifth and finally, culture provides assets for political organization and mobilization. It offers significant material and psychological resources that leaders and groups use as instruments of organization and mobilization. After Hugo Chávez gained approval for the 1999 constitution, one of his first acts was to terminate the practice of financing the election campaigns of political parties. During Punto Fijo, political parties received funds from the National Electoral Council. The Chavista political narrative portraying Punto Fijo parties as corrupt and self-serving dictated eliminating these funds. Electoral organizations fielding candidates supported by the Chavistas received government funds.

Economic good fortune delivered assets to Hugo Chávez's government. When Chávez came to power, a barrel of Venezuelan petroleum sold on the international market for roughly US$10. During the eighteen years of Chavista rule, a barrel of petroleum sold for as much as US$125. This allowed President Hugo Chávez to fund programs known as *Misiones*. These programs bypassed the traditional bureaucracy to assist shantytown residents and other previously excluded groups. They provided health care, housing, and a host of infrastructure improvements. Recipients formed attachments to President Chávez and his government because of them. It was an important reason why Chavistas believed that preservation of the "revolution" had the highest priority. If unfavorable election results threatened Chavista control it was acceptable, even imperative, that they be nullified.

The opposition, not surprisingly, commanded far fewer resources once Hugo Chávez assumed power. AD and COPEI no longer controlled national bureaucracies or state corporations, the source of bloated contracts that had enabled them to nourish their client networks. The power and influence of AD and COPEI evaporated. Some new opposition political parties appeared. Most funding for the newcomers came from entrepreneurs threatened by the government's socialist policies. Middle-class professionals and industrial workers provided votes for opposition political parties.

SOCIAL STRUCTURE, SOCIAL CHANGES, CIVIL SOCIETY, AND INTEREST GROUPS

Historical and Political Economy

The history of Venezuela is one of progressive integration into the North Atlantic area. Crucial in this process were the pacification and development programs initiated by General Antonio Guzmán Blanco (1870–1888) and consolidated by General Juan Vicente Gómez (1908–1935). Over the final decade of Gómez's rule (1925–1935) the commercial bureaucratic system gave way to a "petroleum-based technological imperium." This arrangement was and is the product of opportunities and complexities endemic to petroleum exploitation. Transformation involved creating modern systems of transportation and communication and diffusing industrial technology into the oilfields. It also facilitated the intervention of foreign interest groups and ideologies in Venezuela's internal politics.

The petroleum-based technological imperium enabled Venezuela's journey from primitive dictatorship (1935–1958) through party-centered democracy (1959–1999) to the current "twenty-first century socialism." This journey began in the late 1920s, even before the passing of General Juan Vicente Gómez, who ruled for twenty-seven years (1908–1935). At that time the demands of managing the new extractive economy exceeded the capabilities of the nineteenth-century commercial bureaucratic structures to broker social, economic, and political conflict. This prompted the search for new institutions, and growing US influence throughout the Caribbean led Gómez's successors to experiment with limited political democracy. The elitist tenor of this experiment proved its undoing.

On October 18, 1945, junior military officers joined with working- and middle-class reformers to seize power in a short but bloody coup d'état. Democracy for the few gave way to democracy for the masses. Democratic Action gained control of the government and passed legislation that began to redistribute wealth, power, and cultural authority. The upper and middle classes turned to the military for protection. On November 24, 1948, the armed forces overthrew the popularly elected government of Rómulo Gallegos, outlawed AD, and imposed a military junta to govern the country.

The military held power for a decade. After an initial economic boom fueled by revenue from petroleum the price of oil plummeted. The economic situation became critical in 1957, leading financial elites to criticize the military regime openly. General Marcos Pérez Jiménez, the president, attempted to counter declining support with increased repression. This only stiffened the resolve of his enemies, who received assistance from the US government. Early in the morning of January 23, 1958, after Pérez Jiménez lost control of Caracas, he fled the country.[4]

Fair and open elections occurred at the end of 1958. Rómulo Betancourt (AD) won the presidency and AD gained control of congress. The opportunistic Democratic Republican Union, the Social Christian Party, and the Venezuelan Communist Party elected significant congressional delegations. Those three major political parties agreed to share power. The Pact of Punto Fijo[5] gave to partisans from these three groups bureaucratic positions and a place in the leadership of each major interest group organization (e.g., the Labor Confederation, the Peasant Federation, and professional associations such as the Engineering Guild). The three parties implemented a reformist agenda.

The Petroleum Roller Coaster and Institutional Stress

The flow of revenue from petroleum to Venezuela's central government between 1958 and the present has varied greatly. These ups and downs strongly influenced the development of political institutions. Escalating petroleum revenue helped to consolidate liberal democracy in the 1970s, and declines in the 1980s contributed to its unraveling.

The first government of the 1990s, the second presidency of Carlos Andrés Pérez, began on February 2, 1989. During his presidential campaign, Pérez played on his image as the political leader who presided over boom times in the 1970s. Thus, Venezuelans were stunned when three weeks after his inauguration Pérez announced that foreign reserves were severely depleted, that in 1988 the country had run a fiscal deficit exceeding 9 percent of the GDP, and that the current account of the balance of payments had its largest deficit in history. In addition, all prices in the economy—from interest rates and black beans to medicines and bus fares—were artificially low and impossible to maintain. The president warned that only bitter medicine could cure these maladies. But when he administered the first dose, a week of rioting and looting (an event known as the *Caracazo*) left more than three hundred dead. Fallout from the Caracazo weakened President Pérez and doomed efforts by his successor to restore the regime's legitimacy.

In the immediate aftermath of the February 1989 rioting there was reason to hope that Carlos Andrés Pérez might salvage Punto Fijo democracy. Venezuela settled into a deceptive calm even though conditions screamed that the petroleum-fueled distribution network could no longer sustain existing institutions.[6] President Pérez used this calm to initiate a neoliberal economic package, the Great Turnaround. This radical departure from the past relied on four sets of policies: macroeconomic stabilization, trade liberalization, privatization, and deregulation.

Early in the decade Venezuela's economy set world records. These records, however, masked the deterioration of state institutions. Carried into policy areas such as health care, transportation, housing, and agriculture, poor performance by the state further undermined the quality of life for most Venezuelans. Purchasing power also declined. This damaged the government's legitimacy even more. The societal deterioration that eroded support for Pérez also extended to the armed forces. As early as the 1970s the professional military promotion system was relaxed and politicized. This spurred partisan rivalries inside the officer corps, thereby intensifying incentives for aspiring officers and their protégés to block or even sabotage the career development and possibilities for promotion of their rivals. Until the mid-1980s fiscal downturn, those who lost in this byzantine competition received mid-level executive positions within the myriad of state enterprises.

The crisis broke on February 4, 1992. A group of junior military officers calling themselves the Bolivarian Military Movement attempted a coup that almost succeeded. Although much in the Movement's program was confused, its call for the affluent and dishonest to be tried for crimes against the nation struck a responsive chord. Thus, although the coup failed, it emboldened the opponents of President Pérez, his austerity plan, and even long-forgotten enemies of post-1958 liberal democracy.

The fifteen months that separated the February 1992 coup attempt from President Pérez's suspension from office in May 1993 proved remarkable for their turbulence and intensifying opposition to his government. Former President Rafael Caldera stopped just short of proclaiming that the Bolivarian Military Movement's cause was just. In late November 1992, the military (this time the navy, air force, and marines) mounted a second unsuccessful coup. Venezuela's once-robust macroeconomic indicators faded. The following May, Attorney General Ramón Escobar Salom presented evidence that President Pérez had misused government funds. The Supreme Court then found "merit" in these charges, and the Senate suspended Pérez from office.

The eight months that followed raised more questions than they answered. After AD and COPEI came to an agreement, their senators selected one of their own, Ramón J. Velásquez, as interim president. Velásquez oversaw free and open elections in December 1993 for president, congress, and the state legislatures. However, during his brief stewardship the economy failed to recover, privatization stalled, and bitterness over declining living standards intensified.

Rafael Caldera, Velasquez's elected successor, initially attempted to set the clock back to a past that he viewed positively—the years of his first presidency (1969–1974). He blamed corruption and the neoliberal policies of Carlos Andrés Pérez for the country's ills, and moved against Pérez's backers in the financial community. The unintended consequence of that decision was the collapse of the entire banking system, which severely damaged the government's ability to grow the economy.

In July 1996 Caldera made a complete turnaround and negotiated an agreement with the International Monetary Fund that reinstated many of the neoliberal reforms (as a program called *Agenda Venezuela*) that he had previously criticized. The fruits of Caldera's earlier policies, despite their popularity when first announced, were an inflation rate of 103 percent (1996) and an increase in the foreign public debt to US$26.5 billion. When it came to implementing Agenda Venezuela, President Caldera recentralized the state. He and Luis Alfaro Ucero, the secretary general of AD, allied in the congress to give the national executive new powers to amend the consumer protection law and intervene in the foreign exchange market. This unmasked the AD as the silent partner in an unpopular government.

Blowback and Bolivarianism

Opportunity to change the political regime came with the national elections of December 6, 1998. Voters went to the polls to choose the president and members of congress. COPEI and AD nominated presidential candidates with fatal flaws. Just prior to the presidential voting, these parties abandoned their nominees and threw their support behind the promising but ultimately unsuccessful candidacy of Enrique Salas Römer, the maverick governor of Carabobo. The real story of the presidential election campaign, however, was the meteoric rise of Hugo Chávez.

Chávez won the 1998 election and rewrote the rules of Venezuelan politics. At his February 1999 inauguration, he vowed to replace the existing "moribund" and "unjust" order with a new and responsive democracy. He quickly organized a referendum in which 85 percent of the voters authorized elections that would select delegates to a Constituent Assembly whose charge was to draft a new constitution. Delegates favorable to President Chávez dominated the Constituent Assembly. On December 15, 1999, the government submitted the new constitution to voters for their approval. Seventy-two percent voted in favor, although more than half of the electorate abstained.

Neither President Chávez nor his opponents were totally satisfied with the 1999 constitution. Opponents felt that it gave too much power to the national executive, especially after President Chávez implemented its provisions in ways that allowed his followers to dominate most of the state apparatus. Opposition leaders proclaimed this undemocratic. Conflict between the opposition and the government reached crisis levels after November 2001 when President Chávez enacted a package of forty-nine special laws designed to reverse the neoliberal policies of the 1990s.

Opposition forces attempted an unsuccessful coup, or *golpe del estado* (April 11–13, 2002). Eight months later the opposition attempted to force President Chávez from office through massive demonstrations. With the economy contracting and more violence a real possibility, the government agreed to hold a revocatory referendum. The referendum was held on August 15, 2004, as the economy was beginning to turn around. More than 58 percent of voters expressed the preference for Hugo Chávez to remain as president. Defeat stunned the opposition and allowed President Chávez to increase his domination over the country.

Two subsequent referendums initiated by President Chávez revealed his dissatisfaction with the 1999 constitution. The first referendum took place on December 2, 2007, a year after his election to a second six-year term as president. The paramount political change proposed by this referendum was the abolition of presidential term limits and the allowance of the indefinite reelection of the president (but this was not allowed for any other political post). Other important changes expanded social security benefits

to workers in the informal economy, ended the autonomy of the central bank, prohibited large land estates while allowing the state to provisionally occupy property slated
for expropriation before a court has ruled, reduced the maximum working week from
forty-four to thirty-six hours, prohibited foreign funding for political associations, and
prohibited discrimination based on sexual orientation. In addition, the referendum
provided for reorganization of the country's administrative districts and empowered
the president to control elected state governors and mayors through an unelected "popular power."

Voters narrowly rejected the proposal (51 to 49 percent). It was Hugo Chávez's first
loss at the polls since assuming the presidency. Initially he conceded defeat and congratulated the opposition for this victory. Two days later the president called the results
a "*victoria de mierda*" (shitty victory). Manuel Rosales, the most important opposition
candidate in the 2006 presidential election, had a different response. He proclaimed,
"Tonight, Venezuela has won." Inside the Chavista movement, speculation sprang up
over who would succeed the president when his term expired in February of 2013.
The opposition took heart, waged vigorous campaigns in the subnational elections of
November 23, 2008, and scored some surprising victories. Even more ominously, petroleum prices fell as the global recession deepened. Within the president's inner circle there was concern that economic decline would increase dissatisfaction with the
government.

Seven days after the 2008 subnational elections President Chávez seized the initiative. He announced that he would open discussion on the proposal for allowing postulation without limits for the presidential candidate. The initiative, however, received
a mixed reception. Inside the Chavista camp, individuals with presidential aspirations
grumbled. President Chávez defused this discontent by wording the proposed change
so it applied to all popularly elected positions (state governors, mayors, National Assembly deputies, and state legislators), not only to the president. The National Assembly overwhelmingly approved the proposal, which opened the way for the referendum.

On February 15, 2009, 54 percent of voters (abstention was 30 percent) backed the
amendment. Students and others took to the streets in protest, but the police quickly
dispersed them. Most of the international observers found the voting to have been
clean, transparent, and fair. Success strengthened Chávez's authority within the PSUV
and the armed forces. It also disheartened the opposition. Following passage of this
referendum, President Chávez turned to imposing changes that had been rejected by
voters in 2007.

A series of bills passed by the National Assembly and signed into law by the president during December 2010 changed state institutions. Especially significant was the
Law of Socialist Communes that established communal development districts controlled by the Minister of Popular Power for Communes. The authority of the communes, of which there were nearly 1,500 in 2016, blurred existing boundaries between
local (*municipio*) and regional (state) governments. A related matter still in need of
clarification was the dividing line between the authority of the communes, local governments, and the community councils.

On December 29, 2010, the revised Law of Community Councils went into effect.
The community councils had been created in 2005. They were intended to assume
over time most powers that traditionally were reserved for municipio governments.

The 2010 legislation made the community councils official state institutions and provided a path for them to marginalize the municipios. Finally, the National Assembly established the Federal Council of Government, giving it responsibility for defining relations among the communes, the community councils, the municipios, and regional governments.

The institutional changes legislated in December 2010 were implemented hesitatingly. Delay derived from the uncertainty stemming from President Chávez's two-year struggle with cancer, and the electoral calendar. For eighteen months after the President's first cancer surgery in 2011, he insisted that he had become cancer free. But his physical appearance and additional surgeries belied this assessment. Chávez grew weaker during the 2012 presidential election campaign and never appeared in public after he departed for Havana on December 10, 2012, to undergo a fourth cancer surgery. Between the presidential election of October 7 and voting for governors and regional legislators on December 16, government officials devoted most of their time to electioneering. This was also true of the period between Chávez's death on March 4, 2013, and the presidential election of April 14. Nicolás Maduro, Hugo Chávez's designated successor, won that election. Immediately he began implementing the institutional changes legislated in 2010. However, replacing local and regional governments with community councils and communes proved more difficult than the central government anticipated.

Interest Groups and Civil Society

Hugo Chávez stated on more than one occasion that he viewed the checks and balances of liberal democracy as a smoke screen that allowed the upper and middle classes to perpetuate their domination. Chávez's advocacy of direct democracy reflected his preference for populism and affinity for Rousseau. Nevertheless, interest groups are not without influence even after the years of Chavista rule. The military, along with the church and the landed elite, dominated Venezuela from independence until General Pérez Jiménez fled the country on January 23, 1958. The provisional junta that replaced Pérez faced nationwide strikes supported by interests demanding civilian political rule. The armed forces, confused and dispirited, acquiesced to the election as president of their nemesis, Rómulo Betancourt. The counterinsurgency campaign that defeated the guerrillas forged a bond between the armed forces and civilian democratic leaders.

The affinity between Punto Fijo elites and the military weakened after 1989 for several reasons. First, the army was called out on numerous occasions to maintain order as demonstrations against the Pérez and Caldera governments became more frequent. Neither the officer corps nor the enlisted ranks saw this as one of their primary responsibilities. They resented being asked to function as a police force. Second, the inability of the police to deal with demonstrations raised the issue of how law enforcement budgets were spent and increased suspicions of widespread corruption. In addition, the experience of using force against protesting civilians led many in the military to question their support of an unpopular, party-centered regime dominated by gerontocracies that appeared unscrupulous and isolated. Finally, the opulent lifestyles of young politicians and businessmen during the 1990s, when contrasted with the economic difficulties experienced by junior officers, created resentments in the armed forces against the political and economic establishment.

The military was divided into three factions when Hugo Chávez first assumed the presidency. One supported his Bolivarian Revolution, another was vehemently opposed, and a third argued that the armed forces should remain apolitical and focus on professional enhancement. President Chávez, however, wanted the military to become a pillar of support. He launched Plan Bolívar 2000, a legally questionable program that funneled funds for infrastructure maintenance and development through regional military garrisons. Many officers used the opportunities that accompanied the construction of public works for personal enrichment.

By early 2002, factions in the military opposed to President Chávez viewed his leftward drift with concern. On April 11, a march through Caracas by hundreds of thousands of his government's opponents ended in shootings that killed and wounded more than fifteen individuals. Opposition leaders and government security forces blamed each other. This incident became an excuse for military factions opposed to the president to remove him from office. They replaced Chávez with Pedro Carmona Estanga, president of the umbrella business confederation Venezuelan Federation of Chambers of Commerce (FEDECAMARAS). The perpetrators of the coup could not agree on how to organize a government. This gave Chavistas the opportunity to regroup. In less than forty-eight hours, factions loyal to the president took control and returned him to the presidency.[7]

After the coup, President Chávez purged officers suspected of having sympathized with his removal and marginalized all who were not seen as active supporters. In addition, President Chávez organized militias of reserves among unemployed slum dwellers. On January 29, 2005, the secretary of the National Defense Council announced the adoption of a new military doctrine that gave priority to preparing for asymmetric warfare, an activity in which the militias would have an important role. This gave the government a national security rationale for strengthening forces composed of individuals from the socioeconomic strata most supportive of the president.

On July 31, 2008, President Chávez promulgated a new Organic Law of the Armed Forces. The renamed Bolivarian National Armed Forces boasted a strengthened chain of command that allowed the president unprecedentedly direct control over all four services. The law also enshrined protection of the Bolivarian Revolution as a primary obligation of the armed forces. In addition, the law gave formal recognition to the Bolivarian National Militia and subjected the entire population to mobilization at the discretion of the president. Finally, as Venezuela became a primary location for shipping drugs to the North Atlantic region, President Chávez encouraged the armed forces to become involved. Wealth derived from that involvement cemented the loyalty of the armed forces to Chavismo.

The Roman Catholic Church has operated as a political interest group in Venezuela since independence, but the ecclesiastical hierarchy has enjoyed less influence than in other Latin American countries. During the 1960s, after a two-decade conflict with the AD party over state control of education, the church reached an accommodation with AD.[8] Accommodation did not prevent church leaders from expressing their disapproval of corruption, decay in the judiciary, cronyism, inequality, and moral deterioration in the government. The *Centro Guimilla,* a Jesuit think tank, leveled especially biting criticism at AD and COPEI during the 1970s and 1980s. After the urban riots of February 1989 and two unsuccessful coups in 1992, the Episcopal Conference issued public statements intended to put distance between the church and the neoliberal policies of President Carlos Andrés Pérez.

The bishops viewed the rise of Hugo Chávez with alarm. Nevertheless, the ecclesiastical hierarchy took no official position in the referendum that approved the 1999 constitution. After the unsuccessful coup of April 11, 2002, relations between the ecclesiastical hierarchy and the government deteriorated. President Chávez opined on more than one occasion that the church had supported the coup. Influential clerics condemned government policies for undermining democracy. This led President Chávez into a brief flirtation with evangelical Protestantism. However, his enthusiasm for this option cooled when Rev. Pat Robinson, a well-known fundamentalist preacher in the United States, suggested on his *700 Club* television program that President Bush should use the Central Intelligence Agency to "take out" the Venezuelan leader. President Chávez responded with a novel strategy to weaken established religious interests. He imported *babalaos*, or shamans of the Santería religion from Cuba, and installed them in the shantytowns.

President Maduro has maintained a respectful attitude toward the Catholic Church. However, when bishops criticized the government for human rights abuses, he warned them not to takes sides in the conflict between Chavismo and the opposition. After demonstrations increased in September 2016, Maduro accepted the Vatican as a facilitator of a formal dialogue between his government and the opposition.

Private sector interests in Venezuela are diverse, ranging from local agribusinesses to multinational manufacturers. Two hundred individual groups comprise FEDECAMARAS, but the institution is dominated by four pivotal interests: industry, trade, cattle raising, and agriculture. Each possesses its own chamber: CONINDUSTRIA for industry, CONSECOMERCIO for commerce, FENAGAN for cattle raising, and FEDEAGRO for agriculture. Because these key interests have different and sometimes conflicting priorities, the single-interest or intermediate chambers are as important as centers of political demands as FEDECAMARAS. After 1958, the business community adapted to Punto Fijo democracy and prospered.

President Chávez revealed his sympathy for socialist schemes soon after taking office. Relations between the government and the private sector cooled. When the president of FEDECAMARAS agreed to serve as provisional president during the short-lived military government of April 2002, relations turned frigid. In 2007, following his reelection to a second six-year term as president, President Chávez nationalized numerous private enterprises. President Maduro has placed unprecedented restrictions on the remaining businesses, ranging from the setting of "just prices" at which their products must be sold to determining the percentage of that product that must be channeled to state entities. However, like his predecessor, Maduro signed contracts with selected multinationals to exploit reserves of viscous petroleum in the Orinoco tar belt.

Organized labor and peasants, two associational interest groups, played pivotal roles during Punto Fijo. As part of their strategy to wrest power from the entrenched Andean cabal in the 1940s, AD and COPEI organized workers and peasants. A third interest group, professionals, fell under the domination of political parties in the 1970s. All three groups were subject to party discipline. AD and COPEI exercised decisive power and influence over unionized workers, peasants, and professionals until 1999.

227

The

After approval of the 1999 constitution the dominant labor organization, Venezuelan Confederation of Workers (CTV), opened negotiations with President Chávez. Its leaders offered to eliminate the influence of AD and COPEI in their unions in return for recognition by the government. This was unacceptable to the president, who began organizing his own "Bolivarian" trade unions. Consequently, the CTV joined with FEDECAMARAS and other opponents of the government in the strikes that convulsed the country during 2002 and 2003. In March 2003, after breaking the final and most virulent strike, President Chávez discharged sixteen thousand workers belonging to the Federation of Petroleum Workers (FEDEPETROL), as well as six thousand of the petroleum company's elite staff. Contracts with other CTV unions were simply ignored. Still, the CTV persists. CTV and Bolivarian trade unions marched separately in the May Day parades as recently as 2016. But the CTV now is a shadow of its former self.

Until the early 1980s Venezuela's urban poor were only weakly integrated into the Punto Fijo system. This was largely because the political parties having the greatest appeal to slum dwellers lost out to AD and COPEI. The demand-making structures that crystallized among shantytown inhabitants were different from those that AD and COPEI used with their internal "bureaus" of workers, professionals, and peasants. The most important organization to represent Venezuela's urban poor during Punto Fijo was the Center for the Service of Popular Action (CESAP). However, during the 1980s CESAP settled on the strategy of working within the existing party-centric regime. This choice undermined the legitimacy of CESAP when the second Pérez and Caldera governments adopted neoliberalism.

Feeling abandoned by AD and COPEI, the urban poor turned to Hugo Chávez in the presidential elections of 1998 and 2000. Soon after taking office in 1999, Chávez began organizing shantytown residents into Bolivarian Circles. These circles were multifaceted. On the one hand, they taught young women to sew, manage small businesses, and provide needed child care. On the other, they assisted the government in connecting with its supporters and identifying opponents. Bolivarian Circles remained active in most shantytowns during the first decade of Chavista rule. In 2005, as mentioned earlier, the addition of resource-allocating Misiones, administered directly by President Chávez, gave the government a broad range of programs to reward supporters. In general, the Misiones made a positive difference in the lives of shantytown residents. No Chavista innovation has been more popular among the urban poor.

The Misiones are ad hoc creations. They often have been inefficient and wasteful. The December 2010 legislation of the National Assembly merged the Misiones and traditional bureaucracies into a unified socialist public sector. Nevertheless, during the lead-up to the 2012 presidential election, President Chávez launched a massive public housing program that he implemented through a newly created mission (*Gran Misión Vivienda*). The president's decision to organize the set piece of his campaign for reelection as a Misión attested to their continuing popularity. For this reason, progress in crafting a unified socialist sector has been tentative and disjointed.

POLITICAL PARTIES AND ELECTIONS

Venezuela's contemporary political party system evolved from the anti-party consensus that predominated at the end of the 1990s. This consensus reflected disillusionment with the system of strong political parties that controlled the country. Throughout the 1998 presidential campaign, support for the once dominant AD and COPEI parties hovered in single digits. Hugo Chávez organized a loose grouping—The Fifth Republic Movement (MVR)—to coordinate his run for the presidency. Support for him mushroomed in the second quarter of 1998, after the early frontrunner, beauty queen Irene Sáenz, demonstrated that a single term as mayor does not prepare one for presidential leadership. Concern that a Chávez presidency would smash the structure of power led opponents of the surging candidate to unite behind the bid of Enrique Salas Römer, governor of the industrial state of Carabobo. Salas's campaign, like that of Chávez, projected populism and opposition to established political parties. However, unlike Chávez, Salas Römer had belonged to an established political party (COPEI). To many he appeared as more of the same. Chávez swept the December 1998 presidential election, capturing roughly 57 percent of the total vote.

On July 31, 2000, Venezuela held elections for the first time under the 1999 constitution. In those elections voters chose the president, all governors and mayors, and all members of the new unicameral National Assembly. AD and COPEI declined to contest the presidency. President Chávez's only significant challenger was Lieutenant Colonel Francis Arias Cárdenas, his second in command during the unsuccessful military coup of February 4, 1992. Cárdenas claimed to have split with Chávez over the president's anticlericalism and leftward drift.

The dour Arias was no match for the charismatic Chávez. The president captured 60 percent of the total vote, slightly more than in 1998. The MVR and its allies secured 46 percent of the seats in the National Assembly. AD and COPEI together held only 21 percent. The remaining third of the seats were controlled either by allies of the MVR or regional political parties.

Although Hugo Chávez and his allies controlled the National Assembly, they lacked the two-thirds majority necessary for modifying the constitution. This changed on December 4, 2005, when opposition political parties abstained from the National Assembly elections. Their decision in large part was a reaction to suspicions of fraud in the recall referendum of August 2004 and the municipal elections that followed in October. Opposition leaders anticipated that abstention would discredit the elections and force the government to hold one that would be internationally supervised. This proved a disastrous miscalculation. The rate of abstention approached 75 percent, but without opponents the Chavistas captured all 167 seats in the National Assembly.

There was never any doubt that Hugo Chávez would run in the presidential election of December 3, 2006. After much debate the opposition coalesced and participated. Their unity candidate was Manuel Rosales, governor of the oil-rich state of Zulia. Chávez portrayed the election as a choice between revolutionary progress and a return to Punto Fijo democracy. Rosales attacked the government for its international giveaway programs, especially the discounted sales of petroleum to Cuba. He also promised to reduce crime and replace much of the government's social spending with direct grants to individuals. Rosales made a respectable showing, but Chávez won with almost 63 percent of the popular vote. The rate of abstention fell to 25 percent.

President Chávez moved quickly to advance his revolution after winning. He created a new political party, the PSUV. He tasked the PSUV with organizing the masses, recruiting candidates for political office, and socializing citizens. These challenges were beyond the capabilities of the MVR, the proto-party that had run Chavista candidates for office since the 1998 elections.

The PSUV came together in three phases. The first, which began on March 5, 2007, ended on June 10 with the announcement of a timetable for completing the process. Members of the MVR and the Francisco Miranda Front—President Chávez's personal enforcement organization—worked together in a membership drive that resulted in 5,696,305 people signing up as "aspirants to become militants." This number was roughly 80 percent of the votes that Chávez received in the 2006 presidential election. The second phase began on July 31, 2007, when twenty-two thousand base organizations (known as *batallones socialistas*) held assemblies to organize and elect representatives to the Foundational Congress. The congress, attended by 1,681 delegates, met in Caracas on January 12, 2008. President Chávez subsequently approved a list of sixty-nine candidates for provisional posts in the party. Ninety-four thousand people voted for fifteen from this list in intra-party elections held on March 9, 2008.[9]

The first electoral test for the PSUV came on November 23, 2008, when voters chose twenty-two regional (state) governors, the "High Mayor" of metropolitan Caracas, and mayors of Venezuela's 265 municipios. The PSUV took seventeen governorships and roughly 80 percent of the mayoralties. Opposition candidates won governorships in several populous states (Zulia, Miranda, Carabobo, and Táchira) while also capturing the High Mayor office of metropolitan Caracas. The PSUV gained a level of domination at the regional and local levels that had never been achieved by a single party during the forty years of Punto Fijo.

Four political parties have dominated the opposition since 2008: AD, Justice First (PJ), New Time (TU), and Popular Will (VP). All four belong to the umbrella organization MUD. The opposition parties are strongest in eastern Caracas, the urbanized states of the west, and the Andes. They are weakest in the small towns, rural areas, selected shantytowns, and states of the east. During Punto Fijo, at its height, more than 40 percent of Venezuelans identified with AD. After seventeen years of the Bolivarian Revolution, voter identification with AD hovered around 5 percent. Voter identification with Justice First was roughly the same. It was lower for New Time and Popular Will. In the National Assembly elections of December 2015, as part of the MUD, PJ elected thirty-three delegates and AD elected twenty-five.

The three important opposition political parties formed after Hugo Chávez came to power lack national followings. The middle-class TU has some appeal to unionized workers, especially in the petroleum industry. It is strongest in the western state of Zulia. Manuel Rosales (the leader of TU) attempted to build the party into a national force following his defeat in the presidential election of 2006. He had little success. President Chávez forced Rosales into exile in 2009, soon after he was elected mayor of Maracaibo. When Rosales returned to Venezuela in 2015, the government arrested and imprisoned him.

The second important opposition political party, PJ, appealed initially to young Catholics who reacted against the ongoing internecine warfare between the second-generation leaders of COPEI and the party's founder, Rafael Caldera. PJ attracted a broad spectrum of Catholic youth and professionals in Venezuela's Central Region. The most important leaders of PJ are National Assembly deputy Julio Borges and Henrique Capriles Radonski, mayor of the Caracas municipality of Petare.

The third important opposition political party is Popular Will. Leopoldo López, the mayor of an affluent Caracas municipality, founded PV in 2010. PV self-identifies as a pluralist and democratic movement committed to the realization of social, economic, political, and human rights for every Venezuelan. PV played a central role in the protests that took place in early 2014. On February 18 of that year, López called for a pacific exit from authoritarian government, "within the constitution but in the streets." Two days later the government imprisoned him on charges of damaging public property and association for organizing criminal behavior. Lopez was convicted on all charges and sentenced to forty-four years in prison.

Three elections in 2012 and 2013 configured the contemporary landscape of Venezuela's political party system. The first, a contest for president, took place on October 7, 2012. In that contest, Hugo Chávez notched an eleven-point victory over Henrique Capriles Radonski, candidate of the MUD. An election for regional governors followed on December 9. Candidates of the PSUV took twenty of the twenty-three governorships, which demoralized the opposition. Three months later Hugo Chávez lost his struggle with cancer. In the presidential elections that followed, the opposition again put forward Henrique Capriles. The PSUV nominated interim president Nicolás Maduro, Chávez's choice to lead the government should he pass from the scene. Maduro won by less than 2 percent of the total vote.

Opposition political parties of the MUD supported a single candidate in each district for the National Assembly elections of December 6, 2015. They also agreed to a unified party list. Anticipating a strong challenge, the government modified the basic electoral law. Among the most important changes was the reduction of deputies elected by party lists to 30 percent. In addition, the new law completely separated the winner-take-all district vote and the party list votes. This created a mixed member majoritarian system. The electoral districts were redrawn in ways that critics of the government claimed would favor the PSUV, especially in the assigning of more weight to rural votes.

Gerrymandering election districts and changing election rules did not preserve government majorities in the National Assembly. Economic contraction, extreme Chavista partisanship, and human rights abuses resulted in blowback against Chavista candidates. The PSUV won 41 percent of the total vote and the MUD captured 56 percent. The government gained fifty-five seats and the MUD 109. A defiant President Maduro announced that he would give no quarter to the opposition in spite of his own party's crushing defeat.

A week after the elections, on December 15, 2015, the outgoing National Assembly created the National Communal Parliament. President Maduro stated that he would transfer all legislative power to that body. The communal parliament met twice in January 2016. Delegates came from the community councils and the communes. The Communal Parliament was disorganized and impossible to command. After adjourning the second session the government sent its members home. President Maduro then turned to the Supreme Judicial Tribunal (TSJ), which he controlled. The TSJ, as indicated earlier, had invalidated the election of three MUD deputies elected from the state of Amazonas. When the National Assembly refused to abide by this ruling of the TSJ, the justices declared the National Assembly to be in violation of the constitution. All legislation passed by the National Assembly was declared null and void.

STATE ORGANIZATION AND POLICY

Government Structure

Venezuelan state organization has been in flux since 2000, when the shift toward institutions envisioned by the constitution of 1999 began to take shape. The 1999 constitution provides for a presidential system with five separate branches of government: the executive, the legislative, the judicial, the electoral, and the people's power. Twenty-three states and a capital district comprise the polity in which the Chavistas recentralized many powers that in 1989 and 1993 were allocated to regional and local governments. The 1999 constitution envisioned a Federal Council of Government, presided over by the vice president, which would oversee subnational governments. President Chávez, as discussed earlier, delayed establishing the Federal Council of Government until April 2010. He expected that during a third term, opposition in the regions would be marginalized and the Federal Council would be an important mechanism for exercising control from Caracas.

Venezuela's national executive is a presidential system. Hugo Chávez stretched presidential powers beyond what was envisioned by the framers of the 1999 constitution. President Maduro lacks his predecessor's personal magnetism and suffers from low approval ratings. Maduro has compensated with a more authoritarian style of governing. He has involved the military more in rule enforcement than at any time since the dictatorship of General Pérez Jiménez.

Under the 1999 constitution, the Venezuelan president is chosen by a plurality of the popular vote for a term of six years. The president names the vice president, who assumes the presidency should that office fall vacant. Presidents freely appoint and remove members of the cabinet, which numbered thirty-three as of December 2016. Cabinet positions can be created and eliminated at the pleasure of the president. He or she is commander in chief of the armed forces. Nicolás Maduro named his first cabinet on April 22, 2013. At that time, a majority of his cabinet had been serving in President Chávez's cabinet when he died. Maduro's current cabinet confirms his domination of the government and the PSUV.

The use of numerous Misiones to allocate resources is a unique feature of Venezuela's national executive. In anticipation of the revocatory referendum of August 2004, as discussed earlier, President Chávez established the Misiones, which he oversaw personally. For example, the Ministry of Education was bypassed to establish special programs for literacy (*Misión Robinson*), accelerated high school degree programs (*Misión Ribas*), and revolutionary Bolivarian Universities (*Misión Sucre*). Other high-profile Misiones include programs that provide public health services to the slums (*Misión Barrio Adentro*) and distribute food to the poor at subsidized prices in popular markets (*Misión Mercal*). There is even a program to construct socialist cities (*Misión Villanueva*). In November 2016, the official website of the Venezuelan government listed thirty-six such Misiones. The national executive closely guards their budgets.

The 1999 constitution substituted a unicameral National Assembly for the bicameral congress that under the 1961 constitution was the font of central government lawmaking. Legislation can be introduced into the National Assembly from seven sources: the national executive, the Delegative Commission of the National Assembly, any three members (deputies) of the National Assembly, the Supreme Tribunal of

Justice, the Electoral Power, the Citizen Power, and by petition bearing the signature of 0.1 percent of registered voters. Deputies are elected for terms of five years, and following the referendum of February 15, 2009, are eligible for indefinite reelection. Each state, regardless of population, sends at least three deputies to the National Assembly. The indigenous community, in a departure from tradition, elects three deputies. The president can dissolve the National Assembly and call for new elections. The National Assembly has less autonomy and fewer prerogatives than did congress under the 1961 constitution.

There have been four National Assemblies elected since the 1999 constitution entered into force. In the first (2000–2005), allies of President Chávez gained roughly 55 percent of the seats. The opposition boycotted the 2005 National Assembly election and supporters of the Bolivarian revolution captured all 167 seats. The third election for National Assembly occurred on September 28, 2010. The opposition participated and unified behind the candidates in each district who stood the best chance of defeating the government party. The PSUV won ninety-six seats (out of 165) while receiving 48.1 percent of the vote. The opposition Unity Table received 47.2 percent of the total vote but garnered only sixty-four seats. Elections for the fourth National Assembly occurred in December 2015. The opposition won overwhelmingly. The government, as discussed previously, responded by having the Supreme Judicial Tribunal (TSJ) find the Assembly to be "in contempt" of the constitution—not eligible to legislate.

The 1999 constitution places the TSJ at the apex of the judicial system. Like the Supreme Court of the 1961 constitution, the TSJ meets in several kinds of "chambers": plenary, political-administrative, electoral, and others that deal with civil, penal, and social matters. The National Assembly elects justices to the TSJ for terms of twelve years and they cannot run for reelection. During their term in office, the constitution prohibits justices from engaging in partisan political activity. Indeed, drafters of the 1999 constitution went to great lengths to shield the entire judiciary from the influence of political parties. The twenty TSJ justices initially enjoyed limited autonomy, and in several chambers opponents of President Chávez initially had the majority. After the 2004 recall referendum failed to remove Chávez, he increased the number of justices by twelve. Until 2016 the National Assembly elected individuals as justices who rubber-stamped government positions.

The 1999 constitution, like its predecessor, established separate courts for the military. This practice has its roots in the Castilian tradition of the military *fuero* (right). The fuero shields members of the armed forces from being tried by civilian courts.

The 1999 constitution established the Electoral Power as a separate branch of government in reaction to domination by political parties of the Punto Fijo Supreme Electoral Council (CSE). During Punto Fijo the CSE was the source of funds for the political parties. The CSE also oversaw tabulation of the votes at local polling places prior to the transfer of ballots to a central location by the armed forces. In some polling centers, only AD and COPEI had observers. Evidence exists that on occasion the two divided among themselves the votes of third political parties where those parties had no observers. The worst excesses of this kind occurred in the 1993 presidential elections, but five years later the reorganized CSE eliminated most problems by mobilizing a random sample of citizens as poll watchers. Under the 1999 constitutional regime the Supreme Electoral Tribunal (TSE) supervises all elections. Most observers agree that voting has been generally free and ballots have been counted accurately. However, the TSE has refrained from intervening in disputes during electoral campaigns when opposition parties charge the government with assisting the PSUV.

The Citizen Power, a second new branch of government, was established in reaction to the widely held perception that during Punto Fijo government had become abusive and corrupt. The Citizen Power is a kind of ombudsman and watchdog. The maximum authority of this branch of government is the Moral Republican Council, an institution composed of three individuals: the public prosecutor, the national comptroller, and an official known as the People's Defender. The People's Defender "promotes, defends, and watches out for" constitutional rights and guarantees. By a two-thirds vote, the National Assembly designates the People's Defender, who serves for a single period of seven years. Currently, the People's Defender is highly responsive to the national executive.

Policy Making

In Venezuela, policy making is personalistic and presidentially dominated. The central issue areas of Venezuelan policy making are service delivery, economic development, public order and safety, and foreign and national defense.

Service Delivery

Service delivery immediately and directly affects quality of life. Its diverse components include housing, infrastructure development, health, sanitation, food, environment, social security, education, urban development, culture, and transportation. Until the revolution of 1945, only the upper class enjoyed access to quality services. One of the most attractive dimensions of the AD's early program was its use of the state to extend high-quality services to previously neglected groups. The making and implementation of service delivery policies as Venezuela transitions to twenty-first century socialism is fluid and often inconsistent. Chavismo employs six kinds of service delivery institutions: ministries of the national executive, regional governments, municipal bureaucracies, corporations managed by the state, Misiones, and communal institutions such as community councils. Eliminating duplication is one of the most important challenges facing the Maduro government.

Economic Development Policy

Economic development policy encompasses activities that expand the capacity to produce goods and commodities for internal consumption and export. Its impact on quality of life, while as important as service delivery, is less immediate and direct. The issue areas of economic development policy are highly diverse: mineral extraction, industry, commerce, finance, and planning. Venezuela's private sector coexisted with AD and COPEI governments between 1958 and 1990. Punto Fijo also reserved large areas of the economy for state enterprises. Hugo Chávez's 1998 presidential campaign suggested that he would end the most flagrant abuses of neoliberalism rather than abolish private enterprise. As of 2016, however, only three of Venezuela's top thirteen companies remained in private hands.

Venezuelan mineral extraction industry, despite the importance of gold, iron, and bauxite, revolves around petroleum. Nationalization of the multibillion-dollar oil industry, the product of a broad national consensus, occurred on January 1, 1976. To manage and coordinate the newly nationalized petroleum industry, the government created Petroleum of Venezuela (PDVSA), a state corporation attached to what is now the Ministry of People's Power of Energy and Petroleum. One of President Chávez's first decisions was to replace the president of PDVSA with an individual from his inner circle. In early 2003, PDVSA workers and executives sided with demonstrators seeking to remove President Chávez. After surviving the recall referendum, as we have seen, Chávez discharged almost nineteen thousand PDVSA employees. Petroleum production fell precipitously and never recovered. It is now at a level more than 30 percent below the point considered normal prior to the dismissal.

With PDVSA in turmoil the government looked increasingly to petroleum from the concessions given to multinational companies for exploitation of the Orinoco tar belt's heavy reserves. These concessions themselves became controversial when the soaring price of petroleum allowed the companies to profit mightily from their activities. In 2007, when the Venezuelan government increased the tax rate on these profits, ExxonMobile and Conoco-Phillips rescinded their concessions. However, other multinationals remained. In May 2013 PDVSA and Russia's Rosneft signed an agreement establishing a joint enterprise that anticipated extracting 2.1 million barrels of petroleum per day from the tar belt. China (after the United States) currently is the second most important buyer of Venezuelan petroleum.

Finance and commerce are policy areas that involve especially intensive public-sector/private-sector interaction. The Ministry of People's Power of the Treasury and the Central Bank set the broad financial parameters within which the government pursues economic development. The 1999 constitution gave the national executive limited authority to intervene in the Central Bank, but the Chavistas have pushed intervention far beyond what was envisioned by the constitution's framers. On July 3, 2009, the government assumed control of the influential Spanish-owned Banco de Venezuela. Combined with other state banks, this purchase gave the government control over about 21 percent of deposits, 16 percent of loans, a payroll of 15,000 employees, and 651 bank branches.

Public Order and Safety Policy

Public order and safety policy is the responsibility of the Ministry of People's Power of the Interior and Justice. The vice minister for the System of Integrated Policing directly oversees the National Bolivarian Police (PNB). President Chávez pressed for the creation of this national police force in 2009. At that time, the PNB assumed many of the policing functions that were scattered throughout the national executive and some that were the responsibility of regional and local police forces. In 2011, the Police Reform Commission established the Citizen Police Oversight Committees (CCCPs) to monitor the PNB. By the summer of 2012, forty-four committees had been formed. Additionally, twenty-two committees were monitoring state police forces and twenty-one oversaw municipal police forces. The other important national police force, the Bolivarian Intelligence Service (SERBIN) is also embedded in the Ministry of People's Power of Interior and Justice. It focuses on counterterrorism, intelligence, counterintelligence, government investigations, and background investigations, and provides protection services for high-ranking government officials. Opposition leaders have accused SERBIN of harassing and intimidating opponents of the government.

Police reform has not increased personal security. With some 15,000 killings a year, Venezuela's homicide rate is the fifth highest in the world, according to UN statistics. The murder rate doubled during the fourteen-year rule of the late President Hugo Chávez as cheap access to guns and an ineffective justice system fed a culture of violence in the shantytowns, parts of which have become no-go zones for outsiders, including police. Lack of security was a major issue in the April 2013 presidential election, and one of President Maduro's first initiatives was to dispatch the armed forces to the shantytowns to increase personal security.

Foreign and National Defense Policy

Foreign and defense policy making is centered in the Ministries of People's Power of Defense and Foreign Affairs and in the institutes and government entities attached to them. The Ministry of People's Power of Energy and Petroleum, because of Venezuela's heavy dependence on international petroleum markets, also plays an important role in foreign policy. The focus here is on traditional national and foreign policy concerns: defense of the frontiers, control of the national territory, relations with foreign powers, and an array of nonpetroleum international economic issues.

Despite substantial overlap in the assigned tasks of the ministries of Defense and Foreign Affairs, coordination between them was minimal until the 1980s. The most important explanation for this shortcoming is that historically the critical missions of the armed forces have been internal. Presidents Rómulo Betancourt (1959–1964) and Raúl Leoni (1963–1968) strengthened relations between AD and the military during their successful campaigns against leftist insurgents. Subsequently, until the ascent of Hugo Chávez, the primary mission of the military was to exercise control over the national territory in a manner that discouraged dissidents from waging guerrilla warfare. All four branches of the military (army, navy, air force, and national guard) provided a path for upward mobility. The officer corps attracted middle and working-class youths, while peasants and shantytown residents filled the enlisted ranks.

On July 31, 2008, the new Organic Law of the National Bolivarian Armed Forces took effect. This law committed the military to defending the Bolivarian Revolution and made the National Bolivarian Militia an integral part of the armed forces. The militia, acting with the Defense Committees of the Community Councils, was empowered to determine which citizens are "patriotic." The Organic Law also increased the president's authority over maneuver units of the armed forces and gave him the power to order any citizen to serve in the military. In summary, Chavismo has transformed the military from a professional force to a presidential Praetorian Guard.

Foreign affairs, a constitutionally mandated presidential responsibility, center on the Ministry of People's Power of Foreign Relations. During Punto Fijo, presidents often selected prominent independents for the position of foreign minister as a way of building broad societal support. Over time AD and COPEI each formed a cadre of foreign policy experts. The professional foreign service was co-opted into these cadres, which also managed the Foreign Trade Institute (ICE). Established in the early 1970s, ICE oversees and stimulates Venezuela's nonpetroleum exports. President Chávez appointed some of his most reliable collaborators to the position of Minister of Foreign Affairs. One of the most important charges given early appointees was to purge the foreign service of diplomats with long-standing ties to AD and COPEI.

Venezuelan diplomacy during Punto Fijo gave lip service to reducing the importance of relations with North Atlantic countries. Successes were meager and fleeting. Cooperation within OPEC to set the price of petroleum acquired great importance. It gave Venezuela an influential voice among global producers of petroleum. In the 1980s, coordination with other debtor countries in negotiating repayment terms with OECD-country banks became a priority. Membership in OPEC and coordination with debtor countries gave Caracas opportunities to resurrect rhetoric associated with such anti-European and anti-US themes as Latin American unity, international social justice, and Hispanic cultural superiority. President Hugo Chávez took these themes to new heights.

From the beginning, Hugo Chávez voiced his unease with US influence over Latin America in general and Venezuela in particular. He clashed with President George W. Bush at the April 2001 Quebec summit over free trade in the Americas. He opposed the US invasion of Iraq in 2003 and took the lead in organizing UNASUR (Union of South American Nations), a regional organization designed to resolve political and military conflicts in South America, but without the United States.

Hugo Chávez excoriated Presidents Álvaro Uribe and Barack Obama for signing a treaty on July 16, 2009, that gave the United States access to three Colombian air bases. The United States and Colombia claimed that these bases were to assist in stopping the flow of drugs out of South America. They were a substitute for the Manta facility in Ecuador that President Rafael Correa closed. Chávez charged that US armed forces at Colombian bases could be used to invade Venezuela. He voiced his concern at the August 28 meeting of UNASUR in Bariloche, Argentina, but calls for sanctions against Colombia were rejected. Since then leading Chavistas, including members of the armed forces, have become major players in drug trafficking. Chavista foreign policy has supported efforts sponsored by Cuba to end the decades-long guerrilla war in Colombia.

The final high concern of Venezuelan foreign policy is relations with Cuba. President Maduro has indicated he will continue supporting Cuba's communist regime through sales of petroleum at deep discounts. These sales freed the Castro brothers from accommodating to pressures intended to make Cuba more pluralistic as a condition for increased trade and investment from countries in the North Atlantic. Venezuela and Cuba also formed the Bolivarian Alternative for the Americas (ALBA) trading group, which provides an institutional home for states opposed to the US-supported Free Trade for the Americas Initiative. Other members of ALBA include Antigua, Bolivia, Cuba, Dominica, Ecuador, Nicaragua, Saint Vincent, and the Grenadines.

Important but lesser foreign policy concerns include relations with Argentina, Brazil, and other countries of the Western Hemisphere. Venezuela's desire to reduce US influence in South America and enhance its profile as a continental actor bore fruit when President Chávez played a key role in establishing the Union of South American Nations (*Unión de Naciones Suramericanas*, or UNASUR) as an alternative to the OAS for resolving disputes within the region. Soon after Nicolás Maduro's inauguration as president, he visited key UNASUR countries to gain support for his government after domestic opponents questioned the legitimacy of his election.

CONCLUSION: THE FUTURE

Venezuelan politics changed dramatically when Hugo Chávez Frías passed from the scene. The fallen leader came to power through elections when one of Latin America's longest-running liberal democracies unraveled due to economic deterioration, internecine conflict among its political elites, and corruption. Chávez gave voice to the impoverished and marginalized. Punto Fijo democrats failed to live up to the promise that brought them to power in 1958. Once in control Chávez demonized the liberal democratic system and those who continued to support it. Partisans of the Bolivarian revolution were those who counted—El Soberano. Opponents were *los escuálidos* (the squalid ones).

El Soberano was the majority. In none of his runs for president did Hugo Chávez receive less than 55 percent of the total vote, and his support reached 63 percent in 2006. He was lucky. Income from the foreign sales of petroleum increased dramatically during his time in office. President Chávez had access to more money than all governments of the Punto Fijo era combined. Millions who had fallen into poverty in the 1990s benefited from Hugo Chavez's programs. Millions remain loyal Chavistas.

Challenges to Hugo Chávez's Bolivarian Revolution were always intense and widespread. The political cultures of Chavismo and its opponents differ sharply. Opposition support comes from middle-class individuals, many of whom escaped poverty during the forty years of liberal democratic governments. Political party elites whose power the Chavistas have taken hope for a comeback. Opposition also comes from domestic entrepreneurs and their foreign associates whose businesses can't compete with imports purchased by the government and sold in country below cost. Merchants tied to Chavismo receive lucrative government contracts and prosper. They are known as the Bolivarian oligarchs, and live in exclusive neighborhoods once inhabited by elites who dominated Punto Fijo democracy.

Four years into his presidency Nicolás Maduro finds himself governing a country that is sharply divided between partisans and opponents of twenty-first century socialism. His government no longer commands the economic resources that enabled Hugo Chávez to assist El Soberano and placate others. On December 3, 2016, Venezuela's monthly inflation passed 50 percent and the country's economy entered the world of hyperinflation. Economists and administration critics blame the soaring prices on failed economic policies. These included draconian price and currency controls, which, perversely, have fueled speculation in the black market. President Nicolás Maduro and his lieutenants place the blame on "economic warfare" being waged by shadowy forces. Regardless of who is to blame, Venezuela faces an economic crisis of staggering dimensions. Still, the country sits atop extensive petroleum reserves. Multinational corporations remain interested in extracting Venezuelan oil, as do state enterprises in Brazil, Russia, and China. Venezuela is likely to receive substantial income from the sale of petroleum for the foreseeable future.

The Chavistas will make important choices during the last half of President Maduro's term in office (2017–2019). On one hand, they could intensify the transition to twenty-first century socialism. A critical factor limiting this option is the government's lack of resources to sustain the programs that facilitated Chavismo's rise to power. In order to consolidate the regime, Chavista leaders would have to tighten control over their own movement. They would have to employ authoritarian methods to repress the opposition, reduce the autonomy of subnational governments, and dominate political socialization. In addition, Chavismo's ability to successfully implement the transition to twenty-first century socialism will depend on whether the government can secure over time some minimal level of income from the sale of petroleum. The international political economy will play an important role in determining the viability of partisan regime consolidation. The other option for Chavistas is to seek a modus vivendi with the opposition and reintroduce some tenets of liberal democracy. There could be greater toleration of private enterprise, more acceptance of regional and local autonomy, and conferral of loyal opposition status upon opponents as long as they make demands through peaceful channels. Advocates of both options exist within Chavismo. For its part, the opposition is unlikely to attempt a seizure of power by force given the disastrous outcome of this course of action in 2002 and 2003. Militant demonstrations against the Maduro government fared no better in early 2014. To summarize, the Venezuelan polity stands at a crossroads. It could become an authoritarian leftist hybrid with overtones of Rousseau, a liberal democracy with a strong state sector, or even an authoritarian regime controlled by the military.

SUGGESTIONS FOR FURTHER READING

Carroll, Rory. *Comandante: Hugo Chavez's Venezuela.* New York: Penguin Press, 2013.

Chaplin, Ari. *Chavez's Legacy: The Transformation From Democracy to a Mafia State.* Lanham, MD and New York, NY: University Press of America, 2014

Corales, Javier, and Michael Penfold. *Dragon in the Tropics: Hugo Chavez and the Political Technology of Revolution in Venezuela.* 2nd ed. Washington, DC: Brookings Latin America Initiative Books, 2015.

Coronil, Fernando. *The Magical State: Nature, Money, and Modernity in Venezuela.* Chicago: The University of Chicago Press, 1997.

McCoy, Jennifer L., and David J. Myers, eds. *The Unraveling of Representative Democracy in Venezuela.* Baltimore: Johns Hopkins University Press, 2005.

Morgan, Jana. *Bankrupt Representation and Party System Collapse.* University Park: Penn State University Press, 2011.

Myers, David J. "Venezuela: Politics, Urban Reform and the Challenges of Metropolitan Governance amid the Struggle for Democracy." In *Metropolitan Governance in the Federalist Americas,* edited by Peter Spink, Peter M. Ward and Robert H. Wilson, 209–246. Notre Dame, IN: University of Notre Dame Press, 2012.

Nelson, Brian. *The Silence and the Scorpion: The Coup Against Chávez and the Making of Modern Venezuela.* New York: Nelson Books, 2009.

Tinker Salas, Miguel. *Venezuela: What Everyone Needs to Know.* New York: Oxford University Press, 2015.

Valesco, Alejandro. *Barrio Rising: Urban Popular Politics and the Making of Modern Venezuela*: Berkeley and Los Angeles: University of California Press. 2015.

NOTES

1. Lisa Peattie, *Rethinking Ciudad Guyana.* (Ann Arbor: University of Michigan Press, 1987).

2. For a useful discussion of the variant of "limited pluralism" that prevailed in Venezuela prior to the rise of Chavismo, see José A. Gil Yepes. *The Challenge of Venezuelan Democracy.* (New Brunswick, NJ: Transaction Books, 1981).

3. Marc Howard Ross, "Culture in Comparative Political Analysis," in *Comparative Politics: Rationality, Culture and Structure*, eds. Mark Irving Lichbach and Alan Zuckerman. 2nd ed. (New York. Cambridge University Press, 2009), 137–142.

4. Judith Ewell, *Venezuela: A Century of Change* (Palo Alto, CA: Stanford University Press, 1984), 124–27.

5. Terry Lynn Karl, "Petroleum and Political Pacts: The Transition to Democracy in Venezuela," *Latin American Research Review* 22, no. 1 (1987): 63–94.

6. Moisés Naim, "The Launching of Radical Policy Changes, 1989–1991," in *Venezuela in the Wake of Radical Reform*, ed. Joseph S. Tulchin (Boulder, CO: Lynne Rienner, 1992), Chapter 4.

7. Brian A. Nelson, *The Silence and the Scorpion: The Coup Against Chávez and the Making of Modern Venezuela* (New York: Nation Books, 2009).

8. A more comprehensive discussion appears in Daniel H. Levine, *Popular Voices in Latin American Catholicism* (Princeton, NJ: Princeton University Press, 1992), 65–91.

9. The official website of the PSUV is: www.psuv.org.ve/.

14

URUGUAY: BALANCING GROWTH AND DEMOCRACY

Martin Weinstein and Jorge Rebella

INTRODUCTION

Uruguay is the smallest of the South American republics, but the distinctiveness of its political experience and innovations far transcends its size.[1] It is perhaps best known today as a long-standing democracy that "failed" during the Cold War, but recovered wholly its democratic traditions in 1985 after a twelve-year hiatus. However, it is also a country that in the nineteenth century created democracy out of chaos and translated its traditional corporatist values and realities into democratic institutions. It experienced a profound disillusionment with the modern premises of economic growth and stability, as well as a period of escalating political instability and incremental military intervention. In 1985 Uruguay reestablished democratic government and politics, and since then it has been preoccupied with defining the meaning of "normalcy" in this new context.

Uruguay often has been viewed as a historical exception to the general pattern of politics in Latin America, an isolated instance of enlightened pluralistic politics in a region of corporatist authoritarianism. Uruguayans, in fact, have shared the same corporatist values as most of their neighbors but, almost uniquely, have shaped them into distinctive democratic processes and traditions. They have borrowed selectively from the experiences of Europe and the United States and, as necessary, innovated to suit their own environment. Today Uruguay has reestablished its democratic heritage and revitalized its historic values, and in the process has cautiously explored new forms of organization and reevaluated the failed premises that eroded its traditional democracy previously.

The unique qualities of Uruguayan democracy have been little known, let alone understood, outside the country. Outwardly the country seems to have many similarities with other democracies, including regular and meaningful elections, a rule of law that respects and protects individual liberties and freedoms, and a policy-making process that is responsive to public opinion and scrutiny. Yet these qualities exist within a distinctively Latin American context, which recognizes and incorporates corporatist assumptions in the democratic processes, utilizing such familiar devices as co-optation, parity, coparticipation, and charismatic leadership. Many of the premises, which were the logic of the country's traditional democracy, proved unreliable, and in the mid-twentieth century Uruguay went through a period of sustained political and economic decay, violence, and ultimately authoritarian military rule.

The establishment of Uruguayan democracy originally was the result of an armistice between contentious landowners and provincial *caudillos*, who came to recognize the potential for significant profits from increased exports. The politicians also saw democracy as a way to create political stability and gain political support from a rapidly expanding urban middle class committed to consumerism, consumption, and the benefits of state-provided services and welfare. Uruguayan democracy was based on an important economic assumption: economic growth was inevitable, irreversible, and largely a spontaneous process that could subsidize the expanding and increasingly costly demands of a democratic society.

The political ideas that underlay Uruguayan democracy were forcefully and explicitly articulated by its most influential statesman, José Batlle y Ordóñez, in the first decades of the twentieth century. These included the belief that political stability was essential for prosperity and growth; that it would be achieved only by allowing free but balanced access to political power under a rule of law; that it could be sustained only by responding to the needs and demands of the masses; and that it must be protected from the pernicious influences of ambitious executives, politicians, and international opportunists while guaranteeing a strong role for the state. Batlle was also strongly anticlerical. He believed that the church and Catholicism were an organized threat to secular control and progress, and that the church and state should be totally separated.

What is important about the Uruguayan experience is its relevance to other democracies whose processes, welfare, and stability are based on similar assumptions. The reexamination in Uruguay of fundamental democratic premises and values, particularly within a context of economic stress, was not an easy task, nor were the questions of blame and retribution for individuals and institutions that were culpable for the collapse of the democratic system. The concerns ultimately raised the issue of how normalcy would be defined within the new and reevaluated contemporary context. It is still unclear how much the result will borrow from the past, from neighboring societies in Latin America, or from new premises and new values. Uruguay has dealt with crises and dilemmas that would test any democracy, and for that reason its experience, both the universal and the parochial dimensions, merits careful evaluation.

ECONOMIC HISTORY AND SOCIAL CONTEXT

Uruguayan economic history is particularly important for understanding the country's politics and government. Early in the twentieth century Uruguay became a largely middle-class country with one of the highest standards of living in Latin America, but it subsequently experienced a protracted economic decline that challenged and eventually helped destroy its democratic politics. Uruguayan exports failed to remain viable and competitive internationally; its domestic economy became heavily dependent upon services rather than agricultural and industrial activities; its dependency on imports, particularly for energy, created massive financial problems; and its commitment to consumption rather than productivity distorted national priorities and created an escalating international debt and uncontrolled inflation. Uruguay's economic success and its subsequent decay were both influenced by international economic realities, most of them beyond the country's control.

Uruguay's wealth was generated by the export of traditional commodities, principally cattle, hides, wool, mutton, lamb, and grains. The economy was too small to industrialize rationally or efficiently, and the effort to do so encouraged import-substitution industrialization (ISI) and protectionist trade policies, which in turn created inefficient monopolies, both foreign and domestic, along with equally inefficient state-owned enterprises. The domestic economic situation was complicated by high production costs and profit expectations resulting from high-risk industrial ventures. It was also complicated by modern but unrealistic economic expectations of workers, who effectively organized and created politically influential labor unions.

By the end of the nineteenth century the worldwide demand for Uruguayan exports had grown dramatically. Traditional fibers like wool had not yet been challenged by synthetic ones, and by the mid-1870s the technology of refrigerated ships had made the export of fresh meat possible. The rural sector provided the capital on which the nation's development and wealth were based, thus subsidizing the industrial, commercial, and financial interests of the capital city, Montevideo. Export revenues allowed the importation of consumer goods demanded by the urban dwellers and helped supply the capital for Montevideo's own inefficient industrialization.

However, the workers who the industries employed, concentrated in and around the capital city, grew in number and became more highly organized and politically active than their rural counterparts. For them the process of industrialization was popular. There emerged an inevitable conflict between the rural and urban interests in the country, one in which the capital city eventually prevailed by virtue of its greater population. The situation was a corrosive and dangerous one in which the affluence, growth, and consumption of the urban area were being subsidized by the rural areas, whose economies were slowly deteriorating.

By the end of World War II the demand for Uruguayan exports had begun to decline. Other supplies of fresh meat were available in international markets, particularly for Uruguay's largest trading partner, Great Britain, and wool fibers were being replaced by synthetic ones. Rather than responding to these changes, the traditional rural economy continued producing the same export commodities, and so export revenues decreased within a context of shrinking demand.[2] Uruguay's failure to renovate its export economy and to recognize and respond to major shifts in international demand and new technologies set in motion a slow process of economic decay, which went largely unnoticed by the public until after decades its cumulative effects were clearly visible. The eventual political implications were disastrous.

Rapid industrial growth in Uruguay had run its course by the end of World War II. Based on ISI, local manufactures had become expensive and technologically outdated by the mid-1950s and could not compete in export markets or domestically either in quality or price with imports.

The worsening imbalance between export revenues and import costs, an imbalance seriously aggravated by the sharp rise in the cost of imported energy in the 1970s, severely strained the country's financial solvency and encouraged two further and ultimately disastrous economic decisions. To sustain economic growth and financial liquidity the civilian governments expanded the money supply, inducing rapid and at times rampant inflation, and the country increasingly borrowed money from international sources to subsidize its deteriorating trade deficit.

The first policy eroded the confidence of Uruguayan investors and encouraged an accelerating capital flight along with declines in investment. It also destroyed the ability of the urban middle and working classes to save or maintain (not to mention improve) their living standards, which eventually alienated a substantial portion of the electorate and eroded confidence in the economic system. The second policy created a massive international debt, which by the mid-1980s was equal to about half the annual national per capita income. In the decade from 1977 to 1986 the level of international debt in Uruguay increased by more than 400 percent, one of the highest rates of increase in the hemisphere, and that was largely under a military government committed to economic austerity and willing to endure the response to unpopular policies.

However, economic decay was not an unpredictable, catastrophic experience that instantly devastated living standards and economic activity. It was slow, incremental, and entirely predictable, but the difficult political decisions required to reverse it were not or could not be made, even by a military government. As economic conditions deteriorated following World War II and a brief boom brought on by the Korean War, increasing demands were imposed on the government to provide jobs and to subsidize housing, which in turn created more public spending and inflation, further discouraged domestic and foreign investment, and ultimately reinforced the general pattern of economic decline and the political problems associated with it. Although the country had achieved one of the highest standards of living in Latin America, Uruguay began to face apparently unsolvable economic problems, which continue to frustrate the nation's politics and politicians today.

The country's economic performance in the 1990s was strong by historical standards, thanks for the most part to the creation of the Southern Common Market (MERCOSUR) with its significant increase in intraregional trade. This trend lasted until the end of the decade only. Gross domestic product grew by 35.2 percent between 1992 and 1998, but Brazil's currency crisis put Uruguay in recession in 1999.

When all is said and done, the tiny Uruguayan economy, coupled with the state's historic commitment to welfare policies, allows a homogeneous population of some 3.4 million people to maintain the highest Physical Quality of Life Index (PQLI) in Latin America, according to the United Nations.

The Uruguayan people are themselves a distinctive mixture. During the colonial period the country had virtually no indigenous population. Most immigrants were from Spain and Italy, the latter primarily in the late nineteenth and early twentieth centuries. These were largely middle- and working-class people from urban areas, attracted to the prosperous and expanding Uruguayan economy, who remained in the capital city of Montevideo. They brought with them European political attitudes and economic expectations, which were absorbed into the country's party politics. Today about half the national population resides in the capital city. Rural life, perhaps because of its historic economic importance, spawned a mythology of its own centered around the *gaucho*, but the reality of rural life has little in common with the myths. During the period of economic decay following World War II and the Korean War there was a substantial migration of urban Uruguayans out of the country, many of them to Argentina and Brazil, a process that was reinforced by the turbulent political conditions of the 1960s and the subsequent military dictatorship.

Uruguay was one of the first nations in Latin America to make a major commitment to public education, with the result that a high literacy level was achieved at a relatively early time historically. With literacy came high levels of political awareness and participation along with modern socioeconomic expectations.

POLITICAL ORGANIZATION IN URUGUAY

Uruguay is a highly organized society, with clearly defined interest groups and complex political parties, but the society is organized in organic rather than pluralistic ways. The framework for this organization was devised by José Batlle to achieve political stability out of the chaotic experience of civil wars, international intervention, and party-organized conflict.

The nineteenth century produced two political parties: the Colorado Party and the National Party, more commonly known as the Blanco Party (the parties originally were identified by the color of the brassards and headbands their adherents wore during armed confrontations). After generations of fighting for national hegemony, often with international provocation from Brazil, Argentina, and Great Britain, the possibility of economic prosperity, which came in the 1870s with the potential for a rapid expansion of exports, dramatized the advantages of cooperation rather than armed conflict for advancing the economic interests of both sides. The resolution of the civil conflict was promoted and eventually achieved by José Batlle. He was a descendant of a politically prominent and influential Uruguayan family belonging to the Colorado Party that had produced many important political leaders. He was elected president twice, in 1903 and 1911, and he established the framework for modern Uruguayan politics and government. After defeating the Blancos in the last of the civil wars, he established a political compromise with them based on the concepts of parity and co-participation. Parity recognized the legitimate interests of the Blancos in the rural departments where they were strong, and Batlle all but ceded these departments to their control. He also accepted their participation in the national government, proportional to their share of the national vote, and allowed them a share of government patronage and revenues. The Blanco Party won only three subsequent national elections—in 1958, 1962, and 1989—and became virtually a permanent minority. Batlle's Colorado Party consistently attracted more voters nationally than the Blancos, but it was willing to share with the Blancos the exercise and benefits of power. The 1952 constitution went so far as to formalize coparticipation by awarding three of the nine seats on a collegiate executive branch as well as two of five positions on the boards of all state enterprises to the minority party.

Batlle designed an electoral system that incorporates parity and coparticipation both within and among the nation's political parties. The Uruguayan electoral system regulates parties, elections, and the distribution of legislative seats, establishing *lemas* and *sublemas*, which are equivalent to parties and party factions. Lemas are composed of sublemas, factions that are the supporters or political machines of individual leaders. Anyone can form a sublema, acquire formal identification within a lema, and in effect create a personal political organization with a separate identity. The electoral strength of a sublema and its leader adds to the total vote of a lema, which in turn determines both lema and sublema legislative representation. From this process, ambitious political leaders are thereby permitted into the political system and can exercise political influence proportional to their ability to attract votes. Their organizations are integrated into the larger lema, or party coalition, and they have a vested interest in the success of other sublemas, which they nonetheless campaign against because their representation is determined by their share of the cumulative vote for the lema. Presidential elections used to have the effect of combining a primary election with a general election.

Sublemas in Uruguay form the nucleus of political organization and encourage a clientele relationship between the party leaders and the voters. Constituents with problems can request help from sublema leaders and their organizations, and sublemas maintain neighborhood clubs and organize campaigning all over the country. Through cross-endorsement, cross-listing, and a sharing of candidates, they form additional coalitions among themselves within the lemas, coalitions that constantly shift from one election to another.

The lema system is formalized by proportional representation, which allocates legislative representation according to the size of the popular vote. Campaign costs are also subsidized for sublemas according to the size of their vote. For the voter, the system encourages a general identification with a lema and a personal identification with a sublema. The general electoral system also reinforces the traditional Colorado and Blanco parties and, more recently, the Frente Amplio. They benefit principally from it, and it restrains the growth and success of new or smaller parties.

José Batlle built the Colorado Party into the majority political organization by mobilizing the urban classes of Montevideo and appealing to their interests. He proposed—and implemented while president—vast public programs of education, culture, welfare, and social security. He encouraged industrialization and resisted foreign penetration of the country's economy. The Colorado leader advocated abolishing the presidency as an institution and replacing it with a rotating collegial executive, an idea he borrowed from Switzerland. His reasoning was that the dictatorships that were so common in Latin America were the result of an inevitable greed for power, and because one could not change human nature, the only way to prevent dictatorships was to abolish the presidency and replace it with an institution that dispersed power. Batlle was by profession a journalist, and he used his journalistic interest to further his political objectives, a process that continues today in Uruguay. Opposition to his leadership arose within the Colorado Party, and anti-Batllista factions (sublemas) were formed.

Batlle's ideas were visionary for their time: he initiated a modern welfare state in Uruguay long before it had been tried elsewhere. He was a consummate politician, but his political pragmatism was tempered by his idealism. Batlle believed he could eliminate instability and turmoil by expanding and organizing the political base of the country and by responding to the basic needs of the Uruguayan people.

In spite of his influence and success, Batlle's principles were based on two vulnerable assumptions, both of which proved to be erroneous and eventually contributed to the decay of Uruguayan democracy. The first was the assumption of continued economic growth and prosperity, a common perspective among industrializing nations during the nineteenth century. This assumption was drawn from the experiences of large Western nations and proved inappropriate for Uruguay. The second was the assumption that a collegial executive could prevent authoritarian governments. Uruguay did not experiment with a pure form of the collegial executive until the 1950s, perhaps the worst possible moment because the economy was declining and strong leadership was desperately needed. Ironically, for eight of the fourteen collegial executive years (1952–1966) the government was controlled by the Blanco Party, which was the first time in the twentieth century it had prevailed in national elections. The experiment with a collegial executive, combined with the economic dilemmas for which no answers could be found, contributed to the political paralysis that encouraged a revolutionary group known as the *Tupamaros* and, ultimately, military intervention. The Tupamaros did not succeed in taking power, but they did provoke the military to do so.

By the 1960s several small parties combined with two small dissident liberal sublemas of the Colorado Party to form an electoral coalition, originally known as the Leftist Front of Freedom (FIDEL), and ultimately as the Broad Front. Included in the Broad Front were the Communist Party of Uruguay, the Christian Democratic Party, the Socialist Party, and List 99 of the Colorado Party. By combining the strengths of small parties in the 1971, 1984, and 1989 elections, the coalition posed a serious threat to the two traditional lemas, which in many ways are themselves political coalitions.

Like the political parties, economic interests have been well organized in Uruguay. The organizations include national associations of ranchers, business enterprises, and labor. Workers' organizations emerged very early in Uruguay and were modeled after their European counterparts. The largest labor organization—the National Convention of Workers (CNT), founded in 1966—is Marxist dominated, but its strength has not necessarily translated into votes for Marxist parties. Organized workers were a principal target for José Batlle's policies, and a large proportion used to be Colorado Party supporters in spite of their union's orientation. The CNT was outlawed under the dictatorship, but a new organization, the Inter-Union Workers' Plenary (PIT), formed in the early 1980s and subsequently merged with the CNT after the reestablishment of democracy.

The political scenario that eventually produced a military dictatorship was a long and complex one. Military intervention occurred gradually, although by mid-1973 the military was fully in control of the government. The Tupamaro revolutionary movement, specializing in urban guerrilla tactics in the capital city, became a highly destabilizing influence during the 1960s. The government retaliated with a state of siege, massive arrests, torture, suppression of political leaders and groups, and censorship. However, these actions were ineffective and even counterproductive. The military gradually assumed responsibility for the Tupamaro threat and brought the civilian institutions under its control.

The military regime had both successes and failures in managing the economy, but the experience proved unpopular with Uruguayans and divisive for the military. No single military leader was able to consolidate his control, although one—General Gregorio Álvarez—tried. The military response to the Tupamaros was brutal and, for Uruguay, unprecedented. The movement was crushed before the military took control of the government in June 1973, but at exceptionally high costs to Uruguayan legal and political values. The military ruled until 1985.

By the early 1980s the military leaders had begun to recognize the inevitability of restoring civilian rule and began looking for a way to maximize their continuing influence and minimize any retribution against them—individually and institutionally—after leaving power.

The military regime decided to hold a referendum in 1980 on a new constitution that would protect the military's political influence, a referendum held under conditions of tight control and censorship. The measure was so decisively defeated that the regime had no choice but to acknowledge its failure. At that point military officers began negotiating with civilian political leaders, at least those they were willing to talk with, about conditions for a return to civilian rule. This change was formally achieved in March 1985 after elections the preceding November, in which three of the major presidential contenders, Wilson Ferreira Aldunate of the Blanco Party, Jorge Batlle Ibáñez of the Colorado Party, and Líber Seregni of the Broad Front, were prohibited from being candidates.

The victor in 1985 was a Colorado Party candidate, Julio María Sanguinetti. Party voting and the resulting legislative representation were very similar to what they had been in 1971—the last election before the total military takeover. The Colorado regime encountered difficulties and controversies in its quest for normalization, and in the 1989 elections the Blanco party, for only the third time in history, prevailed, winning a plurality in the two legislative chambers and electing a president, the moderate Blanco leader Luis Alberto Lacalle. In 1994 the Colorados again won the presidency, but only barely, with the Blancos and the Broad Front close behind. National politics seemed to have been transformed by that election, perhaps permanently, to a three-party system.

GOVERNMENT STRUCTURE AND POLICIES

Structure

Uruguay has a centralized government and is divided into nineteen departments, including the capital city of Montevideo. Virtually all decisions in the country are made at the national level. The current constitution was adopted in 1966 in the aftermath of the fourteen-year experiment with a collegial executive. It allows departments to elect local legislatures comprising thirty-one members and an *intendente,* the departmental administrative officer. The president and all legislators are popularly elected for a five-year term in national elections that are held simultaneously. The legislature is bicameral, with ninety-nine representatives in the Chamber of Deputies, elected from districts, and thirty-one in the Senate, with the nation as a single district. They all are elected by proportional representation. The legislature has considerable power and is organized through a system of committees.

In December 1996, after years of discussion, a reform was narrowly approved by the voters in a constitutional plebiscite. Under the new system each party can run only one presidential candidate, who will be chosen by primaries conducted in each party and ratified at a party convention. To be elected president the successful candidate must receive at least 50 percent of the total vote or face a runoff against his nearest competitor.

This constitutional reform, which passed by the barest margin (50.3 percent) in a national referendum, represents a revolutionary change in the electoral system. In brief, the most significant features are:

1. A primary system was established to determine each party's candidate. The successful candidate must obtain at least 40 percent of the primary vote, with a 10 percent difference between the winner and the nearest competitor. If not, a party convention will choose the candidate.
2. Local elections are now separated from national elections. Elections for intendentes of the nineteen departments and their local legislative bodies take place in May of the year following the presidential and congressional elections.

There are several major implications of these reforms. First, the elected president can claim majority support, a result unheard of under the old system. Second, voters sometimes have to choose from candidates not of their party, or even of their liking, in the second round. Third, the primary system can help produce a real party leader as opposed to the historical norm of leaders of party factions. Finally, local governments are elected at a different time from the national government, a change that allowed ticket-splitting for the first time in history. This can generate more power at the local level and, with it, more demands on the central government.

Economic Policies

The Uruguayan economy is a distinctive mixture of private and public enterprises. Most of the economy is privately owned and managed, but about 20 percent of the gross domestic product (GDP) comes from state-owned companies. The largest of the state-owned monopolies is the *Administración Nacional de Combustibles, Alcohol y Portland* (ANCAP), which refines petroleum and manufactures alcohol and cement. That agency alone accounts for 4 percent of the GDP. In the 1970s there was an effort to encourage international banking in Uruguay in order to provide offshore benefits to foreign banks and investors and stimulate economic development by encouraging new investments in the country. The policy was partially successful and was supported by the military regimes and the subsequent civilian governments.

What has historically given Uruguay the appearance of a welfare state has been not so much the direct participation of the government in the economy but the benefits provided by the government. Nowhere is this situation more apparent than in the social security system, which covers a number of people equal to almost one-third of the active workforce. Low population growth means Uruguay has the highest proportion of retired persons of any Latin American nation, and this fact, combined with state-provided retirement benefits, creates an enormous financial burden on the people who are economically active. In fact, some 7 percent of Uruguay's most important revenue—the 22 percent value added tax—is usually destined to subsidize the State Social Security Bank (BPS).

The Military

The Uruguayan military is professional by Latin American standards and, except for the 1973–1984 dictatorship, it stayed out of politics for most of the twentieth century. During the dictatorship, the size of the military grew at least 400 percent, and defense expenditures rose appreciably to a percentage of the GDP far exceeding that of Brazil, Argentina, or Mexico.

One of the principal objectives of normalization following redemocratization was to bring the military under civilian control, and the major issue was how to deal with military leaders who were responsible for human rights violations during the dictatorship. The issue plagued the Sanguinetti government, which was otherwise preoccupied with serious economic problems, and impeded the normalization of national politics. In late 1987 the legislature passed an amnesty bill that prevented prosecution of military and police personnel for human rights violations during the dictatorship. The legislation was very unpopular and provoked a petition campaign to hold a referendum on the question of immunity. The referendum was held in April 1989, but the effort to overturn the immunity legislation failed by a negative vote of 53 percent. Twenty years later, a new attempt to overturn the amnesty law also failed. Nonetheless, since 2005, the controversial law did not prevent a score of military and civilian personnel from being convicted of kidnapping, torture, and murder charges with sentences of up to thirty years. The fate of the disappeared continues to be an issue in Uruguayan politics.

The Uruguayan military never engaged in the mass killings for which their Argentine and Chilean comrades are so infamous. However, they did arrest thousands and subject them to torture while also imposing a draconian rule on Uruguay's citizens from 1973 to 1985. The number of disappeared in Uruguay totaled a few dozen, with some 140 Uruguayans sharing the same fate in Argentina. The whereabouts of these individuals has never been clarified by the Uruguayan military. Children born to captive and subsequently disappeared Uruguayans are being sought by their relatives in much the same manner as the mothers and grandmothers of the Plaza de Mayo in Argentina. In 2000, President Jorge Batlle Ibánez was directly involved in this issue and convened a commission—the Commission for Peace—to investigate and issue a report on the matter. Three years later, on April 10, 2003, it submitted a report in which most of the 260 arrested or missing Uruguayans in Uruguay and other neighboring countries were confirmed. After the final report was produced, a Secretariat for the Follow-up of the Commission for Peace was appointed by President Batlle, and continues to function today.

Recent Administrations

In the first round of 1999 elections, the left, in a historic breakthrough, finished first with some 39 percent of the vote. But, in the second-round runoff, the perennial

Colorado candidate, Jorge Batlle Ibáñez, with the full support of the center-right Blanco voters, prevailed over the Broad Front candidate, Tabaré Vázquez, by 52 to 45 percent.

Uruguay thus began the new century with a wake-up call to its traditional parties. The voters indicated that although a majority still favors the rule of Colorados and Blancos, they wanted more creative solutions to the country's endemic problems of high unemployment and mediocre growth.

2001 was a difficult year for Uruguay even before the events of September 11. President Jorge Batlle Ibáñez had to face a worsening of Uruguay's economic situation exacerbated by an outbreak of foot-and-mouth disease that seriously disrupted Uruguay's meat exports. Moreover, the continued devaluation of Brazilian currency and the deepening economic and political crisis in Argentina had adverse effects on both Uruguayan exports and tourism.

In 2002 Uruguay suffered its worst economic crisis ever due to the financial meltdown in Argentina and the political and economic instability in Brazil caused by the election of the leftist candidate Luiz Inácio "Lula" da Silva. In the first seven months of 2002, Uruguay lost 81 percent of its foreign reserves. The country's sovereign debt abruptly declined from investment grade to junk status during the same period. Uruguay's GDP declined some 20 percent after the recession started in 1999 and unemployment climbed to a record 17 percent. Inflation, which was a mere 3.59 percent in 2001, hit 25.9 percent by the end of the year.[3]

The goodwill president Batlle Ibáñez enjoyed in Washington helped him obtain a US$1.5 billion bridge loan from the United States in order to keep the banking system solvent until more than US$3 billion in funds could arrive from the IMF, the World Bank, and the Inter-American Development Bank (IADB).

The following year proved no less difficult for the Uruguayan economy. In May Uruguay successfully renegotiated its private debt with an innovative bond exchange that stretched out the repayment schedule, thus giving some breathing room for the last two years of the Batlle administration and the first year of the next government. The banking system remained deeply depressed with nonperforming loans running at 25 percent at private banks and a staggering 50 percent at such key public institutions as the Banco de la República and the Mortgage Bank (Banco Hipotecario). The later institution lost US$1.1 billion in 2002 and was technically bankrupt.

2004, however, was an exciting and pivotal time in Uruguay. After nearly four years of sharply negative growth, the economy—aided by recovery in Argentina, strong growth in Brazil, and excellent commodity prices—grew by a robust 13.6 percent in the first half of the year. Unfortunately for the ruling Colorado Party, little of this positive macroeconomic performance filtered down to Uruguay's poor or to the middle class. Unemployment remained above 13 percent, and more than one-third of Uruguayans lived in poverty.

In this context, the presidential and congressional elections that took place on October 31 marked a sea change in Uruguayan politics. The presidential candidate of the Broad Front-Progressive Encounter was Tabaré Vázquez, a sixty-four-year-old oncologist, who had been elected mayor of Montevideo in 1989 in what was a breakthrough election for the left. A Socialist Party militant, Vázquez carefully juggled his coalition, which included social democrats, democratic socialists, socialists, communists, and ex-Tupamaros.

In the election itself, the left received 50.4 percent of the vote, followed by the Blancos (34 percent) and the Colorados (10 percent). Vázquez assumed office on March 1, 2005. This historic victory was seen by many to further strengthen the hand of Brazilian president Lula da Silva as he sought to turn MERCOSUR into the major voice for Latin American economic integration and the chief interlocutor with both the European Union and the United States in trade negotiations.

Five years of leftist rule proved very positive for Uruguay. With the appointment of Danilo Astori as Minister of Economy and Finance, the Vázquez administration quickly signaled its willingness to accept the rules of international finance and investment. Early on Vazquez made it clear that he would keep an eye on budget deficits and inflation.

The country enjoyed four years of exceptionally solid economic growth after the Broad Front victory, with average annual increases of some 7 percent. Inflation continued to be manageable during the same period. Exports boomed due in no small measure to the voracious appetite of China and India for raw materials and foodstuffs, which propelled a hugely successful economic recovery and resulted in the emergence of Argentina and Brazil as major economic players. The good times enjoyed in the Southern Cone translated into a tourist boom for Uruguay. Foreign investments also grew exponentially, thanks in part to a US$1 billion Finnish investment in Uruguay's forestry and paper pulp industry. Both wood and cellulose pulp are among the country's most important commodity exports now. This latter project, however, proved a bone of contention between the Uruguayan and Argentine governments. President Néstor Kirchner fought the paper pulp plant all the way to the International Court of Justice in The Hague. When Argentina lost there, the government continued to support environmental groups that closed the highways and a bridge between the two countries, thereby causing an economic loss estimated at several hundred million dollars for Uruguay. In the end, the plant was completed and is functioning.

The Vázquez government took advantage of its majority in both houses of congress to pass legislation on same-sex partners' rights. In January 2008, Uruguay became the first Latin American country to have a national civil union law, which allows both opposite-sex and same-sex couples to enter into a civil union after they live together for at least five years. Furthermore, a bill passed in 2009 established that same-sex couples could jointly adopt children.

In 2007, Law 18131 created the National Health Fund (Fonasa), which provides health care coverage for all inhabitants. This program is paid for by a specific tax on salaries and pensions. (Note: It levies 4.5 percent on individuals or 6 percent on families if one of the spouses does not work.)

A hard fight in the Broad Front primary in June 2009 resulted in the candidacy of the former Tupamaro leader José Mujica, head of the Movement of Popular Participation (MPP) faction of the Frente Amplio. Mujica turned to his main rival, Danilo Astori, as his vice-presidential choice, but this marriage was not made in heaven. In a second-round runoff held in November 2009, José Mujica beat his Blanco opponent, former president Luis Alberto Lacalle, with 53 percent of the vote, thus keeping the left in power.

In March 2010, Mujica was inaugurated as President of Uruguay, ensuring five more years of rule by the leftist coalition. The coalition continued to enjoy a majority in both houses of the Uruguayan Congress. During his presidential term, Mujica became an internationally recognized icon. He was called the world's "humblest president" due to his sober lifestyle and his donation of a large part of his monthly salary to welfare organizations. In the Mujica years, the major issues were the economy, the reform of the state bureaucracy, port and railway infrastructure, education, advanced social legislation, and relations with neighboring Argentina.

From 2010–2014, Uruguay continued to enjoy solid economic growth thanks to high commodity prices in the international market. The country had a near-record economic expansion—7.8 percent—in 2010, but it grew at a slower pace in the following years as the favorable tailwind brought by international conditions had faded out by 2013. However, GDP expanded 29.9 percent over the five-year period, and most importantly, unemployment remained at a historic low, 6.5 percent on average annually. Exports were at record levels due principally to the increased prices for soy. Sales abroad climbed to US$9.2 billion in 2014 from US$5.4 billion in 2009, though they rose hardly one percent at the end of this period as agricultural commodity prices had fallen.

Some social indicators were very encouraging in that period, however. National income per capita climbed 30 percent and pensions increased 17 percent in 2010–2014, while poverty dropped to 9.7 percent of the population in 2014 from 18.6 percent in 2010.

A strong increase in foreign direct investment (FDI) also took place in the 2010–2014 period, amounting to US$13.2 billion based on an adequate policy and regulatory framework and fiscal incentives to foreign investors. FDI flows peaked at US$3 billion in 2013, equivalent to 5.2 percent of GDP. This included a US$1.9 billion investment—the country's biggest private industrial investment—in the construction of a second cellulose pulp plant by Montes del Plata, a joint venture by Stora Enso (Finland) and Arauco (Chile).

On the other hand, a worrisome indicator was the fiscal deficit, which rose from 1.7 percent of GDP in 2009—at the end of president Vázquez's first term—to 3.5 percent in 2014, the highest since 2002 when Uruguay suffered its worst economic crisis. The main causes were increased public expenditure on social programs, large bailouts of bankrupted private companies through government financial assistance for the formation of workers' co-operatives, and expanded government payrolls.

President Mujica took office promising an in-depth reform of public institutions. One of his main priorities was to wipe out excessive bureaucracy and red tape, but he did not succeed. Ironically, the number of public employees rose 16 percent, from 264,957 at the beginning of his term to 308,091 early in 2015. Another blemish on his administration was the closure of the bankrupt government-owned national air flag carrier Pluna, which he prompted in mid-2012, and which generated various scandals throughout its liquidation.

During his administration, President Mujica spent time and money on unsuccessful attempts to implement some much-needed infrastructure projects that aimed to turn Uruguay into a top logistic player in the Río de la Plata Basin. He planned the construction of a US$1 billion mega-port facility on Uruguay's Atlantic coastline to be located in waters deep enough to allow the docking of super-Panamax vessels, which would load domestic and regional grains and minerals. The multipurpose terminal project turned out to be economically unfeasible because it depended largely on an iron ore mining venture in Uruguay whose Indian investors gave up after international mineral prices had tumbled.

Mujica also highlighted the rehabilitation and expansion of the rundown state-owned railway network to reduce transport costs and increase trade competitiveness. As his idea was to operate the country's public railway utility under private-sector rules to boost efficiency, the railway union opposed it flatly and Broad Front leaders did not give much support to his plan.

In his inaugural address Mujica called for a thorough school reform and remarked, "Education, education, and more education." But, at the end of his term, he had to recognize that his biggest failure as a president was in the area of education. Educational reform is long overdue in a country that, despite significant economic improvement and fiercely middle-class values, finds itself with a very high dropout rate in secondary school, especially among poorer students, compared to much of the region. In this context, Uruguayan students' scores have been below average in the Program for International Student Assessment (PISA), a worldwide study by the OECD that assesses learning accomplishments in math, reading, and science.

President Mujica also failed in his attempt to give autonomy to the *Universidad del Trabajo del Uruguay*, a network of trade and crafts schools, and turn it into a national technological school system. Negotiations did not succeed because neither government authorities, nor teachers' unions, nor political parties knew exactly what they wanted. At the end of his term, Mujica established, at least, the *Universidad Tecnológica* (UTec), which started preparing students for three degrees—two in milk production—in Fray Bentos. It has been expanding slowly but steadily.

Advanced Social Measures

Three laws passed in the Mujica administration made international headlines. They were the legalization of the state-controlled growth, sale, and consumption of marijuana; abortion decriminalization; and same-sex marriage.

In June 2012, President Mujica proposed that the government legalize marijuana and distribute it in order to cut off revenue to drug dealers. After a prolonged debate in Congress, the controversial bill that legalized regulated marijuana production, sale, and consumption across the country was promulgated in December 2013. The subsequent Vázquez administration, however, is still working on implementing the legislation. Its promulgation proved to be difficult and slow, because individuals are allowed to grow a certain amount each year, but the government will control the price of cannabis when it is eventually sold at pharmacies. The law requires consumers, sellers, and distributors to be licensed by the government.

In September 2012, Uruguay's House of Representatives voted to decriminalize abortion during the first trimester. The Senate followed suit in October and President Mujica indicated he would not veto the legislation, unlike his predecessor Vázquez in 2008. Thus, Uruguay became the first country in South America to allow women to have abortions through the first twelve weeks of pregnancy.

After a ten-month debate in congress, President Mujica signed the same-sex marriage bill in May 2013 that took effect three months later. Uruguay thus became the second Latin American country to legalize gay marriage.

President Mujica was again in the international limelight after making two spectacular decisions in 2014. He brought five Syrian refugees to Uruguay and gave asylum to six inmates released from the US prison at Guantanamo Bay. Both measures were more popular abroad than locally, because most of those refugees have given few signs of wanting to integrate themselves into the Uruguayan society.

GLOBALIZATION AND THE CHALLENGES FOR ECONOMIC GROWTH

Globalization

Globalization and regionalization under MERCOSUR, which Argentina, Brazil, Paraguay, and Uruguay created in 1991, have shown mixed results for Uruguay. The neoliberal model adopted by Blanco president Luis Lacalle (1990–1995) and Colorado president Julio Sanguinetti in his second term (1995–2000) brought decent growth and an explosion of consumer credit in the mid- and late 1990s along with a boost in tourism and trade with Argentina and Brazil. As discussed above, the deep economic crisis in the new millennium helped bring the left to power.

China and India may have an increasingly important role to play in Uruguay's future. Already, the Indian software giant, Ta-Ta Consultancy, is guaranteeing a job to all computer science graduates in Uruguay. Additionally, China's huge demand for food and raw materials is already benefiting the Southern Cone, and Uruguay has enjoyed a piece of this export boom. In 2015–2016, Heilongjiang Foresun Agriculture Group, one of China's largest bovine meat producers, acquired two medium-sized locally owned meatpacking plants to expand its participation in Uruguay's meat producing chain.

Relations with Argentina

Although José Mujica and his Argentine colleague Cristina Fernández de Kirchner shared similar leftist ideologies, their countries' opposite economic interests often made them clash and develop ill feelings. Uruguayan–Argentine relations proved thorny in 2012, owing to President Fernández de Kirchner's desire to prevent capital flight. As a consequence, Argentina's demands at the G-20 and the OECD forced Uruguay to sign a bilateral treaty on the exchange of tax information, which has allowed the Argentine tax bureau to learn about Argentine taxpayers' assets in Uruguay, namely in Punta del Este. Despite MERCOSUR treaty obligations, stiff Argentine constraints imposed on manufactured imports hit the Uruguayan industrial sector hard, because it is quite dependent on its neighboring market. Also, Argentina's foreign currency restrictions seriously harmed Argentine tourism to Uruguay for several years.

Fragile bilateral relations suffered a serious setback in 2013 after President Mujica authorized an expansion in production from 1.2 million to 1.3 million tons for the UPM Kymmene cellulose pulp mill without reporting it to the binational Uruguay River Administrative Commission (CARU). The Argentine government retaliated immediately by passing various measures against Uruguayan ports, including a halt on the shared dredging of both the Rio de la Plata estuary and Uruguay River navigation canals. But Fernández de Kirchner's toughest retaliation was a de facto ban on Argentine exporters using Uruguay's ports for transshipping goods, which became effective in November

2013. It made the Montevideo port lose some US$100 million. The ban was finally lifted when Argentina's President Mauricio Macri took office in December 2015.

CONCLUSION: THE SECOND VÁZQUEZ ADMINISTRATION

Uruguay has undoubtedly achieved democratic consolidation. The 2014 national election was the seventh since democracy was restored. During that period, all three major political forces have enjoyed at least one term in the presidential office. Elections are clean, fully contested, and voter fraud is virtually impossible. Since three decades have passed since the 1973–1984 dictatorship, it is clear that the unpleasant rupture of constitutional democracy was an anomaly for Uruguay's proudly democratic political culture and political history.

On November 30, 2014, the candidate of the ruling Broad Front coalition, Tabaré Vázquez, was elected president for his second non-consecutive five-year term (2015–2020). In a second-round election he garnered 56.5 percent of the vote against 43.5 percent for Luis Lacalle Pou—a forty-year-old candidate who is former president Luis Alberto Lacalle's son—of the opposition Partido Nacional. The ruling party enjoyed a slim majority of one vote in both houses of the Uruguayan Congress since it took power in 2005. However, it lost a crucial seat in the House of Representatives at the end of 2016. A Broad Front representative, Gonzalo Mujica, who is no relation to former president José Mujica, confirmed that he would become an independent congressman in December 2016. From now on, the government will have to negotiate the approval of every bill with the opposition in the House of Representatives. The left, however, won only six out of the nineteen governorships in the departmental elections held in June 2015.

Just two days after his clear victory, Vázquez surprisingly announced the names of his cabinet members, disregarding electoral quotas within the ruling party and leaving out representatives from those sectors pushing for a more aggressive left turn in the new administration. His decision disappointed the Popular Participation Movement (MPP), which had received the Broad Front's largest balloting percentage (31.8) in the October 2014 presidential and legislative elections. This Mujica-led faction was placated by the appointment of more of its representatives in the boards of state-owned companies.

Former Vice President Danilo Astori was appointed Minister of Economy and Finance—a position he had enjoyed from 2005–2010—in compliance with an agreement reached between Tabaré Vázquez and José Mujica several months ahead of the national elections. His program combining pro-business policies with an emphasis on social development was first introduced successfully in 2005 when the local economy was favored by a worldwide tailwind.

In his first year in office, President Vázquez had to put the house in order after his predecessor's sloppy management. At the same time, Uruguay's economic situation darkened due to the end of the agricultural price boom that had supported the country's strong GDP growth from 2004–2013. The local economy grew a meager one percent in 2015 and is likely to show a similar expansion in 2016 because of Argentina's slow recovery and Brazil's huge political and economic problems. Hence, the government has implemented a more controlled spending policy and stiffer fiscal discipline than existed under Mujica. Despite minister Astori's efforts to curb the steady rise of the country's fiscal deficit, it reached 3.6 percent in 2015 and is predicted to climb to more than 4 percent by the end of 2016.

After inflation exceeded the maximum target range for several years, reaching 9.4 percent in 2015, the government adopted a stronger anti-inflationary policy. In addition to making price agreements with supermarkets on massive consumer goods, which had relative success in 2015, the Minister of Economy has tried to decouple public- and private-sector wage hikes from inflation through the votes of government delegates in salary council negotiations. This policy has Astori facing strong opposition from the labor federation, the PIT-CNT, which called several work stoppages and two twenty-four-hour general strikes between March 2015 and December 2016. Among other claims, the Marxist-dominated labor movement demanded higher tax rates for wealthier taxpayers, corporations, and financial activities, the proceeds from which could be channeled to the public education system and to public investment to spur Uruguay's sluggish economy.

In spite of greater concern about the local economy's slowdown and higher inflation, the government was forced to postpone its deficit reduction plans due to the demands of Broad Front leftist representatives for larger funds to upgrade social programs and build infrastructure. Instead of a projected US$500 million spending increase for 2015 and 2016 in the Five-Year National Budget Law, public expenditure was raised by US$1.3 billion over that two-year period, and congress will have to readjust the budget legislation in 2017.

The Vázquez administration's ability to govern will be tested in 2017, since the Broad Front lost its slim majority—just one vote—in the House of Representatives. As expected, the internal divisions of the Broad Front often surface between the minority social-democrat faction—to which president Vázquez is closer—which accepts capitalism, provided wealth is distributed more evenly—and the left-wing factions, which aim to head the economy toward socialism. However, there is consensus that the quest to dominate the ruling party's hierarchical structure should not jeopardize the coalition's unity.

At the end of 2015 the opposition's bitter criticism, led by the Blancos, made a considerable dent in the Broad Front's approval rating, which sank to its lowest level in 11 years in power, according to a public opinion survey. The setback was due mostly to the scandal over the US$850 million losses that ANCAP—the state-owned petroleum, alcohol, and cement company—had over 2008–2013, when it was headed by Uruguay's current vice president, Raúl Sendic.

In February 2016, the Senate approved a report prepared by an investigative committee made up by a majority of left-wing senators, stating that there had been no illegal or irregular acts in the management of the state-run oil company through 2000–2014. Uruguayans, however, had been shocked by the declarations in the investigative committee hearings, carried on over four months, in which figures of all political parties, including a few from the Broad Front, denounced former ANCAP president Raúl Sendic's incompetence, excessive spending, and cronyism. Sendic has never acknowledged any responsibility for the state company's technical bankruptcy. After the hearings, President Vázquez dismissed the company's new directorate and named new directors more closely identified with minister Astori's policies. Furthermore, in April 2016, the four opposition parties—the traditional Blancos and Colorados, plus the small center-left Independent Party and the far left Popular Unity—filed criminal complaints against the previous ANCAP directorate on the grounds of multiple irregular contracts involving logistics, publicity, and construction.

Since the appointment of Minister of Foreign Affairs Rodolfo Nin Novoa in March 2015, there has been a shift in Uruguay's foreign policy. The new approach is not based on ideological affinities, but on the country's economic and trade interests as well as on the protection of human rights all over the world.

Because MERCOSUR has failed to be a platform for global integration, Minister Nin Novoa, who is supported strongly by President Vázquez, is seeking to reach bilateral trade accords with countries beyond the region by making some MERCOSUR rules more flexible. Since these reforms have stalled, Uruguay has started to look for some loopholes in the regional bloc's bylaws in order to gain access to the Pacific Alliance countries and the Chinese market. In mid-July, Uruguay reached consensus on an upgraded FTA with Chile. Despite some criticism from labor movement leaders, the new accord was signed in October 2016.

Uruguay's new foreign policy has faced several roadblocks placed by the ruling party's hard-left sectors. Thus, President Vázquez failed in his attempt to have Uruguay join the Trade in Services Agreement (TISA) negotiations, a proposed international trade treaty among more than fifty countries that would cover about 70 percent of global services. In September 2015, the TISA project was rejected by an overwhelming majority of 117 leftist votes against twenty-two moderate ones at the National Plenary, the Broad Front's top permanent authority.

President Vázquez's major victory on the international front took place in July 2016 when an arbitration tribunal of the World Bank's Center for Settlement of Investment Disputes ruled against Philip Morris International in its suit against Uruguay. In 2010 the tobacco company sued Uruguay seeking compensation for economic damages caused by the Uruguayan government policy of implementing strong health warnings that covered more than half the surface of a pack of cigarettes. The tribunal ordered Philip Morris to pay Uruguay US$7 million and to cover all fees and expenses.

Highly encouraging investment news cheered up President Vázquez in mid-2016. UPM-Kymmeme which, as indicated earlier, already owns one paper pulp plant in Fray Bentos, announced its interest in negotiating the construction of its second plant on the Río Negro Basin in the center of Uruguay. The Finnish company said they would invest US$4 billion in that project, provided the Uruguayan government complemented it with a US$1 billion investment in infrastructure improvement, namely road building, railway overhauling, and Montevideo port enlargement. As Uruguay is facing a high fiscal deficit—3.6 percent of GDP in November 2016—the government is going to seek financial assistance from international organizations and private investors as well. An investment of this magnitude will have a significant impact on Uruguay as it continues to set a regional—if not global—standard for democracy and social justice.

SUGGESTIONS FOR FURTHER READING

Alsina, Andrés. *Frente a Frente: La crisis del Frente Amplio.* Montevideo: Fin de Siglo, 2016.
Bentancur, Nicolás, and José Miguel, eds. *El decenio progresista-Las politicas públicas de Vázquez a Mujica.* Montevideo: Fin de Siglo, 2016.

Bergara, Mario. *Las nuevas reglas de juego en Uruguay: Incentivos e instituciones en una década de reformas*. Montevideo: Fin de Siglo, 2016.

Caetano, Gerardo, ed. *En busca de desarrollo entre el autoritarismo y las democracias (1930–2010)*. Montevideo: Planeta, 2014.

Campiglia, Néstor. *Los Grupos de Presión y el Proceso Político*. Montevideo: Arca, 1969.

Finch, Henry. *A Political Economy of Uruguay since 1870*. London: McMillan Press, 1981.

Garcé, Adolfo. *Donde hubo el fuego: el proceso de adaptación del* MLN. *Donde-Tupamaros a la legalidad y la competencia electoral (1985–2004)*. Montevideo: Editorial Fin de Siglo, 2006.

———, and Jaime Jaffe. *La era progresista*. Montevideo: Editorial Fin de Siglo, 2004.

Gillespie, Charles G. "Activists and Floating Voters: The Unheeded Lessons of Uruguay's 1982 Primaries." In *Elections and Democratization in Latin America, 1980–1985*, edited by P. W. Drake and E. Silva, San Diego, CA: Center for Iberian and Latin American Studies, Center for U.S.-Mexican Studies, Institute of the Americas, 1986.

González, Luis E. *Political Structures and Democracy Uruguay*. Notre Dame, IN: University of Notre Dame Press, 1991.

Handelman, Howard. "Prelude to Elections: The Military's Legitimacy Crisis and the 1980 Constitutional Plebiscite in Uruguay." In *Elections and Democratization in Latin America, 1980–1985*, edited by P. W. Drake and E. Silva, San Diego, CA: Center for Iberian and Latin American Studies, Center for U.S.-Mexican Studies, Institute of the Americas, 1986.

Kaufman, Edy. *Uruguay in Transition*. New Brunswick, NJ: Transaction Books, 1978.

McDonald, Ronald H. "Uruguay." In *Political Parties and Elections in Latin America*, edited by Ronald H. McDonald and J. Mark Ruhl. Boulder, CO: Westview Press, 1989.

Mordecki, Gabriela, et. al. "Crisis, recuperación y auge: 15 años de política económica en Uruguay (2000–2014)." Montevideo: Instituto de Economía de la Universidad de la República, 2015.

Rial, Juan. "The Uruguayan Elections of 1984: A Triumph of the Center." In *Elections and Democratization in Latin America, 1980–1985*, edited by P. W. Drake and E. Silva, San Diego, CA: Center for Iberian and Latin American Studies, Center for U.S.-Mexican Studies, Institute of the Americas, 1986.

Weinstein, Martin. *Uruguay: The Politics of Failure*. Westport, CT: Greenwood, 1975.

———. *Uruguay: Democracy at the Crossroads*. Boulder, CO: Westview Press, 1988.

NOTES

1. Much of the earlier versions of this chapter were coauthored with Ronald H. MacDonald. The chapter in this edition has been revised, updated, and coauthored with Jorge Rebella.

2. By comparison, Argentina has been reasonably successful in adjusting its rural exports—balancing cattle and grain exports—as international demand and prices have changed.

3. The discussion in the next several paragraphs is adapted from coauthor Martin Weinstein's entries on Uruguay in the 2002–2004 editions of the Britannica Book of the Year.

15

PARAGUAY: THE UNEVEN
TRAJECTORY

Sebastian A. Meyer

INTRODUCTION

On February 3, 1989, the longest presidential rule in Latin America's history was abruptly put to an end, when Paraguay's General Alfredo Stroessner was overthrown in a violent coup d'état initiated by General Andrés Rodríguez, his longtime aide and right-hand man. Although this coup marked the collapse of Stroessner's thirty-five-year reign, it was not enough to loosen the Colorado Party's tight hegemonic grip over virtually all facets of government. Although the party's dominance over Paraguayan politics did not start or end with Stroessner, the strongman's regime almost perfectly encapsulated the country's singular political challenges, including a high tolerance for corruption, authoritarian or demagogic tendencies among leaders and acceptance thereof by the population, and generally despondent attitudes toward elections.

Paraguay remains one of the most understudied and enigmatic countries in the region. It receives less scholarly attention or outsider interest than perhaps any other country in Latin America, in spite of (or perhaps because of) the fact that it is so rife with puzzles and contradictions, many of which do not conform to other trends seen in the region. Centrally located in South America, it has historically remained isolated from its neighbors and inward-looking, largely left to fend for itself. It was the first to gain independence from Spain and in many ways the first to develop and industrialize;

however, it experienced episodes of such trauma and devastation that two hundred years later it is struggling to keep up.

Paraguay's journey toward democratization, liberalization, and economic growth has seen undeniable progress, even though victories in areas of electoral democracy and civil and political rights have been intertwined with episodes of violence, persistent corruption, and distress. In many respects, Paraguay's future is bright and full of opportunity, but there are also pressing challenges it must overcome if it is to realize its full potential. In the sections that follow, this brief introduction to Paraguay will explore the country's idiosyncratic character and political history, emphasize the importance of these factors in understanding its current state of affairs, and discuss what to expect going forward. Throughout this narrative, certain themes will emerge, including Paraguayans' unique relationship with their leaders, the historical importance of the military, and the centrality of party politics over the last hundred years.

EARLY HISTORY AND POLITICAL CULTURE

Landlocked and sparse, the "Heart of South America" is bordered by Brazil to the east, Argentina to the south and west, and Bolivia to the north. At 406,000 square kilometers, it is larger than Germany and only slightly smaller than California, but with only seven million inhabitants, it is one of the least densely populated countries in the world. With deep, navigable rivers and a semitropical climate, the country owes its name to the Paraguay River, which separates the "Green Hell" of the semi-arid and largely uninhabited western Chaco region from the lush and more developed "Oriental Region."

Asunción, the capital, was settled on the banks of the Paraguay River near the Argentine border, and the city's metropolitan area is now home to around thirty percent of the country's population. Outside of the capital city, most of the population lives in smaller towns or farming communities. The population is extremely homogenous: almost all Paraguayans are *mestizos*, rendering ethnic or racial cleavages virtually obsolete. The country is also one of the few officially bilingual countries in the Western Hemisphere, and while visitors have no trouble getting by with only Spanish, the majority of the population heavily relies on the native Guaraní for everyday use, often resulting in a mixture of the two languages known as *Jopara*.

Paraguay Before Independence (1516–1811)

Before the first European settlers arrived in present-day Paraguay in 1516, several distinct indigenous tribes known for being great warriors inhabited the area. Asunción was founded in August 1537, making it the oldest continuous settlement in the Rio de la Plata Basin. Although Buenos Aires had been founded a year earlier, it was soon abandoned following attacks by indigenous tribes, forcing most Spanish settlers to Asunción. It was from here that they resettled Buenos Aires two generations later and founded a number of other important cities in present day Paraguay, Argentina, and Bolivia. As a result of this historical development, Asunción is often referred to as the "Mother of Cities." It remained the capital of the Governorate of the Rio de la Plata until 1617, after which it waned in importance to a Spanish crown that saw little value in land so far removed from the coast and devoid of precious metals.

In the meantime, the Jesuit order brokered a deal with King Phillip III and the Spanish governor of Asunción in 1609 to develop "reductions," semiautonomous settlements meant to convert indigenous populations to Christianity and establish small agrarian economies. Unlike the *patronato* system adopted throughout much of Central America, however, the indigenous peoples were not enslaved or exploited, but rather allowed to retain a degree of cultural autonomy and economic independence. Indeed, over the 150 years this system lasted, the Jesuits and the indigenous Paraguayans established a symbiotic relationship, working the land and practicing their faith far removed from any central authority structure. The reductions were allowed to form militias to defend themselves from raids by the Portuguese, and developed a remarkable cavalry. An increasingly secular crown expelled the Jesuits in 1767, and today all that remains are the beautiful ruins of two of these missions in southeastern Paraguay, which have been declared UNESCO World Heritage Sites.

Spanish settlers in Paraguay found themselves largely dependent on a subsistence economy built on food crops, tobacco, and the native *yerba mate* holly plant, which is still widely consumed throughout much of South America. Far removed from the political centers of Buenos Aires and Lima, these colonizers grew increasingly politically and economically self-reliant. The Spanish and natives developed their own kinship system, and polygamous practices accelerated the mixing of the races and cultural assimilation into a population that became remarkably egalitarian among those with Spanish ancestry, even if the purely indigenous populations remained relegated to a lower order.

The Formation of a State (1811–1840)

Paraguay's trail-blazing path to sovereignty was sparked by the May Revolution of 1810 in Argentina. Seeing an opportunity arise, the Paraguay Intendancy disavowed Argentina's attempt at independence, and when the junta-backed Argentine revolutionaries tried to invade Paraguayan land they were summarily defeated in two key battles in early 1811. Emboldened by the military victories and likely inspired by Argentina's example, Paraguay proceeded to expel the Spanish administration on May 14 and 15 of 1811. In a matter of months, the country freed itself from both Argentine and Spanish influence and became the first Latin American nation to gain full sovereignty from Spain, all without becoming embroiled in a war for independence.

For most of the next sixty years, Paraguay was ruled by three of the most formidable and influential leaders in its history. A few years after independence, the state came under the control of José Gaspar Rodríguez de Francia, who governed as "Supreme and Perpetual Dictator of Paraguay" from 1814 to 1840. Known as *El Supremo*, Francia was a lawyer, philosopher, and doctor of theology who had been a key ideological figure behind the independence movement. Once *elected* dictator and given control over the nascent state, he combined the enlightenment ideas that he so greatly admired with a ruthless and decisive style of rule to implant his vision into the very fabric of Paraguayan society and government.

During his twenty-six years in power, Francia built a national army, strengthened Paraguay's borders, and instituted a policy of economic development built on self-sufficiency. Under his autocratic regime, the state became involved in nearly every facet of political, economic, and social affairs, including state oversight over farms using lands belonging to the aristocracy and the church, firm control over the flow of people and goods across borders, and policies banning marriage among Spaniards. This last policy only served to accelerate Paraguay's already widespread process of racial mixture. Francia also expelled many non-compliant Spaniards and selectively jailed or executed his most vicious critics. Yet abuses of state power notwithstanding, Francia also turned Paraguay into an increasingly prosperous and self-reliant state that managed to completely shelter itself from the waves of war and instability that crashed against the rest of the region during the early age of independence. After a brief illness that lasted two months, Francia died at the age of seventy-four, leaving no successor.

The López Dynasty and the Great War (1841–1870)

The tradition of fierce independence, military discipline, and authoritarian leadership that Francia established was carried forward by the two leaders that followed—Carlos Antonio López and his son, Francisco Solano López. The father was a statesman and writer who opened up the borders, established diplomatic ties with Europe, liberalized the economy, and sought to establish a political dynasty by grooming his son from an early age. The son was commissioned into the Paraguayan Army at the age of eighteen, became commander in chief while Paraguay engaged in skirmishes with Argentina, pursued military studies in Paraguay and Brazil, and was sent to Europe as Paraguay's envoy to the United Kingdom, France, and Sardinia. While there, he learned military strategy as an observer during the Crimean War and helped his father import technologies into Paraguay.

Although father and son were autocratic strongmen, they were not particularly tyrannical in comparison to many of their contemporaries (or indeed Francia), and though in many ways they diverged from Francia's national project, they sought to carry on his legacy in strengthening Paraguay's borders, consolidating its sovereignty, and ensuring its economic self-sufficiency. Driven by the shared vision of a prosperous, autonomous nation, the López men instituted a number of reforms and sought to import European technology, engineers, and technicians to develop local industries. State-managed lands produced and sold vast quantities of yerba mate and tobacco, and social reforms included a public education system that resulted in the highest literacy rate in the region. By 1864, Paraguay was a regional power unrivaled by any of its neighbors. It was the most industrialized nation in South America, having established the first state-run railroad system, an iron metallurgy facility that produced a ton of metal per day, telegraph lines, heavy artillery, and a merchant fleet with the first steamships built from locally sourced steel. In addition, it was the only country free from external debt in the region.

A swift turn of events changed everything for this nation on the rise. An insurrection in Uruguay backed by Brazil and Argentina quickly escalated into a civil war. As an ally to the standing regime in Uruguay, Solano López declared war on Brazil and requested Argentina's permission to cross the stretch of land separating Uruguay from Paraguay. Argentina's President Bartolomé Mitre refused, and in May 1865 signed a treaty with Uruguay's Venancio Flores and Brazilian Emperor Pedro II. This act converted the Paraguayan War between Brazil and Paraguay into a War of Triple Alliance that lasted until 1870 and proved devastating for Paraguay. Over the next five years, the three countries waged a savage and brutal war against Paraguay which became one of the deadliest in Latin American history.

Estimates vary, but Paraguay is believed to have lost between 60–70 percent of its entire population and 70–90 percent of its adult male population. Another legacy of the war and the decimation of the adult male population is that it forever altered gender norms and the role of the Paraguayan woman in society, who were tasked with rebuilding and repopulating the country from the ground up.

THE RISE OF A PARTY SYSTEM

The Liberal Republic, the Chaco War, and the Barefoot Revolution (1870–1954)

Having already lost most of its population and much of its territory, Paraguay's nationalist autocratic experiment came to a dramatic end when Solano López was killed in battle. These events were so devastating that they are sometimes linked to attitudes held to this day, including a strong sense of pride in country. At the same time, the destruction wrought by the war and the oppression incurred by the occupying powers, who remained until 1876, may well have instilled in the Paraguayan people a perverse admiration of tyranny and a longing for the type of ironclad authority that had guaranteed Paraguay's prosperity and strength for the first half-century of its existence.

The "liberal republic" (1870–1936) that followed was a period of great instability during which attempts to institute liberal democracy in the country repeatedly failed. During the occupation of the allied forces and for several years afterward, military leaders attempted to reconstruct a country in ruins amid a climate of pessimism and distrust. The aftermath of this period saw the formation of Paraguay's party system. Although the current party names were not yet in place, the split between the nationalist conservative Colorado Party and the more centrist Liberal Party is one that by and large persists to the present. Another feature of this period was Paraguay's first experiment with *laissez faire* politics, which at times came to dominate government affairs, with the privatization of capital and concurrent liberalization of the principles underpinning domestic politics. Yet it was also a period of revolts, assassinations, and coups.

The era of party politics began in earnest under the presidency of General Bernardino Caballero, Triple Alliance war hero and Colorado Party founder, who, aided by his Brazilian allies, remained an influential figure throughout most of the first Colorado regime (1887–1904). Following the Revolution of 1904 carried out by Liberal exiles in Argentina, the Liberal Party dominated the political sphere until the *Febrerista* Revolution of 1936.

Although there were only two major party regimes during the half-century following the end of the war, it was a turbulent era for the recovering nation. Paraguay's only presidential assassination took place in 1887, and between 1904 and 1936 there were twenty-three separate governments, averaging one transition of power every year and a half. Paraguay's economy was also transformed during this period, with a major portion of Paraguay's public domain land being sold off following land acts in 1883 and 1885. By one estimate, Paraguay sold 75 percent of its entire area by the end of the century, all for an average of less than three cents an acre. Although these sales helped the state recover from financial ruin, the political climate remained unstable. During the postwar decades, there was a civil war, a revolution, and numerous coups.

Following an 1883 defeat by Chile in the War of the Pacific, Bolivia lost its access to the Pacific coast. Desperate to regain easy access to an ocean (which the Paraguay River could provide), Bolivia claimed rightful ownership of the Chaco. Bolivia's claim rested on colonial land partitions, while Paraguay's claim revolved around sustained occupation and commercialization of the land, ties to Guarani-speaking indigenous populations, and the presence of German and Canadian Mennonite colonies who were granted permission by the Paraguayan government to establish colonies in the region. The discovery of oil in the region may also have played a part in the bubbling dispute, with some scholars suggesting Standard Oil supported Bolivia's efforts while Royal Dutch Shell backed Paraguay's interests. Although Bolivian penetration in the Chaco had started as early as 1885, it did not gather steam until the early twentieth century, when Bolivia built outposts and advanced deeper into the Chaco. Tension escalated after a Paraguayan lieutenant on patrol was captured and killed, and the next five years consisted of failed negotiations, sporadic skirmishes, and a frenetic arms race until the official outbreak of war in 1932.

By the time the war started, all prognosticators expected Bolivia to emerge victorious. It had a larger population, a much bigger army with better equipment and superior German training, as well as a German commander in chief. Confident in its prospects, Bolivia launched a frenetic offensive into Paraguayan territory. However, Paraguay had its own unexpected advantages. First, it had an entirely unified and homogenous population, unlike Bolivia's patchwork army made up of highland natives, mestizo officers, and European leadership. Second, it had the advantage of the Guarani language, which Paraguayans were able to use in radio communications without being understood. Third, Paraguay had soldiers accustomed to the unforgiving terrain, unlike most of Bolivia's men who were from the highlands and had never experienced tropical conditions. Indeed, more Bolivian men died from disease and dehydration than from actual combat. Fourth, Paraguay relied on unconventional tactics, including light and fast units, strategic attacks, and night raids. Finally, Paraguay mobilized the entire country behind the war effort, expanding conscription and moving troops using railroad lines into the Chaco as well as its navy, which played a crucial role. In June of 1935, days after a crushing defeat and with Paraguayan troops only miles from Bolivia's oil fields, a ceasefire was agreed upon. Paraguay emerged as the victor and kept most of the land in dispute, but both sides suffered extensive material damages and casualties in the tens of thousands, and Bolivia ended up keeping most of the oil-rich land in the Chaco.

After the war ended, Paraguay once again found itself shattered and destitute, and the liberal regime could no longer satisfy the needs of the population. Amid rising tensions and discontent, acclaimed Chaco War commander Colonel Rafael Franco saw his star rise as he clashed with sitting president Eusebio Ayala. In 1936, Franco's supporters staged the February Revolution and brought the colonel from exile to serve as president. This movement would eventually transform into the Febrerista Party, which was originally national socialist in the vein of Italy's fascist regime, although this orientation was quickly overtaken by Marxist forces. Eighteen months later the Febreristas were toppled by another military coup, and in 1940 General Jose Felix Estigarribia, another war hero, was asked by the Liberals to abandon his post as ambassador to the

United States and assume the presidency. In his year in office, Estigarribia took advantage of his ties to the United States to secure loans for a highway system, and strengthened the state while expanding civil liberties. With the stated mission of averting total anarchy, he scrapped the 1870 Constitution, dissolved congress, and installed himself as benevolent dictator, assuring the population he would restore democracy as soon as it was feasible. Two months after ratifying the new 1940 constitution, Estigarribia and his wife died in an airplane crash close to the capital city.

The presidency then went to General Higinio Morínigo, who exercised repressive dictatorial control over the republic throughout his eight years in office, while the rest of the world became entangled in World War II. His legacy was a mixed one. On the one hand, he welcomed Nazis who fled to Paraguay after the war, suppressed dissent, and outlawed the Liberal Party, leading to a rebellion and civil war. On the other hand, he is often characterized as a fiercely honest and nationalistic leader who instituted political and economic reforms (following US pressure) and oversaw a period of considerable growth as the country sold its food crops to a global market desperate for agricultural products. In 1947, former President Franco, backed by a considerable number of Morínigo's military officers and the Liberal Party, launched the Barefoot Revolution against Morínigo and his Colorado allies, who had the support of Argentina's Juan Perón. A bloody civil war ensued, and while Morínigo's side won, thousands died and hundreds of thousands fled the country.

The following years saw the Colorado Party take power and entrench itself in the state, forcing party affiliation upon any and all wishing to advance in their civil or military careers. During this time, a number of different military leaders wrested power from each other until 1954, when General Alfredo Stroessner, one of the few officers who had remained loyal to Morínigo, reluctantly seized power after President Federico Chávez abused his powers.

Stroessner's Paraguay (1954–1989)

Although Stroessner was thrust into power and his accession was almost involuntary, it did not take long for him to consolidate his position as the head of state. He took charge of the military and the Colorado Party, forming a state hydra that reached virtually all facets of Paraguayan politics. He exploited and expanded the existing network of *seccionales* (party branches), which penetrated every city, town, and neighborhood, providing clientelistic benefits and patronage in exchange for popular support. In addition, he purged the military of all opposition while establishing a cult of personality across the population, the armed forces, and the bureaucracy. Although he was repressive, autocratic, and a demagogue, he refined his populist appeal, providing the citizenry with a sense of safety, order, and stability.

Having swiftly secured a vast base of mass support, Stroessner continued to bring all sectors of government under his yoke. He separated the officers into a loyal military corps and a secret state police, professionalizing and equipping the former while tasking the latter with carrying out the dirty work, conducting espionage on citizens and, where necessary, quelling seeds of dissent from university students, intellectuals, *campesinos*, unions, and the Catholic Church. Fiercely anti-Communist, he also set up an intelligence network with friendly neighboring regimes in Argentina, Bolivia, Brazil, Chile, and Uruguay. Termed Operation Condor, this multinational network of state repression and terror provided mutual aid in flushing out dissidents, sharing state information, assassinating opponents or making them "disappear," and sharing intelligence on everything from bomb-making to torture tactics. This campaign endured for most of Stroessner's regime, from 1968 to 1989. The 1992 discovery of the Operation's Archives of Terror in Asunción helped shed light on many of their clandestine operations, and also revealed US involvement before and after Jimmy Carter's presidency, as well as providing the basis for estimates of deaths attributed to the partner regimes in the tens of thousands.

Between this regional right-wing alliance, a broad populist appeal among the citizenry, a highly professionalized military, a ruthless and efficient state police force, and the absence of any real opposition, Stroessner's regime was all-encompassing and absolute. In this manner, he held the presidency for eight successive terms (winning elections uncontested or with token opposition), securing the longest presidential rule in the history of the Western Hemisphere. By 1989, however, the aging ruler had become less popular and increasingly out of touch with Paraguayan society. Domestic forces also began to conspire against Stroessner, with the Colorado Party beginning to show signs of an impending fracture. Stroessner loyalists wanted his son, Colonel Gustavo Stroessner, to succeed him, while the party traditionalists proposed a transition free from dynastic tinges. International forces also played a part, with the collapse of right-wing regimes and the spread of democracy in the region, as well as a highly influential visit by Pope John Paul II in 1988 which many credit for shaking the people out of their stupor and revealing the regime's shortcomings and hypocrisies. Months later, longtime friend and confidante General Andrés Rodríguez, who had become a wealthy and influential man during the regime (and whose daughter had married Stroessner's eldest son), staged a bloody but expeditious coup with the support of the military. Faced with no better prospects, Stroessner sought exile in Brazil's capital, where he would remain until his death in 2006.

Road to Democratization (1989–Present)

Although General Rodríguez was no civilian, his savvy and relative lack of political ambition allowed him to initiate Paraguay's democratic transition. He immediately liberalized the country, with measures including allowing non-Communist parties to mobilize, granting the press greater freedom of expression, permitting the return and release of a number of people exiled and imprisoned by Stroessner, abolishing the death penalty and the more repressive security measures, and dissolving the existing legislature. Three months after the coup, he held national elections, pledging that he would only serve for one term if elected. In May 1989, he won the election with 77 percent of the popular vote, a figure which seemed borderline democratic in comparison to Stroessner's more recent vote shares. During his term in office, Rodríguez reestablished diplomatic relations with much of the world and oversaw the passage of a new constitution in 1992 that remains in place today. For all his reforms, Rodríguez also fomented a culture of corruption, doling favors out to politicians and officers and granting them exclusive concessions over a number of illicit activities, including black market operations, drug and arms trafficking, racketeering, money laundering, currency exchange, and smuggling, much as Stroessner had done for him years earlier. Nevertheless, he fulfilled his pledge and did not run for reelection.

In 1993, the first civilian ruler in more than half a century was elected president. Juan Carlos Wasmosy, a wealthy engineer and businessman, represented a new, more progressive incarnation of the Colorado Party, albeit one still unwilling to abandon its close ties to influential business interests and the military. Nevertheless, Wasmosy's election represented a firm step toward democracy. Although instances of Colorado intervention and intimidation were recorded, Wasmosy's 42 percent share of the vote might not have been enough to secure office had the opposition not been split between two candidates. Domingo Laino, who had covertly founded the Authentic Radical Liberal Party (PLRA) in 1978 as the successor to the veteran Liberal Party, received 33 percent, while Guillermo Caballero Vargas of the new social democrat National Encounter Party (PEN) received 24 percent.

Throughout Wasmosy's term in office, his staunchest enemy was General Lino Oviedo, a former aide to Rodríguez, who had risen through the ranks and participated in Stroessner's 1989 ouster. A tense standoff between the two men in 1996 became an attempted coup, with the United States and other partners coming to Wasmosy's aid in the interest of protecting Paraguay's fledgling democracy. Despite this moderate triumph for Wasmosy and the stability of the regime, Oviedo remained a key (and among many factions) popular player in Paraguayan politics.

Indeed, Oviedo began campaigning in earnest for the Colorado Party's nomination to run to be Wasmosy's successor in the 1998 elections, further fracturing the party in the process. Combining his military connections, populist appeal, and natural charisma, Oviedo succeeded in securing the nomination, despite some existing wariness within the party ranks over what this might mean for the party's prospects. However, right before the elections took place, Wasmosy's government ordered Oviedo's arrest for his failed 1996 uprising. Oviedo initially hid from the authorities in the hopes that there might be some kind of reversal, but when he realized his imprisonment was inevitable, he surrendered to the authorities and continued campaigning from prison. Argentina and Brazil both threatened economic sanctions if Oviedo were allowed to run, and his candidacy was eventually declared null. Following these events, the nomination was handed to Oviedo's running mate, Raúl Cubas Grau, who like Wasmosy was an engineer. The vice-presidential nominee became Luis María Argaña, a Stroessner loyalist and sworn enemy of Oviedo. Once again, the PLRA fielded party leader Domingo Laino as the head of a slightly broader Democratic Alliance, yet Colorado strength was such that the unlikely Cubas-Argaña ticket won the presidency with 55 percent of the vote.

Immediately upon succession, tensions began to flare. Despite threats of judicial retaliation through the supreme court, Cubas released Oviedo after taking office. The public perceived Cubas as a "puppet-president," with Oviedo pulling the strings. Seeking to capitalize on this perceived lack of legitimacy, Vice-President Argaña turned on his running mate, exerting his power at every opportunity. The Chamber of Deputies, the lower house of congress, began to consider impeachment proceedings against Cubas, which would have made Argaña his successor as president. Yet in March of 1999, Argaña's chauffeured SUV was blocked off by another vehicle in a quiet street near his home, upon which a group of gunmen released numerous machine gun rounds on the vehicle, killing the vice president and his bodyguard.

Given Cubas's evaporating control over the government and his mentor's avowed enmity with the slain politician, suspicions immediately focused on these two men.

The tide of public opinion turned on Cubas and Oviedo, and congress immediately moved to impeach the sitting president. At the same time, riots and protests erupted throughout the streets of Asunción, with Paraguay's youth demanding transparency and accountability, and clashes between factions breaking into violence. So chaotic was the atmosphere that tanks patrolled the streets and snipers took to the rooftops, killing seven protesters and injuring countless more. Having been impeached and facing certain conviction, Cubas fled to Brazil on March 28. With Cubas and Oviedo exiled in Brazil and Argentina, respectively, and the vice president dead, the vacuum of power meant that senate president Luis González Macchi was next in line.

González Macchi was largely perceived as charismatic and reliable, but uninterested in governing. A year and a half after his new Colorado coalition took office, elections were held to fill the vice-presidential vacancy, with a former surgeon and mayor of nearby Fernando de la Mora, Juan Carlos "Yoyito" Franco of the PLRA, defeating Argaña's son Felix by a razor-thin margin of less than one percent. This historic victory for the Liberals signaled the first executive-level election won by a non-Colorado candidate since Estigarribia's election in 1939.

Emboldened, the PLRA ceased its involvement with the coalition government, while the Colorado factions continued to splinter. While González Macchi clung to power on a do-nothing platform, the country's situation continued to worsen. A wave of kidnappings, heretofore unprecedented within Paraguay's borders, began to shake the nation. One of the most prominent kidnappings was of Cubas's thirty-two-year-old daughter Cecilia, who was found dead after the former president paid a hefty ransom. A general atmosphere of corruption, insecurity, and malaise prevailed, with economic setbacks doing little to improve public mood.

And yet, as a testament to Stroessner's adeptness at fusing the state with the Colorado Party, the increasingly discredited party once again managed to retain control in the 2003 presidential elections. The victor this time was Nicanor Duarte Frutos, a former journalist, lawyer, and education minister. In some ways, Duarte represented a break from tradition, as he had briefly abandoned the Colorado Party amid some controversy, was Protestant rather than Catholic, and had revealed some left-leaning inclinations. Despite these surface differences, Duarte proved to be cut from much the same cloth, making populist appeals when it suited him but enacting policies that largely favored the wealthy and powerful. He was widely suspected of wanting to amend the constitution to achieve reelection, and when he failed, sought to take charge of the Colorado Party. Rather than support his own vice president's candidacy, Duarte endorsed Blanca Ovelar, who like him had held the post of education minister. This infighting introduced yet another strain on the party, and the Colorado primary went to Blanca Ovelar, who defeated Vice President Castiglioni by 0.5 percent.

Meanwhile, the indefatigable Oviedo, who had splintered from the Colorados to form his own party years earlier, ran his own third-party bid. The Liberals, having learned their lessons from splitting opposition votes among two candidates in 1993 and 2003, instead rallied behind Fernando Lugo, a longtime populist Catholic bishop whose rallying cry had been helping the poor. Finally, the tides turned for the country's party politics, with Colorado sympathizers splitting their vote between Ovelar, Paraguay's first female candidate, and General Oviedo, while the long-suffering opposition unified behind a single candidate. In 2008, Lugo was elected as the figurehead of a coalition that included the centrist main opposition Liberal Party as well as a number of leftist and left-of-center groups. These groups, minimally compatible in an ideological sense, had come together in mutual opposition to the six-decade rule of the Colorado Party.

The collective sense of euphoria generated by the end of the Colorado hegemony, particularly among the voiceless and marginalized, did not last long. Lugo's presidency had its share of controversies. The most salacious of these involved a string of accusations by former parishioners—several of whom had been teenagers or young women at the time—that he had fathered their children while still a clergyman, with Lugo recognizing some of these claims as legitimate. Still, he instituted a number of popular measures and reforms. Dressing in sandals and plain clothes, he refused to accept the presidential salary and took on an unassuming demeanor, speaking directly to the people. More importantly, he sought to improve the quality of public health services and education, became a champion of the indigenous tribes, expanded government housing projects, introduced a number of cash transfer programs for Paraguay's poorest, and renegotiated an unpopular energy deal with Brazil.

At the same time, the Liberal party in congress largely abandoned Lugo, and as he entered the last year of his five-year term, he found it increasingly difficult to retain control of his coalition. This situation was further exacerbated by the presence of an increasingly confrontational congress, both chambers of which remained under Colorado control.

Lugo's many detractors seized the opportunity to remove him from power when a violent standoff between police forces and landless peasants claimed seventeen dead, with Lugo bearing the brunt of condemnation for his incompetent handling of the long-gestating situation. Six days later the lower house voted to impeach him for "dereliction of duty." The following day, Lugo was given all of two hours to prepare his defense before the senate voted for removal by a margin of thirty-nine to four. The vice-president (and Lugo's former Liberal ally), Federico Franco, immediately succeeded Lugo as president for the remainder of his original term. Lugo's abortive presidency, which had brought with it a number of firsts, appropriately also ended with a first. He had become the world's first Catholic prelate elected as head of state. Furthermore, his victory marked the first time in Paraguay's history that a peaceful transfer of power to an opposition party had taken place. And as a result of his inability to retain control of his support base, Lugo was also the first elected leader in Paraguay ever to be impeached.

By the time the 2013 elections approached, neither the Colorados nor the opposition seemed poised to present a unified front, with the former still dealing with the thorn in its side represented by Oviedo and his National Union of Ethical Citizens party (UNACE) and the latter once again divided into some of the 2008 coalition's composite parts. However, the Colorado Party's prospects improved when sixty-nine-year-old Lino Oviedo died in a helicopter crash following a campaign rally in Concepción. In a strange twist of fate, Oviedo died on the twenty-fourth anniversary of the Stroessner coup he had helped carry out. When the elections took place, the Colorados regained power. An alliance between the Liberals, Febreristas, and Guasú Front might once again have kept the presidency from the grips of the Colorados, more than likely with a Liberal president this time around.

Instead, Paraguay's current president is Horacio Cartes, a conservative cigarette, airline, and financial services magnate and former soccer executive with nonexistent ties to the Colorado Party until a few years prior to his election. Following tradition, his reputation had been tarnished long before he rose to the presidency, with accusations that ranged from currency fraud (he served a prison term before being cleared by a court), smuggling tobacco into Brazil, money laundering, and ties to drug traffickers. In his three years in office, Cartes has sought to replace bureaucrats with technocrats and appoint younger, more professional people with little to no Colorado ties to high offices. Among his most prominent "youth movement" appointments, he entrusted Public Works to a forty-three-year-old, the Ministry of the Interior to a forty-two-year-old, the Ministry of Finance to a thirty-six-year-old, and Housing to a thirty-one-year-old. At the same time, he has been criticized for a number of gaffes and missteps, for being excessively subservient to business interests, and even for pressuring one of his ministers to switch party allegiance in order to retain his office.

AN INTERNATIONAL LENS

Given its landlocked status, small economy, and cultural insularity, Paraguay has not been a major player in international politics since the end of the War of Triple Alliance. Devoid of geostrategic importance or market power, it must fend for itself in dealing with its regional neighbors and other international players. Yet precisely because of this weakened position and legacy of brutal war and violence, it maintains a keen awareness of the importance of doing its part to maintain peaceful relations with its neighbors. As a result, there is a tension between the citizenry's fierce nationalism and collective memory of past wrongs, and the state's frequent willingness to acquiesce to the demands of regional powers.

The International Political Economy

Considering its deep historical and cultural ties, Paraguay traditionally dealt with Argentina on a more sustained basis than any of its neighbors. The sparse and uninhabited Chaco separates it from Bolivia, and even to this day there is only one highway connecting the two countries. Meanwhile, Brazil maintained weaker ties to Paraguay, as it produced many of the same crops and had a number of other neighbors to trade with. As a result, most of Paraguay's channels to the outside world were through Argentina until the mid-twentieth century.

This began to change under Stroessner's regime, as he sought to develop deeper ties with Brazil. During this time, the "Friendship Bridge" was built connecting the cities of Ciudad del Este (then named Puerto Presidente Stroessner) and Foz do Iguaçu. This tri-border area became a hotbed of commercial activity, with a free-trade port and tax-free status, turning Ciudad del Este into one of the largest commercial cities in the world. By the 1980s, Brazil had replaced Argentina as Paraguay's largest trade partner. Construction of the Itaipú Dam began in 1975, and for most of the thirty-two years since its opening in 1984, Itaipú has been the largest producer of hydroelectric power in the world.

In 1991, the Treaty of Asunción between Paraguay, Argentina, Brazil, and Uruguay established MERCOSUR (Southern Common Market), which rapidly turned into a major trading bloc and customs union and symbol of regional integration. This degree of integration, however, faced a backlash. Over the years, Paraguayans have come to worry about the extent of foreign economic penetration by outside neighbors, Brazil in particular. Surges in both immigration and capital flow began to alarm residents of the country, worried about Brazil's regional ambitions and the ease with which major firms, corporate farms and vast swaths of land came under the control of Brazilian migrants who modified cultural and economic norms throughout the country. Far from resolved, this "economic invasion" continues to trouble many Paraguayans and will likely fuel resentments for years to come.

Given the importance of hydroelectric power to the economy, two of the most significant recent clashes have centered around the issue. The first, which commanded national attention for decades, involved the Itaipú Treaty of 1973 signed between two autocratic military regimes. The legitimacy of the treaty was challenged by Paraguay, which stood to lose the most from its terms. Becasue Paraguay uses only a fraction of the electricity generated by the dam, it sells the excess power to Brazil. However, it does so at a price that was fixed when the treaty was signed, a sum which soon became dwarfed by market price for electricity. Still under Stroessner, Paraguay also agreed to allow Itaipú to sell its electricity below market value to help ward off an economic crisis in the neighboring country. This persisted for four years, and Paraguayan authorities claimed the illegitimate deal further plunged them into debt.

The terms of the treaty were not due to expire until 2023, so during his presidential campaign Lugo capitalized on the issue and made it the centerpiece of his foreign policy platform. Once in office, he made the renegotiation of the treaty one of his priorities, and no doubt aided by his ideological and personal proximity to Brazil's President Lula da Silva, succeeded in changing the terms of the agreement, with Brazil agreeing in 2009 to triple the rate paid and allow Paraguay to sell its electricity directly to energy companies.

The other ongoing dispute involves disagreements over the debt incurred surrounding the construction and operation of the Yacyretá Dam, which is jointly owned by Paraguay and Argentina. Although smaller than Itaipú, this hydroelectric dam built in the 1980s and 1990s is still among the thirty most productive in the world in terms of electricity generation. As with Itaipú, Paraguay only uses a small portion of its share of electricity, selling the rest to Argentina at a reduced rate. Argentina claims that Paraguay owes some US$18 billion from having shouldered much of the financial burden of building and maintaining the dam, while Paraguay counters that the sum does not take into account the real value of the excess energy sold over the years. These disagreements over Yacyretá have at times taken center stage in Paraguayan politics, and President Cartes's legacy will surely be affected by whether the issue is resolved.

Global Relations

With a few notable exceptions, extensive relations with other foreign powers did not begin in earnest until after World War II. For decades following the end of that war, the United States became Paraguay's major partner beyond South America. Although the United States pledged financial and military assistance in exchange for loyalty to the Allies, Paraguay nevertheless became a safe haven for several prominent Nazi officers who managed to flee Europe after Hitler's downfall, including Auschwitz physician Josef Mengele.

Stroessner became a symbol of regional allegiance to the United States during the Cold War, with his regime receiving enormous amounts of material aid and diplomatic legitimacy in exchange for an avowed repudiation of communism. Paraguay voted consistently in line with the United States at the United Nations and Organization of American States, broke ties with Cuba, and outlawed and expelled the Communist Party in 1955. Even in his final election in 1988, Stroessner ran on a campaign of "No Communism, No Communists." Beyond this mutual enmity, relations between Paraguay and the United States were little more than stable, and indeed came under some strain following Jimmy Carter's presidency and the resultant emphasis that US foreign policy placed on human rights violations.

After the transition to democracy, relations with the United States improved dramatically. The United States became a major champion for democracy and reform in Paraguay, defending its institutions and intervening to avert the 1996 coup attempt by Oviedo and avoid further crisis in the transition of power following the Paraguayan March in 1999. US involvement in Paraguay currently emphasizes corruption reform, the drug trade, intellectual property rights, and counterterrorism (particularly in the tri-border area, where terrorist financing is believed to take place).

In addition, Paraguayan relations with Europe and Asia have been deepening. Trade with Western Europe constitutes an important column of the import-export portfolio, and recent rises in emigration to Spain have highlighted the importance of maintaining strong ties with the Iberian nation. Ties with Japan are strong and China's commercial influence in the region is growing. Paraguay maintains a particularly strong connection to Taiwan, having been one of the first countries on earth (and still the only South American nation) to recognize it as a sovereign state. To secure this support, Taiwan frequently provides financial assistance, serving as a major creditor and frequently providing grants for education, housing projects, and even Paraguay's new congress building.

The MERCOSUR Dispute

The proximate event that triggered the unfolding of the MERCOSUR dispute of 2012 was the lightning impeachment of President Lugo that same year. Befitting the nature of his impeachment—the entire process having lasted thirty-one hours—reactions to the events from the international community were swift and decisive. Venezuelan Foreign Minister (and eventual Chávez successor) Nicolas Maduro called the impeachment vote a "new type of coup" and declared that "a truly shameful act has been committed." Cristina Fernández de Kirchner, Argentina's president, called the impeachment a *golpe suave* (soft coup), and implored all regional partners not to recognize Lugo's successor. By June 24, most Latin American states had condemned the impeachment, and those from the left refused to recognize Franco's "illegitimate" government.

Yet geopolitical incentives may have played a bigger part than concerns over rule of law, as Paraguay's standing in MERCOSUR became immediately compromised. Days ahead of a summit meeting, Argentina, in control of the body's rotating presidency, announced that Franco would not be welcome at the summit and that harsher measures were being considered. It did not take long for the real reasons behind much of South America's hostility toward the haphazard democratic transition to surface. As early as 2006 Venezuela had been invited to join MERCOSUR as a full member, but the enthusiasm the prospect of cheap oil imports awakened in the other three founding members was not contagious enough to compel Paraguay's congress to agree to Venezuela's admission. As a *Newsweek* article pointed out:

> Venezuela, long a candidate for full membership in the South American common market, had already won the blessings of Mercosur's three other voting members. The only obstacle was Paraguay's opposition-controlled Senate, which feared that Venezuela's bid might become a vehicle for what Chávez calls the Bolivarian revolution— his dream of spreading "21st-century socialism" throughout the Americas.[1]

Even the election of populist ally Lugo was not enough to shepherd Chávez's entry into MERCOSUR, given that Paraguay's 1992 constitution, wary of excessive executive power following the Stroessner dictatorship, had placed more power within the legislative branch.

The last tense clash over this disagreement took place in December 2011, when at the MERCOSUR summit a special committee was appointed to explore the possibility of approving Venezuela's request for full membership. Then, as always, there were complications because Paraguay's senate had accused Hugo Chávez of being authoritarian and anti-democratic. As a *Time* journalist then pointed out, "They may have a point, but their objection is more than a little ironic since the Senators are from Paraguay's Colorado Party—the lapdog of the brutal 1954–89 Stroessner dictatorship and historically one of South America's most anti-democratic forces."[2]

Seeing an opportunity to finally circumvent Paraguay's veto vote, the remaining three leaders accused it of violating MERCOSUR's "democracy clause," suspended it for one year—urging Paraguay to hold democratic elections—and summarily admitted Venezuela as a full member of the union. Paraguay's foreign ministry immediately went on the offensive, declaring the suspension "not only illegal but illegitimate and in violation of due process."[3]

Nevertheless, the decision stood, and a month later Chávez resurfaced after his bout with cancer and made his first foreign trip since his illness had come to light. In the Brazilian city of São Paulo, Chávez met with the other MERCOSUR leaders in celebration of his country's formal accession into the union as well as the purchase by his state-owned airline of six Brazilian-manufactured airplanes. After Cartes was elected in 2013, MERCOSUR announced that it would readmit Paraguay into the common market, and while Paraguay continued to object to the procedural violations committed in admitting Venezuela, later that same year the Paraguayan congress approved Venezuela's entry into the bloc.

Although the issue has largely been resolved, it perfectly captures the tension between Paraguay's weak international standing and at-times defiant character. Addressing Paraguay's neighbors on the floor of the general assembly of the Organization of American States, Paraguay's ambassador to the OAS ended a speech only two days before Paraguay's suspension from MERCOSUR with these words:

> If your goal is to work in tandem to expel us from all [international] organisms at the same time, go ahead. Paraguay will not disappear. Paraguay will remain a sovereign state, will continue to make itself an object of respect, as it has done historically. This

has not changed and it will not change. If you want to assemble an enlarged Triple Alliance, do it. Paraguay is prepared. It has done so once, it will do so twice, it will do so three times. We are not a country that will subdue before external impositions the likes of which we have suffered throughout the two hundred years since our independence.[4]

PARAGUAY IN TRANSITION

In many ways, Paraguay is well equipped to face the future. It has abundant land, water, food, resources, and energy. Paraguay's economy has also benefited from rising commodity prices and sustained growth in the region. It is a net exporter of electric power, and a powerhouse in its exports of soy, wheat, rice, beef, corn, yerba mate, stevia, and organic cane sugar. It has a young and well-educated population with a high life expectancy, and foreign capital and investments coupled with increased labor productivity have been fueling an unprecedented growth in GDP.

However, Paraguayans generally mistrust the state and its institutions. Recent survey data suggest that Paraguay has one of the lowest levels of pride in the political system and trust in the justice system in the entire region, displaying similar levels as Venezuela on both of these measures.[5] In addition, there are still perceptions that the wealthy are given protections that the rest of the population is not. In August 2004, a well-known Asunción commercial complex caught fire, killing almost four hundred and injuring many more. Although the faulty construction, lack of emergency exits, and poor fire protection systems all revealed poor oversight and lax safety standards, the real spark for outrage was ignited by eyewitness reports that the father-and-son owners ordered the doors locked shut from the outside to prevent theft and looting. More than two years later, the responsible parties were sentenced to a maximum of five years in prison, causing an upheaval inside the courtroom and protests in the streets. In 2008, after demands for a retrial, slightly harsher penalties were assigned, but by 2015, the perpetrators had all been released. This episode is one of many that reveal why there is such lack of trust in the criminal justice system.

In mid-2015, Pope Francis made a stop in Paraguay on his first trip to Latin America since his elevation to the papacy. This marked the first such visit to Paraguay by a pontiff since Pope John Paul II's historic visit in 1988, which had been widely seen as the social catalyst for Stroessner's eventual overthrow less than a year later. Among his stops, Francis scheduled a visit to one of the most impoverished slums in the country, an area beset by flooding from the Paraguay River and inhabited by squatters involved in a prolonged land dispute with the state. In a symbolic gesture, he also scheduled a youth gathering as one of his final events, signaling to this deeply Catholic and traditionalist country that new voices must be heard if progress is to continue.

In late 2016, both President Cartes and former president Lugo signaled their intention to run for reelection, despite a constitutional article stating that the president may not be reelected. In Lugo's case, the argument for running seems based in the fact that his impeachment prevented him from finishing out his full term. As for Cartes, his Colorado backers have instituted institutional reform efforts to allow him to run for reelection. Although the constitution states that such changes cannot be made via amendments, but rather by constitutional reform, Cartes and his supporters hope to exploit what they argue is vague language to do so via an amendment anyway. An initial congressional vote on the proposed amendment failed, but efforts are underway to have another vote, with members of the opposition already threatening to initiate impeachment proceedings against Cartes if such a vote goes through. With tensions on the rise, observers of Paraguayan politics will be paying close attention to the 2018 elections.

CONCLUSION

Augusto Roa Bastos, Paraguay's most prominent novelist, is said to have called Paraguay a "hole in the map," and an Argentine sociologist called it "a graveyard for theories," alluding to Paraguay's seeming unwillingness to conform to predictions or expectations formed on the basis of other Latin American countries. Without a doubt, Paraguay continues to puzzle most political observers.

Although support for coups d'état has been steadily decreasing throughout the region, Paraguayan citizens appear increasingly supportive of the notion that military takeovers may be justified in cases of high crime or high corruption. At the same time, levels of trust are much lower for congress than they are for the executive, relative to other nations in the region. Paraguayans display one of the highest levels of partisan identification in Latin America, but this party support is matched by extremely low levels of ideological identification on a left-right scale. Furthermore, it does not carry over to elections, where partisan voting is extremely low. Paraguay has one of the highest percentages of citizens who believe the economy is the main problem facing the country, yet it is one of the few where there is little to no evidence of economic voting. Finally, although Paraguay is consistently ranked among the most corrupt countries, a recent poll found it to be the happiest country in the world.

Perhaps no country in the history of Latin America has risen so high, only to fall even more precipitously. The last century and a half of Paraguayan politics can be understood as a number of wildly uneven attempts to deal with this tragic reversal of fortunes and forge a national consciousness and state that protect Paraguay's sovereignty from the outside world while frequently failing to contain the turmoil within. The degree of entrenchment of the Colorado Party and prevalence of corruption across most levels of government are clear signals of the enduring legacy of the Stroessner regime. Yet Stroessner was neither cause nor effect, but rather a larger-than-life encapsulation of some of Paraguay's more endemic problems.

An awareness of Paraguay's rich and troubled historical tapestry is critical to an understanding of its current political composition. The Colorado dominance can be traced to the Stroessner regime, which can be linked to the 1947 Revolution, back to the Chaco War, the Liberal republic, the War of Triple Alliance, the age of nationalism, the Spanish colony, and all the way back to Paraguay's topography and insularity. At the same time, this is not an argument for dependency or inevitability. To be sure, the nation has faced a number of junctures at which alternate paths might have been taken. Tragically, and with the benefit of hindsight, it seems more often than not that the wrong choices were made. Yet despite the setbacks, bloodshed, tragedy, and chaos, the small and still-troubled nation stands steadfast, as if defying others to challenge its sovereignty.

Paraguay sends so many mixed signals that it becomes almost impossible to assess its prospects going into the future. There is much to be encouraged about, and an optimistic observer will no doubt find numerous indicators pointing to a fertile soil ripe for progress, reform, and continued democratization. Yet that same stubborn character which lends Paraguayans their proud defiance also renders their more perverse habits and attitudes more deeply entrenched, making it much harder to shed undesirable habits surrounding public attitudes and institutional arrangements. In the end, Paraguay is largely in charge of its own development. If its history is any indication, it will not be an easy journey.

SUGGESTIONS FOR FURTHER READING

Abente Brun, Diego. "The Paraguayan Party System in Transition." In *Party Systems in Latin America*, edited by S. Mainwaring and T. Scully, 298–320. Stanford, CA: Stanford University Press, 1995.

Gimlette, John. *At the Tomb of the Inflatable Pig: Travels Through Paraguay*. New York: Vintage, 2005.

Lambert, Peter, and Andrew Nickson. 2012. *The Paraguay Reader: History, Culture, Politics*. Durham, NC: Duke University Press.

Lambert, Peter, and Andrew Nickson, eds. 1997. *The Transition to Democracy in Paraguay*. New York: St. Martin's Press.

Molinas, José, Aníbal Pérez-Liñán, and Sebastian M. Saiegh. "Political Institutions, Policymaking Processes, and Policy Outcomes in Paraguay." In *Policymaking in Latin America: How Politics Shapes Policies*, edited by E. Stein, M. Tommasi, P. Spiller, and C. Scartascini, 329–369. Cambridge, MA: Harvard University Press, 2008.

Roa Bastos, Augusto. 1986. *I The Supreme*. New York: Alfred A. Knopf.

Thompson, George. 1869. *The War in Paraguay, with a Historical Sketch of the Country and Its People and Notes Upon the Military Engineering of the War*. London: Longmans, Green, and Co.

Whigham, Thomas. 2002. *The Paraguayan War, Volume I: Causes and Early Conflict*. Lincoln: University of Nebraska Press.

NOTES

1. www.newsweek.com/power-shift-venezuelas-chavez-gaining-ground-65647.

2. http://world.time.com/2011/12/22/is-latin-americas-boom-over-a-pall-personal-and -economic-falls-over-a-regional-summit/.

3. www.economist.com/node/21558609.

4. Embajador Bernardino Hugo Saguier Caballero en la OEA. www.youtube.com /watch?v=c_Bkt76kz40. Transcription and translation by the author.

5. 2014 AmericasBarometer, Latin American Public Opinion Project.

16

BOLIVIA: CHANGES, CONTINUITIES, AND CONTRADICTIONS

Miguel Centellas

INTRODUCTION

The December 2005 election of Evo Morales as Bolivia's first self-described indigenous president was a watershed moment in Bolivian politics. From the start, his government proclaimed a "revolution" to radically transform and "decolonize" the country. In a country long recognized as having an indigenous majority, Morales's election represented a profound cultural transformation. Promises of more inclusive social policies, the articulation of an anti-neoliberal economic model, and vigorous emphasis on cultural, socioeconomic, and environmental issues touched upon aspirations of Bolivian and international audiences alike. Whether celebrated or vilified, Morales was included among the "new left" along with Hugo Chávez, Rafael Correa, and Luiz Inácio (Lula) da Silva. A decade since coming to power, the reality is more complex. In many ways, Bolivia under Morales has experienced a significant change from previous governments. In other ways, the trajectory of Bolivia under Evo Morales represents a continuity with prior experience. This suggests some contradictions inherent in contemporary Bolivian politics.

The 2005 election came in the wake of a political crisis that threatened the viability of the Bolivian state itself. Discontent with two decades of neoliberal policies and the party system that managed them, as well as long-standing grievances by excluded popular sectors, merged in the 2003 "gas war." A series of unrelated protests converged on opposition to selling gas to the United States through a Chilean port, then snowballed into a widespread anti-regime protest that left seventy-one dead. On October 17, President Gonzalo Sánchez de Lozada resigned and handed power to his vice president. A respected historian and public intellectual, Carlos Mesa was a political novice who had been selected as Sánchez de Lozada's running mate in 2002 to buoy his party's chances. Forced to work with a bitterly divided legislature, Mesa governed on the strength of public approval. He often threatened to resign as a strategy to overcome congressional opposition; in June 2005 parliament called his bluff, leading to a constitutional crisis. The presidents of both legislative chambers were highly unpopular, and the situation was resolved when they stepped aside in favor of the head of the supreme court, Eduardo Rodríguez Veltzé. The quiet jurist immediately scheduled early elections.

The December 2005 general election reflected a different political landscape. None of the major candidates represented any of the traditional major parties, although many establishment political figures aligned themselves with one of two new parties that emerged: Social Democratic Power (PODEMOS) and National Unity (UN). Of the traditional parties, only the National Revolutionary Movement (MNR) fielded a candidate—though he was an inexperienced outsider—although many career politicians ran as members of the two new parties. From the start, Evo Morales was a frontrunner, though few expected that he would win an absolute majority of the vote. Most expected that the president would be elected by parliament, as in every election since 1985. Without the expectation of a clear majority, few expected Morales's party, the Movement Towards Socialism (MAS), to win enough seats to elect him without support from another political party, a position MAS had expressly rejected.

As a compromise to satisfy demands from the so-called *media luna* lowland departments for departmental autonomy, departmental prefects, previously appointed by presidents, would also be elected in 2005. MAS candidates were expected to do well in the Andean highlands, and non-MAS candidates (who largely represented continuity) were expected to do well in the media luna. Thus, whoever won the presidency would face popularly elected opposition regional governors intent on setting the precedent of their own independent offices. The deep polarization set the scene for tense political confrontation and continued instability.

In the end, Morales won a resounding 53.7 percent of the popular vote—the first majority for any candidate since the establishment of democracy in 1982. MAS could not make radical political changes by itself, however, because it only held a slim majority (55.3 percent) of the seats in the lower house, and held one fewer seat in the senate than the main opposition party, PODEMOS, due to that chamber's seat apportionment rules. At the same time, MAS prefect candidates only won in three of the country's nine departments, with candidates from various opposition parties winning most of the contests, including the three most populous departments: La Paz, Cochabamba, and Santa Cruz. Despite fanfare over his unprecedented victory, Morales was more institutionally constrained than any of his predecessors, all of whom had enjoyed majority (coalition) governments and had appointed all of the departmental executives.

Only six months later in July 2006, a constituent assembly was elected to write a new constitution. That election did not significantly alter the political balance. MAS candidates won a majority of the body's seats, but fell short of the supermajority needed to enact most changes alone. This pushed Morales and his MAS party to pursue strategies aimed at increasing their electoral and support base, building strategic alliances with other parties, and, when necessary, leveraging extraconstitutional measures. Although since 2010 Morales and his MAS party have become increasingly confrontational, the first few years—particularly the adoption of the new 2009 constitution—were marked by significant compromises.[1] It is noteworthy that the final draft of the constitution put before voters in a referendum was not the draft approved by the constituent assembly, but one hammered out in the opposition-controlled senate.

By 2016, Evo Morales had governed Bolivia for more than a decade. During that time, MAS became the dominant political party—though it still faced significant competition in regional and local elections. That decade saw important changes to Bolivia's political institutions, as well as its economic and social structures. But there are also important continuities with the past. A decade under a hegemonic party and single leader has produced the kind of tensions that point to important contradictions—particularly between the government's loftier rhetoric and the realities of governing a socially diverse and economically developing country.

A SOCIETY IN TRANSITION

Bolivian society has undergone profound changes in the last few decades, primarily driven by two important, related forces: changing demographics and modernization. With a population of a little more than ten million, Bolivia is one of the smaller countries in the region. But its population growth rate is among the highest, with an estimated doubling time of only 40 years.[2] This growth is almost entirely driven by the region's second-highest birth rates, which would be higher if not for significant out-migration. Together with rapid urbanization, Bolivia's society is quickly transforming simply because of generational changes and the reality that Bolivia is a markedly younger society than the regional norm, with about a third of the population under fifteen years of age, as well as the consequences of transitioning from a predominantly rural, agrarian society.

Perhaps the most important dimension of social change in Bolivia is internal migration. Along with general migration from the eastern highlands to the western lowlands, urbanization has swelled the population of Bolivia's major cities. In 1950, the lowland departments of Tarija, Santa Cruz, Beni, and Pando accounted for 16.1 percent of the national population. In 2012, the year of the most recent census, that figure was 36.6 percent. That first migration wave began shortly after the 1952 National Revolution, as post-revolutionary MNR governments encouraged migration to more "productive" regions of the country, often offering land. A second wave began in 1985, as neoliberal policies led to the dismissal of thousands of miners. The biggest growth was in the department of Santa Cruz, which saw its population increase from 244,658 in 1950 to 2.1 million in 2012. A rapid influx of migrants from the Andean regions transformed the relatively isolated, rural hinterlands of the eastern interior. But there were also important elements of assimilation, as Andean immigrants adopted the customs and culture of the lowlands. Although not as stark as proponents of the idea of "two Bolivias" suggest, cultural and economic differences between Andean and media luna regions are an important political reality.

The most dramatic sign of the new urbanized Bolivia is the explosive growth of the major cities, especially the cities of El Alto and Santa Cruz. Nearly 70 percent of Bolivians live in urban areas—and those two cities alone account for a quarter of the national population. Before the transition to democracy in 1982, a majority of Bolivians lived in rural areas, and the city of El Alto was only a small underdeveloped shanty town community on the periphery of the capital city of La Paz. Today, the typical Bolivian lives in a major city and is connected to an increasingly globalized mass media and consumer culture. It is ironic that MAS, with its strong agrarian-rural base and rhetoric, rose to power as the demographic weight of rural Bolivians was steadily declining. This explains the increasing tensions between the Morales government and urban voters—even in culturally Andean places like El Alto, which in 2015 elected an opposition candidate for mayor by a wide margin.

Bolivia has one of the largest indigenous populations in the region, making ethnic pluralism an important dimension of society. The fluid nature of ethnicity was underscored by the dramatic drop in indigenous self-identification between the 2001 and 2012 censuses. The oft-reported figure that Bolivia is nearly two-thirds indigenous comes from the 2001 census, the first to ask about ethnic identity. That year, 62 percent of Bolivians over the age of fifteen identified themselves as belonging to one of the various indigenous groups in Bolivia—most identified as either Quechua (30.7 percent) or Aymara (25.2 percent). The 2012 census asked about the ethnic self-identification of all Bolivians (not just those over the age of fifteen) and found that only 41.2 percent identified as belonging to one of the various indigenous communities. Quechua and Aymara population shares dropped the most, to 18.3 and 15.9 percent, respectively. One explanation is slight changes to the question's structure. Perhaps more important is a demographic shift among younger Bolivians.[3] Survey data from sources like AmericasBarometer have long suggested that ethnic identity in Bolivia is complex. Those surveys generally report indigenous population around 10–15 percent, with large *mestizo* (a category not included in the Bolivian census) majorities.

The decline in indigenous self-identification is partly a result of urbanization. The indigenous population share of rural areas remained little changed, and about two-thirds of Bolivia's self-identified indigenous population lives in rural areas. The national-level change was mostly driven by wide swings away from indigenous self-identification in urban areas. Even the highly indigenous city of El Alto saw its self-identified indigenous population drop from 81.3 to 49.2 percent between censuses. The reality is that ethnic identity in Bolivia is more complex than is often portrayed. Although indigenous cultural legacies remain strong—particularly in the Andean highlands—Bolivia's ethnic pluralism is more fluid and shouldn't be reduced to an indigenous and nonindigenous dichotomy.

Bolivia's rapid urbanization was accompanied by other kinds of demographic changes associated with modernization. The education level has risen, even in relatively short periods. By 2012, 58 percent of Bolivians had completed secondary education, a significant improvement over the 40 percent figure only a decade earlier.[4] This trend was consistent throughout the democratic period, with the biggest gains made in the 1980s and 1990s.[5] Health indicators show similar improvements. Although it remains the second highest in the region (after Haiti), infant mortality steadily decreased since 1960, from 173 per 1,000 live births to 30.6 in 2015. Meanwhile, life expectancy steadily improved from 42.1 years in 1960 to 68.3 years in 2014—one of the sharpest improvements in the region. And although the fertility rate remains high relative to the region, it has steadily decreased from 6.7 births per woman in 1960 to a modest 3.03 by 2014. Clearly, Bolivia's population growth is driven mainly by improvements in health outcomes, even as birth rates continue to fall. Given time, Bolivia should undergo the same demographic transition seen in other modernizing societies.

Although Protestantism has made inroads in Latin America in recent decades, Bolivia remains a predominantly Catholic country, with 77 percent of the population identifying as such.[6] However, it is important to note that Catholicism in Bolivia is itself diverse and highly intersected by the country's ethnic pluralism. There is a resurgence of indigenous religious practice, particularly among rural indigenous communities, some of which was actively encouraged by some clergy as a way to ward off Protestantism.[7] Additionally, many Bolivians practice some syncretic form of Catholicism, combining indigenous beliefs and practices. Still, Protestantism has had a significant impact on Bolivian society, primarily because of the political influence of American-backed evangelicals. This active religious minority is disproportionately concentrated socially among the lower and aspirational middle classes, and politically among the conservative opposition.

ECONOMIC DEVELOPMENT

Perhaps in no area are continuities and contradictions more visible than in Bolivia's economy. Despite many important improvements in socioeconomic development indicators, the country's economy continues to be dominated by the export of natural resources. Likewise, although recent decades have seen Bolivia rapidly urbanize, industrialization has lagged behind. Instead, most Bolivians today work in the service sector—often informally—although more than a third continue to work in agriculture. Structurally, this means that Bolivia has mostly transitioned from an agrarian to a service society, largely bypassing industrialization. But it also means that Bolivia remains in a relationship of "dependent development" relative to the global economy.

In some ways, Bolivia has gone backward in terms of the structure of its economy. By 1986, manufacturing accounted for a healthy 20.4 percent of GDP. But this declined to 13 percent by 2014. At the same time, revenues from natural resources (primarily minerals, natural gas, and oil) increased. In 1985, natural resource rents accounted for only 7.6 percent of GDP, and hit a low of 4.1 percent in 1999. Since then, natural resource rents have become a larger share of the economy, peaking at 39.7 percent of GDP in 2008. In the years between 2005 and 2008, only Venezuela's economy relied on natural resource rents more than Bolivia. The recent fall of commodity prices has reduced this, bringing it in line with 1970s levels. Greater emphasis on oil and gas revenues during the Morales presidency has come at the expense of manufacturing and other economic sectors.

The global commodity boom buoyed Bolivia's economy during the early years under President Morales. The economic boom, which began in the late 1990s, made meaningful improvements for many Bolivians. According to the World Bank, poverty steadily decreased from 66.4 percent of the population in 2000 to 39.3 percent in 2014. Additionally, economic inequality decreased significantly. Bolivia has long been one of the most unequal societies in the world. In 2000, Bolivia had a Gini index score of 63, making it the most unequal country in the region. By 2011, that measure fell to 46.3, making it the fifth most equal country in the region. Since then, inequality has crept up again, reaching 48.4 in 2014, but still within the regional average. All the while, GDP per capita (in current US$) has more than tripled, from US$1,007 in 2000 to US$3,124 in 2014.

One worrying sign is the large informal sector, which remains at more than 70 percent of nonagricultural employments. The vast majority of Bolivians work in precarious or ad hoc jobs, with little protection from economic downturns. This also means that much of the country's economic activity remains outside of government regulations or taxation. Less troubling is the country's age dependency ratio, which is the ratio of the working-age population relative to those too young or too old to work. Although it remains one of the highest in the region, it steadily declined to a manageable 63.9 percent by 2015.

Two important sources of external revenue continue to be personal remittances and foreign aid, although both have declined in importance in recent years. Throughout the 1990s, personal remittances from Bolivians living abroad had increased, peaking at eight percent of GDP in 2008, but this has since decreased to 3.6 percent in 2015. Likewise, although foreign development aid remains high (it averaged US$682.8 million since Evo Morales was elected), it fell from 12.1 percent of GNI in 2003 to just over two percent by 2014. Because the overall Bolivian economy has grown, the declining weight of foreign assistance gives the Bolivian government much more flexibility in terms of setting its own policy agendas.

Finally, because of the experience of hyperinflation in the mid-1980s (which peaked at 11,750 percent for the year 1985), it is impossible to discuss Bolivia's economy without addressing inflation. Since 1992, Bolivian annual inflation has averaged a modest 6.2 percent. Although older Bolivians remain wary of the specter of hyperinflation, it is telling that Bolivia has not yet seen the same kind of runaway inflation as Venezuela. One important reason for this has been that, contrary to expectations, the Morales government has followed prudently conservative macroeconomic policies and built up significant foreign reserves. By 2014, Bolivia was holding more than US$15 billion in foreign reserves, one of the largest in terms of share of GDP in the region.

POLITICAL CULTURE

Bolivia's political culture is difficult to assess. The country has a vibrant civil society, marked both by its dense patchwork of neighborhood, occupational, and other social organizations and their propensity to mobilize on behalf of political, social, or economic demands. At the same time the country has the propensity to rally around populist figures, a long history of personalization of politics, and widespread clientelism. A key problem is the lack of strong representative institutions that can channel social demands. Instead, the Bolivian norm is for groups to take their demands immediately to the streets in hopes of forcing the government to dialogue and negotiation. This pattern has continued even under Evo Morales, with the number of protests in Bolivia reaching an average of 50.4 per day in 2010, a number that surpasses the number of conflicts during the economic crisis of 1982–1985.[8]

One way to assess the country's political culture is through the AmericasBarometer, a survey administered by the Latin American Public Opinion Project (LAPOP) biannually since 1998.[9] Although many survey items are inconsistently used, we can use them to assess changes in Bolivian attitudes during and since the election of Evo Morales, and compare these to regional attitudes.

A key element of political culture is social support for and satisfaction with democracy, which, according to LAPOP data, has been consistently modest in Bolivia since 2004, only slightly below the regional average. When asked how democratic they think their country is, Bolivian responses are stable and consistent with regional averages. Still, a significant and growing majority of Bolivians agree that democracy is "preferred to any other system of government." Despite a sharp drop in 2006 to 66.4 percent, agreement with that statement increased from 70.4 percent in 2004 to 81.5 percent in 2014.

Today support for democracy in Bolivia is significantly *higher* than the regional average (77.4 percent in 2014). On the other hand, however, a large number of Bolivians continue to say they would support a military coup under certain circumstances. In 2004, more than a third (34.7 percent) said they would support a military coup in the case of high unemployment and half (49.9 percent) said they would tolerate a coup in the case of "widespread social disorder"—although that figure was *lower* than the regional average (52.5 percent) for that same year. Support for coups has declined, however, to under a fifth (19.7 percent) of respondents saying they would support a coup in the case of high unemployment in 2012, the last year that question was included in the survey. The record, therefore, is mixed: Bolivians seem to support democracy generally in line with regional averages, but a sizeable portion of the population is willing to accept authoritarian interventions—although, again, this is not too far out of line with regional figures.

In terms of support for political institutions, Bolivia remains below the regional average, according to LAPOP data. General overall trust in political institutions vacillated between 1998 and 2014, but with a slight trend of improvement; in 2008 and 2010, the Bolivian average coincided with the regional average. Confidence in political parties in Bolivia remains consistently low, and slightly below the regional average. Confidence in the president is generally higher, and there are some interesting contradictions: confidence in the presidency rose dramatically in 2002 and continued to rise, peaking in 2008, before declining again.

More troubling are signs of low political tolerance among the Bolivian population. The AmericasBarometer survey includes questions related to tolerance, particularly of people who criticize the government. Because these questions have been asked consistently in Bolivia since 1998, we can compare levels of tolerance toward government critics before and after the election of Evo Morales. Support for the right of government critics to vote—a very minimal level of political tolerance—has been markedly tepid. However, support for the right to vote for government critics began increasing in 2000 and peaked in 2010, before declining again back to 1998 levels. Interestingly, support for the right of government critics to protest is not much different from support for their right to vote.

Most of the country's population belongs to or is represented by one or more civil society organizations. Typically, Bolivians belong to an occupational association:

professional unions such as those representing teachers, lawyers, and medical workers, but also more blue-collar occupations such as housekeepers, taxi drivers, and miners. Such organizations extend to informal labor sectors, such as the *gremios* that organize street and market venders, and even shoe-shine boys. Additionally, there are interest-, identity-, and community-based organizations. Protests on behalf of social causes (animal rights or environmental concerns, for example) are not uncommon, particularly across middle-class sectors. Most neighborhoods are organized into neighborhood associations (*juntas vecinales*), which are increasingly important political actors in urban politics. In the countryside, communities are organized either by *ayllu* (a traditional Andean community organization), which heavily emphasize ethnic traditional practices, or a more common rural trade union (*sindicato*) model, which squarely emphasizes labor identity as "peasants" (*campesinos*). Finally, most civil society organizations operate through a highly formalized structure that goes from small units to larger, "peak" associations. For example, at the regional level the neighborhood associations are organized into federations, as are the rural unions. Among the most powerful actors in Bolivian politics today are the Unified Syndical Confederation of Rural Workers of Bolivia (CSUTCB), the National Council of Ayllus and Marks of Qullasuyu (a federation of highland ayllus), the Confederation of Indigenous Peoples of Bolivia (CIDOB, a lowland indigenous organization), and the El Alto Federation of Neighborhood Councils (FEJUVE). Although still powerful, the Bolivian Workers' Central (COB), a sort of "union of unions," now shares space with other organizations.

Bolivia's many civil society organizations are very active in social, political, and economic spheres. They mobilize on behalf of interests, to denounce injustices, or to petition for policies. The problem for Bolivian democracy is not that the public is disengaged from politics, but that public demands are channeled almost exclusively through civil society rather than representative institutions. Trust in political institutions is low, and links between political parties and civil society are weak. Rather than mass parties, Bolivian parties are typically small, ideological organizations that seek to build explicit, formal alliances with civil society organizations—or, like MAS, are organized as confederations of civil society organizations. The result is that civil society organizations are the main conduit for politics, rather than the formal political institutions of representative government.

POLITICAL INSTITUTIONS

Shortly after the election of Evo Morales in 2005, Bolivia began an accelerated process of institutional reforms. The 2009 constitution, approved by voters in a referendum on January 25, significantly restructured and redefined the Bolivian state's formal institutions. This included changes to the state's territorial reorganization as a unitary state "with autonomies," various reforms to the electoral system, and a restructuring of the judicial system. Although many reforms remain not fully implemented, they have had important consequences for Bolivia's contemporary democratic politics.

Perhaps the most significant change has been the recognition of subnational autonomy. The 2009 constitution recognizes four different types of autonomies: departmental, regional, municipal, and indigenous communities. Of these, municipal autonomy is the oldest, dating from the 1994 Law of Popular Participation (LPP). Enacted during the first Sánchez de Lozada presidency (1993–1997), municipal autonomy both granted Bolivian citizens direct election of their local governments and guaranteed equitable funding from the central state. Municipal elections were introduced in 1985, shortly after the country's transition to democracy. But these were limited to major cities and used the presidential ballot to determine the composition of municipal councils. The 1994 LPP extended municipal governance across the whole Bolivian territory and earmarked 20 percent of the state budget for municipal governments, distributed on the basis of population.

The municipal autonomy inscribed in the 2009 constitution is a continuation of the LPP. The introduction of three new types of autonomy represents both a radical departure from the earlier unitary state model, as well as a difficult challenge stemming from the nonhierarchical relationship between the different levels. According to the Article 276, Bolivia's nine departmental governments stand on equal footing with municipalities, regions, and indigenous communities. This complicates jurisdictional issues between the different layers of government, particularly between the new autonomous indigenous communities and regions.

Although indigenous rights are championed by the Morales government, by the end of 2016 only one autonomous indigenous community has been legally recognized and had allowed to govern itself according to traditional customs. Voters in eleven municipalities decided to become autonomous indigenous communities in a series of referendums in 2009, but most are stalled in the difficult process of achieving legal recognition. As of 2016, only Charagua, a predominantly Guaraní municipality in the department of Santa Cruz, had won recognition as an autonomous indigenous community—although it had yet to elect a new government using the new autonomy charter. Regions are unlikely to cause significant jurisdictional conflict, because they must be formed on the basis of joining municipalities and cannot cross departmental boundaries. Autonomous indigenous communities, on the other hand, have no such restrictions. Although they must be formed from "ancestral territories" with "geographic continuity," there is no specified restriction against such communities forming across departmental or municipal boundaries. However, it is telling that the only communities so far to have initiated the process to become autonomous indigenous communities have been entire municipalities. This has posed a challenge, because citizens in those municipalities who do not identify as members of indigenous communities have resisted transforming their municipalities into indigenous communities they fear might exclude them. Despite an official rhetoric of "decolonization," the Morales government has defended the integrity of pre-existing departmental and provincial boundaries— although some territorial disputes have been resolved by splitting existing municipalities into two or more new municipalities.

In practice, the new Bolivian state is a form of de facto "asymmetric" federalism.[10] Because municipal and regional autonomies are nested within autonomous departments, the reality is a Bolivian polity with nine "states," each with its own constellation of federalized subterritories within. This is a radical departure from the previously highly centralized Bolivian state. This change, of course, has had significant consequences for the electoral system, which has also been significantly reformed in recent years.

Elections and Parties

Bolivia's electoral system has undergone significant changes since its transition to democracy, moving from one of the simplest to one of the most complex in the region. Some are extensions of earlier reforms, also introduced in the 1990s under Sánchez de Lozada. Others are new and reflect changes in the broader political structure. The introduction of new autonomous governments necessitated the creation of new, subnational electoral systems. In addition, other elements of electoral system reform were part of the broader redesign of the new "plurinational" Bolivian state.

At its transition to democracy, Bolivia had one of the simplest electoral systems: The single ballot cast for president also determined the composition of the two legislative chambers. Presidential candidates simply headed an electoral list; if no one candidate won a simple majority, the newly elected congress would select a president from among the frontrunners. This "parliamentarized presidential" system was marked by multiparty coalitions, which gave presidents legislative majorities.[11] That system began to lose legitimacy in the 1990s and finally broke down after the 2003 gas war, prompting a series of reforms. The overall trend of Bolivia's electoral reforms has been a move away from a proportionality-based electoral system, toward one that is increasingly majoritarian in nature.

A 1995 electoral reform introduced a mixed-member electoral system, giving Bolivian voters a separate ballot to elect an individual representative in single-member districts (SMDs)—in addition to the presidential ballot, which was still used to determine the composition of the senate and the lower chamber of deputies, after taking into account the number of SMD seats won by the parties. That system was first used in the 1997 election, and just over half of the chamber of deputies (62 of 130) were elected in single-member districts using simple plurality. Prior to the 2005 election, the number of SMD deputies was increased to 70 as part of a negotiated reapportionment (to adjust for changes in population distribution across departments). The 2009 election incorporated reforms introduced in the 2009 constitution, which included the creation of seven "special" indigenous seats, further reducing the list-proportional seats to 53 (of 130).

Another reform introduced in 2009 was the introduction of a "qualified" runoff system for presidential elections. A frontrunner can avoid a runoff if he/she wins at least 40 percent of the vote and has a ten-point advantage over the runner-up. This has had no immediate effect, since Evo Morales has consistently won popular majorities. A similar runoff system was introduced for departmental elections in 2015, but not at regional or municipal levels.

The LPP used a "parliamentarized" formula to elect municipal governments: voters were given a simple party list choice; the top listed candidate for the majority party became mayor; if no party won a majority, the new council chose one of its members to be mayor. The 2009 constitution introduced separate elections for mayors and municipal councils, although these could win by simple plurality. This was consistent with the trend toward increasing direct voter choice. This choice made split-ticket voting possible. In the fluid, multiparty context of Bolivian politics, this meant that nearly a third of the mayors elected in 2015 did not enjoy legislative majorities in their municipal councils.

The nine autonomous departments each have their own electoral systems. Although the election of department executives was introduced in 2005 as a compromise toward calls for departmental autonomy, the 2010 and 2015 elections involved more complex department-level electoral systems. Constitutionally, each department is able to draw up its own electoral system. These systems vary from each other considerably. Interestingly, the lowland departments kept the systems they approved in the 2008 wildcat autonomy referendums. The other five departments used "transitory" electoral systems in 2010, which explains the uniformity of their electoral systems.

Another important area of electoral reform involves efforts to improve women's political representation. Bolivia was an early adopter of gender quotas. The 1997 quota law specified that one-third of all list candidates needed to be women. This led to a significant increase in the number of women elected—although the gains were mostly limited to the lower chamber and the numbers remained far below the quota's target of one-third. Adoption of a gender parity law in 2010 led to more significant gains for women's political representation. The new law is not limited only to list candidacies. Bolivia is one of the few countries with an "alternate" (*suplente*) system. In that system, each "titular" candidate is accompanied by a suplente who will act in his/her stead when necessary. The new gender parity law stipulates that if a candidate is male, his suplente must be female (and vice versa).

Overall, these reforms reflect a trend toward greater inclusion and participation, as well as explicit recognition of the country's cultural pluralism that began in the 1990s. Bolivian voters today have more choices than ever before and the scope of representative politics has widened considerably. Interestingly, despite a move from a purely proportional electoral system to a mixed-member system, the electoral system is no more disproportional than before.

These reforms have also coincided with a dramatic transformation of the party system. Throughout the 1980s and 1990s, Bolivian politics was dominated by three major political parties: the MNR, Nationalist Democratic Action (ADN), and Revolutionary Movement of the Left (MIR). By the 1990s, the three parties converged around a general consensus on neoliberal macroeconomic policy and liberal multicultural policies, making them relatively indistinguishable to many voters. A clear example of this was the 1989 alliance between the leftist MIR and the center-right ADN led by former dictator Hugo Bánzer. The realities of a parliamentarized presidential system required the formation of coalition governments, of course, but voters became increasingly cynical about coalitions that seemed to be less guided by ideological programs than by spoils-sharing. That cynicism fueled the rise of populist parties in the 1990s, as well as the rise of more radical anti-system parties, such as the MAS.

The 2005 election was a break with the past, sweeping away the previous party system. In its place, party politics can now be described as a "MAS+" party system. Although the effective number of parties suggests that Bolivia is a two-party system, it is not a stable two-party system (as the high electoral volatility confirms). In each of the last three elections, MAS has faced a different rival party at the national level. In part, this is also a product of the newly federalized state structure, which has encouraged the formation of distinct departmental and municipal party systems. Thus, in each department MAS faces one or two significant rivals (and sometimes MAS is the second party), but these departmental rivals are different across departments. The loosening of restrictions on party registration—particularly the introduction of two new forms of political representation: "civic associations" and "indigenous communities"—has led to a highly fractured political landscape.[12] The first election after the end of the political parties' monopoly of representation was the 2004 municipal election, which saw 425 different parties campaigning across 327 municipalities. That number decreased in 2010 (191) and in 2015 (147), although the number of department-level parties has increased from eight in 2004 to twenty-three in the 2015 subnational elections.

Judicial Reforms

One other important area of reform emerging from the 2009 constitution was a significant reorganization of the judiciary. The most significant change was the introduction of popular elections for the high courts, including the constitutional and supreme courts, the first such elections in the world. Previously, seats on the courts were filled by presidential appointments with senate approval. The first elections in 2011 were a test of the new system, although not without controversy. Because candidacies were restricted to a slate of candidates nominated by the legislature, which was controlled by MAS, opposition critics suggested the electoral process would be limited to pro-MAS candidates. Rules that restricted the campaign activities of candidates and limited campaign materials to those provided by the government's electoral body (the Plurinational Electoral Organ, OEP) led to additional criticism. A decision by most senior jurists to refuse to participate in the process by not submitting their dossiers to the legislative committee that drew up the list of candidates also led to criticisms that the popular election of judges could lead to the election of many unqualified high court judges.

The 2011 judicial elections filled seats in four different judicial bodies: the Plurinational Constitutional Tribunal (the constitutional court), the Magistracy Council (an administrative organ that oversees the day-to-day functioning of the judicial system), the Agro-Environmental Tribunal (a special agricultural court), and the Supreme Tribunal of Justice (the high appellate court), which elected two members (one principal and one alternate) from each department. The Agro-Environmental Tribunal was a new court designed to deal with land and environmental issues. Additionally, the election applied the principle of gender parity, although this only applied to the rules for candidacies: half of the candidates for each tier had to be women, but only the top candidates were elected. The result was one of the most diverse judiciaries in the country's history. The country's seven-seat constitutional court now includes four women and two indigenous members.

Although it is still too early to fully assess the effects of popular election of high court judges, it is clear that the effects of the election were mixed.[13] An active campaign by the opposition to boycott the election had some effect. Voter turnout was significantly lower than average, and in every department and across every tier, the number of null and blank votes was greater than the number of valid votes.[14] Moreover, the boycott included a refusal by many sitting judges to postulate themselves as candidates, leading to claims that the candidates selected by the legislature were not sufficiently competent and that many candidates had ties to MAS. However, it should be noted that with a legislative supermajority, Evo Morales could have simply appointed members to the judiciary; giving voters a choice made it difficult to manipulate a specific outcome.

PUBLIC POLICY

The last two decades have seen a significant expansion in the state's role in day-to-day public policy concerns. This is a radical departure from the earlier neoliberal restructuring, during which the Bolivian state outsourced large areas of public policy either to the market or to foreign aid agencies. Resulting conflicts over socioeconomic issues produced a cycle of popular mobilization and state repression, which Leslie Gill described as the "armed retreat" of the state.[15] Beginning in the 1990s, the Bolivian state began slowly reincorporating itself into public policy, a trend that accelerated under Evo Morales.

Although the Bolivian state is involved in a number of public policy arenas (health care, education, basic infrastructure), the most noteworthy framework for public policy in Bolivia comes in two extremes: individual-level vouchers (*bonos*) and large mega projects. Building of new highways, airports, and industrial facilities represents significant government expenditure meant to improve social conditions and economic development. Many such projects, however, increasingly look like costly white elephants. One recent example is the sugar refinery in San Buenaventura, as part of the newly created state-owned San Buenaventura Sugar Company (EASBA). The plant cost US$300 million and currently only works at 10 percent capacity because sugar production is far below the 11,000 hectares it was designed to process. Other proposed projects, such as the El Bala hydroelectric dam, have been criticized for high proposed costs and their potential impact on the environment.

One of the most controversial projects—a strategic highway through the Isiboro Sécure National Park (TIPNIS), a national bio-reserve—was halted by social protests spearheaded by the park's indigenous peoples. One of the principle objections was that the project, which environmentalists argued would lead to a destruction of the fragile ecosystem, required "prior consultation" (per the 2009 constitution) of local indigenous peoples. After an initial harsh crackdown on the indigenous protesters, the Morales government agreed to halt construction in 2011. In 2016, however, Evo Morales issued an executive decree that formally opened up Bolivia's national parks to oil and gas exploration and extraction.[16] Such moves highlight a clear dilemma for the Bolivian state, which, despite pro-indigenous and environmentalist rhetoric, continues to pursue extractive, natural resource-based development strategies.

Where the Morales government's policies have more direct and long-lasting impacts is in the individual voucher (bono) programs increasingly used as part of the social safety net. These are a continuation of models begun in the 1990s, during the first Sánchez de Lozada presidency, as part of the government's "capitalization" economic reform. Unlike typical privatization schemes, capitalization allowed the Bolivian government to retain partial ownership of state-owned enterprises, while giving management control to foreign interests. The profits from capitalizing state-owned enterprises were then set aside to fund a universal pension system, the first social security system in Bolivia's history. Established in 1995, the Bonosol gave an annual payment of US$248 to every Bolivian over the age of sixty-five. Although small, the cash payment was about equal to the median monthly household income and had a huge impact on poor households. Bonosol payments were suspended by President Hugo Banzer (1997–2001), although smaller payments (US$60 annually) were eventually made after civil society protests. In 2002, Sánchez de Lozada reinstated the Bonosol as a US$250 annual payment, where it remains. Morales has built upon the popular Bonosol model, and introduced a number of other programs. Most notable are the Bono Juancito Pinto, which gives every child attending public school a direct cash payment of US$28.50 to facilitate their education, and the Bono Juana Azurduy, which provides pregnant women and new mothers with prenatal care, a hospital birth, and health care support for the mother and child up through the child's second birthday.

INTERNATIONAL RELATIONS

Perhaps the most radical changes since the election of Evo Morales have been in terms of international relations. For decades, Bolivian policies were closely aligned with Washington—particularly in the US-led drug war, which tended to frame US-Bolivian bilateral relations. This put coca—which has traditional uses in Andean indigenous culture but is also the primary ingredient in cocaine—in a central place in domestic politics. Additionally, economic assistance and even access to American markets was closely tied to Bolivian efforts to reduce coca production to a US-mandated target of 12,000 hectares. These policies were generally unpopular with large segments of the Bolivian public, which became increasingly frustrated with the forced eradication carried out jointly by Bolivian security forces and US Drug Enforcement Agency operatives. It is not surprising that the election of Evo Morales, the leader of the largest union of coca growers, significantly altered US-Bolivian bilateral relations.

During his first term, Morales was able to chart an independent course for Bolivian foreign policy. Despite tensions with the United States, culminating in the expulsion of the US ambassador in 2008, Bolivia maintained good relations with Europe, Japan, and other donor countries. Moreover, Bolivia became a promoter of regional multilateral organizations, such as Common Market of the South (MERCOSUR) and the Venezuelan-backed Bolivarian Alliance for the Peoples of Our America (ALBA). Finally, Bolivia developed partnerships with countries as diverse as China, India, and Iran. The 2008–2009 recession reduced the role of Europe in Bolivia, which helped push the country further toward "South-South" partnerships. Most especially, of course, Morales developed close ties with other leftist regional leaders—especially Venezuela's Hugo Chávez.

Since 2015, declining prices of commodity exports has put pressure on Bolivia's foreign policy. The collapse of Venezuela's economy and the death of Hugo Chávez allowed Morales to step out of the shadow of the region's most flamboyant populist, but it also reduced an important economic partner. The election of Mauricio Macri in Argentina and the fall of Dilma Roussef in Brazil also left Morales more politically isolated in the region.

One area of continuity that has resurfaced is the historical territorial dispute with Chile. The dispute stems from the 1879 War of the Pacific, in which Chile defeated the combined forces of Bolivia and Peru, taking land from both of them, landlocking Bolivia in the process. Ostensibly settled in a 1904 peace treaty, the issue periodically resurfaces as a salient political issue in Bolivia. During most of the democratic period, the issue laid dormant, except for occasional diplomatic overtures. The issue resurfaced during the 2003 gas war, since one of the objections to the Sánchez de Lozada government was that it planned to export gas through a Chilean port. Carlos Mesa tapped into this sentiment during his brief presidency, encouraging Bolivians to sign a petition, which he sent symbolically to the United Nations. During the first several years in power, Morales rarely mentioned the issue. Only recently has it occupied an important place in the government's discourse, culminating in a legal action taken to the International Court of Justice (ICJ), in an effort to force Chile to renegotiate.

CONCLUSION

In February 2016, Evo Morales narrowly lost a referendum on a constitutional amendment that would have allowed him to run for yet another term. That election came on the heels of the 2015 regional and municipal elections, which saw significant setbacks for Morales and his MAS party. Although Morales himself remains generally popular, he has consistently been more popular than his party, which fares less well when he is not on the ballot. And because the MAS party has been heavily centered around the person of Evo Morales, no credible successor has emerged from within the party.

If MAS campaigns for the presidency in 2019 without Evo Morales, it is unlikely that it or any opposition party will carry an absolute majority of the electorate. This could usher in a return of a multiparty system, which would complicate governing. Much will depend on whether the fragmented regional opposition parties can coalesce around a single candidate. Nevertheless, many of the reforms initiated during the Morales presidency are likely to endure. There is significant social consensus on social policies and decentralization reforms. The 2003–2005 political crisis that led to the rise of Evo Morales also fundamentally reshaped Bolivia's political system in ways that are unlikely to change back.

SUGGESTIONS FOR FURTHER READING

Crabtree, John, and Ann Chaplin. *Bolivia: Processes of Change.* London: Zed Books, 2013.

Faguet, Jean-Paul. *Decentralization and Popular Democracy: Governance from Below in Bolivia.* Ann Arbor: University of Michigan Press, 2012.

Farthing, Linda C. and Benjamin H. Kohl. *Evo's Bolivia: Continuity and Change.* Austin: University of Texas Press, 2014.

Gill, Leslie. *Teetering on the Rim: Global Restructuring, Daily Life, and the Armed Retreat of the Bolivian State.* New York: Columbia University Press, 2000.

Gutierrez Aguilar, Raquel. *Rhythms of Pachakuti: Indigenous Uprising and State Power in Bolivia.* Durham, NC: Duke University Press, 2014.

Hindery, Derrick. *From ENRON to Evo: Pipeline Politics, Global Environmentalism, and Indigenous Rights in Bolivia.* Tucson: University of Arizona Press, 2013.

John, S. Sándor. *Bolivia's Radical Tradition: Permanent Revolution in the Andes.* Tucson, AZ: University of Arizona Press, 2009.

Klein, Herbert S. *A Concise History of Bolivia,* 2nd ed. Cambridge: Cambridge University Press, 2011.

Lazar, Sian. *El Alto, Rebel City: Self and Citizenship in Andean Bolivia.* Durham, NC: Duke University Press, 2008.

Orta, Andrew. *Catechizing Culture: Missionaries, Aymara, and the "New Evangelization."* New York: Columbia University Press, 2004.

Pellegrini Calderón, Alessandra. *Beyond Indigeneity: Coca Growing and the Emergence of a New Middle Class in Bolivia.* Tucson: University of Arizona Press, 2016.

NOTES

1. Miguel Centellas, "Bolivia's New Multicultural Constitution: The 2009 Constitution in Historical and Comparative Perspective," in *Latin America's Multicultural Movements: The Struggle Between Communitarianism, Autonomy, and Human Rights*, eds. Todd S. Eisenstadt et al. (Oxford: Oxford University Press, 2013).

2. Based on data from the Instituto Nacional de Estadística de Bolivia. Available online at: http://www.ine.gob.bo.

3. See Xavier Albó, "Censo 2012 en Bolivia: posibilidades y limitaciones con respecto a los pueblos indígenas," *T'inkazos* 32 (2012): 33–45.

4. INE census data.

5. World Bank, World Development Indicators. Available at http://data.worldbank.org. Unless otherwise specified, the data presented in this chapter comes from this source.

6. "Religion in Latin America: Widespread Change in a Historically Catholic Region," Pew Research Center Report, November 13, 2014. Available at www.pewforum.org/2014/11/13/religion-in-latin-america/.

7. Andrew Canessa, *Catechizing Culture: Missionaries, Aymara, and the "New Evangelization."* (New York: Columbia University Press, 2004).

8. Emily Achtenberg, "In Bolivia, Social Protest is a Way of Life," NACLA Report on the Americas, June 17, 2011. Available at http://nacla.org/blog/2011/6/17/bolivia-social-protest-way-life.

9. AmericasBarometer data is available at www.vanderbilt.edu/lapop.

10. Alfred Stepan, "Federalism and Democracy: Beyond the US Model," *Journal of Democracy* 10 (1999): 19–34.

11. René Antonio Mayorga, "Bolivia's Silent Revolution," *Journal of Democracy* 8 (1997): 142–156.

12. Miguel Centellas, "Bolivia's Radical Decentralization," *Americas Quarterly* 4 (3): 34–38.

13. Amanda Driscoll and Michael J. Nelson, "Ignorance or Opposition? Black and Spoiled Votes in Low-Information, Highly Politicized Environments," *Political Research Quarterly* 67(3): 547–561.

14. OEP-TSE. "Elección de autoridades del Órgano Judicial y del Tribunal Constitucional 2011: Resultados Finales."

15. Leslie Gill, *Teetering on the Rim: Global Restructuring, Daily Life, and the Armed Retreat of the Bolivian State* (New York: Columbia University Press, 2000).

16. Emily Achtenberg, "Morales Greenlights TIPNIS Road, Oil and Gas Extraction in Bolivia's National Parks," *NACLA* Rebel Currents blog, June 15, 2015. http://nacla.org/blog/2015/06/15/morales-greenlights-tipnis-road-oil-and-gas-extraction-bolivia's-national-parks.

17

ECUADOR: CHANGE AND CONTINUITY AFTER TEN YEARS OF NEW LEFT REVOLUTION

Jennifer N. Collins

INTRODUCTION

After a decade in power, on May 24, 2017, Rafael Correa placed the presidential sash on his former vice president and chosen successor, Lenin Moreno, and return to civilian life. Of the crop of new left leaders, only Hugo Chávez and Evo Morales were in power longer. Over the past decade, Correa defined and shaped the political project known as the Citizens' Revolution. What happens after he leaves the scene is an open question, and assessing his impact on Ecuador is complicated and fraught with controversy.

Ecuador is in many ways a substantially different country—better off and more politically stable—than it was when Correa first assumed power in 2007. But 2016 saw increasing challenges stemming from the slowing international economy and the low price of oil, as well as internal events outside of the government's control, namely a major earthquake that devastated Ecuador's coastal region in April 2016. Unlike in Brazil and Venezuela, where economic downturn destabilized and profoundly challenged the new left administrations of Dilma Rousseff and Nicolás Maduro, the political dominance of Correa's party does not appear to be crumbling; in fact, polls in late 2016 showed his party's presidential candidate in the lead. However, the personalism that has characterized his political project combined with a weaker economy raises the question of what aspects of the Citizens' Revolution will survive beyond the end of his term.

Correa's ten years in office brought needed political stability and most notably a high level of social investment that has made the country one of the regional leaders in terms of reducing levels of poverty and inequality. Coming to power as part of the "pink tide," Correa supported regional integration and cooperation with other new left governments, and at home decisively abandoned neoliberal economic orthodoxy. He has generally been a popular president; however, he has also been a polarizing figure, viewed as intolerant of dissent and concentrating power in the executive branch. Although considered part of Latin America's cohort of new left leaders, Correa alienated much of the left in his own country, including most of the country's once-powerful social and indigenous movements.

Possessing significant oil reserves, as well as a historically stratified society, Ecuador has struggled to develop economically and to modernize politically. For much of the twentieth century Ecuador was a seemingly sleepy country in which the dramatic winds of change that buffeted other countries arrived as faint gusts. The entrenched power of elites and long ingrained patterns of racism and discrimination have meant that struggles for inclusion of those at the bottom of society have been long and difficult. However, by the end of the twentieth century new social forces had emerged and political struggle intensified, challenging racism and elitism and opening up formal politics to historically marginalized groups.

These dramatic social and political changes have occurred largely nonviolently. Different than its closest neighbors, Colombia and Peru, both plagued by guerrilla insurgencies and state violence, Ecuador has avoided large-scale internal violence. As a result, civil society and social movements have had greater freedom to organize and participate in the democratic process, although the ability of autonomous social movements to contest government policy has been stifled under Correa.

Ecuador offers the opportunity to examine politics in a developing country where struggles for citizenship rights and political inclusion by indigenous people and Afro-Ecuadorians have produced important successes. The country has also made progress in recent years in reducing poverty and inequality. But these significant social-equity and developmental achievements have been attained through continued heavy reliance on the extractive economy, something that Correa's new left revolution has only further entrenched. Ecuadorian politics showcase competing visions on the left of how to pursue development and social justice in the twenty-first century.

LAND AND PEOPLE

Ecuador takes its name from its location straddling the equator on the northern Pacific coast of South America. It is one of the smaller countries on the continent, but it is the most densely populated, with a population of more than sixteen million. Its diverse geography includes a coastal plain, a mountainous interior known as the Highlands, a flat jungle area to the east that forms part of the Amazon basin, and the Galápagos Islands, which lie approximately six hundred miles due west in the Pacific Ocean. Historically most Ecuadorians resided in the Highlands, but the growth of export agriculture and commerce on the coast led to demographic shifts, so that today coastal and highland populations are roughly equal.

Like its topography, Ecuador's population is diverse, having developed from three main groups: sizeable indigenous populations, people of European ancestry, and a small population of people whose African ancestors were brought over as slaves. According to the most recent census of 2010, 70 percent of Ecuadorians self-identify as *mestizos* or people of mixed race, 7 percent as indigenous, another 7 percent as Afro-Ecuadorian, 7.4 percent as *Montubios* (a coastal culture), and 6.1 percent as white. The census figure for indigenous people belies the importance of this group both historically and contemporaneously. By the end of the twentieth century Ecuador's indigenous movement had emerged as the country's most important social movement and as a leader among a wave of such movements regionally and globally.

HISTORICAL BACKGROUND

During the colonial period the Real Audiencia de Quito, which comprised much of present-day Ecuador, was something of a backwater. It was not a source of gold or silver for the crown; instead its resource base lay in agriculture. The Highland indigenous population became subject to forced labor on the landed estates and textile mills owned by the colonial elite. Thus, class and ethnicity were conjoined early in Ecuador's history, leaving a long legacy of racism.

Ecuador gained independence in 1822. Like most Latin American countries, the new republic was dominated by an elite minority, a propertied upper class uninterested in promoting a broad-based democratization. In Ecuador, the elite was divided by geography and had contending economic interests. In the Highlands, large landowners lorded over traditional haciendas, exploiting Indian laborers who were subjected to exploitative arrangements reminiscent of serfdom. Allied with the Roman Catholic Church, these landed oligarchs formed the Conservative party to defend their interests. On the coast, maritime commerce and tropical export agriculture produced a different, more entrepreneurial upper class. The coastal elite, interested in free trade and secularization, became the bedrock of the Liberal party.

The nineteenth century witnessed violent conflicts between the two parties as they vied to control government. Conservatives ruled with an iron fist till the Liberal Revolution of 1895. Liberal *caudillo* Eloy Alfaro served as president for eleven years and brought important modernizing reforms to the country, including curtailing the power of the Catholic Church, establishing separation of church and state, and building the Trans-Andean railroad to connect the coast and the Highlands. He also established the first public high schools and universities. Ultimately, he proved too liberal for his own party and was ousted from power. He met an ignominious death after he was jailed for trying to foment an antigovernment insurrection and then snatched from prison and lynched by an angry mob in 1912. Alfaro has been embraced by President Correa, who characterizes the Citizens' Revolution as the continuity of Alfaro's legacy.

The cacao boom in the early twentieth century brought wealth and social change to Guayaquil as new middle and working classes emerged. But economic prosperity and social differentiation did not lead to a greater disposition on the part of elites toward democratization and social inclusion. In 1922, when hundreds of workers were killed by police during Guayaquil's first general strike, Ecuador's incipient labor movement got its first taste of how far elites were willing to go to retain control.

In 1925, young military officers seized power from the Liberals. Although the "July Revolution" failed to dismantle the power of traditional elites, it did succeed in establishing a state bureaucracy capable of governing with some autonomy from oligarchic interests. Moreover, it set an important precedent for the military itself. Rather than becoming a reactionary and oppressive force in public life, the armed forces identified itself with reform and never resorted to the kind of brutal repression later practiced by militaries elsewhere in the region. For example, the military government of 1972–1976 declared a "Nationalist Revolution" aimed at modernization, statism, and redistribution through agrarian and labor reforms. However, as was often the case with would-be reformers in Ecuador, the nationalist generals proved unable or unwilling to neutralize elite opposition; as a result, reforms were comparatively timid. By the end of the 1970s, facing increasing economic problems and public pressure to relinquish power, the military retreated peacefully from politics, handing over power to civilians in a negotiated transition in 1979.

SOCIAL CHANGE AND THE RISE OF CIVIL SOCIETY

For much of the twentieth century, challenges to elite rule were relatively impotent. Though elites battled each other bitterly at times for the spoils of power, they also united when necessary to ensure that would-be reformers or revolutionaries were contained. Ecuador's great populist leader, José María Velasco Ibarra, who served five times as president in the decades stretching from 1934 to 1972, was more interested in preserving the status quo than challenging it. Leftist parties never constituted a real electoral threat, nor was there a Cuban-inspired guerrilla insurgency as appeared in many other countries. As a result, Ecuador experienced evolutionary rather than revolutionary change, but change it did. The key factors propelling change included agrarian reform, the oil boom of the 1970s, urbanization, expanding access to education, and democratization.

Agrarian reform was carried out in 1964 and 1973. Although modest in scope, it served to dismantle the feudalistic Highland hacienda system, and in so doing it freed up labor, prompted internal migration, and ultimately empowered indigenous communities. Greater access to land and education, as well as the weakening of local power structures, composed of the landowning families, the church, and the state, all contributed to the growth of autonomous indigenous organizing that would culminate in the formation of the Confederation of Indigenous Nationalities of Ecuador (CONAIE) in 1986.

The oil boom fuelled urbanization. Ecuador went from being a predominantly rural society—in 1950, 71 percent of the population lived in the countryside—to an urban one; today 67 percent of Ecuadorians reside in cities. Oil also rapidly accelerated the integration of the vast Amazonian basin region into the nation. As part of the agrarian reform programs, military governments opened up vast tracts of land in the Amazon to landless Highland peasants, thus initiating a process of migration that continues to up to the present time.

Labor unions have been politically active in Ecuador since the 1920s. They played an important role in the late 1970s in pushing for an end to military rule, and in the

1990s worked together with new social movements in protesting and resisting neoliberal reforms. The decade of popular resistance to neoliberalism arguably created the conditions that helped to propel Correa to the presidency, but under Correa labor and social movements' ability to mount opposition to government policies and their role as autonomous actors have weakened significantly. The labor movement has been divided with some sectors supporting the government and others moving into the opposition. Many argue that laws and decrees passed by the Correa administration have weakened workers' rights and that the president has sought to undercut the autonomy and power of labor federations, especially those critical of his government. In 2016, the Ministry of Education dissolved the National Educators' Union (UNE), which since its founding in 1950 has been the national body representing the country's public school teachers.

Women made progress in Ecuador during the twentieth century. In 1929, Ecuador became the first Latin American country to grant the right to vote to women, and during the following decades other important legal rights were granted, including the right to own property and file for divorce. Organizations advocating for women's rights have been among the rich tapestry of social movements that have played such an important role since the country's democratic transition. As a result of advocacy by the women's movement in 1998, the country adopted gender quotas for legislative elections: today all party lists must have 50 percent women, with men and women alternating down the ballot. The gender quota has significantly increased the percentage of women elected to the National Assembly, where women currently hold 42 percent of legislative seats, among the highest percentages globally. Women's participation in the labor force has increased significantly and currently stands at 55 percent, although underemployment and the wage gap with men remain high. Domestic violence remains a pervasive problem, with estimates of the percentage of women becoming victims of this at some point in their lives ranging from 42 to 60 percent. As a result of pressure from women's organizations, innovative responses to curb violence have been developed, including the establishment of police stations dedicated specifically to dealing with crimes against women.

Although democracy in Ecuador has benefited from a vibrant civil society, recent studies indicate that membership in all groups has declined since a peak in the 1990s. The political power of social movements waned noticeably during Correa's tenure, first of all because he co-opted much of their agenda, but also because he aggressively sought to undermine those who disagreed with him.

POLITICAL DEVELOPMENT SINCE THE DEMOCRATIC TRANSITION

Ecuador achieved universal suffrage for the first time in 1979. Previously literacy requirements disenfranchised the poor, particularly indigenous and Afro-Ecuadorians. As late as 1968 the electorate was estimated to be as small as 15 percent of the population. In the decade after the 1978 constitution finally removed the old barriers, the size of the electorate doubled. Elections since 1979 have been free, fair, and competitive. The country has developed a multiparty system, but most parties had shallow roots in society and instead relied on the popularity of their leader, as well as clientelism, to connect to voters. Ongoing economic austerity and crisis in the 1980s and 1990s made it difficult for incumbent parties to cement strong ties to those who elected them. Ecuador became a country noted for its high incidence of electoral volatility—voter preferences for parties swung, often dramatically, from one election to the next. Correa's presidency changed this pattern. He won three successive elections, and the political movement he founded, PAIS Alliance (AP), emerged as the most powerful party, holding a majority of seats in the legislature for most of the past decade.

Ecuador has a presidential system and uses proportional representation to elect the unicameral legislature. Until Correa, the electoral system produced a fragmented party system. This in turn meant that presidents routinely came into office without a stable legislative majority. Complicating matters further, parties were notoriously weak. Presidents often resorted to under-the-table payments or patronage in order to win support for their legislative agendas. Rocky executive-legislative relations made it difficult to pass reforms and contributed to the public's perception of the political system as corrupt and ineffectual.

Between 1997 and 2005 public dissatisfaction with politics-as-usual turned Ecuador into the leader of a continent-wide syndrome that political scientist Arturo Valenzuela dubbed "presidencies interrupted."[1] Within a ten-year period the country had seven presidents, three of whom were forced to leave office before completing their terms. The phenomenon began with Abdalá Bucaram (1996–1997), the founder and leader of the populist Ecuadorian Roldosist Party (PRE). Known for his raucous campaign rallies in which he sang and danced to popular Ecuadorian music and vociferated against the "oligarchs," Bucaram promised to soak the rich and enact sweeping social assistance. However, once in office he resorted to a familiar recipe of reducing consumption subsidies and increasing taxes along with a convertibility plan aimed at curbing inflation. The call for austerity fell flat as accusations of corruption against him and his family piled up.

By early 1997 a wide array of social sectors began demanding his resignation, including social movements, but also business groups, the major opposition parties, and much of the private media. Thousands of protesters took to the streets in February 1997 and the opposition in congress looked for a way to remove him. Lacking the two-thirds majority necessary for impeachment, congressional deputies declared the president "mentally incapacitated." The military signalled that it was time for him to go and Bucaram fled the country seeking political asylum in Panama.

His unceremonious removal from office set a precedent for resolving government crises, although in a way that deviated from the rules prescribed in the constitution. The next elected president succumbed to a similar dynamic. Not long after taking office in 1998, Jamil Mahuad was faced with a massive banking crisis. Earlier in the decade, following neoliberal precepts, Ecuador's financial sector had been liberalized and deregulated. With scant and ineffective government oversight, Ecuadorian banks engaged in risky, irresponsible, and corrupt practices, which ultimately led to the implosion of the whole sector. As major banks began to fail, Mahuad used government monies to bail them out, eventually spending somewhere between US$1.2–US$1.6 billion in the failed effort. This massive public bailout of the private banks, which involved printing huge quantities of money, quickly resulted in skyrocketing inflation, runs on the banks, and eventually the collapse of the currency; in other words, a full-blown economic crisis. The government took the drastic step of freezing depositors' accounts for a full year. Although depositors were denied access to their savings, many bankers escaped with their personal fortunes intact. The revelation that the owner of one of the major banks involved in the crisis had contributed over US$3 million to Mahuad's electoral campaign confirmed the public's sense that the president had sold out the country to save the skin of the wealthy and corrupt bankers.

The crisis took a devastating toll on the economy and ordinary citizens' pocketbooks: the economy contracted by 7–8 percent, unemployment nearly doubled, and poverty rates soared. Led largely by the Confederation of Indigenous Nationalities of Ecuador, social movements protested government austerity measures throughout 1999. In a last-ditch effort to stabilize the economy, Mahuad announced plans to adopt the US dollar as the country's official currency. The highly controversial dollarization decree triggered a new round of protests in January 2000. CONAIE organized a march and supporters stormed the congress. Supported by dissident junior military officers, the protesters declared the formation of a new "government of national salvation." However, facing strong opposition from the US government and the upper echelons of the military, the new government lasted barely six hours. Nonetheless, the demonstrations were sufficient to force Mahuad's resignation and a succession by his vice president, who kept the controversial dollarization decree in place.

Colonel Lucio Gutiérrez, the leader of the rebellious officers, launched a bid for the presidency in 2003. He turned to the social movements with whom he had joined forces to oust Mahuad, forming an electoral alliance with Pachaktuik (PK), a political party founded in 1996 by the country's most important social movements. Gutiérrez won the election as the crusading anticorruption candidate of the left. Yet his left turn was short-lived. In a familiar turn of events, Gutiérrez acquiesced to International Monetary Fund (IMF) pressures for debt repayments and public spending cuts. After CONAIE and PK withdrew their support, Gutiérrez struck political deals with right-wing parties, eventually making a devil's bargain with Bucaram's PRE, which facilitated the disgraced former president's return from exile and the dropping of all criminal charges against him. Bucaram arrived in Guayaquil in April 2005 pledging defiantly to run again for the presidency.

His return unleashed mass demonstrations in Quito. This time the previous coalition of indigenous, social, and labor movements were not at the forefront of the protests; instead, it was students and the urban middle class who staged vigils and marches with an angry demand aimed at President Gutiérrez and the political class: "¡*Que se vayan todos!*" ("Throw them all out!") When repeated attempts to quell the demonstrations failed, Gutiérrez too fled into exile.

As the 2006 presidential election approached, Ecuadorians were fed up with politicians and their crisis-prone political system. Public opinion polls showed that citizens had virtually no confidence in congress, political parties, or the government at large. Moreover, the poorly performing economy had torn families apart: an estimated three million Ecuadorians had left the country to seek work in the United States or Europe.

Correa and the Citizens' Revolution

Rafael Correa campaigned as a political outsider. Born to a modest middle-class family in Guayaquil, he earned scholarships that eventually led to a doctorate in economics from the University of Illinois and a career as a university professor in Quito. His only major stint in public service came after Gutiérrez's fall when interim President Palacio tapped him as finance minister. Correa's tough stance toward foreign investors and the IMF established his credentials as a fresh new leader on the left. Yet Correa had no formal ties to any party nor a history of involvement with social movements. A devout Roman Catholic, Correa described himself as a "humanist Christian of the left." Tapping into the public's anti-party sentiment, Correa built an independent political movement, as opposed to a party, and enlisted the support of left-leaning intellectuals, technocrats, and leaders from the rebellion that ousted President Gutiérrez.

Young, handsome, and charismatic, the forty-three-year-old Correa proved to be an effective campaigner with a creative campaign team. He blamed the party establishment for virtually all of the country's ills and promised to govern with "clean hands, lucid minds, and passionate hearts," sweeping away corruption, incompetence, and elitism, and refounding the country on the basis of a new constitution. Correa told voters that he would put an end to the "long and sad neoliberal night" by increasing social assistance, rejuvenating the role of the state, and putting foreign creditors and investors on notice that abuses would no longer be tolerated.[2]

As in previous elections, the fragmented multiparty system produced a crowded field of thirteen candidates and no first-round winner. Correa came in second with 22.8 percent of the vote in the first round and then in the second round went head-to-head with Ecuador's richest man and perennial presidential candidate, banana magnate Alvaro Noboa. Whereas Correa promised an end to neoliberalism, Noboa celebrated the merits of business and the free market.

Correa won the second round decisively with 56.7 percent of the vote. Yet his victory was complicated by a crucial decision made during the campaign: in a daring gamble to prove his anti-party credentials, Correa ran without a slate of legislative candidates, arguing that the congress would be irrelevant because he was promising to convene a constituent assembly to draft a new constitution. The gamble paid off, but once in office he faced the dilemma of how to gain the needed consent of a recalcitrant legislature to convene the assembly.

Re-founding the Nation

Like former President Hugo Chávez of Venezuela and Bolivian President Evo Morales, Correa ran for office promising a radical restructuring of politics and economics, and the writing of a new constitution was the crucial mechanism to achieve this end. Correa proved determined to make good on this promise. His willingness to take risks and play political hardball early on in his presidency was supported by the social movements and served to dramatically increase his popularity, but it also led critics to accuse him of being a populist who was willing to bend the institutional rules of the game.

On his first day in office Correa signed Decree 002, which called for a referendum on convening a constituent assembly; the legislature balked. Correa then appealed directly to the public to mobilize in support of the referendum and force the hand of the opposition. This led to a high-stakes showdown with the Assembly that drew in the Constitutional Tribunal and the Supreme Electoral Tribunal. Constitutionally questionable actions were taken by all parties, but ultimately intense public pressure, including massive demonstrations, forced the legislature to acquiesce to the referendum.

The referendum was held in April 2007 and Correa won a huge victory with 82 percent of voters supporting the call to convene an assembly that would not only draft a new constitution, but also assume legislative powers until the new constitution was completed, thus effectively dissolving the incumbent legislature. Correa's ticket won 80 of the 130 seats in the new Constituent Assembly, thus giving his movement majority control. The new constitution was approved by popular referendum in September 2008 with 64 percent approving; this was followed by a general election in January 2009, under the new constitution, in which Correa won reelection, although without a legislative majority. However, in 2013 Correa was decisively reelected yet again, winning 57 percent of the vote in the first round, trouncing the runner-up by nearly 35 percentage points, and his party swept the legislative elections. During his third and last term, his popularity weakened. Although there were points when Correa had enjoyed public approval ratings as high as 87 percent, by August 2016 his approval ratings were down to 40 percent.

CONSTITUTION AND POLITICAL INSTITUTIONS

Ecuador has a long history of constitution writing. The 2008 constitution is the country's twenty-first since its birth as an independent nation in 1830. Often referred to as the Montecristi Constitution, for the coastal city where the assembly met, Ecuador's newest Magna Carta is progressive, and in some respects revolutionary. The result of a highly participatory process that involved extensive interaction between the assembly's working committees and civil society, it combines several strains of progressive and leftist thinking: it is social democratic in its vision of a state empowered to advance the public good and rein in and regulate the market. Postmodern ideas are reflected in its embrace of plurinationalism and collective rights for indigenous and other groups. Finally, there is much attention throughout to environmental sustainability. *Sumak Kawsay,* a Kichwa term roughly translated as "to live well," is a central concept in the document: it emphasizes living in harmony and balance with nature and other human beings, rejecting consumerism and individualism in favor of sustainability and community. It is also the first constitution in the world to recognize nature and the environment as rights-bearing entities.

The constitution grants citizens an expansive array of political and socioeconomic rights, ranging from social security, to free legal counsel and health care, to rights to water and a clean environment, adequate housing, and even the practice of sports. It is not quite as progressive when it comes to reproductive and LGBTQ rights, reflecting Catholic norms and the president's commitment to the church's teachings. Abortion is illegal, except when pregnancy poses a threat to the life of the woman or in cases of rape where the victim is a woman with diminished mental capacities. Women's rights groups and human rights organizations have called for changes that would expand access to legal abortion, at the very least in cases of rape or when the pregnancy is inviable. In terms of LGBTQ rights, marriage is defined as only between a man and a woman and adoption is limited to heterosexual couples. However, discrimination based on sexual orientation is expressly prohibited and civil unions between same-sex couples are legal.

With regards to the economy, the Montecristi Constitution breaks with neoliberal orthodoxy by significantly increasing the power of the state to regulate and intervene in the market. The state is expected to "administer, regulate, control and manage" the strategic sectors of the economy, which include energy, telecommunications, nonrenewable natural resources, transportation, biodiversity, and water. There are provisions designed to protect small farmers and secure food sovereignty. Banks and financial institutions are barred from participating financially in other activities, in particular media ownership. There are also provisions for protecting state sovereignty in interactions with more powerful states and actors, especially the United States.

The 2009 constitution permitted presidential reelection for two successive four-year terms. However, all term limits were removed in 2016 when the National Assembly passed a controversial package of constitutional reforms. The constitution grants the president the power to dissolve the legislature once during his term and call for new elections. Although the president would also have to run in the special election, the reform gives the president a powerful threat to wield in any executive-legislative conflict. Overall, the Montecristi Constitution enhanced the powers of the president relative to other branches of government.

POLITICAL CULTURE AND THE DEMOCRATIC DEBATE IN ECUADOR

Despite his popularity and achievements, Correa has been a polarizing figure in Ecuador, with ardent critics on both the left and the right. His critics accuse him of undermining Ecuadorian democracy in a number of crucial ways. First of all, his political style is combative and he has demonstrated a low tolerance for dissent. Correa regularly uses his bully pulpit to reprimand, chastise, and insult anyone who expresses disagreement with him or opposition to government policy. The private media and social movements have been frequent targets of his hectoring. Beyond verbal aggression the president has aggressively used the courts, which his government has been able to populate with sympathetic judges, to intimidate and silence critical views in the press, civil society, and even on social media. In one of the most widely publicized cases, Correa sued *El Universo*, one of the country's leading newspapers, for libel after one of their columnists wrote an opinion piece accusing Correa of responsibility for civilian deaths during a 2010 police rebellion. The courts, whose independence from the executive was questioned by the opposition, ruled in the president's favor, sentencing the newspaper's owners and the journalist to three years in prison and a financial penalty of US$40 million. After the ruling, the president pardoned all three, thus releasing them from both the prison terms and the fine, which would have surely bankrupted the newspaper. Nevertheless, this case and numerous others have sent a strong signal to the private media that they need to carefully consider the possible consequences before criticizing the president. Many journalists have decried these actions, arguing that they have led to self-censorship and have had a stifling effect on press freedom.

Correa has also clashed with social movements. Although his Citizens' Revolution has pursued an agenda that was shaped initially by Ecuador's dynamic social movements, he distanced himself from the post-developmentalist and environmental wing of the left. The main points of contention revolve around the president's insistence on large-scale mining, which environmentalists warn will have disastrous environmental impacts. Hundreds of activists who have publicly criticized the president or organized protest actions have been charged with crimes ranging from libel, to sabotage, and even terrorism. Although these charges have not led yet to substantial jail time, they are viewed as a way of intimidating those who dare to challenge the president. Human rights organizations have accused the Correa administration of systematically "criminalizing social protest."

For his critics, Correa's presidency has been fundamentally damaging to democracy. But polling data reveals a more complex reality in terms of shifts in Ecuadorian political culture. According to surveys by Latin American Public Opinion Project (LAPOP), citizen support for democracy and for Ecuador's political system increased dramatically over the course of Correa's presidency, from only 37 percent in 2006 (the year before Correa assumed power) to 67.2 percent in 2014. Similarly, 56.5 percent of survey respondents reported being satisfied or very satisfied with the way Ecuadorian democracy was functioning, up from only 36.5 percent in 2006. Also significant is the fact that support for military coups has decreased steadily during these years. Citizen satisfaction in terms of government efforts to combat corruption rose dramatically between 2008 and 2014, and indeed perceptions of actual corruption have decreased. On the negative side of the balance sheet, indicators of tolerance have gone down somewhat during the Correa era.[3]

With the exception of the last measure, these surveys indicate a significant improvement in Ecuadorians' satisfaction with their government, support for democracy, and trust in their institutions, all of which suggests a strengthening of democratic norms and political culture. But how then to make sense of this in light of opposition criticism of Correa as heavy-handed, maybe even authoritarian? After the crises of the 1990s and early 2000s Ecuadorians had lost faith in their political system; they felt betrayed by their elected representatives. Correa changed this dynamic by following through on many of his campaign pledges, including ending the neoliberal policies of austerity and building state capacity and effectiveness. His success in making the government functional again combined with robust economic performance offer the main explanation for the higher levels of citizen satisfaction with their political system and democracy. However, it is also likely that Correa's belligerence toward those who question or challenge his political project has stoked polarization and justified impatience with and intolerance of political dissent, which is concerning. But even with Correa's bare-knuckled political style, it must be emphasized that he has maintained the integrity of the core democratic institutions, the most important of which are free and fair elections. He is also voluntarily stepping down from political power within the period allowed for by the constitution, thus ensuring a stable and orderly democratic transition.

POLITICAL ECONOMY: OIL AND THE QUEST FOR DEVELOPMENT

The discovery in 1967 of massive oil reserves in the Amazon transformed Ecuador from an agro-export economy into a petrostate—a nation whose public finances are extremely dependent on this single mineral export. Much of the country's modern development is thanks to this "black gold." But, similar to other oil-producing countries, Ecuador fell victim to "Dutch Disease," the observed pattern whereby extraordinary revenues from a single and highly valuable natural resource stifle the development of a more diversified and integrated economy.

During the 1980s and 1990s the major challenge faced by all governments was managing the troubled economy. Military governments had borrowed freely during the 1970s. When international interest rates shot up in the 1980s and commodity prices plummeted, Ecuador was ensnared in the "debt trap." In order to avoid defaulting, Ecuadorian presidents accepted IMF offers of new loans, and in exchange promised to apply austerity and neoliberal restructuring, including privatization, deregulation, and opening up to foreign investment. However, when they attempted to implement these reforms they came up against stiff resistance from the public and even the business community. Comparatively, Ecuador was one of the region's most shallow reformers. Nonetheless, the episodic application of stabilization packages evoked the ire of labor unions and social movements, and fed public dissatisfaction with and mistrust of the political class. By the close of the 1990s, an estimated 63 percent of the population was living below the poverty line, and stagnant economic growth had given way to negative growth.

Today, Ecuador is a middle-income country with a Human Development Index ranking of 88, thus putting it in the category of High Human Development. Oil remains the country's most important single export, contributing more than 50 percent of export earnings and up to 35 percent of the public budget. In addition to oil, Ecuador is the world's top banana producer, and exports flowers, shrimp, and cacao; tourism is another important sector. Major deposits of gold, silver, and copper were discovered recently in the southern part of Ecuador, and Correa has aggressively sought to develop large-scale mining. Another important part of Ecuador's economy is remittances, or monies that Ecuadorian migrants living and working abroad send back to their families. These grew dramatically in the early 2000s and have continued apace. In 2014 remittances represented about 3 percent of Ecuador's gross domestic product (GDP).

Since 2000 Ecuador has used the US dollar as its official currency. Although the dollarization decree was highly controversial at first, it has had a stabilizing effect on the economy and there is no serious discussion of ending it, as the costs of doing so would be high. Dollarization severely restricts the government's ability to use monetary policy as a tool of economic management, and it can be problematic for the export sector when the value of the dollar is high relative to a country's trading partners. However, in Ecuador's case these disadvantages have not been as keenly felt, because the United States remains one of the country's most important trading partners and this trade is facilitated by use of the same currency, and because oil as an export is not as sensitive to currency differences as are other products. In the absence of a major economic crisis, it is unlikely dollarization will be abandoned.

The role of extractive industries in the Ecuadorian economy has been a significant source of conflict between the Correa administration and social, indigenous, and environmental movements. Correa has pursued a statist, developmentalist approach, namely doubling down on resource extraction in order to finance social spending and infrastructural development. Many on the left who initially supported Correa now advocate for a shift to a post-extractive economy. They argue that the environmental costs of drilling and mining, especially in the fragile Amazonian ecosystem, are too high. Together with the global environmental movement, they contend that fossil fuels need to stay in the ground if we are to avoid the worst consequences of global warming. Finally, they condemn the way extractive activities violate the human rights of native peoples living in the areas where these resources are located. Activists contend that they pose a grave threat to the physical and cultural survival of Amazonian tribes still living in "voluntary isolation."[4]

Until 2015 Ecuador enjoyed robust rates of economic growth. Between 2007 and 2015 growth averaged 3.9 percent annually, compared to the regional rate of 2.9 percent for the same period. Over the course of Correa's decade in power, the Ecuadorian economy more than doubled in size. However, beginning in 2015 economic growth decreased significantly and the devastating earthquake that hit in April 2016 further exacerbated existing challenges.

In addition to macroeconomic growth, government revenue increased dramatically from 27 percent of GDP in 2006 to more than 40 percent in 2012. This was accomplished through several key initiatives: (1) raising the government's share of oil revenue through hard-nosed negotiations with international oil companies; (2) reforming the tax code and improving tax collection; (3) increasing regulation and taxation of the financial sector, including doing away with Central Bank autonomy and restricting capital flows; and (4) long-term loans from China. The first three measures fly in the face of neoliberal policy prescriptions, which contend that assertive measures by the state will drive away private investment. Ecuador under Correa's leadership appears to offer evidence that there are alternatives to what Thomas Friedman has called the "golden straightjacket," or the imperative that all countries adopt the free-market, neoliberal model if they are to thrive in a globalized marketplace.[5]

Although Correa's record of macroeconomic management appeared quite good, at least until 2015, it is also true that his administration did not adequately prepare for the inevitable end of favorable economic conditions. When the international price of oil was high, instead of building the country's reserves, the Correa administration spent most of the earnings and went into significant debt with China. As a result, the government did not have much of a cushion to fall back on when the price of oil began to fall and economic conditions worsened in the wake of the earthquake.

Ecuador's economy had historically been highly dependent on the United States for trade and investment. One of the most significant changes under Correa has been the diversification of the country's economic relationships. China became the most important new source for capital and markets. The dimensions of the shift have been dramatic. In 2005, the United States was the single major source of foreign direct investment in Ecuador and accounted for 50 percent of the country's export markets, including oil. China, by contrast, did not figure among the top four purchasers of Ecuadorian oil. However, by 2011 China was purchasing a full half of Ecuador's oil exports, directly operating seven oil wells in Ecuador, and participating in various other partnerships, accounting altogether for 40 percent of Ecuador's private sector oil development. This is in addition to Chinese investment in other areas, including mining. China has locked in sales of Ecuadorian oil for years to come in exchange for massive lending. By 2012 Ecuador's debt to China amounted to 22 percent of the country's GDP. Many have suggested that while Correa has reduced Ecuador's economic dependence on the United States, he may have exchanged it for a new dependency on China.

Correa's shift away from the United States was facilitated not only by the pivot to China, but also by surging oil and commodity prices during the first few years of his administration and the fact that he could count on regional allies. However, in recent years the slowing of the Chinese economy, historically low international prices for oil, and the weakening or fall of allied governments in countries like Venezuela, Brazil, and Argentina, have dramatically worsened the international climate for Ecuador, resulting in an economic contraction and a resulting restriction in the country's room to maneuver. On top of all this, on April 16, 2016, Ecuador was hit by a 7.8 magnitude earthquake, the strongest in more than seventy years. The quake killed more than 650 people, injured more than 16,000, and caused an estimated US$3 billion in damages. In order to raise revenue for reconstruction, the Correa administration raised the sales tax, employed a one-time garnishing of wages from higher-paid government workers, and instituted a new wealth tax on millionaires. He has also sought international help and suggested that the state might privatize some of its assets, something that would represent a backsliding toward neoliberalism.

PUBLIC POLICY: PENDULUM SWINGS BETWEEN THE DEVELOPMENTAL AND NEOLIBERAL STATE

During the oil boom years of the 1970s the state dramatically expanded its functions and the services it provided to the population. However, during the neoliberal decades of the 1980s and 1990s, the trend was reversed. Austerity and economic crisis forced governments to privatize, lay off government workers, and dramatically cut spending. During these years, Ecuador had one of the lowest levels of public investment in the region. Correa's administration reversed this trend and oversaw a dramatic expansion in the size and role of the state. Public investment increased by a factor of six, and instead of one of the lowest, Ecuador became one of the countries with the highest levels of public investment in the region. In 2012, the government budget was 160 percent greater than in 2004 and the largest in the country's history.

Until the economic downturn at the end of his presidency, Correa's government invested heavily in road construction; newly paved highways crisscrossing Ecuador's difficult terrain made transportation of goods and people faster and easier. Social spending increased dramatically, with the largest increase for government programs that built thousands of modest homes for low income people. Spending on public education doubled between 2006 and 2009, and in the health-care sector the government spent significant amounts building and updating hospitals and clinics, and equipping them with modern medical equipment. Ecuador's cash transfer program for the poor, the Human Development Stipend, reaches 44 percent of the population, one of the highest levels of coverage of any Latin American country. The public sector has expanded through the hiring of more public school teachers, police, doctors and nurses, as well as government bureaucrats and administrators.

The significant expansion of the welfare state that Correa spearheaded succeeded in reducing poverty and inequality. From the start of his presidency to 2014, the World Bank reports that poverty measured by income fell from 37.5 to 22.5 percent and extreme poverty from 16.9 to 7.7 percent. Wage growth was fastest for the poorest Ecuadorians, which resulted in a significant decrease in inequality: the Gini index fell from

54 at the start of Correa's presidency to 48.7 in 2014. According to the United Nations, Ecuador was one of the leading countries in Latin America in terms of poverty reduction and equitable growth.

The government has also spent vast sums on sophisticated media campaigns to tout its public works. The opposition has repeatedly criticized Correa for wasteful spending on government propaganda, has called some of his infrastructure projects white elephants, and leveled numerous accusations of corruption, although so far none of these have been proven.

NATIONALISM AND INTERNATIONAL POLITICS

Restoring national pride, asserting the country's sovereignty, and fomenting regional integration were key components of Correa's approach to foreign policy. In rhetoric and substance, Correa demonstrated his readiness to distance Ecuador from its traditionally compliant relationships with the United States and international financial institutions, like the World Bank and the IMF. He was also a stalwart supporter of regional efforts to build new institutions that advance cooperation, integration, and a united voice for Latin America on the world stage.

Following through on a campaign promise, Correa refused to renew a lease to the US Air Force for a military base in the coastal city of Manta, forcing the US military to look for other countries willing to host its antinarcotics surveillance operations. In 2009 Ecuador withdrew from the ICSID Convention, an international entity that arbitrates disputes between national governments and foreign investors. This was in compliance with the Montecristi Constitution, which prohibits ceding sovereignty to international tribunals in disputes with foreign companies, and also in anticipation of such disputes after the government raised taxes on foreign oil companies. Correa kicked out several high-ranking foreign diplomats, including a World Bank envoy and US Ambassador Heather Hodges over a WikiLeaks cable.

In terms of regional integration, Correa participated in the creation in 2008 of the Union of South American Nations (UNASUR), an intergovernmental union that aims to integrate the two existing customs unions in South America into a European Union-like structure. In 2010 UNASUR established its permanent headquarters in Quito. In July 2009 Correa announced Ecuador's entry into the Bolivarian Alliance for the Peoples of Our America (ALBA), the attempt of Hugo Chávez to develop an alternative model of integration based on principles of solidarity as opposed to neoliberal market models. In 2011 Ecuador participated along with all thirty-three Latin American and Caribbean states in the founding of the Community of Latin American and Caribbean States (CELAC), which is a potential rival to the Organization of American States (OAS), and is noticeable for its inclusion of Cuba and exclusion of the United States and Canada.

CONCLUSION

Correa's presidency changed Ecuadorian politics in a number of crucial ways. The country has enjoyed a decade of political and economic stability after more than a decade of crisis. Until 2015 the country experienced robust levels of economic growth.

True to his promise to end the "long and sad neoliberal night," he re-empowered and rebuilt the state. Ecuador in 2017 faces difficult challenges stemming from changes in the international economy and fallout from the devastating 2016 earthquake. The country is now also burdened with significant debt. All of these factors suggest that the economy will be challenging for the country's next president.

Although Correa had a positive record in terms of poverty reduction and promotion of more equitable growth, his track record on press freedom, fostering inclusive democratic debate, and working collaboratively with social movements and civil society was problematic. The use of his substantial powers to intimidate, ostracize, and silence opposition voices and the private press alienated many, weakened and divided Ecuador's once powerful social movements, and set a poor example in terms of fostering a political climate of respect for dissent and tolerance. Although Correa's consolidation of executive power appears to have resolved the problem of "presidencies interrupted," it came at the cost of what critics argue is an overly powerful executive branch.

Critics on Ecuador's left also argue that while Correa increased social spending, he failed to alter the country's underlying economic model, which is based on the unsustainable extraction of the country's abundant natural resources. His pursuit of large-scale mining and oil drilling may help maintain high levels of state spending, but it also entails high environmental costs and leaves the country vulnerable to swings in international commodity prices.

Despite significant opposition and a recent economic slowdown, Correa and his Citizen's Revolution bucked the regional trend of the crisis and decline of the left in the 2017 elections. In February Correa's political party, AP, won a decisive victory in legislative elections, securing 74 of 137 or 54 percent of the seats in the National Assembly, Ecuador's unicameral legislative body. Although this represented a decrease of 26 seats compared with the previous term, the AP nevertheless retains an absolute majority. Following this was the second-round presidential election in April. Although the vote was close, AP candidate, Lenin Moreno eked out a win with 51.15 percent of the vote over right-wing challenger and former banker, Guillermo Lasso's 48.85 percent. Most of the opposition to Correa had united behind Lasso in the second round.

Moreno's win removes the immediate threat of a dismantling of Correa's political project by the right. He ran on the promise to protect and deepen many of the social gains achieved by the Citizen's Revolution, but also to govern in a more conciliatory manner. If he is able to mend ties with social movements and parties on the left that moved into the opposition in reaction to Correa, he may be able to strengthen and renew the party. But he will have to govern under more difficult economic circumstances and will certainly face challenges in keeping his party and movement united once the domineering and galvanizing figure of Correa is no longer at the forefront of the political project.

SUGGESTIONS FOR FURTHER READING

Becker, Marc. ¡Pachakutik!: Indigenous Movements and Electoral Politics in Ecuador. Lanham, MD: Rowman and Littlefield, 2011.

De la Torre, Carlos. Populist Seduction in Latin America. 2nd ed. Athens: Ohio University Press, 2010.

De la Torre, Carlos, and Steven Strifler, eds. *The Ecuador Reader: History, Culture, Politics.* Durham, NC: Duke University Press, 2008.

Gerlach, Allen. *Indians, Oil, and Politics: A Recent History of Ecuador.* Wilmington, DE: SR Books, 2003.

Martin, Pamela L. *Oil in the Soil: The Politics of Paying to Preserve the Amazon.* Lanham, MD: Rowman and Littlefield, 2011.

Roitman, Karem. *Race, Ethnicity, and Power in Ecuador: The Manipulation of Mestizaje.* Boulder, CO: Lynne Rienner Publishers, 2009.

NOTES

1. Arturo Valenzuela, "Presidencies Interrupted," *Journal of Democracy* 15, no. 2 (2004): 5–19.

2. Prensa Latina, "Presidente de Ecuador: 'Superaremos la triste noche neoliberal'," www.ecuadorinmediato.com/index.php?module=Noticias&func=news_user_view&id=45376&umt=presidente_ecuador_superaremos_triste_noche_neoliberal, desembre 9, 2006, accessed abril 2013.

3. Juan Carlos Donoso, Daniel Montalvo, Mitchell Seligson, and Elizabeth J. Zechmeister, "Analisis preliminar de la encuesta nacional de LAPOP en Ecuador, 2014," Latin American Public Opinion Project. PowerPoint presentation, Quito, Mayo 2014.

4. "Voluntary isolation" refers to groups of hunters and gatherers who live deep in the forest and have had little or no contact with the outside world.

5. Thomas L. Friedman, *The Lexus and the Olive Tree: Understanding Globalization* (New York: Farrar, Straus and Giroux, 2000).

PART III

The Political Systems of Mexico, Central America, and the Caribbean

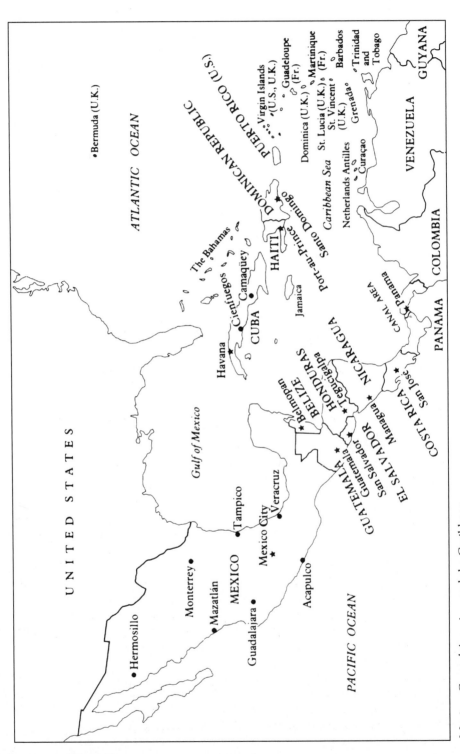

Mexico, Central America, and the Caribbean

18

MEXICO: DEMOCRATIZATION AND VIOLENCE

José Luis Velasco

INTRODUCTION

Since the beginning of the twenty-first century, Mexicans have been able to enjoy something that many previous generations had dreamed of but were unable to achieve: a political regime in which parties and candidates freely compete for office, where the civil and political rights of citizens are guaranteed by law, and where diversity is not only tolerated but often even promoted and applauded. This achievement is far from complete, however. Inequality and poverty seem as intractable as ever, and political corruption as pervasive as it was during colonial times. A wave of criminal violence engulfed much of the country precisely when it had just begun to enjoy the blessings of competitive politics. But even with these problems, Mexico is going through one of the more dynamic and challenging epochs of its long and often convulsive history.

This is not always obvious. To much of the world, Mexico seems a rather exotic country, blessed with some cultural and natural attractions but quite violent and un-predictable. This perception is not unfounded. Mexico is, to begin with, the source of many illicit goods, or at least the place from where they are shipped to the rest of the world, especially the United States. For example, according to estimates made by US authorities, most of the cocaine entering the United States passes through Mexico. The country is also a major producer of marijuana, heroin, and synthetic drugs, most of which are exported, especially to the North American market.

319

Mexico is also a leader in the illicit movement of people. In 2012, 59 percent of all the unauthorized immigrants living in the United States were Mexican nationals. Moreover, located at the northern extreme of Latin America and with precarious law enforcement, Mexico is also a major transit route for illegal migrants of all nationalities trying to enter the United States, a nation with which it shares an almost two thousand mile border.

Mexico is often associated with financial instability. Major cases include the so-called peso crisis of 1982, when it had to default on its sovereign debt—the first Latin American country to do so during that fateful decade. Perhaps even more notorious was the 1995 financial crisis, when, unable to stop the outflow of money, the country was forced to devalue its currency. In what was known as the "tequila effect," this crisis rocked the entire transnational financial system; it was also the first in a series of crises that later affected such emerging markets as the Philippines, Indonesia, South Korea, Russia, and Brazil.

Mexico is also infamous for its blatant inequalities. With a Gini index (the most common indicator of income inequality) of almost 0.5, Mexico is one of the most unequal nations among upper-middle-income countries. Not surprisingly, although it boasts twelve billionaires on the Forbes list of the super-rich (including telecommunications mogul Carlos Slim), more than half of its population lives in poverty. The differences in well-being are especially stark between urban and rural dwellers, between Indians and whites, and between people living in the south and those living in the north of the country.

Mexico is also seen as a paradise of corruption. Large corruption scandals, involving powerful government officials and other high-level politicians, are often aired in the press. But what has given Mexico much of its recent notoriety is the problem of crime and public insecurity, most of which is related to the illegal drug business. The competition between drug trafficking organizations became especially murderous at the beginning of the twenty-first century. Although estimates of the casualties provoked by this violence vary widely, reliable sources estimate that more than eighty-three thousand people had been killed by the end of 2015. Another indicator of this violence is the number of people officially recognized as "disappeared," which totaled almost twenty-eight thousand individuals in 2015.

Yet, Mexico is much more than the sum of its problems. With more than 120 million inhabitants, it is the eleventh most populated country in the world. It has a rich territory, with long coastlines and a variety of climes and ecosystems, from the deserts of the north to the tropical rainforests of the southeast. It has a long and rich history, spanning such classic civilizations as the Aztecs, Zapotec, Maya, and Olmec, three centuries of Spanish colonial domination, and two more centuries of eventful independent existence. And it is deeply integrated into the global economy and society. Since 1994, Mexico has been a member of the Organization for Economic Cooperation and Development (OECD), often considered the "rich-man's club" of nations. Even more significantly, together with the United States and Canada, it is a member of the North American Free Trade Agreement (NAFTA), established in 1994. Partly thanks to this agreement, it is one of the United States' main trade partners. In 2015, US-Mexico trade amounted to almost US$600 billion; Mexico was the second most important destination of US exports and the third most important source of US imports.

This level of trade would not be possible without a large and complex economy. With a total output of almost US$1.2 trillion, Mexico was the world's fifteenth largest economy in 2015. It is also a quite modern one, with less than 3 percent of its product coming from agriculture, almost one-third from industry, and 63 percent from services. Similarly, Mexico is highly urbanized. Almost eight in every ten Mexicans are urban dwellers; almost 40 percent of Mexicans live in metropolitan areas of more than one million inhabitants. Indeed, with more than twenty million inhabitants, Greater Mexico City is the twelfth largest megacity in the world.

Scarcely noticed but extremely important, especially in current years, is Mexico's religious diversity. After the so-called *Cristero* war of the late 1920s, no major religious conflict has developed in the country. This fact is all the more significant because of the religious diversification that the country experienced in the late twentieth century. Although Mexico continues to be a predominantly Catholic country, Catholicism went from being virtually the only religion in 1950 (98.2 percent of all the population) to being only a majoritarian one (82.7 percent in 2010). Perhaps even more significant is the growth in the number of people who claim to profess no religion, which increased from less than 1 percent to almost 5 percent from 1960 to 2010.

Equally noticeable is the ethnic and linguistic diversity of the country. Mexico is an important member of the Spanish-speaking community—indeed, it is the country with the largest number of Spanish speakers in the world. But it is also a country with more than seventy Indian languages, spoken by as much as 7 percent of the population. Closely associated with this ethnic and linguistic diversity is another phenomenon: the cultural richness of the country. Mexico has a powerful popular culture, with many festivals, handicrafts, dances, and songs, in which indigenous and European elements subtly combine to create distinctive national products. A similar, distinctive mix is also present in the works of some of the country's best-known artists, including painters such as Diego Rivera and Frida Kahlo and writers such as Juan Rulfo and Octavio Paz.

Finally, and most important for the purposes of this text, Mexico was able to move, in a relatively peaceful way, from a seven-decade authoritarian regime, controlled by a single political party, to a competitive political system with greater respect for political and civil rights. To be sure, this process was slow and often painful, punctuated by violent outbursts from the opposition and far more lethal repressive attacks from the government—including such notorious massacres as those of 1968 and 1971, as well as the so-called Dirty War of the late 1960s and 1970s. Still, the remarkable fact is that Mexico's political transition required no major break of the institutional order, no large-scale insurrection, no military coup, and no foreign invasion. Instead, the transition took place mainly through a series of institutional changes, beginning with the so-called political reform of 1977 and culminating with the ambitious electoral reform of 1996.

The goal of the ensuing text is precisely to present, within the limitations of a single chapter, the complex, often contradictory, nature of Mexico's society and politics: its progress, well as its setbacks, its problems and its strengths, the weight of its past and the challenges of its present.

BACKGROUND: FROM CONQUEST TO REVOLUTION

Bernal Díaz del Castillo, one of the Spanish conquerors, described the impression that the capital of the Aztecs made upon them in 1519:

> When we gazed upon all this splendour at once, we scarcely knew what to think, and we doubted whether all that we beheld was real. A series of large towns stretched themselves along the banks of the lake, out of which still larger ones rose magnificently above the waters. Innumerable crowds of canoes were plying everywhere around us; at regular distances we continually passed over new bridges, and before us lay the great city of Mexico in all its splendour.

This impression was justified. When the Spaniards arrived, Mexico-Tenochtitlan was one of the world's largest cities, with more than two hundred thousand inhabitants. And although it was the largest, it was not the only city in the territory of present-day Mexico. Archaeologists have identified around one thousand urban centers in Mesoamerica—the region that corresponds to what is now the southern part of Mexico and northern Central America.

Together with the Andes, Mesoamerica was one of the two main cultural areas of the pre-Columbian Western Hemisphere. Archaeologists usually date its history to 2,000 BC, the beginning of the Preclassic period during which the first cities were built. This period was marked by the rise and fall of what has often been called the mother culture, the Olmec, which flourished in the southern part of the Gulf of Mexico. The next period, known as the Classic—approximately from AD 200 to 900—was extremely rich in cities, languages, and civilization. But three cultures were dominant: Teotihuacan, the Zapotec, and the Maya. It was an age of great progress in several fields, especially architecture, mathematics, and astronomy. Among the many achievements of these cultures were the independent invention of the zero, the creation of a very precise calendar, the corbel arch, and a sophisticated system of writing that allowed its users to communicate anything they wanted. It was in this period that Mexico's most famous archaeological sites—Teotihuacan, Palenque, and Chichen Itza—were built.

This broad center of civilization entertained a tense relation with the region to its north, so-called Aridoamerica—a dry, forbidding area thinly populated by roaming tribes. These tribes continuously threatened to override the cities to the south. In fact, it was from this area that the Aztecs came, eager to learn from their civilized hosts and neighbors but also to subdue them. Thanks to this aggressiveness, the Aztecs soon became the dominant force of the Mesoamerican post-Classic period (900 to 1519). At its climax, Mexico-Tenochtitlan—the city that they founded two centuries before the arrival of the Spaniards—dominated almost half of Mesoamerica and enjoyed a sort of military and political hegemony over much of the rest. Its power was felt even in the remote post-Classic Maya territories and in present day El Salvador.

Not surprisingly, when the Spaniards reached current Mexican territory it was this city that they targeted first. The struggle for the Aztec capital was ferocious, but rather brief. It started with the arrival of the Spaniards in November 1519 and ended with the surrender of the city in August 1521. In contrast, the conquest of the rest of the territory was much slower. Organized in a set of mutually independent cities, the Maya could elude full conquest for many decades. Indeed, the last independent Maya kingdom (in current Guatemala) was not conquered until 1697. The struggle against the Chichimeca and other nomadic or seminomadic peoples of Aridoamerica took even longer; in the northern extremes, Spanish dominion remained precarious during the entire colonial period.

But whether rapid or gradual, the conquest was truly devastating for the Indians. The wars of conquest, the forced labor, the demoralization, and, above all, the new illnesses brought by the conquerors proved fatal for the Indians. To give an idea of this destruction, the population of Central Mexico has been estimated to have declined from twenty-five million just before the conquest to just above one million at the beginning of the seventeenth century.[1]

But these first eighty years of Spanish domination—years of conquest and destruction—also set the durable basis for what was eventually to become a new country. The social and political order that they created was highly stratified. The bottom was reserved for Indians and the slaves imported from Africa. The high positions were occupied by the creoles, the descendants of Spanish immigrants. But the true top was monopolized by people born in Spain, the so-called *peninsulares*. The rigid caste system, however, was complicated—and often disrupted—by the growing number of mestizos, who did not always remain within their assigned place (above Indians and slaves but below the creoles).

The bulk of the colonial population lived in the countryside. Agriculture was often organized in the hacienda system, a series of large, almost self-sufficient properties with some form of indentured labor. But the most lucrative activity, by far, was mining. Indeed, the search for precious metals was the single most important motivation of the conquest. Mines were especially important in Guanajuato, San Luis Potosi, Zacatecas, and other places in central-northern Mexico. Gold and, above all, silver were the main minerals extracted.

But urban life was also intense. Mexico, Guadalajara, Guanajuato, Veracruz, Puebla, Merida, Valladolid (current Morelia), and Antequera (current Oaxaca) were the most important cities. Apart from being the political and administrative headquarters of the entire colonial enterprise, they were also its main educational and scientific centers. The intellectual life was dominated by the seminars for the education of the clergy and the Royal and Pontifical University of Mexico—the forerunner of the current National Autonomous University of Mexico (UNAM).

Politically, Mexico was the core of New Spain, which at one time comprised most of the territory from Nicaragua to the south of Canada, as well as Cuba and the Philippines. Presided over by a viceroy, New Spain was divided into a series of provinces (called kingdoms and general captaincies). In theory, life in the colony was meticulously regulated by laws made in Spain. In reality, however, the laws were often hard to follow and enforce in territories that were so far and so different from Spain. Therefore, using a formula developed by medieval lawyers, New Spaniards often declared their obedience to the laws but disregarded them in practice.

The Catholic Church was the only religion allowed in colonial territories. Indeed, paralleling the military and political invasion, there was a "spiritual conquest," aiming to impose the Spanish religion over the defeated Indians. But the result of this spiritual enterprise was not orthodox Catholicism: the ancient gods and their ceremonies often survived under Christian guise. The best-known case is that of the Virgin of Guadalupe, still one of the main religious figures in Mexico and beyond. The church had a territorial organization—a number of dioceses and their respective parishes, all of them under the authority of an archbishop. But there were also several religious orders, like the Dominicans and Jesuits. Indeed, the latter became especially powerful, almost monopolizing the education of the elite and holding large haciendas.

This political and administrative structure underwent many changes during the three centuries of Spanish domination. But the so-called Bourbon reforms, implemented in the late eighteenth century, were particularly important. Seeking to tighten its control over its colonial territories, the Spanish crown reorganized most of New Spain into a series of "intendancies," putting all of them under the watch of reliable administrators sent directly from Spain. Another step in the same direction was the expulsion of the powerful Jesuits.

The resentment created by these centralizing measures was one of the main causes of the independence movement that broke out a few decades later. But independence was also driven by larger factors: the decline of Spain, exhausted by its fight against other European powers; the independence of the United States; the growth of England's economic and naval supremacy; above all, the Napoleonic invasion of Spain in 1808 and the consequent abdication and imprisonment of King Ferdinand VII.

The struggle for independence started as a movement in favor of the imprisoned king. Emblematic of this beginning was the declaration issued by the municipal government of Mexico City in 1808, repudiating the new pro-French metropolitan authorities. In late 1810 Father Miguel Hidalgo, in Guanajuato, exhorted the people to rise up against the authorities collaborating with the French invaders. Soon, the movement turned into a full-grown revolt against the established powers. Although their march seemed unstoppable, the insurgents were defeated at the outskirts of Mexico City. Hidalgo and his main commanders were soon captured and executed, but the popular revolt continued and became even more radical, under the main leadership of another priest, José María Morelos. But after the capture of Morelos, the popular phase of the struggle, which had threatened to upset the entire social and political order, was over.

The small pro-independence bands that survived posed no major threat to the authorities. Their chance came in 1821, in an unexpected way: one year earlier, a military revolt in Spain had forced the king to accept a liberal constitution, opening up a three-year period of constitutional monarchy in the metropolis. Frightened by that change, conservative creoles in the New Spain decided to join forces with the insurgents. The program of this unlikely alliance, known as the Iguala Plan, was profoundly conservative, centering on "three guarantees": Roman Catholicism was to remain the only religion, Mexico was to become a fully independent kingdom, and this kingdom was to be ruled by Ferdinand VII or another king from an "established dynasty."

Yet, conservative as its result was, independence was extremely costly. Approximately six hundred thousand people, 10 percent of the total population, were killed in the war.[2] The economy was ravaged, roads were dangerous and often impassable, villages were decimated, and the entire social fabric seemed to have been torn apart by violence. And yet, beneath this destruction, the social structure seemed to have changed little. Haciendas and mines continued to dominate the countryside; slavery was abolished, but blacks and Indians were still confined to the social bottom, while the white elite's dominion continued unabated; the Catholic Church retained, and even increased, its spiritual and secular influence.

In contrast, politics became chaotic. Because no member of the established European dynasties accepted the crown, Agustin de Iturbide, the conservative creole who had engineered the consummation of independence, became the first monarch of the Mexican Empire—an enormous territory extending from today's US state of Oregon to the Republic of Costa Rica. But the coalition that had made independence possible did not last long; in 1823, Iturbide abdicated and the empire was abolished.

Thus, began a long period of chaos. With the break of colonial political and administrative institutions, factions, personal leadership, and militarism reigned supreme. Revolts, coups d'état, and full-fledged civil wars were almost continuous. This period produced Mexico's paramount *caudillo*, General Antonio López de Santa Anna. In just twenty years (from 1833 to 1855), he managed to be president of Mexico eleven times, in the name of a succession of political programs and ideologies that were not only contradictory but often even incompatible. The last time he occupied this office, he was appointed dictator for life by his conservative supporters (whom he officially described as "the authorities, corporations and most notable people from all districts and towns of the Republic").

Still, alongside these conflicts of individuals and factions, there were also ideological and programmatic struggles. One of these was the opposition between the centralists—partisans of a strong, centralized form of government—and the federalists—seeking more autonomy for the provinces. This cleavage partly coincided with the division between conservatives—who wanted to preserve the old institutions, especially the church, the haciendas, and the army—and the liberals—who wanted to abolish the old privileges and were in favor of individual rights.

At first, liberal federalists appeared to have the upper hand. The first Mexican Constitution, proclaimed in 1824, adopted a federalist model, largely based on that of the United States But the federal republic collapsed ten years later, to be replaced in 1836 by an openly centralist and conservative system. It was not until 1857 that liberal principles became firmly established in a constitution that would last for six decades. The new constitution abolished the privileges of the Catholic Church, ordering the selling of its property; guaranteed such liberal individual rights as freedom of the press, speech, and conscience; and established a federal republic with strong separation of powers.

But the promulgation of the new constitution did not entail the triumph of the liberals. On the contrary, it gave rise to a bitter struggle, known as the War of the Three Years. Although the liberals won this war, their triumph was short-lived. Embittered by their recent defeat, conservatives decided to take a step that they had planned but never dared to undertake for several decades: to transform Mexico into a monarchy, headed by a member of one of Europe's royal families. The man who took up this challenge was Maximilian of Hapsburg, supported by the French government. But, despite its initial success, this Second Mexican Empire did not fare better than the one that preceded it by forty years. The liberal government, headed by Benito Juárez, was expelled from Mexico City and was cornered in the dusty town of Paso del Norte, now known as Ciudad Juárez. But it never ceased to resist the occupation. The conflict ended in

1867 with the withdrawal of French troops, the shooting of the emperor, and the definitive triumph of the liberals.

But political instability was not only domestic. Without the protection of Spain and devastated by its internecine conflicts, Mexico became more vulnerable in the international arena. This resulted in the progressive loss of territory. The first of these losses was also the least violent: the separation of Central America from the Mexican Empire in 1823. The second major loss was the independence of Texas, in 1836, after a short but humiliating war in which President Santa Anna himself was made prisoner. The third loss—including such important territories as Upper California, New Mexico, and Arizona—was the largest, resulting from what is known in Mexico as the US invasion of 1847.

The definitive triumph of the liberals ushered in a long period of stability and progress. This was especially so with the arrival of General Porfirio Diaz to the presidency. Inspired less by classical liberal principles than by the positivist ideal of order and progress, the Diaz administration, which lasted more than thirty years, endeavored to modernize the country. The budget was balanced, the army was downsized and disciplined, foreign debt was renegotiated, foreign investment was attracted in larger sums, and political rivalries were gradually put under the control of the modernizing dictator. In response to these and similar measures, agriculture and industry flourished, as did the export of silver, oil, sisal, cotton, sugar, and other commodities. The progress registered during these years could be illustrated by the growth of railroads. The first major railroad line (Mexico City to Veracruz) was not inaugurated until 1873; in 1879, there were less than one thousand kilometers of railroad in the entire country; by 1910, the railroad system extended from the northern to the southern borders, totaling almost twenty thousand kilometers.[3]

Although progress was rapid, so was the accumulation of problems. Perhaps the gravest of them concerned the distribution of land. Acting on the premise that the noncirculation of landed property is one of the greatest obstacles to national development, liberals not only targeted the church's vast landholdings, they also went against the property of Indian communities and other "dead hands." This led to innumerable abuses: Indians and many other peasants lost the lands that they had occupied for entire generations; large haciendas became even larger; corrupt officials legalized even blatantly abusive land seizures; and many people were reduced to indentured labor, and even slavery, especially in the southern plantations of Oaxaca and Yucatán.

Another social problem—not as large but perhaps even more visible—was labor repression. The rapid industrialization of the country required labor discipline, and the government rushed to impose it with characteristically authoritarian zeal. Wages were usually precarious, often paid in private money only accepted in company stores; unions and strikes were prohibited; workdays were long and labor conditions painful. This situation created a fertile ground for the penetration of anarcho-syndicalism and other radical ideologies. Two strikes were especially notorious: one by miners in Cananea, Sonora, in 1906; the other by textile workers in Río Blanco, Veracruz, the following year. These strikes, both harshly repressed, are usually considered among the most important precursors of the revolution that erupted four years later.

Perhaps even more explosive was the political situation. For many years, Diaz was able to keep political aspirations in check, ordering his subordinates to do "little politics and much administration." But as his death or retirement seemed more imminent, this discipline started to crumble. Two factions emerged: one formed by the new techno-cratic elite, the other by old-style caudillos. By sending General Bernardo Reyes, the leader of the latter faction, into golden exile (disguised as an official mission to study military matters in Europe), Díaz managed to assuage this tension for a time. When, in 1908, he told a US journalist that Mexico was "ready for democracy" and hinted that he was looking forward to his retirement, Díaz himself agitated the political system that he had previously pacified.

This political agitation provided the opportunity that people dissatisfied with the re-gime had long awaited. Yet, it was not radical dissidents, like the Flores Magón broth-ers, who benefited most from it but Francisco Madero, the heir of one of Mexico's richest families. At first, Díaz tolerated Madero's presidential campaign, but he eventu-ally sent him into prison. Soon Madero escaped and fled to the United States, calling on the Mexican people to rise up on November 20, 1910, in the name of "free vote" and against reelection. The Mexican Revolution—an event that would mark the devel-opment of Mexico for the rest of the century—had begun.

Madero's cry for free and fair elections resonated throughout the country, awaken-ing old political resentments. One element that made the rebellion truly popular was the promise to restore to their legitimate owners the lands that had been "abusively" taken from them. Different armed bands sprang up almost everywhere, especially in the north, occupying many villages and even some mid-sized towns. When revolution-ary forces took Ciudad Juárez, Díaz resigned, leaving the government in the hands of an interim president.

This set the scene for an event that was not to be repeated for the rest of the twen-tieth century: a vigorous, competitive and basically fair electoral process, in Octo-ber 1911. Although Madero's electoral victory was overwhelming, his government was shaky. Once its immediate goal—the overthrowing of Porfirio Díaz—had been achieved, the revolutionary coalition began to break up. Popular forces demanded the rapid restitution of lands, and Madero was not eager to fulfill that promise. The first major rebellion occurred in Morelos, under the leadership of Emiliano Zapata. The sec-ond occurred in Chihuahua, headed by Pascual Orozco. Although the latter presented a more serious military threat and was supported by powerful conservatives, it was the Zapatista movement—a truly peasant rebellion—that exposed the contradictions of the revolutionary coalition. Feeling this weakness, former partisans of the Díaz regime began to conspire ever more boldly against the revolutionary government.

This situation involved much more than the usual clash of factions and individuals. The national system of authority had collapsed, leaving the deep fractures of Mex-ican society fully exposed. Even so, Madero managed to remain in power for more than a year, not so much because of his own strength as because of the division of his rivals, who often hated each other more than they hated the president. But the situation changed in February 1913: under the auspices of the US ambassador, anti-revolutionary leaders agreed to join forces against the government. After ten days of fierce combat in Mexico City, the counterrevolutionary forces prevailed, killing the president and vice president and setting up a new government, headed by General Vic-toriano Huerta. But their triumph was ephemeral. With a new enemy in front and enraged by the assassination of Madero, revolutionary forces united again in a broad front, the so-called Constitutionalist movement. Moreover, with the election of Woodrow Wilson to the US presidency, the government of that country shifted sides, decidedly aiding the revolutionaries.

The struggle was merciless, but quite rapid. In August 1914, after losing a string of battles, the decimated Federal Army surrendered to the Constitutionalists. But peace was still far away. Having eliminated its common enemy, the revolutionary coalition broke down again. Factions were numerous, but they coalesced around two large blocs: the followers of the Revolutionary Convention and the followers of Carranza. The former, including the large revolutionary armies commanded by Francisco Villa and Emiliano Zapata, prevailed at the beginning, for some months controlling Mexico City and much of the rest of the country. But their forces, although mighty, were unable to coordinate among themselves, and the political leaders of the Convention's government were wary of their peasant allies. In contrast, the Constitutionalists were tightly united under the political leadership of Venustiano Carranza and the military command of Alvaro Obregón.

After losing decisive battles in the central state of Guanajuato in the spring of 1915, Villa's all-powerful Division of the North disintegrated. Villa's popular appeal did not vanish, however, and he was able to maintain a very aggressive guerrilla force. Angered by the US support for his enemies, Villa crossed the border and attacked Columbus, New Mexico, in March 1916. In reaction, the US sent a "Punitive Expedition," with a strength of almost fifteen thousand soldiers, which for eleven months tried—and failed—to capture or kill him. Although Villa kept the state of Chihuahua in permanent turmoil in the following years, he was unable to resurface as a serious contender for national power; he surrendered in 1920 and was assassinated three years later. The Constitutionalists were also able to contain the other large peasant army—the one commanded by Zapata—assassinating its leader in 1919.

THE POST-REVOLUTIONARY REGIME

The Constitutionalist movement was not free of factional struggles, but in 1920 they managed to get rid of their main leader, Venustiano Carranza, without suffering a major rupture. Thus, one can say that by 1920 the military phase of the Revolution was mostly over. The country, however, was wrecked. According to census data, in 1921 Mexico had 826,000 fewer inhabitants than in 1910. The new constitution, written in 1917, contained many socially progressive measures, but had not been implemented. Armed bands continued to roam the country. With the notable exception of sisal and oil production, most economic activities were disrupted by the ten years of revolution.[4] Moreover, relations with the US were strained. The most controversial issue concerned the property of oil companies, since the new constitution had declared oil and other minerals to be under the "direct dominion" of the state. It was only after lengthy negotiations and many concessions that the United States and Mexican governments reached an agreement (known as the Bucareli Treaty, signed in 1923).

Reconstruction also implied the creation of new roles and institutions, notably the minister of public education in 1921, and the Central Bank (Banco de México) in 1925. Even more important were the efforts to build a truly national army out of the rather disparate Constitutionalist forces. This task was not completed until the end of the 1920s, after several military rebellions, the execution of many dissident generals, and the co-option of many others. It was during this decade that Obregón coined the phrase: "No general is able to resist a cannon ball of fifty-thousand silver pesos."

Reconstruction also required redefining the relations between the state and the Catholic Church. The 1917 constitution mandated a strict separation of state and religion, denying any special status to the church. When the revolutionary government tried to enforce these provisos, the church's hierarchy resisted ever more forcefully. Eventually, the confrontation evolved into a full-fledged military conflict, known as the Cristero war, between 1926 and 1929. Although at the end of this conflict the government had to make several concessions, the church ended up losing many of the privileges it had enjoyed for centuries.

The Cristero rebellion (as well as the intrigues within the revolutionary elite) cost the life of General Alvaro Obregón, the last of the great revolutionary caudillos. The immediate result of this assassination was the enthroning of a new strongman, General Plutarco Elías Calles. But its main effect was the institutionalization of the new regime. Acknowledging his own limitations as a revolutionary leader, Calles declared that Mexico should stop being a country of "one man" and become instead "a nation of institutions and laws." In practice, this meant reuniting the multitude of revolutionary factions into a single official political organization, first known as the National Revolutionary Party (PNR) and eventually as the Institutional Revolutionary Party (PRI).

This party was one of the most original and durable creations of the post-revolutionary regime. Unlike other revolutionary parties across the world, the PRI was scarcely ideological: almost any political program could find accommodation under its often inflamed but always imprecise rhetoric. Despite its name, it never was a truly institutional party; rather, it gladly situated itself as the agent of the president of the republic. But it was not the instrument of a single individual: its loyalty was transferred to whomever was elevated to the presidency. It aimed to encompass most, if not all, of Mexican society. Yet, unlike truly totalitarian parties, it never sought to dominate the thoughts and aspirations of its members. The loyalty that it demanded was never too deep. Moreover, though the PRI mobilized support for the state and, in turn, enjoyed the legal and illegal support of the authorities, it never was a state party in the proper sense of the term, imposing its ideology and policy preferences upon the government. Even so, its presence in the political arena was so strong and so durable that it forced all other parties wanting to cooperate or compete with it to emulate it.

Another major pillar of the post-revolutionary regime was the loyalty of the masses. In the first decades of the post-revolutionary regime, this loyalty was impossible to achieve without one measure: land reform. At first, land reform advanced rather timidly. It was not until the presidency of General Lázaro Cárdenas, the most radical phase of the post-revolutionary regime, that it became a national priority. From 1934 to 1940, the government distributed almost eighteen million hectares to more than eight hundred thousand peasants. Although no other presidential administration would match these figures, land reform remained a major official policy until 1992. In total, from 1934 to 1988, the government distributed more than 86 million hectares to 2.25 million beneficiaries.[5] However, most of the distributed lands were of poor quality, the plots were too small, and the benefited peasants never became their full owners. The fear of losing their plots and the hope of obtaining better and larger ones was a powerful motive behind the loyalty of peasants to the post-revolutionary authorities. This unequal alliance between peasants and state was cemented by the National Peasants' Confederation (CNC), founded in 1938.

Although predominantly rural at the beginning, post-revolutionary Mexico was undergoing rapid urbanization and industrialization. Labor legislation, as outlined in Article 123 of the 1917 constitution, was quite progressive, if difficult to implement. But labor organization was on the ascent. Some groups, like the Regional Confederation of Mexican Workers (CROM), were staunch government allies. Others, like the General Confederation of Workers (CGT), were far more militant, often acting under the guidance of anarchists and communists. In his fight against conservative forces both within and outside the official party, President Cárdenas called on labor to rally behind the government. This call coincided with the Popular Front policy of international communism, which sought the unity of progressive forces against fascism. The main product of this convergence was the Mexican Confederation of Workers (CTM), an umbrella organization that both gave labor a voice in official decision-making circles and served to suppress labor dissent.

President Cárdenas consolidated another pillar of the post-revolutionary regime: nationalism. In other countries, this term is usually associated with expansionist policies and the search for national supremacy. Such was not the case in Mexico. Post-revolutionary nationalism was largely defensive: a desire to fend off foreign intervention, especially from the United States, and a refusal to get entangled in international confrontations.

This peculiar nationalism was especially evident in economic matters. One major measure in this respect was the 1938 nationalization of the oil industry. Twenty years after the promulgation of the 1917 constitution, oil production continued to be dominated by foreign firms. This started to change in 1935, when, with government support, oil workers created a national union, which two years later declared a nationwide strike for better wages and other benefits. Companies refused to grant these demands and instead threatened to stop production. In response, the government nationalized them. Their replacement was PEMEX, a state-owned firm monopolizing the extraction, refinement, and distribution of oil. In the following decades, oil would be a major source of public incomes, often contributing almost half of the state's revenue.

Economic nationalism also took the form of restrictions to foreign trade, with the use of such conventional tools as tariffs and subsidies. Equally important was the development of state property. Large state-owned enterprises proliferated in almost every economic activity. This economic nationalism was part of a large development strategy known as "stabilizing development," the Mexican version of the well-known Import-Substitution-Industrialization model.

Nationalism was also important in security and diplomatic matters. With some minor tensions, relations between Mexico and the United States were largely harmonious during this period. Even the nationalization of the oil industry caused no major trouble, in part thanks to the "Good Neighbor" policy that the United States implemented in that period. During World War II, Mexico, like most of Latin America, supported the Allies, sending a small unit to fight in the Pacific theater. But in subsequent years, unlike many other Latin American countries, Mexico took pains to limit, without eliminating, US influence on its security forces. During the Cold War, the country also strove to maintain its good relations with the Soviet bloc, without alienating the United States.

This effort was especially evident in relation to the Cuban Revolution. Mexico defended Cuban sovereignty in international circles. At the same time, it actively, if quietly, cooperated with US undercover efforts to penetrate and disrupt Soviet and Cuban operations, not only in Mexico but in Latin America as a whole. Thanks to this ambivalent policy, Mexico managed to avoid both the effects of Cuba-assisted insurgency and the risks of US-sponsored counterinsurgency.

Also as part of this orientation, Mexico was a proud promoter of the Tlatelolco Treaty, negotiated in 1967, which prohibited nuclear proliferation in Latin America and the Caribbean. Even more actively, Mexico was a major advocate of the Non-Aligned Movement, through which many developing nations sought to avoid being overwhelmed by the global bipolar confrontation. Even in the 1980s, Mexico played an independent role as a promoter of peaceful solutions to the civil wars of Central America.

Another major component of the post-revolutionary regime was corruption. To be sure, the post-revolutionary regime often used force to suppress political opposition. Even so, compared to that of other developing nations, Mexico's official violence looked rather mild. This feat would not have been possible without the massive use of corruption. Besides being a way for political leaders and their allies to enrich themselves, corruption also served to buy the support of the elite and co-opt emerging leaders. In this sense, corruption was not a perversion of the system, but one of the ways it normally operated.

But although the features mentioned so far would suggest that the post-revolutionary regime was entirely authoritarian, in reality it always claimed to be democratic. On paper, the country was a federal republic, with "free and sovereign" states and autonomous municipalities. At both the state and federal levels, power was divided into the traditional executive, legislative, and judicial branches.

In reality, all the power of the system was vested in a single person: the president. Through the party, the bureaucracy, the army, and the corporatist organizations, he could control not only the entire state apparatus but society as a whole. Still, this person was not simply imposed on the country: he was duly nominated by the PRI and had to campaign against other candidates, and his time in office was carefully delimited, with no reelection allowed. The president could do as he pleased during his six-year term, including deciding who was to be the next presidential candidate of the PRI, and therefore in practice hand-picking his successor. But after the new president had been anointed, control of the entire political machinery was transferred to him. It is in this limited sense that the system was institutional—power belonged to the system, which had its written and unwritten rules, not to the specific individual it temporarily placed at its top.

This system was durable, lasting from the late 1920s to the end of the twentieth century. Perhaps the main indicator of its success was its ability to maintain political stability, avoiding the succession of revolts and military coups that haunted most of Latin America during that period. Equally notable was its capacity to foster economic growth. From 1940 to 1980, while the country's population multiplied by 3.4, its total economic output (expressed in constant Mexican pesos) multiplied by 11.5.[6] Not in vain has this period been called the "Mexican miracle."

But although it may have looked miraculous, this process was far from perfect. As documented in *The Children of Sanchez,* Oscar Lewis's classical anthropological analysis, poverty was the omnipresent companion to economic growth. But active dissent came not so much from the destitute as from apparently well-placed workers. Thus, despite the rigid control exerted by corporatist organizations, there were massive protests: of schoolteachers in 1958, of railroad workers in 1959, and of doctors in 1964–1965.

Although the government was able to repress these movements, often with the extensive help of the police and the army, social discontent did not disappear. On the contrary, it became more radical. In September 1965, inspired by the Cuban Revolution, a group of insurgents attacked a military garrison in the state of Chihuahua. Although the attack was unsuccessful, insurgent movements appeared in several other parts of the country. Even more important were the massive student protests in the summer of 1968, which culminated in the notorious Tlatelolco massacre that left dozens, perhaps even hundreds, dead. This massacre and another attack against students in 1971 encouraged many activists to join the guerrilla movements that operated both in remote rural areas and in some of the most important cities.

The government responded to these rebellions with a characteristic mix of illegal repression, cooption, and concession. While launching a "dirty war" on their radical opponents, the administrations of Luis Echeverría (1970–1976) and José López Portillo (1976–1982) adopted an inflamed populist rhetoric, which often provoked the hostility of the business elite and other conservative forces. But, despite that opposition, this official populism created no major problems, largely thanks to the unprecedented growth of oil revenues. Encouraged by this bonanza, the government felt strong enough to promote a "political reform" in 1977 and decree an amnesty to political rebels in 1978. The goal of both measures was to attract the radical opposition to mainstream politics, facilitating the establishment of new political parties, helping them stay competitive, and offering them new seats in the legislature.

These measures appeared so adequate and the future so bright that President López Portillo affirmed that henceforth the main task was to "administer abundance," predicting that, in a matter of years, Mexico would become a middle power.

But when international oil prices came down, these exalted hopes were frustrated. The huge debts that the country had incurred when interest rates were low were now impossible to repay. Official corruption, which seemed tolerable during the bonanza, now provoked the anger of the public and, especially, of the business sector. The government elite, so far firmly united under the leadership of the president, suddenly split into two major camps: one in favor of the old, inward-looking, state-led development model; the other advocating privatization, deregulation, and trade openness.

Desperate, in 1982 the outgoing López Portillo administration took two controversial measures: suspending payment of the external debt and nationalizing commercial banks. Suddenly, it seemed as if the country were marching toward socialism. In reality, this situation was just the beginning of the transition to the competitive form of capitalism and to the equally competitive political system that still prevail in the country at the time of this writing.

ECONOMIC TRANSITION

The 1980s were a truly lost decade for Mexico. Inflation was relentless; from 1980 to 1990, prices multiplied by a factor of 130. Access to foreign credit was nil; each year from 1982 to 1989, the service of the foreign debt consumed at least 34 percent of the country's exports. Domestic production fell. Measured in per capita units, the economic output of 1990 was 7 percent smaller than ten years earlier.[7] Standards of living suffered accordingly.

To stabilize the economy, the government undertook several difficult measures. It drastically cut public spending, especially for social purposes. It engaged in wage repression with unprecedented aggressiveness. On average, from 1983 to 1988, real wages fell by as much as 7 percent a year.[8] That the official unions were able to keep their members disciplined was a proof of their strength; but by siding so unequivocally with the authorities and employers, they endangered their own legitimacy. Seeking to make the control of wages, prices, and public spending less unilateral, in 1987 the government promoted a "Pact of Economic Solidarity," signed by the top business organizations, the big union corporations, and the government itself. The ensuing economic stabilization seemed so auspicious that the experiment was repeated several times in the following years, until 1995. Moreover, after several attempts at debt renegotiation, in 1989 the Mexican government took advantage of the so-called Brady Plan, in which lenders accepted cuts to either the principal or interest. As a result, the cost of the foreign debt service decreased abruptly and the entry of foreign capital began anew.

But the government not only endeavored to stabilize the economy. It also undertook to dismantle the old, state-led and protectionist model, replacing it with one based on freer market competition. One key measure was the liberalization of foreign trade, which began in the mid-1980s with reductions in tariffs and other restrictions. A second major policy was deregulation: the elimination of government-imposed restrictions to market competition. This included the reduction or elimination of price controls. Finally, a third major change was the privatization of state-owned enterprises and of communal property. Privatization became especially rapid during the administration of President Carlos Salinas (1988–1994). One of the most significant steps in this direction was the privatization of the banks, which began in 1990, eight years after they had been nationalized. Another decisive step was the privatization of the *ejido* system—the communal lands created by decades of land reform—in 1992.

As a result of these changes, in the early 1990s, the Mexican economy appeared not only stabilized but also transformed. Economic growth resumed. And with the signing of NAFTA, which went into effect in 1994, Mexico seemed poised to become a forceful player in the global economy. But the new growth was driven not by domestic savings but by the inflow of foreign capital, especially in the form of short-term investment. With the massive entry of capital, the Mexican peso soon become overvalued, which made the purchase of foreign goods more attractive.

As long as foreign capital kept flowing in, this situation presented no major problem. But when international investors realized that the situation was unsustainable, they fled in increasing numbers, forcing the government to devalue the currency in late 1994. And when it became clear that this measure was insufficient, the International Monetary Fund (IMF) and the US Federal Reserve had to step in with a US$50 billion loan.

For the great majority of Mexicans, the crisis was painful but short-lived. In 1996, the economy began to grow again, as did the inflow of capital. The growth of exports was spectacular, going from 13 percent of GDP in 1994 to almost 27 percent in 1996.

Thus, unlike 1982, the crisis of 1995 did not provoke a major shift in economic model. If anything, it made the new model more radical. Something similar, although less dramatic, can be said about the downturn provoked by the 2008 global crisis.

In sum, in less than twenty years, Mexico had created a more modern, market-driven economy, fully open to external investment and foreign trade.

DEMOCRATIZATION, ELECTIONS, AND THE STATE

Paralleling the transition to competitive markets was a movement toward competitive politics. This process, which began with the political reform of 1977, was quite slow. But by 1994, after several rounds of elections and institutional reforms, the country had a competitive three-party system. This movement toward electoral competitiveness gave rise to pluralization, which gradually transformed the formal structure of power of the country. The PRI lost its two-thirds majority in the Chamber of Deputies in 1988 and the absolute majority in 1997. With some delay, a similar change took place in the Senate. As the PRI lost its monopoly on seats, the legislative branch overcame its subordination to the executive, transforming itself into a truly independent power. Similarly, constitutional reforms in 1994 and 1996 significantly strengthened the judiciary. Moreover, with the triumph of a candidate from the opposition in Baja California, in 1989 the official party's monopoly on state governments was broken. By late 2000, parties other than the PRI ruled twelve of Mexico's thirty-one states, plus Mexico City. A similar process of pluralization took place in state legislatures and municipalities. On the whole, this process severed the partisan links that in fact, though not quite in right, subordinated state and local governments to the president.

Although not as clearly, important progress was made on political rights, civil liberties, and human rights. Voting-related rights showed great improvements as citizens were able to choose among several competing options. Moreover, many legal and institutional reforms sought to enhance respect for human rights and access to public information. Among the most important results of this reformism are the National Human Rights Commission (CNDH), created in 1990, and the National Institute for Access to Public Information (INAI) created in 2003.

The culminating moment of this transition came in 2000, when the PRI for the first time lost a presidential election. The winner was Vicente Fox, from the center-right National Action Party (PAN). Six years later, another candidate from the PAN, Felipe Calderón, won the presidency, very closely followed by Andrés Manuel López Obrador, the candidate from the left-leaning Party of the Democratic Revolution (PRD). It is true that the PRI returned to the presidency in 2012; but this was the result of a competitive election that was very different from the largely ritualistic contests of the post-revolutionary regime.

With all of this, it seemed that democracy had, at last, become the country's new reality. But the transition has been riddled with problems. Since 1997, the party holding the presidency has not had a legislative majority. This was rightly seen as sign of political diversity, but it also provoked a political paralysis. To be sure, this paralysis was broken at certain times. For example, in 2008, the constitution was amended to set the basis for a broad penal reform, aiming to replace the old, accusatory system—where defendants were often treated as if they were already guilty and most proceedings were conducted in writing—with one where defendants and their lawyers would have the opportunity to show their innocence in oral trials. But even that reform was devised so cautiously and divided into so many partial steps that eight years later many of its provisos still remained to be implemented.

This situation seemed to change at the end of 2013, when the leaders of the most important parties signed the so-called Pact for Mexico, widely considered a resounding success. One of its most important outcomes was the reform of the energy sector, which opened the oil industry to private investment. Also crucial was the telecommunications reform, which removed many legal hurdles to competition in that lucrative market. Equally ambitious was education reform, which sought to reinforce government control over the appointment and evaluation of teachers in public schools.

Although each party signing the Pact for Mexico imposed some of its preferred changes, the most important modifications were clearly aligned with the neoliberal reforms of the 1990s. Although they were strongly criticized by the leader of the electoral left, López Obrador, the strongest opposition came not from the ranks of political parties but from social movements. The education reform—announced as an effort to reassert state control over the hiring, tenure, and promotion of teachers through periodic evaluations—was so unpopular among teachers that even the official leadership of the National Union of Education Workers (SNTE), with a long history of collaboration with the government, felt obliged to oppose it. Seeking to weaken this opposition, President Peña Nieto imprisoned Elba Esther Gordillo, the leader of this union and a powerful ally of the PRI. But this move only strengthened the hand of the most radical forces within the union, which launched a series of protests in the summer of 2013.

Determined to defend its reforms, which it saw as its greatest achievement, the Peña Nieto administration sought to deactivate this movement through the usual combination of concessions and repression. By the summer of 2014, things seemed to have calmed down. This calm, however, was suddenly broken in September, when students from the Ayoztinapa Normal School, a teachers' college, were attacked in the city of Iguala, Guerrero. In total, six people were killed and forty-three students were disappeared. This college was well known for its opposition to the government and closely allied with the radical organizations operating in central and southern Mexico.

Initially, the federal government tried to put all the blame for this aggression on corrupt municipal authorities and violent drug traffickers. But although it seems clear that drug traffickers did participate, their real role was much smaller than the government claimed. As diverse reports have made clear, federal authorities—the army, the federal intelligence service, the federal police, and even the navy—were aware of the attacks even before they started, and they freely moved in the streets where the students were being killed or kidnapped. And although the federal government mounted an enormous cover-up operation, directed by the attorney general, it failed to explain why drug traffickers would want to launch such a large attack on well-known dissident students. Neither was it able to substantiate its claim that all of the missing students had been killed and burned to ashes in a garbage dump. Moreover, it was not able to explain how a second-tier drug trafficking organization, known as United Warriors, was able to mobilize local authorities from at least three municipalities and federal agents from at least one powerful corporation (the Federal Police) in a massive operation that covered a radius of more than eighty kilometers. All of this fed the suspicion that political repression, not criminal profit, was the main motivation of the attack.[9]

The event revitalized popular protests. When they subsided in early 2015, they left radical movements, in particular dissident teachers, in a more favorable position. This was the basis from which a new wave of protests was launched in mid-2016 against the implementation of the education reform. This time, the government seemed determined to carry out the reform at all costs. But when the federal and local police killed at least eight protesters in Oaxaca, the movement eventually forced the government to negotiate. The result was that the evaluation of teachers, the most controversial ingredient of the reform, was suspended in four Mexican states and scaled down in the rest of the country.

Important as these episodes of protest and repression are, they are only illustrative of a broader situation: despite the evident progress in the creation of a competitive political regime, large, seemingly intractable problems persist. One of the most visible of these is corruption. Because corruption performed such important functions in the post-revolutionary system, it was tempting to believe that it would be suppressed when that system was dismantled. But this expectation proved unfounded. Large corruption scandals, involving powerful government officials and other high-level politicians, are often aired in the press. Petty corruption, like the bribes that police officers extract from common citizens who want to circumvent a certain regulation, are also common—a sort of regressive tax that, according to one estimate, consumes up to one-third of the income of the poorest households.[10] Not surprisingly, in the influential Corruption Perception Index compiled by Transparency International, which ranks countries from less to more corrupt, Mexico occupies the ninety-fifth place, between Mali and the Philippines.

Another major problem is impunity—the government's incapacity or unwillingness to punish crimes. According to the latest official victimization survey, only 10.5 percent of all crimes committed in the country were reported to the authorities. Of those that were reported, only 60 percent were investigated by the authorities; and less than 10 percent ended up in a trial. In other words, 99.4 percent of the crimes were left unpunished.

Another serious problem, one that also undermines the rule of law and the legitimacy of the political system, is the violation of human rights. As in the case of corruption, it seemed reasonable to expect that respect for human rights would significantly improve with the demise of the post-revolutionary regime. But this, again, has not been the case. On the contrary, at least four major politically motivated massacres of unarmed civilians have taken place since the late 1990s: Aguas Blancas, Guerrero, in 1995; Acteal, Chiapas, in 1997; El Charco, Guerrero, in 1998; and the 2014 attack on students and other individuals in Iguala that was briefly discussed above. Moreover, as shall be mentioned below, government forces also have massacred real or alleged drug criminals.

These massacres are not isolated events but part of a general pattern. As a UN special rapporteur noted in 2014, "Torture and ill-treatment are generalized in Mexico." They are frequently used "in various parts of the country by municipal, state and federal police, state and federal ministerial police and the armed forces."[11] The 2015 human rights report by the US State Department concurred: "There were numerous reports that the government or its agents committed arbitrary or unlawful killings, often with impunity."

Another major problem is the lack of political coordination. The changes of the last decades were far more efficient at disrupting the ties with which, often against the law, the president bound all the lesser authorities than in creating new forms of coordination among authorities answering to different political parties. A case in point, often a very dramatic one but by no means isolated, is that of law enforcement. The Mexican police force is predominately local: state and municipal corporations comprised slightly more than 90 percent of the 471,000 agents registered in mid-2009. But if in terms of manpower the balance is clearly in favor of local governments, with respect to material and organizational capacities the situation is exactly the opposite. The salaries, weapons, training, and organization of local police corporations are far behind those of their federal counterparts. This is especially true of municipal corporations, which together comprise one-third of the country's police force. Not surprisingly, when criminals become particularly aggressive, local and federal authorities spend much of their time and energy blaming each other rather than jointly tackling the problem. Proposals to unify the command of the country's police forces have been on the agenda for almost a decade, with no success.

Finally, although elections are certainly more competitive than under the post-revolutionary regime, and countless legal and institutional safeguards have been laid down to prevent fraud, electoral irregularities—short of outright fraud—remain numerous. Vote buying, illegal campaign funding, illegal government intervention in electoral races, and biased, even defamatory coverage by interested media are all very common. The latest step in a long chain of efforts to control practices like these was to put all elections under the supervision of a single specialized authority—the National Electoral Institute (INE, established in 2014). Yet, the thirteen gubernatorial races held in 2016 still were plagued by the usual electoral irregularities, showing that this centralization was scarcely effective. The importance of these practices is obvious enough: they not only rarify political competition and weaken the legitimacy of the elected authorities but also put democratic competition into question.

SOCIETY: GROUPS, RIGHTS, AND VALUES

The transition to competitive markets and competitive politics was accompanied by equally profound transformations in the social sphere. To begin with, civil society became more independent and plural. This is particularly evident, for example, in the case of the business sector. Dissatisfied with the populist official rhetoric of the 1970s, business organizations became more assertive, less willing to accept the dictates of the government, and more prone to make their complaints public. But important as this change is, it is not too surprising: after all, it concerns a sector that has always enjoyed a privileged position in the public sphere.

But even traditionally subordinated sectors have undergone similar changes. This is especially evident in the case of labor. The big labor organizations, notably the Confederation of Mexican Workers (CTM), were discredited by their uncritical support for the government's policies in the 1980s. Perhaps even more importantly, in the new, market-dominated economy their role became much less important than in the old protectionist model. All of this facilitated the development of independent unions, the most important of which created a new umbrella organization, the National Union of Workers (UNT). More revealingly, even traditional progovernment unions have become more assertive, able and willing to act on their own, defining their own policies and making their own alliances. A case in point is the Teachers' Union (SNTE), which in the early twenty-first century became a powerful political actor, bringing decisive support to even presidential candidates.

But the change goes much beyond the world of business and labor. The so-called "third sector" has acquired a vitality that has no parallel in Mexican history. From the early 1990s, there has been a veritable explosion of nongovernmental organizations, devoted to a variety of themes. As of 2014, the federal government had registered more than twenty-seven thousand civil society organizations, an unprecedented number.[12]

Another major area of change was the revitalization of the media. Key traditional forms of government control and censorship—like the official monopoly on printing paper or the stiff penalties for defamation—were dismantled or at least relaxed. Periodicals multiplied, some of them fiercely independent, like *Proceso* (founded in 1976), *Reforma* (1993), and *La Jornada* (1984). Facing greater competition, even traditionally complacent media became more open to public debate. Other types of media grew as well. The number of radio stations increased from 554 in 1973 to 1,750 in 2015.[13] Even the TV industry—though only two networks still controlled virtually the entire private-sector market—experienced some opening, with more news programs of better quality.

With less government control, newer media, and more competition, freedom of the press and the quality of public debate improved in various senses. Thus, to cite but one indicator, the country's "freedom of the press" score, as estimated by an influential watchdog organization, systematically improved at the close of the century, moving from 60 in 1993 to 36 in 2003 on a scale ranging from 0, "freest," to 100, "least free."[14]

Another important social change is the proliferation of what may be called transnational Mexicans. To be sure, Mexicans from the upper social sectors have always moved at ease in the transnational sphere. But what is most significant is that in the last three decades, this transnationalism has extended to the very lowest sectors, especially through undocumented migration. Overwhelmed by the massive importation of agricultural products and finding few job opportunities in the country, peasants and other poor Mexicans headed for the United States in increasing numbers in the 1990s and early 2000s. On average, as many as 485,000 Mexicans entered the United States without documentation every year from 2000 to 2004.[15]

It is true that after reaching its peak in 2007, the number of undocumented Mexicans living in the United States began to fall rapidly, as a consequence of both the economic crisis of 2008 and the increase in the number of deportations.[16] Still, the social and economic effect of this large movement of people is enormous. In 2015, family remittances from abroad—the immense majority of them coming from the United States—amounted to US$24.8 billion, a figure equal to almost two-thirds of the value of Mexico's agricultural production.[17] Most of these remittances go directly to millions of poor Mexican households, which makes them one of the most perfectly targeted forms of income support. But beyond its narrowly economic relevance, this migration has created a truly transnational community from below—one that includes not only the migrants themselves but also the relatives that they support.

This diversification of Mexican society has been accompanied by a change in culture and values. As shown by numerous sources, there is greater tolerance for sexual diversity, less acceptance of violence against women and children, a strong rejection of violence in teaching, and even a passionate defense of animal rights. To cite a crucial example, according to the World Values Survey (WVS) in 1981–1984, 64 percent of Mexicans affirmed that homosexuality is "never justified"; by 2010–2014, that figure had dropped to 39 percent.

In sum, in a few decades Mexico's civil society became more diverse, independent, participatory, and cosmopolitan. Yet, for all its changes, Mexico remains a very unequal country. This persistent inequality explains why, despite decades of economic growth, poverty remains massive. According to official calculations, fifty-three out of every one hundred Mexicans were poor in 2014, as many as in 1992.[18] This suggests that massive poverty is not a transitory problem; on the contrary, it is a basic aspect of Mexico's social structure.

Moreover, virtually all relevant sources agree that, after 1980, this structure became more rigid. According to the latest survey on social mobility, almost half of the people born within the lowest 20 percent of the income bracket remain there for the rest of their life; of those who did move, most did not get beyond the second lowest quintile. Observed from the opposite extreme, the social structure seems even more rigid: 52 percent of people born into the highest quintile remained there; most of those who did descend did not go below the second highest quintile. In other words, most of those born within the lowest social strata were condemned to remain at the bottom, and most of those born within the highest strata were also "condemned" to remain at the top.[19]

Mexico can be proud of its diverse and vibrant civil society. Yet, this civility stands on a persistently rigid and exclusionary social structure. And it is not alone there: on the same social structure stands a diametrically different kind of society, one that is as violent as the other is tolerant.

VIOLENCE: CRIMINAL AND POLITICAL

The most fearful manifestation of this uncivil society is the high number of so-called executions—homicides attributed to organized criminals, most of which were committed with blatant brutality. According to the most reliable data, from 2001 to 2010 there were between 34,542 and 43,642 executions.[20] This means that, on average, between nine and twelve people were executed every day during this decade. Moreover, executions grew consistently during the period: three Mexicans were executed every day in 2001, compared to as many as forty-two in 2010.

Data on criminal violence became less systematic in subsequent years. Even so, it is quite certain that, after reaching a peak in 2011, the number of executions decreased in 2012. But this decrease was short-lived. According to one estimate, after falling to 7,500 in 2014, the number of executions jumped to 8,100 in 2015.[21] Available information clearly suggests that it continued to grow in 2016.

Although information about this topic is notoriously unreliable, it is clear that most of these executions were perpetrated by drug trafficking organizations as they competed with each other for control of the illegal drug market. This is clear from the geography of drug-related executions, which largely coincides with that of the illegal drug market. Most of these homicides were committed in the state of Tamaulipas and, particularly, Nuevo Laredo, which according to the US National Drug Intelligence Center is "the most lucrative smuggling corridor along the US–Mexico border";[22] the state of Michoacán, particularly the area close to Lázaro Cárdenas, the most important point of entry of pseudoephedrine and other synthetic-drug precursors; Ciudad Juárez, another major transit point between Mexico and the United States; the so-called Golden Triangle, the mountainous zone straddling the states of Sinaloa, Durango, and Chihuahua, which is the main drug cultivation area of the country; Tijuana, another major connecting point between Mexico and the United States; and the state of Guerrero, home to the country's second most important drug cultivation area.

When this violence began to expand, the Mexican government simply tried to ignore it. Yet, when powerful actors (including several business organizations, many social organizations, and even the US Department of State) insisted that the authorities should intervene, the government finally responded by launching Operation Safe Mexico, sending thousands of soldiers, marines, and federal police agents, supported by state and municipal forces, to the most troubled areas in June 2005. In December 2006, after President Felipe Calderón came to office, campaigns of this sort—known as joint operations—multiplied.

These campaigns have had limited impact on the armed capacities of criminal organizations and, in fact, have often exacerbated the violence that they ostensibly sought to combat. Yet, they may have been successful in one basic sense: by preventing drug trafficking organizations from seizing and holding crucial parts of the Mexican territory, they helped maintain drug violence as a criminal problem, instead of becoming a political threat to the state's territorial sovereignty.

Yet, things changed after the inauguration of Enrique Peña Nieto in 2012. Arguing that his predecessor had exacerbated drug violence by paying too much attention to it, Peña Nieto seemed determined to downplay the matter. Although the new administration initiated its own joint operations and maintained many of those that were on course, it did so with obvious reluctance.

Sensing this opportunity, some drug trafficking organizations scaled up their predatory attacks on uninvolved civilians. In reaction, many of the latter decided to create their own "self-defense" armed groups—some of them with the support of other drug trafficking organizations. The problem was especially acute in the state of Michoacán, which in 2013 experienced a veritable civil war between drug criminals and armed civilians. The conflict subsided only when the federal government joined forces with the self-defense groups (and with their not-so-occult criminal allies), eventually killing or capturing the leaders of the predatory Knight Templars "cartel."

In its search for substitutes for the massive use of force that it criticized in its predecessor, the Peña Nieto administration implemented a policy that was even more controversial: the perpetration of spectacular massacres. At least three major cases have been documented: Tlatlaya (June 2014), Apatzingán (January 2015), and Tanhuato (May 2015). These massacres—which should not be confused with the "normal" abuses that the government has always committed in its fight against undisciplined drug traffickers—have an obvious aim: to terrify criminals and persuade the public that the government is willing to combat them with the full force of the state.

Thus, depending on the side from which one observes it, Mexico's society seems either more plural, tolerant, and institutionalized or more violent and disorderly. But this uncivil, murderous faction is not the only one that acts against the laws and institutions. There is also a rebel society, a constellation of insurgent groups and radical social movements that by different means try to subvert the prevailing political order.

The most well-known member of this constellation is the National Zapatista Liberation Army (EZLN), which launched a fairly large attack in the state of Chiapas in early 1994 and which some enthusiast observers hailed as the first "postmodern" or "post-communist" insurgency. In subsequent years, other insurgent groups emerged, not as large and ideologically sophisticated as the EZLN, but some apparently better armed and trained. Among these were the People's Revolutionary Army (EPR), the Insurgent People's Revolutionary Army (ERPI), the Democratic Revolutionary Tendency-Army of the People (TDR-EP), and the People's Revolutionary Armed Forces (FARP). Despite their many differences, all these groups claim to be against social injustice and seek a wholesale social transformation.

Although initial clashes between the government and these rebels were quite bloody, in the following years they became scarcer and less murderous. In part, this pacification was due to the government's actions, which by foul and fair means, managed to contain the threat. Even so, all the insurgent groups remain active, often in alliance with radical social organizations, especially in central and southern Mexico.

FOREIGN RELATIONS

Since the early twentieth century, Mexico's foreign relations have revolved around a single country—the United States This dependence became even stronger in the 1990s following the establishment of NAFTA. The United States is Mexico's largest partner: the main source of its imports, the main destination of its exports, the main origin of its foreign investment, the main destination of its migrants, and the main supporter of its security policies.

This growing economic relationship has also been accompanied by a political shift. Mexico's political leadership is less reluctant to accept this relationship. Unlike their post-revolutionary predecessors, presidents Salinas, Zedillo, Fox, and Calderón willingly proclaimed their desire to earn the goodwill of the US government. Even the armed forces, traditionally wary of their northern counterparts, have openly welcomed their support. This has been especially so after the launching of the Merida Initiative, in 2007, which sought to strengthen cooperation between the United States, Mexico, and the Central American countries against drug traffickers and other organized criminals.

Somewhat surprisingly, the return of the PRI in 2012 threatened to stop this trend. The Peña Nieto administration signaled its desire to limit US intervention in Mexico's law-enforcement institutions. One practical measure was to establish a so-called single window, an office within the Interior Ministry that would handle all contacts between US and Mexican law enforcement and security agencies. Peña Nieto also sought to diversify the country's economic relations. The most visible move in this direction was the decision to put a big infrastructure project—the Mexico City-Querétaro railroad—in the hands of a group of firms headed by a Chinese corporation. This project was soon abandoned when allegations of illegal dealings between the Peña Nieto government and one of the Mexican partners surfaced.

Peña Nieto also tried to mend Mexico's relations with the left-leaning governments of Latin America, especially those of Cuba and Venezuela. Although these efforts have eliminated much of the animosity created by the Fox and Calderón administrations, they have achieved nothing comparable to the active and independent role that Mexico played in Latin American affairs in the late 1970s and early 1980s.

Other tensions have emerged from the US side of the relationship. Like many other foreign observers, the US State Department has been increasingly critical of Mexico's human rights situation. As a consequence of these criticisms, the US State Department withheld part of the Merida Initiative funding to Mexico in 2015. Even more serious were the complaints of the new US president Donald Trump against NAFTA and Mexican immigration during his campaign, often accompanied by racist comments against Mexicans in general. As many surveys and studies have noted, this hostility comes not only from Trump: it reflects the real grievances of large sections of the US electorate, harmed by what they feel is unfair competition from Mexican workers, both in Mexico and the United States.

Mexico's foreign relations will continue to pivot around the United States in the future. This, however, should not lead one to ignore the tensions that exist on such important issues as migration, security, and trade. Sooner or later, these tensions will require serious adjustments in the bilateral relationship—adjustments that will inevitably affect Mexico's relations with all other countries.

CONCLUSION

A long, often traumatic, history has created a peculiar, often incongruent society—proud of its culture, with a modern economy, a vibrant civil society, and a plural and competitive political system, ready to act in the transnational sphere, yet ravaged by criminal violence, undermined by corruption, continuously threatened by political instability, and weakened by its blatant inequalities. The intense political and economic transformations of the past three decades reshaped many of these contradictions but did not eliminate them.

It would be tempting to ignore these disconnects, emphasizing some positive or negative facts and discarding the rest. But, as this chapter has endeavored to show, such an approach would be foolish, for both analytical and practical reasons. The truth about Mexico lies precisely in those incongruities. They are the main source of the country's problems, but also of its potential solutions.

For example, many observers, including top government leaders, have often noted with obvious satisfaction that most victims of illegal drug violence were themselves involved in the illegal drug trade. According to this view, the country should be glad that criminals are killing each other. But this way of seeing the situation is not only egotistic but also myopic. Even if it were true that some drug traffickers are incurably violent individuals, many participants in the competition for illegal drug profits are ambitious people who find no attractive option in the unequal and rigid legal social structure. This ambition is the energy, so to speak, that fuels drug violence. Rather than suppressing this social energy, or simply letting it exhaust itself, Mexico should try to channel it in education, science, sports, and many other fields where the competitive drives of ambitious people can be not only harmless but truly productive.

Similarly, because most Mexicans are poor, it is often assumed that the only way to promote national development is to lure foreign capital with cheap wages and to produce for foreign markets. The wave of protectionism that began gaining momentum in several powerful countries after the 2008 financial crisis is seen as a fatal threat to this development strategy. It seems as if Mexico could not exist, let alone develop, without NAFTA and similar free trade agreements. But although this protectionism poses great challenges, it also creates unique opportunities. Rather than blindly defending a development strategy that seems to require the continuous existence of large numbers of poor, Mexico should take any possible measure to transform them into skillful producers and potent consumers. This does not entail isolating the country from the international economy; on the contrary, it would make Mexico a more energetic participant in global markets.

Measures like these may seem intimidating, because they entail great efforts and require much imagination. But they are not beyond the reach of a country with such a rich past and such a vibrant society.

SUGGESTIONS FOR FURTHER READING

Camp, Roderic A. *The Oxford Handbook of Mexican Politics*. Oxford: Oxford University Press, 2012.

———. *Politics in Mexico: Democratic Consolidation or Decline?* 6th ed. Oxford: Oxford University Press, 2013.

Campbell, Howard. *Drug War Zone: Frontline Dispatches from the Streets of El Paso and Juárez*. Austin: University of Texas Press, 2009.

Gibler, John. *Mexico Unconquered: Chronicles of Power and Revolt*. San Francisco: City Lights, 2009.

Joseph, G. M., and Timothy J. Henderson. *The Mexico Reader: History, Culture, Politics*. Durham, NC: Duke University Press, 2002.

Keller, Renata. *Mexico's Cold War: Cuba, the United States, and the Legacy of the Mexican Revolution*. New York: Cambridge University Press, 2015.

MacLeod, Dag. *Downsizing the State: Privatization and the Limits of Neoliberal Reform in Mexico*. University Park: Pennsylvania State University Press, 2004.

Preston, Julia, and Sam Dillon. *Opening Mexico: The Making of a Democracy*. New York: Farrar, Straus and Giroux, 2004.

NOTES

1. Sherburne F. Cook and Woodrow Borah, *Essays in Population History: Mexico and California*, Volume Three. (Berkeley: University of California Press, 1979), 1.

2. María Eugenia Romero Sotelo and Luis Jáuregui, "México 1821–1867. Población y crecimiento económico," *Iberoamericana* 3, no. 12 (2003), 32.

3. John H. Coatsworth, "Indispensable Railroads in a Backward Economy: The Case of Mexico," *The Journal of Economic History* 39, no. 4 (December 1979), 941.

4. John Womack Jr., "The Mexican Economy during the Revolution, 1910–1920: Historiography and Analysis," *Marxist Perspectives* 1, no. 4 (Winter 1978).

344 JOSÉ LUIS VELASCO

5. Florencio Salazar Adame, "La cuestión agraria en la transición" (Mexico: Secretaría de la Reforma Agraria), 8, www.ordenjuridico.gob.mx/Congreso/CongresoInt/ponencias/FSA.pdf.

6. Author's calculations, based on Abraham Aparicio Cabrera, "Series estadísticas de la economía mexicana en el siglo XX," *Economía Informa,* no. 369 (July-August, 2011), tables 4 and 5.

7. Abraham Aparicio Cabrera, table 5.

8. Nora Lustig and Miguel Székely, México: Evolución económica, pobreza y desigualdad (Washington: The World Bank, 1997), table 1.

9. The best sources on this event are the two reports by the Interdisciplinary Group of Independent Experts (GIEI): *Informe Ayotzinapa: Investigación y primeras conclusiones de las desapariciones y homicidios de los normalistas de Ayotzinapa* and *Informe Ayotzinapa II: Avances y nuevas conclusiones sobre la investigación, búsqueda y atención a las víctimas* (http://prensagieiayotzi .wixsite.com/giei-ayotzinapa/informe-).

10. Transparencia Mexicana, "Indice nacional de corrupción y buen gobierno: informe ejecutivo 2010," www.tm.org.mx/wp-content/uploads/2011/05/INFORME_EJECUTIVO _INCBG2010.pdf.

11. Juan E. Méndez, Report of the Special Rapporteur on torture and other cruel, inhuman or degrading treatment or punishment. Addendum. Mission to Mexico. United Nations, Human Rights Council. Twenty-eighth session. 2014.

12. Indesol, "¿Sabes cuántas OSC existen en México?" *Conecta,* no. 18 (2014) (www.gob.mx /cms/uploads/attachment/file/116272/Conecta_Indesol_Mural_No._18.pdf).

13. Manuel Alejandro Guerrero, "Los medios de comunicación y el régimen político," in *Instituciones y procesos políticos*, eds. S. Loaeza and J. F. Prud'homme (Mexico City: Colegio de México, 2010), 260.

14. Freedom House, Freedom of the Press: Detailed Data and Subscores (1980–2015) (https://freedomhouse.org/sites/default/files/FOTP2015%20Detailed%20Data%20and%20 Subscores%201980-2015.xlsx).

15. Jeffrey Passel, Unauthorized Migrants: Numbers and Characteristics. Background Briefing Prepared for Task Force on Immigration and America's Future (Washington, DC: Pew Hispanic Center, 2010), 10.

16. Ana González-Barrera, More Mexicans Leaving than Coming to the U.S. (Washington, DC: 2015), figure 5.

17. Segob et al., *Anuario de migracion y remesas 2016* (Mexico: BBVA-Bancomer, Conapo, 2016), 130.

18. Coneval, Evolución de las dimensiones de la pobreza 1990–2014 (www.coneval.org.mx /Medicion/EDP/Paginas/Evolucion-de-las-dimensiones-de-la-pobreza-1990-2014-.aspx).

19. Roberto Vélez Grajales et al, *Informe de movilidad social en México 2013* (Mexico: CEEY, 2013), 5.

20. These data come from three sources: CNDH, Informe especial sobre el ejercicio efectivo del derecho fundamental a la Seguridad pública en nuestro país (Mexico City: CNDH, 2008); Mexican Presidency, Base de datos de homicidios presuntamente relacionados con la delincuencia organizada, 2011 (http://presidencia.gob.mx/voceria_seguridad/); and the *Reforma* newspaper (Jan. 2, 2006; Jan. 8, 2007; Jan. 7, 2008; Jan. 1, 2009; Jan. 1, 2010; and Jan. 1, 2011).

21. Kimberly Heinle, Octavio Rodríguez Ferreira and David A. Shirk, Drug Violence in Mexico: Data and Analysis Through 2015 (San Diego: Justice in Mexico, 2016), 6 and 9.

22. National Drug Intelligence Center, South Texas High Intensity Drug Trafficking Area Drug Market Analysis, 2008 (www.justice.gov/archive/ndic/pubs27/27513/border.htm).

19

CUBA: REVOLUTION IN
THE BALANCE?

Juan M. del Aguila, Frank O. Mora, and Brian Fonseca

INTRODUCTION

As the only nation in the Western Hemisphere that adopted revolutionary Communism for its model of political development, Cuba stands separate from other Latin American nations. The revolution of 1959 and its subsequent radicalization attracted the interest of students of politics as well as that of policy makers, journalists, intellectuals, and ordinary people, many of whom have been inspired by the Cuban example. In addition, the central role played by Fidel Castro from the beginning of the revolution is key to understanding developments in Cuba in the years since he and his followers came to power. Under his leadership, Cuba became an influential actor in regional politics engaged in an unusual degree of revolutionary activism. Fidel personified his country to observers the world over, but his own transformation from an impetuous young revolutionary to an aging dictator parallels the course of the revolution itself, despite efforts by his brother and successor, President Raúl Castro, to "adjust" or "update" certain parts of the system.

The politics of revolutionary development have moved Cuba through periods of radical transformation in the economy and the social system, and through phases when pragmatism and moderation shaped domestic priorities and affected social attitudes. In effect, the revolution and its consequences can be understood as an ongoing experiment in the process of achieving mature nationhood, but as with any experiment, Cuba's has been characterized by fits and starts, abrupt policy reversals, intense criticism of the real nature of socialism and revolution, and evident exhaustion. The defining characteristic of the Cuban Revolution in the two decades since the end of the Cold War and the collapse of the Communist bloc and the Soviet Union—a significant source of Cuba's economic sustainability—has been, as Eusebio Mujal-León notes, "chronic economic difficulty and remarkable political durability."[1] What explains this durability is a basic theme of this chapter.

HISTORY, POLITICAL CULTURE, AND EARLY DEVELOPMENT

Cuba, the largest of the Greater Antilles, is located at the entrance of the Gulf of Mexico, some 112 nautical miles (208 kilometers) from the United States. Its 44,218 square miles (114,525 square kilometers) stretch over a varied topography that includes mountain ranges, rolling hills, plains, and hundreds of rivers and streams. The principal mountain ranges lie in the eastern, central, and western provinces, and the highest mountain, Pico Turquino, rises to some 6,500 feet (1,981 meters) in the Sierra Maestra range.

Unlike many other developing countries, Cuba has not experienced a dramatic rise in population, and its demographic growth rates remain stable. Population growth averages around 1 percent, which alleviates the burden on employment and services that plagues many developing countries. Of the country's 11.5 million inhabitants in 2015, 73 percent reside in urban areas and the rest live in small towns and in the less densely populated rural areas.

Caucasians, mulattoes, and blacks are practically the only ethnic groups in the country. Whites account for 60 percent of the population, mulattoes and mestizos are nearly 25 percent, and blacks make up approximately 15 percent. Whites were the dominant ethnic group during the twentieth century, and many are descendants of the creole elite of colonial Cuba. No Indian subcultures exist because for all practical purposes the mostly primitive Indian communities that inhabited the island in precolonial times disappeared early in the colonial period, dying of disease or in conflicts with the colonizers.

Christopher Columbus initially encountered Cuba in 1492, but because the island lacked substantial mineral wealth and an advanced indigenous civilization, it remained sparsely populated well into the eighteenth century. Spanish settlers gradually subdued the roughly fifty thousand native Indians at the time of the discovery under the *encomienda* system. Catholic missions were established and charged with propagating and maintaining the faith, so friars and priests played important roles in the early life of the colony. The Catholic Church subsequently grew in membership, wealth, and influence, and its notions of order, faith, spirituality, and salvation pervaded Cuba's cultural foundation.

Black slaves were brought to Cuba by the thousands, from the 1700s to the middle of the nineteenth century, replacing Indians as laborers on sugarcane plantations, as servants in the larger towns and cities, and as manual laborers in service occupations. A census taken in 1791 showed that out of a total population of 273,000, 56 percent were white and that slaves made up the largest proportion of the black population.

Cuba's economy originally revolved around tobacco farming and subsequently coffee cultivation, but it gradually became a plantation economy geared toward the cultivation, production, and export of sugar. The island's geographical location offers the right temperatures as well as the necessary rainfall for sugar production, and the terrain of the lowlands is suitable for harvesting cane. Indeed, economists and historians maintain that the island's comparative advantage in sugar production was soon realized and that earnings from sugar exports financed the imports of foodstuffs, textiles, machinery, and other capital goods.

The combination of sugar, slavery, and the plantation economy shaped the colonial social structure and laid the foundation for an economy geared to foreign commerce, but it did not produce a society of small landowners and rural proprietors. Differences among *peninsulares, criollos,* slaves, and *libertos* (freed slaves) were evidence of a hierarchical system unmindful of any notion of social equality. As depicted by popular novels, books, and documents of the time, colonial Cuba remained unaffected by changes taking place elsewhere and therefore stayed under the tight control of Spain. On the other hand, the benefits of free trade were strongly felt during the English occupation of Havana in 1762–1763, as new markets were found and the economy was further integrated into regional and international commercial networks. Spain sought to reestablish political control over its colonial domains, including Cuba, in the early nineteenth century, but the impact of liberal ideas, in addition to the introduction of capital and new technology, stimulated new thinking.

STRUGGLES FOR INDEPENDENCE, 1868–1901

The emergence of new political currents in the 1860s stemmed from the need to challenge Spanish domination and to improve Cuba's economic position. A nationalistic and clearly separatist movement advocated confrontation and war against Spain if those were the only means of achieving independence. More moderate elements, represented by the Reformist Party, founded in 1862, advocated representation for Cuba in the Spanish Cortes (the Spanish legislature), administrative reforms, and liberal trade policies. The issue of slavery often divided the creoles, as did class and economic differences between the eastern and western planters. The latter feared a social revolution and tended to be more conservative. Still, Spain's refusal to grant meaningful concessions to the Cubans and its failure to satisfy legitimate political demands led to rebellion in 1868 followed by a decade of bloody and destructive warfare.

Nearly two hundred fifty thousand people on both sides lost their lives in the struggle, and Cuba's infrastructure was devastated. The war cost Spain approximately US$300 million and was both a cause and a consequence of political quarrels among its own elites. Yet Spain and the rebels signed an armistice in 1878 that led to a tenuous peace and a period of self-criticism and questioning on the part of those Cubans who still advocated independence.

A growing dependence on the US market for trade, investment, technology, and industrial inputs characterized US–Cuban relations in the 1880s and 1890s, even while Spain maintained political control. In 1896, US investments in Cuba were estimated at US$50 million, concentrated in mining and sugar holdings. Trade between the two countries was valued at US$27 million in 1897. The United States exported to Cuba manufactured and industrial goods and imported sugar, molasses, tobacco, and a few nonmanufactured products.

The growing penetration of a weak economy dominated by sugar and its derivative production by a growing capitalist, industrial power meant that the colonial regime was subjected to both internal and external pressures. Once again pro-independence forces gathered to challenge Spanish authority and assert claims for independence and sovereignty, and this time they did so with a new and more compelling sense of unity and national purpose. New leaders, principally José Martí, had forged a more mature vision of political emancipation and nationalism, and the issue of slavery had been laid to rest since its abolition in the 1880s. In short, ideologically and organizationally, the separatists were in a stronger position than in the 1860s, whereas Spain vacillated between granting meaningful reforms and reimposing absolutist government. As the founder of the Cuban Revolutionary Party (*Partido Revolucionario Cubano*—PRC) in exile and as the intellectual force and principal civilian organizer of the war effort, José Martí represented a younger generation of Cubans committed to the total liberation of the country.

The war started in 1885 and raged back and forth for three years, with the rebels fighting a guerrilla struggle and Spain following more of a scorched-earth strategy. A military stalemate between rebel and Spanish forces along with sensationalist accounts of the fighting published in the United States led to US military intervention in 1898. The Cuban question had become an important issue in US domestic politics, and Spain as well as the rebels had attempted to influence US public opinion. Spain rejected diplomatic entreaties and offers of mediation from European powers and obstinately refused to accept either military or political defeat. In April 1898, the US Congress passed a resolution granting President McKinley's request for authority to end hostilities in Cuba, but it also disavowed any interest in exercising sovereignty, jurisdiction, or control over Cuba once Spain had been driven out.

The US occupation of Cuba lasted until 1902, and many students of Cuban politics believe that it created a legacy of resentment and frustration because, in part, US intervention prevented the Cubans from achieving a complete victory over Spain. US military authorities partly rebuilt the nation's infrastructure and brought about significant improvements in public health, education, public administration, and finance, but Cuban nationalists and many intellectuals felt a sense of political impotence and frustration. Subsequently, the inclusion of the Platt Amendment in the Cuban constitution meant that Cuba became a US protectorate rather than a sovereign nation because the amendment granted territorial concessions to the United States, placed financial restrictions on the Cuban government, and allowed the United States to intervene in Cuba's internal affairs.

Cuba's foreign economic relations were subsequently shaped by the Reciprocity Treaty (1903), which granted preferential treatment to Cuban sugar in the US market and reduced tariffs on US exports to Cuba. US investments in Cuba's sugar industry, cattle industry, public services, utilities, and other properties had reached US$200 million by 1909, nearly 50 percent of all foreign investment in Cuba. The Platt Amendment and the Reciprocity Treaty facilitated a growing US influence in Cuba and were often perceived as neocolonialist measures aimed at protecting US interests in the island. The US presence created a significant political cleavage, separating those people who felt it to be beneficial and necessary for Cuba's early development from nationalists who saw it as a direct infringement of genuine self-determination. Ramón Ruiz argued that the Platt Amendment limited Cuba's first experience in self-government and "offered the Cubans a facile way out of domestic difficulties. Reliance on the United States eventually engendered among Cubans a loss of faith in their Republic and in their own nationality."[2]

THE POLITICAL DEVELOPMENT OF PREREVOLUTIONARY CUBA

Political competition during the early republican period existed predominantly between the Liberal and Conservative Parties. These parties—and others—were essentially controlled by the political *caudillos* José Miguel Gómez and Mario García Menocal, respectively, and did not articulate clear political philosophies or programs. The political system was based on client arrangements and patronage networks. Electoral fraud and administrative corruption were common. Public office was held in disrepute, politics was used as a means of self-enrichment, and the democratic ideals that had motivated Martí and other revolutionary leaders remained little more than abstractions.

Still, respected intellectuals such as Fernando Ortiz and Enrique José Varona formed part of an emerging democratic intelligentsia that rejected politics as a means to private gain and advocated civic-mindedness, cultural emancipation, and, above all, honest and democratic government. Reformist groups encouraged debate, much of it focused on the need to cleanse political culture and on appeals to the anti-imperialist principles of students, intellectuals, and labor leaders.

Gerardo Machado was elected as a popular president in 1924, but he became a virtual dictator following his contrived reelection in 1928 and his violation of constitutional norms. From that point forward, politics took on a violent character. Government and opposition alike engaged in terrorism, shootings, and political assassinations, indicating that institutions were unable to resolve political conflicts and that force was seen as a legitimate arbiter of political disputes.

The Great Depression had a devastating effect on the economy. Plummeting sugar prices affected the livelihood of hundreds of thousands of families, and unemployment, social misery, and rural banditry reflected a deeper structural crisis. The government sought to alleviate the problems by acquiring new loans from US bankers, but the country's creditworthiness was shaky, and it had previously accumulated substantial debts. The economic picture deteriorated rapidly, helping stimulate and organize opposition to Machado.

Student protesters challenged the police in the streets, but resistance to Machado also involved professionals, middle-class elements, and labor leaders. One of the leading anti-Machado organizations was the University Students Directorate, through which a new generation of activists and revolutionaries advocated a complete and definitive change of regime. A diverse number of other anti-Machado groups with differentiated and often competing agendas emerged to confront the regime, often using violent means; they included the Popular Socialist Party (PSP, Communist Party) and the ABC, a secret organization made up of middle-sector individuals. In short, the opposition was unified in its commitment to driving Machado from power and ending the dictatorship, but it was also tactically and ideologically divided.

The army proved to be a critical contender because its support was essential for either keeping Machado in power or shifting the balance to his adversaries. The army was structured on parochial loyalties rather than merit, and its military competence was questionable. It remained the pillar of order and stability, but it also felt the violent political fragmentation that ultimately ousted Machado. Some lower-rank members, many of whom came from humble backgrounds, viewed the army as a vehicle for self-improvement and social mobility, and they demanded higher pay and an end to the politicization of promotions. Such internal pressure, at a time when a crisis of political authority affected the government's freedom of action and paralyzed decision making, opened the way for an internal revolt led by then Sergeant Fulgencio E. Batista y Zaldívar. Under his leadership, the army sought to contain revolutionary outbursts and directly influence the selection of presidents. This would play a central role during the following decades.

Finally, as had been the case since 1898, the United States played the role of ultimate power broker. In 1933 the new Roosevelt administration, through Sumner Welles as its special ambassador, shaped a resolution to Cuba's political crisis that preserved US interests and restored stability. Through Welles's efforts a weak government under Carlos Manuel de Céspedes succeeded Machado, but that regime was quickly overthrown. A five-member executive committee headed by Ramón Grau San Martín, a physician and university professor, took power briefly, but it too gave way to a more revolutionary government, still led by Grau. Jaime Suchlicki maintains that these events constitute a "turning point in Cuba's history," marking the "army's entrance as an organized force into the running of government and Batista's emergence as the self-appointed chief of the armed forces and the arbiter of Cuba's destiny for years to come."[3] The truncated revolution of 1933 had a profound impact on the succeeding generation's psychological makeup, its social agenda, and the political determination of its most able leaders. The incomplete business of 1933 left a sense of frustration among the protagonists of reform and revolution, but in time the goals were rechristened. The failure to democratize politics, achieve economic sovereignty, and cohesively assert a national will shaped the ethos of future reformers and revolutionaries, for whom "the lessons of 1933" laid the foundation for new departures.

SOCIAL DEMOCRACY AND AUTHORITARIANISM IN THE 1940S AND 1950S

After 1933, Cuba went through a period of realignment and moderate authoritarianism, characterized by the conservative domination of weak and undemocratic regimes supported by Batista and the army. Taking advantage of improved economic conditions and secure from military threats or revolutionary outbursts, the regimes governed by partially satisfying political demands and reintroducing client arrangements. On the other hand, electoral irregularities, corruption, episodic repression, and the subordination of civil authority to military pressures retarded the development of viable governing institutions, so the system remained personalistic.

Economic dependence on the United States meant that domestic capital played an increasingly important role, and Cuban interests gradually acquired a growing share of ownership in the sugar industry. Measures such as the Reciprocity Treaty and the

Jones-Costigan Act, in addition to the policies of the Export-Import Bank, stabilized Cuba's economy and gave confidence to domestic producers, who always looked to the US market as the preferred outlet for Cuban products. US-mandated quotas for sugar guaranteed that Cuba's principal export would enter the United States under a preferential tariff and led to the expansion of acreage and production. The United States supplied 54 percent of Cuba's imports in 1933, a figure that increased to nearly 65 percent at the end of the decade and to some 81 percent by 1950. What Cuba bought was purchased in the United States, and although having a dynamic market close by proved to be convenient, it also slowed Cuba's industrial development.

A major threshold in the process of political development was reached in 1940 following the enactment of a democratic and progressive constitution, itself the result of political compromises among the democratic left, conservatives, and Communists. This constitution established universal suffrage and freedom of political organization, recognized Western-style civil rights, and abolished the death penalty. Women, children, and workers received social protection, and racial and sexual discrimination was outlawed. Public education was mandated, and the needs of rural children in particular were identified. The state was charged with "orienting the national economy." The constitution reflected a complex bargain between the rising middle sectors and traditional interests, and by explicitly framing a tutelary role for the state in economic and social affairs, it incorporated then-current ideas and political philosophies.

The *Partido Auténtico* (Authentic Party) administrations of Ramón Grau San Martin (1944–1948) and his successor Carlos Prío (1948–1952) initiated reforms in agriculture, fiscal management, labor, and education, while they also maintained respect for civil liberties. Public subsidies, bureaucratic employment, and the creation of new state agencies led to gains among middle-class and professional groups, but agricultural development lagged, and the power of foreign interests was not directly confronted. Worst of all, political violence and urban-based gangsterism threatened the integrity of the democratic regimes, and neither Grau nor Prío was able to stem the violence. Corruption was spawned by a vast system of patronage, payoffs, and bribes, and Grau's minister of education turned his office into a powerful political machine and an illegal financial network. Student activists turned the University of Havana into a haven for gun-toting thugs and criminal factions and often paralyzed the institution through intimidation and brutality. An entire system of nepotism, favoritism, and gangsterism predominated. Meanwhile, the reformist zeal of the Grau era degraded further, weakening and delegitimating democratic political institutions. Modernization through reformism did not curb the power of vested interests or foreign capital, and central authority proved weak and incapable of eradicating violence and corruption.

Batista's bloodless but effective coup in March 1952 ended the constitutional regime and restored order superficially through political authoritarianism. Cuba's political development was cut short by the coup, and the system proved vulnerable to force. Proclaiming that worry about the lack of guarantees for life and property had led him to accept "the imperious mandate" to usurp power, Batista and his supporters found little resistance to their actions. During his time in office Batista was unable to legitimate his regime through elections, good relations with the United States, or negotiations with his opponents. Opposition to Batista included moderate, democratic elements sympathetic to the *Auténticos* but willing to entertain confrontational approaches.

Several revolutionary groups, including Fidel Castro's Twenty-Sixth of July Movement, participated in the struggle against the dictatorship. Among these, the Revolutionary Directorate (*Directorio Revolucionario*—DR) stood out because of its uncompromising ferocity and violent strategy aimed at assassinating Batista himself. Led by the charismatic student leader José Antonio Echeverría, the DR was not the vanguard of a social revolution but rather an organization committed to ending the dictatorship.

As one of the founders of the Twenty-Sixth of July Movement and its undisputed leader, Fidel played a central role in the insurrection against Batista's dictatorship. A group led by Fidel attacked the Moncada military garrison in the city of Santiago in 1953, but the attack failed and many of Fidel's followers were either killed or subsequently arrested and shot. Fidel himself was captured and tried for subversion, but as a trained lawyer with oratorical skills, he used the trial to issue an indictment of the government. Portraying his cause as just and inspired by patriotism and Martí's ideals, Fidel called for a return to constitutional government, agrarian reform, profit-sharing arrangements between owners and workers, and social improvements in rural Cuba. He was convicted and sentenced to fifteen years in prison, but he was subsequently released in 1954 under an amnesty program.

Fidel's political beliefs and true intentions before he came to power have been the focus of considerable debate. Some people argue that his commitment to armed struggle reflected the compelling facts that no compromise was possible with Batista and that rebellion itself is justified by lofty principles of Western political theory. Others maintain that Fidel harbored Marxist beliefs during his days at the university but that he kept the Communists away from his movement so that it could appeal to the Cuban middle class.

Fidel was neither a member of the Communist Party nor a doctrinal Marxist prior to coming to power. Rather, he was committed to a radical revolution whose final outcome could not have been foreseen but which placed him in the center of power. In addition, one of his top lieutenants, the Argentine revolutionary Ernesto "Che" Guevara, was a committed Marxist, as was Fidel's younger brother, Raúl. Indeed, the Twenty-Sixth of July Movement itself was divided between moderates who rejected Communism and radicals such as Guevara who believed that the solution to the world's problems lay behind the Iron Curtain. A radical minority led by Fidel saw themselves as the self-anointed vanguard of an epic political struggle against capitalism, the Cuban middle class, and US influence in Cuba, and this group launched a mass movement that created an unstoppable momentum.

The guerrilla phase of the insurrection ended successfully for the rebels in December 1958. Domestic isolation, rebel victories in eastern Cuba, and loss of support from Washington convinced Batista that his regime could survive only if the guerrillas were defeated. The army, however, was poorly led, partly because some of its top generals were corrupt and frightened; when a forty thousand–man army disintegrated in the face of several popular uprisings, this demonstrated a profound loss of morale and an alarming unwillingness to fight a few hundred guerrillas. Cornered and without options, Batista and many of his closest allies fled at dawn on January 1, 1959, paving the way for a total victory by the guerrilla forces.

THE CUBAN REVOLUTION

Neither the insurrection against Batista nor the social revolution that the new regime began to carry out stemmed from deep-seated popular dissatisfaction with the development pattern of Cuba's dependent capitalism. The evidence shows that Cuba had reached a moderate degree of modernization by the late 1950s. Indicators such as literacy rate (75 percent), proportion of the population living in urban areas (around 57 percent), life expectancy (approximately 60 years), and the size of the middle class (between 25 and 30 percent of the population) suggest that Cuba's level of development was comparable to that of other, more advanced Latin American nations.

Still, urban-rural contrasts were marked and the quality of life for the average *guajiro* (peasant) family was well below that of the average urbanite. Health services and educational opportunities were much better in Havana and other large cities than in the small provincial towns or isolated rural communities, and the best jobs and occupations were not available in rural Cuba. Seasonal unemployment also affected the rural areas disproportionately, and a rural proletariat dependent on the mills for employment saw its economic situation deteriorate once the sugar harvest ended. In effect, neither the model of Cuba as a chronically underdeveloped society nor that of an idyllic island characterized by social harmony, a sound economy, and a bustling population fits reality.

The success of the revolution can be better explained by political factors than by socioeconomic criteria. The failure of prerevolution governments to develop and nourish viable ruling institutions or to sustain a national ethos of civic-mindedness left those regimes vulnerable to force and strongman rule and to subversion from within. Legal and constitutional norms were not fully developed, and too many people viewed politics and public office as ways to obtain private, selfish gains. No idea of the public good had taken root, and the political culture revolved around traditional notions of order, loyalty, patrimony, and authority.

The new regime was originally divided among advocates of liberal democracy and a mixed economy and the more radical sectors around Fidel and Guevara who called for a social revolution. The radicals believed that the basic capitalist system needed to be abolished and the social system uprooted so that the power of vested economic interests, some of them foreign-based, could be reduced. Policy making was shaped by statist practices, antimarket doctrines, and the goal of eradicating economic evils associated with a dependent capitalist system, and the revolutionary elite was fully aware that to increase state power meant to increase its own. The agrarian reform of 1959 satisfied the long-standing claims of peasants and rural workers, and it also made sense politically. The urban reform of 1960, which socialized Cuban-owned businesses and privately owned real estate, adversely affected the private sector's strength. This collectivization produced a massive transfer of power and resources from the private economy into the public sector, which was precisely the intended effect.

Structural changes combined with populist, redistributive measures signaled willingness to incur domestic costs and foreign anger so as to accelerate the process of radicalizing the revolution. The revolutionary elite believed that to slow down was to court disaster; that momentum itself was proof that the masses supported the regime and enthusiastically joined the assault on capitalism and the private sector. Huge rallies commanded the attention of the populace, and during marathon speeches Fidel often mesmerized crowds. The regime realized that social mobilization could serve as a form of explicit consent. For this purpose, it established mass organizations such as the Committees for the Defense of the Revolution, the Federation of Cuban Women, and the Union of Communist Youth to reach the grassroots.

Once it became evident that a radical social revolution committed to socialism was in the making—led by individuals seeking total power—an opposition emerged that attempted to restrain or defeat the revolutionary elite. As often happens in revolutionary situations, a decisive struggle between radicals and moderates ensued, between people committed to some form of democracy and those who would settle for radical socialism and nothing else. Both sides knew that only one would prevail, that no compromise was possible, and that personal risks were involved. The opposition included Catholic organizations, disaffected cadres from Fidel's own ranks, respected democratic figures, and other anti-Communist elements.

Fidel's relationship with the PSP stemmed from his desire to limit the damage inflicted on his regime by the defection of non-Communist revolutionaries as well as from the need to enlist Soviet support. The party shrewdly provided organization when Fidel's own was being shaken up, and it offered a dialectical explanation for the society's troubles. Andrés Suárez believes that "the Communists played no role, neither in the political leadership of the country nor in the leadership of the students or of the trade unions," but that the party's discipline, support of "national unity," and foreign connections facilitated understandings with Fidel.[4] By the mid-1960s revolutionary changes restructuring class, property, political, and foreign policy relationships had eliminated a dependent capitalist order replete with US influence and moved the country toward radical socialism. The state took over the basic means of production as well as domestic and foreign commerce, industry, transportation, and utilities. Agriculture was reorganized into collective and state farms, but peasants could produce some goods on small, privately owned plots. The mass media were under state control, as was the national system of telecommunications. Party cadres supervised the information network, and Marxism-Leninism shaped the content of public discussion. Dissident intellectuals, nonconformists, and political opponents of the regime were arbitrarily imprisoned, scorned, or forced to leave the country.

The educational system was radically reorganized and centralized, and education was treated as a key to the process of political socialization. National literacy campaigns pushed literacy rates to the mid-90th percentile, but the quality of instruction left much to be desired. Much of Cuba's history was revised and rewritten, and patriotism and national virtues were highlighted. US influence over Cuba's destiny was made the root of many ills.

Considerable resources also were devoted to public health. Most basic medical services were provided free under a government-run health system that included preventive care, specialized services, and even advanced treatment for common or rare diseases. Over the years hundreds of clinics, hospitals, and specialized-care facilities were built and staffed by thousands of graduates in medicine, nursing, and health-related fields. As a result, life expectancy and infant mortality ranked among the best for developing countries.

Regime consolidation came about through sustained mobilization, direct exhortation, and a top-to-bottom direction of an ongoing revolutionary agenda rather than through elections. Rewards and sanctions were utilized to elicit compliance with revolutionary policies, but care was exercised not to alienate key sectors of the working class, peasantry, and urban proletariat. These sectors formed the class basis for the new regime once the middle class had been destroyed and the upper strata had either left the country or accepted a dramatic loss in privilege and status. Daily life became intensely political.

INSTITUTIONALIZATION AND CRISIS: ECONOMY, GOVERNMENT, AND SOCIETY, 1976–2006

Needing to regularize the political process and establish national ruling institutions through which stability could be preserved, the revolutionary elite succeeded in reorganizing the state and the Communist Party and created ruling councils at the local level. Fundamental changes in government became evident, especially in the manner in which central authority was exercised, in Fidel's role as chief decision maker, in the critical role of the Revolutionary Armed Forces (*Fuerzas Armadas Revolucionarias*—FAR) and the Cuban Communist Party (*Partido Comunista de Cuba*—PCC), and in the organization of social forces. A new socialist constitution was enacted in 1976 outlining the powers of a number of other key national and provincial institutions. This period of institutionalization, after more than a decade and a half of ad hocism and voluntarism, did not mean, however, that institutions gradually replaced the power and influence of Fidel and his lieutenants.

Economy

A new economic model, the System of Direction and Economic Planning (SPDE), framed policies in the late 1970s and mid-1980s, taking into consideration criteria such as efficiency, rationality, prices, and other economic mechanisms. This framework accepted the validity of material incentives and market processes. From this, the government introduced wage differentials, production norms, monetary controls, and taxes. Under the SPDE the emphasis would shift from building socialist consciousness through voluntarism and ideological appeals to the satisfaction of consumer demands through market mechanisms.

The collapse of orthodox Communism in the former Soviet Union and Eastern Europe prompted the Cuban leadership to declare a Special Period in Peacetime in the early 1990s. A strategy of economic survival took shape under conditions of severe austerity and hardship, largely because the US$5–US$6 billion subsidy from former Communist allies was no longer available. During the Special Period, consumption dropped dramatically, services and subsidies provided by the state were reduced or altogether eliminated, and the standard of living for the average individual or household fell precipitously.

Economic hardships multiplied under this strategy. Reliable studies show that Cuba's gross domestic product fell 35 to 50 percent between 1989 and the mid-1990s, plunging the economy into a depression. For the government, catastrophic losses meant downsizing the state bureaucracy, shutting down factories and industries, and reducing or eliminating subsidies to the transportation system, agriculture, construction, housing, and other sectors. Unable to secure oil supplies due to lack of hard currency, the government imposed draconian measures throughout the economy, causing total or partial blackouts on a regular basis. Energy supplies dwindled while unemployment rose as workers saw their jobs and standard of living adversely affected.

As Cuba entered the new century, growth rates were erratic. Cuba's unproductive and uncompetitive economy was simply unable to generate the material or financial resources needed to sustain its eleven million people. The annual growth rate for 1990–2000 was 1.2 percent—the worst in Latin America. A very modest rebound started with 3.0 percent growth in 2001, 1.5 percent in 2002, 2.6 percent in 2003, and roughly 2.0–2.5 percent in 2004. Declines in the price of nickel and the failure to improve agricultural or industrial production lay at the root of the crisis, which was further exacerbated by damaging hurricanes. One explanation for the economy's abysmal performance was the catastrophic collapse of the sugar industry. Total output in the 1990s stood at around four million metric tons per harvest, but by 2006 it had declined to about 1.4 million tons; this had a significant impact on generating adequate levels of hard currency. Nickel exports, revenue from services provided by Cuban professionals abroad, and tourist dollars have since replaced sugar exports as Cuba's main sources of hard currency during the first decade of the twenty-first century.

An important source of revenue that compensated for austerity and the decline of the sugar industry is tourism, which generates badly needed hard currency. Nearly two million tourists reportedly visited Cuba in 2006, with net earnings estimated to be between US$400–US$600 million. Cuban exiles are another source of hard currency; during the second term of US President George W. Bush's administration, they sent anywhere from US$400 million to US$800 million annually in remittances to their relatives—although estimates vary greatly and some analysts put the total figure at around US$1 billion.

A central question faced by the Cuban regime regarding the economy is the degree to which the satisfaction of consumer demands is essential for regime legitimacy and stability. The economic crisis of the 1990s brought into focus the lack of resources and the adoption of ill-advised policies that deepened austerity. Promises that socialism would produce abundance and prosperity were not fulfilled; in fact, enormous scarcity of basic goods and services emerged. Such a dramatic deterioration in economic conditions inevitably produces resentment and political disaffection, weakening the social contract between the regime and the masses.

Revolutionary Armed Forces (FAR)

The small guerrilla force that Fidel Castro commanded in the Sierras in the late 1950s, known as the Rebel Army, quickly became the most dominant institution of the revolution after its triumph in 1959.[5] Scholars of Cuban politics generally agree that the FAR embodied the values associated with the struggle against the dictatorship of Fulgencio Batista. Unlike the socialist bloc in Europe, not only did the FAR predate the Communist Party, but it became the true vanguard of the revolution. Some analysts have argued that the party was often subordinate to the FAR during the nearly fifty-seven years of the revolution.

The revolutionary regime and leadership emerged from a military struggle that continued even after its triumph, when the level of societal militarization was enhanced. The FAR became the preeminent institution of the early stages of the revolutionary process by virtue of the important responsibilities it assumed. For the regime, the FAR has the highest degree of legitimacy and reliability in terms of historical background, prestige, honesty, and loyalty, all critical to guaranteeing the survival of the revolution.

During the early period of consolidation, the FAR played a pivotal role in providing internal and external defense as well in socialist development, working in the administrative and economic sectors. Until the 1980s, the FAR was at the vanguard of proletarian internationalism, serving as a critical instrument of the regime's foreign policy objectives in the Third World. By the mid-1980s, however, the political and economic costs of supporting revolutionary causes proved simply too great for Cuba and the FAR. In the late 1980s, as a result of a growing ideological and economic crisis brought on by Mikhail Gorbachev's reforms in the Soviet Union and the waning of the Cold War, the Cuban leadership announced a defensive campaign that led to deinstitutionalization and a return to the military-mobilization approach of the 1960s that placed the FAR at the center of the process. As the edifice of Cuban Communism seemed to begin to crumble, the response was for the trusted military to assume a greater role in areas considered by the government to be vital to its survival: the economy and state security.

The critical role played by the military in Cuba's bureaucracy and economy, particularly in the early years, produced what Jorge Domínguez described as "civic-soldiers": "military men who govern large segments of both military and civilian life . . . bearers of revolutionary tradition and ideology . . . who have educated themselves to become professional in political, economic, managerial, engineering, and educational as well as military affairs."[6] Frank Mora described these figures of the post–Cold War era of the Special Period, when some special skills and revolutionary reliability were required, as "technocrat-soldiers": "a manager and administrator, in addition to being a soldier. He is implementing modern organizational and technical business practices and methods to enhance the efficiency and productivity of military and civilian industries, responding to market demands and relying on principles of financial engineering and complex telecommunications."[7] The FAR was not spared the shock of the Special Period. The military budget declined by half and expenditures as a percentage of GNP declined from 3.9 percent in 1987 to 1.6 percent in 1995. Troop strength and resources available for training, fuel, spare parts, and other equipment were cut dramatically as a result.

In the late 1980s, the military was once again given a decisive role in helping the regime weather a difficult period of crisis. The technical capabilities of a disciplined institution, under the unquestionable authority of the (then) longest-serving minister of the FAR (MINFAR) and first-generation revolutionary leader Raúl Castro, contributed to the regime's decision to rely on the FAR in implementing Raúl's proposal for economic modernization. The leadership had to rely on the FAR because all other institutions, the PCC above all, were failing to perform. The absence of a civil society and independent entrepreneurs placed the burden of the economy on the military.

The process of economic modernization was led by and largely implemented within the FAR. Through the *sistema de perfeccionamiento empresarial* (SPE, business improvement system), the regime sought to increase self-sufficiency within the FAR, increase the efficiency and productivity of military industries, and provide a model that could be adopted elsewhere in the economy.[8] By the early 2000s, as a result of this new mission, the FAR's technocrat-soldiers controlled the most dynamic, strategic sectors or industries of the Cuban economy, such as tourism, retailing, and transportation. By one estimate, MINFAR's holding company, Grupo de Administracion Empresarial (GAESA), managed by the late General Julio Casas Regueiro, is estimated to have invoiced US$1 billion in 2000.[9]

The Cuban Communist Party (PCC)

The PCC has undergone significant transformations since the early 1960s, when Castroites took effective control of its organization and eliminated political adversaries. Inaugurated in 1965, the party-building process went through a rocky period.[10] The party atrophied in the 1960s, and by 1969 membership was only fifty-five thousand. Lip service was paid to its leading role, but in fact the rambunctious politics of the period and the ad hoc manner in which policies were framed forced the party to the sidelines. The "microfaction affair" in 1968, in which orthodox former PSP cadres led by Aníbal Escalante attempted to sow division in the ranks and provoke Fidel's downfall, led to a bitter internal struggle. Purges followed and the guilty party members were sent to jail.

The PCC was never really the vanguard of the revolution, despite its legal standing and rhetorical pronouncements by Fidel and others in the ruling class about the party's role. The top Cuban leadership held high party positions, such as in the Political Bureau (Politburo), the highest body of the PCC, which directs the general orientation of the government and enacts policies, but their influence and power came from their relationship and loyalty to Fidel (and more recently Raúl) and not as a result of their standing in the party. Within this *partido fidelista*, "the PCC was responsible for administering the party-state bureaucracy and coordinating mass organizations that organized, directed and channeled participation in Cuban society"—often acting as a transmission belt for mobilizing and socializing the public.[11] Since the First Party Congress (1975), when the PCC was "institutionalized," there have been six congresses: 1980, 1986, 1991, 1997, 2011, and 2016.

In the mid-1980s, the PCC began to decline as a result of two key events: Fidel's rectification campaign, which dismantled SPDE and centralized economic decision making, and the end of the Cold War and collapse of the Communist bloc. Substantive questions emerged in the 1980s regarding the ideological rigor of the cadres, their discipline, and their willingness to lead through example and sacrifice. Instances of corruption in the party were common in the late 1980s. It suffered from scandals, poor leadership, careless management, lack of discipline, and other deficiencies. Many (perhaps thousands of) party leaders, members, and militants were purged in the late 1980s and early 1990s when the quality of their work was found wanting and abuses of authority and cases of personal corruption were discovered.

Some of the negative tendencies in the party's performance stemmed from its failure to monitor the illegal activities of high officials—many of whom were party members—in the Ministry of the Interior, the armed forces, and elsewhere. In addition, party members were embroiled in the arrest, trial, and execution of division general Arnaldo Ochoa and three other officers in 1989. General Ochoa, a decorated veteran of the Angolan war and a "Hero of the Revolution," was found guilty of corruption and involvement in drug trafficking. Several officers received long sentences, while others, such as the powerful minister of the interior, General José Abrantes, were subsequently removed from their positions.

After much public debate (and internal wrangling), a series of limited economic reforms were approved during the Fourth Party Congress in order to make the party more responsive to popular concerns. It was clear to Fidel and his ruling cohort that Cuba had to tread very carefully in instituting deep economic reforms for fear that their "contaminating" social and political impact (i.e., the creation of dangerous islands of autonomy) could further weaken or even derail the regime, as it did in the Communist bloc. The strategy seemed to be just enough economic reform to weather the crisis but not so much as to threaten or question the political legitimacy of the revolutionary project. The Fifth Party Congress reaffirmed the limited economic reform strategy and its strong opposition to any political liberalization, as illustrated by its tough reaction against dissent inside and outside the regime. As the Cuban leadership could have predicted, economic reforms instituted in the early 1990s did weaken the PCC's monopoly, but it was a price that Fidel was prepared to pay because, in the end, the party was never the ultimate source of power and legitimacy in Cuba.

GOVERNMENTAL FRAMEWORK

Cuba's highest-ranking executive organ is the Council of Ministers (CM), composed of the head of state and government, several vice presidents, and "others determined by law," as the constitution specifies. Raúl Castro formally succeeded his brother Fidel as its president in 2008; he also serves as first secretary of the Communist Party (since 2011) and commander in chief. In short, all lines of authority now converge on Raúl. The CM has the power to conduct foreign relations and foreign trade, maintain internal security, and draft bills for the National Assembly. It has an executive committee whose members control and coordinate the work of ministries and other central organizations. All of its members belong to the Communist Party.

The Council of State (CS) functions as the executive committee of the National Assembly between legislative sessions. The CS issues decrees and exercises legislative initiatives. Additionally, it can order general mobilization and replace ministers. It has some twenty-nine members, including several of the seventeen members of the Political Bureau elected at the Seventh Congress of the PCC in April 2016. In addition to Raúl, the CS includes influential party and military leaders such as Miguel Diaz Canel, first vice president of the Council of Ministers and the Council of State; Jose R. Machado Ventura, a vice president of the Council of Ministers and the Council of State, and second secretary of the PCC; Salvador Mesa Valdes, secretary general of the Central Workers' Union; and General Álvaro López Miera, vice minister of MINFAR and chief of the General Staff of the FAR. As of the Seventh Party Congress, all four are members of the Politburo.

The National Assembly of People's Power (NA) is the national legislature. Deputies are elected for five-year terms, but the Assembly holds only two brief sessions per year. In the 2008–2013 *quinquenio* (five-year term) each of its 612 deputies stood for roughly nineteen thousand inhabitants. The people directly elect deputies, but there is only one candidate for every seat. Among the NA's formal powers are deciding on constitutional reforms, discussing and approving (but not disapproving) the national budget, planning for economic and social development, and electing judges. In practice, legislative initiative is not exercised as the NA cannot challenge the political leadership, and it is, in fact, a rubber-stamp body. The next election is scheduled for February 2018.

At the conclusion of the National Assembly session in February 2012, Miguel Diaz Canel, former party provincial leader and minister of higher education, was elected to the post of first vice president of the CS. In his speech before the assembly, Raúl Castro announced his retirement in five years, anointing fifty-two-year-old Diaz-Canel, an electrical engineer and former longtime member of the Youth Communist League (UJC), as his successor, signaling the start of a long transition to younger leadership.

THE INTERNATIONAL ARENA

The key factors framing Cuba's role in the world, particularly until the early 1990s, are revolutionary messianism, an anti-American and anti-imperialistic stance, a legacy of defiance, and Marxist-Leninist ideology. Fidel Castro's revolutionary convictions as well as his shrewdness and episodic demagogic outbursts—often in the midst of crisis and bipolar confrontations—made Cuba an influential actor in regional politics and in parts of the developing world, a pattern that, to a lesser extent, Raúl has maintained.

In the 1960s, Cuba's revolutionary messianism led it to support guerrilla movements in Venezuela, Bolivia, Guatemala, Nicaragua, and other nations. Cuban support varied according to political circumstances and the country's own capabilities, but in practically all cases it involved either training guerrillas in Cuba and sending them out or supplying weapons and logistical assistance to such groups.

Through a vigorous assertion of proletarian internationalism, Cuba once maintained thousands of cadres abroad on various missions. The regime's view had been that through proletarian internationalism Cubans fulfilled their self-imposed revolutionary duties and advanced the cause of socialism and Marxism-Leninism. The policy has had explicit geopolitical aims. In the late 1980s, approximately eighty-five thousand Cubans were stationed abroad either as combat troops (in Angola and Ethiopia) or as technical and economic advisors. Contingents included doctors, nurses, and other health-care personnel as well as construction workers, teachers, agronomists, and other professionals. Intelligence people, political operatives, and security personnel also served abroad—often disguised as *internacionalistas* (internationalist workers). In some cases, Cuba earned hard currency as a result of these missions, because countries such as Libya and Angola paid Cuba in dollars for its services, while the Cuban government paid its people's salaries in pesos.

On occasion, fulfillment of these international duties led to war or confrontation with status quo powers (such as in South Africa) or, as was the case in Grenada in 1983, direct clashes with US forces. In Angola, Cuba supported the Marxist dictatorship, and in Ethiopia it backed a brutal Marxist regime. The Angolan war started in the wake of the Portuguese collapse in southwestern Africa in the mid-1970s, and Cuban forces helped turn the tide for Angola's Popular Movement for the Liberation of Angola (MPLA). Cuban forces remained in Angola until 1991.

As the late 1980s approached, changes began to surface in Cuban foreign policy. In the 1980s, Cuba resumed diplomatic relations with influential Latin American states such as Argentina, Brazil, and Peru. Havana began to prefer normalization of state-to-state relations to active support for guerrilla movements. Meanwhile, key Latin American governments were seeking ways to bring Cuba back into the Latin American community.

By the early 1990s, Cuba's once ambitious foreign policy of proletarian internationalism was considerably downsized as a result of economic hardships and the end of the Cold War. The government looked inward, focused on addressing the severe economic and social impacts of the Special Period. Cuba's foreign policy was quickly restructured to develop the greater political and especially economic space needed to help confront the two key challenges to the regime: continued US aggression and economic austerity.[12]

In the economic realm, Cuba sought to expand and diversify its economic relations by negotiating a number of bilateral agreements with western Europe and Latin American and Caribbean countries, building upon the diplomatic inroads established in the 1980s. International realignment and limited economic change were enough for the regime to at least muddle through.

One relationship that helped Cuba create the necessary economic and political space started in the late 1990s with President Hugo Chávez of Venezuela. Beginning in 2000, Venezuela provided Cuba with 53,000 barrels of oil per day; by 2005 the figure had reached nearly 100,000 barrels per day. This energy lifeline was considerable if one considers that Cuba consumes approximately 140,000 barrels per day, while it produces about 60,000 barrels per day, allowing it to re-export the surplus. Today, Venezuela has cut its exports back down to about 65,000 barrels a day. Because payment terms are so favorable to Cuba, analysts estimate that Venezuela provided Cuba with a total "gift" of US$6–US$8 billion over the next fifteen years. In exchange, Cuba provided Venezuela with approximately thirty thousand technical staff, largely medical doctors, teachers, sports coaches, and a number of military, political, and intelligence advisors.[13] In short, the relationship went beyond just ideological affinities and solidarity—there were real domestic material and political advantages, especially for Cuba.

In the 1990s and 2000s, Cuba continued to reach out in search of diplomatic allies, as Washington enhanced its efforts to pressure and isolate the island. Cuba established relations with the European Community in 1989 and in 1998 the country welcomed a visit from Pope John Paul II. Fidel Castro established personal friendships with a number of leaders in the Americas, such as Brazilian president Luiz Inácio "Lula" da Silva, Venezuela's Hugo Chávez, and President Néstor Kirchner of Argentina, who defended Havana from human rights criticism emanating from Europe and the United States. Meanwhile, Cuba intensified its use of multilateral institutions, particularly emerging Latin American blocs such as the Bolivarian Alliance for the Americas (ALBA) and the Community of Latin American and Caribbean States (CELAC).

In terms of the United States, formal diplomatic relations were broken in 1961, but "interest sections" opened in Washington and Havana in 1977. Issues raised by the United States included Cuba's strategic relationship with the Soviet Union, its revolutionary activism in Africa and Latin America, and problems in the area of human rights. Historical grievances, nationalism, the US economic embargo, and Cuban insistence on sovereignty and on earning its powerful neighbor's respect have shaped Cuba's outlook.

The 1990s did not see much of an improvement after a period of open hostility during the 1980s when the Reagan administration tightened the economic embargo and called out Cuba as the source of instability in Central America and the Caribbean. Restoring relations with Cuba was not a high priority for the George H. W. Bush and William J. Clinton administrations. In fact, economic pressures were intensified in the form of the Cuba Democracy Act (1992) and the Democracy Solidarity Act (1996), known as the Helms-Burton Act, which prohibited foreign-based subsidiaries of US companies from trading with Cuba, travel to Cuba by US citizens, and family remittances to Cuba. Though largely driven by domestic political considerations, the objective of US policy was clear: regime change.

The means by which Washington pursued its policy objectives during the George W. Bush administration intensified. Three months into his first term President Bush expanded travel restrictions, and in 2003 he announced fresh measures designed to hasten the end of Communist rule in Cuba, including cracking down on illegal cash transfers and a more robust information campaign aimed at Cubans. Cuba's response followed the script it had consistently resorted to when confronted with intense pressure from Washington: mobilize the Cuban nation around nationalist and anti-imperialist measures and messages while rallying the international community against "determined efforts from the superpower to destroy a beacon of freedom and justice for the oppressed."

Thawing of US-Cuba Relations

On December 17, 2014, US President Barack Obama and Cuban President Raúl Castro simultaneously announced, via split-screen broadcasts in the US and Cuba, the full restoration of diplomatic ties, ending more than five decades of confrontation between the two nations. Rapprochement centered on the exchange of prisoners, including the return of American USAID contractor Alan Gross, the easing of travel and communications restrictions, and the movement of money and certain goods between the two nations. For Obama, changes in the views of Cuban Americans provided the space to shift policy toward a long-term strategic approach to deepen people-to-people exchanges.[14] The number of Americans traveling to Cuba increased from 91,000 in 2014 to 150,000 in 2015, and that number will grow because direct flights by American carriers were launched in 2016.[15] Remittances doubled from 2014 to 2015, reaching US$1.4 billion.[16]

Many countries throughout the region had long criticized the United States for its outdated policy toward Cuba. Thus, the timing of Obama's strategic policy shift was driven in part by a desire to improve the image of the United States in the region prior to the April 2015 Summit of the Americas meeting in Panama.[17] US-Cuba rapprochement proved effective in quieting the anti-American tone that had characterized the previous summit meeting in Cartagena four years earlier. At the 2015 summit, Obama and Raúl held a joint news conference and reaffirmed their desire to fully restore diplomatic relations, both acknowledging the complexities of overcoming decades of confrontational policy.[18] It became difficult for countries throughout the region to criticize the United States after Raúl complimented Obama for his leadership in changing the trajectory of US-Cuba relations.

Eight months after US Secretary of State John Kerry raised the flag at the re-opening of the US embassy in Havana, President Obama became the first sitting US President to visit Cuba since Calvin Coolidge in 1928. Obama's March 2016 visit was an incredible success for US foreign policy; however, it was unsettling for the Cuban government. For the first time since the 2014 announcement, the Cuban government visibly showed concerns about the impact that engagement with the United States would have on its ability to preserve power. One media outlet wrote, "While state media treated Obama with cautious distance, there was no mistaking the thrill of ordinary Cubans as the president toured local sights, watched a baseball game, and drove through Havana with his family and entourage. They dubbed the president Santo Obama. 'He's more popular than the Pope!'"[19]

Immediately following Obama's trip, Fidel published an open letter in *Granma* criticizing the "coercive" behavior of the United States.[20] The visit underscored the United States' strategic intent to foster change by both removing the United States as the adversary in Cuba's ideological narrative and increasing people-to-people exchanges. Cuba is hedging that it can solicit US assistance while controlling the texture and pace of US engagement and its subsequent impact on Cuba's political and social order. Since the announcement, the United States has been aggressive with its attempts to engage Cuba and Cuba has been reluctant to reciprocate on a number of issues.

Human rights and the US embargo remain contentious issues going forward. The United States, along with the Cuban diaspora, criticizes Cuba for the mass detention of political dissidents. The Cuban government detained just as many political activists in 2015 and 2016, more than eight thousand, as it did in 2014.[21] In response, the Cuban government criticizes the United States for its alleged human rights violations against terrorist suspects being housed at the Guantanamo Bay Detention Camp, a US military prison located within Guantanamo Bay Naval Base. As for the embargo, Cuba argues that the embargo has cost its economy about US$125 billion over the last fifty-five years.[22] Although the embargo will remain in place until the US Congress votes to lift it, Obama has taken a number of measures to facilitate greater bilateral commercial, scientific, and educational ties. However, as of early 2017, President Donald Trump, prior to and since the 2016 election, has been very clear that his intention is to reverse President Obama's policy change. If he does so, it will likely have a dramatic impact on US–Cuban relations, probably returning to the previous policy of isolation and confrontation.

FROM FIDELISMO TO RAULISMO:
CHANGE OR CONTINUITY?

In July 2006, Fidel Castro suddenly fell gravely ill from a severe intestinal ailment and delegated all executive functions to his brother Raúl on a provisional basis. Fidel recovered his health but not the same power and influence he had exercised before. In February 2008, Raúl assumed full authority within the government, becoming president of the Council of Ministers and Council of State, in addition to commander in chief of the FAR. Within a year, Raúl made a number of personnel changes including the appointment of a new number two, Miguel Diaz Canel, while also taking the more important step of removing young leaders associated with the hardline ideological stance taken during the "battle of ideas" that Fidel had launched to mobilize youth. Raúl treaded carefully, so as not to seem like he was criticizing his brother, but it was clear that he was interested in charting a different course, one that emphasized pragmatism, efficiency and productivity, and accountability, specifically in the economic realm. As in the past, political liberalization was kept to a minimum; in fact, a campaign of low-intensity, arbitrary preventive detentions and violent suppression of dissidents and other opponents intensified. According to the dissident Cuban Human Rights and National Reconciliation Commission and other local and international human rights organizations, the number of arbitrary, temporary detentions rose significantly from 2010–2016.

Raulismo

If Fidelismo was characterized by voluntarism and mobilization, Raulismo is more focused on strengthening key governing institutions, such as the Communist Party, so as to have legitimacy and responsibility for policy rest in the institution and not on the charismatic leader. The party had not convened a congress since the Fifth Party Congress in 1997 when Cuba was in midst of the Special Period. In the 1997 congress, Fidel doubled down on socialism, refusing to institute any reforms. On the other hand, in late 2010 during the run-up to the long overdue Sixth Party Congress (April 2011), Raúl presented 313 guidelines designed to update the economy, culminating with their formal approval at the Party Congress. However, the Congress did not "settle the uncertainties regarding the pace and scope of the economic reforms," as conservative elements within the party and bureaucracy feared the impact of the reforms on patronage. Raúl insisted on "order, discipline and exigency," but the bureaucracy slow-rolled the changes, guaranteeing their failure.[23] In the end, the conflict between ideological purity and economic necessity could not be reconciled. In the choice between maintaining political control and enhancing standards of living through economic reform, the regime, as it always did, chose the former. This policy contradiction created bottlenecks and inefficiencies that impeded the modest economic measures instituted during the party congress from truly bearing fruit during the following five years.

The run-up to the Seventh Party Congress (April 2016) did not have the fanfare and public discussion that led up to the previous congress. In fact, the work of the congress seems to have been continuity. According to a report of the congress, only 21 percent of the Sixth Party Congress guidelines had been implemented. There was some rhetoric about continuing reform and the need to enhance efficiencies, but the Cuban leadership made it clear that Cuba was not heading toward capitalism. Moreover, the conservative approach adopted by the congress seemed to signal a backlash against recent warming of relations and the March visit by President Obama to Havana, with much criticism of the Obama administration for attempting to move Cuba from its socialist roots.

The documents approved by the congress did signal support for limited market mechanisms while making it very clear the "PCC would not relinquish its tight political grip on political control and the distribution of most resources and services."[24] Many observers believed a new, younger cohort of leaders would be introduced into the higher echelons of the party. Raúl Castro announced age limits for party leadership, opening greater opportunities for younger generations; however, a majority of previous Politburo members were ratified. If the Sixth Party Congress was character-ized by more change than continuity, the latest Congress saw a conservative approach, underscoring how the regime always opts for playing it safe, even at the expense of economic necessity.

The core of Raulismo is to reorient the bases of the regime's legitimacy away from voluntarism and charismatic mobilization toward bolstering the government's popular-ity and legitimacy by improving the economic lot of normal Cubans. Raúl spoke of up-dating and modernizing the economy but "without haste in order to avoid mistakes." Some of the reforms proposed in 2010 included the rise and expansion of self-employ-ment, the legalization of home and car sales, and boosting private farming by granting land in usufruct to farmers and cooperatives.[25] No other industry has seen as much liberalization as agriculture, with a steady rollout of incentives for farmers. Raúl was explicit on the need for agricultural reform: increasing efficiency and food production to replace imports that cost Cuba hundreds of millions of dollars a year was a matter of "national security."

It was already clear by 2010, however, that economic reforms had not had their de-sired effect. Economic growth remains relatively low despite measures taken to incen-tivize small private enterprises and liberalize agricultural production. As the *New York Times* noted, "by most measures, the project has failed. Because of waste, poor man-agement, policy constraints, transportation limits, theft and other problems, overall efficiency has dropped: many Cubans are actually seeing less food at private markets. That is the case despite an increase in the number of farmers and production gains for certain items."[26]

The nonagricultural sector has not fared better. The number of private sector jobs is not increasing at the pace required to hire the five hundred thousand to 1.3 mil-lion state sector employees the government was expected to slash by 2015. There are a number of reasons for the failure of these reforms, such as poor infrastructure, waste, inability to access capital, and policy constraints, but in the end, it is a result of politics that impeded economic modernization and progress. As in the past, the government continues to fear the emergence of independent, private economic activity that in other countries contributed to unleashing the forces of political liberalization. By 2015, it was clear to all that the Cuban economy was faltering and that expectations of improvement in the standards of living were dashed. In April 2016, Raúl delivered a grim report on the state of the economy, acknowledging that the hundreds of changes launched in 2010 had failed to stimulate the stagnant centrally controlled economy. The unwilling-ness to implement key structural reforms (e.g., eliminating the double currency system) needed to increase production of goods and services and expand exports—all measures containing potentially dangerous political consequences—meant that Raúl's attempts at expanding growth would fail. In the end, Raúl's government remains committed to a pervasive system of social controls even at the cost of improving the economic lot of Cubans.

With respect to the FAR, there has been far more institutional continuity than change. Raúl appointed General Julio Casas Regueiro as Minister until the latter's death in 2011. Casas Regueiro was among Raúl's closest allies. Since Casas Regueiro's death, General Leopoldo Cintra Frías has served as Minister of FAR. Despite leader-ship changes in the ministerial position, there seems to be no visible shift in the FAR's influence on Cuba's social, economic, and political fabric. In fact, some would argue that Raúl's ascension to the presidency has elevated the profile of the FAR. Raúl remains surrounded by loyal generals in control of key ministries and enterprises in strategic sectors of the economy administered by the armed forces. Several of these generals started out as guerrilla fighters under Raúl's command in the Second Front during the struggle against Batista. An increasing number of senior officers, such as Raul's former son-in-law, Brigadier General Luis Alberto Rodriguez Calleja (head of GAESA), are taking over leadership of key economic sectors.

CONCLUSION

Cuba's political development following its independence was characterized by clientelism, strongman rule, and military intervention in politics. The legitimacy of these early regimes seldom rested on popular consent. In the 1940s and 1950s, democratic reformism failed to develop viable institutions, and as a result, corrupt governments undermined public support for political democracy. Authoritarian regimes alienated the rising middle sectors and relied on coercion rather than consent, thus seldom ruling with popular support. Economic dependency made national development difficult, resulting in a social system that lacked cohesion.

Structural transformation uprooted capitalism and reordered the political system through mobilization and charismatic rule. Egalitarianism, unity, and social militancy became the supreme values of the new Marxist order. Private education was abolished, and the state reshaped the entire educational system, expanding health services as well. State control of industry, commerce, telecommunications, agriculture, and even small-scale production created a large bureaucracy, which in turn led to a new technocracy composed of administrators, planners, and managers, many from the Cuban military.

Many predicted the collapse of Cuban socialism during the Special Period. These predictions about its demise or about the implementation of major transformations that would be necessary for the system to survive were not realized. Contrary to what many experts, social scientists, and regime opponents have held, the system has proved to be more resilient than anticipated. Limited economic reforms placed a bottom under what could have been an economic cataclysm, blunting the edge of social pressures that could have exploded into political disorder.

Broadly speaking, that resiliency is rooted in nationalism, not quite yet a spent force. The loyalty and relative cohesion of strategic elites such as the party apparatus, the armed forces, and younger, proven cadres involved in administration and management limit the probability that a reformist faction might shake up the system. A survival strategy of adaptation introduced in the early 1990s and intensified under President Raúl Castro—combining major ideological reversals with limited macroeconomic changes and a partial opening for foreign capital—generated sufficient resources to maintain social stability and elite cohesion, one of the crucial determinants of the regime's survival. The 2016 death of Fidel Castro is unlikely to change the current course taken by his brother. Maintaining the status quo, however, will be a challenge once the first generation of revolutionary leaders, led by Raul Castro, passes from the scene. Renewed relations with the United States were challenging the social and elite cohesion that had persisted in Cuba over the last several decades. However, a return to the previous policy of isolation and confrontation under President Trump may very well offer the cohesion that will allow the regime to survive in the face of economic distress.

SUGGESTIONS FOR FURTHER READING

del Aguila, Juan M. *Cuba: Dilemmas of a Revolution*. 3rd ed. Boulder, CO: Westview Press, 1994.

Dominguez, Jorge I., Omar Everleny Perez Villanueva, Mayra Espina Prieto, and Lorenia Barbeira, eds. *Cuban Economic and Social Development Policy Reforms and Challenges in the 21st Century*, Cambridge, MA: Harvard University Press, 2012.

Dominguez, Jorge I. *To Make a World Safe for Revolution: Cuba's Foreign Policy*. Cambridge, MA: Harvard University Press, 1989.

———. *Cuba: Order and Revolution*. Cambridge, MA: Belknap Press, 1978.

Erikson, Daniel. *The Cuba Wars: Fidel Castro, the United States, and the Next Revolution*. New York: Bloomsbury, 2008.

Frank, Marc. *Cuban Revelations: Behind the Scenes in Havana*. Gainesville: University Press of Florida, 2015

Klepak, Hal. *Cuba's Military, 1990–2005: Revolutionary Soldiers During Counter-Revolutionary Times*. New York: Palgrave Macmillan, 2005.

———. *Raul Castro and Cuba: A Military Story*. New York: Palgrave Macmillan, 2012.

LeoGrande, William M., and Peter Kornbluh. *Back Channel to Cuba: The Hidden History of Negotiation Between Washington and Havana*. Chapel Hill: University of North Carolina Press, 2014.

Mesa-Lago, Carmelo, and Jorge Perez Lopez. *Cuba Under Raul Castro: Assessing the Reforms*. Boulder, CO: Lynne Rienner Publishers, 2013.

Mesa-Lago, Carmelo. *The Economy of Socialist Cuba*. Albuquerque: University of New Mexico Press, 1981.

Pérez, Louis A. *Cuba: Between Reform and Revolution*. 4th ed. New York: Oxford University Press, 2010.

Perez-Stable, Marifeli. *The Cuban Revolution: Origins, Causes and Legacy*. 3rd ed. New York: Oxford University Press, 2011.

Schoultz, Lars. *That Infernal Little Cuban Republic: The United States and the Cuban Revolution*. Chapel Hill: University of North Carolina Press, 2011.

Smith, Wayne S. *The Closest of Enemies: A Personal and Diplomatic Account of US-Cuban Relations Since 1957*. New York: W. W. Norton, 1987.

Szulc, Tad. *Fidel: A Critical Portrait*. New York: Harper, 2000.

NOTES

1. Eusebio Mujal-León, "Survival, Adaptation and Uncertainty: The Case of Cuba," *Journal of International Affairs* 65, no. 1 (Fall/Winter 2011): 150.

2. Ramón Ruiz, *Cuba: The Making of a Revolution* (New York: W. W. Norton, 1968), 31.

3. Jaime Suchlicki, *Cuba: From Columbus to Castro,* 5th ed. (Washington, DC: Pergamon-Brassey's, 2002), 114.

4. Andrés Suárez, *Cuba: Castroism and Communism 1959–1966* (Cambridge, MA: MIT Press, 1967).

5. Frank O. Mora, "The FAR and Its Economic Role: From Civic to Technocrat Soldier," ICCAS Occasional Paper Series, June 2004, University of Miami, Coral Gables, FL.

6. Jorge Dominguez, *Cuba: Order and Revolution* (Cambridge, MA: Belknap Press, 1978), 342.

7. For a discussion of the FAR's restructuring during this period, see Domingo Amuchaste-gui, "Cuba's Armed Forces: Power and Reform," *Cuba in Transition* 9 (1999).

8. Brian Latell, "The Cuban Military and Transition Dynamics," 2003, Cuba Transition Project, Institute of Cuban and Cuban American Studies, University of Miami, Coral Gables, FL.

9. Gerardo Fernandez and M. Menendez, "The Economic Power of the Castro Brothers," *Diario 16* (Madrid), June 24, 2001.

10. William LeoGrande, *The Cuban Communist Party and Electoral Politics: Adaptation, Succession, and Transition*, 2002, Cuba Transition Project, Institute of Cuban and Cuban American Politics, University of Miami, Coral Gables, FL, 3.

11. Mujal-León, "Survival, Adaptation and Uncertainty," 157.

12. Michael Erisman and John M. Kirk, eds., *Redefining Cuban Foreign Policy: The Impact of the Special Period* (Gainesville: University Press of Florida, 2006).

13. Javier Corrales, "The Logic of Extremism: How Chávez Gains by Giving Cuba So Much," working paper presented at the meeting "Cuba, Venezuela, and the Americas: A Changing Landscape," Washington, DC, September 14, 2005. Mujal-León, "Survival, Adaptation and Uncertainty," 155.

14. Florida International University, "2016 Cuba Poll," 2016.

15. Danielle Renwick, Brianna Lee, and James McBride, "U.S.-Cuba Relations," Council on Foreign Relations, September 7, 2016. www.cfr.org/cuba/us-cuba-relations/p11113.

16. Ibid.

17. Ibid.

18. Eric Hershberg and William M. LeoGrande, eds. *A New Chapter in US-Cuba Relations: Social, Political, and Economic Implications* (New York: Palgrave Macmillan, 2016).

19. Ann Louise Bardachi, "Backlash in Cuba," *Politico Magazine* (June 10, 2016).

20. Fidel Castro, "El hermano Obama," *Granma*, March 28, 2016.

21. Renwick, Lee, and McBride, "U.S.-Cuba Relations."

22. VOA, "Cuba says US embargo cost it $4.6 billion last year," Voice of Americas, September 9, 2016. www.voanews.com/a/cuba-says-us-embargo-cost-it-four-point-six-billion-dollars-last-year/3501327.html.

23. Mujal-León, "Survival, Adaptation and Uncertainty," 157.

24. Albright Stonebridge Group, "Cuba's Seventh Party Congress," (20 April 2016).

25. For an assessment of Raúl's economic reforms, see Carmelo Mesa-Lago and Jorge Perez-Lopez, *Cuba Under Raul Castro: Assessing the Reforms* (Boulder, CO: Lynne Rienner Publishers, 2013).

26. Damien Cave, "Cuba's Free-Market Farm Experiment Yields a Meager Crop," *New York Times,* December 8, 2012.

20

COSTA RICA

Mitchell A. Seligson

INTRODUCTION

Virtually all the studies comparing Central American nations contain the phrase "with the exception of Costa Rica." Travelogues—and even many academic studies—refer to Costa Rica as the "Switzerland of Central America." And in many ways, it is, with an enviable tradition of respect for civil liberties and broad access to advanced social services, not to mention its many mountaintops that make the references to Switzerland more than just fanciful. In recent years, however, citizens have grown increasingly discontent as, for many, expectations have exceeded the limitations of the economy of this small nation, and voters have become disillusioned by the disappointing performance of their elected leaders. Despite those concerns, in broad strokes Costa Rica is indeed different from its neighbors in three fundamental ways.

First, levels of social and economic development are far higher in Costa Rica than elsewhere in Central America.[1] Life expectancy at birth for Costa Ricans was seventy-nine years in 2014, matching that of the United States, higher than any other country in Latin America, and substantially higher than the Latin American average of seventy-five years. The under-five infant mortality, a universally used measure for comparing development, stood at nine per one thousand live births in 2011–15, compared with nineteen in Nicaragua and twenty-four in Guatemala. In terms of the gross college enrolment ratio, by 2014 Costa Rica nearly surpassed even Switzerland, with 50 percent enrolled versus 56 percent in Switzerland. Costa Rica's rate was more than 2.5 times higher than Guatemala (18 percent), and substantially higher than El Salvador (29 percent), its closest competitor in Central America in the area of college enrollments.

Second, Costa Rica has the longest and deepest tradition of democratic governance of any nation in Central America. Indeed, for many years experts have rated Costa Rica as the most democratic country in all of Latin America.[2] Civil liberties, including freedom of press, speech, and assembly, are widely respected and protected, and, unlike a number of other countries in the region, journalists do not live in fear. After a rough start in the nineteenth century, free and open elections have long been the hallmark of Costa Rica's style of politics, with observers throughout the world seeking to copy elements of an electoral system that faithfully guarantees against voting fraud and corruption. Human rights, so often brutally abused in other Central American nations, are carefully respected, and one rarely hears even of allegations of their violation.

Third, Costa Rica is a peaceful island in a violent region. It abolished its army nearly seventy years ago, and is constitutionally prohibited from forming another one. Although there have been minor incursions and incidents over the years along Costa Rica's northern and southern borders, security units, now organized into a national police force (*Fuerza Pública*) of some twelve thousand members, have been adequate to cope with these international conflicts. Strikes and protests are rarely violent, and negotiation is the most common mechanism for resolving disputes. Terrorism is almost unknown.

Costa Rica, then, stands out from its neighbors as being more advanced socially, economically, and politically, and more democratic and peaceful. There have been many scholarly attempts to determine why Costa Rica diverges from the regional pattern. Some studies have focused on historical accidents as an explanation, others on the mixture of resources (especially land and labor), and yet others on questions of ethnic homogeneity. To date, no comprehensive explanation has been established, yet partial explanations incorporating each of the aforementioned features seem plausible. In this short introduction to Costa Rica, these elements will be highlighted as factors that seem to explain Costa Rican distinctiveness.

HISTORY AND ECONOMIC DEVELOPMENT

Costa Rica, the southernmost country in the group of five colonies that united into a loose federation shortly after gaining independence from Spain in the early 1820s, developed in isolation from its neighbors to the north. This isolation was partially a result of historical factors, because politics pivoted around Guatemala, the colonial seat of power and the area of greatest indigenous population. It was also partially the result of a geographic factor—namely, that the bulk of Costa Rica's population resided in San José, Cartago, and Heredia, towns located on the *meseta central* (central plateau), and thus was largely cut off from both the Pacific Ocean and the Caribbean Sea as well as from Nicaragua to the north and from Panama to the south.

Although Costa Rica can boast that it is more than twice the size of El Salvador, its 19,650 square miles (50,900 square kilometers) make it less than half the size of Guatemala and Honduras and only slightly more than one-third the size of Nicaragua. In US terms, it is tiny—about the size of West Virginia. The usable territory is further reduced by the presence of a mountain chain that cuts through the center of the country, running from north to south. The mountain chain is studded with active volcanoes, and periodic eruptions and earthquakes have caused considerable damage to crops, and on some occasions, such as the earthquake in 2012, some loss of life, although enforced antiseismic codes have limited loss of life and property damage considerably. The net effect of the mountains, volcanoes, and other natural formations is a reduction of arable land to an estimated 53 percent of the total land area.

Costa Rica's early development was further weakened by the absence of large Indian populations widely found further north in Central America. In Guatemala, for example, the conquering Spaniards were able to rely on a large supply of Indians to undertake heavy labor in the mines and in the fields. Population estimates for the precolonial period are widely disputed. Some accounts report a population for the entire Central American region as high as six million. The Costa Rican portion of the region has been characterized as having low to medium indigenous population density.[3] Although there is some limited evidence that prior to the conquest there were perhaps as many as 400,000 Indians living in the territory that was to become Costa Rica, by the end of the sixteenth century there were fewer than 20,000, and according to some estimates as few as 4,500 by 1581.[4] Isolation, mountains, volcanoes, earthquakes, and the absence of a sizable indigenous workforce do not seem to add up to a very promising basis for the impressive developments that Costa Rica was eventually to achieve. Paradoxically, however, what seemed like disadvantages turned out to be significant advantages. Isolation proved a blessing because it removed the country from the civil wars and violence that so rapidly came to characterize postindependence Central America. Later, the dictatorial rule and foreign invasions that plagued the rest of the region had little direct impact on Costa Rica. Furthermore, in contrast to its neighbors to both the north and the south (Nicaragua and Panama), Costa Rica's relative political stability meant that it was never subject to an invasion by US marines. The mountains provided the altitude and the volcanoes the rich soil for what was to prove to be a highly successful coffee industry. Finally, the absence of a large indigenous population meant that the repressive labor systems (especially the encomienda system) that predominated in much of the rest of Latin America could not prosper in Costa Rica. The *encomiendas* that were established faced a rapid decline in population as the Indians died from disease.

The colonial period in Costa Rica was one of widespread poverty. Early explorers found little of the gold and silver that so strongly stimulated Spanish migration to the New World. Had they discovered major mines, no doubt they would have found ways of importing a labor force to work them. But significant mines, while long rumored, were never found, the labor was not imported, and the flood of colonizers who settled elsewhere proved to be only a trickle in Costa Rica. There are reports that as late as 1675 there were only five hundred to seven hundred Spanish settlers in Costa Rica, and by 1720 the number barely exceeded three thousand. Estimates are that in 1778 the total population of Costa Rica was less than twenty-five thousand, of which only 8 percent was Indian.[5] It was not until the mid-1850s that the total population of the country had grown to more than one hundred thousand.

The small population, both indigenous and immigrant, together with the absence of major gold and silver mines, meant that agriculture became the principal source of economic activity throughout the colonial period. Although the soil was rich in many parts of the country, and a wide variety of crops grew well, farming was directed toward subsistence agriculture. As a result, Costa Rica had little to trade in exchange for needed goods that were not available locally. The initial poverty reinforced itself by placing beyond the reach of the settlers the farm tools and other implements needed for a more productive economy.

Throughout the colonial period efforts were made to add vitality to the fragile local economy. Attention was focused on export agriculture, especially cacao and tobacco. Both crops grew well and fetched high prices on the international market, but both eventually failed in Costa Rica. In the case of cacao, which was grown in the tropical lowlands bordering on the Caribbean Sea, marauding Indians from Nicaragua, in league with British pirates, systematically raided the plantations and stole the crop as it was being prepared for export. Tobacco grew in the highlands and therefore was protected against such coastal raids, but Spain declared a monopoly on tobacco exports and drove down profit margins for producers to the point where the cultivation of tobacco no longer proved worth the effort. By the end of the colonial period Costa Rica had not been able to find a way out of its poverty.

Independence was delivered as a gift to Costa Rica in 1821 when the isthmus, under the leadership of Guatemala, became independent from Spain. Costa Rica and the rest of Central America briefly (1822–1823) came under the rule of the Mexican Empire headed by Augustín de Iturbide. In 1824 Costa Rica joined with the other nations of Central America into a short-lived federation, which rapidly crumbled and effectively ceased to exist in 1839. Costa Rica then began the process of establishing itself as an independent country, and by 1848 Costa Rica was a fully independent republic. Very early on in the postcolonial period the fledgling government took critical steps to help develop a stronger economic base for the country. One of these was a kind of "Homestead Act," which granted land to farmers who were willing to plant coffee on it. As a result, coffee cultivation increased dramatically in the first half of the nineteenth century, and by the 1840s direct exports of Costa Rican coffee to the markets in Europe had begun. The product was well received by buyers and quickly achieved a reputation for its high quality, one that it still holds today.

Coffee exports soon became the principal engine of economic growth for Costa Rica. The income from these exports made it possible for coffee producers to import new work tools and building materials, and the government was also able to invest funds in critical infrastructure projects, especially roads and ports to facilitate the production and export of coffee. The largest and most consequential project that grew out of the effort to facilitate coffee exports was the construction of a railroad to the Caribbean port of Limón. Until the completion of this project, virtually all coffee exports had been shipped to Europe via the Pacific coast port of Puntarenas, around the tip of South America, and then to Europe. Early on in this process the coffee was repackaged in Chile, and shipped to Europe as if its origin had been Chilean, thereby denying Costa Rica its brand recognition. The high shipping costs of the lengthy voyage, furthermore, reduced profits for the producers. The railroad project to the Caribbean therefore promised to cut those costs, while ensuring the establishment of brand recognition for Costa Rican coffee.

The railroad construction was financed by a series of foreign loans, the interest and principle of which Costa Rica found itself unable to repay during the construction process. As a result, in an effort to raise cash, the US-owned firm that had contracted to build the railroad began to plant bananas to subsidize its construction. From this small start, the United Fruit Company developed, and it became the major economic influence in the Caribbean tropical lowlands of Costa Rica up through the 1930s, after which time the company moved its operations to the Pacific coastal lowlands. Banana cultivation provided employment for the railroad workers who had migrated to Costa Rica from Jamaica and later for job-seekers from Costa Rica's highlands. As a result, these black Jamaicans came to be a significant ethnic minority in the country. Today, however, according to the 2011 population census, they account for just 1 percent of the non-indigenous population, with the indigenous comprising 104,143 people out of a total population of 4,301,712, or about 2.4 percent.

Coffee and bananas proved to be the mainstays of the economy through the middle of the twentieth century. Over the years, coffee fields were expanded to cover a wide area along the chain of mountains that runs through the country, an expansion caused by farmers in search of new land on which to grow coffee. As the territory suitable for coffee-growing shrank, settlers moved to other areas where they planted basic grains, and in the higher mountain regions they grew vegetables or raised dairy cattle. In the province of Guanacaste, annexed from Nicaragua in 1824, the broad flatlands proved suitable for cattle raising, and a major export industry of fresh beef developed between Costa Rica and the United States. When the United Fruit Company left the Caribbean lowlands because of the onset of debilitating banana diseases there, those banana fields lay largely abandoned until the 1950s, when the discovery of new, resistant varieties allowed other companies, some of them domestic, to reinitiate the banana industry in that area.

Although agriculture has been the traditional base of the economy, Costa Rica's entry in the Central American Common Market in the early 1960s led to significant industrialization, especially of the assembly-type industries, such as packaging bulk products for local consumer distribution. By the 1980s the economy of Costa Rica rested on the export of coffee, bananas, and beef, with some industrialization. More recently, however, notable shifts have occurred. The recent introduction of nontraditional crops, such as pineapples, flowers, melons, tropical fruits, and vegetables, began to produce significant export earnings. Yet agriculture was in a steady decline as the traditional mainstay of the economy. What was overshadowing agriculture, both traditional and new, was tourism, especially ecotourism, drawing on Costa Rica's natural beauty accompanied by a wise policy of establishing a large network of national parks. Tourists come from all over the world to visit Costa Rica's incomparable beaches, rainforests, and volcanoes. Today tourism earns more foreign exchange than bananas and coffee combined. Even more recently, the economy has expanded in the area of high technology, especially the manufacture of software and computer components for such giants as Intel (although Intel decided to halt chip manufacturing in Costa Rica in 2014, diminishing its presence there).

By 2013 agriculture had declined to less than 5 percent of the GDP, industry produced around 25 percent, while services, including tourism, had risen to 70 percent. The growth of industry has paralleled the growth of urbanization, and according to the 2011 census, more than 72 percent of the population is urban. For many years, Costa Rica's entry into the Dominican Republic, United States, Central American

Free Trade Agreement (CAFTA-DR) with the United States was stalled by opposition in the legislature, but a national referendum held in 2007 gave a narrow edge to the pro-agreement side, and in late 2008 the final pieces of legislation were put in place for Costa Rica to join. This legislation paved the way for several market liberalization measures, including the introduction of competition into the telecommunications and insurance industries, which up until that point were closely held state monopolies. The jury is still out on the balance of costs and benefits of CAFTA-DR for Costa Rica, but there have been important increases in exports, a growing sophistication of export products, and marked expansion of internet and cell phone availability, while labor groups have complained bitterly about unfair competition.

POLITICS AND PARTIES

Colonial poverty and the absence of a ruling class that derived its power from a slave or Indian population are factors that favored the development of democracy in Costa Rica. Local government had its origins in colonial Costa Rica when local *cabildos* (city councils) were established in 1812. When independence was announced, a procedure was established that involved the popular election of delegates to a constitutional convention, and thus indirect, representative democracy was established in the first constitutional arrangements. A weak presidency was created, with the term of office limited to only three months, within a rotating directorate.

But all was not favorable for democratic rule. The system was weakened by regional rivalries between the two major population centers, San José and Cartago, and civil wars punctuated the first twenty years of independence—as did coups, assassinations, and invasions. In 1844 a new constitution was drafted and approved, dividing the government into three separate branches: legislative, executive, and judicial. Voting rights were established, but restrictions were many: to be eligible to vote, one had to be married, male, a property owner, and at least twenty-five years of age. Less than 3 percent of the population voted in the first elections under this new constitution. However, even this limited form of democracy was extinguished by a coup within two years of its establishment.

Additional efforts at constitution making, more coups, and countercoups occurred until 1890. In that year, a period of relative political stability and democratic rule was initiated, and this one lasted largely unbroken, except for a period of dictatorship in 1917–1920, until 1948. Direct elections were instituted in 1913, and a new constitution drafted in 1917 granted numerous social guarantees to the working population. Although this document was to be replaced in 1919, in the years that followed, Costa Ricans made continual improvements to the election laws and procedures. In 1925, the secret ballot was instituted, and in 1927 the Civil Registry, a verifiable voter registration system, was established.

Political parties were first organized in the nineteenth century, but until 1940 they were little more than loose, personalist coalitions built around the leading economic interests with narrow popular bases. In that year, the coffee oligarchy, under the banner of the Republican Party, elected Rafael Angel Calderón Guardia to power and was surprised when he quickly moved in a populist direction. Calderón, a physician who had developed a large following among the urban poor, embarked on a major program to introduce modern social legislation. In 1942, he began a social security program and approved a minimum wage law. He also established an eight-hour workday and legalized unions. In 1943, after the Nazi invasion of the Soviet Union, he formed an electoral alliance with the Costa Rican Communist Party, known as the Popular Vanguard Party. This party, organized in 1929, had attempted to run candidates for local office in the 1932 elections, but after it was barred from doing so it became increasingly involved in labor protests that took place during the Great Depression, especially among banana workers.

The alliance between Calderón and the Communists caused great concern and division within Costa Rica, but in the 1944 elections the alliance forces won, supporting a candidate of Calderón's choosing. With World War II over and the Cold War beginning, the wartime alliance of convenience with the Communists became the target of increasingly strong protests within Costa Rica, and in 1948 a coalition of the traditional coffee oligarchy in league with young reformist social democrats defeated Calderón, who was once again running for the presidency. The legislature, however, had the responsibility of declaring the results of the vote, and with Calderón's supporters in the majority, it annulled the election.

The reaction to the maneuver was swift and violent. An armed group led by José (Pepe) Figueres Ferrer organized in the mountains to the south of the capital and began a series of skirmishes with government forces, aided by unionized banana workers loyal to the Vanguardia Popular party. After a brief but bloody civil war, Figueres triumphed. He took over the government and ran it for a year and a half, during which time a new constitution was drafted and approved. Although it was a modern constitution, guaranteeing a wide range of rights, it outlawed parties that were perceived as threatening to democratic rule, such as the Communists, thus causing deep divisions in the electorate that persisted for decades.

Four major consequences of the civil war of 1948 have served to shape Costa Rican politics ever since. First, the new constitution abolished the army and replaced it with a civilian police force. Without an army, it is far more difficult for dissenting forces to engineer a coup, and indeed, there have been no successful attempts to dislodge civilian rule since 1948. Further, the absence of an army prevented the draining away of state budgets, allowing those funds to be used for education, health, and welfare. Second, Figueres did what no other successful leader of a coup in Latin America has ever done: he voluntarily turned control of the government over to the victor of the annulled election. By doing so he firmly established a respect for free and fair elections that had been growing in Costa Rica since the turn of the century. Third, the civil war largely marginalized the Communist Party, and since that time, even after the elimination of the constitutional prohibition on Communist candidates running for office, the voting strength of the Communist Party has not exceeded 3 percent of the total presidential vote. Fourth, Figueres ushered in with him a group of social reformers who, somewhat ironically, in many ways merely expanded on programs begun by Calderón. As Figueres relinquished power he began to build the bases for a new party, called the National Liberation Party (PLN), to compete in the 1953 elections, which he won handily with 64.7 percent of the valid vote, in an election in which only two parties fielded candidates; Calderón and his Republican Party were banned from running. From the moment of that election through 1998, the presidency oscillated between control by the PLN and control by a coalition of opposition forces, since 1986 running as the *Partido Unidad Social Cristiana*, PUSC.

Since 1998, however, party politics in Costa Rica have been shifting. New political parties, especially the *Partido Acción Ciudadana* (PAC), often in coalitions with other minor parties, have entered the electoral arena in force. At the same time, electoral abstention has been increasing substantially. The result has been that the PLN has lost much of its firm grip on the presidency. In 2002, for the first time ever, elections went into a second round because of a strong run by a third party. In that year, PUSC won 38.6 percent of the first-round votes, PLN 31.1 percent, and the new PAC 26.2 percent. PUSC eventually won easily in the second round, 58.0 percent to the PLN's 42.0 percent. In 2006 Oscar Arias, allowed to run for office a second time as a result of a supreme court (Sala IV) decision, won a close election by only a 1 percent margin (40.9 percent to the PAC's 39.8 percent). The PUSC won only 3.5 percent, having been mired in a major corruption scandal. It was worrisome that abstention increased to almost 35 percent of registered voters. But in 2010 the PLN regained strength and elected Laura Chinchilla Miranda, Costa Rica's first female president, by a strong 46.9 percent vote total, followed by Ottón Solís of the Citizen Action Party (PAC) with 25.1 percent, and Otto Guevarra of the Movimiento Libertario (ML) with 20.9 percent. The once powerful PUSC, still rocked by corruption scandals, received only 3.8 percent of the votes. Abstention declined somewhat from its high point in 2006 to 30.9 percent, but was still far higher than the norm for the 1962–1994 period, where only about one-fifth of the registered voters stayed home. The PLN won twenty-three of the fifty-seven seats in the unicameral legislature, far exceeding PAC's twelve, but still necessitating coalition formation to achieve a majority. Women took nearly 37 percent of the seats, the highest total in history, and Chinchilla appointed women to two-fifths of ministerial positions. In 2014, after a close first round in which the PAC edged the PLN 30.6 to 29.7 percent, with a surprisingly strong turnout by a new party, the *Frente Amplio* (with 17.3 percent), the PAC won its first presidential victory in the runoff. The PLN candidate withdrew from the race in the middle of the runoff, giving the PAC 77.8 percent to the PLN's 22.2 percent in that race. Abstention in the runoff was an unprecedented 43.5 percent, compared to the first round's rate of 31.8 percent. Luis Guillermo Solís, whose background had been largely in academia, assumed the presidency in 2014. The legislature suffered from a broad division of power, with the PAC winning only 13 seats, the PLN 18, the Frente Amplio 9, and the PUSC 8, with five other parties splitting the remaining seats.

Turnout at the local level (Costa Rican municipalities are called *cantónes*), where elections for mayor were held for the first time in 2002, has been far lower than for the presidential/legislative elections, running about 25–30 percent of the electorate. Those mayoral elections had been conducted at a separate time from national elections, resulting, not surprisingly, in reduced turnout. In 2016, for the first time mayoral and council elections were held simultaneously, partially in an effort to increase interest and turnout. The PLN has frequently dominated in local elections: they won fifty mayoral races in 2016, followed by fifteen for the PUSC. Unfortunately, 65 percent of the registered voters abstained, disappointing those who had hoped for much higher turnout.

One of the most serious problems to confront Costa Rica in recent history is the growing number of high-level incidents of corruption. Two former presidents have been convicted of taking bribes, and both were given five-year sentences, although various appeals and rulings have complicated the outcomes. In recent years, accusations of high-level corruption have been commonplace. The most recent AmericasBarometer surveys carried out by the Latin American Public Opinion Project (LAPOP) show declining support for the system, increased concern about corruption, and growing doubts about the legitimacy of the regime. Some observers are suggesting that Costa Rican exceptionalism is fast eroding and that in the not-too-distant future Costa Rica will look very much like its Central American cousins.

GOVERNMENT STRUCTURE

Since 1949 Costa Rica has operated under the constitution that grew out of the 1948 civil war. Power is shared among the president, a unicameral legislature, and the courts. Members of the legislature and the president are elected every four years. Candidates for the legislature, representing each of the seven provinces of the country, are selected by party conventions. The ability of a sitting president to implement programs has always depended on the strength of congressional support.

In order to implement the wide range of social and economic development programs envisioned by the leaders of the PLN, numerous autonomous and semiautonomous agencies have been created. Hence, one agency handles electric and telephone services, another water supply, and yet another automobile and home insurance. These agencies have been a positive force for development and have spawned many creative ideas. For example, the automobile and home insurance agency also runs the fire department, which guarantees that it is in the insurance agency's interest to have an efficient fire-fighting service. The autonomy of these agencies has helped to isolate them from partisan political pressure. Yet along with their autonomy has come the problem of an excessive decentralization of control. As a result, central planning and budgetary control have become extremely difficult as agencies and their functions have proliferated over the years. The free trade agreements, however, have served to reduce the power of these agencies, and now insurance, cell phones, and other similar services have become subject to market competition.

ECONOMIC AND SOCIAL POLICY MAKING

The modern state that Costa Rica has evolved into can be largely credited with the achievements that were noted at the beginning of this chapter. The high standard of living that has been attained, however, has been built on an economy that has limited industrial capacity. Most industrialization is of the assembly type, and as much as ninety cents of each dollar of output derives from imported materials. For decades, a continuously growing government and parastatal bureaucracy further increased costs without adding to production.

By the mid-1970s it was beginning to become clear that the growth model of the post–civil war period was running out of steam and that the economy could no longer support the expense of widespread social welfare programs and a bloated public sector.

Yet little was done to correct the system under successive PLN presidents. Then beginning in 1980, under the leadership of an opposition president, the system began to come apart. In order to shore up local production and consumption—and taking advantage of cheap loans being offered by foreign banks that were awash in petrodollars as a result of the dramatic rise in world petroleum prices—Costa Rica began to borrow wildly. Over a very short span of time the country's foreign debt grew to the point at which it exceeded the equivalent of the total annual national production, and by 1982 Costa Rica had one of the highest per capita foreign debts in the world. The local currency was devalued again and again, inflation and unemployment rose, and the system seemed headed for a crash.

By late 1981 the future seemed grim indeed. Yet while similar circumstances have led to coups in other Latin American countries, Costa Ricans waited patiently for the elections of 1982 and once again voted in the PLN. A dramatic plan for recovery was put in place by the victorious president, and the plan proved successful in stabilizing the economic picture. Inflation dropped, employment rose, the currency was revalued, and an effort was made to rationalize the foreign debt. These actions restored confidence in the system, but they did not return to the citizens the benefits of the growth that had been lost during the 1980–1982 period. Belts had to be tightened, taxes were increased, and prices rose. Economic growth picked up a bit, but there was no dramatic recovery.

Throughout the 1980s Costa Rica followed a slow path to economic recovery. Under the competent leadership of the central bank's president, Eduardo Lizano, the PLN conducted a strenuous and ultimately successful effort to renegotiate important components of the foreign debt. The recovery would have been stronger if it had not been for the precipitous decline in coffee prices brought on by the collapse of the International Coffee Organization's system of quotas and prices. Throughout the period and on into the 1990s, when the opposition again took office as a result of the 1990 election, Costa Rica operated under a strict International Monetary Fund (IMF) mandate to cut public expenditures and hold down inflation. Although the IMF goals were not always met, by 1993 the economy had essentially recovered to its pre-1980 levels, and it enjoyed modest growth in the 1990s and strong growth, often more than 6 percent annually, in the new millennium. For the entire period from 2000 to 2013, growth averaged 4.5 percent annually. The global financial meltdown that began in 2008, however, threatened to greatly weaken the economic outlook for Costa Rica, driving down tourism and threatening exports. Yet prudent anticyclical policies, such as reducing the cost of internal tourism to replace the decline in international tourism, helped restore the economy to reasonably good health. Despite this positive outlook, growing inequality and persistent poverty are serious problems that recent governments have not been able to overcome.

THE INTERNATIONAL ARENA

In 1986, the PLN won the national election, breaking the pattern of electoral victory that had normally oscillated between the PLN and the opposition party. It did so under the leadership of Oscar Arias Sánchez, and Arias took power in an increasingly threatening international environment brought on by crisis in Nicaragua.

When the Sandinista revolutionaries were fighting in Nicaragua to overthrow the Somoza dictatorship in the late 1970s, they found extensive support in their neighbor to the south. Although Costa Rica remained officially neutral in that conflict, there was a long-standing antipathy for Somoza and the harsh dictatorial regime that he represented. Public support for a Sandinista victory was overwhelming, and there is much evidence that the government of Costa Rica did what it could to help.[6]

Once the Sandinistas took power, however, relations between Costa Rica and the new regime rapidly deteriorated. Costa Ricans perceived the revolution as having a Marxist-Leninist orientation, and as such, it presented two threats to Costa Rica. First, it was a threat because of the fear that Communist expansionism would mean an eventual attempt by Nicaragua to take over Costa Rica. Second, it presented a threat to internal stability because it was feared that disgruntled Costa Ricans, especially among the university youth, would turn to revolutionary activity. In fact, in a small way the second expectation was realized. Terrorism, which had been almost unknown in Costa Rica, erupted with a number of ugly incidents in which lives were lost, and several clandestine "people's prisons" were discovered that were apparently designed to hide victims of political kidnappings. With the Reagan administration in the White House, yet a third fear gripped Costa Ricans: that the United States would invade Nicaragua, possibly using Costa Rican territory as a base of operations. Such an event would have thrust Costa Rica into an international military conflict for which it was not prepared and that it did not want. Indeed, as the Iran-Contra hearings in the United States were later to demonstrate, a clandestine airstrip was built in Costa Rica to help ferry arms to the Contra rebels, and a plan was developed for a so-called southern strategy involving Costa Rican territory.

On top of all of these concerns was the growing problem of Nicaraguan refugees. As the Contra war grew in ferocity and the Nicaraguan economy deteriorated, waves of refugees joined those already in Costa Rica who had fled the initial takeover of the Sandinistas. In short, Costa Ricans mortally feared being caught up in an impossible international conflict that could only result in deep harm to their country's national economy and society.

Upon assuming office, Oscar Arias dedicated himself to bringing peace to the region. Doing so was not only appropriate for a country that had long been noted for its internal peace and lack of an army but also urgently needed if Costa Rica hoped to avoid the problems noted above. Arias managed to draw together the leaders of all of the Central American countries and develop a peace plan that not only would involve Nicaragua but also would serve to end the civil war in El Salvador and the guerrilla war in Guatemala. For his efforts, Arias was awarded the Nobel Peace Prize.

Unfortunately, tensions between Costa Rica and its northern neighbor, Nicaragua, have boiled up in recent years. A long-standing dispute over navigation and other rights on the Río San Juan, which separates the two countries, reemerged as a flashpoint in Costa Rica's external relations in 2015–2016. Armed Costa Rican police forces have been sent to the northern border, while international diplomatic efforts have attempted to forestall violent clashes. Costa Rica has built an emergency access road near the border and periodically border incidents erupt to continue to darken relations between the two countries.

CONCLUSION

Costa Rican democracy, buffeted by political and economic changes worldwide and in the Central American region, nonetheless continues on a strong footing. Free and fair elections shift power but do not threaten the continuity of democratic rule. In the 1990 elections, the PLN lost the presidency to an opposition coalition led by the son of Calderón Guardia. Within a few months of this loss, the Sandinistas in Nicaragua were defeated in an upset election. These two elections saw the new decade emerging with new leadership in these two Central American neighbors. The dominant parties of the decade of the 1980s, the PLN in Costa Rica and the Sandinista National Liberation Front in Nicaragua, were being asked by the voters to take a backseat in order to allow fresh faces to try their hand at economic development, democratization, and peace. The dramatic changes in the Soviet Union and Eastern Europe did not go unnoticed in Central America, as capitalism and democracy rapidly began to replace socialism and dictatorship. New elections in 2002 brought the opposition Social Christian Party (PUSC) to power with the election of Abel Pacheco, a physician who had participated in an attempt to overthrow Figueres in 1955. Elections in 2006 and 2010 returned the PLN to power, yet voter frustration meant that in 2014 the PAC won for the first time. These shifts in political control are signs of a healthy democracy.

In the region, however, youth gangs and narco-traffickers have produced an explosion of criminal violence. Costa Rica has not been immune to this new challenge, with crime rates growing. In this context, peaceful, democratic Costa Rica once again faces challenges and opportunities for regional leadership as the one country in Central America with a long tradition of democracy. On the domestic scene, the ability of the economy to continue to grow remains a major challenge. Democratic rights were expanded as a result of the creation of the Sala IV, a constitutional court, which has been augmenting individual liberties at a rapid pace. Yet many Costa Ricans wonder if this movement has gone too far, granting individual rights that end up weakening the state. In the new century, Costa Rica has had incidents of mass protest that it had not experienced before. As already noted, voting abstention, historically never very high, increased to around one-third of the electorate, a sign for some of growing disenchantment with the political system. Political leaders have been sensitive to this shift in voter sentiment and have begun a new process of institutional reform that promises to keep Costa Rican politics on an even keel, but many believe that the old parties are not capable of real democratization. Corruption scandals have become more widespread and have reached higher than ever before, souring citizens on their government.

Costa Rica's open, democratic style of governance has enabled the country to withstand crises that would cause others to wilt. If the past is any guide to the future, Costa Rica will rise to the test and overcome its problems.

SUGGESTIONS FOR FURTHER READING

Alfaro-Redondo, Ronald, and Mitchell A. Seligson. *Cultura política de la democracia en Costa Rica y las Américas, 2014: Gobernabilidad democrática a través de 10 años del Barómetro de la Américas.* San José, Costa Rica: Estado de la Nación, 2014.

Bell, John Patrick. *Crisis in Costa Rica*. Austin: University of Texas Press, 1971.

Biesanz, Mavis Hiltunen, Richard Biesanz, and Karen Zubris Biesanz. *The Ticos: Culture and Social Change in Costa Rica*. Boulder, CO: Lynne Reinner Publishers, 1999.

Booth, John A. *Costa Rica: Quest for Democracy*. Boulder, CO: Westview Press, 1999.

Booth, John A. and Mitchell A. Seligson. *The Legitimacy Puzzle in Latin America: Democracy and Political Support in Eight Nations*. Cambridge: Cambridge University Press, 2009.

Cruz, Consuelo. *Political Culture and Institutional Development in Costa Rica and Nicaragua: World-making in the Tropics*. New York: Cambridge University Press, 2005.

Edelman, Marc, and Joanne Kenan, eds. *The Costa Rica Reader*. New York: Grove Weidenfeld, 1989.

Gudmundson, Lowell. *Costa Rica Before Coffee: Society and Economy on the Eve of the Export Boom*. Baton Rouge: Louisiana State University Press, 1986.

Hall, Carolyn. *Costa Rica: A Geographical Interpretation in Historical Perspective*. Boulder, CO: Westview Press, 1985.

Hall, Carolyn and Héctor Pérez Brignoli. *Historical Atlas of Central America*. Norman: University of Oklahoma Press, 2003.

Lehoucq, Fabrice Edouard. *The Politics of Modern Central America: Civil War, Democratization, and Underdevelopment*. Cambridge: Cambridge University Press, 2012.

Lehoucq, Fabrice Edouard, and Iván Molina Jiménez. *Stuffing the Ballot Box: Fraud, Electoral Reform, and Democratization in Costa Rica*. Cambridge Studies in Comparative Politics. New York: Cambridge University Press, 2002.

Palmer, Steven, and Iván Molina, *The Costa Rica Reader: History, Culture, Politics*. Durham, NC: Duke University Press, 2004.

Seligson, Mitchell A. *Peasants of Costa Rica and the Development of Agrarian Capitalism*. Madison: University of Wisconsin Press, 1980.

———. "Ordinary Elections in Extraordinary Times: The Political Economy of Voting in Costa Rica." In *Elections and Democracy in Central America*. Edited by John A. Booth and Mitchell A. Seligson, 158–184. Chapel Hill: University of North Carolina Press, 1989

Seligson, Mitchell A., and John A. Booth, "Trouble in Central America: Crime, Hard Times and Discontent," *Journal of Democracy* 21, no. 2 (April 2010): 123–135.

——— and John A. Booth. "Institutional Legitimacy in Central America: 2004–2010." In *The Routledge Handbook of Central American Governance*. Edited by Diego Sánchez-Ancochea and Salvador Martí i Puig, 149–162. New York: Routledge, 2014.

Seligson, Mitchelle A., and Juliana Martínez Franzoni. "Limits to Costa Rican Heterodoxy: What Has Changed in 'Paradise'?" In *Democratic Governance in Latin America*. Edited by Scott Mainwaring and Timothy R. Scully, 307–337. Palo Alto: Stanford University Press, 2010.

Seligson, Mitchelle A., and Edward N. Muller. "Democratic Stability and Economic Crisis: Costa Rica, 1978–1983." *International Studies Quarterly* 31 (September 1987): 301–326.

Vargas-Cullell, Jorge, Luis Rosero-Bixby, and Mitchell A. Seligson. *La Cultura política de la democracia en Costa Rica, 2004*. San José, Costa Rica: Centro Centroamericano de Población, 2005.

Wilson, Bruce M. *Costa Rica: Politics, Economics and Democracy*. Boulder, CO: Lynne Rienner, 1998.

Yashar, Deborah J. *Demanding Democracy: Reform and Reaction in Costa Rica and Guatemala, 1870s–1950s*. Stanford, CA: Stanford University Press, 1997.

NOTES

1. The data in this paragraph are drawn from World Bank data available online.
2. See the various years of the Freedom House index.

3. See Carolyn Hall, Héctor Pérez Brignoli, and John V. Cotter, *Historical Atlas of Central America* (Norman: University of Oklahoma Press, 2003), 63.

4. This section draws on Mitchell A. Seligson, "Costa Rica and Jamaica," in *Competitive Elections in Developing Countries,* eds. Myron Weiner and Ergun Ozbudun (Durham, NC: Duke University Press, 1987).

5. Hall, et al., *Historical Atlas of Central America,* 86.

6. See Mitchell A. Seligson and William Carroll, "The Costa Rican Role in the Sandinista Victory," in *Nicaragua in Revolution,* ed. Thomas W. Walker (New York: Praeger, 1982), 331–344.

21

NICARAGUA: AN UNCERTAIN FUTURE

Richard L. Millett

INTRODUCTION

Nicaragua, largest in area of the Central American republics, has a history marked by unfulfilled promises, frustrated hopes, and violent internal conflicts and external interventions. Obsessed with the past and dominated by conflicting personal ambitions, Nicaragua's political system offers few solutions to the nation's overwhelming social and economic problems.

Despite—or perhaps because of—this history, Nicaragua has enjoyed disproportionate attention from US scholars and political activists. Ruled briefly in the nineteenth century by an American named William Walker (a filibuster, or irregular military adventurer), occupied twice by US Marines in the first third of the twentieth century, and the scene of a nearly decade-long conflict between a Marxist regime and US-sponsored counterrevolutionary insurgents in the 1980s, the nation has frequently been the subject of fierce policy debates. The United States and other nations have also been interested in Nicaragua's potential as an interoceanic canal route. In addition, the Sandinista revolution in 1979 seemed to present an opportunity to test both the potential for social revolution in Central America and the possibility of creating a less dogmatic socialist state. Such hopes, like Nicaragua's aspirations to be the site of a canal, remain unfulfilled.

HISTORY

From the colonial period until the present Nicaragua has been the scene of international rivalries. Its indigenous population was decimated in part to provide labor for the mines of Peru. The British waged a prolonged conflict over the rule of its Caribbean coast and competed with the United States for control over the potential transisthmian canal route. The nineteenth-century filibustering expedition of William Walker reflected rivalries over control of the isthmian transit route as well as plans to annex lands for the expansion of slavery. It also was a product of the interminable civil conflicts between the Liberal Party and the Conservative Party, both of which at times preferred foreign intervention to defeat at the hands of their domestic opponent.

Washington's decision to build a canal through Panama rather than Nicaragua damaged relations and led to the 1912 Marine intervention. Fearing that Nicaragua's Liberals might grant a canal concession to some other nation, the United States entered into a de facto alliance with the Conservatives, with the presence of a small Marine unit ensuring Conservative rule until the mid-1920s.

The United States then attempted to withdraw the Marines, but this only contributed to another civil conflict and a much larger intervention in 1927. Washington imposed a peace settlement on Nicaragua's warring factions, providing for general disarmament, US supervision of the next two presidential elections, and the creation of a US-officered and trained constabulary force to be known as the National Guard. One Liberal general, Augusto César Sandino, rejected these terms and launched a guerrilla war against the Marines and the National Guard. Sandino's resistance endured until the last Marines departed at the start of 1933. Sandino then negotiated peace terms, but a year later he was murdered by the National Guard.

That Guard's commander, General Anastasio Somoza García, used that force to propel himself into the presidency in 1936, inaugurating more than forty-two years of family rule. The Somozas used three basic instruments—control of the National Guard, manipulation of the Liberal Party, and the image of a close alliance with the United States—to perpetuate themselves in power. In the process, they amassed vast wealth and established a network of corruption. The dynasty's founder was assassinated in 1956, but his sons Luís and Anastasio Somoza Debayle managed to hold on to power. They provided the United States with the launching pad for the abortive 1961 invasion of Cuba, and, in turn, Fidel Castro supported the creation of an anti-Somoza insurgency. When the Somozas used the devastating 1971 earthquake that leveled Managua to further enrich themselves and their cronies, popular discontent increased. A Marxist guerrilla movement, the Sandinista Liberation Front (FSLN), in existence since the early 1960s, began to attract support from wider elements of society. When opposition leader Pedro Joaquín Chamorro was murdered in early 1978, popular discontent exploded. Political and economic pressures exerted by business leaders, with support from the Carter administration, failed to oust President Anastasio Somoza Debayle, and national and international support coalesced around the Sandinistas. After a prolonged struggle, the Sandinistas forced Somoza into exile and occupied the capital in July 1979.

Sandinista leaders initially convinced non-FSLN politicians and business leaders to cooperate in forming a broad-based government. However, it soon became clear that real power lay with the nine-member Sandinista national directorate, which was intent on creating a controlled economy, supporting other Central American insurgency movements, and establishing close ties with Cuba and the Soviet Union. Internal political conflict increased, and in 1981, the United States began to support armed resistance to Sandinista rule. Known as Contras, these forces inflicted significant economic damage, but they were never able to seriously challenge Sandinista power. Elections were held in 1984, but, protesting conditions that they claimed made effective participation impossible, major elements of the political opposition boycotted the process. The FSLN used these elections to consolidate control, installing party leader Daniel Ortega as president and adopting a new constitution that incorporated the aims and principles of a socialist revolution. However, a combination of the costs of the ongoing Contra war, the impact of a US economic boycott, and the FSLN's own economic mismanagement ultimately devastated the economy and undermined FSLN efforts to consolidate their control.

A combination of mediation by Central America's presidents and a decision by the George H. W. Bush administration to pursue negotiated solutions to Central America's conflicts led to internationally supervised elections in 1990. To the surprise of the FSLN, these were won decisively by a fourteen-party coalition headed by Violetta Barrios de Chamorro, widow of Pedro Joaquín Chamorro. The FSLN, however, remained the largest bloc in the legislature. To govern effectively, the Chamorro administration made working agreements with the FSLN, including leaving General Humberto Ortega, brother of ex-president Daniel Ortega, in command of the military. This, however, broke up Chamorro's coalition and created problems with the US Congress.

Under the Chamorro administration Nicaragua experienced six years of political turmoil, economic crisis, and citizen insecurity. Determined to "govern from below," the FSLN obstructed legislation and resisted military reforms. Jobless and landless, former members of both the Contra and Sandinista forces again took up arms, returning some rural areas to a virtual state of war. Despite all this, some progress was made. Annual inflation, which under FSLN rule had surpassed 30,000 percent, fell to under 20 percent. The strength of the military was greatly reduced, the police were brought under government control, and the draft was ended. Most contras disarmed and some refugees returned. Humberto Ortega was eventually replaced as military commander, demonstrating a loss of FSLN control over the armed forces.

After a bitter fight the constitution was amended to reduce executive powers, protect private property, depoliticize the military, and bar the reelection of the president or any close relative. Finally, the Chamorro administration conducted reasonably fair—if far from perfect—elections in 1996 and peacefully transferred power to another party. The 1996 elections produced more than twenty candidates but quickly became a race between Daniel Ortega of the FSLN and an alliance of Nicaragua's factionalized Liberals, headed by Managua mayor José Arnaldo Alemán. Alemán won with 51 percent of the vote to 37.7 percent for Ortega. His administration managed to improve relations with the United States, but the economy remained a disaster and charges of corruption engulfed the regime. By the end of his term Alemán was seeking means to ensure immunity from future prosecution. Constitutional amendments approved by the legislature at the start of 2000 reduced the role of smaller parties, undercut the independence of the comptroller general's office, and made it more difficult to convict a president.

A combination of the changes in the electoral system and fears of a Sandinista return to power ensured the victory in the 2001 elections of Alemán's hand-picked candidate, his vice president, Enrique Bolaños Geyer. Once in office, however, President Bolaños turned on his predecessor, actively seeking his prosecution for corruption. He succeeded in getting Alemán convicted and imprisoned, but this cost him the support of the Liberal Party, leaving him with only a small minority of support in congress. Alemán continued to control the party even while under house arrest and, in alliance with the FSLN, gained control of the legislature and used it against Bolaños. Nicaragua entered into a prolonged period of political paralysis as various factions maneuvered to gain an advantage in the scheduled 2006 elections.

A deeply divided opposition opened the way for a return to power by Daniel Ortega and the FSLN in the 2006 elections. The Liberals split between pro- and anti-Alemán factions. A dissident group of Sandinistas formed their own party, the Sandinista Renewal Movement (MRS), and for a time appeared to be a major factor. The Nicaraguan constitution had been amended to give victory to anyone with a plurality in excess of 35 percent, and in the election Ortega and the FSLN won 38 percent to 28.3 percent for the anti-Alemán Liberals; the Alemán faction received 27.1 percent and the MRS 6.3 percent. The FSLN also won thirty-eight of the ninety-two seats in the National Assembly.

President Ortega governed by making deals with Aléman and by manipulating the courts and local and legislative elections. He benefited from close ties with the Venezuelan government, obtaining petroleum on favorable terms and receiving other assistance. As the 2011 elections approached, the Nicaraguan supreme court, packed with his supporters, ruled that the constitutional ban on reelection did not apply to Daniel Ortega, setting the stage for him to win another term. Aided by a divided opposition and an improving economy, Ortega won reelection with more than 60 percent of the vote, and his supporters gained a majority of the seats in the National Assembly. He further consolidated his political power in the 2012 municipal elections, when the FSLN gained control of almost every major town.

The second Ortega term produced economic growth, some expansion of social programs, and continued harassment of the fractured political opposition. The FSLN solidified control over the courts and the Supreme Electoral Council. Aided at first by economic assistance from Venezuela, it reduced poverty and gave the president high levels of public approval. The highlight of this term was the announcement of plans for a Chinese financed transisthmian canal, with the potential to transform Nicaragua's economy. Ortega chose his wife, Rosario Murillo, as his running mate in 2016. Widely viewed as the greatest influence on the president and, in the style of Evita Perón, directly linked to popular social and economic policies, her nomination also generated heated criticism abroad and from the domestic political opposition. This had little effect on the overwhelming victory of Ortega (72.5 percent) and the FSLN in the 2016 elections. The FSLN also took 71 of the 92 seats in the National Assembly with the Constitutional Liberal Party (PLC) finishing a distant second with 15 seats.

SOCIAL STRUCTURE

In 2015 Nicaragua had a population of approximately six million, most of whom were mestizos. Some Indians along the Caribbean coast remain ethnically distinct, and there is also a strong Afro-Caribbean influence on that coast, where much of the population emigrated from the British Caribbean. Because of its ethnic makeup and its isolation from the rest of the nation, the Caribbean coast was granted a measure of political and cultural autonomy in 1987.

The majority of Nicaraguans are Roman Catholic, but Protestant groups have made major inroads, so the nation today is about 22 percent evangelical Christian, and an evangelical political party finished third in the 1996 elections, though it later disappeared. There is also a significant Mennonite presence on the Caribbean coast.

Nicaragua is the largest Central American nation in area, and its economy is heavily dependent on agriculture. Nevertheless, it is also the region's most urbanized nation. Flows of refugees from conflict in the countryside exacerbated this situation in the 1980s and 1990s, and today the nation is more than 60 percent urban. Unemployment and underemployment remain high in urban areas. Nicaragua has the hemisphere's second-lowest GNP per capita.

Both business and labor are relatively well organized in Nicaragua. Many of the largest labor and peasant organizations are controlled by the FSLN. The major business group, the Superior Council of Private Enterprise (COSEP), was a center of anti-Sandinista opposition, but in recent years this has significantly decreased as much of the business sector has profited from the relative security and economic growth provided by the Ortega administration.

In contrast to most of the hemisphere, the military has never been a truly autonomous actor in Nicaraguan politics. It was first the tool of traditional parties, then the instrument of a foreign intervention, then the guardian of a prolonged family dynasty, and finally the bulwark of support for a revolutionary political project. Today, its ties to the FSLN have weakened, and it is becoming more like a traditional Central American military. Several regular changes of command have taken place, any fears that it would intervene in the political process have largely evaporated, and its size has been greatly reduced. Changes in the military code in 2014 expanded the institution's powers and gave it a greater role in internal security. The police have been separated from the military. The military has the highest level of popular confidence of any Nicaraguan institution, while the police have a somewhat lower level but still enjoy majority support. Contemporary issues include the growing degree of FSLN influence over the institution and plans to acquire new weapons from Russia.

Nicaragua's mass media have always been highly politicized. Under the Somozas and then again under the Sandinistas, the newspaper *La Prensa,* controlled by the Chamorro family, became a symbol of resistance to the regime in power. Over the last forty years, radio has become even more important than print media in efforts to boost support for or mobilize opposition to a particular regime. Television, too, has steadily increased its influence. Television was largely government-controlled until the 1990s, but today both national channels and widely available foreign programming reflect a broad variety of views. There is no formal censorship, though the government does exert significant economic pressures.

According to the 2014 survey of the Latin American Public Opinion Project a small majority (52.7 percent) of Nicaraguans are satisfied with the state of democracy in their country. Overall support for democracy is higher (68.4 percent), but has declined somewhat since 2010. The government's ability to maintain public security and provide some economic benefits and growth overcome any concerns about possible authoritarian tendencies.

POLITICAL INSTITUTIONS AND PARTIES

Nicaragua is governed under the Sandinista-authored constitution of 1987, but this was significantly altered by a series of amendments adopted in 1995 and by others added in 2014. In many ways, the government structure follows traditional Central American patterns, with a unicameral legislature, a theoretically independent electoral authority, a supreme court, and numerous autonomous agencies. Local government consists of two levels, departmental and municipal. There are fifteen departments plus the two semiautonomous regions along the Caribbean coast. Outside of these coastal regions, departments are generally dominated by the central government, but municipal governments have had a growing degree of autonomy. These, however, are chronically underfunded. Political parties are more vehicles for individual ambition than disciplined advocates of coherent positions. Popular culture still inclines to traditional patron-client relationships and to hopes for personal rewards. The president (and in the current case, his wife) are viewed as the dispensers of benefits and the creators of public policy, with the National Assembly, the courts, and the constitution relegated to much lesser roles.

Beginning in 1990 Nicaraguans elected municipal officials directly. The powers of municipal government were strengthened, and mayors became the most important local political figures. At least fifteen Nicaraguan cities have populations greater than fifty thousand, and metropolitan Managua's population is more than two million.

Under the rule of the Somoza family the executive branch was totally dominant, and the legislature and courts generally rubber-stamped whatever the president wanted. The FSLN's 1987 constitution then strengthened executive authority even further. In both cases, there was an extraconstitutional power that controlled the government. Under the Somozas this was the Somoza family and the National Guard. Under the Sandinistas it was the FSLN's nine-member national directorate. Today, political power is largely in the hands of elected officials. The president and vice president are elected for five-year terms. Presidential powers are broad, including the right to propose a budget, appoint cabinet members and other high officials, and, prior to 1995, to rule by decree. Thanks, in part, to the 2014 constitutional amendments, the president has great independent authority, especially if a state of national emergency is declared.

Nicaragua's unicameral legislature has ninety-three members. Complex constitutional provisions provide that twenty seats be elected from national party lists and seventy be elected departmentally under a system of proportional representation. In addition, defeated presidential candidates who win more than 1 percent of the vote are given a seat. This encouraged a proliferation of parties, with eleven winning one or more seats in 1996. However, in 2001 only the Liberal alliance, the FSLN, and the Conservatives (who won just one seat) gained seats in the legislature. Electoral law reforms in 2000 had changed the system, curbing the proliferation of smaller parties but also concentrating power in the hands of the two dominant parties. The splintering of the Liberal Party since then has further complicated the system and ensured a majority for the president's party. The revised constitution gives the assembly broad powers, including the ability to amend the constitution with a 60 percent majority. This became a reality in 2014 with presidential powers further enhanced, unlimited reelection allowed, and only a plurality needed for presidential elections.

As in much of Latin America, a weak judicial system presents a significant obstacle to efforts at democratic consolidation. Nicaragua has little tradition of an independent judiciary, and partisan efforts to manipulate the supreme court are constant. In recent years, the court has been a compliant instrument of presidential initiatives. Lower courts are poorly staffed and often overwhelmed by the rising crime rate. Conviction rates in criminal cases have been less than 5 percent. One result is that prisoners are often incarcerated for prolonged periods before coming to trial. Prisons are overcrowded and conditions fall well below minimal international standards. Despite such problems, Nicaragua still has a much lower crime rate than Guatemala, Honduras, or El Salvador and has significantly fewer issues with youth gangs and/or international organized crime. Citizen confidence in the police is also higher in Nicaragua.

A fourth power is the Supreme Electoral Council (CSE), which not only runs elections and certifies the results but also controls the Civil Register and issues citizens their identity cards (*cédulas*). In January 2000, an agreement between the Liberals and the FSLN reformed the electoral law, eliminating provisions requiring broad representation of political parties in the administration of local polling stations and giving the CSE virtual carte blanche in the appointment of these officials. The seven members of the CSE would be appointed by the Assembly and would need the approval of 60 percent of those voting. This ensured that the smaller parties would have no effective voice in the process. To gain a place on the ballot, any party that failed to win 3 percent of the vote in the previous general election must obtain the signatures of 3 percent of eligible voters. Only the Liberal alliance, the FSLN, and the Nicaraguan Christian Way (CCN) qualified for exemption from this provision. Nicaragua's Conservative Party managed to gain a spot on the 2001 ballot, but its presidential candidate garnered only 1.4 percent of the vote. Following President Ortega's 2011 reelection the FSLN gained control of the CSE. The results of the 2016 elections guarantee that this state of affairs will continue. Suffrage is universal for those sixteen and older and there are few claims of eligible voters being denied their rights. In presidential elections, the 2014 constitutional amendments eliminated the possibly of a residential runoff election with only a simple plurality required to win.

Among the most important of the autonomous governmental institutions are the central bank and the office of the comptroller. Both have been the scene of bitter partisan fights and as a result are now largely arms of the executive power.

Nicaragua has dozens of political parties, many of which exist only to promote individual ambitions and have no national structure. The political scene is dominated by the two major Liberal factions and the FSLN. The PLC is dominated by former president Alemán and merges three elements of Nicaragua's traditional Liberal Party. Because this party was long the vehicle of the Somoza dynasty, it is frequently accused of having ties with elements of that regime. The party has support among Nicaragua's upper and middle classes. It is pro-business and generally supportive of the United States in international affairs, and it has traditionally been strongly anti-Sandinista. Its strength, however, has declined. A dissident Liberal faction, the Independent Liberal Party (PLI), began emerging as Nicaragua's major opposition party. However, the Ortega administration utilized a compliant supreme court to oust the party's president before the 2016 elections, replacing him with an Ortega ally. Fifteen PLI deputies in the assembly who refused to accept this were also ousted. As a result, most PLI supporters boycotted the election. This enabled the PLC to finish second with 15.7 percent of the presidential and 14.7 percent of the assembly votes.

The FSLN has modified its Marxist rhetoric and now portrays itself as more of a social democratic party. It has strong support within the labor movement and in other mass popular organizations. It advocates increased government control over the economy, expanded social welfare policies, and an independent foreign policy. Its support has been damaged by a reputation for corruption derived from the massive looting of state resources at the end of its period in power, by deep internal divisions that resulted in the defection of some of the leadership before the 1996 elections, and by personal scandals revolving around the party's leader, former president Daniel Ortega, and his wife, Rosario Murillo. None of this, however, has reduced Daniel Ortega's control over the party. Several smaller parties, including the remnants of the traditional Conservative Party, retain legal status but have little if any power and must seek alliances with one of the Liberal factions to compete in elections. Political parties have limited popular support, having the lowest confidence rating (37 percent) of all national institutions.

PUBLIC POLICY

Nicaragua's public policies are a strange mixture of the revolutionary heritage of the Sandinistas and the personal ambition of Daniel Ortega. The prevailing climate of corruption has jeopardized many international aid sources and held up agreements with the International Monetary Fund. Industry has lagged behind other sectors in the limited economic recovery that has occurred, exacerbating the high rate of urban unemployment. Foreign investment in real estate grew under Bolaños, but has slowed under Ortega. Investment in other areas such as telecommunications has continued to grow. Remittances from Nicaraguans in the United States and elsewhere are a significant source of foreign exchange. The economy continues to grow at a rate of more than 4 percent and poverty has been reduced.

Nicaragua's external debt totals more than US$6 billion. Nicaragua was included in the World Bank's Highly Indebted Poor Countries program, thus making it eligible for the forgiveness of up to 80 percent of its debt, but this has been limited by concerns over internal politics. The ratio of debt to GDP has remained relatively stable in recent years. The nation consistently runs a deficit in its current accounts and depends on external aid to cover this. Venezuela's assistance to Nicaragua declined 25 percent in 2015 and the US House of Representatives approved a bill in 2016 that could jeopardize

Nicaraguan access to World Bank and Inter-American Development Bank funds. If the Trump administration supports this effort it could damage prospects for future economic growth.

The project of a Nicaraguan canal, financed by Hong Kong billionaire Wang Jing, is a central element of Nicaragua's future economic prospects. Severe economic losses by Wang Jing, combined with environmental issues and uncertain economic prospects, have thrown this effort into doubt. Virtually nothing has been done to advance the project since 2015 and prospects are clouded at best.

Nicaragua has little in the way of a regular civil service. Most government positions, at both the national and local levels, are seen as rewards for political support. The bureaucracy has been reduced from the massive levels it reached in the 1980s, but it is still inefficient and widely viewed as corrupt. Disputes over political patronage are a constant theme because apportioning positions is both a major motivation for and a constant source of tension in the formation and maintenance of political alliances and of internal party unity.

FOREIGN POLICY

Nicaragua's foreign policy revolves around four principal foci: relations with the United States; an alliance with other left-wing governments in Latin America, notably Venezuela; the constant search for foreign assistance and debt relief; and relations with other Central American nations, notably Honduras and Costa Rica. As throughout the hemisphere, Nicaragua has striven to expand economic ties and become more fully integrated into the global economy.

Initiatives in these areas are, at times, openly contradictory. The Bolaños administration was a strong supporter of free trade arrangements with the United States (CAFTA), but the Ortega administration placed greater emphasis on ties with the Venezuelan-sponsored ALBA group. Relations with Costa Rica have been complicated by disputes over rights along the San Juan River, especially as this relates to plans for a Nicaraguan canal, and by issues involving Nicaraguan immigrants to Costa Rica. Foreign policy is further hampered by the tendency to make major appointments on the basis of domestic political considerations rather than competency, by the deteriorating international image of the Ortega regime, and by persistent property disputes dating back to the 1979 revolution.

Despite open US efforts in the 1980s to topple the Sandinista regime, formal diplomatic relations were never broken off. The inauguration of President Chamorro ended these tensions, but other issues soon arose. Conservative circles in the United States opposed the Chamorro administration's working arrangements with the FSLN and made a constant issue of property claims against the government advanced by Nicaraguans living in the United States. Relations improved somewhat under the Alemán administration. Progress was made in resolving the property issue, and military-to-military contacts were established. The Bolaños administration attempted to improve relations with the United States, even sending troops to Iraq in 2003, but its efforts were handicapped by domestic political turmoil and by the emerging issue of disposal of surface-to-air missiles. The United States openly opposed Ortega in the 2006 elections, but initially relations with the Ortega administration were not hostile. But Ortega's manipulation of the constitution to allow himself a second term damaged relations, as did his administration's close ties to Venezuela. Criticism escalated prior to the 2016 elections. Relations with the Trump administration could deteriorate still further. US policy on migration will have a significant impact, although less than that on Nicaragua's northern neighbors, while congressional efforts to block access to international lending could prove a more important factor.

Nicaraguan governments over the past quarter century had generally good relations with Europe and with some of the international financial institutions. The Scandinavian nations were especially forthcoming with assistance. Spain and other members of the European Union also provided vital assistance. Hurricane Mitch in 1998 did produce a new outpouring of assistance, but increased evidence of corruption, the failure of the government to undertake needed economic reforms, and constant political conflict caused nations such as Denmark and Sweden to end aid disbursements, and in 2008 the European Union likewise suspended its assistance. Nicaragua's decision to recognize the tiny Russian puppet states taken from Georgia then further damaged relations with Europe. In addition, European assistance has increasingly moved from Latin America to Africa. So long as Ortega remains in office, relations are likely to remain cool but correct.

Relations with other Central American states were very tense during the Sandinista years; however, a regional initiative, led by Costa Rican president Oscar Arias, helped resolve the tensions and end the Contra war.

Under Ortega, relations with Honduras were severely strained over the ouster of President Zelaya. Tensions with Costa Rica have increased, in part because of border disputes related to the possible canal construction. Nicaraguan migration to Costa Rica has also become an issue. Relations with Venezuela remain close, despite that nation's political crisis. A recent World Court decision confirmed Colombian sovereignty over Caribbean islands disputed by Nicaragua, but significantly expanded the maritime areas under Nicaraguan control.

Like much of Latin America, Nicaragua has sought to increase trade with China. It still formally recognizes the government of Taiwan, but this could easily change in the near future. The canal issue will be a major factor in dealings with China. Ortega has also sought closer ties with Russia.

CONCLUSION: AN UNCERTAIN FUTURE

Nicaragua's future is uncertain. On the positive side, the economy has grown steadily, with annual increases between 4 and 5 percent over the past four years. Exports have risen at a constant pace, debt has been reduced, and reserves have grown. There seems little danger of a return to the open violence of previous decades, although the Ortega administration is increasingly inclined to use the courts to manipulate the political system. Politics remains mired in bitter conflict, reflecting both personal rivalries and past disputes. Transparency International's index of corruption gives Nicaragua the third-highest ranking in the Western Hemisphere. The population seems increasingly cynical about the entire process, as they see little hope offered by any party. The nation's reservoir of international sympathy and goodwill, generated by the events of the 1970s and 1980s and reinforced by the impact of Hurricane Mitch, seems exhausted, and both the United States and the European Union have suspended most assistance. Despite recent improvements poverty is endemic, much of the infrastructure is inadequate and worn out, and both human and financial capital tends to seek foreign prospects. The uncertain political future in Venezuela imperils the assistance from that nation, which has helped fuel recent economic growth. The canal project seems increasingly in jeopardy.

Nicaragua is not without important assets. Rural areas are generally not overpopulated, and the nation has some of the best soils in the hemisphere. Its geographic position offers several advantages, especially if the current canal project ever reaches fruition. International contacts forged in the past two decades, along with the considerable resources of the Nicaraguan diaspora, notably those in Miami, are significant potential assets. The current tendency toward increasingly authoritarian rule is a major issue, but given global trends toward populist rule this may be a smaller problem than previously anticipated. Ultimately, global economic trends, combined with the outcome of the canal project, will do more to shape Nicaragua's future than will internal political dynamics.

SUGGESTIONS FOR FURTHER READING

Literature on Nicaragua is extensive, but much of that produced in recent decades is highly partisan and of limited value. There has also been a sharp drop-off in scholarly work on Nicaragua in the past decade. The following are recommended as starting points for a fuller understanding of Nicaragua's past and present.

Booth, John A. *The End and the Beginning: The Nicaraguan Revolution*. Boulder, CO: Westview Press, 1985.

Cajina, Roberto. "Security in Nicaragua: Central America's Exception." Inter-American Dialogue working paper, Washington, DC, January 2013.

Christian, Shirley. *Revolution in the Family*. New York: Vintage, 1986.

Close, David. *Nicaragua: Navigating the Politics of Democracy*. Boulder, CO: Lynne Rienner, 2016.

———. *Nicaragua: The Chamorro Years*. Boulder, CO: Lynne Rienner, 1999.

Colburn, Forrest D. *Post-Revolutionary Nicaragua*. Berkeley: University of California Press, 1986.

European Union Election Observation Mission. "Nicaragua: Final Report: General Election and Parlacen Elections 2011." Available at www.eueom.eu/files/dmfile/moeue-nicaragua-final-report-22022012_en.pdf.

Gilbert, Dennis. *Sandinistas: The Party and the Revolution*. Malden, MA: Basil Blackwell, 1988.

Kirk, John M. *Politics and the Catholic Church in Nicaragua*. Gainesville: University Press of Florida, 1992.

Lean, Sharon. "The Presidential and Parliamentary Elections in Nicaragua, November, 2006." *Electoral Studies* 26 (December 2007): 828–832.

Macaulay, Neill. *The Sandino Affair*. Durham, NC: Duke University Press, 1985.

Millett, Richard. *Guardians of the Dynasty*. New York: Orbis, 1977.

Pastor, Robert. *Condemned to Repetition: The United States and Nicaragua*. Princeton, NJ: Princeton University Press, 1987.

Seligson, Mitchell, and John Booth, eds. *Elections and Democracy in Central America Revisited.* Pittsburgh: University of Pittsburgh Press, 1995.

Spalding, Rose. *Capitalists and Revolution in Nicaragua: Opposition and Accommodation, 1979–1993.* Chapel Hill: University of North Carolina Press, 1995.

Staten, Clifford, *The History of Nicaragua*, New York: Greenwood, 2010.

Walker, Thomas W., and Christine J. Wade, *Nicaragua: Emerging from the Shadow of the Eagle*, 6th edition. Boulder, CO: Westview Press, 2016.

Walter, Knut. *The Regime of Anastasio Somoza, 1936–1956.* Chapel Hill: University of North Carolina Press, 1993.

EL SALVADOR: CIVIL WAR TO UNCIVIL PEACE

Christine J. Wade

INTRODUCTION

In 1992 El Salvador experienced one of the region's most profound political and social transformations. Years of war and violent oppression that killed more than seventy-five thousand people and displaced one million more gave way to peace and democracy in one of the United Nations' most successful peacekeeping endeavors. The peace accords resulted in a restructuring of the country's armed forces, a new civilian police force, and judicial and electoral reforms. The 1994 "elections of the century" were the first truly democratic elections in the country's history. In 2009 the country witnessed the first peaceful transfer of power from one party to another, which many heralded as a milestone in the consolidation of democracy.

Yet El Salvador's peace has been an uneasy one for most Salvadorans. Institutions remain highly politicized and political parties are deeply polarized. Although many socioeconomic indicators have improved since the war's end, more than two decades of neoliberal policies have failed to invigorate the Salvadoran economy, now deeply dependent on remittances from abroad. The country suffers from a legacy of impunity and excessively high levels of social violence. For the past decade, "peacetime" El Salvador has had one of the highest homicide rates in the world. Some Salvadorans refer to the current situation as "not war," and public opinion polls frequently reveal that many believe that conditions are worse than during the war.[1] Although much progress has been made, the story of El Salvador is a cautionary reminder about the limitations of peace-building and democratization in postwar societies.

HISTORICAL BACKGROUND

Called Cuzcatlán by its indigenous inhabitants, El Salvador is the smallest and most densely populated country in Central America.[2] The only country in the region without a Caribbean coast, El Salvador had few natural resources. Instead, El Salvador's early economic development was characterized by the development of a monocrop economy with repeating patterns of development and decline. This pattern had a significant negative impact on the distribution of resources and created conflict between communal lands and private property. Throughout the nineteenth century, more and more communal land was taken over by Europeans and turned into private property.

The development of *haciendas* led, in turn, to the creation of new relationships between landowners and indigenous folk or peasants that could be characterized, for the most part, as feudal. The eighteenth-century expansion of haciendas had the added effect of concentrating land in a decreasing number of hands, primarily through usurpation of communal lands without compensation to the former owners. Meanwhile, the *hacendados* (landowners) had come to exercise increasingly firm control over the political life of the colony by the late eighteenth century, establishing a pattern of economic and political control that would continue for one hundred and fifty years.

Independence and the Repressive, Exclusionary State

The struggle for independence in El Salvador coincided with movements elsewhere in Central America during the second decade of the nineteenth century. In July 1823, the Federal Republic of Central America was created by the five former Central American colonies, and a year later Manuel José Arce, a Salvadoran, was elected its first president. This experiment lasted for fifteen years, then broke apart in the wake of a liberal-conservative struggle that was exacerbated by regional economic woes.[3] The principles on which the new Salvadoran republic was founded were those of classical liberalism—namely, that the role of the state was to maintain order, and economic policy was strictly laissez-faire, with the sanctity of private property its guiding principle. During this period emerged the basic policies that would shape the Salvadoran nation: encouragement of coffee production, construction of railroads to the ports, elimination of communal lands, laws against vagrancy that permitted the state to force peasants to work for hacendados at low wages, and repression of rural unrest. From the latter part of the nineteenth century into the early twentieth century most Salvadoran presidents were both generals and major coffee growers.

The 1886 constitution guaranteed that the liberals' policies would be pursued without obstacle. It established a secular state, decentralized state authority by allowing for the popular election of municipal authorities, and confirmed the inviolability of private property. The notion that the state has some responsibility for the health, education, and general well-being of the people it governs was not a part of Salvadoran political culture.

Landowners employed private armies to deal with rebellious peasants. Elements of these armies would become the Rural Police and the Mounted Police, created by decrees in 1884 and 1889, respectively, in the western coffee-growing departments. An 1895 decree extended these two forces over the entire country, and the Rural Police eventually became the National Police. In 1912 the National Guard was created to eliminate the hacendados' private armies and their excesses. Within a few years, however, the National Guard gained a reputation for being the "most cruel, most barbaric" security force.[4] A third security force, the Treasury Police (Policía de Hacienda), was created in 1936.

By the late 1920s coffee was central to the economic life of the country. Production expanded rapidly, while other crops and industries stagnated. This, coupled with growing business acumen and sophistication, moved the national economy from depression to boom. Coffee averaged between 75 and 80 percent of all exports between 1900 and 1922, then soared to 92 percent during the remainder of the 1920s. In 1919, 70,000 hectares were planted in coffee; by 1932 the figure had increased 34 percent to 106,000 hectares.[5] Despite the boom, the average Salvadoran's living conditions deteriorated during this period. This resulted in an increasingly militant labor union movement, which had begun as World War I ended, and a flirtation with authentic electoral democracy at the beginning of the 1930s that ended in a coup d'état, stolen local elections, a disastrous peasant uprising known as *La Matanza* that left thirty thousand dead, and a political division of labor under which the army assumed control of the state for the next sixty years while the oligarchy continued to control the economy.

Between 1932 and 1948 El Salvador was ruled by a succession of generals whose chief concern was to maintain order and protect elite interests. The ouster of General Salvador Castañeda Castro in the 1948 coup led to an extended period of institutionalized military rule from 1948 to 1979, wherein a cycle of alternating liberalizing and repressive regimes dominated the political landscape. The political system opened significantly following a reformist coup in 1960, allowing for the growth of popular organizations and opposition parties, most notably the Christian Democrats (*Partido Demócrata Cristiano*, PDC), a social democratic party. The Christian Democrats won seats in the assembly during the 1960s as well as mayoralties of the three largest cities, including San Salvador, in 1968. PDC victories presented a growing challenge to traditional interests. In 1972 the PDC coalition ticket, headed by José Napoleón Duarte, was denied electoral victory by the army.

This event, and subsequent fraud in the 1977 elections, led some Salvadorans to choose a revolutionary alternative that included political (mass, grassroots organizing) and military (armed struggle) dimensions. During the 1970s five revolutionary organizations, which had their roots in peasant uprisings of the previous century, in labor organizations of the 1920s, and in the Salvadoran Communist Party (PCS), began working among urban laborers and peasants. Divided over ideology and strategy for a decade, the five came together in the Farabundo Martí National Liberation Front (*Frente Farabundo Martí para la Liberación Nacional*, FMLN) in October 1980. In January 1981, the FMLN initiated military operations that would plunge El Salvador into eleven years of civil war.

The Civil War

In October 1979, a group of junior officers in the armed forces overthrew Carlos Humberto Romero. The goal of the coup was to remove military conservatives, derail the revolutionary movement, and institute long-overdue socioeconomic reforms. A number of prominent civilian opposition leaders who had been forced into exile after 1972 returned to participate in the new government. It soon became clear, however, that a group of extremely conservative officers had displaced the progressive coup leaders, and two months after the coup most of the civilians resigned. The United States encouraged the Christian Democrats to join the military in a new government. This, however, split the party, as some leaders—notably José Napoleón Duarte, the former mayor and exiled presidential candidate—accepted the military's offer while others left the party and created the Popular Social Christian Movement (MPSC), which allied itself with other center-left opposition parties, labor unions, and nongovernmental organizations (NGOs) to create the Democratic Revolutionary Front (FDR) in the spring of 1980. The FDR formed a political alliance with the FMLN and served as its international political voice for much of the next decade.

The United States, fearing another revolution in Central America, increased its involvement via a two-track policy. Politically, reforms and elections were emphasized; militarily, the Salvadoran armed forces were trained in counterinsurgency. Meanwhile, in May 1979 the generals informed their old allies in the oligarchy that they had to begin taking care of themselves.[6] This had two effects. One was the creation of paramilitary death squads, funded by wealthy members of the oligarchy in collaboration with sympathetic elements in the armed forces. The second was the creation in 1981 by some of these same oligarchs of their own political party, the Nationalist Republican Alliance (*Alianza Republicana Nacionalista*, ARENA).

Elections for a constituent assembly that would write a new constitution were held in 1982. ARENA won a plurality of the seats and effective control of the assembly. Only intervention by the US ambassador prevented ARENA from electing its founder, Roberto D'Aubuisson—a man closely tied to the death squads and identified ten years later by the United Nations' Truth Commission as the intellectual author of Archbishop Oscar Romero's assassination in March 1980—as interim president of the country.

In the 1984 presidential elections, the man who had been denied in 1972, José Napoleón Duarte, defeated D'Aubuisson. This and subsequent elections in the next decade—for the legislative assembly in 1985, 1988, and 1991 and for president in 1989—provided a "democratic government" that rarely exhibited the conditions of a functioning democracy: freedom of speech, the media, and party organization; freedom for interest groups; the absence of state-sponsored terror; the absence of fear and coercion among the population; and subordination of the military to civilian rule. Indeed, the armed forces continued to wield effective political control of the country. Duarte, elected on a platform of economic reform and peace negotiations with the FMLN, delivered neither. The PDC, rent by corruption and internal squabbles, split again in 1988. They lost the 1989 presidential election to ARENA's Alfredo Cristiani.

Peace

President Cristiani pledged in his June 1989 inaugural address to pursue peace negotiations with the FMLN. The flaw was that ARENA and the US government, now headed by President George H. W. Bush, who wanted to extract the United States from Central America as expeditiously as possible, assumed that the only thing to negotiate with the FMLN was its surrender. The government's failure to negotiate in good faith and several assassinations of leftist political leaders in the fall of 1989 convinced the FMLN that it had to demonstrate its power. The FMLN launched an offensive on November 11, 1989, bringing the war to San Salvador for the first time. This revealed both the FMLN's inability to provoke a general uprising and the army's incompetence. It also exposed the bankruptcy of US policy: despite nine years of training and more than US$2 billion in US military aid, the army could not rout the FMLN from the capital. The army's murder of six Jesuits and two other people in San Salvador during that struggle had an impact at least as great as the offensive itself. Together they marked the beginning of the end of the war.

The United Nations served as mediator of the negotiations, which began in 1989 and ended in 1991. The aims of the Chapúltepec accords were unprecedented: no previous civil war had ended with an agreement not simply to stop shooting but to restructure society. The accords established a precise calendar for implementation during the cease-fire period. They mandated demilitarization, including halving the size of the armed forces, eliminating the state security forces and the FMLN's guerrilla army; legalizing the FMLN as a political party; amending the constitution; reforming the electoral and judicial systems; settling the land distribution issue, one of the root causes of the war; and establishing independent commissions to identify those responsible for major human rights abuses and to purge the army of its most serious human rights violators. The United Nations Observer Mission in El Salvador (ONUSAL) was created to verify the implementation of the agreements, and its mission was later expanded to observe the 1994 elections.

By 1993 a new police force, the National Civilian Police (*Policía Nacional Civil*, PNC), had replaced the old security forces; a new governmental institution, the National Council for Human Rights (*Procuraduría de Derechos Humanos*, PDDH), was created to receive citizen complaints about governmental abuses; the army was reduced in size and sent to its barracks, with all its special units disbanded and its officer corps purged; the virtually nonfunctioning judicial system was experiencing the first steps toward reform; and the FMLN was a legal political party. Perhaps most significant was the transformation of El Salvador's political culture: it was no longer acceptable to kill people for political reasons.

SOCIAL AND CLASS STRUCTURE, AND INTEREST GROUPS

Social and Class Structure

El Salvador's poverty has generally declined over the past two decades, fluctuating between 30 and 40 percent. In 2014, 31.8 percent of Salvadorans lived below the poverty line, with 7.6 percent in extreme poverty. A new multidimensional poverty indicator first used by the Salvadoran government in 2014 suggested the national poverty rate was 35.3 percent with rural poverty at 58.5 percent. Though El Salvador ranks below the Latin American average in human development, there have been significant improvements in various development indicators in recent years. With a GDP per capita in 2014 of US$4,120, El Salvador ranked second highest in Central America. In 2015 fourteen infants died for every thousand live births, and the death rate for children under five was seventeen per thousand live births. The average Salvadoran completes six and a half years of education. The literacy rate, at 88 percent nationwide and 79 percent in the countryside, is one of the lowest in Latin America. Inequality has persisted in El Salvador despite overall reductions in poverty in recent years. According to the World Bank, in 2013 the richest 20 percent of the population consumed 49.8 percent of national income, while the poorest 20 percent consumed 5.5 percent. El Salvador's Gini coefficient was 43.5.[7]

The Churches and Social Change

The development of Christian Base Communities (*Comunidades Eclesiales de Base*, CEBs) in the late 1960s and 1970s throughout the region was a reflection of and a means of teaching the tenets of liberation theology to people. Key documents, including those originating in the Second Vatican Council (1962) and the 1968 bishops' conference at Medellín, Colombia, called on the church to denounce injustice and established a "preferential option for the poor." In El Salvador, the message of social justice offered through CEBs was labeled "Communist" and "subversive" by the right. Between 1972 and 1989 eighteen Catholic priests, one seminary student, one Lutheran minister, three nuns, and a lay worker from the United States were murdered or disappeared for their work in defense of the poor and human rights.

Although he was selected in 1977 by the Vatican for the post because he was thought to be conservative, San Salvador's new archbishop, Oscar Arnulfo Romero, soon became a champion of social justice and called for an end to the violence that was consuming the country. His assassination while delivering mass on March 24, 1980, served as a catalyst for many to join the guerrillas. The murder of three Maryknoll nuns and a lay worker in December underscored the danger faced by religious workers. After Romero's death, dozens more priests and nuns were driven into exile, while a handful continued their ministries in guerrilla-controlled areas. Despite the violence, the Catholic Church, along with the Anglicans and Lutherans, pushed for a negotiated end to the war throughout the 1980s. Ironically, it was this targeted violence against the church that ultimately helped end the war. On November 16, 1989, the US-trained Atlacatl Battalion entered the grounds of the Jesuit Universidad Centroamericana José Simeón Cañas and killed six Jesuit professors (including the rector), their housekeeper, and her daughter. The murders caused the United States to suspend military aid, and El Salvador's new president, Alfredo Cristiani, was forced to the negotiating table.

Many of the CEBs disrupted by the violence have not recovered, and a change in archbishops has hindered their regrowth. The 1994 appointment of Spanish-born Fernando Sáenz Lacalle, a member of Opus Dei, following the death of Romero's successor, Archbishop Arturo Rivera Damas, was seen as a blow to human rights and social justice. In December 2008 José Luis Escobar Alas was appointed to replace Sáenz Lacalle as archbishop.

Evangelical Protestants came to play an increasingly important role in politics. The evangelical movement, which gained momentum during the war, represented a conservative social counterpoint to the Catholic lay community. Powerful figures, such as Edgar López Bertrand (Brother Toby), of the Baptist Biblical Tabernacle Friends of Israel, drew considerable crowds to their services. They also had increasing political clout. President Tony Saca, himself an evangelical Protestant, invited Brother Toby to deliver the prayer at his inauguration. Presidential candidates for the 2009 elections, both Catholic, aggressively courted evangelical congregations, which broke for ARENA in 2004.

The appointment of the first Latin American pope marked some speculation as to whether he could popularize Catholicism in the country again. Shortly after being elected, Pope Francis advanced Archbishop Oscar Romero for sainthood in 2013. He was declared a martyr for the faith in February 2015. Romero was beatified in May 2015, thirty-five years after his assassination, in a large public ceremony in San Salvador.

Elites and Business

During the 1990s, significant disagreement emerged among the economic elite over economic policy as well as between important parts of the elite and the government. El Salvador's once monolithic oligarchy disappeared. A generation earlier the monolith had two parts: the traditional agricultural sector, whose wealth was exclusively in the land—coffee, cotton, and/or sugar cane—and the landowners who had diversified into finance and industry. By the middle of the decade there were four clearly identifiable sectors: financial, commercial, industrial, and agricultural. In each of the first three sectors there was a small subsector that controlled the overwhelming majority of the capital within that sector. The result was not only intersectoral conflicts but intrasectional disputes, as smaller players battled to stay in the game.

Two of the most prominent NGOs in El Salvador came to represent the triumph of new industrial and commercial elites over the traditional agrarian sector. The National Association of Private Enterprise (ANEP), established in 1966, has played a very influential role in economic and public policy. Its membership comprises the country's most prominent businesspeople and associations, transnational corporations, and public servants. Former Salvadoran president Tony Saca served as president of ANEP from 2001 to 2003. The group was very critical of the Funes administration (2009–2014), the FMLN's first presidential administration. The Salvadoran Foundation for Economic and Social Development (FUSADES) was created in 1983 with a large grant from the United States Agency for International Development (USAID) to promote neoliberal reforms. Like ANEP, the think tank has also enjoyed significant influence over economic policy. When Cristiani, one of the original members of the board of directors, was elected president in 1989 he appointed several members of FUSADES to his cabinet and other positions.

Women

Women's participation in public life has grown significantly in recent decades. During the Cristiani administration, two of his most competent ministers, those heading the planning and education ministries, were women. Two women were members of the FMLN's negotiating team at the peace talks, and the party later adopted a rule that one-third of all its candidates for office must be women. In 1999, the FMLN's vice presidential nominee was a woman, and in 2004 the vice-presidential nominees of ARENA and the CDU-PDC coalition tickets were women. The ARENA victory in 2004 gave El Salvador its first female vice president. Neither ARENA nor the FMLN had women on their presidential or vice presidential tickets in 2009 or 2014. In the 2015–2018 legislative assembly, twenty-seven of eighty-four deputies (32 percent) were women.

In preparation for the 1994 elections a broad coalition of women's organizations hammered out an agenda called *Mujeres '94* (Women '94), which it asked every party to adopt as part of its platform. Only the FMLN agreed, thanks to the pressure of its women members. By the mid-1990s women's organizations had formulated legislative bills to guarantee workers' rights in the *maquiladoras*, make rape a public crime and no longer require a witness (other than the victim) to the rape in order to press charges, require men to prove they are *not* the father of a given child, and ensure inclusion of articles that protect women in the new penal code. A new education law guaranteed equal access for girls, barred discrimination based on gender, and proscribed sexist stereotypes in textbooks. In 2009 President Funes introduced the *Cuidad Mujer* (City for Women) project, which creates safe zones in urban areas for women to access social services. In 2011 the assembly passed the Law of Equality, Equity and the Eradication of Violence Against Women, which guarantees equal access to education, equal pay, and various protections against discrimination. Despite this, violence against women, both public and domestic, remains high. The ban against abortion, which provides for no exceptions, is the most stringent in the region. Beyond simply banning the procedure, El Salvador's law criminalizes it, imposing harsh jail sentences for both the provider and the woman. The ban led to the rise of back-alley abortions, mostly among poor women. As of 2016, seventeen women had been convicted of "intentional" miscarriages.[8] In 2016 the FMLN introduced legislation to repeal the abortion ban, which if passed would legalize abortion in cases of rape, incest, risk to the life of the mother, or an unviable fetus.

POLITICAL PARTIES AND ELECTIONS

Presidential elections are held every five years, while elections for the eighty-four deputies in the legislative assembly and the 262 mayors are held every three years. Elections and electoral reforms are overseen by the Supreme Electoral Tribunal (TSE), an electoral commission created by the peace process. Though no election cycle has been without some irregularities and many necessary reforms still linger, elections since 1994 have generally been considered free and fair.

Political parties did not emerge in El Salvador until the 1920s. The first modern party was the Communist Party (PCS), which was banned following the 1932 uprising. From 1932 until 1944 General Maximiliano Hernández Martínez governed through the Pro-Patria National Party, the only legal party at that time. The party changed its name to the National Conciliation Party (PCN) in 1961, dominating elections until 1982. The PCN and the center-right Christian Democratic Party (PDC), founded in 1960, were disbanded in 2011 for failing to meet the required minimum vote threshold in the 2004 elections.

The current Salvadoran party system is dominated by former wartime rivals the right-wing ARENA and the left-wing FMLN. Whereas smaller right-wing parties have at times benefited from ARENA's declining vote share, centrist parties struggle to survive. Parties must win 3 percent of the vote (or 6 percent in coalition races) to remain registered political parties. Electoral reforms permitted independent candidates to run for office for the first time in 2012.

The 1994 elections were hyperbolically dubbed the "elections of the century" because they were the first to occur after the war's end, because the FMLN was participating for the first time as a legal party, and because a president (who serves for five years), assembly deputies, and mayors (groups that serve three-year terms) were all being elected. Although ARENA won the largest vote share in the 1994 elections and its candidate, Armando Calderón Sol, won the presidency, the FMLN's fortunes increased significantly in the coming years. In the 2000 elections, the FMLN won more seats than ARENA in the legislative assembly.

Although the FMLN steadily increased its vote share in legislative and municipal elections in 1997, 2000, and 2003, it struggled in presidential contests. Internecine political battles within the party created the impression that the party could not govern at the presidential level and resulted in candidates without broad national appeal. As a result, ARENA handily won presidential contests in 1999 and 2004.

The 2009 elections were the first time since 1994 that elections for all offices would be held during the same year. However, the TSE implemented reforms that separated polling days for the legislative and municipal and presidential elections by more than a month. It was a contentious campaign, pitting ARENA's Rodrigo Avila, a former PNC director, against popular television journalist Mauricio Funes for the FMLN. Twenty years of failed ARENA policies left it vulnerable to the FMLN's moderate candidate. Funes, who had not been a guerrilla and was not a member of the FMLN, carved out a centrist position and easily rebuffed ARENA's fear campaign of previous election cycles. Unlike prior US administrations, the new Obama administration vowed to work with the victorious party.

The January legislative and municipal elections promised to be a preview of the presidential elections. The FMLN won 35 seats, ARENA 32, PCN 11, PDC 5, CD 1, and FDR none. The FMLN also increased its share of mayoralties from 58 to 96 (75 on its own and 21 in coalitions), although it lost San Salvador. ARENA, which won San Salvador for the first time since its loss in 1997, suffered a number of losses, dropping from 148 to 122 municipalities. The PCN and PDC lost 14 and 16 municipalities, respectively. Following the legislative and municipal elections, the PDC and PCN withdrew their presidential candidates and lent their support to ARENA. Most of the FDR, which failed to win any seats in the legislative assembly, supported the FMLN.

Funes defeated Avila, 51 to 48 percent. On June 1, 2009, Tony Saca transferred power to Mauricio Funes, the first transfer of power from one party to another since the signing of the peace accords. In the aftermath of the election, former president Alfredo Cristiani, who initiated ARENA's dominance in 1989, returned to head the party—a clear sign that the party was regrouping.

ARENA's electoral fortunes improved in the March 2012 legislative and municipal elections, capturing the most seats in the assembly, 33, and the most municipalities, 116. The FMLN won 31 seats in the Assembly and 95 municipalities, 10 of those in coalitions. Smaller parties picked up the remainder of the seats, but the most prominent of these was the new Grand Alliance for National Unity (GANA). GANA was created by former members of ARENA, including former president Tony Saca, following the 2009 elections. The defections, which included more than a dozen deputies, shifted the balance of power in the assembly away from ARENA. The party, which had been working in coalition with the FMLN since the 2009 defections, won 11 seats in the assembly and 18 municipalities in its first electoral contest.

In 2012 and 2013 the Supreme Electoral Tribunal (TSE) passed a number of reforms that had long been stalled by the partisan body. These changes included a shift from voting by last name to residential voting, the right of Salvadorans living abroad to vote overseas, a quota system requiring that 30 percent of all candidates be women, voting for candidates rather than slates, and replacing the winner-take-all system with proportionality in municipal council elections.[9] Those changes would take effect in the 2014 and 2015 elections.

In December 2012, former president Tony Saca announced his intention to run for president in the 2014 election on the GANA ticket, making him the first democratically elected president to run for a second term. Saca faced the FMLN's Salvador, Funes's vice president, Salvador Sánchez Cerén, and ARENA's Norman Quijano, the mayor of San Salvador, in the February 2014 president elections. Saca won enough votes (11.4 percent) to force a second round between Quijano (38.96 percent) and Sánchez Cerén (48.93), who narrowly missed the 50 percent of the vote required for a first round victory.

The March 2014 runoff was particularly contentious. In particular, Quijano launched a massive ground campaign to rally voters. His strategy worked—voter turnout increased by 5 percent between the first and second rounds. Both candidates claimed victory before the results were announced, and Quijano even threatened that the military would intervene to protect democracy. ARENA demanded a vote by vote recount and rallied its supporters into the streets with allegations of fraud. The final vote count gave Sánchez Cerén 50.11 percent to Quijano's 49.89 percent, a margin of victory of about 6,300 votes. Not only was it the closest margin in a presidential election, but Sánchez Cerén was elected with the most votes of any president. Also noteworthy, the 2014 elections were the first in which Salvadorans living abroad were permitted to vote. Approximately 22.5 percent of registered overseas voters participated in the second round of voting, 60 percent favoring Sánchez Cerén.[10]

There was also controversy surrounding the 2015 legislative and municipal elections as the result of a failure of the TSE's computer system. It took a full month to hand count the votes. ARENA won 35 seats, the FMLN won 31 seats, and GANA won 11 seats, with the PCN and PDC winning 6 and 1 seats respectively.

POSTWAR GOVERNMENT AND PUBLIC POLICY

The Cristiani and Calderón Sol administrations implemented most of the key elements of the peace accords, though not always with transparency or as intended by the accords. Electoral and judicial reforms must be approved through the legislative assembly under the auspices of the 1983 constitution, which gave ARENA significant control over the content and implementation of the reforms. The Cristiani administration failed to accept the findings or implement the recommendations of the Truth

Commission, which assigned most of the blame for abuses during the war to the state. The 1993 amnesty law limited victims' access to justice in El Salvador, though the law was ruled unconstitutional in 2016.

Beginning with the Cristiani administration, four successive ARENA administrations pursued neoliberal economic policies as recommended by international financial institutions. Much of these reforms focused on the privatization of state-owned enterprise, tariff reduction and elimination, a new value-added tax (IVA), and the liberalization of monetary policy. The banks, coffee, and sugar were privatized under Cristiani, who became a major stakeholder in Banco Cuscatlán as a result of the sale. Armando Calderón Sol, the first president elected after the signing of the peace accords, oversaw the privatization of the state-owned telephone and electric companies and an increase in the IVA to 13 percent, which disproportionately affected the poor and working class. Between December 1991 and August 1999 minimum daily salaries declined from 28.18 to 27.37 *colones*.[11] In another measure, GDP per inhabitant grew dramatically over the decade, from US$1,002 in 1991 to US$2,258 in 2003. Most of that increase, however, was lost to inflation. Running as high as 19.9 percent in 1992, the cumulative inflation rate was 186 percent by 1998. By the turn of the century the government had inflation under control, although it continued to exceed growth.

Calderón Sol's successor, Francisco Flores, demonstrated an unwavering commitment to the neoliberal model, as well as an unwillingness to engage in dialogue with civic groups or members of the opposition. Objecting to government plans to privatize the health system, the Social Security Institute Union (STISSS) began a strike in November 1999. President Flores refused to negotiate, and the strike continued until thirty-six hours before the March 2000 elections, when a marathon session resulted in an agreement to return to work. It was a political fiasco for Flores. A second major health care strike, collectively referred to as the "white marches," erupted in October 2002 over the privatization of services. The strike ended nine months later following government assurances that the health care system would not be privatized.

By 2000, El Salvador's economy was in deep trouble. GDP growth declined throughout Flores's tenure, from 3.4 percent in 1999 to 2.2 percent in 2002 and to 1.8 percent in 2003. In 2003 the annual rate of inflation was 2.5 percent, with less than 2 percent growth. Inflation doubled in 2004 while growth lagged at a mere 1.5 percent. In January 2001 Flores's Law of Monetary Integration, which dollarized the economy, was passed by the legislature. The policy has had a disproportionate impact on the standard of living of the poor, as rounding up prices from the conversion became a common practice among vendors in the informal sector.[12] Thus, inflation for the poor was higher than for the general population.

The Flores government was also confronted with growing public insecurity. In 1999 El Salvador's murder rate was sixty-five per hundred thousand, the highest in the hemisphere. Flores cited the influx of criminal street gangs from the United States, such as *Mara Salvatrucha* (MS-13) and the 18th Street gang, as the reason for El Salvador's insecurity. Flores's *mano dura* (iron fist) legislation targeted gang activity, but it did little to address the growing problem of social violence.

ARENA's fourth consecutive president, Antonio Elías Saca, promised to promote social and economic security. Shortly after taking office in 2004, Saca imposed *super mano dura* in a further effort to crack down on gang violence. Although mano dura and its successor were very popular with the public, they did little to stem the violence. By July 2005 El Salvador's murder rate climbed to twelve per day, nearly double that of the previous year. Saca also sought to control social protest through the 2006 Special Anti-Terrorism Law (*Ley Especial Contra Actos de Terrorismo*). The law criminalized common means of protest, including demonstrations and marches. More than a dozen prominent social activists were arrested in the town of Suchitoto in July 2007 en route to the town to protest water privatization. Although the charges were ultimately dropped, the arrests revealed the government's intention to quash its opposition.

Economic growth (the GDP increased 4.2 percent in 2006 and 4.7 percent in 2007) was insufficient to keep pace with the rising cost of living. Despite increases in the minimum wage for industrial and agricultural workers in 2006, real wages were still lower than their 1996 levels—and lower than they had been before the war. Saca also announced the creation of a multipoint poverty reduction program. Economic problems were exacerbated by the 2008–2009 global recession, which retarded growth and resulted in a dramatic increase in poverty.

Mauricio Funes inherited a myriad of problems, but growing criminal violence was the most serious. In 2009 El Salvador had one of the highest homicide rates in the world, at seventy-one per hundred thousand. Although murders decreased slightly in 2010, they rose by almost 10 percent in 2011. Authorities continued to blame gangs, though it was increasingly clear that organized crime and drug cartels were also responsible for the violence. In 2010 the assembly passed a controversial law criminalizing gang membership, reminiscent of the initial mano dura policy. Funes authorized joint patrols by the police and military, and in 2011 he named retired general and former minister of national defense David Munguía Payés as the minister of justice and public security and then in 2012 retired general Francisco Ramón Salinas Rivera as the director of the PNC. El Salvador's supreme court later ruled those appointments were a violation of the peace accords.

In March 2012 members of MS-13 and the 18th Street Gang agreed to a truce in exchange for better prison conditions for incarcerated members and other benefits. Though the truce was mediated by a Catholic bishop and former FMLN legislator, it was later revealed that Funes and Munguía Payés had played a significant role in the truce. In December 2012, the truce was expanded to include "safe cities" in ten municipalities where the gangs would cease operations. The truce effectively ended in 2014 after Munguía Payés, the presumed intellectual author of the truce, was forced to resign.

Homicides continued to rise in 2014 and 2015. In July 2015 gang members sought to force the government to negotiate a new truce by imposing a week-long transport strike throughout San Salvador, crippling the capital. By the end of 2015 El Salvador's homicide rate skyrocketed to 104 per 100,000, the world's highest by far. The Sánchez Cerén government redoubled the government's militarized approach to public security. In April 2016, the legislative assembly passed new anti-gang legislation that criminalized negotiations with gang members and classified gang members as terrorists, among other things. In addition to concerns about the efficacy of such policies, allegations of state abuses included extrajudicial killings and death squads in rural areas as police-gang violence grew in 2016. In May twenty-one people involved in the 2012 gang truce, including chief mediator Raul Mijano, were arrested. At the time of this writing, no high-ranking member of the Funes administration had been arrested for their role in the truce. Some suggested the arrests were politically motivated and counterproductive.

Also troubling were revelations, caught on video, that members of the Funes administration and ARENA party officials had met with leaders of the MS-13 and 18th Street gangs in February 2014 to offer inducements to mobilize gang members to vote for their candidates in the 2014 elections.

Those revelations came amid heightened attention to government corruption. In May 2014 Francisco Flores was accused of diverting $15 million in earthquake relief donations from Taiwan following the 2001 earthquakes. After several months on the run, he turned himself in to authorities in September and was placed under house arrest. Flores died of a cerebral hemorrhage in January 2016 at the age of fifty-six. Past presidents Tony Saca and Mauricio Funes were also investigated for corruption. Tony Saca was arrested in October 2016 on charges of corruption. Saca and several members of his administration were accused of embezzling nearly $250 million. Funes, who was being investigated for illicit enrichment, was granted asylum for political persecution by Nicaragua in September 2016 though no charges had been brought against him at the time. Funes maintained, through numerous Twitter posts, that the investigation was politically motivated. In addition to the past presidents and members of their administrations, other public officials, including former attorney general Luis Martinez, and private businessmen were also arrested on corruption charges in 2016.

The cost of violence had a significant impact on the Salvadoran economy. The country's Central Bank estimated that violence cost approximately $4 billion annually, or about 16 percent of GDP.[13] Additionally, the Salvadoran economy, heavily dependent on the United States, was affected by the global recession. Growth fell more than 3 percent in 2009 and averaged only 1.85 percent between 2010 and 2015. By 2016 the country was in a serious fiscal crisis, unable to pay its bills. A political stalemate between ARENA and the FMLN compounded the crisis.

GLOBALIZATION AND INTERDEPENDENCE

Unlike other Central American countries, the United States demonstrated relatively little interest in El Salvador until the 1979 military coup. US interest in the country accelerated under the Reagan administration, which saw the civil war in El Salvador as an extension of the revolution in Nicaragua and Soviet expansion in the hemisphere. Soon El Salvador became one of the most important countries in the US sphere of influence. El Salvador has remained one of the United States' strongest allies in the region, committing troops to the US-led coalition in Iraq and participating in CAFTA and the Partnership for Growth initiative.

El Salvador has become a transnational society. More than one million Salvadorans fled the country during the war, at least half of them to the United States, though they were not eligible for asylum during that time. Salvadoran migration to the United States has increased dramatically in recent years. In 2010, the Census Bureau estimated that there were 1.8 million people of Salvadoran origin in the United States, making them the fourth-largest Latino population in the United States. Approximately 250,000 of the Salvadorans in the United States were under temporary protected status (TPS), a special program that allowed individuals from specified countries to register to work legally in the United States.

In 2014, a surge of unaccompanied minors—almost fifty-two thousand—from El Salvador, Guatemala, and Honduras revealed the desperation of the region's youth in fleeing violence. In 2016 the Obama administration announced that it would allow a limited number of Central Americans to apply for asylum.

The steady flow of Salvadoran emigrants has been vital to sustaining the Salvadoran economy. In 1991 US$790 million was sent to families in El Salvador; by 2004 that figure had increased to US$2.5 billion, or 17 percent of El Salvador's GDP. In 2008 remittances totaled US$3.8 billion, nearly 20 percent of GDP. Though remittances declined in 2009 as a result of the global economic recession, they rebounded, reaching US$4.3 billion in 2015. Approximately one-third of Salvadoran households received remittances, which were commonly used for housing, education, and consumer goods.

The Salvadoran community in the United States was very active in promoting transnational issues, including immigration reform, labor rights, and the right of Salvadorans living abroad to participate in overseas voting.

CONCLUSION

Although it is clear that El Salvador has made significant progress toward the consolidation of democracy in the more than twenty years since the "elections of the century," many challenges remain on El Salvador's road to lasting peace and democracy. High rates of social violence, corruption, poverty, inequality, impunity, and political polarization have challenged successive governments and continue to undermine the quality of peace. Gang violence, and the policies used to combat it, threatened hard-won democratic principles, including due process and human rights. Many Salvadorans, devoid of economic opportunity and security, made their way to the United States in even greater numbers than during the war.

Despite the difficulties, there were some positive developments in postwar El Salvador. In November 2009, President Mauricio Funes awarded the National Order of José Matias Delgado to the Universidad Centroamericana Jesuits in a public act of atonement for mistakes by past governments. At a ceremony in January 2010 celebrating the eighteenth anniversary of the peace accords, Funes offered the first formal apology for the war by a Salvadoran president. In his apology, he acknowledged the human rights abuses that had occurred during the war and asked the Salvadoran people for forgiveness. In 2014 President Sánchez Cerén published, for the first time, the Truth Commission's report detailing abuses committed during the war. Although the 2016 revocation of the 1993 Amnesty Law has yet to result in any convictions, there was renewed hope of justice for the war's victims. In March 2017 a judge reopened the case of the El Mozote massacre, where more than one thousand civilians were killed by the army. These important advances were tempered by present-day realities for most Salvadorans, for whom the end of war failed to deliver peace.

SUGGESTIONS FOR FURTHER READING

Boyce, James K., ed. *Economic Policy for Building Peace: The Lesson of El Salvador.* Boulder, CO: Lynne Rienner, 1996.

Ching, Erik. *Stories of War in El Salvador: A Battle Over Memory.* Chapel Hill: University of North Carolina Press, 2016.

Ladutke, Larry. *Freedom of Expression in El Salvador: The Struggle for Human Rights and Democracy.* Jefferson, NC: MacFarland, 2004.

Montgomery, Tommie Sue. *Revolution in El Salvador: Origins and Evolution.* Boulder, CO: Westview Press, 1995.

Moodie, Ellen. *El Salvador in the Aftermath of Peace.* Philadelphia: University of Pennsylvania Press, 2010.

Popkin, Margaret. *Peace Without Justice: Obstacles to Building Rule of Law in El Salvador.* University Park: Pennsylvania State University Press, 2000.

Stanley, William. *The Protection Racket State: Elite Politics, Military Extortion, and Civil War in El Salvador.* Philadelphia: Temple University Press, 1996.

Wade, Christine J. *Captured Peace: Elites and Peacebuilding in El Salvador.* Athens: Ohio University Press, 2016.

NOTES

1. For a discussion of postwar violence and attitudes toward peace, see Ellen Moodie, *El Salvador in the Aftermath of Peace* (Philadelphia: University of Pennsylvania Press, 2010).

2. Portions of this section are drawn from Tommie Sue Montgomery, *Revolution in El Salvador: From Civil Strife to Civil Peace* (Boulder, CO: Westview Press, 1995), 25–28, 30–32, and Tommie Sue Montgomery, "El Salvador," in *Political Parties of the Americas 1980s to 1990s,* ed. Charles Ameringer (Westport, CT: Greenwood Press, 1992), 281–301.

3. Latin American conservatives and liberals bear little resemblance to liberals and conservatives in the Anglo-American political tradition. Conservatives were aristocrats and monarchists who wished to keep church and state tied closely together and were dedicated to preserving the church's wealth and privileges. Liberals were anticlerical and often antireligious. They were inclined to support free trade, while conservatives preferred to erect tariff barriers to protect local textile production. Within El Salvador the differences were smaller than in other countries because the church did not have much wealth that could be confiscated. The liberals succeeded in abolishing monastic orders, establishing civil marriage, and taking some initial steps toward removing education from control by the clergy and creating a state education system.

4. Robert Varney Elam, "Appeal to Arms: The Army and Politics in El Salvador 1931–1964," Ph.D. dissertation, University of New Mexico, 1968, 9.

5. Max P. Brannon, *El Salvador: Esquema estadística de la vida nacional* (San Salvador: n.p., 1936), 22–24. By 1950 there were 115,429 hectares, or 75 percent of the total land, under cultivation; in 1961, the figure was 139,000 hectares, or 87 percent of the total. Eduardo Colindres, *Fundamentos económicos de la burguesía salvadoreña* (San Salvador: UCA Editores, 1978), 72.

6. Laurie Becklund, "Death Squads: Deadly 'Other War,'" *Los Angeles Times,* December 18, 1983.

7. The Gini coefficient measures inequality of income distribution on a scale of 1 (perfect equality) to 100 (perfect inequality).

8. Nina Liss-Schultz, "This Salvadoran Woman Served 4 Years for Having a Miscarriage," *Mother Jones,* July 12, 2016. www.motherjones.com/politics/2016/07/las-17-el-salvador-women-prison-abortion-miscarriage.

9. Christine J. Wade, *Captured Peace: Elites and Peacebuilding in El Salvador* (Athens: Ohio University Press, 2016), 79.

10. Ibid., 78–79; 107–109.

11. "Balance económico," *Proceso,* no. 884 (December 30, 1999), www.uca.edu.sv/publica //oproceso/proc844.html.

12. Marcia Towers and Silvia Borzutzky, "The Socioeconomic Implications of Dollarization in El Salvador," *Latin American Politics and Society* 46, no. 3 (Autumn 2004): 29–54.

13. Margarita Peñate, Kenny de Escobar, Arnulfo Quintanilla y César Alvarado,"Estimacion del Costo Economico de la Violencia en El Salvador 2014," Banco Central de Reserva. www.bcr .gob.sv/bcrsite/uploaded/content/category/1745118187.pdf.

23

GUATEMALA: BREAKING FREE FROM THE PAST?

Michael E. Allison

INTRODUCTION

Like several of its neighbors, Guatemala experienced a series of dictatorships, coups, alternating periods of repression and accommodation, and foreign intervention during the twentieth century. The violence culminated in the region's longest and bloodiest civil war. Although the civil war officially ended in 1996 with the signing of a peace agreement between the government and the Guatemalan National Revolutionary Unit (URNG), the country's transition to democracy began in 1985 when the military handed power over to an elected civilian government. Thirty years later, Guatemala's democratic institutions remain weak and designed to reinforce the power of Guatemalan elites at the expense of the masses.

Some consensus exists today around the most important goals of the state: strengthening democratic institutions, promoting security and the rule of law, tackling corruption, and furthering broad-based economic development. However, these goals are far from being realized for the great majority of the Guatemalan people. Poverty burdens more than half the population; corruption remains deeply embedded; and violent crime threatens the security of all Guatemalans, but especially women and the poor. Transnational criminal organizations engage in drug, human, and arms trafficking, which undermines democratic consolidation. The lack of economic opportunities, pressures for family reunification, and heightened insecurity at home cause tens of thousands to emigrate to the United States each year.

Guatemala has recently begun to make progress in the fight against corruption and in favor of transitional justice for victims and survivors of the country's thirty-six-year internal conflict. Investigations and prosecutions have laid bare what many have long suspected about the nature of the Guatemalan state: it had been co-opted by organized crime. However, the forces that benefit from the absence of a rule of law continue to thwart reform efforts during the current Jimmy Morales administration. The road ahead is a long and potentially treacherous one.

HISTORICAL BACKGROUND

Prior to the arrival of the Spanish, the people that occupied present-day Guatemala were part of a Maya civilization that spanned geographically from Chiapas and the Yucatán Peninsula in Mexico southward to El Salvador and Honduras. There are a great many unanswered questions about the people who lived in this area during precolonial times because of the destruction of most primary materials during the conquest.[1] Surviving evidence indicates, however, that the Maya developed a complex culture (see the *Popol Vuh*, the Maya creation story originally written in K'iche'). Along with 250 men, Spanish conquistador Pedro de Alvarado arrived in the western highlands of modern Guatemala in 1524. With the support of several thousand México soldiers, the Spaniards eventually established control over the K'iche', Kaqchikel, Mam, Tz'utujil, and others. Political, social, religious, economic, and territorial reforms were introduced by the Spanish to maintain control over the newly conquered people. Although the people were required to provide for themselves and the Spanish crown, they were granted a semblance of limited political and economic autonomy. Guatemala became the political, spiritual, cultural, and economic center of the Spanish Kingdom of Guatemala, a region that stretched from Chiapas to Costa Rica. Although the region did not have many of the precious metals prized by Spain, it did supply the crown with valuable textiles, mahogany, cacao, and dyes.

At least fifty serious riots, including more than one dozen between 1810 and 1821, were launched against the crown in the century prior to independence.[2] Upon independence from Spain, Guatemala became part of the short-lived Mexican empire of Augustín Iturbide. After he was deposed, Central America, minus Chiapas, declared its independence from Mexico. The former kingdom remained united as the United Provinces of Central America from 1823 to 1840. Guatemala's political leadership alternated between Liberal and Conservative governments after the federation's collapse. The Liberal faction was led by middle-class urban and provincial elites who sought to reduce the power of the Catholic Church and autonomy of indigenous groups. Conservatives from Guatemala City's colonial merchant and governmental aristocracy sought to maintain the vestiges of power from the colonial period—racial hierarchy and the Catholic Church. After Conservative leader Rafael Carrera led Guatemala's withdrawal from the United Provinces, he then presided over the country until his death in 1865. Liberal governments then took control of national politics beginning with the administration of Justo Rufino Barrios (1873–1885). Barrios embarked upon the modernization of the country by investing in a national bureaucracy, transportation infrastructure, and the army. Liberal reforms promoted the country's export potential, particularly in regard to coffee and bananas, and opened the country to international investors. The government passed laws to help private businesses compete in export markets. The *mandamiento* decree (1877) and vagrancy and debt peonage laws required communities to provide plantations with free and forced labor during harvest times for export goods, such as coffee, sugar, bananas, and cotton.

Following 1929's global economic crisis, Jorge Ubico y Castañeda assumed dictatorial powers. The last of the long-term Liberal dictators, Ubico pursued national development by repressing unions and political dissent while centralizing state power. During Ubico's term, the country underwent a period of infrastructure modernization (railways, highways, and utilities) and military professionalization. During the hostilities of World War II, German-owned lands were confiscated and indigenous people were forced to work a certain number of days each year on plantations through vagrancy laws. General Ubico's presidential term linked the country's military to its landed oligarchy, but his policies alienated labor, the emerging middle-class, and the United States. Protests forced President Ubico to resign in June 1944. A short-term military government ended when October elections ushered in "Ten Years of Spring."

TEN YEARS OF SPRING

Teacher and former exile Juan José Arévalo won the presidency and served from 1945 to 1951. Arévalo, a self-described "spiritual socialist," pursued a Guatemalan version of FDR's New Deal. The government instituted social security, adopted a more just labor code, professionalized the military, and invested in public education and health. He sought political and economic reforms to establish a modern capitalist society. Arévalo's reforms were consistent with those simultaneously adopted in neighboring El Salvador, Nicaragua, Honduras, and Costa Rica. Although the reforms did undermine some power of the landed oligarchy and military, Arévalo avoided substantial agrarian reform, a policy which when enacted led to his successor's overthrow.

Jacobo Árbenz Guzmán, a young army officer who participated in the 1944 protests, was elected president in 1950. Árbenz sought to deepen the reforms that had begun under the previous administration. Two policies in particular led to conflict with conservative forces in the Guatemalan military, business community, and Catholic Church and United States. He legalized the communist Guatemalan Labor Party (PGT). Although there were few communists in the government and the country overall, the fact that members of a Communist party took leadership roles in the second reform alarmed conservatives in Guatemala and the United States. The 1952 Agrarian Reform Law confiscated, compensated, and redistributed farmland to approximately 100,000 farmers. The land reform caused a backlash from the country's landed economic elite and Catholic Church, and the United States' United Fruit Company (UFCO), the country's largest landholder. The United States feared that the reforms would threaten their economic interests and that Árbenz was likely to move Guatemala into a deeper relationship with the Soviets. Critics point out that there were few communists in Guatemala, even fewer with ties to the Soviet Union; the government offered compensation for the fallow land it was to redistribute; and the arms from Czechoslovakia were entirely small arms purchased after the United States foiled Guatemala's efforts to purchase weapons from Canada, Germany, and elsewhere.

Eisenhower authorized the CIA to help Colonel Carlos Castillo Armas lead a small invasion force in June 1954. In the aftermath of Operation PBSUCCESS, Árbenz was exiled; labor and peasant movements disbanded; thousands of supporters of the previous regime killed, arrested, or exiled; the Agrarian Reform Law revoked; and political opening closed. The nonviolent path to economic and political development reform via the democratic process was effectively killed in Guatemala and elsewhere in the region.

THIRTY-SIX YEARS OF WAR

After President Castillo Armas was assassinated in 1957, the Guatemalan army chose General Miguel Ydígoras Fuentes as the next president. Active-duty military officers from across the political spectrum rebelled against Ydígoras Fuentes on November 13, 1960, because of government repression of those protesting military rule, corruption, and support for the training of individuals who would launch the US Bay of Pigs invasion of Cuba. After the rebellion's defeat, some of its moderate and leftist-inclined surviving officers joined with remnants of the PGT and student groups to form the Rebel Armed Forces (FAR). The FAR's establishment in 1962 would mark the beginning of a violent conflict that would last until a peace agreement was signed in December 1996.

More than 200,000 Guatemalans, mostly indigenous civilians, were killed in one of the most brutal civil wars of the Cold War in Latin America. The violence reached its highest levels in the late 1970s in urban areas and then in the early 1980s in rural areas. General Efraín Ríos Montt assumed power through a March 1982 coup and escalated the barbarous counterinsurgency policies begun by his predecessors. Ríos Montt launched a rural pacification strategy against the rebels, who in 1982 united under the banner of the Guatemalan National Revolutionary Unit (URNG), and their real and perceived civilian support base. The repression against the largely civilian indigenous population provoked charges of a systematic campaign of genocide and isolation of Guatemala from the world community. In spite of an arms embargo levied against Guatemala by the United States in 1977, the Guatemalan government continued to receive economic and military support from the United States and its allies. Thirty years later in 2013, Ríos Montt would stand trial on charges of genocide and crimes against humanity in Guatemala.

THE TRANSITION TO CIVIL RULE

Following overwhelming violence against revolutionary and nonrevolutionary internal enemies, which resulted not only in their severe weakening but the regime's international isolation, political, economic, and military elites agreed to embark upon a transition toward civilian government. The 1984 constitution paved the way for the election of the first civilian president in sixteen years, Christian Democrat Vinicio Cerezo. Cerezo entered into discussions with the remaining guerrillas, but their positions were far enough apart to prevent any significant movement toward peace. The transition to democratic rule was temporarily disrupted in 1993 when President Jorge Serrano

Elías illegally suspended the constitution and dismissed the legislature and supreme court. Civil society, sectors within the military and economic elite, and the international community organized to counter his power play. Although he is still sought by Guatemalan authorities, Serrano now lives in exile in Panama.

After ten years of negotiations, the URNG and the government led by President Alvaro Arzú signed peace accords in December 1996. The Accord for a Firm and Lasting Peace not only sought to end the war, but also to help the Guatemalan people and international community better understand the causes of the conflict and the behavior of parties during the war, and to lay out several recommendations for how the country could move forward in its process of democratization. The Commission for Historical Clarification (CEH) found that more than two hundred thousand people were killed, 83 percent of whom were Mayan, and that the vast majority of human rights violations, 93 percent, were carried out by forces aligned with the state. A 1999 referendum designed to institutionalize many of the peace accords' recommendations was defeated at the ballot box. Post-transition civilian administrations subsequently have lacked the political and economic resources needed to tackle the country's most pressing problems, and still all too frequently resort to repression and other undemocratic procedures. Thirty years after the military returned to their barracks, the consolidation of democracy remains elusive.

SOCIAL AND ECONOMIC STRUCTURE AND CIVIL SOCIETY

Guatemala stands out from its Central American neighbors in a number of significant ways. Guatemala has a population of approximately sixteen million, eight million more than Honduras, the second most populous country. Two million inhabitants crowd the only major urban center, Guatemala City; approximately six million live within the larger metropolitan area.[3] A much larger percentage of Guatemala's population is indigenous, more than one-half of the population. One has historically spoken about two groups of Guatemalans, indigenous and Ladino (non-Indian), although this is not entirely accurate because of the different ethnic groups along the Caribbean coast and the fluid meaning of what it means to be Ladino. Twenty-four languages are spoken, including Spanish.

Today, key social and economic indicators continue to disadvantage the indigenous people. Fifty-nine percent of the population lives below the national poverty line: approximately 75 percent of the country's indigenous and 35 percent of its non-indigenous people.[4] Although Guatemala sustained economic growth during many of the civil war and post–civil war years, it was the only country in the region that failed to reduce poverty from 2003 to 2012.[5] Among other factors, the state has failed to collect sufficient revenue to invest in public services and infrastructure. Guatemala's economic situation would be direr today if not for the fact that its citizens abroad sent more than US$6billion dollars in remittances back to their families in 2015—a figure representing 10 percent of the country's economy.[6]

Roman Catholicism was the official religion of Guatemala during the colonial period. During those years, Mayan traditional practices were often incorporated into Catholic ceremonies. Today, Roman Catholics comprise just under half of the population. Protestant adherents have grown to approximately 40 percent of the country, helped in part by the country's counterinsurgency program of the 1970s and 1980s and by the support of an international network of evangelicals. Former heads of state Efraín Ríos Montt (1982–1983) and Jorge Serrano Elías (1991–1993) were Protestant.

Similar to its neighbors, Guatemala is a young country with nearly 40 percent of its population under fifteen years old.[7] Unfortunately, an estimated 800,000 young Guatemalans neither work nor go to school.[8]

Government repression prevented the emergence of many civil society organizations during military rule. However, human rights, environmental, labor, and women's organizations have grown increasingly active ever since the return to civilian rule. Likewise, indigenous organizations have become better organized and more active, particularly around issues of land ownership and usage. Although the brutal repression of previous years is no longer the norm, indigenous groups still too frequently suffer violence at the hands of the state rather than accommodation and compromise. Likewise, civil society continues to suffer intimidation, harassment, and arbitrary arrest and detention at the hands of state security forces and other powerful interest groups.

POLITICAL SYSTEM

Even in a region with weakly institutionalized political parties, Guatemala's party system stands apart. During the nineteenth and twentieth centuries, the Liberal and Conservative parties engaged in machine politics, dispensing patronage in return for loyalty. In many ways, not much has changed today. Since the transition to civilian rule in the 1980s, no single political party has been able to establish much of a partisan following that would enable it to be competitive for more than a single election or two. In fact, no political party has won more than a single presidential election and no political party founded with the return to democracy exists today. Today's political parties tend to lack a political platform bearing much resemblance to a consistent ideology. Instead, the parties emerge around a single presidential candidate and tend to die once that leader dies or becomes irrelevant. In recent elections, voters have typically chosen from among fifteen parties, many of which would not survive to see the next election. Politicians regularly change party identification, and parties that contested elections as adversaries in one election might act as a coalition in the next. Elected president in 2015, Jimmy Morales only joined the military-veteran-dominated National Convergence Front (FCN) in 2013. Eleven congressional seats were won by Morales's FCN; however, one year later, its congressional bloc had more than tripled to thirty-five members.

Surprisingly, one of the oldest surviving political parties is the party of the former guerrillas, the URNG (now the URNG-MAIZ). Although it is one of the more institutionalized political parties, with a coherent ideology and permanent members and organization, it has had a difficult time garnering significant support.

Unfortunately, to an extent only seen in neighboring Mexico and Honduras, campaigns are all too often marred by assassinations of political candidates and their family members and other political figures. Votes are counted and the results respected, however, which might contribute to Guatemala's relatively strong record of voter turnout: 71 percent turned out in 2015's first round and 56 percent in the lopsided second round. However, in a 2015 report by the International Commission Against Impunity in Guatemala (CICIG), investigators found that around half of political party financing came from corruption. As a result, elected officials often respond to the interests of organized crime and wealthy elites before those of the country's citizens. There are also significant concerns that Guatemalans frequently turn out to vote in expectation of some form of patronage rather than out of civic duty or an embrace of democratic practices and principles.

THE STATE

The Liberal reforms of the late nineteenth century sought to usher in a modern, centralized state structure. In *El Señor Presidente*, Miguel Angel Asturias, winner of the Nobel Prize for Literature in 1967, writes of an unidentified dictator believed to be modeled after Manuel Estrada Cabrera, leader of Guatemala from 1898–1920. Estrada Cabrera modernized the country's highway, railroad, and seaport infrastructure. However, brute force proved more effective than the rule of law during his interim presidency and four presidential terms. Like Estrada Cabrera, President Jorge Ubico Castañeda (1931–1944) single-handedly ruled the country, making the legislature and judiciary nearly irrelevant. Other than the Ten Years of Spring, there was little effort to establish anything other than a counterinsurgent state.

Guatemala's 1985 constitution establishes three main branches of government. In addition to the executive, legislative, and judicial branches, the constitution created an independent Supreme Electoral Tribunal (TSE) to monitor elections. The president and vice president are elected to four-year terms and, in what has become a rarity in Latin America, there is no reelection.[9] A majority runoff system is utilized to elect the president and vice president. Every election since the turn toward more democratic forms of governing in 1985 has required a second round.

The unicameral congress consists of 158 members elected from a closed party list proportional representation electoral system. Members are elected from a two-tiered system: thirty-one from a single nationwide district and 128 across the twenty-two departments and the capital of Guatemala City. Parties that cannot muster 5 percent of the national vote or win a seat outright from a departmental list lose their registration and cannot compete in the next election. Like the president and vice president, members are elected to serve four-year terms.

Congress elects thirteen justices to the Supreme Court of Justice. Candidates are screened by a thirty-four-member postulation commission comprising representatives from university presidents and law school deans, the national bar association, and appellate court judges. A separate Constitutional Court exercises judicial review of legislative acts to ensure their conformity to the constitution. The president and his cabinet, congress, the supreme court, the main public university, and the national bar association each appoint a justice and a substitute justice to the Constitutional Court. The selection processes are designed to reduce corruption and prevent the appointment of unqualified judges. Justices on both courts serve concurrent five-year terms.

The constitution guarantees judicial independence, but even after years of reform, the courts remain weak and prone to political manipulation and threats. Partly as a result, a unique hybrid institution backed by the United Nations, the International Commission Against Impunity in Guatemala (CICIG), was established in 2006. CICIG works with its Guatemalan counterparts to investigate organized crime and corruption and strengthen the judicial system. The strengthening of the attorney general's office under the leadership of two women, Claudia Paz y Paz and Thelma Aldana, has been one of the most significant developments in establishing the rule of law.

Following the 1996 peace agreement between the URNG and President Álvaro Arzú of the National Advancement Party, the military began to take a less public role in governing the nation. It accepted deep cuts in its budget and subordinated itself to civilian command. Unfortunately, clandestine organized criminal networks of active and retired military officers proliferated and subverted democracy following the peace. The overt presence of active and retired military officials increased with the elections of Otto Perez Molina (Patriotic Party) and Jimmy Morales (National Convergence Front). The use of troops on the streets of rural and urban areas to fight crime and insecurity has also increased.

There is no doubt that greater political freedom exists in Guatemala today than before the return to civilian rule in 1985. Political exiles have returned home, exhumations from the war occur, and victims and survivors lodge complaints and pursue justice through the courts. However, Guatemala remains one of the region's most dangerous countries for journalists, environmentalists, and human rights advocates. Opinion polls show that the percentage of Guatemalans who prefer democracy to any other regime only reached 33 percent in 2015.[10] Freedom House, an organization that measures civil rights and political freedoms around the world, rates Guatemala as "partly free."

PUBLIC POLICY

Otto Pérez Molina won the 2011 presidential election as the candidate of the rightist Patriotic Party. Although Pérez Molina and populist competitor Manuel Baldizón both campaigned on promises to get tough on crime, the retired general's background was more convincing to Guatemalans wearied by public insecurity. Despite his hardline stance and the cloud over his past career as a military officer linked to human rights abuses, Pérez Molina called for a seemingly progressive approach to international drug policy. He also advocated for increased royalties paid by mining companies. Pérez Molina's term came to an unceremonious end in 2015 following weeks of sustained citizen mobilization that forced his resignation. In what is referred to as the *La Linea* corruption scandal, authorities accused him and his vice president, Roxana Baldetti, who had resigned months earlier, of defrauding the state of untold millions of dollars. The former president and vice president and dozens of other individuals are currently in jail awaiting trial.

Designing and financing effective policies to tackle violent crime, boost economic growth, improve education, increase meaningful employment opportunities, and provide adequate health care remain significant challenges. Historically, government programs have been designed and implemented primarily to benefit specific constituents, elites, or voters, rather than in pursuit of a common national project. Like many Latin American governments at the time, the administration of center-left president Álvaro Colom expanded access to various social programs during his presidency (2008–2012). Although these programs did seem to deliver tangible benefits to the country's poor, the programs were undermined because of their politicization, not least because his wife and intended 2011 presidential candidate Sandra Torres was tasked with overseeing the programs. During the 2011 elections, during which then ex-first lady Torres's candidacy was deemed ineligible by the Constitutional Court, candidates from across the political spectrum promised their own social programs if not to help the country's poor majorities, at least to further the interests of their party's supporters.

Street gangs, organized criminal groups, drug traffickers, and other criminal actors, combined with a weak state and the availability of weapons, have made Guatemala and its Northern Triangle neighbors (El Salvador and Honduras) one of the world's most violent regions. Although Guatemala's homicide rate has decreased every year since 2009, its homicide level of just under thirty per one hundred thousand people still means that it is nearly three times the level that the World Health Organization considers "epidemic." Street gangs known as *maras,* exported from Los Angeles to Central America, are active in many urban areas of the country and stretch the already thin resources of law enforcement. Violence, corruption, and insufficient budgets have made it impossible for the state to exercise full control over its territory. The absence of legitimate state authority has also led citizens to take matters into their own hands through the lynching of suspects. The country is also overrun with private companies that provide security for a price, a price that ordinary Guatemalans cannot pay. Protection has become a privilege for the few who can afford it. Although there has been improvement in recent years, the vast majority of crimes continue to go unpunished.

The delivery of health and education services, some of the worst in the region, and national and international investment are undermined by violent crime and government corruption, thereby corroding public confidence in the state (which, according to opinion polls, stands at 18 percent in Guatemala, again the lowest number in Latin America). Low levels of confidence contribute to extremely low levels of tax collection required to strengthen institutions and combat crime.

INTERNATIONAL ENVIRONMENT

Similar to the rest of Spain's colonial possessions, Guatemala was kept relatively isolated from the world when it came to trade. After independence Guatemala's foreign relations were limited mainly to securing foreign investment and resolving boundary disputes with neighbors Mexico and Belize. At the turn of the nineteenth century, Guatemala sought international investment and showcased what the country had to offer at the 1893 World Columbian Exposition in Chicago. Guatemala drew attention from the United States during and between the world wars because of the relatively large number of Germans who had moved from the old to the new world. Guatemala's Ten Years of Spring and civil war occurred during the Cold War, bringing the United States and its allies (Argentina, Israel) and Cuba (less so the Soviet Union) into the conversation.

Today, globalization presents complex opportunities and challenges for the people of Guatemala. With the transition toward more democratic forms of government in the 1980s and the success of the Central American Peace Process, Guatemala and its neighbors made a renewed push for integration. Along with El Salvador, Honduras, and Nicaragua, Guatemala is a member of the Central America Four (CA-4), four countries that adopted common internal borders and passports. It is also a member of the

Central American Integration System (SICA), an organization that promotes regional peace, political freedom, democracy, and economic development. Guatemala entered into the Central American–Dominican Republic Free Trade Agreement (CAFTA-DR) in 2006 and has free trade agreements with the European Union, Colombia, Taiwan, Panama, Chile, Mexico, the Dominican Republic, and Peru.[11] These trade agreements built on the economic liberalization that occurred with Guatemala's entry into the World Trade Organization in 1995.

Forty-one percent of Guatemala's exports goes to the United States, Mexico, and Canada, while another 29 percent goes to its Central American neighbors.[12] Given Guatemala's high rates of poverty and overall poor political and economic conditions, its economy is heavily dependent on aid from the United States. Assistance is tied to achievement of political and economic reforms aimed at democratic institutionalization and transparent government. More recent aid is dependent upon Guatemala's efforts to stem illegal immigration to the United States. Violence, the lack of economic opportunity, and desires for family reunification are strong motivators for immigration.

Although Guatemala's geographic location brings it close to one of the world's most important trade markets, its location also brings with it some drawbacks. Drug, human, animal, and arms trafficking are all too common. Guatemala is a transit country for drugs going from South America to the United States. Local drug traffickers have battled with the Zetas and other Mexican and regional drug trafficking organizations (DTOs) over lucrative routes. These battles have left thousands of victims in their wake, including by way of several massacres reminiscent of the Cold War. Subsequent states of siege have been criticized for further undermining the rule of law and serving as pretext for targeting political enemies involved in local grassroots organizing around human rights issues.

In addition to its economic variant, globalization has in recent years promoted such values as democracy, transitional justice, indigenous rights, and anticorruption. Mostly in a positive way, Guatemala has been forced to defend its record on these issues before foreign governments, the United Nations, and international human rights organizations in addition to domestic civil and political groups.

CONCLUSION

For the last thirty years, Guatemala has regularly held competitive elections through which civilian candidates have ascended to the congress and the presidency. There have also been reforms that have strengthened the rule of law and extended protection to vulnerable groups, both identity- and profession-based, since the brutal counterinsurgency period. However, civilian rule has been undermined by former military officials and traditional and emergent elites who have demonstrated little support for a true deepening of democracy. Freedom of speech, assembly, and the press and basic due process guarantees remain limited because of racism toward the country's indigenous people, poverty and economic inequality, corruption, and elevated levels of crime and insecurity.

In a potential sign of progress, criminal investigations launched by the CICIG and attorney general's office and the unprecedented postwar mobilization of citizens have put criminal entities, both inside and outside of government, on notice that they will no longer be free to operate with impunity in Guatemala. The battle is an uphill one and it remains to be seen whether the Morales administration will prove a step forward toward a brighter future or a step backward toward a much darker past.

SUGGESTIONS FOR FURTHER READING

Goldman, Francisco. *The Art of Political Murder*. New York: Grove Press, 2007.

Grandin, Greg, Deborah T. Levenson, and Elizabeth Oglesby. *The Guatemala Reader*. Durham, NC: Duke University Press, 2011.

Menchú, Rigoberta. *I Rigoberta Menchú: An Indian Woman in Guatemala*. Edited by Elisabeth Burgos-Debray. Translated by Ann Wright. 2nd ed. New York: Verso, 2009.

Schlesinger, Stephen, and Stephen Kinzer. *Bitter Fruit: The Story of the American Coup in Guatemala*. Revised ed. Cambridge, MA: Harvard University, David Rockefeller Center for Latin American Studies, 2005.

Stoll, David. *Rigoberta Menchú and the Story of All Poor Guatemalans*. Expanded ed. Boulder, CO: Westview Press, 2007.

Weld, Kirsten. *Paper Cadavers: The Archives of Dictatorship in Guatemala*. Durham, NC: Duke University Press, 2014.

Wilkinson, Daniel. *Silence on the Mountain*. Boston, MA: Houghton Mifflin Company, 2002.

NOTES

1. Greg Grandin, Deborah Levenson, and Elizabeth Oglesby, *The Guatemala Reader*. (Durham, NC: Duke University Press, 2011), 11–12.

2. Ibid., 101.

3. Population figure from World Population Review. Available at http://worldpopulation review.com/countries/guatemala-population/.

4. Poverty figure from "Pobreza sube a 59.3%: son 9.6 millones de guatemaltecos los afectados." Available at www.prensalibre.com/economia/se-dispara-a-593-la-pobreza-96-millones -de-guatemaltecos-viven-en-pobreza. Breakdown of the poverty rate from "Guatemala's Indigenous Peoples Endure Poverty and Contested Land Rights." Available at www.worldpoliticsreview.com /trend-lines/19711/guatemala-s-indigenous-peoples-endure-poverty-and-contested-land-rights.

5. Statistics from "Guatemala's poor getting poorer." Available at www.dw.com/en /guatemalas-poor-getting-poorer/a-17917809.

6. Remittance statistics from "Guatemala: Remittances Up 13% in 2015." Available at www .centralamericadata.com/en/article/home/Guatemala_Remittances_Up_13_in_2015.

7. Age distribution figure from The World Bank. Available at http://data.worldbank.org /indicator/SP.POP.0014.TO.ZS.

8. Youth statistic comes from "800,000 Guatemala youths neither work nor study." Available at http://latino.foxnews.com/latino/news/2016/10/08/800000-guatemala-youths -neither-work-nor-study/.

9. Amendments changed the original length of terms served by elected officials, in addition to other changes.

10. Figure from the 2015 Latinobarómetro online analysis tool. Available on the Web at www.latinobarometro.org.

11. Information on Guatemala available at www.sice.oas.org/ctyindex/GTM/GTMAgree ments_e.asp.

12. Guatemala's Top 15 Import Partners. Available at www.worldstopexports.com /guatemalas-top-15-import-partners/.

24

HONDURAS: DEMOCRACY IN PERIL

J. Mark Ruhl

INTRODUCTION

Honduras seems an unlikely candidate for democracy. The country has been ruled throughout most of its history by dictatorial political bosses or military strongmen. After the power of the armed forces receded in the 1990s, the nation appeared to build a procedural democracy with a series of free and fair elections. Its democratic progress was abruptly halted in June 2009, however, when a constitutional crisis that set leftist President Manuel "Mel" Zelaya against most of the rest of the Honduran civilian political elite sparked a military coup. Elections a few months later restored a semblance of democratic government, and winning National Party candidate Porfirio Lobo negotiated the 2011 Cartagena Accord that permitted Zelaya to return from exile and form a new Liberty and Refoundation (*LIBRE*) party. But Honduran politics remained polarized and volatile. The National Party's Juan Orlando Hernández won the 2013 presidential contest over Zelaya's wife Xiomara Castro and several other candidates, but leaders from LIBRE and the newly formed Anti-Corruption Party (PAC) alleged electoral fraud.

The consolidation of democracy requires that both political elites and the mass public accept the democratic process as legitimate and as "the only game in town." Honduran civilian and military elites had appeared to have learned to abide by democratic rules by the late 1990s, but the illegal 2009 coup and the illegal actions by President Zelaya that precipitated it proved otherwise. In the years since the coup, Honduran leaders have continued to show scant regard for the rule of law: supreme court justices have been unconstitutionally ousted by Congress, a sacrosanct constitutional bar to presidential reelection has been discarded by judicial fiat, and threatened economic and political elites have been quick to use lethal violence against critics in the media and civil society.

Most ordinary Hondurans have become disillusioned with democratic governance. Despite the promises of neoliberal economic reforms, nearly two-thirds of the population still lives below the poverty line. Embezzlement and bribery on a huge scale have discredited one democratically chosen government after another. Elected leaders also have been unable to stop an explosion of urban gang violence and organized crime. In desperation, Hondurans have welcomed a renewed military role in law enforcement in spite of the institutional regression that this represents. Democracy's future is very much in doubt in Honduras.

POLITICAL CULTURE AND HISTORY

Honduras is a Pennsylvania-sized country of more than 8.5 million people. Nearly half of the population lives in rural areas where illiteracy is common. More than 80 percent of Hondurans are mestizos, but there are significant Afro-indigenous Garifuna concentrations on the north coast as well as some remaining indigenous communities. A slim majority of Hondurans profess Roman Catholicism, but evangelical Protestant congregations are spreading. With a per capita GDP of under US$5,000 at purchasing power parity, Honduras is one of Latin America's three poorest countries. Its economy is dependent on remittances from more than 600,000 Hondurans working in the United States (US$3.7 billion in 2015), *maquiladora* factory production for the US market, and unstable tropical exports such as coffee and bananas.

Authoritarian governments traditionally ruled Honduras; however, Honduran rulers were less repressive of popular sector groups than their counterparts in neighboring nations. Whereas many powerful families in other Central American countries made their fortunes as members of an arrogant coffee oligarchy, Honduran elites of the late nineteenth and early twentieth centuries focused on small-scale cattle ranching and silver mining ventures.[1] Neither of these activities posed a threat to the peasantry in a country where agricultural land was widely available. Although there was little political friction between peasants and large landowners, constant battles for power among rival landed caudillos rendered the nation chronically unstable. These warring political bosses fought over the spoils of office rather than public policy. They promoted a clientelist and patrimonial political culture in which constitutional and electoral rules were regularly violated.

At the beginning of the twentieth century, American banana companies established plantations on the sparsely populated north coast. Hondurans who worked for the banana giants eventually formed the strongest trade union movement in Central America. Dictator Tiburcio Carías Andino (1932–1949) of the National Party was a staunch ally of United Fruit, but some leaders of the weaker Liberal Party were closer to labor. In addition, a commercial-industrial elite with an important Arab-Honduran element that formed on the north coast often backed the banana workers.[2]

Created with US assistance in the 1940s, the Honduran armed forces became an important political actor independent of the feuding Liberal and National parties. The military first intervened in politics in 1956 to depose an unpopular provisional president. Before relinquishing control, senior officers demanded constitutional guarantees of the armed forces' political autonomy. Elected with the support of unions and reformist business elements, Liberal president Ramón Villeda Morales (1957–1963) introduced an urban social security system, a progressive labor code, and a limited agrarian reform. When the Liberal candidate to succeed Villeda Morales threatened to rescind the military's autonomy, the armed forces staged a preemptive coup in 1963 in alliance with the National Party.

Armed forces commander General Oswaldo López Arellano dominated Honduran politics from 1963 to 1975. During the López era, peasants mobilized to press for land reform in response to land scarcity caused by rapid population growth and the expansion of commercial agriculture. López evicted eighty thousand Salvadoran peasants living in Honduras in order to make more land available. After the subsequent 1969 war with El Salvador, the general broke with the National Party to form a progressive alliance with peasants, unions, and the north coast business community. López's more conservative military successors in the presidency re-allied with the National Party and large landowners, but some land redistribution continued and unions remained important political players. While neighboring Central American nations drifted into catastrophic civil wars in the 1970s and 1980s, the Honduran military's more accommodative posture encouraged popular sector organizations to continue to press their demands within established political channels.

Democratic Elections and the Decline of the Military

Encouraged by the United States, the armed forces permitted an elected civilian, Liberal Roberto Suazo Córdova (1982–1986), to become president in 1982. In spite of the new democratic veneer, the armed forces grew stronger as US military aid rose to unprecedented levels in return for permission to base anti-Sandinista Nicaraguan guerrillas in Honduras. President Suazo became the junior partner in an alliance with repressive armed forces chief General Gustavo Alvarez Martínez. After Alvarez's fall from power in an internal coup, the military continued to maintain its supremacy over elected civilian authorities. Corruption within the armed forces reached new extremes as some officers became rich by protecting drug traffickers.

The democratic electoral process was strengthened in 1990 when Suazo's Liberal successor José Azcona (1986–1990) passed the presidential sash to National Party leader Rafael Callejas. This ceremony marked the first democratic turnover of power between competing political parties in nearly sixty years. During the rest of the decade, the electoral process became institutionalized with regular presidential and legislative elections every four years.

With the end of the Cold War and the Central American civil wars, the United States no longer needed the Honduran military as an anti-Communist ally. American military aid was slashed, and the US embassy supported Honduran human rights organizations, student groups, unions, and reformist business leaders as they combined to challenge the military's prerogatives. The political influence of the military rapidly declined under Liberals Carlos Roberto Reina (1994–1998) and Carlos Flores (1998–2002). Reina passed constitutional reforms that ended obligatory military service and stripped the armed forces of control over the national police. He also trimmed the military budget and removed the nation's telecommunications system and other sources of illicit funding from armed forces management. In early 1999, President Flores passed a constitutional reform that formally ended the military's political autonomy, placing the armed forces under a civilian defense minister for the first time since 1957.

The 2009 Military Coup and its Aftermath

Unfortunately, the polarization of civilian elite politics during the tenure of Liberal President Manuel Zelaya (2006–2009) ushered the armed forces back onto the political stage.[3] Although a center-right politician throughout his career, President Zelaya unexpectedly allied himself with radical populist Hugo Chávez of Venezuela and brought Honduras into the Bolivarian Alternative for the Americas (ALBA). Zelaya's sudden shift to the left alienated most of the nation's civilian political class, including other Liberal politicians. When the Honduran chief executive began to campaign for a constituent assembly to revise the constitution, his opponents suspected that he intended to abolish the constitutional ban on presidential reelection and somehow remain in power beyond the conclusion of his term in early 2010. The national congress, the supreme court, the supreme electoral tribunal, and the attorney general united in ruling his actions illegal. President Zelaya, nevertheless, continued with preparations to hold a nonbinding referendum on adding the constituent assembly issue to the November ballot. When the president ordered the armed forces to assist with the referendum, the Chief of the Joint General Staff General Romeo Vásquez refused, citing the poll's illegality. President Zelaya immediately dismissed Vásquez and personally led a crowd of supporters onto an air force base to take possession of referendum materials stored there. The supreme court, which had reinstated General Vásquez, ordered him to arrest the president. Military units deposed Zelaya then illegally expelled him from the country. Right-wing National Congress President Roberto Micheletti became head of a de facto civilian government with broad congressional approval.

The Organization of American States (OAS) suspended Honduras while the international community clamored for Zelaya's reinstatement. For several months, crowds of Zelaya supporters competed with Micheletti partisans for control of the streets. Repressive measures by the security forces caused the deaths of at least twenty coup opponents. Ultimately, neither external nor internal pressures proved sufficient to put the ousted president back in office. Despite its initial support for Zelaya's return, the United States accepted the results of the previously scheduled November 2009 presidential elections, which transferred power to National Party candidate Porfirio Lobo.

President Lobo (2010–2014) stabilized the political situation by negotiating the reintegration of Zelaya and his followers via the 2011 Cartagena Accord. He also appointed a balanced Truth and Reconciliation Commission that blamed both Zelaya and his adversaries for the coup. But rule-breaking by top officials continued. In late 2012, when Lobo and Congress President Juan Orlando Hernández saw their police reform plans blocked by the supreme court, they engineered a quick and unconstitutional removal of four of its justices.

Hernández's own presidential term (2014–2018) has been marked by shocking revelations of criminal activity at the highest levels of politics and society. Hondurans learned that National Party officials at the Honduran Institute of Social Security

(IHSS) had stolen more than US$300 million via kickbacks from suppliers and had spent almost a third of that sum in the 2013 electoral campaign. Huge anticorruption marches of the *indignados* (outraged) erupted, demanding Hernandez's resignation and the creation of a UN-backed International Commission against Impunity in Honduras to emulate a highly successful anticorruption institution in neighboring Guatemala. Hernández denied knowledge of the illicit campaign funding and, instead, persuaded the OAS to sponsor a less powerful Mission to Support the Fight Against Corruption and Impunity in Honduras (MACCIH).

In 2016, investigative journalists revealed that senior national police officials in the pay of drug traffickers had orchestrated the assassinations of the nation's top counter-narcotics official and a former senior advisor. After repeated failed efforts to purge the police of criminal elements, this discovery spurred the creation of a Special Police Purification Commission that began its work by dismissing more than one-third of the top-ranking police officials. Also during this period, the US government publicly targeted Honduras's two main drug trafficking organizations (DTOs) as well as the associated money laundering activities of the influential Grupo Continental led by wealthy former Liberal vice-president Jaime Rosenthal. US agents, the new Military Police of Public Order (PMOP), and other units dismantled both DTOs as Honduran officials seized the assets of Grupo Continental. These actions significantly disrupted narcotics traffic in what had become the principal transshipment country for moving cocaine from South America to Mexico and the United States.

INTEREST GROUPS AND CIVIL SOCIETY

The fragmented Honduran private business sector encompasses several competing financial groups that contribute to political campaigns and vie for influence over government economic decisions. The business community is also split by region (north coast San Pedro Sula-based versus Tegucigalpa-based enterprises), ethnicity (Arab-Honduran-owned companies versus others), and economic sector. The principal umbrella organization for the private sector is the Honduran Private Enterprise Council (COHEP). Foreign investors in the maquiladoras and the banana industry also seek to influence government policy. With some notable exceptions (left-leaning Globo TV), most of the Honduran mass media are owned by a few conservative business families.

The armed forces regained political influence in 2009 when the clash between President Zelaya and his civilian opponents prompted both sides to attempt to enlist military support. Internal factional squabbling among *promociones* (military academy graduating classes) had divided the officer corps in the past, but the military was unified behind the 2009 coup. The armed forces control intelligence-gathering and once again play a major internal security role. Under President Lobo, military units gained the authority to carry out searches, collect evidence, and make arrests. Distrusting the thoroughly corrupt national police, Lobo and his successor Hernández collaborated to establish the Military Police of Public Order (PMOP). Reports of increased human rights abuses including torture have accompanied the expanded use of soldiers in law enforcement. President Hernández also placed many retired and active-duty military officers in leadership positions within his administration.

Honduras once was home to the strongest independent labor movement in Central America, but its unions have suffered from ideological divisions, harassment, and internal leadership conflicts. Only about one-tenth of wage and salary employees are unionized today. The moderate, AFL-CIO-linked Honduran Workers' Confederation (CTH), which includes most banana workers, is the country's leading labor federation. The other major national labor organizations are the Social-Christian General Confederation of Workers (CGT) and the leftist Unitary Confederation of Honduran Workers (CUTH). Labor unions that organize public school teachers and health-care workers have successfully used strikes to win economic concessions from the government. Most trade unionists backed President Zelaya before and after the 2009 coup because of his enactment of generous minimum wage increases and other pro-labor policies.

Honduran civil society has expanded in the last quarter century as indigenous and environmental groups have joined existing peasant organizations in a series of intense struggles over land. The Civic Council of Popular and Indigenous Organizations (COPINH) mobilizes opposition to hydroelectric projects and mining in indigenous and environmentally sensitive areas in western Honduras. In 2016, employees of the corporation building the Agua Zarca dam were implicated in the assassination of internationally recognized indigenous (Lenca) COPINH leader Berta Cáceres. Activists in OFRANEH (the Black Fraternal Organization of Honduras), which fights to protect traditional Garifuna coastal lands from takeover by north coast tourism developers and others, have also been targeted. The most violent land dispute in the country, however, has involved peasant groups such as the United Farmworkers of the Aguán (MUCA) who are battling wealthy landowner Miguel Facussé over control of palm oil–producing plantations in the Bajo Aguán valley in northern Honduras. More than ninety people were killed in this conflict between 2012 and 2014.

Human rights proponents such as the Committee for the Defense of Human Rights in Honduras (CODEH) and traditional actors like the Catholic Church continue to pressure government officials on a range of issues. In addition, student groups and women's organizations as well as organized urban slum dwellers have become more active. Since the late 1990s, unions, peasant organizations, and indigenous groups have increasingly resorted to direct action (protest marches, land occupations, road blockages) to press their demands. Newly mobilized middle class and youth elements played the leading role in the 2015 anti-corruption marches.

POLITICAL PARTIES AND ELECTIONS

Traditionally, relatively few Hondurans entered politics to serve the public interest. The Liberal and National parties are both patron-client political machines primarily organized to compete for state jobs, contracts, and other resources. Each party is divided into competing personalist factions. Both parties choose their presidential candidate in a national primary election that pits factional contenders against one another. The Nationals and the Liberals are center-right, multiclass parties that benefit from hereditary party identification. Honduras became a multiparty system in 2013 when radical populist LIBRE (divided between clientelist former Liberals and radical left groups) and a new middle-class Anti-Corruption Party (PAC) led by television celebrity Salvador

Nasralla made major inroads into traditional party support. Several older minor parties also participated in the election but garnered few votes.

From 1982 through 2013, the Honduran president was elected by simple plurality to a single four-year term. The unicameral national congress is selected at the same time as the president by open list proportional representation by department. Honduran elections are supervised by the Supreme Electoral Tribunal (TSE) chosen by congress. Beginning in the early 1980s, Honduras held seven consecutive democratic general elections that were accepted as legitimate by the losing parties. Results of the two elections that have taken place since the 2009 coup, however, have been disputed. Anti-coup forces boycotted the 2009 race, and LIBRE claimed to have been defrauded of victory in 2013. Although international observers from the European Union and OAS and a partial TSE recount confirmed National Party candidate Hernández's triumph, there was considerable evidence of vote-buying and other irregularities in this election and in the primaries that preceded it. Later revelations about Hernández's corrupt campaign funding have further delegitimized the 2013 contest.

Hernández won with 36.9 percent of the vote on a promise to aggressively attack urban gangs and drug traffickers. Xiomara Castro of LIBRE, running on a socialist platform, came in second with 28.8 percent, followed by Liberal Mauricio Villeda Bermúdez with 20.3 percent and Nasralla (PAC) with 13.4 percent. The National Party won 48 seats in the 128-member Congress and formed a legislative majority with the Liberals (27 seats) on most issues. LIBRE with 37 seats and PAC with 13 frequently collaborated in opposition. Women filled 26 percent of the seats in the new Congress (about average for Latin America); their representation will likely increase in the 2017 elections when half of the candidates must be female.

GOVERNING INSTITUTIONS

The Honduran governmental system is highly centralized, with power concentrated in the presidency. The president directs the activities of executive branch agencies and introduces most legislation. If the chief executive heads a majority coalition of party factions in the National Congress, his policy initiatives generally become law. The National Congress historically did not play a significant policy role, but it recently has become more important in policy making and executive oversight. This has been true especially when the National Congress has been controlled by party factions not affiliated with the president (as under Zelaya in 2008–2009) or when the National Congress President (Hernández, 2010–2013) has harbored ambitions to become chief executive. As president, Hernández lost in his bid to convince congress to place the new Military Police under direct presidential authority, but he won congressional approval for most of his other initiatives.

The National Congress appoints the fifteen justices of the Honduran Supreme Court for a seven-year term from a list of candidates approved by a nominating committee composed of civil society representatives. The eight Nationals and seven Liberals currently on the court were selected in 2016 after a protracted and highly politicized congressional selection process that involved allegations of bribery. The high court played a key role in the ouster of President Zelaya in 2009, but the limits of its power were made clear in 2012 when the National Congress unceremoniously dismissed four justices without legal justification. In 2015, in accordance with President Hernández's wishes, the court's five-member constitutional panel abolished the constitutional prohibition on presidential reelection that traditional elites had defended so vehemently in their battle against leftist President Zelaya in 2009. Supreme Court justices appoint all lower court judges. Corruption and incompetence are endemic at all judicial levels in Honduras. Few high-ranking officials or major drug traffickers have been prosecuted successfully, although an unusually large number of senior public officials have recently been indicted.

LIMITS OF DEMOCRACY

Honduras made important democratic strides after formal civilian rule was restored in the 1980s. Four peaceful turnover elections (1989, 1993, 2001, and 2005) appeared to demonstrate that the electoral system had become institutionalized. By the late 1990s, the long-dominant military also seemed to have accepted a limited and subordinate role. But the 2009 coup showed how fragile these achievements actually were.

Freedom House[4] places Honduras among the least democratic nations in the Americas and classifies it as only "partly free." Although all adults can vote, only one-third of Hondurans believe that their elections are clean. The most recent contest in 2013 was tainted by the winning party's use of millions of dollars in stolen social security institute funds, vote buying, and other irregularities. No laws regulate campaign finance in a country where drug traffickers needing political protection are awash with cash. Basic civil and political liberties are also in jeopardy in Honduras. More than fifty journalists[5] have been murdered since 2009, making this nation one of the hemisphere's most dangerous media environments. Assassinations of human rights, environmental, indigenous, union, peasant, and LGBTQ activists also occur frequently; few of the perpetrators are ever pursued, much less punished. Active-duty and former police and military personnel have been suspected in many of these cases. In addition, although the military has not reassumed its former dominant status in Honduran politics, its expanded influence in internal security is a step backward for democracy. Most Hondurans express greater trust in the military than in any civilian political institution.

The mass public's unhappiness with the quality of democratic governance in Honduras was clearly indicated in the 2015 *Latinobarómetro* survey,[6] in which only 34 percent of Hondurans expressed satisfaction with the functioning of democracy in their country. Just 40 percent of Honduran respondents preferred democracy to any other type of political system, the second-lowest level of democratic support among all Latin American nations.

PUBLIC POLICY

Effective policy making is difficult in Honduras. Resources are scarce, the state bureaucracy is notoriously inefficient, and the political class is driven by spoils rather than policy goals. A 2014 secrecy law also makes it easy for government officials to prevent public scrutiny of their actions. Some Honduran presidents, such as Liberal reformer Carlos Reina, have come into office with clear policy objectives; however, the enactment of public policies to address national problems more often is driven by external pressure or by acute internal crisis.

President Rafael Callejas (1990–1994) began neoliberal economic reform in 1990 in the face of an international credit boycott orchestrated by international financial institutions and the United States. He cut the size of the nation's chronically high fiscal deficit by shrinking the bureaucracy and increasing taxes. He also liberalized trade, devalued the currency, and persuaded foreign investors to establish new maquiladora factories. His successors, with the exception of leftist Manuel Zelaya, have largely maintained these International Monetary Fund-mandated policies. President Ricardo Maduro (2002–2006), a Stanford-educated economist, signed the Central America Free Trade Agreement (CAFTA-DR) with the United States, and his fidelity to neoliberal principles won the country more than US$4 billion in debt relief.

President Zelaya's alliance with Venezuelan populist leader Chávez initially stimulated the economy with low-interest loans, reduced oil import costs, and generous development assistance, although it raised investors' suspicions. Zelaya granted hefty wage increases to public sector employees and demonstrated less financial discipline than Maduro as inflation climbed to more than 11 percent. Through 2007, the Honduran economy continued to grow at the 6 percent rate Maduro achieved, but it contracted sharply with the 2009 constitutional crisis and a world recession.

President Lobo's (2010–2014) return to neoliberal orthodoxy and his political reconciliation efforts helped engineer a modest economic recovery, although excessive public spending produced a large fiscal deficit by the end of his term. Incoming President Hernández instituted a strict austerity program that brought government spending and inflation back under control and produced GDP growth rates in the 3.4 percent range, which exceeded the Latin American average in a period of low commodity prices.

Although Hernández and most of his predecessors have won praise from international financial institutions for their efforts to reform and expand the nation's economy, most ordinary Hondurans have seen only a small improvement in their miserable living conditions. Many of those who are able have left for the United States. Honduras is the second most unequal country in Latin America, and its current 63 percent poverty rate[7] remains one of the region's highest. Conditional cash transfer (CCT) programs of income subsidies to poor families have expanded significantly under Presidents Lobo and Hernández, but they have been marred by inefficiency and a partisan pattern of benefit distribution. No president has revived the agrarian reform program that the Callejas administration ended.

Hondurans have also been disillusioned by the extraordinarily high level of government corruption. In 2015, Transparency International[8] rated Honduras as one of the five most corrupt countries in Latin America. Yet, for many, the greatest disappointment has been their democratically elected leaders' inability to stop the crime wave that has enveloped the country since the 1990s. President Maduro, whose son was killed by kidnappers, made attacking crime his highest priority, but his zero-tolerance policies directed against the Mara Salvatrucha (MS-13) and Barrio 18 street gangs had limited success. An estimated twelve thousand gang members[9] still terrorize urban Honduras, extorting money from businesses, buses and taxis, homeowners, teachers, and schoolchildren (thousands of whom have tried to flee to the United States). By 2011, the Honduran homicide rate (86 murders per 100,000 persons) became the highest in the world. Working with Honduran drug transporting organizations, the Sinaloa cartel and other Mexican DTOs have become deeply involved in the country. Approximately two hundred tons of cocaine from South America pass through Honduras each year.

With US assistance, President Hernández employed his new Military Police and other units to dismember Honduran DTOs and recapture some urban neighborhoods from gang control. Under a 2014 law, major drug traffickers and compromised senior police officers are being extradited to the United States. The homicide rate fell to 60 per 100,000 in 2015.[10] However, drug trafficking networks are reorganizing, and it is too soon to know if the benefits of Hernández's aggressive security policies will be more than temporary.

THE INTERNATIONAL ENVIRONMENT

Few Hondurans base their opinions about government performance on foreign policy, although this is an area of major concern to Honduran presidents and the nation's political elite. Honduran foreign policy officials traditionally have devoted more attention to their relations with the United States than to their ties with the rest of the world combined. Their principal goals have been to secure economic resources, security support, trade preferences, and favorable immigration policies by demonstrating loyalty to the United States. President Zelaya broke with this tradition by joining the anti-US ALBA alliance, but Presidents Lobo and Hernández returned to the American fold.

Although only about a quarter of Hondurans use the Internet,[11] the country is highly integrated into the global economic and cultural network. According to the KOF Index of Globalization,[12] Honduras ranked roughly in the most globalized third of the world's nations in 2016. The Honduran economy depends heavily on exports to the United States and the European Union and on remittances from the many Hondurans who work in the United States. Moreover, the nation's current internal security crisis has been driven by the demand for cocaine in the United States and US deportation of thousands of gang members back to Central America since the 1990s. Hondurans are also fully integrated within American popular culture via US television programs and the Honduran news media, which extensively cover events in the United States. In contrast, Honduras has little impact on the global community.

CONCLUSION: DOUBTFUL DEMOCRATIC PROSPECTS

A constitutional crisis caused Honduras's democracy to collapse in 2009. Although the semblance of a democratic political process has been reestablished, its roots are shallow. Neither the political and economic elites who control the traditional parties nor the radical populists who lead LIBRE can be trusted to respect democratic rules when the political stakes are high. President Hernández played a key role in emasculating the Supreme Court, and its constitutional panel later abolished the once ironclad no reelection rule, which may enable him to run again in 2017. Former President Zelaya's path may also become clear to seek the presidency a second time. Both politicians, one on the right and the other on the left, are more authoritarian than democratic in temperament; they fit comfortably within Honduras's unfortunate *caudillo* tradition. The Honduran mass public's attachment to democracy and its values is also tenuous. In a context of economic weakness, social misery, and rampant crime, substantial segments of the population appear willing to follow Hernández, Zelaya, or some other future patrimonial political boss who promises to improve their security or their material well-being. Although civil society is strengthening and tolerance for corruption is in decline, Honduras remains an unpromising context for democracy.

SUGGESTIONS FOR FURTHER READING

Euraque, Darío A. *Reinterpreting the Banana Republic: Region and State in Honduras, 1870– 1972.* Chapel Hill: University of North Carolina Press, 1996.
Mahoney, James. *The Legacies of Liberalism: Path Dependence and Political Regimes in Central America.* Baltimore: Johns Hopkins University Press, 2001.
Reichman, Daniel R. *The Broken Village: Coffee, Migration, and Globalization in Honduras.* Ithaca, NY: Cornell University Press, 2011.
Schulz, Donald E., and Deborah S. Schulz. *The United States, Honduras, and the Crisis in Central America.* Boulder, CO: Westview Press, 1994.

NOTES

1. The historical section of this chapter draws on J. Mark Ruhl, "Honduras: Militarism and Democratization in Troubled Seas," in *Repression, Resistance, and Democratic Transition in Central America,* eds. Thomas Walker and Ariel Armony (Wilmington, DE: Scholarly Resources, 2000).

2. Darío A. Euraque, *Reinterpreting the Banana Republic: Region and State in Honduras, 1870–1972* (Chapel Hill: University of North Carolina Press, 1996), 96–97.

3. For a fuller discussion of the 2009 military coup, see J. Mark Ruhl, "Honduras Unravels," *Journal of Democracy* 21, no. 2 (April 2010): 93–107.

4. https://freedomhouse.org/country/honduras.

5. Peter J. Meyer, "Honduras: Background and U.S. Relations," *Congressional Research Service* (May 23, 2016): 18. www.crs.gov.

6. Latinobarómetro, Informe 1995–2015, 36, 40, 64. Americanuestra.com/wp-content /uploads/2015/09/INFORME-LB-2015-3.pdf.

7. Data/worldbank.org/country/honduras.

8. Transparency International, Corruption Perceptions Index, 2015. www.transparency.org.

9. Aaron Korthuis, *The Central American Regional Security Initiative in Honduras,* Woodrow Wilson Center Working Paper, The Wilson Center, Washington, DC (September 2014): 6.

10. National Autonomous University of Honduras (UNAH), Observatorio de la Violencia, *Boletín Nacional,* 40 (February 2016).

11. Elizabeth J. Zechmeister et al., "Internet in the Americas: Who's Connected?" *Americas Quarterly* 9, no. 2 (Spring 2015): 71.

12. Globalization.kof.ethz.ch/media/filer_public/2016/03/03/rankings_2016.pdf.

25

PANAMA: POLITICAL CULTURE AND THE STRUGGLE TO BUILD DEMOCRACY

Orlando J. Pérez

INTRODUCTION

Few countries in the world have been more defined by geography than Panama. Since the Spaniards initiated the conquest of the isthmus in the sixteenth century, Panama has been described as the "crossroads of the world." The national motto is *Pro Mundi Beneficio* (At the Service of the World). The isthmus was at the heart of Spain's colonial empire. It was where Simón Bolívar sought to establish the capital of a unified Latin America. During the nineteenth century, the Trans-Isthmian Railroad was central to the exploration and exploitation of the Western United States. The completion of the Panama Canal in 1914 symbolized the might of the United States, and Panama was vital to US strategic plans during and after World War II. After taking control of the Panama Canal in 1999 and following the canal's expansion in 2016, Panama hopes to continue to play an important role in world commerce well into the twenty-first century.

Panamanians exhibit a transactional political culture. Panama's elites were predominantly merchants; doing business is a deeply ingrained custom. Deal making, transacting for the purpose of advancing an agenda or one's economic or political interest is a vital component of Panamanian culture. Since the US military invasion of 1989, the transactional nature of Panama's political culture has contributed to democratization by promoting dialogue and compromise among political elites.

However, the very culture of transaction that enables elites to seek compromise also promotes corrupt deal making. Instrumental rationality dictates that "the ends justify the means," therefore cheating, or as Panamanians say "*juega vivo,*" generates a tendency to cut corners and do what is necessary to succeed, even if it means violating the rules.

HISTORICAL ROOTS OF THE POLITICAL CULTURE

The New Nation, 1903–1968

The common understanding is that Panama's independence from Colombia in 1903 was the product of US geopolitical machinations. Certainly, the United States played a significant role, but by the beginning of the twentieth century Panamanian elites were convinced that only independence could further their commercial interests. But US support came at a price: the United States was granted the rights to build and control the interoceanic canal. The emergence of the United States as the dominant power on the isthmus led to the development of an economy that was at the service of US financial interests.

Between 1903 and 1968 Panama had a political system controlled by an urban commercial elite allied with US military, economic, and political interests. For the United States, this alliance provided the necessary political stability for the smooth operation of the Panama Canal. For Panamanian elites, the alliance secured their right to govern the country through a system of tight social and political networks that excluded popular sectors from political participation and from enjoying the benefits of the transit route.

US dominance was evidenced by a number of steps taken to integrate Panama's economy into the US global economic network. The first step was the adoption of the US dollar as the legal currency. The dollar was chosen as the currency to comply with the wishes of William Howard Taft, then US Secretary of War and acting director of the Isthmian Canal Commission. Taft wanted currency compatibility between Panama and the Canal Zone.

Panama's status as a tax haven began in 1919 with the registry of foreign ships to help Standard Oil avoid US taxes and regulations. The shipping registry was designed to minimize taxes, regulations, and disclosure requirements in order to attract foreign owners wanting to escape their home jurisdictions. US ship owners wishing to sell alcohol to passengers used Panama's registry to avoid prohibition. The registry grew after World War II as ship companies sought to avoid higher wages and improved working conditions mandated by US law. Before that J. P. Morgan had helped Panama introduce incorporation laws in 1927 that permitted anyone to start tax-free, anonymous corporations, thus paving the way for Panama's role in offshore finance. The registry of ships was the primary activity of Panama's financial service economy until the 1970s.

The Military Regime, 1968–1989

In 1968, a sector of the Panamanian commercial elite together with the United States supported the overthrow of an elected civilian president by the National Guard, ushering in twenty-one years of military-dominated politics. The military government sought to broaden the ruling alliance by incorporating previously excluded sectors such as labor and the peasantry, while continuing to maintain the support of the urban commercial elite. The military regime pursued labor rights, control of the interoceanic waterway, and broadening of the commercial economy through the development of the international banking center and the Free Trade Zone in the city of Colón.

In 1970, Cabinet Decree 238 established the National Banking Commission and laid the foundation for the country's banking and financial center. To attract offshore investments the decree forbade the investigation of the private affairs of any bank client except under a court order. That year there were twenty-one banks with assets of US$898 million; by 1982 Panama had 125 banks with assets of US$49 billion. By the 1980s Panama's dollarized economy, secrecy laws, low tax environment, and substantial commercial links to the United States had become a magnet for those who sought to launder illicit capital and traffic drugs across the world.

As part of its effort to rally popular support, the military regime sought to renegotiate the terms by which the United States controlled the Panama Canal. Those negotiations culminated in 1977 with the signing of the Torrijos-Carter Treaties (named after Panamanian strongman General Omar Torrijos and US president Jimmy Carter) by which the United States agreed to gradually draw down its military presence on the isthmus and transfer the Panama Canal to Panamanian hands on December 31, 1999.

After signing the Torrijos-Carter Treaties, General Torrijos announced a "return to the barracks" for the military and the beginning of a process of liberalization that would lead to open presidential elections by 1984. As part of the political opening, political parties were legalized and the regime created the *Partido Revolucionario Democratico* (PRD). The organizational efforts of the party were facilitated by the increased number of state employees resulting from the government's populist policies. The PRD would serve as the political expression of the multiclass alliance that had backed the regime's efforts to negotiate the Torrijos-Carter Treaties. In effect, the party brought together urban and rural workers, businessmen, and government employees in a political coalition aimed at dominating future electoral contests and perpetuating the "revolutionary process" in power. Like the Institutional Revolutionary Party (PRI) of Mexico, the PRD was not born as a political organization to attain political power, but rather it was born *in* power. And like its sister party, the PRD sought to create a corporatist structure by which functional groups in society were represented within the state via the party. Until the United States military invasion, however, the PRD served as the political arm of the National Guard (later the Panamanian Defense Forces).

Panama's post-1969 period of political stability ended with General Torrijos's death in an airplane accident on July 30, 1981. The next several years saw considerable turmoil both in the National Guard and among the political leadership, as various individuals jockeyed to fill the void created by Torrijos's untimely death. Ultimately, Colonel Manuel Antonio Noriega, the former head of military intelligence, emerged as the regime's strongman. One of his first acts was to have the Legislative Assembly approve a bill to restructure the National Guard, which thereafter would operate under the name of Panamanian Defense Forces (PDF) (*Fuerzas de Defensa de Panamá*, or FDP). Nominally, the president of the republic would head the PDF, but real power would be in the hands of Noriega.[1] General Manuel A. Noriega used Panama's government and banking system as a criminal enterprise in the service of Colombian drug cartels.

The consolidation of power by General Noriega, his illicit activities, and the changing geopolitical environment ushered in a period of political turmoil and significant changes in US-Panamanian relations. The United States, which had worked closely with the military government, now saw it as a threat to its strategic interests in Central America. The distancing between the United States and the military precipitated a rupture of the alliance between the commercial elite and the military. The former sought to mobilize opposition to the regime by organizing civil society. The United States sought to push General Noriega from power by imposing economic sanctions. Opposition to the regime was organized around the National Civic Crusade, an amalgamation of civic, business, and popular groups that sought to defeat the government through peaceful protest and electoral politics.

The presidential elections of May 7, 1989, were held under an atmosphere of intimidation and violence. Despite the best efforts of the regime, the opposition managed to mobilize significant support and was on its way to winning when the government stopped the count and annulled the results. In the months that followed, the United States sought to broker a deal that would lead to the removal of General Noriega and recognition of the opposition's victory. In retrospect, negotiations were doomed to fail. On the one hand, the opposition groups were reluctant to support any concessions toward General Noriega. On the other hand, General Noriega feared the legal consequences of abandoning power and never quite believed the United States would remove him violently. By the end of 1989 the domestic situation and US-Panama relations had deteriorated to the point that the United States saw little option but to intervene. For the United States, the December 20, 1989, invasion was aimed at (1) protecting US assets on the isthmus, particularly the Panama Canal; (2) showing geopolitical resolve in the face of a small, regional actor that had challenged US hegemony; and (3) establishing a nominally democratic government politically and economically friendly to the United States.

In the decades since the invasion Panamanians have successfully established the institutional foundations of a liberal democracy. Since 1990, Panama has held five free and competitive elections. In each case a candidate representing opposition parties has emerged victorious. Another major accomplishment is the dismantling of the military apparatus and the creation of a new security structure that promotes civilian control. Moreover, there are clear signs that Panamanian elites have learned to behave in a more democratic and conciliatory fashion, thus promoting the necessary agreements to establish democratic rules of the game.

DEMILITARIZATION AND DEMOCRATIZATION

In 1994, Panama took an important step in securing democracy by constitutionally prohibiting armed forces. After the US invasion, the Panamanian Defense Forces (PDF) was dissolved, its command was destroyed, and its personnel were the subject of a massive reorganization. From the ashes of the PDF emerged a *Fuerza Pública* (Public Force) of twelve thousand men and women. Three factors were decisive in demilitarizing public security. First, the invasion destroyed the operational capabilities of the Panamanian Defense Forces. Second, the looting and ensuing anarchy dramatized the urgent need for an organization that could ensure public security. Third, the country required a new security apparatus independent of the party in power.

The new Public Force was composed of three services: the National Police, the National Air Service, and the National Maritime Service. These units were almost completely demilitarized in terms of their structure, philosophy, weapons, and training—though not in terms of their personnel, who were largely recruited from the former PDF. The new security forces were subordinated to civilian authorities through direct control by the Ministry of Government and Justice and budgetary oversight by the Office of the Comptroller General as well as the Legislative Assembly.[2]

The institutional success of demilitarization in Panama is bound to the internal changes in the PRD. Without acceptance by the PRD hierarchy of the preeminence of civilian authority, along with the constitutional and institutional changes undertaken since December 1989, it is doubtful demilitarization would have been consolidated.

The embrace of demilitarization was the result of internal structural changes within the party that purged the influence of former members of the PDF and their most ardent supporters, but more importantly of a change in attitudes toward the role of the military within the state. The latter was perhaps more due to political convenience than real conviction, but was important nonetheless. The PRD stopped short of totally repudiating its military past, picking out the elements that shored up popular appeal while remaining within the norms of the new political order. It accepted the new rules of the game and made no call or attempt to orchestrate disturbances or destabilize the reforms. The PRD that was victorious in the 1994 elections was clearly different from the party that had previously done little but rubber-stamp the policies of the military regime. Supporting the institutionalization of the demilitarization process allowed the PRD to consolidate its new credentials. The victory in the 1994 general election vindicated this approach and demonstrated to party members that they did not need the support of the security forces in order to gain political power. Civilian politicians within the PRD were no longer subordinated to the armed forces and for the first time since the creation of the party in 1978 were in control both of the party and of the government. What is more, by voting for the constitutional amendment that institutionalized the demilitarization of Panama, the PRD had nothing to lose because the PDF had already been dissolved.

ELECTORAL POLITICS

Since 1990, Panama has held five presidential and legislative elections (1994, 1999, 2004, 2009, and 2014), plus three referenda (1992, 1998, and 2006). Each election has been judged to be fair, free, and competitive. Freedom House has ranked Panama's political system as an "electoral democracy" since 1994, and the rankings for the indexes used by the organization (political liberties and civil rights) for 2016 were 1 and 2,[3] respectively.[4]

With few exceptions, political parties remain weak and are mostly vehicles for the promotion of individual political careers. The exceptions are the PRD and the *Panameñista* party. The former has adapted to the democratic game, participating in all post-invasion elections and winning the presidency in 1999 and 2004. The party claims to represent a social democratic ideology, but presidents serving under its banner have implemented structural adjustment policies favored by neoliberalism. The Panameñista party was the vehicle for the advancement of the political ideology and ambition of

Arnulfo Arias, one of Panama's great political leaders of the twentieth century.[5] Populist in inclination, the party is generally conservative but espouses certain ideas closer
to the center-left. The newest party is *Cambio Democrático* (Democratic Change). This
party is nonideological and was formed in 2004 to serve as the political vehicle for the
presidential ambitions of Ricardo Martinelli.

An interesting characteristic of Panamanian electoral politics is that there are few
viable options on the left of the political spectrum. The Communist Party, historically called the *Partido del Pueblo*, is no longer a legally recognized party because of its
small membership and poor electoral results—parties must have a certain number of
registered members and receive at least 5 percent of the presidential ballot in order to
survive as a legal entity. The left has been represented by some independent candidates
and in the 2014 elections by an amalgamation of labor groups under the banner of the
Frente Amplio para la Democracia (FAD). The FAD received less than 1 percent of the
vote and lost its legal standing.

The weakness of the left is a result of Panama's economic structures. The dominance
of the service sector and foreign commercial interests has led to a rather small industrial
proletariat. Thus, the basis for labor mobilization is small and labor unions tend to be
weak in relation to commercial and elite interests. Furthermore, the preeminence of the
transit economy has developed a near-unanimous acceptance of neoliberal economic
policies. Nearly every party, including the PRD, accepts the ideology associated with
an open free economy. In fact, it was a PRD-led government between 1994 and 1999
that implemented the harshest and most controversial neoliberal structural adjustment
policies, including the privatization of major state industries. The left's weakness results in a rather narrow political spectrum. The major parties all tend to agree on the
basic nature of the economic system and only differ on the emphasis of their sectoral
appeal—some are more rural and others focus on the urban middle classes—and on
personalities. This consensus has facilitated the conduct of elections because fundamental differences are small and anti-system forces too weak to be a real threat.

The 1994 elections were perhaps the most challenging test for the new electoral
institutions. The elections were the first after the US invasion and the first under an
electoral tribunal not controlled explicitly by the government. The PRD had not been
banned after the invasion and thus was going to contest elections under a free and competitive system for the first time in its history. Some in the movement that opposed the
Noriega regime had advocated banning the party and were wary of its commitment to
democratic electoral contestation. There were those who feared violence and manipulation. For their part, the PRD sought guarantees that they would be able to campaign
freely and that if they won they would be allowed to take office.

From the start of the campaign the UNDP and civil society sought to bring the
parties together in a dialogue to establish clear ground rules for the electoral contest.
These efforts led to the signing of the *Compromiso Etico de Santa María la Antigua*,
named after the university where it was signed by representatives of the various political
parties and those of the Catholic Church's Justice and Peace Commission (*Comisión de
Justicia y Paz*). The document set forth basic and practical rules for the campaign, such
as not defacing another party's propaganda. The ethical pact established precedent-
setting norms which would instruct future electoral contests. Although not always totally successful, the ethos of the *Compromiso* shaped the consciousness of political elites

to the extent that the potential moral sanction of violating the pact served to moderate partisan behavior.

For the first time since 1960, the presidential vote actually dictated the succession; losing incumbents and other candidates accepted defeat. Outgoing President Guillermo Endara promised a smooth transition, despite the fact that his party had lost. The winner, Ernesto Pérez Balladares of the PRD, graciously visited rival candidates and party leaders. The electoral tribunal presented credentials to the winners eight days after the election, and President-elect Pérez Balladares took office, as expected, on September 1, 1994.

The victory of the PRD marked a significant step forward for the party and Panamanian democracy. The party now seemed to have shed its dubious past and become an active supporter of democratic rule.

Although the 1994 elections were important because they illustrated the capacity of Panamanians and their government to hold free and competitive elections, the May 1999 elections were also important for several reasons: first, the government elected in May 1999 would receive the keys to the Panama Canal on December 31, 1999, and thus become responsible for showing the world that Panamanians were capable of managing that important global interoceanic waterway. Second, the ability to hold two free and competitive elections in a row would help to assure the world community that Panama was capable of building a democratic regime. Third, many in Panama and the United States questioned whether the PRD was capable of moving beyond its checkered past and committing itself to honest and clean electoral politics. Therefore, the PRD's performance in the 1999 elections—ones they would preside over—was closely watched.

The year before the 1999 elections was consumed with the debate over a referendum to approve or disapprove a package of constitutional amendments, among which was one that would allow the president to seek reelection. The debate was bitter, with the opposition claiming that President Pérez Balladares and the PRD wanted to institute a civilian dictatorship. The vote became a referendum not on constitutional reforms, but on the performance of the incumbent administration. In the end, the voters rejected the proposed reforms by a vote of 63 percent against and 34 percent in favor (the remaining ballots were either blank or null). Having lost the possibility of supporting the reelection of Ernesto Pérez Balladares, the PRD chose the son of the party's founder General Omar Torrijos, Martin Torrijos Espino, as their standard bearer. The opposition was led by Mireya Moscoso—the widow of Arnulfo Arias. In the end, Moscoso defeated Torrijos by more than one hundred thousand votes, becoming the country's first female president.

The next elections were held in May 2004 and pitted the PRD's Martín Torrijos—running for a second time—against a fractured set of political opponents. The Moscoso administration had been characterized by a series of corruption charges including nepotism, misappropriation of government resources, and bribery of congressional members. By the election, the government was among the most unpopular in Panama's history and a victory for the opposition was almost assured. Vying for the support of voters loyal to the incumbent government were ex-President Guillermo Endara, former Minister of Foreign Affairs, José Miguel Alemán, and businessman Ricardo Martinelli, representing his new political party, Cambio Democrático (CD). Martin Torrijos of the PRD won by a wide margin. The PRD had thus proven it could win, lose, and win again with little disruption to Panama's underlying political system. By the end of the third electoral contest Panama's electoral system, while not perfect and subject to significant debate,[6] was consolidated enough to be considered an electoral democracy.

The elections of May 2009 marked the emergence as a major political force of Ricardo Martinelli's Cambio Democratico. Martinelli had developed the party as a vehicle for his electoral ambitions, receiving about 5 percent of the vote in the 2004 elections. He spent the next five years growing the party and polishing his image. Martinelli is an interesting character. One of the wealthiest men in Panama, he had served in the Moscoso administration and had cultivated an image as a philanthropist and capable businessman. Panama's political culture is susceptible to the rise of business leaders, particularly those engaged in commerce. Although many voters are suspicious of wealthy elites and the origins of their money, they also admire the ability to amass wealth. Even if they think such wealth was obtained through shady deals, the culture of juega vivo feeds a certain admiration for the skills and success of the rich. Martinelli also played up his macho, strongman image (he is a notorious *bon vivant* and has been equated with Silvio Berlusconi of Italy).

The PRD nominated Balbina Herrera, a former minister of housing and legislator. The election centered on personal attacks between the candidates. Herrera was accused of being a radical leftist who had received support from Hugo Chávez, the controversial president of Venezuela. Martinelli sought to exploit Herrera's past links to General Manuel Noriega's regime and strong anti-US statements. Martinelli's campaign also emphasized the need for change after five years of PRD-led government. For her part, Herrera accused Martinelli of being mentally unstable; rumors have abounded for years that Martinelli is bipolar. She also tried to use Martinelli's wealth and business practices against him. Martinelli turned the charges in his favor by adopting the campaign slogan "the crazies are more" (*los locos somos más*). Herrera countered with the slogan "the poor are more" (*los pobres somos más*). In the end, the desire for change, despite robust economic performance during the last three years of Torrijos's administration, and Herrera's campaign mistakes led to a landslide victory for Martinelli, who captured 60 percent of the votes. His coalition also won a majority of seats in the legislature.

The most recent elections were held in May 2014. The campaign was framed around the theme of continuity versus change. The government touted social spending, infrastructure investments and economic growth. Panama's economy saw average GDP growth rates of 7 percent during the Martinelli administration, with significant increases in foreign direct investment and infrastructure spending—particularly around the expansion of the Panama Canal. There were two leading opposition candidates: Juan Carlos Navarro, a former mayor of Panama City and the candidate of the PRD, and Juan Carlos Varela, representing the Panameñista party. Mr. Varela had served as vice-president and foreign minister until August 2011 when President Martinelli removed him from the government.

Panama's constitution prohibits immediate presidential reelection. However, the nomination of the first lady, Marta Linares de Martinelli, as the vice-presidential candidate on the government party's ticket was seen as a sign of the president's desire to remain influential after the elections. Despite polls showing the CD's José Domingo

Arias leading, Juan Carlos Varela won the elections with 39 percent of the votes. Arias received 31 percent and Navarro 28 percent. The victory of Varela marked the fifth election in a row in which a candidate representing an opposition political party has won the presidency.

Despite losing the presidency, the CD won 30 of 71 legislative seats, with the PRD winning 25 seats and the Panameñistas 12 seats. The situation in the National Assembly remained fluid months after the elections as numerous allegations of corruption and use of government funds for campaign purposes were raised against several legislators. In subsequent investigations, the Electoral Tribunal overturned the election results in ten legislative districts, requiring those districts to hold new elections. Out of the 10 districts, CD won 4, Panameñistas 4, and PRD 2.

EXECUTIVE-LEGISLATIVE RELATIONS

Prior to the US invasion, the Panamanian legislature acted as a rubber stamp for the executive, which in turn was dominated by the military.

Today, the president has extensive legislative powers. The constitution gives the president exclusive authority to formulate and introduce laws relating to the national economy and expenditure of funds. In matters of treaties and international agreements the legislature can only approve or disapprove the measure, it cannot make any changes to the proposed document. If the legislature does not approve the national budget by a certain date, the budget submitted by the executive becomes law without legislative action. This means that if the president does not want the legislature to change his or her budget, he or she can work with his or her allies in congress to block legislative action.

The lack of budget initiative means legislators are at the mercy of the executive to satisfy constituent needs. Without significant powers to affect the national budget (probably the most important policy statement a government can make) the legislature cannot hope to become an active and effective branch of government.

Legislative autonomy has increased during the post-invasion period, but presidents continue to hold significant sway over the legislature. Only President Guillermo Endara (1989–1994) had to deal with an assembly controlled by an opposition hostile to his policies. Every other chief executive has either had majorities of their party in control of the legislature (Ernesto Perez Balladares 1994–1999, Martin Torrijos 2004–2009, Ricardo Martinelli 2009–2014, and Juan Carlos Varela 2014–2019) or was able to use executive power to obtain support from nominal opposition legislators (Mireya Moscoso, 1999–2004). President Moscoso's efforts to acquire legislative support received significant attention for being brazen and overtly corrupt. For example, on January 16, 2002, PRD legislator Carlos Afu appeared on TV waving a large wad of cash, which he claimed was a US$6,000 down payment on a US$20,000 bribe to vote for infrastructure projects and sanction the appointment of supreme court justices. As a result of these accusations and the scandal they generated, Article 155 of the constitution was amended in 2004 to allow the supreme court the authority to investigate sitting legislators. The episode with Deputy Afu illustrated the effect of corruption on executive-legislative relations. Presidents routinely use state resources to obtain majorities in the National Assembly.

ORLANDO J. PÉREZ

During his term of office, President Martinelli used the distribution of government contracts and spending to "persuade" PRD legislators to either support his policies or cross the aisle and join his party. Nine of the PRD's twenty-six lawmakers shifted their allegiances, giving a legislative plurality to Martinelli's Democratic Change—which was only the third-biggest party in the Assembly following the 2009 elections—and leaving it just three seats short of an absolute majority. President Juan Carlos Varela (2014–2019) has also used the resources available to the executive to cobble together a working majority in the assembly. Ironically, both Martinelli and Varela built majorities by cooperating with the PRD—the old party of the military. The PRD has thus become the center of political coalitions in the assembly. This is partly because the party has held a relatively large number of seats since 1994 and also because its deputies have shown an ability to set aside partisan differences so they could advance their personal and political interests.

"JUEGA VIVO": THE CULTURE OF CORRUPTION

The inability to restrain corrupt practices, and in fact their increase, is perhaps the most significant weakness of Panama's post-invasion democratization. Panama was ranked 72 out of 168 countries and territories surveyed in Transparency International's 2015 Corruption Perceptions Index.[7] A probe into the purchasing practices of the National Assistance Program (PAN), a highly touted welfare program started by former President Martinelli, now involves the ex-president, dozens of congressmen, and several cabinet members. The investigation centers on allegations that government officials inflated contracts and took bribes to favor certain suppliers. Two former PAN directors have been arrested for allegedly skimming US$60 million dollars from contracts. Prosecutors have indicted 120 people and seized US$22 million in connection with the case. More than a billion dollars in contracts issued between 2010 and 2014 have come under close scrutiny due to poor accounting records.[8] The magnitude of the money and the number of people involved in the allegations against former President Martinelli are significant even by Panamanian standards. In early 2015, the Supreme Court of Panama lifted the immunity from prosecution of the former president and named a special prosecutor to investigate the charges.

The recent revelations of the Panama Papers,[9] and the activities they represent, are a manifestation of juega vivo on a grand scale. Panama's low tax environment and open economy, plus its sophisticated banking system, lends itself to use as a platform for avoiding taxation or cleaning illicit gains.

After the US invasion, confidence in Panama's financial services industry returned and by 2015 the system reported US$118 billion in assets, close to US$10 billion more than in 2014. Today, financial services make up about 8 percent of Panama's GDP. Regulating such a large sector of Panama's economy, employing thousands of people, and generating wealth for some of Panama's most prominent businessmen is very difficult. Despite some efforts in the past five years to increase transparency and accountability, the system remains prone to abuse. In fact, many Panamanians see the latest revelations in the Panama Papers as an attempt to smear the good name of the country and undermine its growing economy. In the end, the government is walking a fine line between meeting the demands of the international community, improving the image of Panama, and preserving one of the pillars of the economy.

A DUAL ECONOMY: DEVELOPMENT, INEQUALITY, AND THE PANAMA CANAL

Although Panama is categorized by the World Bank as having an upper-middle-income economy because of its relatively high per capita income level of US$11,800 (2014 estimate), and its economy grew an average of 8 percent since 2003—the fastest rate in Latin America—the country's major economic challenge remains a highly skewed income distribution. According to the UN Economic Commission for Latin America and the Caribbean, Panama's poverty rate was almost 37 percent in 2002, but declined to about 26 percent in 2009 and 2010. Extreme poverty also fell from 18.6 percent in 2002 to 11.1 percent in 2009, although it increased to 12.6 percent in 2010. In the indigenous areas poverty reaches 90 percent and in rural areas more than 60 percent. Indigenous communities—such as the *Ngäbe Buglé*—have mobilized to oppose mining and hydroelectric projects on their land, as the government continues to seek to develop Panama's mineral reserves. The mobilization of indigenous communities is perhaps the most signficant civil society movement since the one that organized against the military regime in the late 1980s. Indigenous communities are challenging the basic premise of Panama's economic development strategy, which relies heavily on foreign direct investement and privatization of land holdings. In 2016, the Varela government reached a deal with indigenous leaders that would allow completion of a controversial hydroelectric plant, Barro Blanco, in exchange for concessions, such as providing a percentage of the income from the sale of power from the project to indigenous communities. But some residents remain adamantly opposed to the project and have vowed to continue fighting it.

Panama's economic development is intimately linked to the Panama Canal. The country was born as a result of the dispute around which superpower would gain the right to build the interoceanic waterway. For Panama's elite the building of the canal was the culmination of their dream to postion the country at the heart of the global economic system. The evidence suggests that Panama's post-1999 management of the canal has been exemplary. The canal has been profitable and has provided significant funds to the national treasury, and the management has been free of corruption.

The growth of the national economy in the past decade has largely been attributed to the investment of US$5 billion dollars in a project to expand the waterway. The expansion, the largest project at the canal since its construction, created a new lane of traffic through the construction of a new set of locks, doubling the waterway's capacity. Building the new locks allowed for so-called neo-Panamax ships, with a capacity nearly three times (14,000 containers instead of just 5,000) that of Panamax ships, to travel the canal. The expanded canal opened in June 2016. Although most Panamanians celebrated the conclusion of the project, concerns remain about the impact of a decline in global demand for maritime commerce, the environmental consequences of the large amounts of water needed to run the new waterway, and the impact of a design process that perhaps focused too much on cutting costs.[10]

CONCLUSION

Although the US invasion was highly contested, the undeniable consequence was the dismantling of the old military and the opportunity to establish civilian control over security forces. The process was consolidated because most political actors, despite their partisan affiliations prior to the invasion, eventually supported the elimination of the armed forces. Another important transformation was that undertaken by the Democratic Revolutionary Party. The PRD has accepted and played by the democratic rules of the game, winning two national elections since the invasion and twice handing power to their opponents.[11]

Corruption remains the most significant challenge facing Panama's democracy. A political culture that condones, often encourages, and seldom punishes the use of state resources for private gain weakens the rule of law and undermines public trust in state institutions.

Finally, no single challenge compares with the necessity to manage the country's most important asset, the Panama Canal, in an effective, independent, and transparent manner. The Canal Authority is consistently the most trusted national institution. Just as the birth of the nation depended on the building of the interoceanic waterway, any future economic prosperity and the consolidation of democracy depend in great measure on the success of the expanded canal.

SUGGESTIONS FOR FURTHER READING

Conniff, Michael. *Panama and the United States: The End of the Alliance*. 3rd ed. Athens: University of Georgia Press, 2012.

Greene, Julie. *The Canal Builders: Making America's Empire at the Panama Canal*. New York: Penguin Press, 2009.

Guevara Mann, Carlos. *Political Careers, Corruption, and Impunity: Panama's Assembly 1984–2009*. Notre Dame, IN: University of Notre Dame Press, 2011.

Maurer, Noel, and Carlos Yu. *The Big Ditch: How America Took, Built, Ran, and Ultimately Gave Away the Panama Canal*. Princeton, NJ: Princeton University Press, 2011.

Pérez, Orlando J. *Political Culture in Panama: Democracy After Invasion*. New York: Palgrave Macmillan, 2012.

Sanchez, Peter M. *Panama Lost? US Hegemony, Democracy, and the Canal*. Gainesville: University of Florida Press, 2007.

Szok, Peter. *Wolf Tracks: Popular Art and Re-Africanization in Twentieth-Century Panama*. Jackson: University Press of Mississippi, 2012.

NOTES

1. Law No. 20 of September 29th, 1983, reorganized the National Guard in an attempt to strengthen its organizational and professional base. The law went on to concentrate power in the hands of the commander in chief of the new Panamanian Defense Forces (PDF) (Ley 20 de 29 de septiembre de 1983, Gaceta Oficial, Organo del Estado, No. 19.909, viernes, 30 de septiembre de 1983, Panama, Republica de Panama, p. 1–8).

2. "Decreto de Gabinete No. 38 de 10 de febrero de 1990," Gaceta Oficial, no. 21, 479 (20 de febrero de 1990).

3. The indexes go from 1 to 7, with 1 being the best score and 7 the worst. Scores of 1 and 2 place Panama in the "free" category among the nations of the world.

4. Panama's score on the index for political rights was 1 until 2014, when it was changed to 2 because of corruption charges against President Martinelli and intimidation of journalists investigating such cases.

5. Arnulfo Arias was a founding member of a group known as *Acción Comunal*. Founded in 1926, the basic ideological tenants of Acción Comunal were nationalist and fervently anti-United States; their slogan was *"Patriotismo, Accion, Equidad y Disciplina"* (Patriotism, Action, Equality, and Discipline). In 1931, Acción Comunal spearheaded the first violent overthrow of a sitting president in Panamanian history. In 1940, Arnulfo Arias founded the National Revolutionary Party (precursor to the Panameñista movement). His program called for a new governing alliance, composed of the most dynamic sector of the bourgeoisie (i.e., the industrial), small agricultural producers, and rural peasants. Arnulfo Arias became the great *caudillo* of Panamanian politics. He ran for the presidency five times (1940, 1948, 1964, 1968, and 1984): three times (1948, 1964, and 1984) he was denied his electoral victory through fraud, and three times (1941, 1951, and 1968) he was overthrown by the military.

6. Many questioned the manner in which legislators were elected, which tended to over-represent rural areas, placed high entry costs on independent or small party candidates, and encouraged celebrity or lone wolf candidates in the single-member districts. Additionally, some observers also advocated for a second-round balloting for the presidential election.

7. Transparency International. 2015. *Corruption Perceptions Index 2015: Results*. www.trans parency.org/cpi2015/.

8. Ereida Prieto-Barreiro. 2015. "El coleccionista de casas," *La Prensa*. 14 de abril. www. prensa.com/locales/coleccionista-casas_0_4185331634.html; Tracy Wilkinson, 2015. "In Panama, corruption inquiries grow after president's tenure ends," *The Los Angeles Times*, May 23, 2015. /www.latimes.com/world/mexico-americas/la-fg-panama-corruption-20150523-story .html#page=1.

9. https://panamapapers.icij.org/.

10. A key design concern is that the distance left to maneuver a post-Panamax ship through the locks is too small when considering the size of the ship, the length of the locks, and the tugboats used to move the ships through the waterway.

11. Some argue that just as a "leopard cannot change its spots," the PRD still encompasses militaristic or authoritarian tendencies. Although I accept that some in the PRD may not have fully embraced democracy, and, to a certain extent, those who do have done so for instrumental reasons, the fact remains that the party leadership has contested every single election since the invasion and accepted their losses without conflict or violence.

26

THE DOMINICAN REPUBLIC: DEMOCRACY, STILL A WORK IN PROGRESS

Lilian Bobea

INTRODUCTION

As happened with most Caribbean societies that evolved from being colonized subjects to having republican systems of governance, the Dominican Republic became part of the international economic and political community as a peripheral actor. Since the last century, however, the country has followed a path of modernization through social and economic changes, international exposure via commercial exchange and migration, cultural transformation to become more urbanized and transnational, political diversification with the emergence of a more competitive plural party system, and institutional strengthening. Each one of these transformations has improved considerably the level and quality of life in the Dominican Republic, and has furthered the country's emergence in the international arena. Despite its size, the Dominican Republic currently constitutes a relevant political agent in the Western Hemisphere.

BACKGROUND

The Dominican Republic shares with Haiti the island known by its indigenous population, the Tainos and Arawaks, as *Quisqueya*, later renamed Hispaniola by the Spanish conquistadores that took possession of the territory in 1492. Hispaniola would eventually become a subject of the great power rivalry between France and Spain. The conflict was finally resolved through the signing of the Treaty of Aranjuez (1777), through which the eastern two-thirds of the island was ceded to the original Spanish colonizers, with France acquiring the western portion.

By the middle of the nineteenth century, the Dominican Republic began participating in the world economy: as with any peripheral country, first through the export of raw materials such as tropical hardwoods, tobacco, coffee, and sugar. It wasn't until well into the twentieth century that the country left behind this extractive economic model to reposition itself within the international economy through another externalized structure, this time based on tourism, remittances, free industrial zones, and services.

The political and social trajectory of the Dominican Republic has been one of difficulty and resilience, change and continuity. Situated in the center of the Caribbean, the country has historically been exposed to the threat of invasions, hurricanes, pirate incursions, and illicit trafficking. In 1844, the country obtained its independence, paradoxically enough not from the original colonizer Spain, but from the first black republic in the new world. The Republic of Haiti emerged in 1804 from the triumphant slave rebellion of the so-called Black Jacobins[1] under the command of the Haitian leader Toussaint L'Ouverture. Following Haiti's independence there were several attempts by the Haitian political leadership to take control of the western part of the island as a way to insure their own security against an eventual invasion from France. By 1822, under the presidency of Jean-Pierre Boyer, the occidental side of Hispaniola finally fell under the control of the Haitian government in an occupation that lasted for twenty-two years, opening a long period of resistance from a national independence movement. At the time of the Dominican Republic's independence in 1844, the new nation was a fundamentally rural society.

The territorial and political fragmentation of the time translated into the absence of a central administrative body that could be characterized as a functional institutional framework recognizable as a modern state. Much to the contrary, the very local political rivalries constantly threatened not only the cohesiveness of the nation but also its sovereignty. Members of the political and commercial elites in what might be called a protostate won political power only by the armed control they exerted over their rivals. *Caudillismo* was the name that reflected this atomized political landscape and social order. The caudillo paradigm was distinctive; it was characterized by a patronage approach to public goods and a lack of institutionalized means of succession. Caudillos used political violence to fill the vacuum of power in the absence of the rule of law. They also developed informal mechanisms to gain the favor of the popular masses, through patron-client relationships.[2]

Later in the nineteenth century, modernizing regimes attempted to centralize administrative functions and connect internal territories into a national state entity that would serve the interests of an emerging capitalist elite and of international investors. They all eventually benefited from the concessions given by successive governments aimed at increasing the construction of roads, bridges, and railroads. Under the US customs receivership (1905–1940) and the American military occupation (1916–1924), the creation of transportation and telecommunications systems to facilitate centralization moved apace, as noted below.

THE MAKING OF A REPUBLIC

During the long nineteenth century, the country endured several regressive experiments, including an attempted re-annexation to Spain by an influential political figure, General Pedro Santana. There was a period of virtual civil war, plagued by rebellion and conspiracy between the two main parties of the time: *Azules* (Blue) and *Colorados* (Red). The Azules, more inclined to liberal views, represented the tobacco growers and merchants of the northern Cibao. The Colorados, much more conservative, represented the interests of the northwest, south, and east. The Azules produced Ulises Heureaux (popularly known as Lilis), who by the end of the century would become a key figure in enabling the administrative and infrastructural architecture required for the country's incipient modernization. The Heureaux administration (1882–1899) welcomed third-party actors to the country: the private foreign investors incarnated in first the Westendorp Corporation of Holland, succeeded by the San Domingo Improvement Company (SDIC), with its headquarters on Wall Street in New York, which took over Dominican finances by buying the foreign debt that the Dominican state had with European stakeholders in 1893.[3]

The impact of foreign capitalists was mixed. On one hand, the SDIC did help the ambitious president Ulises Heureaux to promote an export-oriented economy; implement the gold standard, even though this was ephemeral; and build much-needed infrastructure. On the other hand, most of these investments were granted to the SDIC in the form of concessions, giving the company the prerogative of establishing a monopolistic dominance in the country. Even worse, the majority of the capital raised through bond issues in Europe was in fact used to keep Heureaux in power. Eventually, the SDIC and Lilis were together responsible for the collapse not only of Dominican government finances, but ultimately of the economy itself, flooded by a depreciated local currency and an incommensurable debt. That crisis led to the eventual intervention of the United States, under the presidency of Theodore Roosevelt, which would experiment with new mechanisms to stabilize, rationalize, and reinforce geopolitical supremacy over the Dominican Republic. The Roosevelt administration accomplished this in 1905 by taking control of the Caribbean nation's finances through a customs receivership to ensure the payment of their debts to hegemonic powers and avoid intervention by any European power, a policy later known as "dollar diplomacy."[4]

These developments had two remarkable outcomes: first, the repositioning of the Dominican Republic as a strategic objective of the United States, and second, the increasing political volatility of the country, precisely the opposite of what dollar diplomacy and the customs receivership were meant to accomplish. For a few years after the receivership was installed, the country enjoyed relative peace under a liberal and reformist president, Ramon Caceres. However, when he was assassinated in 1911, a series of revolts and revolutions destabilized the country and gave the United States the pretext to occupy it from 1916 to 1924.

The influence of external forces in a nation's internal process of social change has been the subject of exhaustive study. The Dominican state lacks administrative and political centralization, a condition that reflected the incapacity of the political elites to produce a strong and competitive party system. According to a study by Ellen Tillman, the American occupiers assumed "that a centralized state could be militarily imposed and . . . that such a structure would resolve the major complications of Dominican government."[5] But the newly centralized state and more powerful military created the conditions that allowed Rafael Leonidas Trujillo Molina to come to power in 1930 and terrorize his countrymen until his assassination more than three decades later.

Trujillo was a product of the military academy installed in the country before US troops left the Dominican Republic in 1924. His predecessor, President Horacio Vazquez, made Trujillo one of the country's top military officers, which helped him to consolidate the loyalty of the rank and file. In the election of 1930, Trujillo used intimidation and political violence against the man who had elevated him to command the military, and with the defeat of Horacio Vazquez, democratic institutions disappeared for the next three decades. Once in power, Trujillo created one of the most violent, personalist, and enduring dictatorships in Latin American history, even changing the name of Santo Domingo, the oldest European settlement in the New World, to Ciudad Trujillo. The establishment of order became a priority. Under his totalitarian mandate, Trujillo imposed social control and discipline by regulating internal flows of migration, severely punishing dissidence, terrorizing the masses, and creating a ubiquitous intelligence apparatus at the national level. In the 1930s, Trujillo established the Dominican Party (*Partido Dominicano*) as the only legal political party in the country.

One key to Trujillo's megalomaniacal dictatorship was his government's fierce anti-Communism and close ties to the United States. Although some State Department officials despised the dictator, Trujillo carefully cultivated his image as a steadfast American ally in the Cold War and treated members of congress who visited his nation as royalty. Only after Fidel Castro won power in neighboring Cuba in 1959 and Trujillo attempted to assassinate the president of Venezuela, Romulo Betancourt, did US policy makers begin to reevaluate their support of Trujillo.

Trujillo headed one of the longest dictatorships in Latin America and the Caribbean, ruling the Dominican Republic for thirty years through persecution, extermination, incarceration, torture, and intimidation of most of his opponents and the subjugation of the whole population to his rule. Trujillo was assassinated in 1961 by a group of military officers with support from sectors of the Dominican middle class.

THE POST-TRUJILLO POLITICAL ORDER
AND STATE-SOCIETY RELATIONS

Wilfredo Lozano, a Dominican sociologist, has divided this long period from 1961 to the present into eras characterized by key political actors, the institutional arrangements they promoted, and the politics of representation orchestrated around the possibilities of governance within Dominican democracy. According to Lozano, the period between 1961 to 1978 reflected the authoritarian pattern of governability, dominated by Trujillo protégé Joaquín Balaguer, who became president after Trujillo's assassination; the second cycle (1978–1996) was the populist period; and the final and current one, from 1996 to 2016, is the corporatist period, based on the predominance of effective clientelistic practices.

These three stages have been anything but linear. The period that immediately followed the downfall of Trujillo's dictatorship was marked by a convoluted transition in which a call for elections allowed the center-left party, the *Partido Revolucionario Dominicano* (PRD), at the time headed by the well-known, center-left intellectual Juan Bosch, to win the election over organized sectors of the Dominican oligarchy. The conservative group, the *Union Civica Nacional* (UCN), however, was strongly supported by influential sectors of landowners, industrialists, merchants, and the military, and eventually by the administration of US President Lyndon Johnson. Fearing that Bosch would lead the country toward socialism as Fidel Castro had done in neighboring Cuba, Johnson sent US troops to the island in 1965, marking the second time the Americans played a role in the establishment of the nation's institutional architecture. The military occupation, which lasted until 1966, forced the creation of a transitional government that organized new presidential elections for 1966. The winner of those elections, supervised by the US occupiers, was none other than Trujillo's protégé Joaquin Balaguer, thus beginning the "*doce anos*" (1966–1978) of unbroken political control by Balaguer's authoritarian government, which has been variously called "Caesarist" and "Bonapartist," as well as sultanistic.[6]

At a time when Latin America was undergoing complex period of popular resistance to military dictatorial governments, Balaguer's authoritarian and fraudulent model was showing signs of exhaustion. The ideological fragmentation among the vernacular political and economic elites, as well as within the *campesinato* (peasantry), which was Balaguer's popular constituency, forced him to open the political arena by letting opposition parties became legal and allowing the return of political figures who were either in jail or in exile. This in turn became the opportunity for the country to hold for the first time in more than a decade a more pluralistic and participative election.

The year 1978 marked a watershed for democracy with the defeat of Balaguer, who lost the election to a renewed PRD led by Antonio Guzman (1978–1982), who won a popular mandate with a social democratic orientation. Internal confrontations within the original PRD had earlier culminated in the organization's fragmentation, giving birth in 1974 to the more neoliberal Dominican Liberation Party (*Partido de la Liberacion Dominicano,* PLD), headed by Juan Bosch and a group of his followers who had left the PRD.

The coming to power of the social democratic PRD in the nonfraudulent and open elections of 1978 was the beginning of a new era of competitive politics. This transition also marked a more populist state/society relationship, with major growth of social movements, community-based organizations, and organized labor movements that were able to exert their demands in favor of the improvement of their working conditions, salaries, and social policies. During the first government of the PRD there were several hundred protest actions. The major riots of 1984, triggered by the government's agreement to an austerity program with the International Monetary Fund during the presidency of Jorge Blanco (1982–1986), one of the founders of the PRD, accelerated the collapse of this progressive administration and the deterioration of popular confidence in the social democratic alternative.

One of the most important effects of this transition was the demilitarization of public life. The military lost the central role it enjoyed under Trujillo and Balaguer, as became evident when President Guzman purged the armed forces after conservative military officers attempted to overthrow his government.

The second consequence of the transition toward a populist and liberal democracy was the change to an administrative model that included social expenditures as part of the government's budget. This decision balanced the process of corporatization of the entrepreneurial sector, which goes back to the 1970s and 1980s when state policies protected private capital. The state assumed some of the expansion of social benefits for working- and middle-class professionals via public employment policies. However, this model showed limitations as important sectors of the economy became more and more privatized. In addition, the system for taxing lime phosphate, which favored private capital, along with protectionist policies that favored the private sector, increasingly weakened the state.

In the political arena, competition among emerging parties was propelled by their particular agendas and by internal tensions within those parties. The PRD, which was the predominant political force throughout the 1970s and into the mid-1980s, saw confrontation between Antonio Guzman, who represented agricultural interests, and Salvador Jorge Blanco, a candidate more inclined to favor the industrialists and commercial bourgeoisie. In social terms, this period also was marked by the mobilization of the urban masses, who had become better organized through various associations and institutions, modifying, as Lozano (2016) points out, the terms of negotiation between political power and its social base. In institutional terms, not only the entrepreneurial class became more corporatist and independent from the influence of the state; but also the congressional representatives enhanced their independence from the executive power, allowing political parties to cut deals around their particular interests.

By the end of the PRD's second term, the import-substitution industrialization model was already in crisis. The declining economy brought with it the deterioration of the popular trust in the populist alternative. Not only was the traditional export economy declining, along with serious deficits in the production of energy needed for industrialization, but the international debt also became a heavy burden for the government to carry. As the working class and popular masses became more active in demanding the improvement of social conditions, many felt betrayed by the PRD's social democratic alternative.

In the 1986 elections Joaquin Balaguer was once again elected president, an outcome that was seen by many as punishment for the PRD's previous performance. Balaguer, the uncontested leader of the Reformist Social Christian Party *(Partido Reformista Social Cristiano,* PRSC) hoped to retain power for two more consecutive electoral periods, by fraud if need be. His reelection in 1990 was widely seen as fraudulent, and over the next few years the legitimacy of Balaguer's government was increasingly challenged. In the 1994 elections Balaguer hatched an intricate plot to prevent the PRD and its presidential candidate, Jose Francisco Pena Gomez, from coming to power. As several analysts (Lozano 2013; Graham 2011; Diaz 1996) have noted, the 1994 elections were manipulated from the beginning, using fraudulent means, such as changing the district where people were supposed to vote, duplicating names to create confusion, "buying" and sequestering votes. These maneuvers compromised the integrity of the Junta Central Electoral, and thereby prevented thousands of Dominicans from voting. These political tensions brought the country to the verge of violence. Balaguer once again "won" reelection, but to defuse the crisis he was forced to negotiate a constitutional amendment with the PRD that shortened his term in office from four years to two years. The constitutional revision also recognized the dual citizenship of Dominicans living outside of the country, allowing them to vote in national elections. It further created an inclusive mechanism for electing judges to the highest courts, such as the *Consejo Nacional de la Magistratura,* and a new procedural code that changed the court system in favor of an adversarial procedure.

Despite all these efforts in favor of institutionalization, the PRSC succeeded in orchestrating an accord with Leonel Fernández from the PLD, as well as other conservative forces constituting the so-called Patriotic Front (*Frente Patriótico*). Eventually, this Frente Patriótico would evolve into what was known as the "Pact for Democracy," an alliance that made it possible for Leonel Fernández to win the 1996 elections. Balaguer's maneuver displaced the PRD and elevated the PLD, not as rival of the PRSC, but as a partner. In effect, the octogenarian leader of the PRSC transferred power to the PLD more or less democratically while also effectively undermining the chances of the PRD to win the 1996 elections. With this final act of his sixty-year political career, Balaguer facilitated the reemergence of the Dominican Liberation Party, now led by Juan Bosch's pupil Leonel Fernández, as the main actor in Dominican national politics. From that moment forward, the political system heavily relied on a single-party arrangement, transforming the political landscape for years to come. Fernández and the PLD remain dominant forces in the nation's political life to this day.

In economic terms, since the conservative government of the Reformist Party returned to power in the mid-1980s, the country had evolved new points of insertion into the international economy. Tourism rapidly became a new source of international currency, along with remittances sent home by the hundreds of thousands of Dominicans living abroad (mainly in the United States and Spain), as well as the development of free trade zones where investors were generally exempted from taxes and were protected from the formation of labor unions. This new development model was as externalized as the previous one and even more vulnerable to competitive conditions of international supply and demand.

This cycle of political, economic, and social arrangements among the traditional party elites came to its end with the deaths of Jose Francisco Peña Gomez in May 1998; Juan Bosch in November 2001 (at the time he still was considered a messianic leader of the PLD) and Joaquin Balaguer in mid-2002. The passing of the three leaders who had dominated post-Trujillo politics was recognized as "the end of the caudillos."

Even the closing of a political era did not put an end to the caudillo's relationship to the political parties and the patron-client relationship between the party leadership and its constituencies. This pattern of exercising power also was reflected in the relationship between the Dominican state and society. The paternalistic approach that distinguished Balaguer's relationship with a mostly agrarian and rural population evolved toward a prebendalist, yet still clientelistic, interaction with a more complex, urbanized society. By the end of the twentieth century, Dominican society comprised a growing middle class, a significant sector of the population that depended on the remittances sent by family members from the diaspora, and a large socially and economically marginalized population located in the expansive slums of the metropolitan areas of Santo Domingo, the National District, Santiago, and La Romana.

Even before the physical passing of the caudillos, Leonel Fernández, a disciple of Juan Bosch, had emerged as the new leader of the PLD. From 1996 to 2000 he embraced the mantra of modernization of the state, a sort of new social pact with society, with a clear agenda of strengthening his party to remain in power for years to come.

Despite the institutional modernization promoted by Fernández and the growing economy, inequality among urban sectors of the population, stagnation on the political front, and clear evidence of corruption weakened the PLD in the 2000 elections. This time, a renewed PRD supported the candidacy of agronomist Hipólito Mejía, a member of Santiago's agrarian oligarchy and a defender of the agro-industrial sector, who won the elections with a neopopulist agenda. During Mejía's administration, a national social security plan was approved thanks in part to the control that the PRD had over the lower house of congress. Mejía's emphasis on the promotion of agriculture led him to support approval of the US-Central America Free Trade Agreement (DR-CAFTA), intended to promote internal production in more favorable competitive conditions in international markets. Several issues clouded Mejía's administration. For one thing, a new constitutional amendment to allow the possibility of reelection exacerbated conflicts within the PRD, setting off fractures within the party organization. Moreover, corruption was at its height, and embezzlement that involved banking fraud linked to one of Mejía's bodyguards led a major bank to collapse, bringing the national economy to a crisis that affected all social classes. After this economic catastrophe, the PRD was so delegitimized that in 2004 there was little question that the PLD would win.

When Leonel Fernández returned to power in 2004, he was basically without serious political rivals. The electorate was truly disappointed in his major competitor, the PRD, and the PRSC post-Balaguer had been reduced to a third force that only functioned as a strategic ally of the larger parties, not as an option in itself.

In his second term, Fernández and the PLD expanded their reform agenda from their first government. Fernández implemented a fiscal reform aimed at generating resources for public investments such as road construction, which in turn would stimulate employment in the construction sector. He also expanded social security, retirement, and health coverage for workers in the public sector. One of the major contributions of this period was implementation for the first time of a national public security strategy. The *Plan de Seguridad Democratica*, or PSD (Democratic Citizen Security Plan), was conceived as an integral, holistic, and preventive public policy. It had several components, including police and judicial reform, establishment of a national criminal policy, reform of the prison system, social investment, and interventions focused in the most violent neighborhoods.

With Leonel Fernández facing reelection in 2008, the political system became more presidential and personalist than ever, especially because the PLD retained majorities in both houses of congress. After Fernández won a third term in office, the four years that followed were marked by rumors and highly publicized cases of corruption. Several constitutional reforms were implemented as byproducts of this competitive politics. Some of them introduced important institutional innovations, but most reforms were intended to facilitate particular political interests to the detriment of constitutional principles. For example, the 2003 constitutional amendment promoted by Hipólito Mejía of the PRD sought to lift the ban on successive reelection and allow a president to serve two full terms. Although Mejía hoped to benefit from that change, he paradoxically helped Fernández win reelection in 2008. In 2010, Fernández proposed a new "reform" of the constitution to permit a president to serve three times consecutively. The constitution was modified literally overnight and secretly, because of the PLD's control of congress.

The consequence of all these maneuvers was heightened factional rivalry that ended up splitting both the PRD and the PLD. In the end, the PLD faction led by Danilo Medina, former Secretary of the State under Fernández, went on to win the 2012 election. Medina, an economist and founding member of the PLD, had an understated personality, yet he succeeded in mobilizing the party rank and file with the motto, "To fix what is wrong, maintain what is right, and to do what never has been done." He won support as a pragmatic, approachable figure who appeared at public places and governmental project sites without previous notice, just to get a sense of what was really going on under his administration.

In the 2016 election, Medina led a coalition of party organizations to confront a new political organization, the Modern Revolutionary Party (PRM), whose candidate, Luis Abinader, attracted part of the constituency of the old PRD, intellectuals and sympathizers from the center-left. While facing external pressure from opposition constituencies that were against the practice of reelection, Medina and his partisans were fostering internal tensions by attempting to reform the constitution once again to allow presidential reelection. Ultimately the Fernández faction opted for party cohesion and agreed to accept Medina's reelection.

In the midst of these political nuisances, Medina's administration faced a more serious issue that emerged from a decision of the constitutional court (*tribunal constitucional*) to strip most of the Haitians residing in the Dominican Republic of their Dominican citizenship, even those who were born or grew up in the Dominican Republic. This controversial verdict sharply divided the Dominican public around questions of national sovereignty, national identity, and especially racism. The measure was widely reviled by the international community and human rights organizations, as well as the Haitian-Dominican community and citizens who advocate for a better understanding among the two societies. This situation also has been a major disgrace for the two-term Medina government.

SUPPORT FOR DEMOCRACY

The Dominican Republic was one of the first countries in Latin America and the Caribbean to experience the transition from an authoritarian regime to a democratic one in the 1970s. This transition was imperfect, however; it carried with it a series of features from the old regimes. Among the most relevant characteristics of premodern political schemes is the predominance of personalism, which in some cases assumes messianic tones, and most of the time incarnates a hyper-presidentialist pattern of government. Likewise, clientelism has become almost a systemic condition of Dominican politics, especially in the many ways political parties relate to civil society. Contrary to what happened in other countries of the hemisphere, the articulation between state and society was based on a precarious process of institutionalization that promoted informal mechanisms of social mobilization and power influence throughout the political party system.

According to the Latin American Public Opinion Project (LAPOP), Dominican citizens' opinions of the democratic project reveal decreasing support for the political system and its institutions, from 35.2 percent of respondents in 2006 to 29.4 percent in 2014. The country shows a low level of trust in political parties (29.4 percent). The same pattern applies to the justice system, in which only 38.5 percent of respondents declared confidence, versus 46.7 percent in 2006. Regarding trust in the national legislature, fewer than half of the respondents (42.8 percent) declared confidence in 2014 in comparison with more than half (52.9 percent) in 2006. Only trust in the president has increased in 2014 (71.1 percent) compared to 2008 (62.8 percent), a curious reflection of the persistent presidentialism that defines the Dominican political landscape. One of the most striking indicators is the fact that the Dominican Republic places among the countries with the lowest ranking of citizens' trust in elections (42.5 percent), above only Honduras (42.2 percent) and Brazil (34.0 percent), and below Venezuela (44 percent) and Chile (62.5 percent).

Over the last years, support for democracy has fluctuated between 78.7 percent of citizen responses in 2006, to 68.5 percent in 2010, rebounding to 72.5 percent in 2014. The commitment that citizens express toward democracy is very closely related to the performance of government institutions, especially with regard to the provision of social services, the enhancement of economic conditions, and the legitimacy and credibility of the president.

Interestingly enough, civil society entities enjoy more legitimacy than public institutions. The Catholic Church and the evangelical churches garner 62.7 percent and 58.9 percent of the public's support, respectively, followed by neighborhood councils.

SOCIETY AND SOCIAL ISSUES

More than a century and half since its independence and its constitution as a republic, and almost four decades since its transition to democracy, the Dominican Republic is still a highly divided nation in social terms, including racial, ethnic, and class configurations.

The current Dominican population of approximately ten million people is predominantly young, with an average age of 26.5 years (only 6.7 percent is over sixty-five), with almost 70 percent residing in cities. As a product of multiple migration flows, the Dominican Republic has a heterogeneous racial composition of black, mulatto, and white populations, coming from an ethnic mixture of Europeans (predominantly Spaniards and Italians) and African descendants. Since the nineteenth century, the Dominican Republic was a destination country for Japanese, Chinese, and Middle Eastern migrants. Despite this diversity, race and ethnicity still are sources of tension among Dominicans, as is the relatively low tolerance of homosexuality. In 2008, the AmericasBarometer found very low social tolerance of diverse values, attitudes, and ways of life, especially regarding sexual preference.

However, these trends also show signs of evolving: by 2014 the AmericasBarometer found that 34.5 percent of Dominicans supported the idea of homosexuals running for public office. Also, 22 percent of those interviewed approved of same-sex couples' right to marry, an increase of 4 percent from three years before.

Issues related to race, identity, and ethnic origins have historically contributed to intolerance against Dominicans of Haitian heritage, as well as Haitians living in the country for decades, along with their descendants. Regarding racial identity, 58 percent of Dominicans interviewed in 2013 identified as mestizo or indigenous (even though there are no scientific traces of the indigenous population since their extermination by the end of the seventeenth century). Only 15.8 percent of respondents identified as black, and just 12.4 percent as mulatto or mixed-race.[7]

Because two countries share the island of Hispaniola, with population flowing almost exclusively from Haiti to the Dominican Republic, the immigration issue has been the center of a major social, political, and cultural debate for more than a century. In recent years, it has become a national and international human rights issue. The decision of the constitutional tribunal to strip citizenship from Haitians who couldn't produce documents to prove their nationality, even if they were clearly born in the country, reopened a wound that had never properly healed. Despite the contentious situation, it is important to recognize that 61 percent of those interviewed by LAPOP in 2014 agreed that the government should offer social services to undocumented immigrants (nearly all of Haitian origin). More than 52 percent agreed that Haitians in the Dominican Republic should have access to jobs, but only 41.3 percent supported the government providing work permits to undocumented Haitians.

Dominicans of Haitian origin are not the only group that suffers hardship. Social inequality remains stark in a country that in recent years has shown healthy economic growth when compared with other Latin American and Caribbean nations. The Dominican Republic is considered an upper-middle-income country by World Bank standards, but its Gini index in 2013 was calculated as 47.7.[8] This is a systemic condition: for the last twenty-seven years, the coefficient has oscillated between 52.9 and 45.68. This unequal distribution of wealth is reflected in the fact that 40 percent of Dominican citizens are considered to be living in poverty. The high levels of underemployment explain why the overall unemployment rate is only 13 percent, meaning that the informal and unregulated economy compensates for the lack of stable job opportunities, especially among the youngest sector of the population, 30 percent of whom are unemployed as of 2016.

THE RISE OF CRIME, VIOLENCE, AND CITIZENS' INSECURITY

Crime, violence, and insecurity, along with inequality and the deterioration of social citizenship, are among the major problems affecting the daily lives of Dominicans over the last ten to fifteen years. Institutional weakness, corruption, and lack of trust in the political leadership and fundamental institutions are the major challenges for the Dominican state and democracy.

Since 2000, violent crime has increased dramatically. In fact, the number of homicides and other serious crimes has spiked since the economic crisis of 2004. In just four years (2000–2004), the Dominican Republic went from a homicide rate of 10 per 100,000 inhabitants to 25 per 100,000 inhabitants. Common street crime and property crime also escalated, as did the number of victims of rape, domestic violence, and gang violence. Much of the criminal activity has been associated with drug trafficking, due to the country's location, which makes it a major transit point for drugs coming from South America to North America and Europe, as well as the active role that Dominican organized criminal groups play in transnational criminal networks. As early as the mid-1990s, this illicit economy opened up new channels for black market goods as well as illegal local markets and related criminal activities. In the Dominican Republic, not only did drug trafficking became an important source of income, especially for unemployed and underemployed youth; it also was a way to get rich quickly for a corrupt elite of military, police, and judicial public servants, as well as private entrepreneurs.

The impacts of these trends are reflected in the AmericasBarometer, according to which 27 percent of Dominicans interviewed in 2010 declared that someone in their household was a crime victim. By 2014 that rate had grown to 36 percent, among the highest in Latin America and the Caribbean, along with Peru, Ecuador, and Venezuela.[9] Institutional violence constitutes another major problem, because the police engage in the common practice of killing suspected perpetrators while in hot pursuit. The rate of killings by police for the last decade has oscillated between 2 to 4 victims per 100,000, a record comparable only to Brazil and Jamaica. This institutionalized violence undermines the legitimacy and professionalism of the police force and demonstrates the inability of the criminal justice system to confront the problem.

The recent upsurge of violence correlates with the use of guns in the commission of crimes against persons and with confrontations among armed actors competing for emerging drug markets. The presence of gangs in many urban settlements was reported by 48 percent of the LAPOP respondents in 2012, with a slight decrease of five points in 2014.[10] The growing participation of corporative criminal networks, which include Dominican criminal groups outside and inside the country, is responsible for establishing more sophisticated businesses that promote illicit flows into and out of the country. In addition, the involvement of corrupt officials and bureaucrats in illicit activities has exacerbated violence and fostered more complex crime. The press now reports "entrepreneurial" crimes that previously were rare, with mafia-style murders, "*sicariatos*" (hitmen), kidnappings, and score-settling among drug dealers. In 2015 and 2016, the Attorney General and the National District Prosecutor have both publicly denounced the involvement of public servants in criminal activities such as extortion and drug-related crimes. Equally alarming is the fact that the new criminals seem to have formed links with government officials, not only rank-and-file police officers, but also high military officials, bureaucrats, and even members of the Dominican congress.

In the face of increased drug trafficking, crime, and violence, Fernández's second administration implemented the Democratic Security Plan (PSD) in 2005. The plan was well received by the general population and created lots of expectations among middle- and lower-class Dominicans. It worked fairly well for its first two years, even though the results were mostly felt in the urban areas of the two main cities, Santo Domingo and Santiago. Administrative and political issues imposed serious limitations on the implementation of the plan. For one thing, the funding to improve police work conditions and salaries and to modernize the communication and research component of the system was precarious and never met the needs of the sector. Second, institutional disorganization undermined the integrated approach necessary for coordinated action. Finally, there was confusion about the role that the executive gave to the military in crime fighting while the police were experiencing their own institutional reforms. These factors limited the effectiveness of the PSD and lessened the public's confidence in the government's ability to address the new challenges that Dominicans were facing in the realm of insecurity.

THE INTERNATIONAL ENVIRONMENT

The Dominican economy is not only the largest in the Caribbean region but also the fastest growing in the Americas, at a rate of 7 percent for the past two years. According to Franco Uccely, JP Morgan's chief economist, "tourism is looking bright; remittances are quite robust and foreign investment is through the roof."[11] The United States is the most important commercial ally of the Dominican Republic, because nearly 85 percent of Dominican trade is oriented toward the United States. However, from the Dominican side there is also a negative exchange balance. Over a period of ten years (2006–2016), the balance of exchange went from US$818 million to US$2.8 billion in favor of the US.[12] According to the US Census, in 2014, total exports from the United States to the DR amounted to more than US$7.9 billion, while the amount of Dominican goods imported to the United States totaled US$4.5 billion. Likewise, in 2016, the United States exported US$7.1 billion to the Dominican Republic, while only importing a total value of US$4.3 billion from the DR.[13]

The Dominican Republic-Central America Free Trade Agreement (CAFTA-DR), approved by the US Senate in June 2005, is the first trade agreement between the United States and a group of small, developing countries to create exchange opportunities by eliminating tariffs and opening markets. (The Dominican Republic falls in the middle rank of countries that export commercial goods under CAFTA-DR, which the DR joined in 2007.) In 2009, the estimated two-way trade amounted to US$37.9 billion.[14]

Under CAFTA-DR, 100 percent of US goods exported to Central America and the Dominican Republic were exempted from tariffs beginning in 2015, which resulted in a liberalization of trade in goods and services. Despite high expectations and positive predictions during the initial signing, some Dominican investors from the agro-industrial and textile manufacturing sectors saw the agreement as detrimental to the country, based on the negative exchange balance that resulted from it. This opinion contradicts governmental sources, such as the economy ministry that see a stable trade relationship over the ten years since the signing of the treaty. According to the ministry, since 2011 the country has exported between US$4.1 and US$4.6 billion to the United States. Nevertheless, garment exports decreased from US$1.9 billion to US$851 million over the same period. National economists interpret these trends as indicative of a change in the Dominican export matrix, which tends to be more diverse and less dependent on the textile economy.

CONCLUSION: CHALLENGES, RISKS, AND OPPORTUNITIES

The political trends described here have important consequences for Dominican democracy and the well-being of Dominican society.

Power has become progressively centralized while political parties became corporatized machines, meaning that they accumulate economic and social rent for the benefit of those who monopolize resources and have the capacity to manipulate basic institutions of the precarious democracy.

The excessive personalism reflected in the clientelist and neo-patrimonial model before and after the democratic change has given too much power to the executive, while becoming a major challenge to the separation of powers and the independence of the legislature and the judiciary. Also, the lack of relative autonomy of institutions tends to reinforce a major deficit of transparency and accountability in the public sector. As result of this lack of transparency, corruption has become an endemic condition, at least in the perception of 80 percent of the Dominican population polled by Gallup in February 2016. Among these, 46 percent perceived greater corruption, including 32 percent of those who sympathized with the party in power, the PLD.

Personalism, clientelism, and corruption impede attempts to modernize the Dominican state and to democratize social and political conditions that could provide Dominicans with a more comprehensive social citizenship. Moreover, these political problems as well as patterns of behavior tend to foment attitudes among Dominican citizens and the bureaucracy that reinforce authoritarian practices and discourses.

The Dominican political party system exhibits a paradox. On one hand, political parties are still considered the main conduit for individual supporters and for collective rewards and bargaining. On the other hand, the legitimacy of the two main contending parties, the PRD and the incumbent PLD, has deteriorated as both have shown serious signs of internal fractures and corrupt practices among the upper and middle leadership. Like Venezuela, Turkey, and Russia, the Dominican Republic is a democracy that holds regular elections, but the quality of the democratic process has been seriously undermined, leading to widespread disenchantment among voters. In the coming years, Dominican political parties will struggle to recapture the legitimacy that they have lost.

SUGGESTIONS FOR FURTHER READING

Betances, Emelio. *State and Society in the Dominican Republic.* Boulder, CO: Westview Press, 1995.

Bobea, Lilian. *Violencia y Seguridad Democratica en Republica Dominicana.* Santo Domingo: FLACSO, 2011.

Cassa, R. *Capitalismo y Dictadura.* Santo Domingo: Editora de la Universidad Autonoma de Santo Domingo, 1982.

Faxas, Laura. *El Mito Roto: Sistema Politico y Movimiento Popular en Republica Dominicana, 1961–1990.* Mexico: Siglo XXI Editores, 2007.

Hartlyn, Jonathan. *The Struggle for Democratic Politics in the Dominican Republic.* Chapel Hill: The University of North Carolina Press, 1998.

Latin American Public Opinion Project (LAPOP). *Political Culture of Democracy in the Dominican Republic and in the Americas, 2014: Governance across 10 Years of the Americas Barometer.* Nashville, TN: Vanderbilt University, 2014.

Lozano, Wilfredo. *El Reformismo Dependiente.* Santo Domingo: Ed. Taller, 1985.

———. (2013). *La Razon Democratica; Cultura Politica, Desarrollo y Clientelismo en la Democracia Dominicana.* Santo Domingo: Ed. Buho.

Tillman, Ellen D. *Dollar Diplomacy by Force; Nation-Building and Resistance in the Dominican Republic.* Chapel Hill: University of North Carolina Press, 2016.

Veeser, Cyrus. *A World Safe for Capitalism: Dollar Diplomacy and America's Rise to Global Power.* New York: Columbia University Press, 2002.

Wiarda, Howard J., and Ester Skelley. *The 2004 Dominican Republic Elections: Post-Election Report.* Washington, DC: Center for Strategic and International Studies, 2004.

NOTES

1. In his 1938 book, *The Black Jacobins: Toussaint L'Ouverture and the San Domingo Revolution,* the Trinidadian historian C. L. R. James recounted the process and universalist values of freedom, liberty, and equality embraced by the Haitian revolution between 1791 to 1804, in the context of the French revolution.

2. See Emilio Betances, *State and Society in the Dominican Republic* (Westview Press, 1995), 2.

3. For more details of this period and these issues see Cyrus Veeser, *A World Safe for Capitalism, Dollar Diplomacy and America's Rise to Global Power* (New York: Columbia University Press, 2002).

4. Ibid.

5. See Ellen D. Tillman, *Dollar Diplomacy by Force: Nation Building and Resistance in the Dominican Republic* (Chapel Hill: University of North Carolina Press, 2016), 104–105.

6. These qualifying statements have been made by Lozano, 1985, and J. Hartlyn, 2008.

7. See Latin American Public Opinion Project, LAPOP, 2014:126.

8. The Gini coefficient is a statistic measure of dispersion that represent the income and/ or wealth distribution and as such is generally used to measure inequality. A Gini coefficient of zero represent perfect equality, while a coefficient of 1 means the maximum inequality among the values

9. LAPOP, 2014:137.

10. LAPOP, 2014:143.

11. See *The Economist,* "Hispaniola: The Dominican Republic and Haiti: one island, two nations, lots of trouble. One is about to hold elections. The other has not had a proper government for months. The differences go deeper than that." Port-au-Prince and Santo Domingo, May 14, 2016. www.economist.com/news/americas/21698805-one-about-hold-elections-other -has-not-had-proper-government-months.

12. *"Foreign Trade-U.S. Trade with Dominican Republic."* https://www.census.gov/foreign -trade/balance/c2470.html.

13. www.census.gov.

14. Office of the US Trade Representative. Retrieved January 2016. https://ustr.gov /countries-regions/americas/dominican republic.

27

HAITI: SEARCHING FOR DEMOCRATIC GOVERNANCE

Georges A. Fauriol

INTRODUCTION

Few factors have had a more lasting impact on Haitian development than the violent transition from colonialism in the late eighteenth century. This brought initially little more than nominal independence. Haiti's early status as an outcast among the community of nations further increased its vulnerability to both internal and external threats. At the beginning of the twentieth century, this overlap of factors ultimately generated direct US military and political administration (1915–1934). The follow-up years to the Duvalier dictatorships after 1986 triggered direct engagement from the international community, while the twenty-first century so far has brought more political breakdowns.

This multivariate legacy of instability has generated a frustrating search for political change and democratic governance—framed by weak political institutions, an absence of coherent economic policy making, and an overburdened social infrastructure. Arguably, Haitian institutional independence is now commingled with extensive participation from the nongovernmental (NGO) and humanitarian communities, and since 2004 a quasi-permanent multinational presence anchored by United Nations peacekeeping forces. The January 2010 earthquake that destroyed much of the national capital's infrastructure only reinforced this reality. Breakdowns of the two succeeding electoral cycles (2010–2011 and 2015–2016) underscore the profound discomfiture of the Haitian polity and the somewhat feckless attitudes of international actors that frame it.

HAITI AND THE CULTURE OF DYSFUNCTIONAL POLITICS

Characterizing this polity is therefore a challenge. Baseline analyses suggest urbanized political and economic elites often at odds with each other in maintaining a fragile status quo, exploiting a limited enclave of export-oriented commercial activity. Some have described this environment as a "kleptocracy," a "predatory state," and giving rise to the "politics of squalor." Recognizing the salience of Haiti's large rural populations leads to a characterization of Haitian society as "colonial" or "self-colonized." Connected to that is a strain of analysis that places Haiti's development failures at the crossroads of a core-periphery paradigm of capitalism and notably American imperialism. Others borrow from development literature and assess Haiti in the context of a "transitional society."

The arrival on the political scene in the late 1980s of Jean-Bertrand Aristide, a Roman Catholic priest espousing liberation theology and populist politics, gave currency to notions of "deliberative" democracy. More recent characterizations draw attention to Haiti's status as a "failed state" as well as notions of an exhausted *habitus*, that is, of a governance repertoire in such disrepair that it can no longer generate coherent action. All of these characterizations incrementally add to a rich if disjointed conceptual mosaic, while individually, each is unable to provide a satisfactory explanation of Haiti's experience.[1]

The challenges facing the Haitian state trace back to a flourishing plantation colony characterized by extraordinary wealth and deep social and racial divisions. Saint-Domingue, as Haiti was then known, was the crown jewel of France's overseas empire, fueled by the importation of more than 800,000 African slaves. This untenable socio-economic mix of slaves and sugar came crashing down after 1789, triggered partly by the explosions of the French Revolution. What followed was Haiti's own revolution and war of independence (1789–1804). In the ensuing confrontation blacks, lighter-skinned mulattoes, and whites built shifting alliances, intermittently supported by the intervention of warring British, Spanish, and, naturally, French forces.

After independence Haiti faced the traditional threat patterns of nineteenth-century power politics regarding small states, and as a spiritual heir to the French Revolution, it provided a serious challenge as the first non-European postcolonial state in the modern world. According to diplomatic historian Rayford Logan's characterization, Haiti started out as a "power and enigma," turned into an "anomaly," became a "threat," and ultimately was an "outcast" among the nations of the earth.[2] Nonetheless, the nation survived mostly on the shoulders of a remarkable collection of powerful personalities who over time defined Haiti's style of governance—authoritarian figures anchored to coercive power: Jean-Jacques Dessalines (1804–1806), Haiti's first emperor and efficient exterminator of the colonial white power structure; Henri Christophe (1807–1820), Haiti's first crowned king; Alexandre Pétion (1807–1818), Haiti's first president for life; and Jean-Pierre Boyer (r. 1818–1843), who ruled over an increasingly crippled nation.

At midcentury, another extraordinary figure emerged—Faustin Soulouque (1847–1859), later Emperor Faustin I. He ordered a general massacre of the mulattoes, led the country in several abortive campaigns into the neighboring Dominican Republic, and further precipitated Haiti's decline. Of the twenty-two presidents who served between 1843 and 1915, one finished his term in office, three died a natural death while in office, one was blown up with the presidential palace, another one was probably poisoned, one was hacked to pieces, and one resigned. The fourteen others were overthrown.

The effects of nineteenth-century economic expansionism nurtured the seeds of Haitian instability. France was the underwriter for all external loans between 1825 and 1896, and owned the national bank—while also negotiating ruinous long-term payments to indemnify France of its loss of Saint-Domingue. The Germans initially controlled key trading houses, while imports increasingly came from the United States, and after 1900 US influence expanded into banking. Washington, in a pattern seen elsewhere in the region at the time, perceived the sorry state of Haitian finances as a Trojan horse for European interference in the Caribbean. Without any clearly defined endgame, in 1915 US Marines landed in Haiti following political violence in the capital, Port-au-Prince. The initial security rationale for the landing mutated into a policy to promote Haitian political stability, financial rehabilitation, and economic development.

Instead, Haiti became one of the United States' least successful interventions. Although a minimum of financial order was established, debt was reduced, and the administrative infrastructure was improved, the US presence did not lead to the emergence of democratic political virtues or national development coherency. Nationalist backlash forced a review of US policy in 1930. Faced with similar problems in Nicaragua, President Herbert Hoover and his successor, Franklin D. Roosevelt, were determined that the United States would exit from Haiti's tropical imbroglio as quickly as possible, and did so in 1934.

What ensued was initially hopeful, anchored to an energized political and cultural effort to institutionalize the foundations of a modern nation. Ironically, the most visible product of the US occupation—the *Garde d'Haiti*, trained by US Marines—later transformed into Haiti's armed forces, undermined these hopes, and gave way to the decaying weight of presidential excesses. This period came to an uninspired end with the 1957 elections that brought François Duvalier to power in a period of brutal family rule that was to last until his son's downfall in 1986.

GOVERNANCE AND POLICY MAKING

The real tragedy of the period following the US occupation (1915–1934) is that it provided the backdrop for François Duvalier's sinister regime (1957–1971). With the hindsight of what was to follow with his son's tenure (1971–1986) and the Aristide presidencies (1990–1995, 2001–2004), this was "at best a missed opportunity, and at worst a complete failure."[3] The intellectual class that had emerged in the 1920s was nationalist in character, subscribing to varying forms of progressive social change later tinged with Marxism, and was anchored to the reevaluation of the country's African tradition—*noirisme* or black nationalism. This somewhat messy ideological brew also held hope for a potentially vibrant environment of political change, an incipient modern civil society, a labor movement, political party development, and cultural revival. The high point of these hopes was the Dumarsais Estimé presidency (1946–1950), which, however, floundered under conflicting ideological tensions and radicalization.

Unlike many of his predecessors, François Duvalier ("Papa Doc" became president for life in 1964) was never a military man and shrewdly played up his image as a soft-spoken physician and part-time ethnologist. He also successfully cultivated US concerns with Communism in the Caribbean, which generated somewhat reluctant support from Washington. He ruthlessly suppressed opponents, real or imagined. The influence of the mulatto elite was eroded, the political power of the Roman Catholic Church was reduced, and the army was purged and brought into line. A powerful paramilitary organization (*Volontaires de la Securité Nationale*, or VSN—the infamous Tonton Macoutes) was established to protect the regime and enforce its directives.

Following his father's death, Jean-Claude "Baby Doc" Duvalier assumed office in April 1971 at age nineteen and initially confounded political predictions. A superficial commitment to an "economic revolution" implied greater solicitation of assistance from major donor countries (notably the United States) and multilateral lending agencies. Nonetheless, the aimless nature of Baby Doc's style of governance ultimately led to his downfall in 1986 after facing hardened Catholic Church militancy and a reluctance by the army to defend the regime. What also played a part was Washington's declining interest in supporting "friendly" dictators like Duvalier and others, such as Chile's Pinochet, the Philippines' Marcos, and South Korea's Chun Doo Hwan.

US policy initially shifted with the Carter administration's emphasis on human rights followed by a broader global theme of freedom and democracy under the Ronald Reagan presidency. Haiti also drew the attention of an emerging Congressional Black Caucus and others on Capitol Hill, driven in part by the differentiated treatment of Haitian refugee flows—as opposed to Cuban refugees—in the early 1980s. Ultimately, Duvalier left on board a US military transport plane for exile in France on February 6, 1986 (returning to Haiti in 2011, where he died in 2014). What followed was not, however, what either Haitians or the international community had hoped for.

Governmental authority passed to the military-led Council of National Government, headed initially by General Henri Namphy. The ensuing near-anarchy subsided temporarily and US foreign aid flows increased, as did support from other donors. Some progress was even achieved in stabilizing the economy. However, the foundations upon which this stability was constructed were flawed. International policy designs were tied to notions of democratic consolidation, when the reality on the ground visibly lacked the political consensus to achieve that objective. The first casualty was the bloody election of November 1987, halted in the first hour of balloting by armed thugs linked to the army and Duvalierist allies. A truncated election in January 1988 brought to power an exiled academic turned politician, Leslie Manigat. He received little international support and was overthrown by the military in June. The political situation unraveled further with a succession of intra-military coups. Under international pressure this process gave way to an interim consensus government that in turn led to elections in December 1990.

By an overwhelming majority, Haitians chose a charismatic ordained priest and proponent of liberation theology, Jean-Bertrand Aristide, as president in what was regarded by most observers as the nation's first modern election. However, the 1990 elections presaged a fifteen-year period of intermittent euphoria as well as a succession of spectacular failures during which Aristide was the principal political variable. His capacity to speak the political language of Haiti's overwhelmingly poor population and convey an almost mystical message of hope was his most singular attribute. This was encapsulated most vividly by Aristide's signature concept, *Lavalas*, the cleansing flood that would lead Haiti's masses "from misery to poverty with dignity." Often accused of holding a questionable commitment to Western-based notions of representative democracy, Aristide sustained a political marathon lasting through two presidencies, two constitutional interruptions, and periods of exile.

Within eight months of his 1990 election, Aristide was ousted in a coup. Whether it was a result of the army's paranoia, Aristide's inflammatory rhetoric, or the reaction to violence directed at Aristide's political opposition, the crisis that ensued endured through several phases of an interim military regime and only concluded with an international military intervention that returned Aristide to power in October 1994. He was succeeded in 1995 by his protégé, René Préval, whose only achievement was to complete his five-year mandate. His term (1996–2001) was highlighted by increasing distrust between Aristide's Lavalas movement and the rest of Haiti's political actors, let alone portions of the international community, all of which led to political paralysis.

Aristide's return to office in early 2001 was quickly undermined by disputes over the credibility of the previous year's cycle of local and national elections. What was a serious but manageable technical breakdown morphed into a political crisis and ultimately violence. Diplomatic mediation by the OAS failed, and by 2003 the political atmosphere reached a point of no return. A disjointed coalition of Aristide's former supporters turned against him along with an assortment of gangs, former military, and renegade police. Large segments of Haiti's urban civil society also began mobilizing, and in an increasingly violent standoff, and under pressure from Washington and Paris, Aristide left the country (some argue was forced out) in late February 2004 for exile in South Africa—returning to Haiti in 2011. In a repetition of the recent past, René Préval once again became Aristide's successor (2006–2011).

Preval's second presidency ended tragically. With its epicenter in the Port-au-Prince region, the January 12, 2010, earthquake devastated the nation's core infrastructure, killed about three hundred thousand people, and left another one million or more homeless. The impact was overwhelming and affected the 2010 electoral cycle. The ensuing breakdowns were initially linked to a partially destroyed national elections machinery, but politics was ultimately the main culprit. This mix of factors became the backdrop to controversies surrounding the results of the first round of presidential elections in late 2010. The political standoff lasted for several tense weeks and was only resolved with direct engagement from the international community. Through what some observers considered a heavy hand, a partial vote recount analysis became the basis for an imposed solution to the crisis. This switched the results of the presidential candidates in the second and third positions for a spot in the two-person runoff, and ensured Michel Martelly's victory in the March 2011 elections.

Martelly's tenure became the basis for a new electoral breakdown. A popular musician with no formal political background, "Sweet Mickey" was perceived by some as a game changer following the turbulent Aristide and Préval presidencies. Demonstrating something of a populist streak and mass appeal, notably among youth, his presidency (2011–2016) presided over some post-earthquake reconstruction successes but also growing political impotence. Parliamentary elections and the first round of presidential elections were delayed until late in 2015, yet his tenure ended with no elected successor because of disputes over these elections—a dynamic reminiscent of the 2010–2011 electoral fiasco. The "provisional" government that stepped into the breach quickly lost momentum, and with an increasingly thin layer of constitutional or political credence, was forced to repeat the late 2015 cycle of presidential elections. The ensuing late November 2016 election results, although contested by some, essentially repeated the disputed 2015 outcome in favor of Jovenel Moïse—a protégé of Martelly with little political experience.

ECONOMIC AND SOCIAL CHANGE

Approximately the size of the state of Maryland, Haiti lies at a crossroads of historical trading passages and strategic interests—bound by the Windward Passage to the west, the open waters of the Atlantic Ocean on the north, and the Caribbean Sea to the south. Haiti is the poorest country in the Western Hemisphere, with a GDP per capita estimate in the US$700 range and essentially unchanged over the past decade, a ranking that places Haiti 163rd out of 188 countries on the UN Human Development Index, an estimated population of 10.7 million with a life expectancy that ranks 167th out of 201 in UN data, and a mountainous topography coupled with land-management neglect that has reduced further an already negligible productive potential.

Revenues from a few odd exports as well as apparel manufacturing and offshore assembly have had limited economic impact—despite having been significant sectors in the 1970s–1980s—leaving much of the workforce on the margins of economic life. The estimated unemployment of 40 percent of the labor force is compounded by the probable underemployment of two-thirds of those who are nominally working. As a result, Haiti's surplus talent keeps leaving for other shores. The current US population of Haitian origin is estimated to be more than 1.5 million, and their remittances and other economic flows contribute by some accounts perhaps one-third to half of Haiti's GDP. Approximately 20 percent of the country's national government budget comes from foreign assistance and related direct budgetary support, while an indeterminate portion of the economy is dependent on drug trafficking and contraband trade.

What in the past made life somewhat bearable for the average Haitian was the fact that government had historically not intruded too much into their lives. After 1957, however, the Duvalier regimes modernized notions of government by introducing a more formal and occasionally brutal local presence. Neither modern law enforcement nor much of an effective local administrative structure emerged. Nonetheless, government administration has constituted a center of influence, if for no other reason than that it has represented the source of jobs, money, and patronage, if not outright access to the national treasury. At its most senior echelon are the lucky few whose authority is derived from ties to the presidential palace. This dysfunctional structure is not only inefficient and corrupt but also further weakened by the absence of a capable second and tertiary layer of public administration.

Despite these hard facts, Haiti has not lost the basic fabric of its national character. Its roots lie in a hybrid of African ethnicity and culture, the legacy of French eighteenth-century colonialism, an evolving brand of Catholicism, and the aftereffects of the United States' strategic sweep in the Caribbean region. The African cultural and spiritual features have been foundational for a majority of the population since they were first imported in the seventeenth century. Haiti remains ethnically and culturally distinct, with about 85 percent of its people of direct African descent, and is the only independent French-speaking nation in the Caribbean region. These characteristics have survived despite economic adversity and the extraordinary failures of political leadership in advancing national development.

Established religious institutions are numerically and culturally important in the Caribbean generally, and in Haiti coexist with indigenous cults and practices derived from tradition and folklore. Voodoo has a deeply engrained national persona, enriched by both ancestral African rites and Christianity. It has sociocultural relevance in the contemporary environment by providing a link to an ancestral past, and shapes a sense of fatalism perceived as prevalent in Haitian culture.

POLITICAL INSTITUTIONS

In its more than 200 years Haiti has never succeeded in establishing the structures of a civilian society capable of minimizing conflict. Instead, the rule of force through the consolidation of political power in the hands of strongmen has been the baseline institutional characteristic. The US occupation's legacy, the Garde d'Haiti and the successor Haitian armed forces, for a while gave all of this a somewhat coherent if colonial institutional tone. Yet, this was in turn gradually undermined during the Duvalier dictatorships, followed into the 1990s by the collapse and ultimate political dismemberment of the army in the aftermath of the first Aristide presidency and ensuing US-led military intervention.

There has been a rolling series of efforts to create a professional national police force in the post-Duvalier years, but this has been undermined by politicization of the force, let alone intimidation and corruption. Worse yet, the intersection of a politicized police and the impact of drug trafficking have created additional pressures and were factors in the downfall of the second Aristide presidency (2001–2004). Understandably, the reintroduction of a professional military force has remained a sensitive topic, although the continued presence of an international UN-led security presence has provided a cap on the ambitions of those Haitian proponents of such a force.

The overall poverty of the nation has centralized national authority into a small urban constituency, while the cumulative ravages of crises since the 1980s have undermined the reservoir of political leadership. The political party structure, anchored more by personalities than by viable agendas, remains weak. In order to appeal to a wider public, national leadership has been tempted by populist solutions that often lack any practical policy deliverables. In contrast, more traditional political parties have oscillated between legalistic political platforms and well-intentioned technocratic proposals—often appropriate solutions for Haiti's challenges but devoid of any contextual meaning for the average citizen.

Modern social or political pressure groups typical of democratic environments (for example, human rights organizations, local community interests, women's groups, students, labor unions, and the media) have found some space to prosper since the 1990s. Many of these are tied to an expanding multinational network of donors and an NGO community, as well as an increasingly active US-based Haitian diaspora; the latter is both a source of remittances and an as yet unrealized potential source of political influence. Significantly, a politicized civil society and business community played a salient role in the collapse of the Aristide presidency in 2004. For its part, a small modern business sector—generally living a life very different from that of the average Haitian citizen—remains cautious and is in part co-opted by changing political winds.

The Catholic Church has since the mid-nineteenth century fulfilled an important educational mission and provided isolated communities with the rudiments of continuity and linkage to the outside world. As elsewhere in the region, the Catholic clergy has in recent times split between conservative and liberal contingents, and has played decisive roles in political transitions. Pope John Paul II's 1983 visit to Haiti legitimized opposition to and partly enabled the ultimate demise in 1986 of the Jean-Claude Duvalier regime. Under pressure from the Vatican, the church subsequently pulled back from a formal political role, but its engagement continued to be the conduit through which human rights and sociopolitical concerns were exposed. The grassroots or *Ti Legliz* movement in the 1980s, which was the basis for Aristide's arrival to power in 1990, highlighted splits within the church hierarchy and more generally within Haitian society. The expanding grassroots involvement of evangelical Protestant denominations also has translated into political movements with national presence.

Explanations of Haiti's experience point to the historically exploitative character of Haiti's elites: the mulatto (lighter-skinned) minority generally associated with the country's commercial activity, and the black elite, representing the political governing class. Paradoxically, despite the modernizing sociopolitical influences of the urbanized elites, the emotional heart of Haiti remains in its inner country—rural, poor, dedicated to basic agricultural production, and sometimes living in socioeconomic conditions often reminiscent of past centuries. Long periods of isolation have made this part of Haiti a conservator of African traditions, and it is in this milieu that traditional spiritual influences remain strong.

This duality is exacerbated by geographical separation of the elite from the masses and of the urban population from the rural one, with significant political and social implications. The peasantry has until recently played no formal role in national decision making. Language use underscores the point: the lingua franca is Creole, yet national debates take place partly in French, a language that the vast majority of the population does not speak or read. Significantly, the use of English is expanding due to the growing influence of Haiti's US diaspora and the sociocultural influence of the United States.

The dysfunctional character of socioeconomic development has triggered a movement of populations to larger cities, particularly Port-au-Prince. The nation's capital is now an unsightly, crowded, and chaotic urban region that encompasses by some estimates almost one-third of Haiti's population. This demographic urbanization has created an expanding universe of slum-like communities and a subculture with its own political and social dynamics. Arguably, in the past twenty-five years a new paradigm has therefore emerged, at the heart of which is a political contest to determine the direction and control of these communities. As a populist leader, Aristide's support after 1990 was based in part on the mobilization of these urban constituencies, and a related appeal to Haiti's peasant heartland. Similarly, Michel Martelly's background as a popular musician and band leader—with little political experience—provided an effective populist character to his unlikely presidency (2011–2016).

THE INTERNATIONAL ENVIRONMENT

The period since the 2004 collapse of the second Aristide government has been framed by a succession of efforts to return the country to normalcy, backed up by a robust international presence. Unfortunately, two sets of events have so far punctured these efforts—first, the 2010 earthquake that upended Haiti's already desperate infrastructure, and second, paralyzing electoral breakdowns in 2010 and 2015–2016.

With its epicenter in the Port-au-Prince region, the January 12, 2010, earthquake devastated the nation's core infrastructure, killed about three hundred thousand people, and left another one million or more homeless. The earthquake upended Haiti's already desperate infrastructure—the dysfunctional nature of Haitian governance and its overwhelming inadequacies were compounded by the material and human damage that also affected the UN and other parts of Haiti's international development apparatus.[4] In the aftermath of the earthquake, the country's dependence on foreign assistance increased further with a multiyear commitment of about US$9 billion, in addition to significant targeted bilateral aid (such as electoral assistance) and private international aid. To add insult to injury, a cholera epidemic, originating from within the UN peacekeeping contingent, emerged in late 2010 and spread in a vulnerable post-earthquake environment. Only recently has the UN recognized responsibility for this additional calamity.

Nature and Haiti's convoluted politics also combined to create two successive electoral breakdowns—2010–2011, that led to Martelly's election but also the seeds for the 2015–2016 debacle. Both drew in the international community with substantial financial support but also growing skepticism. The reported US$70+ million price tag of the failed 2015 balloting led the United States to withhold further electoral assistance, forcing the Haitian government to cobble together the needed financing from other sources. To make matters worse, in early October 2016 Hurricane Matthew slammed into Haiti's southwest peninsula, causing enormous damage and postponing the elections for another month. Nonetheless, all of this may have had the salutary effect of forcing Haitian leadership to own up to their collective failures and responsibilities. Although many international actors appear resigned to resolving Haiti's recent political stalemates through expediency, there was hope that the November 2016 elections had enough credibility to sustain the Jovenel Moïse presidency commencing in 2017.

The scale of the post-earthquake reconstruction effort has significantly strained patterns of political and economic interaction, and in its wake broadened a long-lasting debate about who actually shapes Haiti's domestic priorities. One strain of thinking has questioned the logic of pressing for democratic governance when Haiti's economic and social institutions are so weak, also pointing to the dysfunctional character of state institutions and rule of law, and the near absence of political accountability. The ensuing void has been partially filled by a politically divided civil society and a large informal economy. To have such an outcome after three decades of continuous international assistance has led some critics to highlight Haiti's limited capacity to manage what has been described as the "chaos of good intentions" that descends on the country with regularity—most recently after the 2010 earthquake, and earlier after the 1994 return of President Aristide.

GEORGES A. FAURIOL

The reverse side of these arguments has called into question the capabilities, if not the intentions, of the international community to achieve change on the ground. Sharp criticism of Haiti's post-2010 earthquake reconstruction efforts has raised questions about the actual beneficiaries of foreign assistance. A panoramic indictment issued by the World Bank in 2015 noted that over a forty-two-year period (1971–2013) Haiti's per capita income averaged a yearly decline of 0.7 percent. Despite the considerable amounts of foreign aid, the government still could not perform many basic functions.

It is not for a lack of trying or of resources. Much of the international intervention since the late 1980s has been on a grand scale with a full panoply of diplomatic resources, economic development packages, and security policy tools drawn from across the globe. This includes specialized financial support packages from the IMF and international lending institutions, let alone the resources in varying overlapping forms of the often-maligned humanitarian and NGO communities. Likewise, despite the frustrations, US response has been exemplary, recently after the 2010 earthquake as well as with several trade preferences laws (Haitian Hemispheric Opportunity Through Partnership Encouragement Act—HOPE, and follow-on HELP) and a mosaic of efforts over the last three decades in connection with peacekeeping operations, refugee crises, and drug interdiction efforts.

CONCLUSION: CRITICAL QUESTIONS

Haiti's contemporary experience is built on domestic political foundations that lack a working consensus, compounded by conflicting expectations among international actors. What has been achieved in its place is a quasi-permanent international peacekeeping presence and parallel multinational governance infrastructure that underscores the depth of the international community's commitment to Haiti's development process. Remarkably, little of this has consolidated democratic governance or improved the socioeconomic well-being of most Haitians.

This dismal record could reenergize those voices, in Haiti and beyond, who either question the international community's discipline in effectively engaging Haiti's problems, or alternatively see nothing but continuous meddling in the nation's affairs. The idea that even well-meaning donors can undermine the emergence of competent Haitian political national leadership should be given some attention. The record shows that foreign actors have often sought expediency over the obvious challenges of holding Haitian political and electoral leadership accountable; this has not served Haiti well. Haiti's political experience since the 1980s is essentially a sequence of elections joined by political crises with each succeeding presidency achieving very little.

Some change may be discernable. The disputed role of the international community in forcing a solution to the 2010–2011 electoral imbroglio contrasts somewhat with the more hands-off response to the 2015–2016 breakdown. Either way, the resolution of Haitian governance challenges is ultimately the responsibility of Haitian leaders. That can be achieved—in the wake of the 2015–2016 electoral crisis, the United States withdrew support for another round of elections, forcing Haiti's authorities to find alternative ways to fund the process.

The context of the reoccurring crises has been a predictable brew familiar to observers of Haitian affairs: an elections machinery, some of it mandated by the 1987 constitution, that has retained its "provisional" status for almost three decades, as well as an administrative structure essentially rebuilt with more sophisticated technologies (and expanding costs) after each election cycle and ensuing national crisis. This dysfunctional dynamic has been sustained by political interference as much as weak political leadership, managerial incompetence, uneven follow-through from foreign donors, and over time, material losses.

The catastrophic scale of the 2010 earthquake has been seen by some as providing the basis for a makeover of Haiti's political and economic map. So far that has not really happened, with Haitian leadership making political promises with few returns, economic activity with little growth, and sustained international support undermined by either misuse or misallocation of foreign assistance. Nonetheless, Haiti retains a reservoir of individual skill and political acumen, and the challenge lies in the pooling of these human resources and the development of relevant economic and political organizations. There may be egalitarian and cooperative features in the nation's peasant environment, yet Haiti's traditional political culture and linguistic bifurcation are profound obstacles to the development of a modern democratic society.

Likewise, although the components of a modern civil society have emerged, its effectiveness has been squeezed by the absence of credible government interlocutors at both the national and local levels, and undermined by varying layers of corruption and violence. The historically dubious interest of some elites in collaborating in the economic, political, and cultural integration of the nation has been an additional disappointment. Still, the multiple crises of the last two decades have also generated a more mature, socially conscious universe of competing political and economic elites, a potentially salient development if channeled in a constructive direction.

Another component in Haiti's makeover might lie in the mobilization of its diaspora, notably in the United States. More than just a source of remittances, this community has begun to successfully participate in the US political process, suggesting points of contact, interest, and influence regarding Haitian affairs. Although the potentially beneficial impact of the diaspora on Haiti's politics has so far been unsubstantiated, it is beginning to emerge as a significant variable.

These factors represent a fragile basis upon which Haiti's future is to be built. With the nation's catastrophic social and ecological collapse—worsened almost yearly by hurricanes—any Haitian government faces a daunting task. Fears of political crisis will continue to attract external interest, exacerbated by concerns with their humanitarian implications. This is particularly true for Washington, whose vision of regional strategic interest is amplified by a concern that any crisis in Haiti will affect the United States directly. This will define Haiti's continuing search for what has so far been an elusive national consensus toward generating politically democratic governance and socially measurable economic development.

SUGGESTIONS FOR FURTHER READING

Abbot, Elizabeth. *Haiti: The Duvaliers and Their Legacy.* New York: McGraw-Hill, 1988.

Deibert, Michael. *Notes from the Last Testament: The Struggle for Haiti.* New York: Seven Stories Press, 2005.

Fatton, Robert. *Trapped in the Outer Periphery.* Boulder, CO: Lynne Rienner, 2014.

Fauriol, Georges A., ed. *Haitian Frustrations: Dilemmas for U.S. Policy.* Washington, DC: Center for Strategic and International Studies, 1995.

Girard, Philippe R. *Clinton in Haiti: The 1994 U.S. Invasion of Haiti.* New York: Palgrave Macmillan, 2004.

Heinl, Gordon Debs Jr., Nancy Gordon Heinl, and Michael Heinl. *Written in Blood: The Story of the Haitian People 1492–1995.* Rev. ed. Lanham, MD: University Press of America, 1996.

Schmidt, Hans. *The United States Occupation of Haiti, 1915–1934.* New Brunswick, NJ: Rutgers University Press, 1971.

Trouillot, Michel-Rolph. *Haiti, State Against Nation: The Origins and Legacy of Duvalierism.* New York: Monthly Review Press, 1990.

Wilentz, Amy. *The Rainy Season.* New York: Simon and Schuster, 1989.

NOTES

1. Compare, among others, David Nicholls, *From Dessalines to Duvalier: Race, Colour, and National Independence in Haiti* (Cambridge: Cambridge University Press, 1979); Robert I. Rotberg, *Haiti: The Politics of Squalor* (Boston: Houghton Mifflin, 1971); Robert Fatton, *The Roots of Haitian Despotism* (Boulder, CO: Lynne Rienner, 2007); and Laurent Dubois, *Haiti: The Aftershocks of History* (New York: Metropolitan Books, 2012).

2. Rayford W. Logan, *The Diplomatic Relations of the United States with Haiti, 1776–1891* (Chapel Hill: University of North Carolina Press, 1941).

3. Matthew J. Smith, *Red and Black in Haiti: Radicalism, Conflict, and Political Change, 1934–1957.* (Chapel Hill: University of North Carolina Press, 2009).

4. In one of many assessments following the 2010 earthquake, see Jonathan M. Katz, *The Big Truck That Went By: How the World Came to Save Haiti and Left Behind a Disaster* (New York: Palgrave Macmillan, 2013).

ABOUT THE EDITORS AND CONTRIBUTORS

COEDITORS

HARVEY F. KLINE is Professor Emeritus at the University of Alabama. He has studied Colombia for more than fifty years, during which he received three Fulbright fellowships to do research and teach there. He has written nine books on Colombian politics, including *Colombia: Democracy Under Assault* (Westview Press, 1995), *State-Building and Conflict Resolution in Colombia* (University of Alabama Press, 1999, Choice Outstanding Academic Book for 1999), *Chronicle of a Failure Foretold* (University of Alabama Press, 2007), *Showing Teeth to the Dragons* (University of Alabama Press, 2009), *Historical Dictionary of Colombia* (Scarecrow Press: 2012), and *Fighting Monsters in the Abyss* (University of Alabama Press, 2015).

CHRISTINE J. WADE is Professor of Political Science and International Studies at Washington College where she is also the curator of the Louis L. Goldstein Program in Public Affairs. She is a specialist in the domestic and international affairs of Central America. Her most recent books include *Captured Peace: Elites and Peacebuilding in El Salvador* (Ohio University Press, 2016), *Nicaragua: Emerging from the Shadow of the Eagle* (6th ed. Westview Press, 2016), coauthored with Thomas W. Walker, and *Understanding Central America* (6th ed. Westview Press, 2014), coauthored with John A. Booth and Thomas W. Walker.

HOWARD J. WIARDA was a member of the political science department of the University of Massachusetts-Amherst from 1965–2003, leaving to become the founding head of the Department of International Affairs at the University of Georgia and the Dean Rusk Professor of International Relations. He was the author and/or editor of more than one hundred books and the author of more than three hundred articles, book chapters, op-eds, and congressional testimony. His many books include *The Dominican Republic: Nation in Transition*, *Politics in Iberia: The Political Systems of Spain and Portugal*, *Corporatism and Comparative Politics*, *The Soul of Latin America*, and *Divided America on the World Stage: Broken Government and Foreign Policy*.

CONTRIBUTORS

MICHAEL E. ALLISON is Professor and Chair of Political Science and Coordinator of Education for Justice at the University of Scranton in Pennsylvania. His teaching and research interests include the comparative study of civil war and civil war resolution, particularly as it relates to the transformation of armed opposition groups into political parties in Latin America. His work has appeared in *Latin American Politics and Society*, the *Journal of Latin American Studies, Democratization, Conflict Management and Peace Science*, and *Studies in Comparative International Development*.

LILIAN BOBEA teaches sociology at Bentley University in Massachusetts, with a Ph.D. from Utrecht University. Her areas of specialization include security and defense issues, civil-military relations, and violence and citizen security in Latin America and the Caribbean. She is the author of *Violencia y Seguridad Democrática en República Dominicana* (FLACSO, 2011), and editor of *Soldados y Ciudadanos en el Caribe* (FLACSO, 2002), *Entre el Crimen y el Castigo: Seguridad Ciudadana y Control Democrático en América Latina y el Caribe* (Nueva Sociedad, 2003), and *La Gobernabilidad de la Seguridad en el Caribe: Iniciativas de Reformas y Cooperación* (Woodrow Wilson International Center for Scholars, 2010), among other publications.

JULIO F. CARRIÓN is Associate Professor of Political Science and International Relations at the University of Delaware. His most recent publications are "The Fearful Citizen: Crime and Support for Democracy in Latin America" (with Lauren M. Balasco), *Revista Latinoamericana de Opinión Pública*; "Democracy and Populism in the Andes: A Problematic Coexistence," in Richard Millet, Jennifer Holmes, and Orlando Pérez, eds., *Latin American Democracy: Emergent Reality or Endangered Species?* (2nd ed. Routledge, 2015); and *Cultura Política de la Democracia en Perú y en las Américas, 2014: Gobernabilidad Democrática a Través de 10 Años del Barómetro de las Américas* (Lima: Vanderbilt University-Instituto de Estudios Peruanos, 2015; coauthored with Patricia Zárate).

MIGUEL CENTELLAS is Croft Instructional Assistant Professor of Sociology and International Studies at the University of Mississippi. His teaching interests include democracy and democratic institutions in Latin America and other new democracies, with a research focus on Bolivia. His recent publications are "The Santa Cruz Autonomía Movement: A Case of Non-Indigenous Ethnic Popular Mobilization?" (*Ethnopolitics*); "Cycles of Reform: Placing Evo Morales's Bolivia in Context" (*Latin American Research Review*); and "Bolivia's New Multicultural Constitution: The 2009 Constitution in Historical and Comparative Perspective," in Todd Eisenstadt and Michael S. Danielson, eds., *Latin America's Multicultural Movements* (Oxford University Press, 2013).

LINDA CHEN is Associate Vice Chancellor for Academic Affairs and Dean of Undergraduate Studies and Professor of Political Science at Indiana University South Bend. She has published in the areas of democratic transition in Latin America and the enduring legacy of corporatism in Argentina.

JENNIFER N. COLLINS is an Associate Professor of Political Science at the University of Wisconsin-Stevens Point. Her research examines political participation by indigenous and social movements in Ecuador and Bolivia and new left political projects in both countries. She is the recipient of two Fulbright fellowships and has published several articles and book chapters. Her most recent article reexamined the concept of populism in light of the new left and was published in the *Journal of Latin American Studies*. She is currently working on a book manuscript that explores the role of social movements and their relationships with the Correa and Morales administrations.

BRITTA H. CRANDALL is an adjunct assistant professor of Latin American Studies at Davidson College. She is the author of *Hemispheric Giants: The Misunderstood History of U.S.-Brazilian Relations* (Rowman and Littlefield, 2011). Prior to teaching, she was associate director for Latin American sovereign risk analysis at Bank One in Chicago and worked as a Latin American program examiner for the Office of Management and Budget.

JUAN M. DEL ÁGUILA received his doctorate from the University of North Carolina at Chapel Hill in 1979 and subsequently taught and carried out research as an associate professor at Emory University in Atlanta for thirty-two years. He now is retired and living in South Florida. During his career, he authored one book and many articles and chapters on Cuban politics and Latin American politics. He also published dozens of book reviews and served as the book review editor for *Cuban Affairs*, an online academic journal.

GEORGES A. FAURIOL is Vice President, Programs—Grants Operations and Evaluation at the National Endowment for Democracy. He is also a Senior Associate at the Center for Strategic & International Studies, and teaches in Georgetown University's Democracy and Governance graduate program. He has extensive field experience, including sixteen election observation missions. He is the author or coauthor of more than seventy publications, including most recently, "Haiti Policy: Now for Something Totally Different" (CSIS, 2016), and "Engaging the Caribbean: From Relations to Actual Strategy" (CSIS, 2016).

BRIAN FONSECA is the Director of the Jack D. Gordon Institute for Public Policy and Adjunct Professor at the Kimberly Green Latin American and Caribbean Studies, Steven J. Green School of International and Public Policy, Florida International University. He is coauthor (with Jonathan Rosen) of *US Security in the Twenty-First Century* (Palgrave, 2017) and coeditor (with Eduardo Gamarra) of *Culture and National Security in the Americas* (Lexington, 2017).

SEBASTIAN A. MEYER is a Ph.D. student at Vanderbilt University. A native of Paraguay, he is a research affiliate at the Latin American Public Opinion Project and the Center for the Study of Democratic Institutions.

RICHARD L. MILLETT is Professor Emeritus at Southern Illinois University at Edwardsville. Among his books are *Guardians of the Dynasty* (Orbis, 1977), *Searching for*

Stability: The U.S. Development of Constabulary Forces in Latin America and the Philippines (Fort Leavenworth, KA: Combat Studies Institute Press, 1977) and *Latin American Democracy: Emerging Reality or Endangered Species?* (coeditor, 2nd ed., Routledge, 2015).

FRANK O. MORA is Director of the Kimberly Green Latin American and Caribbean Center and Professor of Politics and International Relations at Florida International University. He is the author of several articles and edited volume contributions on Cuban politics and the Cuban military. He served as Deputy Assistant Secretary of Defense for the Western Hemisphere (2009–2013).

DAVID J. MYERS is Professor Emeritus of Political Science at Penn State University. He has published extensively in the areas of political party systems, public opinion and urban policy making. He is the author or editor of more than fifty articles and eight books. His most recent publications include "Liberal Democracy, Populism and Beyond: Elite Circulation in Bolivarian Venezuela," *Latin American Research Review*, 2014; and "Venezuela: Politics, Urban Reform and the Challenges of Metropolitan Governance amid the Struggle for Democracy," in Peter K. Spink, Peter M. Ward, and Robert Wilson, eds., *Metropolitan Governance in the Federalist Americas: Case Studies and Strategies for Equitable Integrated Development.* (University of Notre Dame Press, 2011). Professor Myers has held faculty positions at the United States Military Academy (West Point), the Instituto de Estudios Superiores de Administración (Caracas, Venezuela), Universidad del Norte (Barranquilla, Colombia), and the Central University of Venezuela.

DAVID SCOTT PALMER is Professor Emeritus of International Relations and Political Science in the Pardee School of Global Studies at Boston University, where he was also Founding Director of the Latin American Studies Program. He's the author of books on Peruvian politics, guerrillas, and border disputes; US-Latin American relations; and Latin America's long-range future. His book chapters and journal articles cover these and other Latin America-related topics. The most recent of these include "A Road Less Traveled: Peru's Difficult Post-Conflict Reconciliation Process," in *Revista: Harvard Review of Latin America*; and "The Influence of Maoism in Peru," in Alexander Cook, ed., *Mao's Little Red Book* (Cambridge University Press, 2015).

ORLANDO J. PÉREZ is Associate Dean, College of Arts, Humanities & Social Sciences, Millersville University of Pennsylvania. He is the author of *Political Culture in Panama: Democracy after Invasion* (Palgrave, 2011); *Civil-Military Relations in Post-Conflict Societies: Transforming the Role of the Military in Central America* (Routledge, 2015); and coeditor (with Richard L. Millett and Jennifer Holmes) of *Latin American Democracy: Emerging Reality or Endangered Species?* (2nd ed. Routledge, 2015).

JORGE REBELLA is a Uruguayan educator and journalist who specializes in political and economic reporting. He worked for Business International from 1968–1986 and was a reporter for *El País*, Uruguay's major newspaper, from 1996–2012. Currently he is a press correspondent for *The Economist Intelligence Unit*. He is the author of hundreds of articles on politics, economy, business, sociology, and the environment in

Uruguay and Latin America published in *El País* (Montevideo), *Economist Intelligence Unit* (London), *America Economia* (Santiago, Chile), *Bloomberg News*, *TelePress* (São Paulo), and *Business Latin America* (New York).

J. MARK RUHL is the Glenn E. and Mary L. Todd Professor of Political Science at Dickinson College in Carlisle, Pennsylvania. He is the coauthor of *Party Politics and Elections in Latin America* (Westview Press, 1989) and has written extensively on problems of democratization in Latin America with a special emphasis on the Central American countries. His most recent articles have appeared in *Latin American Politics and Society*, *Journal of Democracy*, and *Security and Defense Studies Review*.

MITCHELL A. SELIGSON is the Centennial Professor of Political Science, courtesy Professor of Sociology, and the Alexander Heard Distinguished Service Professor of Political Science at Vanderbilt University. He is founder and senior advisor of the Latin American Public Opinion Project (LAPOP). His most recent books include *The Legitimacy Puzzle in Latin America: Democracy and Political Support in Eight Nations*, coauthored with John Booth (Cambridge University Press, 2009), and *Development and Underdevelopment: The Political Economy of Global Inequality*, coedited with John T. Passé-Smith (4th ed. Lynne Reinner Publishers, 2014).

PETER M. SIAVELIS is Professor in the Department of Politics and International Affairs at Wake Forest University, where he is also the director of the Latin American and Latino Studies program. He has researched and published widely on many aspects of Latin American and Chilean politics including candidate selection, presidencies, and informal institutions. His most recent edited book is *Democratic Chile: The Politics and Policies of a Historic Coalition* (with Kirsten Sehnbruch) and he has published in journals including *Comparative Politics*, *Comparative Political Studies*, *Latin American Research Review*, and *Electoral Studies*.

JOSÉ LUIS VELASCO is a researcher at the Institute of Social Research of the National Autonomous University of Mexico (UNAM). He holds a Ph.D. in Political Science from Boston University and is the author of several articles and book chapters, and two books: *Insurgency, Authoritarianism, and Drug Trafficking in Mexico's "Democratization"* (Routledge, 2005) and *El debate actual sobre el federalismo mexicano* (Mexico: Instituto Mora, 1999). His current work focuses on the politics of drug violence in Mexico.

MARTIN WEINSTEIN is Professor Emeritus of Political Science at the William Paterson University of New Jersey. He is the author of *Uruguay: The Politics of Failure* (Greenwood Press, 1975) and *Uruguay: Democracy at the Crossroads* (Westview Press, 1988). He also edited *Revolutionary Cuba in the World Arena* (ISHI Press, 1979) and most recently coedited, with Abraham F. Lowenthal, *Kalman Silvert: Engaging Latin America, Building Democracy* (Lynne Rienner Publishers, 2016). He has authored dozens of book chapters and encyclopedia entries on Uruguay's political, economic, and social development, as well as on human rights and US–Latin American relations.

INDEX

abortion, 42, 258, 307, 402
Abrantes, José, 359
Acccord for a Firm and Lasting Peace, in
  Guatemala, 415
AD. *See* Democratic Action
ADN. *See* Nationalist Democratic Action
AFPs. *See* Pension Fund Administrators
Afu, Carlos, 443
agrarian reform. *See* land reform
agriculture, 10, 38–39, 60–61
  in Costa Rica, 371–373
  in El Salvador, 397
  in Mexico, 323
  in Peru, 202
  in Venezuela, 231
Aguas de Tunari, 65
Aguirre Cerda, Pedro, 147
ALBA. *See* Bolivarian Alliance for the People
  of Our Americas
Alemán, José Arnaldo, 385–386
Alessandri, Jorge, 146, 147, 149
Alexandre Pétion (Emperor), 466
Alfaro, Eloy, 301
Alfaro Ucero, Luis, 227
Alfonsín, Raúl, 94, 110
Alfonso the Wise, 52
Alianza IMP. *See* Initiative of Colombian
  Women for Peace
Allende, Salvador, 79, 92, 141, 146,
  149–152
Alliance for Progress, 78, 79, 201
Alternative Democratic Pole (PDA), in
  Colombia, 173
Álvarez, Gregorio, 252
Alvarez Martínez, Gustavo, 425
Amazon basin, 11

American Popular Revolutionary Alliance
  (APRA), in Peru, 43, 196, 198, 206,
  208
Amnesty International, 42
Anderson, Charles, 29, 30
ANEP. *See* National Association of Private
  Enterprise
Anti-Corruption Party (PAC), in Honduras,
  423, 428–429
AP Ecuador. *See* PAIS Alliance
AP Peru. *See* Popular Action; Popular
  Alliance
APRA. *See* American Popular Revolutionary
  Alliance
Árbenz, Jacobo, 78
Árbenz Guzmán, Jacobo, 413
Arce, Manuel José, 396
ARENA. *See* Nationalist Republican Alliance
Argaña, Luis María, 273
Argentina, 10, 26, 47, 50, 52, 56, 64
  Bolivia and, 296
  civil war in, 94
  constitution of, 111, 115
  democracy in, 110, 116–118
  economy of, 25, 103–122
  ethnicity in, 113
  Falkland Islands and, 75–76, 109–110
  foreign policy of, 120–121
  globalization and, 120–121
  government of, 115–116
  history of, 103–113
  human rights in, 110
  inflation in, 110, 117, 120
  institutions in, 115–116
  military coups d'état in, 108
  military rule in, 32, 108–110

Argentina *(continued)*
  Paraguay and, 267
  political parties in, 104, 105, 106–107,
    113–115
  public policy in, 118–120
  revolution in, 23
  social structure of, 112–113
  Uruguay and, 249, 256, 259–260
Arias, José Domingo, 442–443
Arias Sánchez, Oscar, 376, 378–379
Aristide, Jean-Bertrand, 81, 466, 468–469
Armas, Carlos Castillo, 78
Army of National Liberation (ELN), in
    Colombia, 178, 190
Arzú, Alvaro, 415
assembly plants *(maquiladoras)*, 66
Astori, Danilo, 256
AUC. *See* United Self-Defense Forces of
    Colombia
Austral Plan, in Argentina, 110
Authentic Party *(Partido Auténtico)*, in Cuba,
    351
Authentic Radical Liberal Party (PLRA), in
    Paraguay, 273
authoritarianism, 15–16
  in Argentina, 107
  in Cuba, 350–352
  in Peru, 195–216
  presidency and, 49–50
  See also military rule
autonomous state agencies, 54–55
AV. *See* Green Alliance
Avila, Rodrigo, 403
Azcona, José, 425
Azeredo da Silveira, Antônio, 136
Aztec, 20, 322
Azules, in Dominican Republic, 451

Bachelet, Michelle, 41, 161–162
Balaguer, Joaquín, 452, 453–455
Baldetti, Roxana, 418
Balladares, Ernesto Perez, 443
Balmaceda, José Manuel, 144
Barbosa, Joaquim, 130
Barco, Virgilio, 179, 180
Barefoot Revolution, in Paraguay,
    269–271
Barrantes, Alfonso, 197, 206
Barrios, Justo Rufino, 412–413
Barrios de Chamorro, Violeta, 41, 89, 385

Batista y Zaldívar, Fulgencio E., 77, 78,
    350–352
Batlle, José, 249–251
Batlle Ibáñez, Jorge, 252, 254, 255
Bay of Pigs, 78
Belaúnde Terry, Fernando, 197, 202
Bergoglio, Jorge Mario, 35
Betancourt, Rómulo, 225, 229, 452
Betancur, Belisario, 180
birth control, 34–35, 174
Black Jacobins, 450
Blanco, Jorge, 453
Blanco Party, in Uruguay, 251
BNDES. *See* Brazilian Development Bank
Boff, Leonardo, 34
Boland Amendment, 80
Bolaños Geyer, Enrique, 386, 390, 391
Bolívar, Simón, 23
Bolivarian Alliance for the People of Our
    Americas (ALBA), 313, 361
Bolivia, 10, 17, 21, 56, 66, 67, 283–297
  Chile and, 143
  courts in, 294
  democracy in, 97, 289
  drug trade in, 94
  economy of, 287–288
  foreign policy of, 296–297
  indigenous people in, 40, 41
  institutions in, 290–294
  interest groups in, 289–290
  Law of Mother Earth in, 71
  MNR in, 43
  modernization in, 285–287
  Paraguay and, 270
  political culture in, 288–290
  political parties in, 284–285, 284–295,
    292–294
  presidency of, 50
  public policy in, 295–296
  revolution in, 30
  water privatization in, 65
  women in, 41
Bolivarian Alliance for the People of Our
    Americas (ALBA), 66, 391, 426, 432
Bolivarian Military Movement, in
    Venezuela, 226
Bonaparte, Napoleon, 22, 125
Borges, Julio, 217, 234
Bosch, Juan, 456
Boyer, Jean-Pierre, 450, 455

Bracero program, 84
Brady Plan, 203, 333
Brazil, 11, 21, 26, 51, 56, 69
    Bolivia and, 296
    corruption in, 91, 128–130
    courts in, 52
    economy of, 13, 25, 130–133
    elites, elitism in, 123–138
    foreign policy of, 136–137
    history of, 124–127
    hyperinflation in, 123
    institutions in, 127–128
    military coups d'état in, 79
    military in, 31
    military rule in, 32
    as monarchy, 23, 24
    NGOs in, 42
    Paraguay and, 268, 276
    political culture in, 127–128
    political parties in, 44
    Portugal and, 3, 10
    presidency of, 50
    social structure of, 133–135
    Uruguay and, 249
    violence in, 135–136
Brazilian Development Bank (BNDES), 132
Brazilian Social Democratic Party (PSDB),
    128
Brazil, Russia, India, China, and South
    Africa (BRICS), 136–137
British Guiana, 76
Broad Front
    in Peru, 201
    in Uruguay, 251, 252, 260–261
Bucaram, Abdalá, 304
buen vivir ("good living"), 71
Bulnes, Manuel, 143
bureaucracy, 53
    in Argentina, 107
    in Uruguay, 257
    See also institutions
bureaucratic-authoritarianism. *See* military
    rule
Bush, George H. W., 66, 81, 385, 398–399
Bush, George W., 81, 82, 356
Bushnell, David, 170

CA-4. *See* Central America Four
Caballero, Bernardino, 269
Cabral, Pedro, 124

Cabral, Sérgio, 136
Cáceres, Berta, 428
Caceres, Ramon, 451
CACM. *See* Central American Common
    Market
CAFTA. *See* Central American Free Trade
    Association
CAFTA-DR. *See* Central America-
    Dominican Republic-United States
    Free Trade Agreement
Caldera, Rafael, 221, 226–227
Calderón, Felipe, 334, 340
Calderón Guardia, Rafael Angel, 375–376
Calderón Sol, Armando, 403, 405
Callejas, Rafael, 425, 431
campesinos. See peasantry
Cámpora, Héctor, 108, 113
Cano Isaza, Guillermo, 180
Capriles Radonski, Henrique, 234
Cárdenas, Lázaro, 329–330
Cardoso, Fernando Henrique, 129, 131–132,
    137–138
Carías Andino, Tiburcio, 424
Carmona Estanga, Pedro, 230
Carranza, Venustiano, 328
Carrera, Rafael, 412
Cartagena Accord, 426
Carter, Jimmy, 79–80, 437, 468
Cartes, Horacio, 276, 280–281
Casas Regueiro, Julio, 358
Castañeda, Jorge, 90
Castañeda, Luis, 199, 209
Castañeda Castro, Salvador, 397
Castaño, Carlos, 183
Castillo Armas, Carlos Castillo, 414
Castro, Fidel, 17, 345–366, 453
    attempted assassination of, 78
    FTAA and, 66
    Nicaragua and, 384
Castro, Raúl, 345, 352, 357, 360, 362–366
Catholic Church, 5, 16, 22, 23, 33–35
    in Argentina, 105, 107, 108
    in Bolivia, 287
    in Brazil, 135
    in Chile, 143, 148, 166
    in Colombia, 176
    in Ecuador, 301
    in El Salvador, 400–401
    in Guatemala, 412, 415–416
    in Haiti, 468

Catholic Church *(continued)*
in Honduras, 428
in Mexico, 321, 323–324, 329
in Nicaragua, 387
in Venezuela, 230–231
Cauas, Jorge, 153
caudillos. See landowners
CCTs. *See* conditional cash transfer
programs
CEBs. *See* Christian Base Communities
CELAC. *See* Community of Latin American
and Caribbean States
CELAM. *See* Latin American Council of
Bishops
Center for the Service of Popular Action
(CESAP), in Venezuela, 232
Central America Four (CA-4), 419–420
Central America-Dominican Republic-
United States Free Trade Agreement
(CAFTA-DR), 66, 373–374, 420, 431,
461
Central American Common Market
(CACM), 63, 373
Central American Confederation, 23
Central American Free Trade Association
(CAFTA), 36, 391
Central American Integration System
(SICA), 420
Central Intelligence Agency (CIA), US, 78,
79, 149, 152, 153, 231, 414
Cerezo, Vinicio, 415
CESAP. *See* Center for the Service of
Popular Action
CGE. *See* General Economic Confederation
CGT. *See* General Confederation of Labor;
General Confederation of Workers
Chaco War, in Paraguay, 269–271
Chamber of Deputies
in Argentina, 115–116
in Chile, 149
Chamorro, Pedro Joaquín, 79, 385, 391
Chamorro, Violeta de, 80
Chávez, Federico, 271
Chávez, Hugo, 17, 44, 90–93, 98, 218, 220,
221–241
Bolivia and, 296
Cuba and, 361
democracy and, 82
FTAA and, 66
Honduras and, 426, 431

Kirchner, Néstor and, 121
Peru and, 199
Chicago Boys, 141, 153, 154
The Children of Sanchez (Lewis), 331–332
Chile, 21, 44, 51, 56, 79, 141–168
Bolivia and, 296–297
constitution of, 142–143, 145–148,
154–155
democracy in, 142–148, 156–167
economy of, 13, 25, 152–156
government of, 157–165
human rights in, 159
military coups d'état in, 151–152
military rule in, 32, 152–156
oligarchy in, 24, 142–144, 148
Parliamentary Republic of, 144–145
political parties in, 157–158
populism in, 26
presidency of, 50
revolution in, 23
social structure of, 147–148
Socialist Party of, 79
Chilean Development Corporation
(CORFO), 147
Chilean Socialist Workers Party, 145
China, 7, 32, 69, 171, 278, 392
Brazil and, 132, 134
in BRICS, 136–137
Ecuador and, 311–312
Uruguay and, 259
Chinchilla, Laura, 41
Chinchilla Miranda, Laura, 376
Chlimper, José, 201
Christian Base Communities (CEBs), in El
Salvador, 400
Christian Democratic Party, 44
in Chile, 147, 148, 149
in El Salvador, 397, 402–404
in Uruguay, 251
in Venezuela, 221, 223–224, 226, 227,
232, 233–235
Christianity, 16, 20, 52
in El Salvador, 400–401
in Haiti, 471
See also Catholic Church; Protestantism
CIA. *See* Central Intelligence Agency
CICIG. *See* International Commission
Against Impunity in Guatemala
Citizen Action Party (PAC), in Costa Rica,
376

Citizen Power, in Venezuela, 238
Citizen's Revolution, in Ecuador, 305–306
Civic Option, in Colombia, 173
civil society organizations. *See* interest groups
civil unions. *See* same-sex marriage
civil wars, 93–94
    in Costa Rica, 375–376
    in El Salvador, 397–398
    in Guatemala, 411, 414
    in Paraguay, 268–269
    in US, 76
Civilista Party, in Peru, 196
class structure. *See* social structure
climate change, 6, 72
Clinton, Bill, 81, 82
Clinton, Hillary, 85
CNC. *See* National Peasants'
    Confederation
CNT. *See* National Convention of
    Workers
Cold War, 7, 32, 77–80, 78, 346
Colom, Álvaro, 418
Colombia, 24, 26, 40, 42, 52, 56, 67
    civil war in, 93–94
    corruption in, 191–192
    crime in, 190–191
    democracy and, 97
    drug trade in, 82, 94, 179–182
    economy of, 170–171
    ethnicity in, 170–171
    geography of, 170–171
    guerrilla revolution in, 178, 184–190
    history of, 175–177
    legislature in, 51
    LGBTQ in, 191
    military in, 33
    Panama and, 436
    paramilitary in, 178–179, 182–184
    political culture in, 171–172
    political parties in, 172–173, 172–173
        (table)
    public policy in, 190–192
    social structure of, 170–171
    violence in, 170, 176–192
    women in, 41, 174–175, 174 (table), 191
colonization, 11–12, 21–22, 59–60
    of Brazil, 125
    of Costa Rica, 370–372
    of Cuba, 347–349
    of Dominican Republic, 449–450

    of Guatemala, 412–413
    See also France; Portugal; Spain
Colorado Party
    in Dominican Republic, 451
    in Paraguay, 265, 269, 273–276
    in Uruguay, 249–251
Columbus, Christopher, 9, 19, 20, 346
COMINTERN. *See* Communist
    International
Common Market of the South
    (MERCOSUR), 118, 121
    Bolivia and, 296
    Brazil in, 137
    Paraguay and, 276–2780
    Uruguay and, 248, 256, 262
Communist International (COMINTERN),
    in Chile, 147
Communist Party, 43
    in Chile, 145, 146, 148, 157
    in Costa Rica, 375
    in Cuba, 44, 349, 358–359, 364
    in El Salvador, 397, 402
    in Paraguay, 278
    in Uruguay, 251
    in Venezuela, 221, 225
Community of Latin American and
    Caribbean States (CELAC), 313, 361
CONAIE. *See* Confederation of Indigenous
    Nationalities of Ecuador
conditional cash transfer programs (CCTs),
    56, 70, 132, 431
conditionality, 64
Confederation of Indigenous Nationalities of
    Ecuador (CONAIE), 302, 305
Confederation of Mexican Workers (CTM),
    337
Congregation for the Doctrine of the Faith,
    34
conquistadors, 11
Conservative Party
    in Argentina, 105
    in Chile, 143–144
    in Colombia, 173, 176
    in Nicaragua, 384, 389
constitutions
    of Argentina, 111, 115
    of Chile, 142–143, 145–148, 154–155
    of Ecuador, 307–308
    of El Salvador, 396
    of Mexico, 325, 328

constitutions *(continued)*
  of Nicaragua, 385–386
  of US, 23–24
  of Venezuela, 227, 236, 237–238
co-optation/repression, 30
COPRI. *See* Promotion of Private Investment
CORFO. *See* Chilean Development
    Corporation
Correa, Rafael, 98, 299–314
corruption, 56, 118, 358–359, 386
  in Brazil, 91, 128–130
  in Colombia, 191–192
  in El Salvador, 398
  in Guatemala, 417, 419
  in Honduras, 425, 426–427
  in Mexico, 320, 331, 335–336
  in Panama, 443–444
  in Paraguay, 274, 281
Cortés, Hernán, 20
COSENA. *See* National Security Council
COSEP. *See* Superior Council of Private
    Enterprise
Costa Rica, 26, 50, 51, 56, 63, 67, 369–380
  Christian-Democratic party in, 44
  civil war in, 375–376
  colonization of, 370–372
  democracy in, 370
  economy of, 370–374, 377–378
  foreign policy of, 378–379
  geography of, 370–371
  government of, 377
  history of, 370–374
  PLN in, 43
  political culture in, 374–377
  political parties in, 374–377
  social structure of, 377–378
coups d'état. *See* military coups d'état
courts, 52
  in Bolivia, 294
  in Honduras, 429–430
  in Mexico, 334–335
  in Nicaragua, 389
CR. *See* Radical Change Party
crime, 6, 85
  in Colombia, 190–191
  in Dominican Republic, 459–461
  in El Salvador, 395–396, 405–407
  in Guatemala, 419
  in Honduras, 431–432
  in Mexico, 336

  in Peru, 212
  in Venezuela, 240
  See also drug trade
Cristero war, in Mexico, 329
Cristiani, Alfredo, 398
CROM. *See* Regional Confederation of
    Mexican Workers
CSE. *See* Supreme Electoral Council
CTM. *See* Confederation of Mexican
    Workers
CTV. *See* Venezuelan Confederation of
    Workers
Cuba, 50, 66, 77, 345–367
  authoritarianism in, 350–352
  Cold War and, 78, 346
  colonization of, 20, 23, 347–349
  Communist Party in, 44, 349, 358–359,
    364
  democracy in, 350–352
  economy of, 355–356
  emigration from, 84, 355
  foreign policy of, 360–363
  geography of, 346
  government of, 359–360
  guerrilla revolution in, 26, 32, 78,
    353–355
  Mexico and, 331, 342
  political culture in, 346–347
  political parties in, 351
  social structure of, 346
  Soviet Union and, 78, 346, 355
  Spain and, 347–349
  US and, 76, 78, 347–352, 361–363
Cuban Adjustment Act, 84
Cuban Revolutionary Party (PRC), 348
Cubas Grau, Raúl, 273–274

DACA. *See* Deferred Action for Childhood
    Arrivals
DAPA. *See* Deferred Action for Parents of
    Americans and Lawful Permanent
    Residents
D'Aubuisson, Roberto, 398
de Alvarado, Pedro, 412
de Céspedes, Carlos Manuel, 350
de la Cuadra, Sergio, 153
de la Mora, Fernando, 274
de la Rúa, Fernando, 111
de Ojeda, Alfonso, 175
de Soto, Hernando, 92

DEA. *See* Drug Enforcement Agency
death squads, in El Salvador, 80
debt, 63–65, 123, 202
  of Argentina, 119, 121
  of Mexico, 320, 332–333
Declaration of Principles, 81
Deferred Action for Childhood Arrivals
  (DACA), 85
Deferred Action for Parents of Americans and
  Lawful Permanent Residents (DAPA),
  85
delegative democracy, 89, 97–98
Delgado, José Matias, 408
democracy, 3, 14–15, 89–99
  in Argentina, 110, 116–118
  in Bolivia, 97, 289
  in Brazil, 126–127
  in Chile, 142–148, 156–167
  in Costa Rica, 370
  in Cuba, 350–352
  in Dominican Republic, 91, 451–452,
    457–458
  in Ecuador, 308–309
  in Honduras, 423–426, 430, 432–433
  in Mexico, 334–337
  in Nicaragua, 9, 89–90, 388
  in Panama, 438–439
  in Paraguay, 272–276
  in Peru, 197, 207
  in Uruguay, 245–263
  US and, 81–82, 92
  See also interest groups; political parties
Democratic Action (AD), in Venezuela, 43,
  221, 223–224, 225, 227, 232, 233–235
Democratic Center, in Colombia, 173
Democratic Republican Union (URD), in
  Venezuela, 221, 225
Democratic Revolutionary Front (FDR), in El
  Salvador, 398
Democratic Revolutionary Tendency-Army of
  the People (TDR-EP), in Mexico, 341
Democratic Security Plan (PSD), in
  Dominican Republic, 460
Democratic Union, in Argentina, 105
Democratic Unity Table (MUD), in
  Venezuela, 217–218, 222, 235
dependency theory, ISI and, 63
los desaparecidos ("the disappeared ones"),
  108–109
Dessalines, Jean-Jacques, 466

Development, Relief, and Education for Alien
  Minors Act (DREAM), 85
DGTASD. *See* General Direction of Labor
  and Direct Social Action
Díaz, Porfirio, 25, 326–327
Diaz Canel, Miguel, 360, 363–364
Díaz del Castillo, Bernal, 322
DINA. *See* National Intelligence Directorate
"the disappeared ones" (*los desaparecidos*),
  108–109
diversity, in Latin America, 3–5, 9
dollarization, in Ecuador, 310
Dom João (King), 23, 125
Dom Pedro (Emperor), 125
Domínguez, Jorge, 357
Dominican Liberation Party (PLD), 453,
  455–457
Dominican Republic, 449–462
  CCTs in, 56
  colonization of, 20
  corruption in, 56
  democracy in, 91, 451–452, 457–458
  economy of, 25
  foreign policy of, 461
  history of, 449–450
  political parties in, 451, 453–457
  presidency of, 50
  Roosevelt Corollary and, 77
  social structure of, 458–459
  US and, 76
DREAM. *See* Development, Relief, and
  Education for Alien Minors Act
Drug Enforcement Agency (DEA), US, 82,
  180, 201
drug trade, 6
  in Brazil, 135–136
  in Colombia, 82, 94, 179–182
  in Cuba, 358–359
  in Dominican Republic, 460
  government and, 94
  in Guatemala, 420
  in Honduras, 427, 430, 432
  local government and, 54
  in Mexico, 82, 94, 319, 335, 339–341
  in Paraguay, 272
  in Peru, 94, 201–202, 214
  rule of law and, 83, 90
  US and, 82–83
Dry Corridor, 72
Duarte, José Napoleón, 80, 397, 398

Duarte Frutos, Nicanor, 274
Dulles, Allen, 78
Dulles, John Foster, 78
Durán, Julio, 148
Duvalier, François, 467, 468
Duvalier, Jean-Claude "Baby Doc," 468

Echeverría, Luis, 332
ECLAC. *See* Economic Commission on Latin
    America and the Caribbean
Economic Commission on Latin America and
    the Caribbean (ECLAC), of United
    Nations, 62, 70, 203
economy, 11–15, 24–25, 59–73
    of Argentina, 103–122
    of Bolivia, 287–288
    of Brazil, 13, 25, 130–133
    of Chile, 13, 25, 152–156
    of Colombia, 170–171
    in colonization, 11–12, 21, 59–60
    of Costa Rica, 370–374, 377–378
    of Cuba, 355–356
    debt in, 63–65
    of Ecuador, 303–304, 309–312
    of El Salvador, 401, 406
    exports in, 60–62, 61 (table)
    in Great Depression, 12, 25–26
    of Guatemala, 415–416
    of Haiti, 470–471
    of Mexico, 13, 25, 332–334
    of Panama, 445
    of Peru, 202–204
    sustainable development in, 69–72
    of Uruguay, 247–249, 253–254, 257
    of Venezuela, 238–239
    See also globalization;
        import-substitution-industrialization
Ecuador, 33, 56, 64, 66, 67
    Citizen's Revolution in, 305–306
    constitution of, 307–308
    corruption in, 56
    democracy in, 97, 308–309
    economy of, 303–304, 309–312
    foreign policy of, 313
    geography of, 300–301
    history of, 301–302
    indigenous people in, 40
    institutions of, 307–308
    nationalism in, 24, 313
    political culture in, 308–309

political parties in, 44, 303
poverty in, 10
presidency of, 50
public policy in, 312–313
revolution in, 23, 299–314
social structure of, 301
Ecuadorian Roldosist Party (PRE), 304
education
    in Bolivia, 286
    in Ecuador, 312
    in El Salvador, 399–400
    in Mexico, 335
    in Uruguay, 258
Eisenhower, Dwight, 78, 414
El Niño, 72
El Salvador, 35, 44, 56, 63, 68, 395–408
    civil war in, 94, 397–398
    constitution of, 396
    death squads in, 80
    economy of, 401, 406
    elites, elitism in, 401
    exports of, 67
    FMLN in, 80
    globalization and, 407–408
    government of, 404–406
    guerrilla revolution in, 80
    history of, 396–399
    military coups d'état in, 397–398
    nationalism of, 23
    political parties in, 397, 402–404
    poverty in, 10
    presidency of, 50
    public policy in, 404–406
    religion in, 400–401
    revolution in, 79
    social structure of, 399–400
Election Observer Mission, of OAS, 207–208
Elías, Jorge Serrano, 35
elites, elitism, 14, 15–16, 36–37
    in Argentina, 105, 113
    in Brazil, 123–138
    in Chile, 147
    in Colombia, 171
    in Ecuador, 302
    in El Salvador, 401
    in Panama, 436
    in Venezuela, 242
ELN. *See* Army of National Liberation
emergency contraception, 42
emigration. *See* immigration/emigration

encomienda system, 60
Endara, Guillermo, 90, 443
Enlightenment, 22
Enterprise for Americas Initiative, 66
Environmental Defense Fund, 42
environmentalism, 71–72
    in Bolivia, 294
    in Ecuador, 307
    in Honduras, 428
    in Uruguay, 256
EPL. *See* People's Liberation Army
EPR. *See* People's Revolutionary Army
ERPI. *See* Insurgent People's Revolutionary
    Army
Escalante, Aníbal, 358
Escobar, Pablo, 181–182
Escobar Alas, José Luis, 400
Escobar Salom, Ramón, 226
Estigarribia, Jose Felix, 270–271
Estimé, Dumarsais, 467
ethnicity. *See* race and racism; social structure
exports
    from Chile, 145
    from Colombia, 171
    from Costa Rica, 372
    from Ecuador, 310
    from El Salvador, 397
    globalization and, 66–67, 67–68 (table)
    from Guatemala, 413, 420
    liberalism and, 60–62, 61 (table)
    from Mexico, 333–334
    from Peru, 204
    from Uruguay, 247–248, 256
EZLN. *See* National Zapatista Liberation
    Army

Falkland Islands, 75–76, 109–110
family-planning agencies, 54
Faoro, Raymundo, 126
FAR. *See* Rebel Armed Forces; Revolutionary
    Armed Forces
Farabundo Martí National Liberation Front
    (FMLN), in El Salvador, 80, 399
FARC. *See* Revolutionary Armed Forces of
    Colombia
FARP. *See* People's Revolutionary Armed
    Forces
fascism, 26
Fatherland and Country (PyL), in Chile, 151
FCN. *See* National Convergence Front

FDR. *See* Democratic Revolutionary Front
Febrerista Party, in Paraguay, 270–271
Federal Republic of Central America, 396
femicide, 70
Ferdinand VII (King), 324
Fernández, Leonel, 456
Fernández de Kirchner, Cristina, 41, 103,
    112–113, 115–118, 120–121
Ferreira Aldunate, Wilson, 252
feudalism, 4, 11–12, 14, 15, 21–22, 48
FIDEL. *See* Leftist Front of Freedom
Fifth Republic Movement (MVR), in
    Venezuela, 233
Figueres Ferrer, José (Pepe), 375
Flores, Carlos, 425
Flores, Francisco, 405
Flores Nano, Lourdes, 198
FMLN. *See* Farabundo Martí National
    Liberation Front
FONASA. *See* National Health Service
foreign aid, 35
    to Bolivia, 288
    to Haiti, 468, 470
    from US, 77, 468
foreign investment
    in Argentina, 104
    in Colombia, 171
    in Dominican Republic, 451
    globalization and, 66
    in Honduras, 427
    in Mexico, 326
    in Peru, 293
    in Uruguay, 256, 257
foreign policy
    of Argentina, 120–121
    of Bolivia, 296–297
    of Brazil, 136–137
    of Costa Rica, 378–379
    of Cuba, 360–363
    of Dominican Republic, 461
    of Ecuador, 313
    of Honduras, 432
    of Mexico, 341–342
    of Nicaragua, 391–392
    of Paraguay, 276–280
    of Peru, 213–214
    of Venezuela, 240–241
    See also globalization
Fox, Vicente, 334
FP. *See* Popular Force

France, 3
  Dominican Republic and, 450
  Haiti and, 59, 466, 467
  Mexico and, 324–325
  Napoleonic Code of, 52
Francia, José Gaspar Rodríguez de, 267–268
Francisco Miranda Front, in Peru, 222
Franco, Juan Carlos "Yoyito," 274
Franco, Rafael, 270, 271
Frank, Andre Gunder, 63
Free Trade Area for the Americas (FTAA), 66
Freedom House, 90, 418, 430
Frei Montalva, Eduardo, 147, 148–149
Frei Ruiz-Tagle, Eduardo, 159–160
FrePaso. *See* Front for a Country in Solidarity
Friedman, Milton, 141, 153
Front for a Country in Solidarity (FrePaso),
  in Argentina, 111
FSLN. *See* Sandinista National Liberation
  Front
FTAA. *See* Free Trade Area for the
  Americas
Fujimori, Alberto, 81, 92, 195, 198, 202,
  207, 211–212
Fujimori, Keiko, 195, 199–201
Funes, Mauricio, 401–408

Galán, Luis Carlos, 181
Galtieri, Leopoldo, 109–110
GANA. *See* Grand Alliance for National
  Unity
García, Anastasio Somoza, 77
García Menocal, Mario, 349
García Pérez, Alan, 197–199, 202, 211
Gaviria, César, 181
gay people. *See* lesbian, gay, bisexual,
  transgender, and queer
gender. *See* women
General Confederation of Labor (CGT), in
  Argentina, 106, 109
General Confederation of Workers (CGT), in
  Mexico, 330
General Direction of Labor and Direct Social
  Action (DGTASD), in Argentina, 106
General Economic Confederation (CGE), in
  Argentina, 106
Generation of 1842, in Chile, 143
geography, 10–11
  of Chile, 141
  of Colombia, 170–171

  of Costa Rica, 370–371
  of Cuba, 346
  of Ecuador, 300–301
  of Venezuela, 218–219
Gill, Leslie, 295
globalization, 3–4, 7
  Argentina and, 120–121
  China and, 69
  El Salvador and, 407–408
  employment and, 68
  exports and, 66–67, 67–68 (table)
  foreign investment and, 66
  Guatemala and, 419–420
  Honduras and, 432
  Uruguay and, 259
  Washington Consensus and, 64–65
Gómez, José Miguel, 349
Gómez, Juan Vicente, 224
González, Florentino, 60
"good living" (*buen vivir*), 71
Good Neighbor Policy, 77
Gordillo, Elba Esther, 335
Gorriti, Gustavo, 93
GOU. *See* Group of United Officers
Goulart, João, 131
government, 49–55
  of Argentina, 115–116
  of Chile, 157–165
  of Costa Rica, 377
  of Cuba, 359–360
  drug trade and, 94
  of El Salvador, 404–406
  of Guatemala, 417–418
  of Haiti, 467–470
  history of, 47–48
  of Honduras, 429–430
  of Panama, 443–444
  regional and local, 52–54
  of Uruguay, 252–253
  of Venezuela, 236–238
  See also institutions
Grand Alliance for National Unity (GANA),
  in El Salvador, 403–404
Grau San Martín, Ramón, 351
Great Britain, 75–76, 109–110, 249
"Great Chain of Being," 16
Great Depression, 12, 25–26, 62, 84, 104,
  145, 349
Green Alliance (AV), in Colombia, 173
Gross, Alan, 362

Group of United Officers (GOU), in
　Argentina, 105
Gruber, Mireya Moscoso de, 41
Guantanamo Bay, Cuba, 363
Guatemala, 23, 63, 78, 411–421
　civil war in, 94, 411
　colonization of, 412–413
　corruption in, 56
　economy of, 415–416
　globalization and, 419–420
　government of, 417–418
　history of, 412–413
　interest groups in, 30
　military coups d'état in, 62, 78
　political culture in, 416–417
　poverty in, 10
　presidency of, 50, 92
　Protestantism in, 35
　public policy in, 418–419
　remittances in, 69
　revolution in, 79
　social structure of, 415–416
　Ten Years of Spring in, 413–414
Guatemalan Labor Party (PGT), 413
Guatemalan National Revolutionary Unit
　(URNG), 411, 414
guerrilla revolutions, 40
　in Colombia, 178, 184–190
　in Cuba, 26, 32, 78, 353–355
　in Ecuador, 300
　in El Salvador, 80
　in Mexico, 341
　in Peru, 204
　in Uruguay, 251–252
Guevara, Ernesto "Che," 352
Gueverra, Otto, 376
Gutiérrez, Lucio, 305
Guzán Blanco, Antonio, 224
Guzman, Antonio, 453–454
Guzmán, Julio, 201

Haiti, 3, 67, 68, 81, 465–475
　colonization of, 20, 59
　corruption in, 56
　economy of, 470–471
　emigration from, 84
　foreign aid to, 468
　government of, 467–470
　institutions in, 471–472
　military coups d'état in, 469

political culture in, 466–467
　poverty in, 10
　public policy in, 467–470
　Roosevelt Corollary and, 77
　slavery in, 23
　social structure of, 470–471
　US and, 76
Haya de la Torre, Víctor Raúl, 43, 197
Hay-Bunau-Varilla Treaty, 77
Health Institution Providers (ISAPRES), in
　Chile, 154
Heavily Indebted Poor Countries initiative
　(HIPC), 65
Henri Christophe (Emperor), 466
Heredia, Nadine, 209
Hernández, Juan Orlando, 423, 426–427,
　429–433
Hernández Martínez, Maximiliano, 402
Hidalgo, Miguel, 324
HIPC. *See* Heavily Indebted Poor Countries
　initiative
Hispaniola, 20, 449–450, 459
Hitler, Adolf, 77
Hodges, Heather, 313
Homestead Act, in Costa Rica, 372
hometown associations (HTAs), 68
homosexuality. *See* lesbian, gay, bisexual,
　transgender, and queer
Honduras, 10, 23, 56, 63, 66, 423–433
　democracy in, 423–426, 430, 432–433
　foreign policy of, 432
　government of, 429–430
　history of, 424–427
　interest groups in, 427–428
　military coups d'état in, 82, 90, 426–427
　political culture in, 424–427
　political parties in, 423, 424, 428–429
　presidency of, 50
　public policy in, 430–432
　remittances in, 68
Hoover, Herbert, 467
Hoyos, Carlos Mauro, 180–181
HTAs. *See* hometown associations
Huerta, Victoriano, 327
Humala, Ollanta, 199, 200, 204, 209, 212
human rights, 29, 32, 34, 90
　in Argentina, 110
　in Chile, 159
　in Cuba, 363
　in Ecuador, 309

human rights *(continued)*
  in El Salvador, 399
  in Guatemala, 415, 416
  in Honduras, 428, 430
  in Mexico, 83, 334, 336–337
hyperinflation, 64, 110, 123, 242

IADB. *See* Inter-American Development
    Bank
IAPI. *See* Institute for Production and
    Trade
Ibáñez, Carlos, 145–146
Illegal Immigration Reform and Immigrant
    Responsibility Act (IIRIRA), in US,
    84–85
IMF. *See* International Monetary Fund
immigration/emigration
  to Argentina and, 104
  in Bolivia, 285
  from Cuba, 84, 355
  from El Salvador, 408
  from Guatemala, 412
  from Mexico, 84, 85–86, 320, 338
  Uruguay and, 249
  US and, 84–86
import-substitution-industrialization (ISI),
    12, 27, 36, 62–63
  in Argentina, 106
  in Brazil, 131
  in Chile, 147
  in Uruguay, 247–248
Inacio da Silva, Luís (Lula), 126–127, 132,
    136, 255, 361
Inca, 20
Independent Democratic Union (UDI), in
    Chile, 158
Independent Liberal Party (PLI), in
    Nicaragua, 390
Independent Party, in Uruguay, 262
indigenous people, 5, 10, 12, 16, 40–41, 53
  assimilation of, 9
  in Bolivia, 286, 291
  Christianity and, 20
  in Colombia, 175
  in Costa Rica, 371
  in Dominican Republic, 449, 459
  in Ecuador, 301, 302, 310–311
  in Guatemala, 414
  in Honduras, 428
  in Mexico, 20, 321, 322, 323

  in Paraguay, 266
  in peasantry, 38
  women of, 70
Industrial Revolution, 20, 22, 48, 62
industrialization, 12, 14, 36–37
  in Chile, 147
  in Mexico, 330
  in Paraguay, 265
inequality, 5, 39, 70, 92–93
  in Bolivia, 287–288
  in Brazil, 133–134
  in Dominican Republic, 459
  in Ecuador, 312–313
  in El Salvador, 400
  in Mexico, 320
inflation, 64
  in Argentina, 110, 117, 120
  in Bolivia, 288
  in Brazil, 131
  in Chile, 150
  in Ecuador, 304
  in El Salvador, 405
  in Mexico, 332
  in Peru, 202–203
  in Uruguay, 261
informal sector, 71–72
  in Bolivia, 288
Initiative of Colombian Women for Peace
    (Alianza IMP), 175
Institute for Production and Trade (IAPI), in
    Argentina, 106
Institutional Revolutionary Party (PRI)
  in Mexico, 44, 329, 334
  in Panama, 437
institutions, 5–6, 47–55, 48 (table)
  in Argentina, 115–116
  in Bolivia, 290–294
  in Brazil, 127–128
  of Ecuador, 307–308
  in Haiti, 471–472
  in Nicaragua, 388–390
  in Peru, 206–210
  in Venezuela, 228–229
Insurgent People's Revolutionary Army
    (ERPI), in Mexico, 341
Inter-Amazon Services Program (PIAS), 212
Inter-American Democratic Charter, of OAS,
    92
Inter-American Development Bank (IADB),
    255, 391

Inter-American Treaty of Reciprocal Assistance (Rio Treaty), 77
interest groups, 29–42
  in Bolivia, 289–290
  in Guatemala, 30
  in Honduras, 427–428
  in Mexico, 337–339
  in Peru, 30
  in Venezuela, 229–232
  See also specific groups
International Commission Against Impunity in Guatemala (CICIG), 416–417
International Labour Organization, 71–72
International Monetary Fund (IMF), 64, 65, 92, 121, 255, 378
  Brazil and, 123, 132
  Ecuador and, 305, 310
  Mexico and, 333
  Venezuela and, 226–227
Inter-Union Workers' Plenary (PIT), in Uruguay, 251
ISAPRES. *See* Health Institution Providers
ISI. *See* import-substitution-industrialization
Iturbide, Agustin de, 325, 372
IU. *See* United Left

Jiménez de Quesada, Gonzalo, 175
John Paul II (Pope), 272, 280, 361, 472
Johnson, Lyndon, 453
Jones-Costigan Act, 351
José de Sucre, Antonio, 23
Juárez, Benito, 325
Justice First (PJ), in Venezuela, 217, 235
Justicialist Party, in Argentina, 114

Karl, Terry Lynn, 95
Kennedy, John F., 78
Kerry, John, 363
Kirchner, Néstor, 103, 111–121, 256, 361
Kissinger, Henry, 79, 136
Kubitschek, Juscelino, 130–131, 132
Kuczynski, Pedro Pablo, 201–202

Labor Party, in Argentina, 105
labor unions, 5, 15, 30, 38
  in Argentina, 104, 105, 109
  in Bolivia, 290
  in Chile, 152–153
  in Ecuador, 302–303
  in Guatemala, 413

  in Honduras, 428
  ín El Salvador, 397
  in Mexico, 326, 337–338
  in Nicaragua, 91, 387
  in Uruguay, 251
  in Venezuela, 231–232
Lacalle, Luis Alberto, 252, 256, 259
Lacalle, Sáenz, 400
Lagos, Ricardo, 160–161
Laino, Domingo, 273
land reform, 35–36, 55, 134, 372
  in Mexico, 326, 329–330
  in Paraguay, 269–270
landowners (*caudillos*), 31, 35–36, 53, 104, 396–397, 450
LAPOP. *See* Latin American Public Opinion Project
Lara, Rodrigo, 181
Latin America, 12, 52–54, 102
  authoritarianism in, 15–16
  colonization of, 21–22
  constitutions in, 23–24
  courts in, 52
  debt in, 63–65
  democracy in, 3, 14–15, 89–99
  diversity in, 3–5, 9
  economy of, 24–25, 59–73
  geography of, 10–11
  government of, 49–55
  history of, 19–27
  institutions in, 5–6, 47–55, 48 (table)
  legislatures in, 51
  military conquest of, 10, 19–21
  military rule in, 26–27, 79
  modernization in, 4, 12 (table), 17
  political culture in, 4–5, 15–17
  public policy in, 6–7
  race and racism in, 9–10
  social structure of, 5, 14–15
  US and, 75–86
Latin American Council of Bishops (CELAM), 148
Latin American Public Opinion Project (LAPOP), 289, 309, 377, 388, 458
Lavín, Joaquín, 160
Law of Community Councils, in Venezuela, 228–229
Law of Mother Earth, in Bolivia, 71
Law of Popular Participation (LPP), in Bolivia, 290–291

Leftist Front of Freedom (FIDEL), in
    Uruguay, 251
legislatures, 51, 115–116, 429, 443–
    444
  in Cuba, 359–360
  in Nicaragua, 388–389
  in Venezuela, 236–237
Leguía, Augusto B., 196
lemas, in Uruguay, 250
lesbian, gay, bisexual, transgender, and
    queer (LGBTQ), 6, 56
  in Chile, 166
  in Colombia, 191
  in Ecuador, 307
  in Honduras, 430
  in Mexico, 339
  See also same-sex marriage
Let's Change alliance, in Argentina, 114
Lewis, Oscar, 331–332
LGBTQ. See lesbian, gay, bisexual,
    transgender, and queer
liberal democracy, 95–97, 96–97 (table),
    138, 220, 438
Liberal Party
  in Chile, 143–144
  in Colombia, 173, 176
  in Honduras, 424
  in Nicaragua, 384, 386
  in Paraguay, 269, 275
liberalism
    exports and, 60–62, 61 (table)
    See also neoliberalism
liberation theology, 34–35
Liberty and Refoundation Party (LIBRE),
    in Honduras, 423, 428–429, 432
Lobo Porfirio, in Honduras, 423, 426,
    427, 431
Logan, Rayford, 466
López, Andrés Manuel, 334
López, Carlos Antonio, 268
López Arellano, Oswaldo, 425
López de Santa Anna, Antonio, 325
López Obrador, Andrés Manuel, 335
López Portillo, José, 332
L'Ouverture, Toussaint, 450
Lozano, Wilfredo, 452, 454
LPP. See Law of Popular Participation
Lugo, Fernando, 90, 274–275
Lula. See Inacio da Silva, Luís

M-19. See 19th of April Movement
Machado, Gerardo, 349–350
Macri, Mauricio, 103, 112, 114, 118,
    120–121, 296
Madero, Francisco, 327
Maduro, Nicolás, 217–218, 220, 229, 231,
    235, 242
Maduro, Ricardo, 431
Mahuad, Jamil, 304–305
Mancuso, Salvatore, 183
Manifest Destiny, 76
Manigat, Leslie, 468
MAPU. See Popular Unitary Action
    Movement
maquiladoras (assembly plants), 66
María Argaña, Luis, 274
Mariátegui, José Carlos, 196
marijuana legalization, in Uruguay, 258
Martelly, Michel, 469–470
Martí, José, 348
Martinelli, Ricardo, 443
Martínez de Hoz, José, 109
Marulanda Vélez, Manuel, 178, 183
Marxism, 17, 34, 38, 39, 63
  in Chile, 141, 149
  in Cuba, 354, 360
  in Haiti, 467
  in Nicaragua, 383
  in Peru, 197
  in Uruguay, 251
MAS. See Movement Towards Socialism;
    Wide Social Movement
Maya, 20, 322, 412, 415
MDGs. See Millennium Development Goals
Media Law, in Argentina, 118
Medina, Danilo, 457
Mejía, Hipólito, 456
Méndez Montenegro, Julio César, 91
Mendoza, Veronika, 201
Menem, Carlos, 110–111, 114, 119
Mengele, Josef, 277
MERCOSUR. See Common Market of the
    South
Mérida Initiative (Plan Mexico), 83
Mesa, Carlos, 284
mestizo, 10
Mexico, 40, 52, 56, 64, 68, 83, 319–343
    civil war in, 93
    constitution of, 325, 328
    democracy in, 334–337

drug trade in, 82, 94, 319, 335, 339–341
economy of, 13, 25, 332–334
emigration from, 84, 85–86, 320, 338
foreign policy of, 341–342
history of, 322–328
interest groups in, 337–339
manufacturing in, 66
military conquest of, 20, 322–323
military in, 32
NGOs in, 42
Nueva España in, 47
political parties in, 329, 334
presidency of, 50
PRI in, 44
revolution in, 12, 25, 30, 325–328
social structure of, 337–339
US and, 76
violence in, 339–341
Meximilian of Hapsburg, 325
Miami Summit, 66
Micheletti, Roberto, 426
middle class, 14, 37–38, 242, 428
    in Argentina, 104, 113
    in Uruguay, 247, 248
military, 10, 19–21, 31–33
    in Brazil, 130
    in Chile, 151
    Costa Rica and, 370
    in Cuba, 350
    in Honduras, 424, 427
    in Mexico, 328–329
    in Paraguay, 271–272
    in Uruguay, 254
    in Venezuela, 230, 240–241
military coups d'état, 32
    in Argentina, 108
    in Brazil, 79
    in Chile, 151–152
    in El Salvador, 397–398
    in Great Depression, 12
    in Guatemala, 62, 78
    in Haiti, 469
    in Honduras, 82, 90, 426–427
    in Paraguay, 89, 265, 272, 281
    in Venezuela, 44, 82, 226, 230
military rule, 26–27, 32, 79
    in Argentina, 108–110
    in Brazil, 126
    in Chile, 152–156
    in Cold War, 79

in Colombia, 177
in El Salvador, 397
in Guatemala, 414
in Panama, 436–438
in Peru, 196–197
in Uruguay, 251–252
in Venezuela, 221, 225
Millennium Development Goals (MDGs), of
    United Nations, 69, 70
MIR. *See* Movement of the Revolutionary
    Left
mixed races, 14
    in Brazil, 134–135
    in Dominican Republic, 466–467
    in Ecuador, 301
ML. *See* Movimiento Libertario
MNR. *See* National Revolutionary
    Movement
Modern Revolutionary Party (PRM), in
    Dominican Republic, 457
modernization, 4, 12 (table), 17, 35
    in Bolivia, 285–287
    in Chile, 153
    in Cuba, 351, 357–358
    in Dominican Republic, 456
    in Guatemala, 413
Moïse, Jovenel, 470
Molina, Carlos, 82
Monroe Doctrine, 75–77
Montesinos, Vladimiro, 207
Montt, Efrain Rios, 35
Montt, Manuel, 143
Morales, Evo, 17, 41, 98, 283–285, 288–297
Morales, Jimmy, 35, 412, 416, 418
Morales Bermúdez, Francisco, 197
Morelos, José María, 324
Moreno, Lenin, 299
Morínigo, Higinio, 271
Moro, Sérgio, 130
Mothers of the Plaza de Mayo, 109, 110
Movement of Popular Participation (MPP), in
    Uruguay, 256, 260
Movement of the Revolutionary Left (MIR)
    in Bolivia, 293
    in Chile, 150, 151
Movement Towards Socialism (MAS), in
    Bolivia, 284–285, 293
Movimento Sem Terra (MST), in Brazil, 134
Movimiento Libertario (ML), in Costa Rica,
    376

MPP. *See* Movement of Popular
   Participation
MPSC. *See* Popular Social Christian
   Movement
MRTA. *See* Túpac Amaru Revolutionary
   Movement
MST. *See Movimento Sem Terra*
MUD. *See* Democratic Unity Table
Mujal-León, Eusebio, 346
Mujica, José, 256–259, 260
Munguía Payés, David, 406
MVR. *See* Fifth Republic Movement

NAFTA. *See* North American Free Trade
   Agreement
Namphy, Henri, 468
Napoleon Bonaparte, 22, 125
Napoleonic Code, of France, 52
Nasralla, Salvador, 429–430
National Action Party (PAN), in Mexico, 334
National Assistance Program (PAN), in
   Panama, 444
National Association of Private Enterprise
   (ANEP), in El Salvador, 401
National Civic Crusade, in Panama, 438
National Conciliation Party (PCN), in El
   Salvador, 402
National Convention of Workers (CNT), in
   Uruguay, 251
National Convergence Front (FCN), in
   Guatemala, 416
National Encounter Party (PEN), in
   Paraguay, 273
National Endowment for Democracy (NED),
   82
National Front, in Colombia, 176
National Health Service (FONASA), in
   Chile, 154
National Intelligence Directorate (DINA), in
   Chile, 153
National Office of Revenue Administration
   (SUNAT), in Peru, 211
National Party
   in Chile, 148
   in Honduras, 424
   in Peru, 209
   in Uruguay, 249–250
National Peasants' Confederation (CNC), in
   Mexico, 330
National Renewal (RN), in Chile, 158

National Revolutionary Movement (MNR),
   in Bolivia, 43, 284
National Revolutionary Party (PNR), in
   Mexico, 329
National Secretariat of Social Welfare
   (SENDAS), in Colombia, 177
National Security Council (COSENA), in
   Chile, 154–155
National Union of Ethical Citizens
   (UNACE), in Paraguay, 275
National Union of Workers (UNT), in
   Mexico, 338
National Unity (UN)
   in Bolivia, 284
   in Peru, 198
National Zapatista Liberation Army (EZLN),
   in Mexico, 341
nationalism, 22–24
   in Cuba, 347–349
   in Ecuador, 313
   of indigenous people, 40
   in Mexico, 330
Nationalist Democratic Action (ADN), in
   Bolivia, 293
Nationalist Republican Alliance (ARENA),
   in El Salvador, 398, 402–406
Navarro, Juan Carlos, 442
NED. *See* National Endowment for
   Democracy
neoliberalism, 64–65, 66, 93, 141, 431
   in Argentina, 111, 119
   in Ecuador, 312–313
   in Venezuela, 226–227
New Granada, 24
New Time (TU), in Venezuela, 235
NGOs. *See* nongovernmental organizations
Nicaragua, 10, 23, 40, 56, 66, 77, 383–393
   in CACM, 63
   Christian-Democratic party in, 44
   constitution of, 385–386
   Costa Rica and, 379
   democracy in, 9, 89–90, 388
   foreign policy of, 391–392
   FSLN in, 79
   history of, 384–386
   institutions in, 388–390
   labor unions in, 91, 387
   political parties in, 384, 388–390
   public policy in, 390–391
   remittances in, 69

revolution in, 30, 79
Sandinista revolution in, 17
US and, 76, 79–80
women in, 41
19th of April Movement (M-19), in
Colombia, 178
Nisman, Alberto, 118
Nixon, Richard, 79, 82
nongovernmental organizations (NGOs),
15, 42, 338, 398, 401, 465
Noriega, Manuel Antonio, 90, 437–438
North American Free Trade Agreement
(NAFTA), 36, 66, 320, 333,
341–342
Nueva España, in Mexico, 47
Núñez de Balboa, Vasco, 21

OAS. *See* Organization of American States
Obama, Barack, 82, 85, 127, 361–362, 364,
403, 408
Obregón, Alvaro, 328
OceanaGold, 71
Ochoa, Arnaldo, 358–359
Ochoa, Fabio, 181
O'Donnell, Guillermo, 97
OECD. *See* Organization for Economic
Co-operation and Development
oil, 64, 120, 132, 270, 295
in Ecuador, 300, 302, 309–312
in Mexico, 330, 332
in Venezuela, 224, 225–227,
238–239
oligarchy, 31–36
in Argentina, 104
in Chile, 24, 142–144, 148
in Ecuador, 301
in El Salvador, 398
Olmec, 322
Olney, Richard, 76
Olney Doctrine, 76
Olympics, in Brazil, 123, 132, 134
OPEC. *See* Organization of Petroleum
Exporting Countries
Operation Safe Mexico, 340
Organization for Economic Co-operation and
Development (OECD), 171, 320
Organization of American States (OAS),
77–78, 81, 92, 207–208, 313
Haiti and, 469
Honduras and, 426, 429

Organization of Petroleum Exporting
Countries (OPEC), 64
Orozco, Pascual, 327
Orsini, Deborah, 92
Ortega, Daniel, 80, 93, 385, 386, 390–392
Ortega, Humberto, 385
Ortiz, Fernando, 349
Os Donos do Poder (Faoro), 126
Ovelar, Blanca, 274
Oviedo, Lino, 273–274

PAC. *See* Anti-Corruption Party; Citizen
Action Party
Pachaktuik (PK), 305
Pacifying Police Unions (UPPs), in Brazil,
136
Pact for Mexico, 335
Pact of Economic Solidarity, in Mexico, 333
Pact of Punto Fijo, 221–222, 223
PAIS Alliance (AP), in Ecuador, 304
Palma, Arturo Alessandri, 145
PAN. *See* National Action Party; National
Assistance Program
Panama, 40, 50, 56, 76–77, 435–446
democracy in, 438–439
economy of, 445
government of, 443–444
political culture in, 436–443
political parties in, 437
US and, 435–436, 438
Panama Canal, 76–77, 435, 445
Panama Papers, 444
Paniagua, Valentín, 198
Paraguay, 10, 21, 40, 50, 56, 265–282
democracy in, 272–276
foreign policy of, 276–280
future for, 280–281
history of, 266–269
military coups d'état in, 89, 265, 272, 281
military in, 271–272
Uruguay and, 270
Paraguayan War (1864–1870), 31, 268
paramilitary, in Colombia, 178–179,
182–184
Parliamentary Republic, of Chile, 144–145
Partido Auténtico (Authentic Party), in Cuba,
351
Partido Unidad Social Cristiana (PUSC), in
Costa Rica, 376
Party for Democracy (PPD), in Chile, 157

Party of National Liberation (PLN), in Costa Rica, 43, 375
Party of the Democratic Revolution (PRD)
 in Dominican Republic, 453–457
 in Mexico, 334
 in Panama, 437, 439–443
patria chica, 53
patronage, 16, 133, 146, 417
PCN. *See* National Conciliation Party
PDA. *See* Alternative Democratic Pole
PDVSA. *See* Petroleum of Venezuela
peasantry (*campesinos*), 5, 12, 15, 21, 38–39, 231
 from El Salvador, 397
 in Honduras, 425, 428
 in Mexico, 329–330
Pedro II (Emperor), 268
PEN. *See* National Encounter Party
Pena Gomez, Jose Francisco, 454
Peña Nieto, Enrique, 86, 335, 340, 341–342
Pension Fund Administrators (AFPs), in Chile, 154
People's Defender, in Venezuela, 238
People's Liberation Army (EPL), in Colombia, 178
People's Revolutionary Armed Forces (FARP), in Mexico, 341
People's Revolutionary Army (EPR), in Mexico, 341
Pérez, Carlos Andrés, 225–226, 231
Pérez Jiménez, Marcos, 221, 223, 225
Pérez Molina, Otto, 418
Perón, Eva, 106–107, 114
Perón, Juan Domingo, 26, 105–107, 114, 177, 271
Peronist Party, in Argentina, 106–107, 110–111, 113–114
Peru, 40, 41, 50, 56, 69, 92
 APRA in, 43
 authoritarianism in, 195–216
 Chile and, 143
 democracy in, 197, 207
 drug trade in, 94, 201–202, 214
 economy of, 25, 202–204
 foreign policy of, 213–214
 institutions in, 206–210
 interest groups in, 30
 military rule in, 32, 196–197
 political culture in, 196–202

 political parties in, 196, 197, 198, 206–209
 public policy in, 210–213
 social structure of, 204–205
Peru Possible (PP), 198
Petroleum of Venezuela (PDVSA), 239
PGT. *See* Guatemalan Labor Party
Phillip III (King), 267
PIAS. *See* Inter-Amazon Services Program
Piñera, José, 154
Piñera, Sebastián, 163–165
Pinochet, Augusto, 79, 141, 151, 153–156
PIT. *See* Inter-Union Workers' Plenary
PJ. *See* Justice First
PK. *See* Pachaktuik
Plan Colombia, 83
Plan Mexico (Mérida Initiative), 83
Plan of Action, 81
Plata, Río de la, courts in, 52
Platt Amendment, 76, 348–349
PLD. *See* Dominican Liberation Party
PLI. *See* Independent Liberal Party
PLN. *See* Party of National Liberation
PLRA. *See* Authentic Radical Liberal Party
PNR. *See* National Revolutionary Party
PODEMOS. *See* Social Democratic Power
police, 239–240, 337, 379
 in El Salvador, 396–397, 399
 in Honduras, 425, 427, 430, 432
political culture, 4–5, 15–17
 in Bolivia, 288–290
 in Brazil, 127–128
 in Colombia, 171–172
 in Costa Rica, 374–377
 in Cuba, 346–347
 in Ecuador, 308–309
 in Guatemala, 416–417
 in Haiti, 466–467
 in Honduras, 424–427
 in Panama, 436–443
 in Paraguay, 266–269
 in Peru, 196–202
 in Uruguay, 249–252
 in Venezuela, 220–224
political institutions. *See* institutions
political parties, 30, 42–45
 in Argentina, 104, 105, 106–107, 113–115
 in Bolivia, 284–285, 292–294
 in Brazil, 128
 in Chile, 142–144, 157–158

in Colombia, 172–173, 172–173 (table)
in Costa Rica, 374–377
in Cuba, 351
in Dominican Republic, 451, 453–457
in Ecuador, 44, 303
in El Salvador, 397, 402–404
in Honduras, 423, 424, 428–429
in Mexico, 329, 334
in Nicaragua, 384, 388–390
in Panama, 437
in Paraguay, 269–276
in Peru, 196, 197, 198, 206–209
in Uruguay, 249–251
in Venezuela, 217, 221–222, 232–235
See also specific political parties
Polk, James, 76
Popular Action (AP), in Peru, 206
Popular Alliance (AP), in Peru, 197
Popular Christian Party (PPC), in Peru, 208
Popular Force (FP), in Peru, 208
Popular Social Christian Movement (MPSC),
in El Salvador, 398
Popular Unitary Action Movement (MAPU),
in Chile, 150
Popular Unity
in Chile, 149, 151
in Uruguay, 262
Popular Will (VP), in Venezuela, 234–235
populism, 26, 89
in Argentina, 106–107
in Venezuela, 229
Portales, Diego, 142–143
Portugal, 3, 10, 11–12, 19–21, 47, 59–60
Brazil and, 124–125
Catholic Church and, 33
poverty, 5, 10, 56, 70
in Argentina, 119
in Bolivia, 287
in Brazil, 134
in Chile, 165–166
in Colombia, 171
in Costa Rica, 371
in Ecuador, 312–313
in El Salvador, 399–400, 406
in Mexico, 320, 332
in Peru, 211
in Venezuela, 242
PP. *See* Peru Possible
PPC. *See* Popular Christian Party
PPD. *See* Party for Democracy

PR. *See* Radical Party
Prats, Carlos, 151, 153
PRC. *See* Cuban Revolutionary Party
PRD. *See* Party of the Democratic
Revolution
PRE. *See* Ecuadorian Roldosist Party
Prebisch, Raul, 62
presidency, 48–50, 49–50 (table)
of Argentina, 116, 118
of Brazil, 130–131
of Chile, 79, 143, 152
of democracy, 92
of Ecuador, 304
of El Salvador, 80
of Honduras, 82, 429
of Mexico, 331
of Nicaragua, 388
of Panama, 443–444
of Paraguay, 273
of Peru, 199–202
of Uruguay, 254–258
of Venezuela, 236
See also specific individuals
Préval, René, 469
PRI. *See* Institutional Revolutionary Party
Prieto, Joaquín, 142
Prío, Carlos, 351
privatization, 55, 92, 111, 226
in Bolivia, 65
in El Salvador, 405
in Mexico, 333
in Peru, 211
PRM. *See* Modern Revolutionary Party
PRO. *See* Republican Proposal
Promotion of Private Investment (COPRI), in
Peru, 211
Protestantism, 5, 15, 35
in Bolivia, 287
in Brazil, 135
in El Salvador, 400–401
in Guatemala, 416
in Nicaragua, 387
in Venezuela, 231
PRSC. *See* Reformist Social Christian Party
PRSD. *See* Radical Social Democratic Party
PSD. *See* Democratic Security Plan
PSDB. *See* Brazilian Social Democratic
Party
PSUV. *See* United Socialist Party of
Venezuela

PT. *See* Workers Party
public policy, 6–7, 55–56
  in Argentina, 118–120
  in Bolivia, 295–296
  in Colombia, 190–192
  in Ecuador, 312–313
  in El Salvador, 404–406
  in Guatemala, 418–419
  in Haiti, 467–470
  in Honduras, 430–432
  in Nicaragua, 390–391
  in Peru, 210–213
  in Uruguay, 252–253
  in Venezuela, 238–240
Puerto Rico, 20, 23
PUSC. *See Partido Unidad Social Cristiana*
PyL. *See* Fatherland and Country

Quijano, Norman, 404

race and racism, 9–10, 134–135
  See also indigenous people; mixed races
Radical Change Party (CR), in Colombia,
  173
Radical Civic Union (UCR), in Argentina,
  104, 108, 110, 111, 113–114
Radical Party (PR), in Chile, 144, 146, 147,
  148–149
Radical Social Democratic Party (PRSD), in
  Chile, 157
Ramírez, Joaquín, 201
Ratzinger, Joseph, 34
Reagan, Ronald, Nicaragua and, 79–80
Real Plan, in Brazil, 131–132
Rebel Armed Forces (FAR), in Guatemala,
  414
Recabarren, Luis Emilio, 145
Reciprocity Treaty, 348–349, 350–351
Red Cross, 42
Reformist Social Christian Party (PRSC), in
  Dominican Republic, 454
Regional Confederation of Mexican Workers
  (CROM), in Mexico, 330
Reid, Michael, 129
Reina, Carlos Roberto, 425–426,
  430–431
religion
  in Brazil, 135
  in El Salvador, 400–401
  in Haiti, 471

  See also Catholic Church; Christianity;
    Protestantism
remittances, 68–69, 288, 424
Republican Proposal (PRO), in Argentina,
  114
Resolution 1080, of OAS, 81
Revolutionary Armed Forces (FAR), in Cuba,
  356–358, 365–366
Revolutionary Armed Forces of Colombia
  (FARC), 94, 169, 173, 178, 184–190
revolutions, 79
  in Ecuador, 23, 299–314
  in Mexico, 12, 25, 30, 325–328
  in Paraguay, 269–271
  See also guerrilla revolutions
Reyes, Bernardo, 327
Rio Treaty (Inter-American Treaty of
  Reciprocal Assistance), 77
Ríos Montt, Efraín, 414, 416
Rivadavia, Bernardino, 104
RN. *See* National Renewal
Roa Bastos, Augusto, 281
Robinson, Pat, 231
Rodríguez, Andrés, 272, 273
Rodriguez Calleja, Luis Alberto, 366
Rodríguez Veltzé, Eduardo, 284
Roett, Riordan, 126
Rohter, Larry, 137
Rojas, María Eugenia, 177
Rojas Pinilla, Gustavo, 173–174, 177, 178
Romero, Óscar, 80, 398, 400, 401
Roosevelt, Franklin D., 77, 467
Roosevelt, Theodore, 76, 451
Roosevelt Corollary, 76–77
Rosales, Manuel, 228
Rosas, Juan Manuel de, 104
Rosenthal, Jaime, 427
Rossi, Marcelo, 135
Rousseff, Dilma, 41, 51, 123, 127–129, 132,
  138, 296
Ruiz, Ramón, 349
rule of law, 6–7, 83, 90, 336

Saca, Tony, 35, 400–401, 403, 404,
  405–406
Salinas, Carlos, 333
Salinas Rivera, Francisco Ramón, 406
same-sex marriage (civil unions), 117, 166,
  256, 258, 307
Samper, Ernesto, 182

San Martín, José de, 23
Sánchez Cerén, Salvador, 404, 408
Sánchez de Lozada, Gonzalo, 284, 291, 295
Sandinista National Liberation Front
    (FSLN), in Nicaragua, 17, 79,
    384–386, 388
Sandino, Augusto César, 384
Sanguinetti, Julio María, 252, 259
Santana, Pedro, 451
Santos, Juan Manual, 169–170
SAPs. *See* structural adjustment policies
Schmitter, Philippe, 95
Schneider, René, 149
Scioli, Daniel, 120
SENDAS. *See* National Secretariat of Social
    Welfare
Sendero Luminoso (Shining Path), in Peru, 94,
    212, 214
Serrano Elías, Jorge, 92, 415–416
sex discrimination, 42
Shining Path (*Sendero Luminoso*), in Peru, 94,
    212, 214
SICA. *See* Central American Integration
    System
Siete Partidas (Alfonso the Wise), 52
Silva, Marina, 124, 129
slaves and slavery, 9, 11, 23, 125, 323,
    346–347
Slim, Carlos, 320
Smith, Adam, 60
Smith, Peter, 43, 95
SNTE. *See* Teachers' Union
El Soberano, in Venezuela, 242
Sobrino, Jon, 34
Social Christian Party, in Venezuela, 225
Social Democratic Power (PODEMOS), in
    Bolivia, 284
social structure, 5, 14–16
    of Argentina, 112–113
    of Brazil, 133–135
    of Chile, 147–148
    of Colombia, 170–171
    of Costa Rica, 377–378
    of Cuba, 346
    of Dominican Republic, 458–459
    of Ecuador, 301
    of El Salvador, 399–400
    of Guatemala, 415–416
    of Haiti, 470–471
    of Mexico, 337–339

    of Peru, 204–205
    of Uruguay, 247–249
    of Venezuela, 220, 224–232
    See also elites, elitism; middle class;
        peasantry; race and racism; working
        class
socialism, 17
    in Cuba, 26, 364
    See also Marxism
Socialist Party, 43
    in Chile, 79, 145, 146, 157
    in Peru, 196
    in Uruguay, 251
Solano López, Francisco, 268
Solís, Ottón, 376
Somoza Debayle, Anastasio, 9, 79, 379, 384
Somoza García, Anastasio, 79, 384
Soulouque, Faustin, 466–467
Soviet Union, 78, 80, 89, 346, 355
Spain, 3, 10, 11–12, 19–24, 47, 59–60
    Catholic Church and, 33
    Costa Rica and, 370–372
    Cuba and, 347–349
    Dominican Republic and, 449–450
    Guatemala and, 412–413
    Mexico and, 322–324
    Paraguay and, 267
Spanish-American War, 76
Stroessner, Alfredo, 89, 265, 271–272, 278
structural adjustment policies (SAPs), 64
Suazo Córdova, Roberto, 425
sublemas, in Uruguay, 250
Suchlicki, Jaime, 350
SUDENE. *See* Superintendence for the
    Development of the Northeast
SUNAT. *See* National Office of Revenue
    Administration
Superintendence for the Development of the
    Northeast (SUDENE), in Brazil, 132
Superior Council of Private Enterprise
    (COSEP), in Nicaragua, 387
Supreme Electoral Council (CSE), in
    Nicaragua, 389
Supreme Electoral Tribunal (TSE)
    in El Salvador, 402, 404
    in Honduras, 429
Supreme Tribunal of Justice (TSJ), in
    Venezuela, 218, 237
sustainable development, in economy,
    69–72

Taft, William Howard, 436
TDR-EP. *See* Democratic Revolutionary
   Tendency-Army of the People
Teachers' Union (SNTE), in Mexico, 338
Temer, Michel, 129, 138
Ten Years of Spring, in Guatemala, 413–414
Tillman, Ellen, 451–452
Tilly, Charles, 94
TISA. *See* Trade in Services Agreement
Tlatelolco Treaty, 331
Toledo, Alejandro, 198–199, 207, 212
Tomic, Rodimoro, 149
Torrealba, Jesús "Chúo," 217
Torres, Camilo, 176
Torres, Sandra, 419
Torrijos, Martin, 443
Torrijos, Omar, 437
Townley, Michael, 153
Trade in Services Agreement (TISA), 262
Transparency International, 56, 431, 444
Treaty of Aranjuez, 450
Treaty of Paris, 76
Trujillo, Rafael, 77, 78, 91
Trujillo Molina, Rafael Leonidas, 452
Trump, Donald, 85, 363
Truth Commission, 212, 404–405, 408,
   426
TSE. *See* Supreme Electoral Tribunal
TSJ. *See* Supreme Tribunal of Justice
TU. *See* New Time
Túpac Amaru Revolutionary Movement
   (MRTA), in Peru, 197
Twenty-Sixth of July Movement, in Cuba,
   352

Ubico y Castañeda, Jorge, 413
UCC. *See* Union of the Center
UCR. *See* Radical Civic Union
UDI. *See* Independent Democratic Union
UFCO. *See* United Fruit Company
UN. *See* National Unity
UNACE. *See* National Union of Ethical
   Citizens
UNASUR. *See* Union of South American
   Nations
Union of South American Nations
   (UNASUR), 137, 313
Union of the Center (UCC), in Chile, 158
Unitary Party, in Argentina, 104
United Fruit Company (UFCO), 62

United Left (IU), in Peru, 206–207
United Nations, 62, 69, 70, 203, 395, 399,
   465
United Self-Defense Forces of Colombia
   (AUC), 183
United Socialist Party of Venezuela (PSUV),
   222, 234, 235, 237
United States (US), 32, 41, 48 (table), 49,
   75–86, 92
   Brazil and, 137
   Chile and, 150
   civil war in, 76
   Cold War and, 77–80
   Colombia and, 171, 181
   constitution of, 23–24
   Cuba and, 76, 78, 347–352, 361–363
   Dominican Republic and, 451, 461
   drug trade and, 82–83
   Ecuador and, 311–312
   El Salvador and, 407–408
   foreign aid from, 77, 468
   Guatemala and, 420
   Haiti and, 467
   Honduras and, 432
   immigration and, 84–86, 338
   Mexico and, 76, 320, 328, 340
   Nicaragua and, 383, 391–392
   Panama and, 76–77, 435–436, 438
   Panama Canal and, 435
   Paraguay and, 277–278
   Peru and, 199, 214
United States Agency for International
   Development (USAID), 401
Universal Benefit for Children (*Universal por
   Hijo*), in Argentina, 117
UNT. *See* National Union of Workers
UPPs. *See* Pacifying Police Unions
urbanization, 35, 285–286, 302, 330
URD. *See* Democratic Republican Union
Uribe, Álvaro, 98, 174
URNG. *See* Guatemalan National
   Revolutionary Unit
Uruguay, 10, 26, 32, 50, 56
   Argentina and, 249, 256, 259–260
   democracy in, 245–263
   economy of, 247–249, 253–254, 257
   globalization and, 259
   government of, 252–253
   military in, 254
   political culture in, 249–252

political parties in, 249–251, 269–276
public policy in, 252–253
social structure of, 247–249
US. *See* United States
US Citizenship and Immigration Services
(USCIS), 85
USAID. *See* United States Agency for
International Development
US-Colombia Free Trade Agreement, 171

Valencia, Guillermo León, 178
Vanguardia Popular Party, in Costa Rica,
375
Varela, Juan Carlos, 442–443
Vargas, Getúlio, 26, 44, 126, 130
Vargas Lleras, Germán, 173
Varona, Enrique José, 349
Vásquez, Romeo, 426
Vazquez, Horacio, 452
Vázquez, Tabaré, 255–256, 260–262
Velasco Alvarado, Juan, 197, 204
Velasco Ibarra, José María, 302
Venezuela, 26, 43, 51, 56, 76, 97, 217–243
ALBA and, 66
Bolivia and, 296
Christian-Democratic party in, 44
constitution of, 227, 236, 237–238
crime in, 240
Cuba and, 361
economy of, 25, 238–239
foreign policy of, 240–241
geography of, 218–219
government of, 236–238
institutions in, 228–229
interest groups in, 229–232
Mexico and, 342
military coups d'état in, 32, 44, 82,
226, 230
military in, 240–241
nationalism of, 24
oil in, 64, 224, 225–227, 238–239
police in, 239–240
political culture in, 220–224
political parties in, 217, 221–222,
232–235
presidency of, 50
public policy in, 238–240
revolution in, 23
Roosevelt Corollary and, 77
social structure of, 220, 224–232

Venezuelan Confederation of Workers
(CTV), 232
Videla, Jorge Rafael, 108, 109, 110
Villa, Francisco, 328
Villeda Morales, Ramón, 425
Viola, Roberto, 109
violence, 90
in Brazil, 135–136
in Colombia, 170, 176–192
Costa Rica and, 370
in Dominican Republic, 459–461
in Ecuador, 300, 303
in El Salvador, 395–396, 405–407
in Guatemala, 419
in Mexico, 339–341
in Peru, 212
voting rights, 91, 128, 207–208, 303, 389,
416
in Argentina, 104, 114
in Dominican Republic, 454
VP. *See* Popular Will

Walker, William, 383, 384
Wang Jing, 391
War of the Confederation, 143
War of the Pacific, 144, 196, 270
War of Triple Alliance, 268
Washington Consensus, 64–65, 111, 119
Wasmosy, Juan Carlos, 273
Welles, Sumner, 350
Wesson, Robert, 93
Wide Social Movement (MAS), in Chile,
157
Williamson, John, 64–65
WILPF. *See* Women's International League
for Peace and Freedom
women, 5, 41–42, 70
in Argentina, 109
in Colombia, 174–175, 174 (table), 191
in Costa Rica, 376
in Ecuador, 303
in El Salvador, 401–402
in Guatemala, 416
in Honduras, 429
in Paraguay, 269
voting rights of, 91, 114, 303
Women's International League for Peace and
Freedom (WILPF), 175
Workers Party (PT), in Brazil, 123, 126–127,
128, 133

working class, 14, 37, 104, 113, 240, 248
World Bank, 42, 65, 92, 255, 262, 391, 459
World Cup, in Brazil, 132, 134
World Values Survey (WVS), 339
World War I, 62

World War II, 12, 26, 62, 77, 248, 277, 413
WVS. *See* World Values Survey

Zapata, Emiliano, 327–328
Zelaya, Manuel, 82, 90, 423, 428–433